ST. FRANCIS SEMINARY
THE LIBRARY
SALZMANN
LIBRARY
Milwaukee, Wis. 53207
De Sales Prep Seminary
3501 S. Lake Drive
Milwaukee, Wis. 53207

D1269399

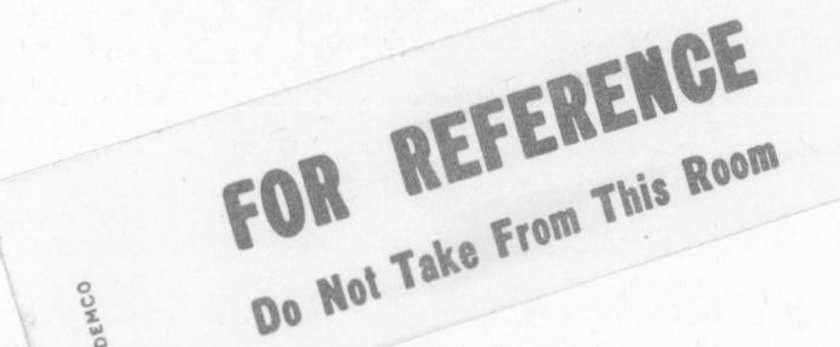
FOR REFERENCE
Do Not Take From This Room
DEMCO

MUIR'S HISTORICAL ATLAS

ANCIENT, MEDIEVAL AND MODERN

Comprising Muir's Atlas of Ancient and Classical History and Muir's Historical Atlas—Medieval and Modern

EDITED BY

R. F. TREHARNE, M.A., PH.D.

PROFESSOR OF HISTORY, UNIVERSITY COLLEGE OF WALES, ABERYSTWYTH

AND

HAROLD FULLARD, M.SC.

CARTOGRAPHIC EDITOR

BARNES & NOBLE INC.

BOOKSELLERS . PUBLISHERS . FOUNDED 1873

105 FIFTH AVENUE NEW YORK 3 N Y

CONTENTS OF
ANCIENT AND CLASSICAL ATLAS

** Maps marked with an asterisk are coloured physically*

***1** THE WORLD AS KNOWN TO THE ANCIENTS 1: 70M.
World according to Herodotus c. 450 B.C.
World according to Eratosthenes c. 200 B.C.
World according to Strabo c. 18 A.D.
World according to Ptolemy c. 150 A.D.

2A THE CRADLES OF CIVILISATION IN THE XV CENTURY B.C. 1: 25M.
B *Achaean Greece according to Homer c. 1200 B.C. 1: 8M.*
C *Troy 1: 500,000*
D *The Assyrian Empire in the First Half of the VII Century B.C. 1: 15M.*

3A THE NILE AND EUPHRATES VALLEYS *c.* 1200 *B.C.* 1: 10M.
B *Ancient Egypt 1: 5M.*

4A ISRAELITE CONQUEST OF CANAAN 1: 2M.
B *Jerusalem before the Exile 1: 50,000*
C *Syria and the Hebrew Kingdoms 1: 5M.*
D *Palestine in the time of Christ 1: 2M.*
E *Jerusalem before 70 A.D. 1: 50,000*
F *Paul's Missionary Journeys 1: 30M.*

5A PHOENICIAN AND GREEK COLONIES 1: 20M.
B *Persian Empire c. 500 B.C. 1: 20M.*

***6-7** ANCIENT GREECE 1: 2M.
A *Acropolis 1: 15,000*
B *Ancient Athens 1: 50,000*
C *The Shores of Propontis 1: 3M.*
D *Crete 1: 3M.*

8 GREECE AND THE AEGEAN IN THE V CENTURY B.C. 1: 3M.

9A PELOPONNESIAN WAR 1: 8M.
B *Empire of Alexander the Great 1: 20M.*
C *Empires of Alexander's Successors c. 300 B.C. 1: 40M.*

***10-11** ROMAN EMPIRE 1: 15M.
A *Imperial and Senatorial Provinces c. 14 A.D. 1: 40M.*
B *Roman Conquest of the Mediterranean 1: 30M.*
C *Republican Rome 1: 60,000*
D *Imperial Rome 1: 60,000*

***12** ANCIENT ITALY: NORTHERN SECTION 1: 3M.

***13** ANCIENT ITALY: SOUTHERN SECTION 1: 3M.
A *Republican Forum 1: 15,000*
B *Imperial Fora 1: 15,000*

14A ITALY UNDER THE ROMAN REPUBLIC 1: 5M.
B *Latium 1: 2½M.*
C *Racial Distribution c. 400 B.C. 1: 15M.*

15 WEST ROMAN EMPIRE IN THE TIME OF AUGUSTUS 1: 10M.

16 EAST ROMAN EMPIRE IN THE TIME OF AUGUSTUS 1: 10M.

ANCIENT AND CLASSICAL ATLAS

First Edition	1938
Second Edition	1956

MEDIEVAL AND MODERN ATLAS

First Edition	1911
Second Edition	1914
Third Edition	1917
Fourth Edition, Enlarged	1920
Fifth Edition	1923
Sixth Edition, Revised and Greatly Enlarged	1927
Seventh Edition	1947
Eighth Edition	1952
Reprinted	1956
Ninth Edition, Completely Redesigned	© 1962

PRINTED IN GREAT BRITAIN BY GEORGE PHILIP AND SON, LIMITED, LONDON

INTRODUCTION

THE ANCIENT WORLD

Plate 1 shows the area within which the whole drama of ancient history was played—the development not only of the civilisation of the West, upon which our attention is mainly concentrated, but of the remote and independent civilisations of China and India. But by far the greater part of the area shown on this map—the whole of northern Europe and Asia and the whole of Africa south of the Atlas mountains, except the narrow valley of the Nile—was practically untouched by the influence of the various civilisations, and was known to them, vaguely, as the region from which incursions of barbarians broke into the more civilised regions.

The small maps at the foot of the page give a diagrammatic illustration of the expansion of human knowledge about the earth's surface among the Greeks and Romans between the time of Herodotus (c. 450 B.C.) and the time of Ptolemy (c. 150 A.D.). Herodotus knew of the existence of India, but knew nothing of its shape, and the great civilisation of China lay altogether beyond his horizon. Ptolemy knew that China existed, but no more than that. The expansion of knowledge about the world and its peoples among the Greeks and Romans was thus very slight during the six centuries covered by these diagrams.

The beginnings of civilisation in the western part of the region covered by the main map took place in the two riverine districts of Egypt and Mesopotamia. The relations between these two regions are more clearly illustrated in **Plate 3.** They were brought into contact with one another at an early date ; the wanderings of Abraham ranged from Ur of the Chaldees, which was probably the chief centre of the Sumerian or Euphratic civilisation, through Syria to Egypt. Which of these two centres of development was the older, scholars are not yet ready to affirm with confidence. They probably had independent beginnings, but contributed something to each other's development. Excavators are beginning to reveal to us a third riverine civilisation, on the lower Indus, which was probably an offshoot from Sumer, but it seems to have had almost no influence upon the development of Indian civilisation, which seems to have been of much later origin. In distant China another riverine civilisation grew up, in the basins of the Hwang-ho and (later) of the Yang-tse-kiang. No direct contact seems to be traceable between the civilisation of China and those of Egypt and Babylonia. Isolated by the huge mountain-mass which is shown on the map, and by the great deserts of the north-east, the marvellous civilisation of China seems to have had from the first an isolated existence, though its influence spread over the Indo-China peninsula to the south-west of China, and over Japan, Korea and Manchuria in the north.

In the west, the riverine stage of civilisation was followed by a marine stage, when first the Minoans (whose brilliant civilisation has only recently been discovered,) and later the Phœnicians, the Greeks and (to some extent) the Etruscans made the Mediterranean the centre of the rising European civilisation, which was to be unified by the conquests of Rome. Throughout the "classical" era, and down to the great discoveries of the fifteenth and sixteenth centuries, the Mediterranean and the countries bordering upon it remained the arena of western civilisation ; these lands are, indeed, the only part of the wide area shown in the main map of which the classical geographers had any real knowledge.

Meanwhile, from Egypt, and still more from Babylonia, the impetus to progress in civilisation had passed to the uplands of the Near East : to the Hittites and the Lydians in Asia Minor, to the Assyrians in upper Mesopotamia, to the Persians and the Medians on the high ground that looks down upon Mesopotamia in the East. Here arose huge but short-lived empires which strove for the control of the Fertile Crescent that curves round the Syrian deserts from Palestine to Mesopotamia. With these wide empires first the Greeks and then the Romans were brought into contact and conflict ; and it was in struggles against them that the nascent European system of freedom-under-law underwent its first ordeals. For a time, under Alexander and his successors, this wide region of the Near East was brought under the influence of the European civilisation. But this influence was short-lived. The Romans only succeeded in preserving control over the western fringes of this area. But this was enough to ensure that Christianity, born in Palestine, should be one of the most powerful moulding influences in the development of the European civilisation.

As for India, the real beginning of her distinctive civilisation may be traced to the coming of the Aryans, about 2,000 years before Christ. But this civilisation, though it was temporarily influenced by the coming of Alexander, and by a series of barbarian irruptions from Central Asia, had its own independent existence, almost as isolated as that of China. There was, indeed, always a thin stream of trade between India and Europe, and an intermittent trickle even from China to Europe ; but the European civilisation in effect knew nothing of the great civilisations of the East, at any rate until the later middle ages.

If by the "Ancients" we mean the Greeks and the Romans, the world really known to them was but a small fragment of the wide area represented in this map.

Plate 2 illustrates the ancient civilisations of the Near East which preceded the rise of Greek and Roman civilisation. The date 1400 B.C. is chosen for the first map, **2*a***, because by that date the main powers of the Near East had got themselves into position. (1) *Egypt*, whose records date back to at least 4,000 B.C., had reached a great height of development in the Early and Middle Kingdoms before 2000 B.C. Its development had then been interrupted by the conquest of the Hyksos (c. 1800–1600), who were probably Hittites (*see* below) with a following of Semitic tribes. The expulsion of the Hyksos (1580 B.C.) was followed by a great imperialist period, when Egypt conquered Nubia and Syria, especially under Thutmose III., c. 1500 B.C. The Egyptian empire was at the height of its power under Amenhotep III. at the date of the map ; all the Semitic tribes of Syria were obedient to it ; and the other empires were all in relation with it. (2) In *Babylonia* the beginnings of civilisation were as ancient as in Egypt. The Sumerians, a non-Semitic people who lived near the mouth of the Euphrates, had invented cuneiform writing, which was adopted by all the peoples of the Near

East. Their power was subsequently merged in that of the Semitic Akkadians of Babylonia, whose empire reached its height under the great codifier Hammurabi, c. 2200 B.C.—the Amraphel of Genesis and the contemporary of Abraham. But the development of Babylon, like that of Egypt, had been checked by a barbarian irruption—that of the Aryan Kassites (c. 1800–1200 B.C.): on all sides the barbarian irruptions of c. 1800 B.C. mark an epoch like the later barbarian irruptions into the Roman Empire. (3) The *Semitic* peoples, who probably sprang from Arabia, occupied the whole area (coloured green on the map) from the mountains of Persia and Armenia to the Mediterranean: a wide crescent of settled ground, from Palestine through Mesopotamia to the Persian gulf, curving round the great desert whence Bedouin movements continually sprang. Apart from Babylonia, the greatest of the Semitic peoples were the *Assyrians*, who were beginning to be active at the date of the map, and were later (*see* 2*d*) to unite nearly the whole Semitic area under their rule; the *Amorites*, who stretched from Syria into Northern Mesopotamia; the *Canaanites*, who occupied the coastlands of Syria, and were beginning to be active in trade in the Phoenician cities; and a multitude of smaller tribes, among whom the Habiru (? Hebrews) are mentioned as giving trouble in the Amarna letters. The Semitic peoples drew their civilisation partly from Babylon, partly from Egypt, and linked the two. (4) The *Hittite* empire, whose greatness has only recently been disclosed by archaeological research, had its centre in south-east Asia Minor (Cappadocia) and the Taurus mountains, whence they waged frequent war against the

FIG. 1.—THE MINOAN CENTRES IN CRETE

Egyptians and other Powers. Their greatness was at its height at the date of the map, 1400 B.C. They had only recently emerged, and had probably been the chief disturbing factor in the irruptions of c. 1800 B.C. There were also scattered Hittite tribes in Syria and Palestine: Abraham bought his grave from a Hittite clan. It is not known to what stock the Hittites belonged, but they were not Semites. Their neighbours and rivals were the people of *Mitanni*, in North Mesopotamia—an Indo-European tribe, probably related to the Medes. (5) In Crete and the Aegean Sea a brilliant civilisation, known as *Minoan*, was at its height at the date of the map. Its existence has only been disclosed in the twentieth century by archaeological research. The Minoans were not Greeks; their downfall was probably due to the invasions of the Greeks from the north; but Greek civilisation owed much to them. *Cnossus*, in Crete, was the centre of a sea-empire of which Greek legends and Egyptian monuments preserve traces. *Mycenae* in European Greece was a secondary centre of Minoan civilisation, and *Troy* (2*c*), at the mouth of the Dardanelles, was another. The influence of the Minoans spread as far west as Sicily and South Italy, where their relics have been discovered.

The second map, 2*b*, illustrates the geography of Greece as it is described by Homer, for the period of the Trojan War (c. 1200 B.C.). The first wave of Greek conquest, that of the "Achaeans," had displaced the Minoan kingdom, while still keeping its Greek centre, Mycenae, as its capital; and the Trojan War was an expedition of all the Achaean chiefs. The second wave of Greek conquest, that of the Dorians (c. 1000 B.C.) brought about a complete reconstruction of the political geography of Greece, which governed the great age of Greek history. The Homeric poems (? c. 850 B.C.) preserve the memory of the older geography, here represented.

The third map, 2*d*, shows, at its height, the empire of the Assyrians, who were the dominating factor in the Near East from c. 1000 B.C. to c. 600 B.C., the older Powers of Egypt, Babylonia, and the Hittites having fallen into decrepitude. Between the date of the first map on this plate, and the date of this, the Israelites had settled in Palestine, and had reached the culminating point of their power in the empire of David (c. 1000 B.C.: *see* **Plate 4**). The history of the divided kingdoms of Israel and Judah was dominated by the struggle against Assyria, which forms the background of the greater part of the Old Testament. The great age of Assyrian history began with Tiglath-Pileser III. (745), and reached its height under Sennacherib (705) and Esarhaddon (681). These monarchs ruled over the whole of Mesopotamia and Syria, thus uniting the whole Semitic stock outside Arabia; they also occupied Egypt for a time. Their most dangerous enemies were, in the north, the *Medes* (Indo-European peoples in the uplands of Iran), the kingdom of *Urartu* (in Armenia: another ancient Power recently rescued from oblivion by archaeology); and in the south the ancient realm of *Elam*, and the *Chaldaeans* who were reviving the civilisation of ancient Babylonia. At the end of the seventh century B.C. the Medes and the Chaldeans united and rapidly overwhelmed Assyria (fall of Nineveh, 612 B.C.), which was more completely ruined than any other empire in history. For a short time a Chaldaean Empire took the place of the Assyrians, reaching its height under Nebuchadnezzar (605 B.C.); while the Medes extended their conquests in the north, and overthrew the empire of *Phrygia*, which had been built up in central Asia Minor by invaders from Europe. But both the Median and the Chaldaean empires were short-lived; in the middle of the sixth century both were overthrown and incorporated by Cyrus in the vast Persian empire (*see* **Plate 5*b***).

Plate 3. This map gives a fuller treatment of the region in which the first civilisations arose, and the lands between them. It shows, in brown, the wide desert regions which separated Babylonia from Egypt—the most difficult of geographical obstacles to intercourse. The deserts were, of course, crossed by caravan routes, using the oases, some of which are marked on the map. Round them curves the Fertile Crescent, with its agricultural (green) and pastoral (yellow) regions, which was the home of the chief Semitic peoples. A glance at this map is enough to show why Palestine was the inevitable clash-point in the constantly renewed conflict between the Egyptian Empire and the successive empires of the Euphrates and Tigris valleys—Babylonia, Assyria, Persia; and why Megiddo was the natural scene of their Armageddon.

The second map (3*b*) illustrates in greater detail the area of the Egyptian Empire; though it is necessary to check this map by the main map, which shows how narrow was the peopled region of Egypt south of the delta, and how inaccessible except from the north. Egypt, indeed, may be compared to a lily, with the well watered region of the delta as the flower, the Nile valley as the stem, and the region of the Fayoum, round lake Moeris, as a bud. The true Egypt—occupied by a white-skinned people who gave birth to the Egyptian civilisation—extended only as far south as the First Cataract, where "Nubia," the land of black-skinned peoples, began. During the period of the Egyptian Empire's greatest power, its sway was extended as far southwards as the Sixth Cataract, but this region (part of the modern Sudan) was never fully incorporated in Egypt. The flat and well-watered lands of the delta never played so great a part in history as the narrow valley of the river; and there was always a clear distinction between Upper Egypt, with its capital at Thebes (temples of Karnak) and Lower and Middle Egypt, with its capital at Memphis (modern Cairo, where the pyramids declare the greatness of its rulers). But these two regions were, according to legend, united as early as the First Dynasty, perhaps 5,000 years B.C. Lower Egypt controlled the western part of the Sinai Peninsula, with its copper and turquoise mines; upper Egypt had ports on the Red Sea, whence trade was carried on in gold, gems, spices and hides. From the ports of the delta trade was carried on with the peoples of Syria and the western Mediterranean, including the Greeks. Protected by the desert and the sea, Egypt could live an isolated life in security. The ambitions of her rulers tempted them to conquer an external empire, and for about 500 years, from the 17th to the 12th century B.C., they controlled most of Syria, and gave civilisation to its peoples. But this empire was broken by the attacks of the Hittites from the north, and of the "peoples of the sea" (probably Minoans) a section of whom, known as the Philistines, were allowed to settle on the coast of Palestine, under the nominal suzerainty of the Pharaohs. After this period of imperialism, Egypt was the victim of successive conquests, first by the Assyrians, then by the Persians, then by Alexander the Great and his Macedonians, and ultimately by the Romans. Egypt was drawn into the common life of the Mediterranean world, and her great Greek port in the Mediterranean, Alexandria, became one of the principal centres of Greek thought and later of Christianity. Her own civilisation became stagnant, though she contributed to the ferment of mystical religious thought which marked the first century of the Christian era. But through all these conquests the life of her people went on unchangingly.

Plate 4 illustrates the history of the Israelites down to the time of Christ.

The first map illustrates the slow conquest of parts of Palestine by the tribes of Israel, and their long struggles with the Semitic Canaanites, whom they gradually absorbed, and with the non-Semitic Philistines. Their piecemeal conquests divided them into four separate blocks. Two tribes, Judah and Simeon, seem to have come in from the southern desert: Simeon melted away among the Bedouin tribes; Judah had a hard struggle to establish a foothold on the high ground above the Dead Sea, and could not even conquer Jerusalem from the Canaanites until the time of David. The other tribes entered the country from the east of the Jordan; the tribes of Reuben and Gad, and half of the tribe of Manasseh settled on the further side of Jordan and formed a second block. The most powerful tribes—Ephraim, Benjamin and half of Manasseh—occupied the highlands round Mounts Ebal and Gerizim, with Shechem as their holy place, but only slowly conquered the fertile plain of Jezreel and the sea coast. In the north—in Galilee and northwards—the four tribes of Dan, Naphtali, Issachar and Zebulun established themselves with difficulty. First Ephraim, under Gideon and Abimelech, then Benjamin, under Saul, strove to bring these divided clans under a single control, and to keep the surrounding tribes at bay. Finally, about 980, Judah under David established for the first time the unity of the Children of Israel.

The second map illustrates (*a*) the consolidated kingdom of David, with its capital in the recently conquered city of Jerusalem, and its control over neighbouring tribes; (*b*) the wide extension of the Davidic empire under Solomon which almost amounted to a hegemony of Syria; and (*c*) its rapid collapse after his death, and the formation of the tiny kingdoms of Israel and Judah.

The third map shows the political condition of Palestine at the time of Christ: it is now a Roman province, including several vassal States held by the family of Herod, one of which contained Galilee. Two small plans show respectively Jerusalem as it was under David and Solomon and down to the exile, and as it was in the time of Christ; and a final small map shows the chief journeys of St. Paul.

Plate 5. The first map on this Plate (5*a*) illustrates the work of three sea-going peoples who brought the Western Mediterranean into contact with the civilisation of the Eastern Mediterranean. First among these, in order of time, were the *Phoenicians*—Canaanites from the cities of the Syrian coast, especially Tyre. Their greatest period was between the fall of the Egyptian Empire in Syria, and the conquest of Syria by the Assyrians—c. 1200–750 B.C.; Solomon's ally, Hiram of Tyre, ruled at the period of their greatest splendour, c. 950 B.C. They are said to have established themselves in Southern Spain (Tarshish or Tartessus) as early as 1100 B.C. They planted colonies in Cyprus, Western Sicily, Malta, Sardinia, Corsica, and along the north coast of Africa. The greatest of these, Carthage, traditionally dates from 813 B.C. It became the centre of the Punic Empire when Tyre fell under the dominion of Assyria and Persia. There was constant conflict between the Phoenicians and the Greeks when the latter began (in the eighth century B.C.) to invade their monopoly of sea-going trade.—The *Etruscans* appear to have migrated from Asia Minor to Western Italy at an unknown date. The Greeks, in the eighth century, found them planted, with twelve thriving cities, in Etruria; they also occupied the Po valley; they later (seventh century) conquered Latium and Campania; and their pirate-ships dominated the Tyrrhenian or Etruscan sea, where they frequently fought the Greeks.—The *Greeks* spread outwards from continental Greece in two great stages: (1) At a very early date, say from 1200 B.C. onwards, Achaeans and Aeolians, and later Ionians, settled in the Aegean islands and the coast of Asia Minor; the Achaeans or Aeolians in the north; the Ionians farther south (Phocaea, Chios, Samos, Ephesus, Miletus); after the Dorian migration into Greece, Dorian colonists spread to the southern islands, to Crete, and to the southern part of the west coast of Asia Minor. (2) Between 750 and 550 B.C. there was a remarkable outburst of colonising activities. Some hundreds of Greek colonies were planted (*a*) on the north shore of the Aegean (mainly by Chalcis and Eretria, cities of Euboea); (*b*) in the sea of Marmora, the Bosporus, and all round the Black Sea (mainly by Miletus and Megara); (*c*) in the Ionian Islands and the coast of Epirus (mainly by Corinth); (*d*) in Southern Italy, which came to be known as Magna Graecia (mainly by the Achaeans of the Gulf of Corinth, but also by Chalcis, which founded Cumae, whence the alphabet spread to the Latins); (*e*) in Sicily (mainly by Chalcis in the north-east, and by Corinth, Megara, and other Dorian cities in the south-east and south); (*f*) in the Western Mediterranean, from the Alps to the Pyrenees, in Corsica and on the west coast of Spain, notably Massilia (Marseilles) (mainly Phocaean); (*g*) on the north coast of Africa, in Cyrenaica (the island of Thera).

The rapid expansion of these three naval Powers represents the first extension of civilisation into the west.

The second map (5*b*) illustrates the gigantic Persian Empire, which with incredible swiftness incorporated all the civilisations of the East in a single vast dominion, in the second half of the sixth century B.C. The Persians

FIG. 2.—BATTLE OF SALAMIS

were an Indo-European people, akin to the Medes: their home, Persia proper, corresponds to the modern district of Fars. The Persian Cyrus, ruling over a little kingdom called Anshan, rebelled in 549 against the Medes, and made himself master of their whole vast empire; overthrew and annexed the Lydian Empire of Croesus (546), with its capital at Sardes, and then came in contact with the Greeks of Ionia, whom he forced to submit; captured Babylon (539) and made himself master of the whole Babylonian Empire, including Phoenicia and Syria where he restored the Jews to Jerusalem; and also extended his sway widely over the countries to the east, possibly as far as Bactria and Afghanistan. Cyrus' son Cambyses conquered Egypt (525), and the whole eastern world was brought under a single rule. The next king, Darius (521–486), had at first to deal with revolts; but he suppressed them and gave to his empire an efficient organisation under twenty satrapies or viceroyalties; he extended his power eastwards as far as the Indus and sea of Aral; he invaded Europe by the Bosporus, and crossed the Danube; and it was this gigantic Power which, from 490 B.C. onwards, menaced the very existence of the little Greek states.

The double-page **Plate 6-7** is intended to illustrate the whole history of Greece proper. The boundaries shown are those of the fifth century B.C. The map is coloured physically, to bring out the mountain features which naturally split up continental Greece into a large number of separate city-states, each with its dependent countryside. The map shows the relationship of Greece Proper to the northern realm of Macedonia, which was to be the means, under Alexander, of disseminating Greek culture over a great part of Asia. The map shows only European Greece: the islands of the Aegean and the Greek-settled coastland of Asia Minor, are shown in the next map, **Plate 8.**

The smaller maps on this plate show (*a*) the principal buildings of ancient Athens, clustered round the great fortified rock of the Acropolis; on which stood the Parthenon and the Erechtheum; (*b*) the extent of Athens in the time of Pericles, with the Long Walls, planned by Themistocles, which linked it to the port of the Piræus, thus making the centre of a maritime empire independent of attacks on the mainland; (*c*) the Propontis, through which the main trade of Greece with the Black Sea passed, and the numerous Greek settlements on its shores. One interpretation of the Trojan war is that it was a struggle for the control of this important trade-route, which could be interrupted by Troy (Ilium); (*d*) the island of Crete, which was the centre of the prehistoric Minoan Empire, but played an unimportant part in Greek history.

Plate 8 is a supplement to **Plate 6-7**, showing not only continental Greece, but the islands of the Aegean and the wealthy Greek cities on the coast of Asia Minor, through which the Greeks were brought into conflict with the Persians. The map is coloured to show the four racial or linguistic groups which the Greeks recognised among themselves. Green is the colour of the Ionians, whose only representative on the mainland was Athens, the natural capital of the Ionian peoples, though in the earliest period this pre-eminence might have been claimed by the great colonising city of Miletus in Asia Minor. A mere glance at the distribution of the green colour in this map is enough to show why Athens became the capital of a maritime empire. Of these four races: (1) the *Achaeans* represent the ruling race of the heroic age, displaced by later migrations; (2) the *Dorians* were the latest Greek immigrants in the tenth century B.C.; Sparta, the greatest Dorian centre, retained leadership throughout the classic period; (3) the *Ionians* were in the classic age the chief rivals of the Dorians and the chief source of Greek art and thought, first in Asia Minor and later in Athens; they were probably, in the main, not only pre-Dorian but pre-Achaean; (4) the *Aeolians* broadly represent all the other pre-Dorian Hellenic peoples. These divisions have not much historical value, except that they counted for a good deal among the Greeks themselves—especially the distinction between Dorian and Ionian, which was brought into sharp antithesis by the conflict of the Spartans and the Athenians.

Plate 9*a* shows the division of Greece between the two sides in the Peloponnesian War. The Athenian Empire, beginning as a confederacy of maritime states for common action against the Persians after the Persian invasion, developed into an empire when the treasury of the league was transferred from the sacred island of Delos to Athens (450 B.C.). Its members were later grouped into five districts, (1) Ionia. (2) Hellespont, (3) Thrace, (4) Caria, (5) the islands. Direct Athenian settlements or *cleruchies* were made in Euboea, Andros, Naxos, Aegina, Melos, Scyros, Imbros, Lemnos, Sinope, several cities in Chalcidice, and the island of Lesbos. The critical struggle for Syracuse is illustrated by **Fig. 3.**

The principal map on **Plate 9*b*** shows the huge empire of Alexander, who brought all Greece under his sway and then conquered the Persian Empire (334–323 B.C.). This conquest was the means of extending the influence of Greek civilisation over the East, as far as the Indus valley;

and this period of expansion is known as the " Hellenistic " period. Alexander's conquering march is shown on the map. An empire which was so swiftly created could not be expected to last long. It broke up into sections under

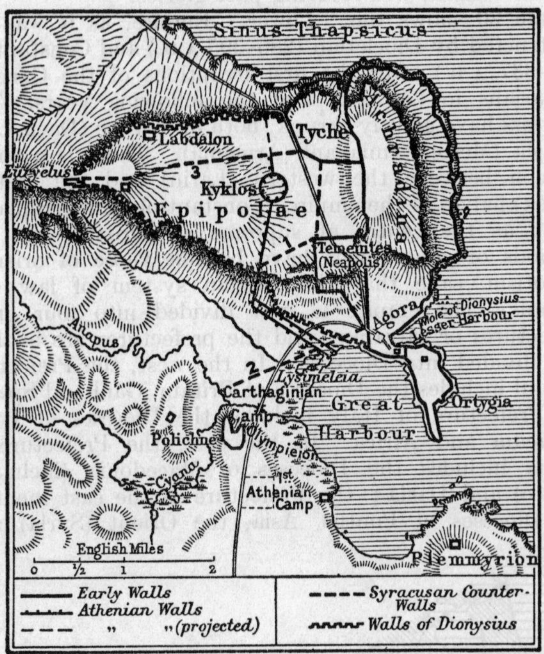

FIG. 3.—SYRACUSE

Alexander's generals, who are known as the Diadochi or successors. This division is shown in the smaller map, **9***c*. The chief of these kingdoms were : (1) Asia Minor and Syria under Seleucus and his successors the Seleucids; (2) Egypt under the Ptolemies ; (3) Macedonia under the successors of Antigonus Gonatas ; (4) Pergamum under the Attalids. It was with these Powers that the expanding empire of Rome was brought into conflict ; their weakness made its conquests easier, and they were gradually merged in the Roman Empire.

Plate 10–11. This double-page plate is intended to illustrate the whole history of Rome and her Empire. On the main map, which is meant for general reference, note the way in which the empire was linked together by great roads, only the principal of which can be shown. It is probable that transport on these great roads was as swift and efficient as at any period in European history down to the coming of the railway ; while the sea formed an equally valuable means of holding this Mediterranean empire together. Note, secondly, the distinction between the limits of the empire as they were when the empire was first systematically organised under Augustus, and the extensions subsequently made down to the time of Trajan : these extensions, shown by a scarlet line, include, in the west, Britain and Mauretania ; in the centre, Dacia ; in the east Cappadocia, Armenia, Mesopotamia and inland Syria. If Augustus' attempt to subjugate northern Germany had not been disastrously defeated, the Roman Empire might have had a shorter and more defensible frontier, along the line of the Elbe, the Bohemian mountains and the Carpathians.

The first of the smaller maps (**11***b*) shows (*a*) the area of the Carthaginian Empire, which was the first external foe of Rome, then (240 B.C.) a purely Italian power ; and (*b*) the stages in the growth of the Roman Empire. The first advances were due to the Punic wars, of which the first gave to Rome the islands of Corsica and Sardinia, and the second Sicily and the Carthaginian coast of Spain. Then came a period of strenuous warfare, extending over eighty years (201–120 B.C.), which gave to Rome Cisalpine Gaul, bringing Italy up to the Alps, the greater part of Spain, south-eastern Gaul (Narbonensis), the home-territory of Carthage (which became the province of Africa), Macedonia, Greece, and the province of Asia (western Asia Minor) : by this time (120 B.C.) Rome had become the dominant power in the Mediterranean. The third stage—the last century of the Republic, down to the death of Julius Cæsar, 44 B.C.—saw Cæsar's conquest of Gaul, the conquest of the African coast (Numidia and Cyrenaica), Syria, and the north and south coasts of Asia Minor. Before his death (14 A.D.) the emperor Augustus had completed the conquest of Spain, subjugated the Alpine regions of Rhaetia, Noricum and Pannonia, and the Balkan regions of Illyricum and Moesia, thus securing the whole line of the Danube as a frontier ; he had annexed Egypt, and had brought the central part of Asia Minor under his control ; the boundaries of the empire had been rounded off. His successors added Britain, Mauretania Thrace, Cappadocia and inland Syria ; the final conquests, which were to be impermanent, included Dacia, in Europe, and Armenia and Mesopotamia in Asia.

The second of the smaller maps (**10***a*) shows how Augustus divided the empire between himself and the Senate for administrative purposes, keeping for himself the warlike frontier provinces where armies had to be maintained, and leaving to the control of the Senate the more peaceful provinces.

Finally, this Plate contains two plans of the city of Rome, one for the Republican, the other for the Imperial period.

Plate 12-13. This large double plate, like the corresponding plate of Greece, is intended for general reference in studying the whole history of Italy. It shows (by underlining) the numerous Greek colonies of " Magna Graecia." It also shows, in different symbols, the Roman and the Latin colonies by means of which the country was held down as it was conquered ; and the great network of roads by which it was held together, and all its parts were made swiftly accessible. Note how the organising genius of Augustus extended the northern boundary of Italy, the heart of the empire, from the indefensible foothills of the mountains to the watershed.—The two plans, which show the forum of republican Rome, and the grandiose fora of imperial Rome, may be regarded as supplements to the plans of the city on the preceding plate.

Plate 14 is a politically coloured supplement to **Plate 12-13**, meant to illustrate, in particular, the methods whereby Rome conquered Italy. The process begins with the unification, after much fighting, of Latium, of which a more detailed map is given in the inset, **Plate 14***b*. The second inset, **14***c*, is meant to illustrate roughly the distribution of the racial stocks in Italy at an early date : the flood of conquered slaves which later poured into the peninsula turned it into a *colluvies gentium*. In the main map the Roman and Latin colonies are indicated, in most cases with the dates of their foundation. Note that Italy Proper excluded the whole valley of the Po and its tributaries. This, the most fertile part of Italy, had once been largely occupied by the Etruscans, while in the east and west the Venetian and Ligurian races remained distinct. Conquered by the invading Gauls, this district became known as Gallia Cisalpina, and even after it was conquered, it was administered as a provincia until Augustus revised the imperial system. Its boundary was the little river Rubicon, which Cæsar crossed when he declared war upon the republic.

Plates 15 and **16**, coloured politically, show more clearly than is possible in **Plate 10–11** (with which they should be compared) Augustus' division of the Empire into provinces. The post-Augustan provinces are coloured buff. The whole coast of the Black Sea was under imperial control, but only the Crimean peninsula was organised as a province.

Plate 17, while primarily designed to illustrate the Roman occupation of Britain, also gives the names and distribution of the British tribes whom the Romans found in the island ; and, being coloured physically, it shows how hills, forests, and marshes broke up the country—obstacles which the Roman roads largely overcame. Though the Romans held Britain for nearly four centuries, little is known about their organisation : it is not even possible to give the boundaries of the provinces into which the island was divided. But note (1) the system of fortification against the northern savages—more fully shown in the inset, 17*b* ; (2) the road-system, with London as its centre, because London was the lowest crossing-place on the Thames for the roads coming from the south-east coast ; (3) the location of the three main armies of occupation (legions), at York, Chester, and Caerleon ; (4) the few organised towns—Colchester, Gloucester, Lincoln, York, and St. Albans ; (5) the Saxon shore (from the Wash to the Severn), fortified during the fourth century as a protection against the German pirates.

Plate 18–19. This plate is intended to illustrate the geographical relations between western civilisation with the Roman Empire as its guardian, and the other civilisations which existed in the world before the breakdown of the Roman Empire began. The map is coloured to show broadly the character of the soil, and of its natural products. Note that there are three fertile and productive regions, each of which gave birth to a civilisation of its own—Europe in the west, India and China in the east. But note also that they are separated from one another by huge barriers of mountains, deserts, or semi-desert countries, which occupy the central area in the map. Out of this region nomadic tribes burst in at intervals upon each of the great civilisations, which strove in vain to keep them at arm's length. For this purpose, the frontier-fortresses of the Roman Empire may be compared with the Great Wall of China. About 200 A.D., the date of this map, the Chinese Empire, which was probably the most advanced of these civilisations, had extended its nominal sway over a vast region of Central Asia, in the hope of keeping the barbarians in check. India (then passing through one of her periodic phases of disorder), saw a large part of her richest territories under the control of a Central Asiatic dynasty ; Rome had pushed out her frontiers to the north and east in the hope of reducing the danger, but was soon to lose these gains. But between these rival civilisations—all threatened, from the same source, by a common danger—there was practically no contact.

The two insets show two stages in ancient history of India. In 250 B.C., when Rome had not yet begun the conflict with Carthage that was to make her the predominant power in the Mediterranean, almost the whole of India was under the enlightened and tolerant rule of the great Asoka, one of the noblest of monarchs. In 400 A.D., when the Roman Empire was already in ruins, a new Indian Empire had arisen under the Guptas and for a moment it promised to reduce the whole sub-continent to subjection ; but before the English conquest India was never to know unity. At the same period of collapse in the west, the Sassanid kingdom, heir of the Parthians and of the Persians, was reviving past glories.

Plate 20 shows the " Lower " Empire, as it was reconstructed by Diocletian (286–305 A.D.) and Constantine (306–337 A.D.) after the first irruptions of the German barbarians in 250 A.D. and the following years. The frontiers have greatly shrunk, both in Europe (Dacia) and in Asia (Mesopotamia and Armenia). There is a sharp division between the western (Latin) and the eastern (Greek) halves of the empire. Constantinople has replaced Rome as the centre of supreme authority ; and the methods of government have become those of oriental despotism, save that the Roman system of law still prevails. The empire is now divided into four great Prefectures or satrapies, and the prefectures are in their turn divided into Dioceses. In the west, the Prefecture of Gaul includes the Dioceses of Britain, Gaul and Spain ; the Prefecture of Italy includes the Dioceses of Italy, Illyricum and Africa. In the east, the Prefecture of Illyria includes the Dioceses of Macedonia (including Greece) and Dacia ; the Prefecture of the east includes the Dioceses of Pontus. Asia, the Orient (Syria) and

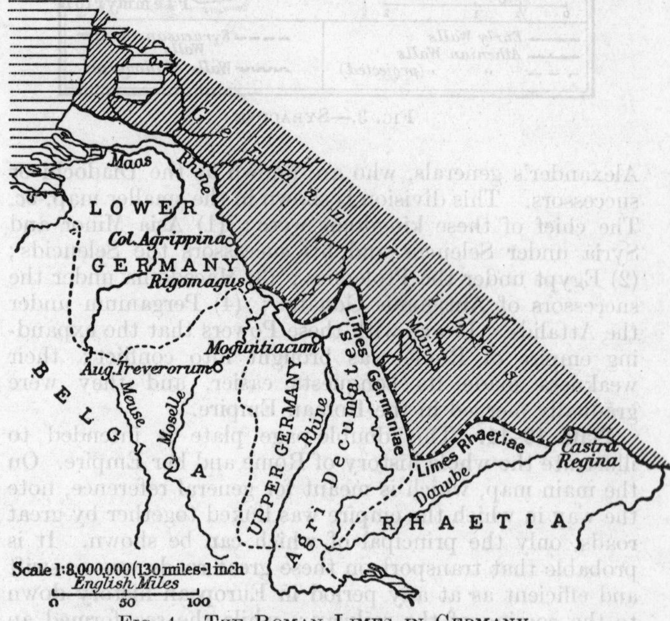

FIG. 4.—THE ROMAN LIMES IN GERMANY

Egypt. Along the weak northern frontier the German tribes are always dangerous and the fortifications of the Limes between the Rhine and the Danube have not availed to prevent the occupation of the angle between the two rivers by the Allemanni and Suevi. These barbarians were being enlisted in large numbers to fill the depleted ranks of the legions. Some of them had been converted to Christianity, which had become, under Constantine, almost the official religion of the empire. Their real veneration for the great structure of civilised society did not prevent them from desiring to enrich themselves by overrunning it ; and the downfall of the Empire under whose shelter the civilisation of Europe had absorbed the learning of Greece, the law of Rome, and the religion of Christianity was at hand. " Ancient " history had reached its term.

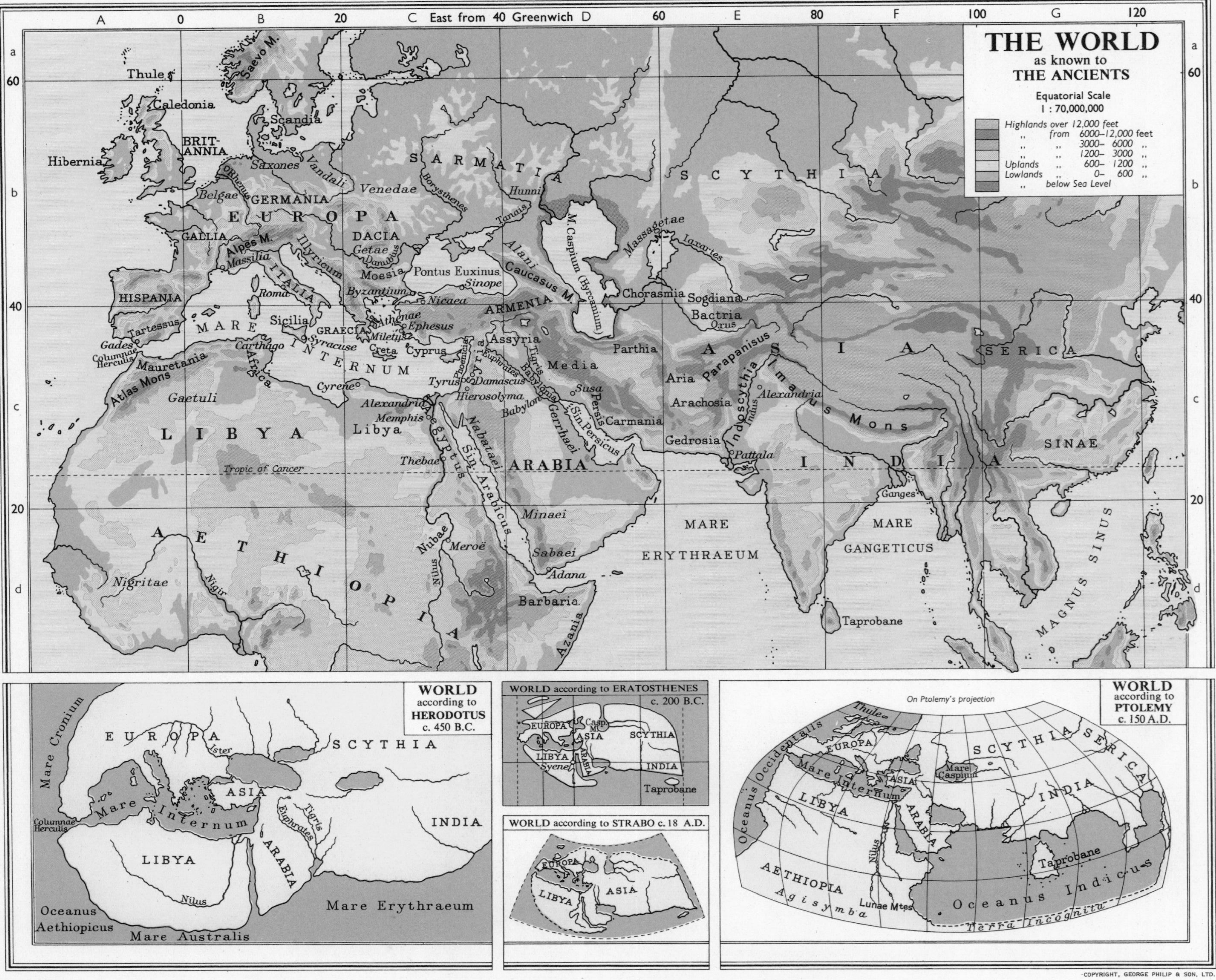
THE WORLD
as known to
THE ANCIENTS
Equatorial Scale
1 : 70,000,000
Highlands over 12,000 feet
,, from 6000–12,000 feet
,, ,, 3000– 6000 ,,
,, ,, 1200– 3000 ,,
Uplands ,, 600– 1200 ,,
Lowlands ,, 0– 600 ,,
,, below Sea Level
East from 40 Greenwich
EUROPA
SCYTHIA
SARMATIA
ASIA
INDIA
SERICA
SINAE
LIBYA
AETHIOPIA
ARABIA
MARE INTERNUM
MARE ERYTHRAEUM
MARE GANGETICUS
MAGNUS SINUS
Thule
Caledonia
BRITANNIA
Hibernia
Scandia
Saevo M.
Saxones
Vandali
Venedae
GERMANIA
Belgae
Rhenus
GALLIA
Alpes M.
Massilia
HISPANIA
Tartessus
Gades
Columnae Herculis
Mauretania
Atlas Mons
Gaetuli
ITALIA
Roma
Illyricum
DACIA
Getae
Danubius
Moesia
Byzantium
Pontus Euxinus
Sinope
Nicaea
Borysthenes
Tanais
Hunni
Alani
Caucasus M.
ARMENIA
M. Caspium (Hyrcanium)
Massagetae
Iaxartes
Chorasmia
Sogdiana
Bactria
Oxus
Parthia
Aria
Parapanisus
Arachosia
Gedrosia
Indoscythia
Indus
Alexandria
Imaus Mons
Pattala
Ganges
Taprobane
Carmania
Persis
Sin. Persicus
Susa
Media
Assyria
Tigris
Euphrates
Babylonia
Babylon
Gerrhaei
Syria
Phoenicia
Tyrus
Damascus
Hierosolyma
Nabataei
Sin. Arabicus
Minaei
Sabaei
Adana
Barbaria
Azania
Sicilia
GRAECIA
Athenae
Ephesus
Miletus
Syracuse
Creta
Cyprus
Carthago
Africa
Cyrene
Alexandria
Memphis
Libya
Aegyptus
Thebae
Tropic of Cancer
Nubae
Meroë
Nilus
Nigritae
Nigir

WORLD according to HERODOTUS c. 450 B.C.
EUROPA
Ister
SCYTHIA
Mare Cronium
ASIA
Mare Internum
Columnae Herculis
Euphrates
Tigris
INDIA
LIBYA
ARABIA
Nilus
Oceanus Aethiopicus
Mare Australis
Mare Erythraeum

WORLD according to ERATOSTHENES c. 200 B.C.
EUROPA
Casp. M.
ASIA
SCYTHIA
LIBYA
Syene
ARABIA
INDIA
Taprobane

WORLD according to STRABO c. 18 A.D.
EUROPA
LIBYA
ASIA

WORLD according to PTOLEMY c. 150 A.D.
On Ptolemy's projection
Thule
Oceanus Occidentalis
EUROPA
Mare Internum
ASIA
Mare Caspium
SCYTHIA
SERICA
INDIA
LIBYA
ARABIA
Nilus
Taprobane
AETHIOPIA
Agisymba
Lunae Mtes
Oceanus Indicus
Terra Incognita

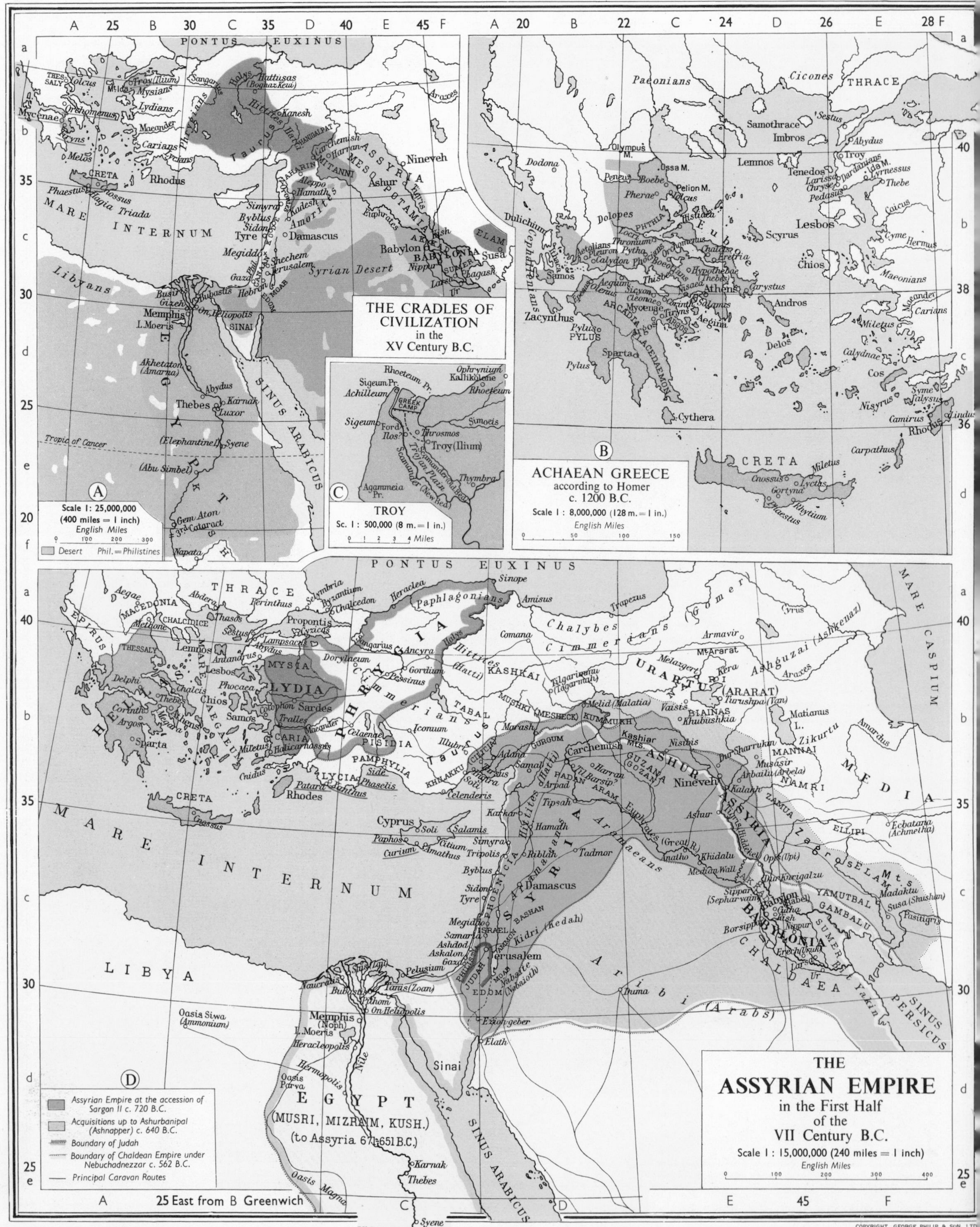
THE CRADLES OF CIVILIZATION
in the
XV Century B.C.
Scale 1: 25,000,000
(400 miles = 1 inch)
English Miles
0 100 200 300
Desert Phil. = Philistines
TROY
Sc. 1 : 500,000 (8 m. = 1 in.)
0 1 2 3 4 Miles
ACHAEAN GREECE
according to Homer
c. 1200 B.C.
Scale 1 : 8,000,000 (128 m. = 1 in.)
English Miles
0 50 100 150
THE
ASSYRIAN EMPIRE
in the First Half
of the
VII Century B.C.
Scale 1 : 15,000,000 (240 miles = 1 inch)
English Miles
0 100 200 300 400
Assyrian Empire at the accession of Sargon II c. 720 B.C.
Acquisitions up to Ashurbanipal (Ashnapper) c. 640 B.C.
Boundary of Judah
Boundary of Chaldean Empire under Nebuchadnezzar c. 562 B.C.
Principal Caravan Routes
25 East from B Greenwich

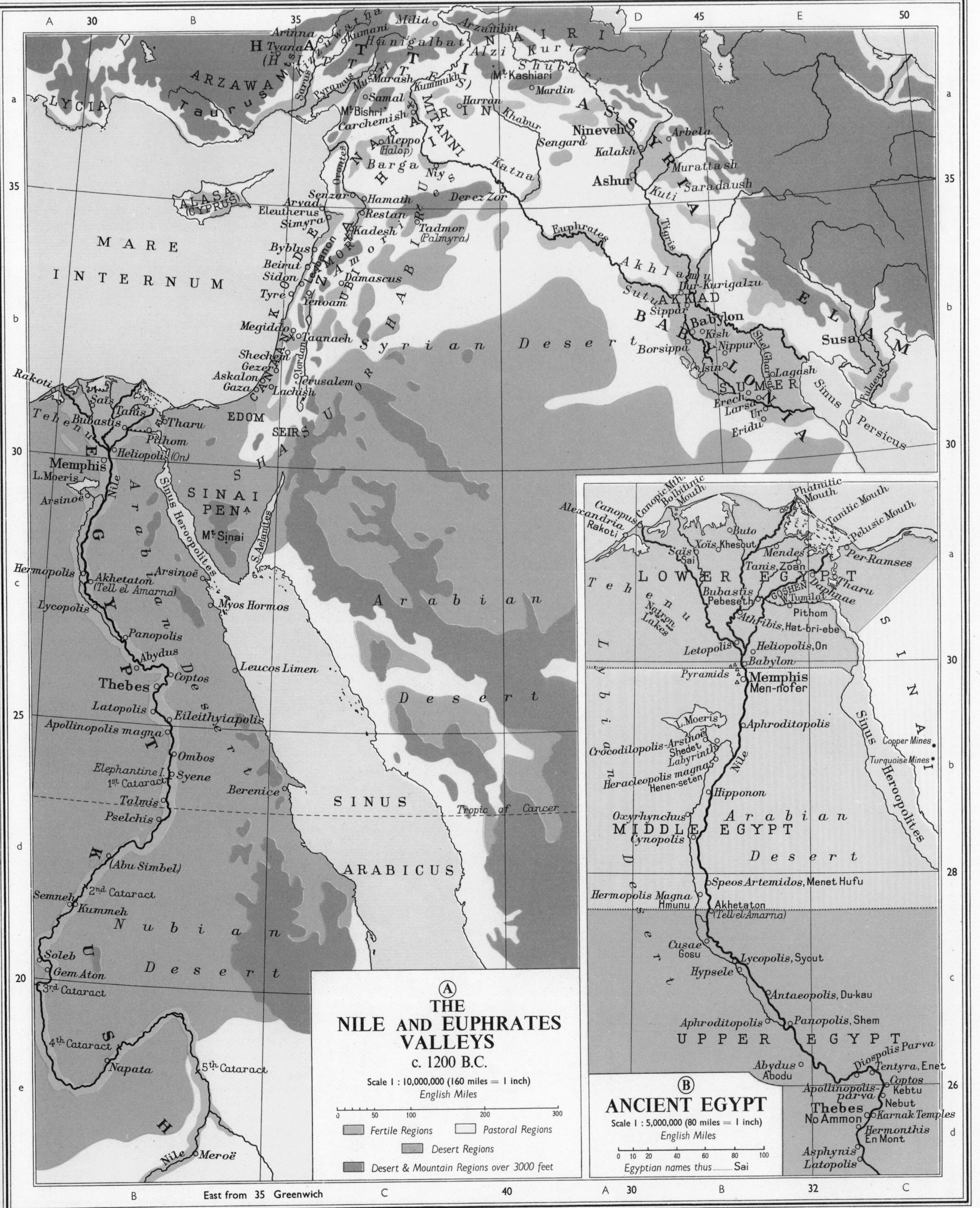
A
THE
NILE AND EUPHRATES
VALLEYS
c. 1200 B.C.
Scale 1 : 10,000,000 (160 miles = 1 inch)
English Miles
0 50 100 200 300
Fertile Regions
Pastoral Regions
Desert Regions
Desert & Mountain Regions over 3000 feet
East from 35 Greenwich
MARE INTERNUM
Syrian Desert
Arabian Desert
Nubian Desert
SINUS ARABICUS
Tropic of Cancer
SINAI PENA
Mt Sinai
EDOM
SEIRS
Memphis
Thebes
Babylon
Nineveh
Ashur
Susa
Sinus Persicus
B
ANCIENT EGYPT
Scale 1 : 5,000,000 (80 miles = 1 inch)
English Miles
0 10 20 40 60 80 100
Egyptian names thus.........Sai
LOWER EGYPT
MIDDLE EGYPT
UPPER EGYPT
Arabian Desert
Libyan Desert
Sinus Heroopolites
Copper Mines
Turquoise Mines

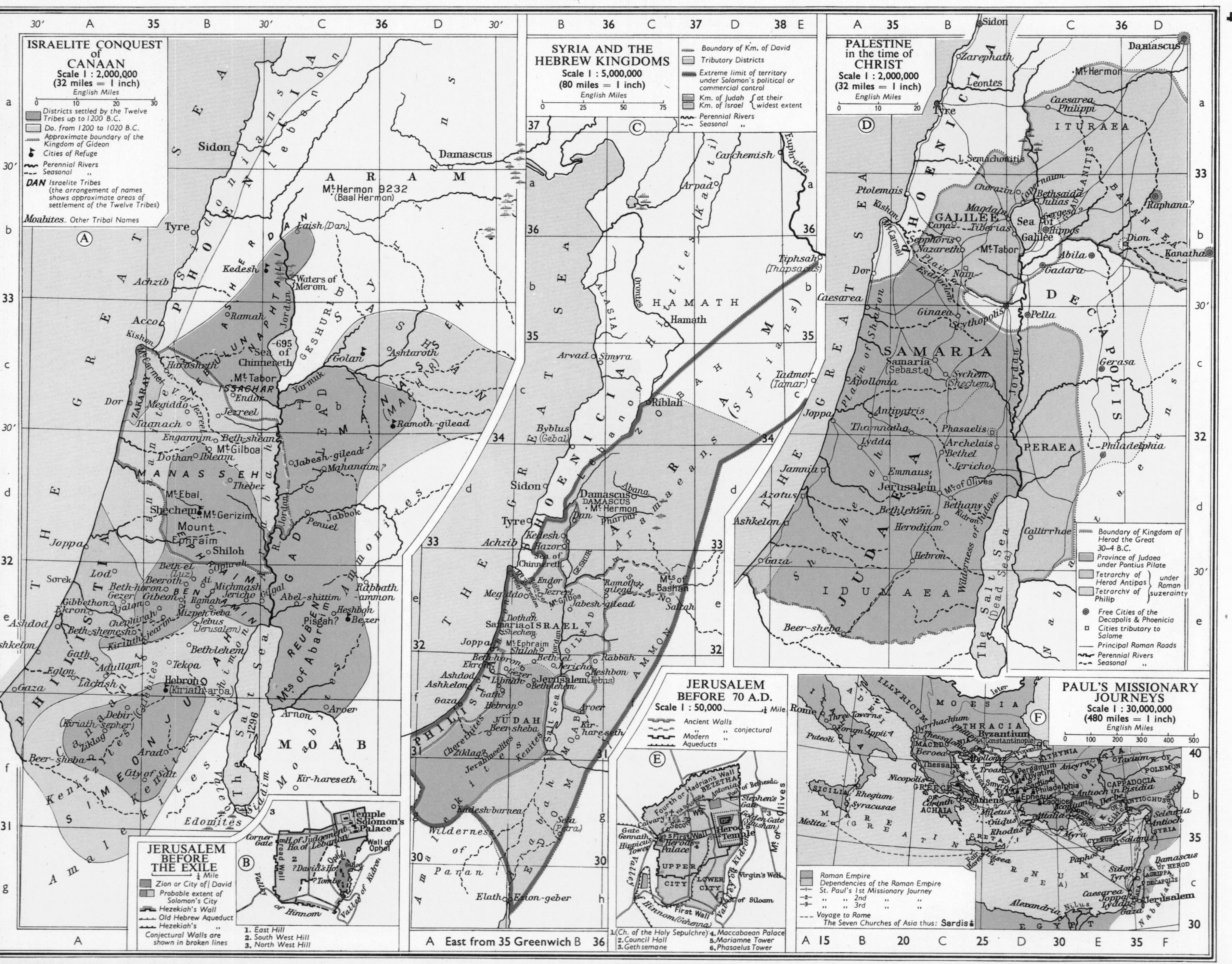
ISRAELITE CONQUEST of CANAAN
Scale 1 : 2,000,000
(32 miles = 1 inch)
English Miles
Districts settled by the Twelve Tribes up to 1200 B.C.
Do. from 1200 to 1020 B.C.
Approximate boundary of the Kingdom of Gideon
Cities of Refuge
Perennial Rivers
Seasonal
DAN Israelite Tribes (the arrangement of names shows approximate areas of settlement of the Twelve Tribes)
Moabites.. Other Tribal Names
JERUSALEM BEFORE THE EXILE
¼ Mile
Zion or City of David
Probable extent of Solomon's City
Hezekiah's Wall
Old Hebrew Aqueduct
Hezekiah's
Conjectural Walls are shown in broken lines
1. East Hill
2. South West Hill
3. North West Hill
SYRIA AND THE HEBREW KINGDOMS
Scale 1 : 5,000,000
(80 miles = 1 inch)
English Miles
Boundary of Km. of David
Tributary Districts
Extreme limit of territory under Solomon's political or commercial control
Km. of Judah
Km. of Israel
at their widest extent
Perennial Rivers
Seasonal
East from 35 Greenwich
JERUSALEM BEFORE 70 A.D.
Scale 1 : 50,000
¼ Mile
Ancient Walls
conjectural
Modern
Aqueducts
1. Ch. of the Holy Sepulchre
2. Council Hall
3. Gethsemane
4. Maccabaean Palace
5. Mariamne Tower
6. Phasaelus Tower
PALESTINE in the time of CHRIST
Scale 1 : 2,000,000
(32 miles = 1 inch)
English Miles
Boundary of Kingdom of Herod the Great 30–4 B.C.
Province of Judaea under Pontius Pilate
Tetrarchy of Herod Antipas
Tetrarchy of Philip
under Roman suzerainty
Free Cities of the Decapolis & Phoenicia
Cities tributary to Salome
Principal Roman Roads
Perennial Rivers
Seasonal
PAUL'S MISSIONARY JOURNEYS
Scale 1 : 30,000,000
(480 miles = 1 inch)
English Miles
Roman Empire
Dependencies of the Roman Empire
St. Paul's 1st Missionary Journey
2nd
3rd
Voyage to Rome
The Seven Churches of Asia thus: Sardis

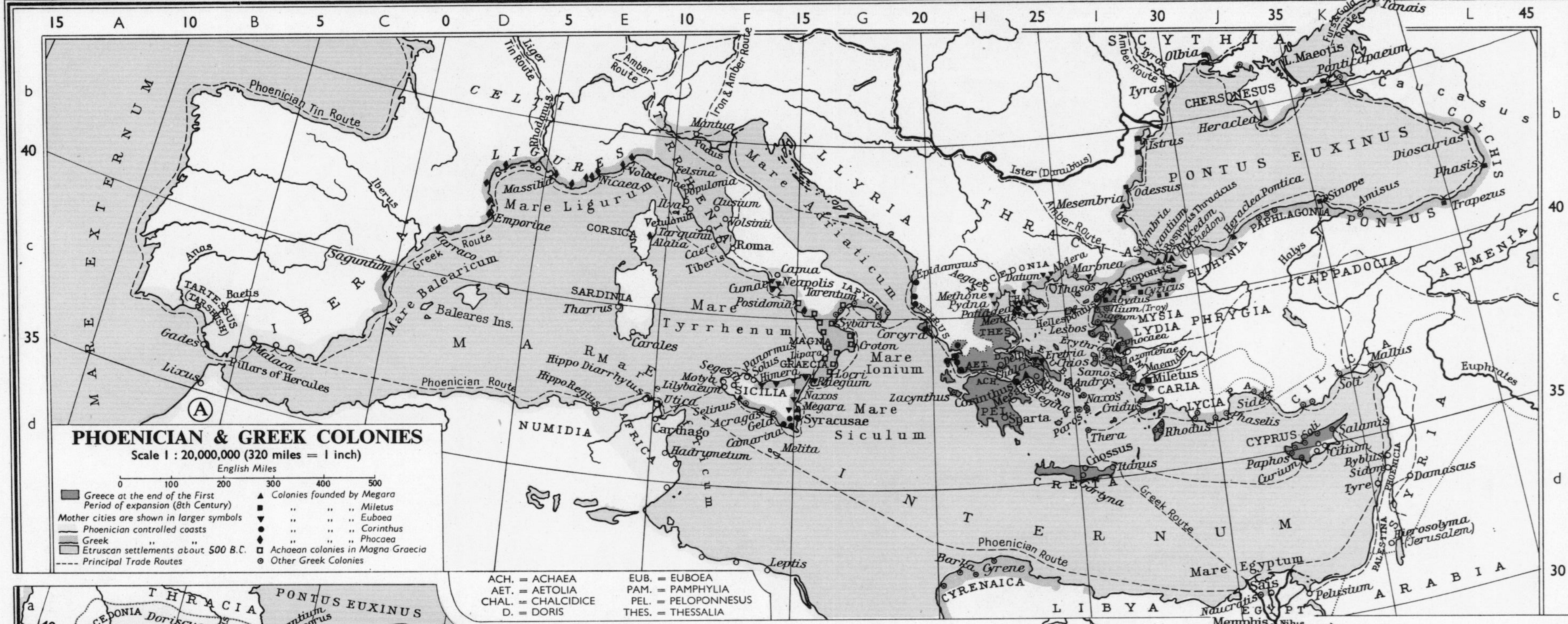

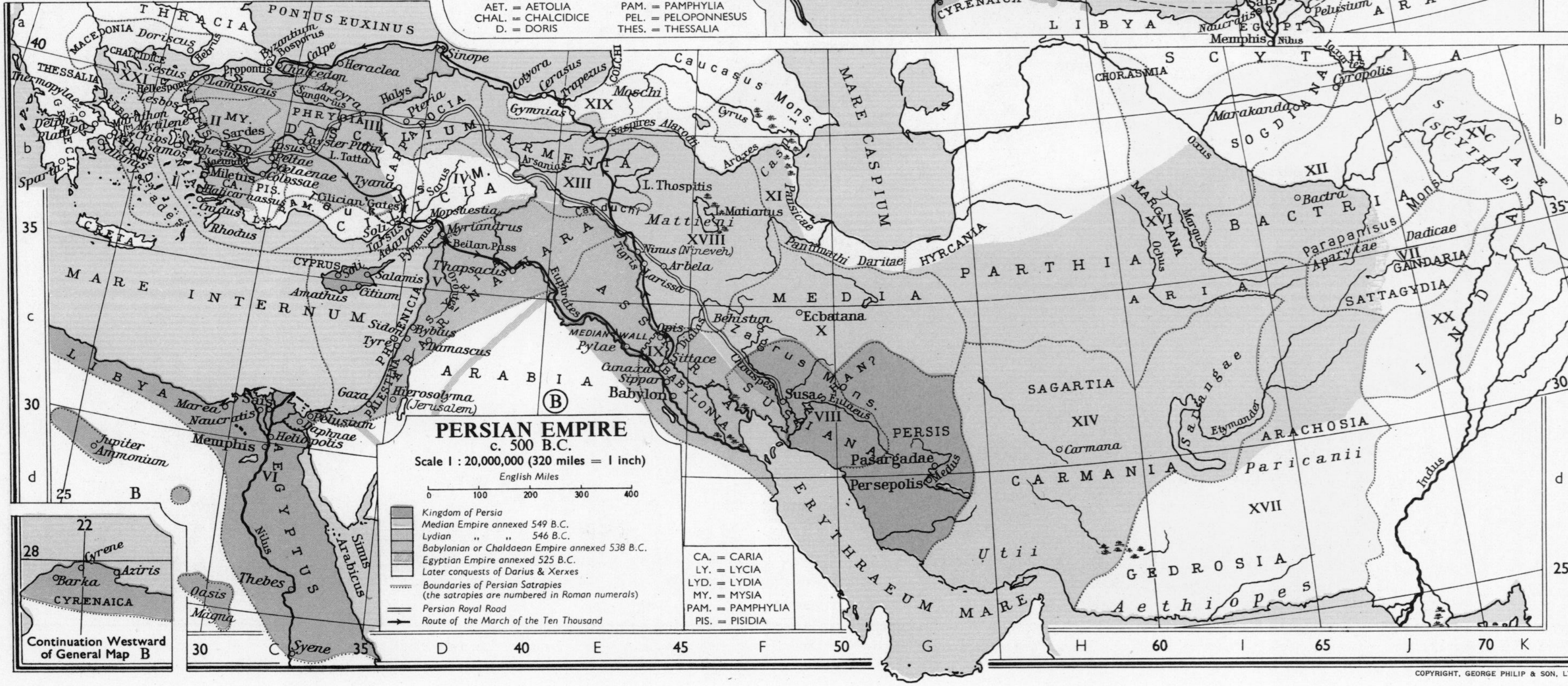

PHOENICIAN & GREEK COLONIES
Scale 1 : 20,000,000 (320 miles = 1 inch)
English Miles
0 100 200 300 400 500
Greece at the end of the First Period of expansion (8th Century)
Mother cities are shown in larger symbols
Phoenician controlled coasts
Greek
Etruscan settlements about 500 B.C.
Principal Trade Routes
Colonies founded by Megara
Miletus
Euboea
Corinthus
Phocaea
Achaean colonies in Magna Graecia
Other Greek Colonies
ACH. = ACHAEA
AET. = AETOLIA
CHAL. = CHALCIDICE
D. = DORIS
EUB. = EUBOEA
PAM. = PAMPHYLIA
PEL. = PELOPONNESUS
THES. = THESSALIA
MARE EXTERNUM
CELTI
LIGURES
IBERI
TARTESSUS (TARSHISH)
Mare Ligurum
Mare Balearicum
Baleares Ins.
CORSICA
SARDINIA
Mare Tyrrhenum
SICILIA
ILLYRIA
Mare Adriaticum
Mare Ionium
Mare Siculum
MARE INTERNUM
NUMIDIA
AFRICA
CYRENAICA
LIBYA
THRACIA
SCYTHIA
PONTUS EUXINUS
CHERSONESUS
COLCHIS
PONTUS
PAPHLAGONIA
BITHYNIA
CAPPADOCIA
ARMENIA
MYSIA
LYDIA
PHRYGIA
CARIA
LYCIA
CILICIA
CYPRUS
SYRIA
ARABIA
CRETA
Mare Egyptum
Phoenician Tin Route
Phoenician Route
Greek Route
Amber Route
Iron & Amber Route
Tin Route

PERSIAN EMPIRE
c. 500 B.C.
Scale 1 : 20,000,000 (320 miles = 1 inch)
English Miles
0 100 200 300 400
Kingdom of Persia
Median Empire annexed 549 B.C.
Lydian ,, 546 B.C.
Babylonian or Chaldaean Empire annexed 538 B.C.
Egyptian Empire annexed 525 B.C.
Later conquests of Darius & Xerxes
Boundaries of Persian Satrapies (the satrapies are numbered in Roman numerals)
Persian Royal Road
Route of the March of the Ten Thousand
CA. = CARIA
LY. = LYCIA
LYD. = LYDIA
MY. = MYSIA
PAM. = PAMPHYLIA
PIS. = PISIDIA
Continuation Westward of General Map B
CYRENAICA
PONTUS EUXINUS
THRACIA
MACEDONIA
THESSALIA
GRAECIA
CRETA
MARE INTERNUM
LIBYA
AEGYPTUS
Sinus Arabicus
ARABIA
PHOENICIA
PALESTINA
CILICIA
CAPPADOCIA
ARMENIA
Caucasus Mons.
MARE CASPIUM
MEDIA
HYRCANIA
PARTHIA
ARIA
MARGIANA
CHORASMIA
SOGDIANA
BACTRIA
SCYTHIA
SAGARTIA
CARMANIA
PERSIS
ARACHOSIA
GEDROSIA
INDIA
SATTAGYDIA
GANDARIA
BABYLONIA
SUSIANA
ERYTHRAEUM MARE
Persepolis
Pasargadae
Babylon
Ecbatana
Susa
Sardes
Memphis

East from 22 Greenwich
THRACIA
Rhodope M.
Nestus
Abdera
Thasos
Neapolis
Crenides (Philippi)
Acontisma
Oesyme
Apollonia
Pangaeus M.
Myrcinus
Amphipolis
Eion
Strymon
Sinus Strymonicus
Athos M.
Nymphaeum Pr.
Sithonia
Torone
Sinus Singiticus
Sinus Toronaicus
Pallene
Potidaea
Mende
Scione
Olynthus
CHALCIDICE
MYGDONIA
ANTHEMUS
Therma
Sinus Thermaicus
CRESTONIA
Odomanti
EDONES
Drabescus
Droi
Doberus
PAEONIA
Axius
Pella
EMATHIA
Europus
Cyrrhus
Aegae
BOTTIAÏS
Berrhoea
ALMOPIA
Haliacmon
Pydna
Methone
Dium
Olympus M.
Heracleum
Ossa M.
Larissa
Pherae
Crannon
THESSALIA
Pharsalus
Tricca
Gomphi
Ithome
Thebes
Sinus Pagasaeus
PHTHIOTIS (ACHAEA)
Othrys M.
Lamia
Oeta M.
Heraclea
Thermopylae
Elatea
Peparethus
Sciathus
Icus
DOLOPES
Polyaegus
Scyros
MARE THRACICUM
MARE AEGEUM
Cerinthus
Lyncestis
PELAGONIA
Heraclea Lyncestis
Bryges
Lychnidus
Lychnites L.
ILLYRIA
Scardus M.
Amphaxitis
Epidamnus
Taulantii
Apsus
Antipatria
Eordaicus
Dassaretae
Orestis
ELIMEA
Tymphe M.
Bolus Mons
EPIRUS
Aous
Antigonia
Amantia
Oricus
Phoenice
Buthrotum
Onchesmus
Corcyra
Cassiope
Istone M.
Amphipagus Pr.
Paxos
Sin. Thesproticus
THESPROTIA
Dodona
Pandosia
Elaea
Ephyra
Buchetium
Nicopolis
Actium
Anactorium
Ambracia
Leucas
Argos Amphilochicum
Athamania
Dolopes
Dryopes
AETOLIA
ACARNANIA
Arachthus
Achelous
Stratus

ANCIENT GREECE
Scale 1 : 2,000,000 (32 miles = 1 inch)
English Miles
Highlands over 6000 feet
from 3000–6000 feet
1200–3000
Uplands 600–1200
Lowlands 0–600
Ionian Greeks
Dorian
Aeolian
CRETE
Scale 1 : 3,000,000 (48 miles = 1 inch)
THE SHORES OF THE PROPONTIS
Scale 1 : 3,000,000 (48 miles = 1 inch)
English Miles
ANCIENT ATHENS
Scale 1 : 50,000
1 Stoa Attali
2 Forum
3 Prytaneum
4 Eleusinium
5 Odeum Herodis
6 Theatrum Dionysi
7 Porta Diocharis
8 " Melitensis
9 Parthenon
ACROPOLIS
Scale 1 : 15,000
1 Athene Promachos
2 Sacra Via
3 Asclepieum
4 Clepsydra
5 Caves of Apollo & Pan
6 Athene Nike
7 Templum Romae et Augusti
8 Templum Athene
9 Stoa of Eumenes
IONIUM
MARE MYRTOUM
MARE AEGEUM
PONTUS EUXINUS
CYCLADES
PROPONTIS
THRACIA

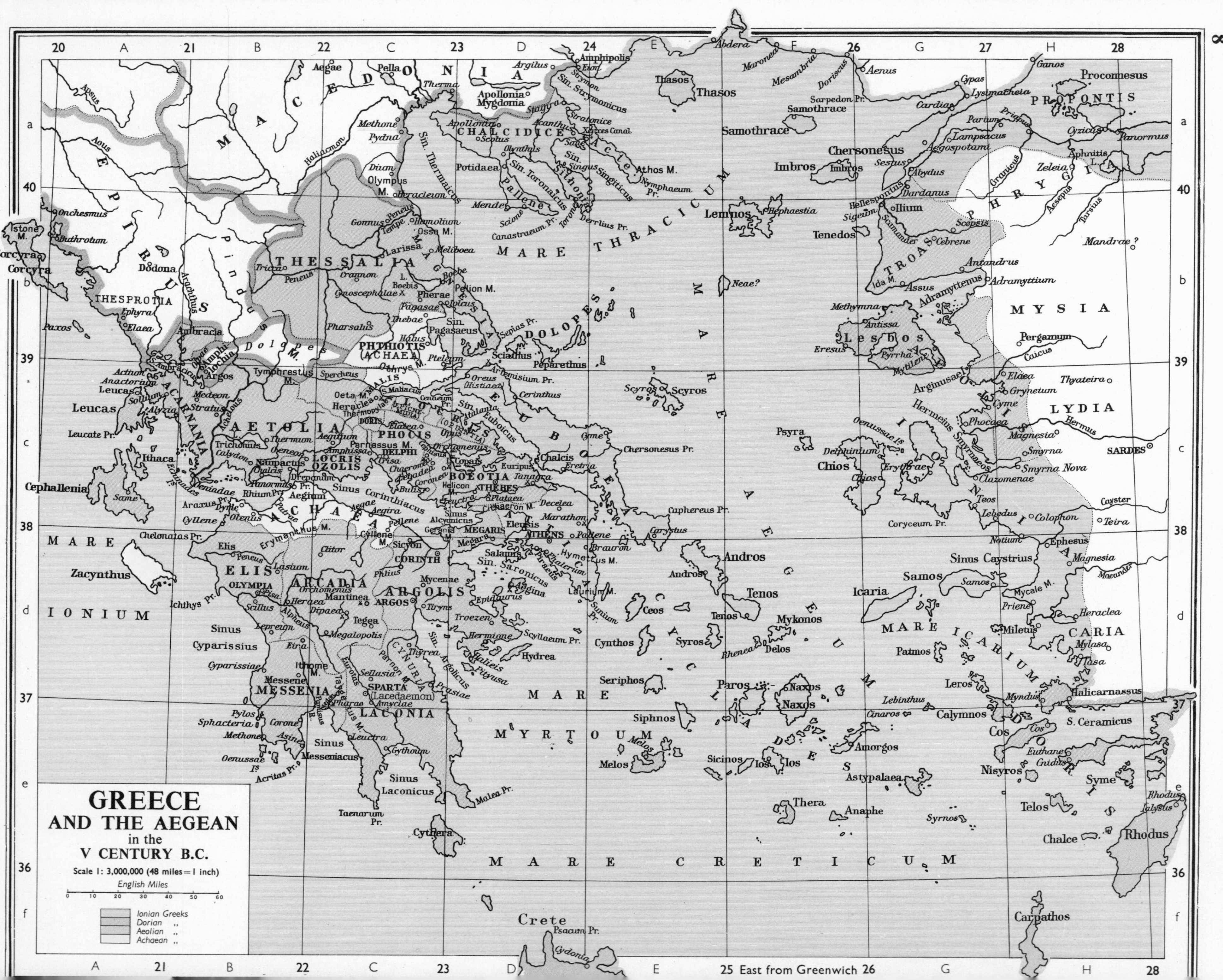
GREECE
AND THE AEGEAN
in the
V CENTURY B.C.
Scale 1: 3,000,000 (48 miles = 1 inch)
English Miles
0 10 20 30 40 50 60
Ionian Greeks
Dorian ,,
Aeolian ,,
Achaean ,,
25 East from Greenwich 26
MACEDONIA
EPIRUS
THESPROTIA
THESSALIA
MAGNESIA
CHALCIDICE
PHTHIOTIS (ACHAEA)
DOLOPES
AETOLIA
ACARNANIA
PHOCIS
LOCRIS OZOLIS
BOEOTIA
EUBOEA
ATTICA
MEGARIS
ACHAEA
ELIS
ARCADIA
ARGOLIS
MESSENIA
LACONIA
CYNURIA
TROAS
PHRYGIA
MYSIA
LYDIA
IONIA
CARIA
DORIS
PROPONTIS
MARE THRACICUM
MARE AEGEUM
MARE MYRTOUM
MARE ICARIUM
MARE CRETICUM
MARE IONIUM
CYCLADES
Sinus Corinthiacus
Sin. Saronicus
Sin. Thermaicus
Sin. Strymonicus
Sinus Laconicus
Sinus Messeniacus
Sinus Cyparissius
Sinus Caystrius
Corcyra
Leucas
Ithaca
Cephallenia
Zacynthus
Thasos
Samothrace
Imbros
Lemnos
Tenedos
Lesbos
Chios
Samos
Icaria
Scyros
Andros
Tenos
Ceos
Cythnos
Syros
Mykonos
Delos
Seriphos
Siphnos
Paros
Naxos
Melos
Ios
Thera
Amorgos
Patmos
Leros
Calymnos
Cos
Nisyros
Telos
Syme
Rhodus
Carpathos
Cythera
Crete
Hydrea
Chersonesus
Hellespontus
ATHENS
THEBES
CORINTH
ARGOS
SPARTA (Lacedaemon)
OLYMPIA
DELPHI
SARDES

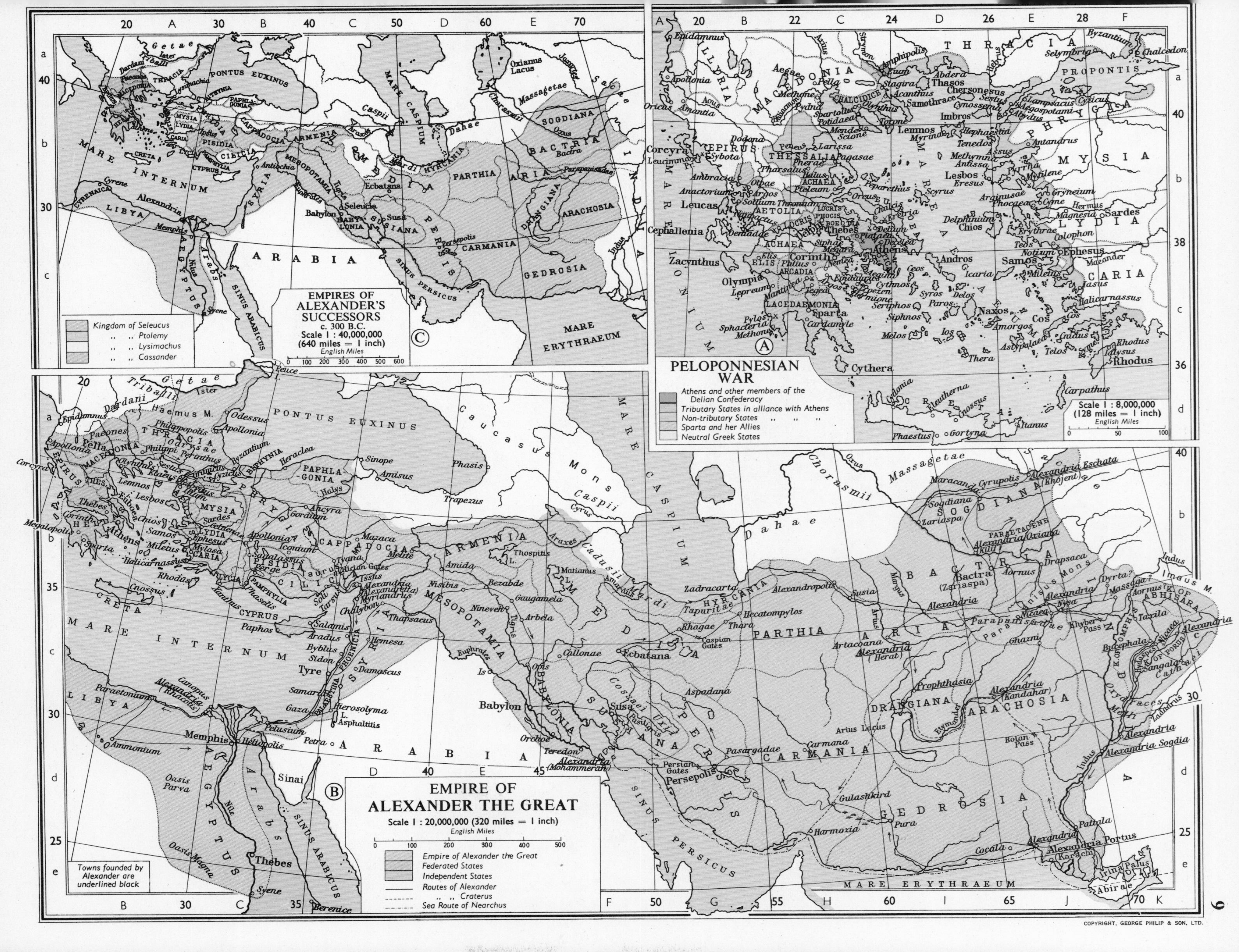

EMPIRES OF ALEXANDER'S SUCCESSORS
c. 300 B.C.
Scale 1 : 40,000,000
(640 miles = 1 inch)
English Miles
0 100 200 300 400 500 600
Kingdom of Seleucus
,, ,, Ptolemy
,, ,, Lysimachus
,, ,, Cassander
PELOPONNESIAN WAR
Athens and other members of the Delian Confederacy
Tributary States in alliance with Athens
Non-tributary States ,, ,, ,,
Sparta and her Allies
Neutral Greek States
Scale 1 : 8,000,000
(128 miles = 1 inch)
English Miles
0 50 100
EMPIRE OF ALEXANDER THE GREAT
Scale 1 : 20,000,000 (320 miles = 1 inch)
English Miles
0 100 200 300 400 500
Empire of Alexander the Great
Federated States
Independent States
Routes of Alexander
,, ,, Craterus
Sea Route of Nearchus
Towns founded by Alexander are underlined black
MARE INTERNUM
PONTUS EUXINUS
MARE CASPIUM
ARABIA
MARE ERYTHRAEUM
SINUS PERSICUS
SINUS ARABICUS
AEGYPTUS
LIBYA
MESOPOTAMIA
ARMENIA
PARTHIA
BACTRIA
SOGDIANA
ARACHOSIA
GEDROSIA
CARMANIA
PERSIS
MEDIA
THRACIA
MACEDONIA
ILLYRIA
PROPONTIS
MYSIA
LYDIA
CARIA
PHRYGIA
Babylon
Alexandria
Athens
Sparta
Persepolis
Ecbatana
Memphis
Thebes
Tyre

OCEANUS GERMANICUS
OCEANUS HIBERNICUS
OCEANUS BRITANNICUS
OCEANUS ATLANTICUS
MARE CANTABRICUM
MARE SUEVICUM
MARE INTERNUM
MARE TYRRHENUM
MARE IONIUM
MARE ADRIATICUM
CALEDONIA
Vallum Antonini
Maeatae
Vallum Hadriani
Brigantes
Eburacum
Deva
Lindum
BRITANNIA
Silures
Isca
Iceni
Dumnonii
Tamesa
Aquae Sulis
Londinium
Camulodunum
Lugdunum Batavorum
Bolerium Pr.
P. Lemanis
Fretum Gallicum
HIBERNIA
Frisii
Chersonesus Cimbrica
Saxones
Cherusci
Suevi Semnones
Rugii
Gutones
Burgundiones
Osii
Veltae
Sugambri
Chatti
Hermunduri
Marcomanni
Quadi
Cobini
Carpatus
GERMANIA
Colonia Agrippina
GERMANIA (INFERIOR)
Aduatuca
Gesoriacum
Samarobriva
Menapii
Nervii
BELGICA
Remi
Durocortorum
Treveri
Aug. Treverorum
Mogontiacum
Divodurum
Tullum
Argentoratum
Lutetia
Agedincum
Cenabum
Senones
LUGDUNENSIS
Veneti
Liger
Limonum
GALLIA
Mediolanum Santonum
Augustodunum
Bibracte
Vesontio
Helvetii
GERMANIA (SUPERIOR)
Agri Decumates
Limes
Danubius
Vindelicia
Aug. Vindelicorum
RHAETIA
Brigantium
Lauriacum
Vindobona
Carnuntum
NORICUM
Noreia
Virunum
Teurnia
Savaria
Aquincum
PANNONIA
Poetovio
(SUPERIOR)
(INF.)
Iazyges
Napoca
Potaissa
Apulum
Sarmizegethusa
Marisus
DACIA
Montes
Burdigala
AQUITANIA
Augustonemetum
Lugdunum
Garumna
Aginnum
Cebenna
Tolosa
Nemausus
Rhodanus
Arausio
Arelata
Massilia
Narbo Martius
NARBONENSIS
Vienna
Allobroges
Octodurus
Eporedia
Segusia
A.C.
A.M.
Mediolanum
Gallia
Taurinorum
Padus
Verona
Tridentum
Aquileia
Pola
Siscia
Savus
Sirmium
Singidunum
Viminacium
Ratiaria
Oescus
Naissus
MOESIA (SUPERIOR)
Serdica
Placentia
Genua
Nicaea
Forum Iulii
Pisae
Bononia
Ravenna
Ariminum
Ancona
Perusia
Spoletium
ITALIA
Roma
Ostia
Corfinium
Bovianum
Capua
Beneventum
Venusia
Brundisium
Tarentum
Neapolis
Tarracina
Thurii
Croton
Rhegium
Messana
Mylae
Salonae
Liburnia
Dalmatia
ILLYRICUM
Epidaurus
Scodra
Lissus
Dyrrhachium
Apollonia
Pella
Pydna
Thessalonica
MACEDONIA
Philippi
Corcyra
Buthrotum
EPIRUS
Nicopolis
Actium
Larissa
Pharsalus
Cephallenia
Zacynthus
Patrae
Corinthus
ACHAEA
Sparta
Cythera
Gortyn
CORSICA
Mariana
Aleria
SARDINIA
Cornus
Sulci
Caralis
SICILIA
Panormus
Lilybaeum
Agrigentum
Gela
Catana
Syracusae
Melite I.
Brigantium
Lucus Augusti
Bracara Aug.
Durius
Gallaecia
Asturica Aug.
Astures
Cantabri
Vascones
Pyrenaei Montes
Pallantia
Numantia
TARRACONENSIS
Salmantica
HISPANIA
LUSITANIA
Scallabis
Olisipo
Tagus
Norba
Emerita Augusta
Toletum
Caesaraugusta
Iberus
Ilerda
Emporiae
Barcino
Tarraco
Dertosa
Oretani
Anas
Laminium
Castulo
Corduba
BAETICA
Baetis
Hispalis
Gades
Munda
Malaca
Pr. Sacrum
Fretum Gaditanum
Carteia
Columnae Herculis
Saguntum
Valentia
Saetabis
Ilici
Carthago Nova
Baleares Iae
Minor
Maior
Pityusae Iae
Tingis
Volubilis
Rusaddir
Siga
Caesarea
Cartenna
Saldae
Sitifis
Cirta
Lambaesis
Hippo Regius
Hippo Diarrhytus
Utica
Carthago
AFRICA
vetus provincia
Theveste
Hadrumetum
Leptis Minor
Thapsus
Zama Regia
Thaenae
Capsa
Tritonis L.
Syrtis Minor
Oea
Leptis Magna
Tripolitana
Syrtis Maior
Nasamones
CYRENAICA
Ptolemais
Arsinoë
Pentapolis
Barka
Apollonia
Cyrene
MAURETANIA TINGITANA
MAURETANIA CAESARIENSIS
NUMIDIA
AFRICA
CRETA
A.C. Alpes Cottiae
A.M. Alpes Maritimae
A.P. Alpes Penninae
Highlands over 12,000 feet
6000-12,000
3000- 6000
Uplands 1200- 3000
600- 1200
Lowlands 0- 600
below Sea Level
East from
IMPERIAL & SENATORIAL PROVINCES
c. 14 A.D.
Scale 1 : 40,000,000
(640 miles = 1 inch)
English Miles
0 200 400 600
Imperial Provinces
Senatorial
HIBERNIA
BRITANNIA
OCEANUS GERMANICUS
MARE SUEVICUM
OCEANUS ATLANTICUS
GERMANIA
SARMATIA
LUGDUNENSIS
BELGICA
GALLIA
AQUITANIA
NARBONENSIS
RHAETIA
NORICUM
PANNONIA
DALMATIA
DACIA
MOESIA
PONTUS EUXINUS
TARRACONENSIS
(HISPANIA CITERIOR)
HISPANIA
LUSITANIA
BAETICA
CORSICA
SARDINIA
Roma
ITALIA
SICILIA
MACEDONIA
THRACIA
ACHAEA
BITHYNIA
PONTUS
ASIA
GALATIA
CAPPADOCIA
CILICIA
LYCIA
PAMPHYLIA
CYPRUS
SYRIA
JUDAEA
PARTHIA
CRETA
CYRENAICA
AEGYPTUS
ARABIA
MAURETANIA
AFRICA
MARE INTERNUM

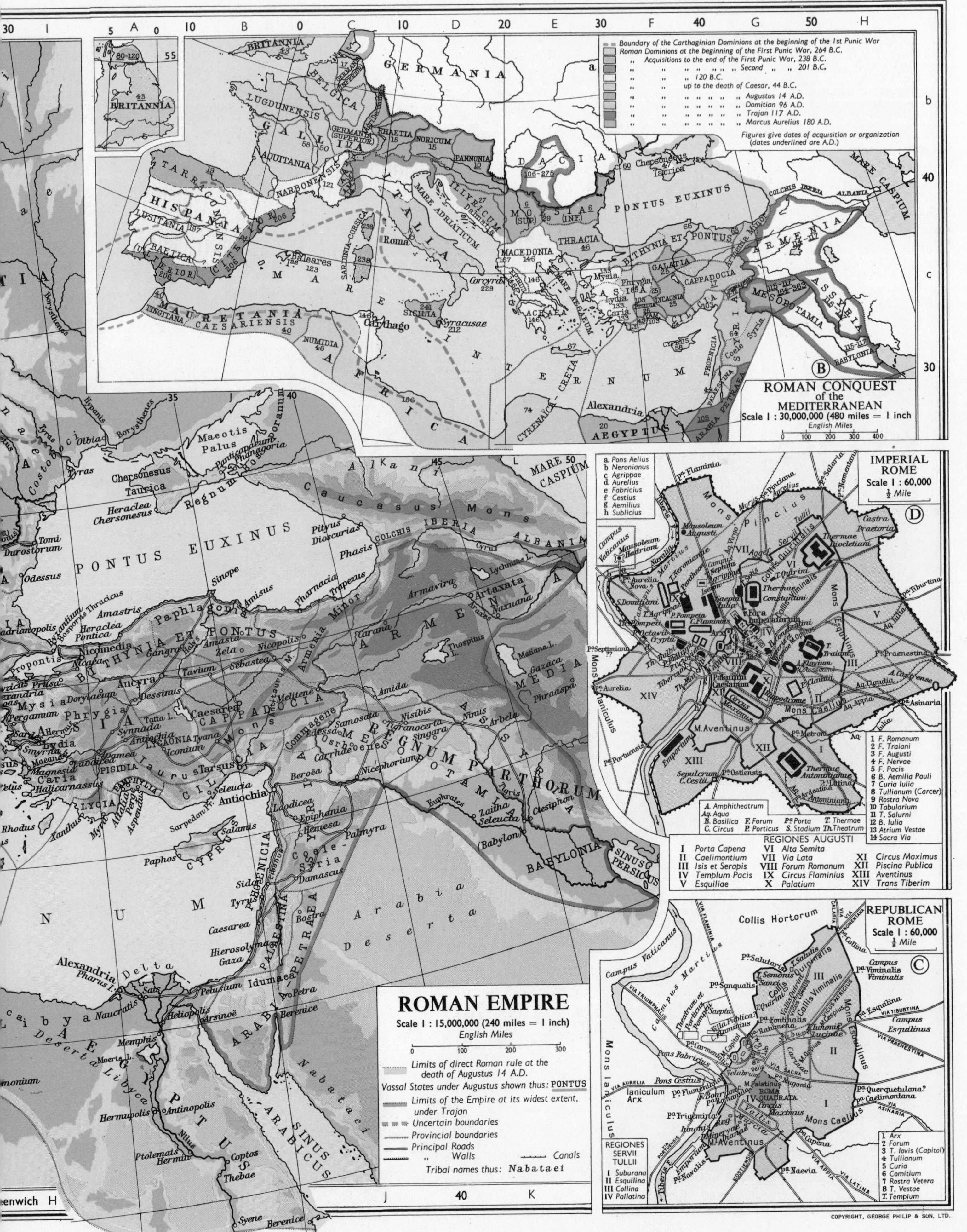
ROMAN CONQUEST of the MEDITERRANEAN
Scale 1 : 30,000,000 (480 miles = 1 inch)
English Miles
0 100 200 300 400
B
Boundary of the Carthaginian Dominions at the beginning of the 1st Punic War
Roman Dominions at the beginning of the First Punic War, 264 B.C.
,, Acquisitions to the end of the First Punic War, 238 B.C.
,, ,, ,, ,, ,, Second ,, ,, 201 B.C.
,, ,, ,, 120 B.C.
,, ,, up to the death of Caesar, 44 B.C.
,, ,, ,, ,, ,, ,, Augustus 14 A.D.
,, ,, ,, ,, ,, ,, Domitian 96 A.D.
,, ,, ,, ,, ,, ,, Trajan 117 A.D.
,, ,, ,, ,, ,, ,, Marcus Aurelius 180 A.D.
Figures give dates of acquisition or organization (dates underlined are A.D.)
BRITANNIA
GERMANIA
BELGICA
LUGDUNENSIS
GALLIA
AQUITANIA
NARBONENSIS
RHAETIA
NORICUM
PANNONIA
DACIA
HISPANIA
TARRACONENSIS
LUSITANIA
BAETICA
MAURETANIA
TINGITANA
CAESARIENSIS
NUMIDIA
AFRICA
ITALIA
ILLYRICUM
MARE ADRIATICUM
SARDINIA-CORSICA
SICILIA
Roma
Carthago
Syracusae
MACEDONIA
THRACIA
MOESIA
ACHAEA
ASIA
BITHYNIA ET PONTUS
GALATIA
CAPPADOCIA
CILICIA
ARMENIA
MESOPOTAMIA
ASSYRIA
BABYLONIA
SYRIA
PHOENICIA
CYPRUS
CRETA
CYRENAICA
AEGYPTUS
Alexandria
ARABIA PETRAEA
PONTUS EUXINUS
MARE CASPIUM
MARE INTERNUM
ROMAN EMPIRE
Scale 1 : 15,000,000 (240 miles = 1 inch)
English Miles
0 100 200 300
Limits of direct Roman rule at the death of Augustus 14 A.D.
Vassal States under Augustus shown thus: PONTUS
Limits of the Empire at its widest extent, under Trajan
Uncertain boundaries
Provincial boundaries
Principal Roads
,, Walls
Canals
Tribal names thus: Nabataei
PONTUS EUXINUS
Maeotis Palus
Chersonesus Taurica
Caucasus Mons
IBERIA
ALBANIA
COLCHIS
MARE CASPIUM
Sinope
Trapezus
Paphlagonia
BITHYNIA ET PONTUS
Nicomedia
Ancyra
CAPPADOCIA
Caesarea
ARMENIA
Artaxata
MEDIA
REGNUM PARTHORUM
MESOPOTAMIA
Ctesiphon
Seleucia
Babylon
BABYLONIA
SINUS PERSICUS
Antiochia
Palmyra
Damascus
Coele-Syria
PHOENICIA
CYPRUS
Tyrus
Caesarea
Hierosolyma
Gaza
PALAESTINA
ARABIA PETRAEA
Petra
Arabia Deserta
Nabataei
SINUS ARABICUS
Alexandria
Delta
Memphis
AEGYPTUS
Thebae
Syene
Berenice
Libya Deserta
Tarsus
CILICIA
LYCIA
PISIDIA
Rhodus
NUMIDIA
IMPERIAL ROME
Scale 1 : 60,000
½ Mile
D
a Pons Aelius
b Neronianus
c Agrippae
d Aurelius
e Fabricius
f Cestius
g Aemilius
h Sublicius
A. Amphitheatrum
Aq. Aqua
B. Basilica
C. Circus
F. Forum
P. Porticus
Pa Porta
S. Stadium
T. Thermae
Th. Theatrum
1 F. Romanum
2 F. Traiani
3 F. Augusti
4 F. Nervae
5 F. Pacis
6 B. Aemilia Pauli
7 Curia Iulia
8 Tullianum (Carcer)
9 Rostra Nova
10 Tabularium
11 T. Saturni
12 B. Iulia
13 Atrium Vestae
14 Sacra Via
REGIONES AUGUSTI
I Porta Capena
II Caelimontium
III Isis et Serapis
IV Templum Pacis
V Esquiliae
VI Alta Semita
VII Via Lata
VIII Forum Romanum
IX Circus Flaminius
X Palatium
XI Circus Maximus
XII Piscina Publica
XIII Aventinus
XIV Trans Tiberim
REPUBLICAN ROME
Scale 1 : 60,000
½ Mile
C
Collis Hortorum
Campus Vaticanus
Campus Martius
Mons Ianiculus
Collis Quirinalis
Collis Viminalis
Mons Esquilinus
Mons Caelius
M. Aventinus
REGIONES SERVII TULLII
I Suburana
II Esquilina
III Collina
IV Pallatina
1 Arx
2 Forum
3 T. Iovis (Capitol)
4 Tullianum
5 Curia
6 Comitium
7 Rostra Vetera
8 T. Vestae
T. Templum

ANCIENT ITALY
Northern Section
Scale 1 : 3,000,000 (48 miles = 1 inch)
English Miles
0 10 20 30 40 50 60
Roman boundary before the reign of Augustus
Roman boundary after the reign of Augustus
Roman Colonies
Latin Colonies
218 Dates (B.C.) of foundation of Colonies
Antipolis Greek Colonies are underlined
Roman Roads
Highlands over 12,000 feet
from 6000–12,000 feet
3000– 6000
1200– 3000
Uplands 600– 1200
Lowlands 0– 600
East from 11 Greenwich
MARE ADRIATICUM
Sinus Ligusticus
GALLIA TRANSPADANA
GALLIA CISPADANA
LIGURIA
VENETIA
ISTRIA
ETRURIA
UMBRIA
PICENUM
SAMNIUM
CORSICA
Alpes Carnicae
Alpes Rhaeticae
Alpes Penninae
Alpes Maritimae
Alpes Venetae
Caruanca M.
ROMA
Ravenna
Ariminum
Pisaurum
Ancona
Aquileia
Mediolanum
Cremona
Placentia
Parma
Mutina
Bononia (Felsina)
Genua
Luna
Pisae
Verona
Patavium
Tergeste
Spoletium
Perusia
Clusium
Tarquinii
Ostia
Antipolis
Nicaea
Ilva (Aethalia)
Aleria (Alalia)
Mariana
Via Aemilia
Via Flaminia
Via Cassia
Via Aurelia
Via Postumia
Via Julia
Via Clodia
Via Salaria
Via Valeria
Via Latina
Via Appia

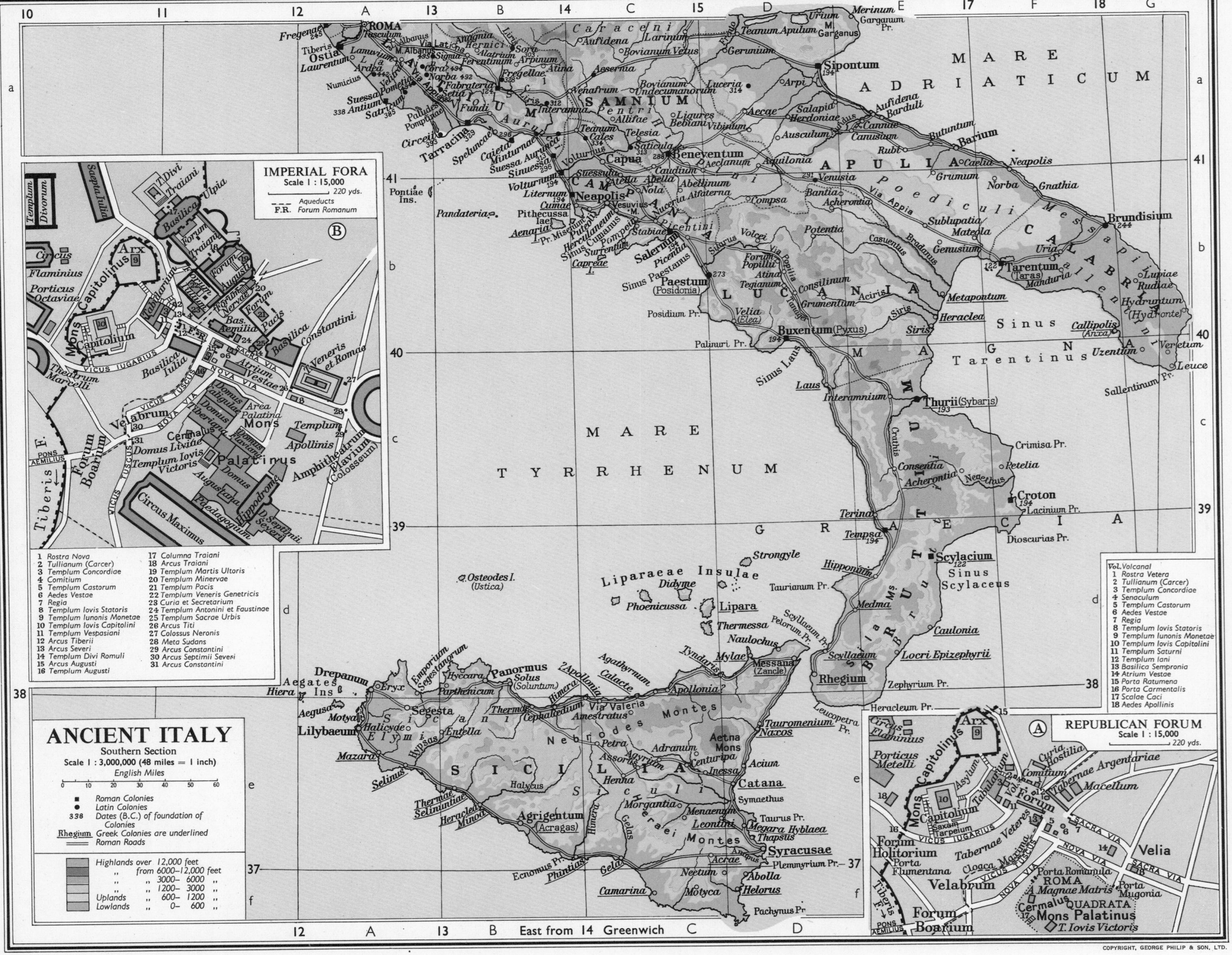

ANCIENT ITALY
Southern Section
Scale 1 : 3,000,000 (48 miles = 1 inch)
English Miles
0 10 20 30 40 50 60
Roman Colonies
Latin Colonies
338 Dates (B.C.) of foundation of Colonies
Rhegium Greek Colonies are underlined
Roman Roads
Highlands over 12,000 feet
,, from 6000–12,000 feet
,, ,, 3000– 6000 ,,
,, ,, 1200– 3000 ,,
Uplands ,, 600– 1200 ,,
Lowlands ,, 0– 600 ,,
East from 14 Greenwich
MARE ADRIATICUM
MARE TYRRHENUM
SAMNIUM
APULIA
CALABRIA
LUCANIA
CAMPANIA
LATIUM
BRUTTIUM
MAGNA GRAECIA
SICILIA
Sinus Tarentinus
Sinus Scylaceus
Liparaeae Insulae
Aegates Ins.
Aetna Mons
Nebrodes Montes
Heraei Montes
ROMA
Ostia
Neapolis
Capua
Beneventum
Brundisium
Tarentum (Taras)
Sipontum
Barium
Paestum (Posidonia)
Thurii (Sybaris)
Croton
Rhegium
Messana (Zancle)
Panormus
Syracusae
Agrigentum (Acragas)
Lilybaeum
Catana
IMPERIAL FORA
Scale 1 : 15,000
220 yds.
Aqueducts
F.R. Forum Romanum
1 Rostra Nova
2 Tullianum (Carcer)
3 Templum Concordiae
4 Comitium
5 Templum Castorum
6 Aedes Vestae
7 Regia
8 Templum Iovis Statoris
9 Templum Iunonis Monetae
10 Templum Iovis Capitolini
11 Templum Vespasiani
12 Arcus Tiberii
13 Arcus Severi
14 Templum Divi Romuli
15 Arcus Augusti
16 Templum Augusti
17 Columna Traiani
18 Arcus Traiani
19 Templum Martis Ultoris
20 Templum Minervae
21 Templum Pacis
22 Templum Veneris Genetricis
23 Curia et Secretarium
24 Templum Antonini et Faustinae
25 Templum Sacrae Urbis
26 Arcus Titi
27 Colossus Neronis
28 Meta Sudans
29 Arcus Constantini
30 Arcus Septimii Severi
31 Arcus Constantini
REPUBLICAN FORUM
Scale 1 : 15,000
220 yds.
Vol. Volcanal
1 Rostra Vetera
2 Tullianum (Carcer)
3 Templum Concordiae
4 Senaculum
5 Templum Castorum
6 Aedes Vestae
7 Regia
8 Templum Iovis Statoris
9 Templum Iunonis Monetae
10 Templum Iovis Capitolini
11 Templum Saturni
12 Templum Iani
13 Basilica Sempronia
14 Atrium Vestae
15 Porta Ratumena
16 Porta Carmentalis
17 Scalae Caci
18 Aedes Apollinis

ITALY
under the
ROMAN REPUBLIC
Scale 1: 5,000,000 (80 miles = 1 inch)
English Miles
Roman boundary before the Punic Wars
Roman boundary before the reign of Augustus
Roman Colonies
Latin Colonies
Greek Colonies are underlined
Principal Roman Roads
LATIUM
Scale 1: 2,500,000 (40 miles = 1 inch)
English Miles
RACIAL DISTRIBUTION c. 400 B.C.
Scale 1: 15,000,000 (240 miles = 1 inch)
English Miles
Itali
Etrusci
Ligures
Veneti
Messapii and Bruttii
Istri
Celti
East from Greenwich
R H A E T I A
N O R I C U M
Alpes Rhaeticae
Alpes Carnicae
Alpes Venetae
Alpes Penninae
Helvetii
Lepontii
G A L L I A   C I S P A D A N A
L I G U R I A
Sinus Ligusticus
E T R U R I A
U M B R I A
P I C E N U M
S A M N I U M
L A T I U M
C A M P A N I A
A P U L I A
L U C A N I A
C A L A B R I A
B R U T T I U M
M A R E   A D R I A T I C U M
M A R E   T Y R R H E N U M
M A G N A   G R A E C I A
Sinus Tarentinus
Mare Ionium
CORSICA
SARDINIA
SICILIA
Fretum Gallicum
Roma
Mediolanum
Aquileia
Bononia (Felsina)
Ariminum
Ravenna
Genua
Pisae
Neapolis
Capua
Beneventum
Brundisium
Tarentum (Taras)
Rhegium
Messana (Zancle)
Syracusae
Agrigentum (Acragas)
Panormus
Carthago
Utica
Hippo Zarytus
Cossyra
Liparaeae Ins.
Aegates Ins

ROMAN EMPIRE
in the time of
AUGUSTUS
I. ITALIA &
WESTERN PROVINCES
Scale 1 : 10,000,000 (160 miles = 1 inch)
English Miles
0 50 100 150 200 250
Limits of direct Roman rule at the death of Augustus 14 A.D.
Territories subsequently acquired
Provincial boundaries
Chief Roads
„ Walls
Tribal names thus: HELVETII
A.C. Alpes Cottiae
A.M. Alpes Maritimae
A.P. Alpes Penninae
West from 5 Greenwich
East from 5 Greenwich
OCEANUS GERMANICUS
OCEANUS HIBERNICUS
OCEANUS BRITANNICUS
OCEANUS ATLANTICUS
MARE CANTABRICUM
MARE SUEVICUM
MARE INTERNUM
BRITANNIA
GERMANIA
GERMANIA INFERIOR
GERMANIA SUPERIOR
BELGICA
LUGDUNENSIS
GALLIA
AQUITANIA
NARBONENSIS
RHAETIA
NORICUM
HISPANIA
Citerior
LUSITANIA
BAETICA
TARRACONENSIS
MAURETANIA TINGITANA
MAURETANIA CAESARIENSIS
NUMIDIA
AFRICA
Vetus provincia
CORSICA
SARDINIA
SICILIA
Baleares Iae
Pityusae Iae
Gallia Cisalpina
Liguria
Etruria
Cimbrica Chersonesus
Scandiae Iae
Eburacum
Lindum
Deva
Ratae
Venta Icenorum
Camulodunum
Londinium
Verulamium
Glevum
Isca Silurum
Aquae Sulis
Venta Belgarum
Isca Dumnoniorum
Regnum
Vectis
Mona
Monapia
Lugdunum Batavorum
Noviomagus
Vetera
Colonia Agrippina
Aduatuca
Bagacum
Gesoriacum (Bononia)
Tarvenna
Nemetacum
Samarobriva
Rotomagus
Iuliobona
Durocortorum
Lutetia
Augusta Treverorum
Divodurum
Mogontiacum
Confluentes
Tullum
Argentoratum
Agedincum
Augustobona
Cenabum
Caesarodunum
Avaricum
Condate
Suindinum
Iuliomagus
Portus Namnetum
Limonum
Mediolanum Santonum
Burdigala
Aginnum
Tolosa
Narbo Martius
Nemausus
Arelate
Massilia
Forum Iulii
Nicaea
Lugdunum
Vienna
Geneva
Vesontio
Bibracte
Alesia
Augusta Rauricorum
Aventicum
Brigantium
Cambodunum
Augusta Vindelicorum
Iuvavum
Virunum
Celeia
Aemona
Aquileia
Tridentum
Verona
Patavium
Mediolanum
Cremona
Placentia
Augusta Taurinorum
Genua
Ravenna
Ariminum
Ancona
Bononia
Florentia
Pisae
Arretium
Perusia
Clusium
Spoletium
Roma
Ostia
Antium
Tarracina
Capua
Puteoli
Neapolis
Mariana
Aleria
Olbia
Cornus
Sulci
Carales
Tarraco
Dertosa
Ilerda
Barcino
Emporiae
Caesaraugusta
Pompaelo
Numantia
Clunia
Pallantia
Asturica Augusta
Lucus Augusti
Brigantium
Bracara Augusta
Conimbriga
Olisippo
Emerita Augusta
Toletum
Segobriga
Saguntum
Valentia
Saetabis
Ilici
Carthago Nova
Castulo
Corduba
Hispalis
Italica
Astigi
Munda
Gades
Malaca
Abdera
Calpe M.
Columnae Herculis
Fretum Gaditanum
Tingis
Zilis
Lixus
Rusaddir
Siga
Portus Magnus
Cartenna
Iol Caesarea
Icosium
Rusgonia
Saldae
Sitifis
Igilgili
Cirta
Hippo Regius
Lambaesis
Theveste
Aurasius M.
Sicca
Zama Regia
Utica
Carthago
Tunes
Hadrumetum
Leptis Minor
Thapsus
Thusdrus
Thaenae
Capsa
Syrtis Minor
Lilybaeum
Drepanum
Panormus
Selinus
Pyrenaei Montes
Alpes
Cebenna M.
Apenninus
Sudeti Mts
Rhenus
Danubius
Albis
Viadua
Rhodanus
Liger
Garumna
Padus
Tiberis
Iberus
Durius
Tagus
Anas
Baetis
Minius
HELVETII
SEQUANI
AEDUI
ARVERNI
SENONES
PICTONES
BITURIGES-CUBI
VENETI
TREVERI
REMI
NERVII
MENAPII
BATAVI
FRISII
CHAUCI
BRUCTERI
SUGAMBRI
CHATTI
CHERUSCI
LANGOBARDI
HERMUNDURI
MARCOMANNI
SUEVI-SEMNONES
VANDALI
LUGII
BURGUNDIONES
RUGII
SAXONES
TEUTONES
ANGLII
AVIONES
CANTABRI
ASTURES
VASCONES
ILERGETES
VACCAEI
CELTIBERI
CARPETANI
ORETANI
BASTETANI
CONTESTANI
EDETANI
ALLOBROGES
BRIGANTES
ORDOVICES
SILURES
ICENI
MAEATAE
CYNAETES
VALLUM ANTONINI
VALLUM HADRIANI
LIMES

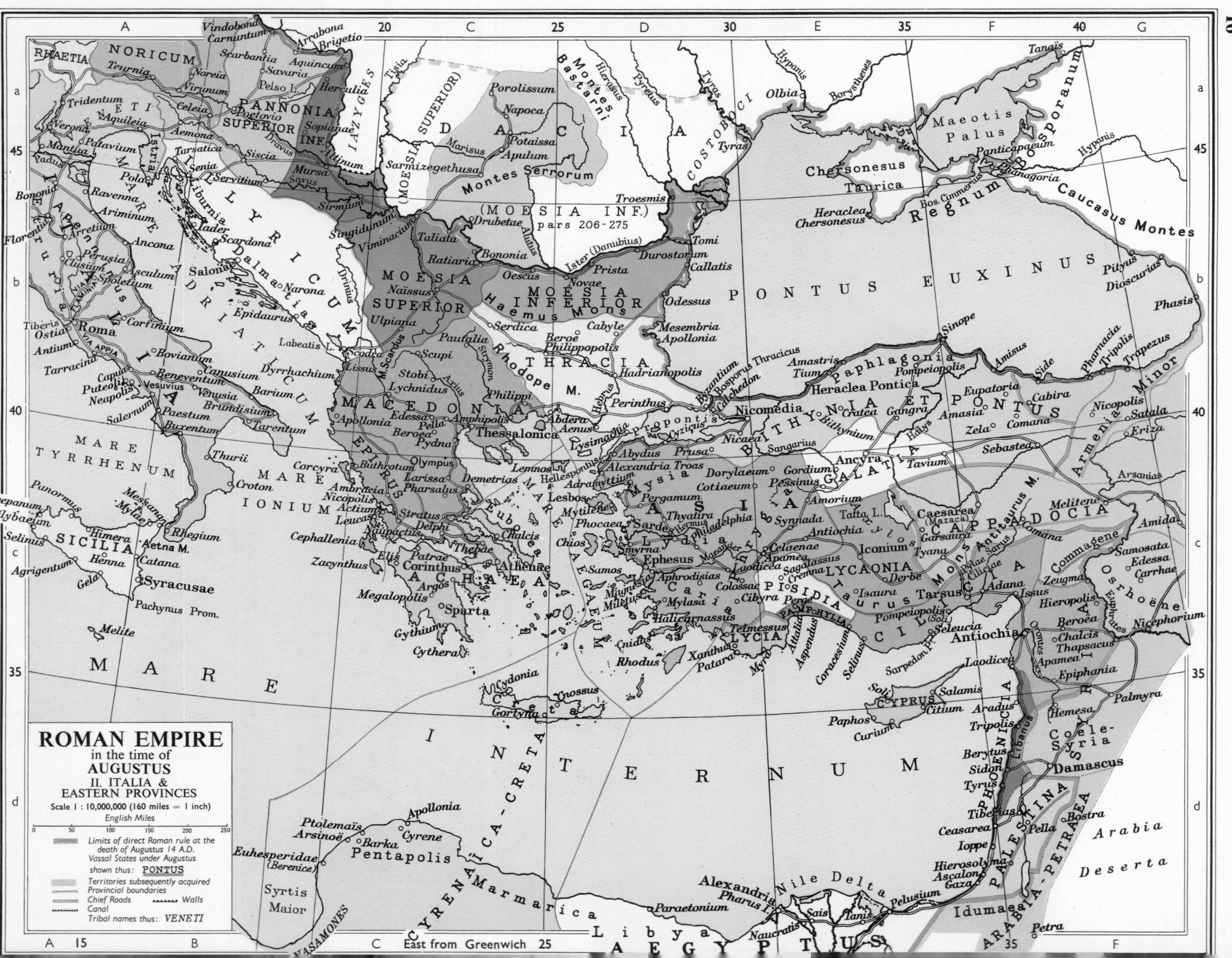
ROMAN EMPIRE
in the time of
AUGUSTUS
II. ITALIA &
EASTERN PROVINCES
Scale 1 : 10,000,000 (160 miles = 1 inch)
English Miles
0 50 100 150 200 250
Limits of direct Roman rule at the death of Augustus 14 A.D.
Vassal States under Augustus shown thus: PONTUS
Territories subsequently acquired
Provincial boundaries
Chief Roads
Walls
Canal
Tribal names thus: VENETI
East from Greenwich
PONTUS EUXINUS
MARE INTERNUM
MARE TYRRHENUM
MARE IONIUM
MARE AEGAEUM
MARE ADRIATICUM
NORICUM
PANNONIA SUPERIOR
PANNONIA INF.
ILLYRICUM
DACIA
MOESIA SUPERIOR
MOESIA INFERIOR
(MOESIA INF.) pars 206-275
THRACIA
MACEDONIA
EPIRUS
ACHAEA
ASIA
BITHYNIA ET PONTUS
GALATIA
CAPPADOCIA
LYCAONIA
CILICIA
LYCIA
PISIDIA
SYRIA
PALESTINA
ARABIA PETRAEA
Arabia Deserta
AEGYPTUS
CYRENAICA-CRETA
Regnum Bosporanum
Caucasus Montes
Roma
Athenae
Byzantium
Antiochia
Alexandria
Damascus

INDEX

Note—Each Map in the Atlas is divided into Squares by the lines of latitude and longitude, and these Squares are indicated by Reference Letters in the map borders. These Reference Letters, following each name in the Index, indicate the Square, and the succeeding Numeral indicates the Number of the Map in which each place will be found. Thus:—"Babylonia, Fc, 9*b*" shows that Babylonia will be found on Map 9*b*, and in the Square indicated by the Reference Letters "Fc".

The following abbreviations are used:—A., *Amphitheatrum* (Amphitheatre); Aest., *Aestuarium* (Estuary); Aq., *Aquaeductus* (Aqueduct); C., *Castellum* (Castle); E., East(ern); F., Fl., *Flumen* (River); Ins., *Insula(ae)* (Island(s); I(s). *Island(s)*; K., *Kingdom*; L., *Lacus* (Lake, Loch); M., *Mons* (Mountain); Mtes., *Montes* (Mountains); Mt(s). *Mountain(s)*; N., North(ern); Pa., *Porta* (Gate); Pr., *Promontorium* (Promontory); R., River; S., South(ern); Th., *Theatrum* (Theatre); Val., *Valley*; W., West(ern).

Abana, R., Cd, 4*c*
Abarim, Mts. of, Ce, 4*a*
Abar-Nahara, Db, 5*b*
Abdera (Hispania), Be, 15
Abdera (Thracia), Hb, 5*a*; Da, 9*a*
Abella, Cb, 13
Abellinum, Cb, 13
Abel-shittim Ce, 4*a*
Abergavenny (Gobannium), Ce, 17
Abhira, Ec, 18*b*
Abhisara, Kingdom of, Kc, 9*b*
Abila, Cb, 4*d*
Abirae, Je, 9*b*
Abodu (Abydus), Bc, 3*b*
Abolla, Df, 13
Abone, De, 17
Abravannus Sinus, Bb, 17
Abu Simbel Bd, 3*a*
Abus, Cb., 15
Abus Fl., Fc, 17
Abydus (Abodu), Bc, 3*b*
Abydus (Mysia), Db, 16
Acanthus, Eb, 6
Acarnania, Cd, 6
Accho, Bc, 4*a*
Acelum, Fb, 12
Acerrae, Db, 12
Achaea, Cd, 7
Achaea, Phthiotis, Dc, 6
Achaia, Ed, 18
Achaici, M., Dd, 6
Acharnae, Ed, 7
Achelous, F., Cd, 6
Acherontia (Bruttium), Ec, 13
Acherontia (Lucania), Db, 13
Achilleum, Inset, 2*c*
Achmetha (Ecbatana), Fc, 2*d*
Achzib, Bb, 4*a*
Aciris, F., Eb, 13
Acium, De, 13
Acontisma, Fb, 6
Acrae, Ce, 13
Acragas, Fc, 5*a*
Acritas Pr., Cf, 7
Acropolis, Inset, 7*a*
Acroria, Ce, 7
Acte, Argolis, Ee, 7
Acte, Chalcidice, Fc, 15
Actium, Bd, 6
Ad Novas, Fd, 12
Adana, Arabia, Gf, 18
Adana, Syria, Dc, 2*d*
Addua, F., Db, 12
Adramyttenus, Gb, 8
Adramyttium, Cc, 7*c*
Adranum, Ce, 13
Adria, Ba, 4*f*
Aduatuca, Db, 15
Adula Mons, Ca, 12
Adullam, Ae, 4*a*
Aebudae, Inset, 17*a*
Aecae, Da, 13
Aeclanum, Da, 13
Aedes Apollinis, Inset, 13*a*
Aedes Magnae Matris, Inset, 13*a*
Aedes Vestae, Inset, 13*a*
Aedui, Cc, 15
Aegae (Achaea), Dd, 7
Aegae (Euboea), Ed, 6
Aegae (Macedonia), Ca, 9*a*
Aegates, Ins., Ad, 13
Aegilia, Eg, 7
Aegina, Ee, 7
Aeginium, Cc, 6
Aegira, Dd, 7
Aegitium, Dd, 6
Aegium, Dd, 7
Aegospotami, Ea, 9*a*
Aegosthena, Ed, 7
Aegusa, Ae, 13
Ægyptus, Fe, 18
Aeminium, Ad, 15
Aemona, Aa, 16
Aenaria Ins., Bb, 13
Aeneum Pr., Db, 6
Aenus, Cb, 7*c*
Aenus, F., Ec, 15
Aeolis, Bb, 5*b*; Bb, 9*b*; Gc, 8
Aequi, He, 12
Aesepus, F., Dc, 7*c*
Aesernia, Ca, 13
Aesica (Great Chesters), Inset, 17
Aesis, Hd, 12
Aesis, F., Hd, 12
Aestii, Ha, 10
Aethalia, Ee, 12
Aethiopes, Id, 5*b*
Aethiopia, Bd, 1
Aetna M., Ce, 13
Aetolia, Bb, 9*a*
Aetolians, Bb, 2*b*
Africa, Dd, 18
Africa, Diocese of, Eg, 20
Africa (*vetus provincia*), De, 15
Agammeia Pr., Inset, 2*c*
Agathyrnum, Cd, 13
Agedincum, Cc, 15
Agger Servii Tullii, Inset, 11*d*
Aginnum, Cd, 15
Agisymba, Inset, 1
Agora, Inset, 7*b*
Agrae, Inset, 7*b*
Agraei, Cd, 6
Agri Decumates, Dc, 15
Agrigentum (Acragas), Be, 13
Agrinium, Cd, 6
Agrippae, Inset, 11*d*
Agyrium, Ce, 13
Ai, Be, 4*a*
Ajalon, Be, 4*a*
Ajodhya, Fc, 18*b*
Akeman Street, Ee, 17
Akhetaton (Tell-el-Amarna), Bc, 3*b*
Akhlamu, Db, 3*a*
Akkad, Db, 3*a*
Alalia (Aleria), De, 12
Alani, Gc, 18
Alasa (Cyprus), Ba, 3*a*
Alasia, Cb, 4*c*
Alatrium, Ba, 13
Alba, Cd, 15
Alba Fucentia, He, 12
Alba Pompeia, Cc, 12
Albania, Gb, 11*b*
Albanus, L., Aa, 13
Albanus, M., As, 13
Albis, R., Fc, 20
Albium Ingaunum, Cc, 12
Albium Intemelium, Bd, 12
Albona, Jb, 12
Alchester, Ee, 17
Aleppo (Halap), Ca, 3*a*
Aleria (Alalia), De, 12; Dd, 10
Alesia, Cc, 15
Alexandreia Troas, Cc, 7*c*
Alexandretta (Alexandria), Db, 9*b*
Alexandria Aegyptus, Ed, 18
Alexandria, Asia, Ec, 1
Alexandria (Alexandretta), Db, 9*b*
Alexandria (Bactria), Ib, 9*b*
Alexandria (Gedrosia), Jd, 9*b*
Alexandria (Herat), Ic, 9*b*
Alexandria (India), Jb, Kd, 9*b*
Alexandria (Kandahar), Jc, 9*b*
Alexandria (Mohammerah), Fc, 9*b*
Alexandria (Porus), Kc, 9*b*
Alexandria (Rhacotis), Bc, 9*b*
Alexandria Eschata (Khojent), Ja, 9*b*
Alexandria Oxiana (Kilif), Jb, 9*b*
Alexandria Portus (Karachi), Jc, 9*b*
Alexandria Sogdia, Kd, 9*b*
Alexandria Troas, He, 11
Alexandropolis, Hb, 9*b*
Aliphera, Ce, 7
Allemanni, Ed, 20
Allifae, Ca, 13
Allobroges, Dc, 15
Almopia, Db, 6
Alope, Dd, 6
Alpes, Ed, 20
Alpes Carnicae, Ga, 12
Alpes Cottiae, Ab, 12
Alpes Maritimi, Bc, 12
Alpes Montes, Dc, 15
Alpes Penninae, Ba, 12
Alpes Rhaeticae, Ea, 12
Alpes Venetae, Ga, 12
Alpheus, F., C, 7
Alpis Graia, Ab, 12
Alpis Pennina, Bb, 12
Alsium, Gf, 12
Alta Semita, Inset, 11*d*
Altinum Venetia, Gb, 12
Altinum Pannonia, Ba, 16
Alutus, F., Gd, 10
Alyzia, Bd, 6
Alzi, Ca, 3*a*
Amalekites, Bf, 4*a*
Amantia, Aa, 9*a*
Amardus, F., Fb, 9*b*
Amasia, Fb, 16
Amastris, Cd, 11
Amathus, Cc, 5*b*
Amboglanna (Birdoswald), Inset 17
Ambracia, Bb, 9*a*
Ameria, Ge, 12
Amestratus, Ce, 13
Amida, Gc, 16
Amisia, F., Db, 15
Amisus, Fb, 16
Amiternum, He, 12
Ammon, Ce, 4*c*
Ammonites, Cd, 4*a*
Ammonium, Bd, 9*b*
Amor, Cb, 3*a*
Amorgos, Fe, 8
Amorites, Cb, 3*a*
Amorium, Ec, 16
Ampelus Pr., Da, 7*d*
Amphaxitis, Ca, 6
Amphilochia, Cc, 6
Amphipagus Pr., Bc, 6
Amphipolis, Ca, 9*a*
Amphissa, Dd, 6
Amphitheatrum Flavium, Inset, 13*b*
Amphylia, Eb, 4*f*
Amyclae, De, 7
Anactorium, Bb, 9*a*
Anagnia, Ba, 13
Anaphe, I., Fe, 8
Anapus, F., De, 13
Anas, R., Bf, 20
Anatho, Ec, 2*d*
Anauni, Ea, 12
Anavio, Ec, 17
Ancaster (Causennae), Fd, 17
Ancona, Hd, 12
Ancus, Kc, 12
Ancyra (Phrygia), Cb, 2*d*
Andania, De, 7
Andematunnum, Dc, 15
Anderida (Pevensey), Gf, 17
Anderida Silva, Fe, 17
AAndhra, Jf, 19
ndhra, Kingdom of, Cc, 18*a*
Andros, Fe, 7
Angli, Ec, 20
Anglii, Db, 15
Anio, F., Gf, 12
Anneianum, Fb, 12
Anping, Nd, 19
Anshan, Fc, 5*b*
Antaeopolis (Du-kau), Bc, 3*b*
Antandrus, Eb, 9*a*
Anthedon, Ed, 6
Anthemus, Eb, 6
Antiachia, Ie, 11
Anticyra, Dd, 7
Antigonia, Bb, 6
Anting, Md, 19
Antinopolis, Ig, 11
Antioch (Pisidia), Eb, 4*f*
Antiochia, Fd, 18
Antiochia (Syria), Fc, 16
Antiochus, Kingdom of, Fb, 4*f*
Antipatria, Ab, 6
Antipatris, Ac, 4*d*
Antipolis, Bd, 12
Antirrhium Pr., Cd, 7
Antissa, Eb, 9*a*
Antitaurus M., Fc, 16
Antium, Aa, 13
Antonia, Inset, 4*e*
Antoniniana Aq., Inset, 11*d*
Anxa, Fb, 13
Anxanum, Je, 12
Aornus (Abhisara), Kc, 9*b*
Aornus (Bactria), Jb, 9*b*
Aous, F., Ab, 6
Apamea (Phrygia), Ec, 16
Apamea (Syria), Fc, 16
Aparytae, Jb, 5*b*
Aperantia, Cd, 6
Aphidnae, Ed, 7
Aphnitis,L., Db, 7*c*
Aphrodis ias, Dc, 16
Aphroditopolis (Middle Egypt), Bb, 3*b*
Aphroditopolis (Upper Egypt), Bc, 3*b*
Apodotia, Cd, 6
Apollinopolis magna Bd, 3*a*
Apollinopolis-parva (Nebut), Cd, 3*b*
Apollo and Pan, Caves of, Inset, 7*a*
Apollonia (Edones), Fb, 6
Apollonia (Illyria), Aa, 9*a*
Apollonia (Judea), Ac, 4*d*
Apollonia (Macedonia), Bb, 16
Apollonia ((Pentapolis), Cd, 16
Apollonia Phrygia), Cb, 9*b*
Apollonia (Sicilia), Cd, 13
Apollonia (Thracia), Db, 16
Apollonia Mygdonia, Eb, 6
Appia, Aq., Inset, 11*d*
Apsorus, Jc, 12
Apsus, F., Ab, 6
Apuli, Cb, 14*c*
Apulia, Ea, 13
Apulum, Ca, 16
Aquae, Inset, 17*a*
Aquea (Buxton), Ec, 17
Aquae Flaviae, Ad, 15
Aquae Populoniae, Ed, 12
Aquae Sextiea, Dd, 15
Aquae Statiellae, Cc, 12
Aquae Sulis (Bath), De, 17
Aquae Tarbellicae, Bd, 15
Aquileia (Etruria), Fd, 12
Aquileia (Rhaetia), Ec, 15
Aquileia (Venetia), Hb, 12
Aquilonia, Da, 13
Aquincum, Ba, 16
Aquitania, Dd, 20
Arabah, Bg, 4*c*; Cd, 4*a*
Arabia, Ge, 18
Arabia Deserta, Lh, 20
Arabia, Felix, Fe, 18
Arabian Desert, Bc, 3*a*; Cc, 3*a*
Arabia, Petraea, Fe, 18
Arabs (Aribi), Ec, 2*d*
Arachosia, Id, 18
Arachthus, F., Cc, 6
Arad, Bf, 4*a*
Aradus, Dc, 9*b*
Aram, Db, 4*a*
Aramaeans (Syrians), Cd, 4*c*
Arar, F., Cc, 15
Ararat, Mt., Eb, 2*d*
Ararat (Urartu), Eb, 2*d*
Arausio, Cd, 15
Araxes, F., Fb, 9*b*
Araxus, Pr., Cd, 7
Arbailu (Arbela), Eb, 2*d*
Arbela, Gd, 18
Arbela (Arbailu), Eb, 2*d*
Arcadia, Cc, 9*a*
Archelais, Bd, 4*d*
Arcus Augusti, Inset, 13*b*
Arcus Constantini, Inset, 13*b*
Arcus Septimii Severi, Inset, 13*b*
Arcus Severi, Inset, 13*b*
Arcus Tiberii, Inset, 13*b*
Arcus Titi, Inset, 13*b*
Arcus Traiani, Inset, 13*b*
Ardea, Aa, 13
Ardeatina, Pa., Inset, 11*d*
Arden, Forest of, Ed, 17
Arduenna Silva, Db, 15
Area Palatina, Inset, 13*b*
Arelate, Cd, 15
Areopagus, Inset, 7*a*
Argentarius, M., Fe, 12
Argentoratum, Dc, 15
Argethia, Cc, 6
Argilus, Eb, 6
Arginusae, Eb, 9*a*
Argolis, De, 7
Argos, De, 7
Argos (Amphilocia), Bb, 9*a*
Aria, Id, 18
Aribi (Arabs), Ec, 2*d*
Aricia, Ab, 14*b*
Ariminum, Gc, 12
Arinna, Ca, 3*a*
Ariolica (Transpadana), Ab, Eb, 12
Arius, F., Ib, 9*b*
Arius Lacus, Hc, 9*b*
Arjunayana, Ec, 18*b*
Armavir, Ea, 2*d*
Armavira, Kd, 11
Armenia, Ke, 11
Armenia Minor, Fb, 16
Armorica, Bc, 15
Arne, Dc, 6
Arnissa, Cb, 6
Arnon, R., Cf, 4*a*
Arnus, F., Ed. 12
Aroer, Bf, 4*c*
Arpad, Da, 4*c*
Arpi, Da, 13
Arpinum, Ba, 13
Arrabona, Ba, 16
Arretium, Fd, 12
Arsanias, F., Db, 5*b*
Arsinoé (Aegyptus), If, 11
Arsinoé (Egypt), Bc, 3*a*
Arsinoé (Pentapolis), Cd, 16
Artacoana, Ic, 9*b*
Artaxata, Gc, 18
Artemisium, Ec, 6
Artyma, L., Eb, 7*c*
Arurias, F., Aa, 14*a*
Arvad, Bc, 4*c*
Arverni, Cc, 15
Arx, Insets, 13*a*, *b*
Arzanibiu, Ca, 3*a*
Arzawa, Ba, 3*a*
Arzus, F., Da, 7*c*
Ascalon, Ad, 4*d*
Ascania, L., Fb, 7*c*
Asclepieum, Inset, 7*a*
Asculum, He, 12
Ashdod, Ae, 4*a*
Asher, Bb, 4*a*
Ashguzai (Ashkenaz), Fb, 2*d*
Ashkelon, Ae, 4*a*
Ashkenaz (Ashguzai), Fb, 2*d*
Ashtaroth, Dc, 4*a*

INDEX

Ashur, Da, 3a
Ashur (Assyria), Eb, 2d
Asia, If, 20
Asia, Diocese of, If, 20
Asinaria, Pa., Inset, 11d
Asine (Argolis), De, 7
Asine (Rhion), Cf, 7
Askalon, Bb, 3a
Asopus, Df, 7
Asopus, F., De, Ed, 7
Aspadana, Hd, 18
Aspendus, Ec, 16
Asphaltitis, L., Dc, 9b
Asphynis, Cd, 3b
Assera, Eb, 6
Assisium, Gd, 12
Assorus, Ce, 13
Assus, Eb, 9a
Assyria, Da, 3a
Astacus (Acarnania), Cd, 6
Astacus (Phrygia), Fb, 7c
Atella, Cb, 13
Astigi, Ae, 15
Astures, Ad, 15
Asturica Augusta, Ad, 15
Astypalaea, I., Ge, 8
Asylum, Inset, 13a
Atalante, Ed, 6
Atavi, Cb, 18
Aternum, Je, 12
Aternus, F., He, 12
Ateste, Fb, 12
Athamania, Cc, 6
Athenae, Hf, 20
Athene Nike, Inset, 7a
Athene Promachos, Inset, 7a
Athens, Ancient, Inset, 7b
Athesis, F., Fb, 12
Athos, M, Fb, 6
Athribis (Hat-bri-ebe), Ba, 3b
Atina (Latium), Ba, 13
Atina (Lucania), Db, 13
Atlas, M., Cg, 20
Atrebates, Ee, 17
Atrium Vestae, Inset, 13a, b
Atropatene, Mf, 20
Attalia, Db, 4f
Attica, Cb, 9a
Attidium, Gd, 12
Attium Pr., Ce, 12
Aufidena (Apulia), Ea, 13
Aufidena (Samnium), Ca, 13
Aufidus, F., Ea, 13
Aufinum, He, 12
Augusta Praetoria, Bb, 12
Augusta Rauricorum, Dc, 15
Augusta Taurinorum (Turin), Bb, 12
Augusta Treverorum, Dc, 15
Augusta Vagiennorum, Bc, 12
Augusta Vindelicorum, Ec, 15
Augustobona, Cc, 15
Augustobriga, Bd, 15
Augustodunum, Cc, 10
Augustodurum, Bc, 15
Augustonemetum, Cc, 15
Augustoritum, Cc, 15
Aulis, Ed, 7
Aunedonnacum, Cc, 15·
Aurasius, M., De, 15
Aurelia, Pa., Inset, 11d
Aurelia Nova, Pa., Inset, 11d
Aureliani, Dd, 20
Aurelius, Inset, 11d
Aureus M., De, 12
Aurunci, Ba, 13
Ausculum, Da, 13
Auser, F., Ec, 12
Australe Pr., Inset, 17a
Autricum, Cc, 15
Auximum, Hd, 12
Avaricum, Cc, 15
Aveia, He, 12
Avenio, Cd, 15
Aventicum, Dc, 15
Aventinus, Inset, 11d
Aventinus M., Inset, 11c; 11d
Avernuslacus, Cc, 14b
Aviones, Db, 15
Axius, F., Ca, 9a
Axylos, Ec, 16
Azania, Gg, 18
Azania, De, 7
Aziris, Inset, 5b
Azotus, Ad, 4d

Baal Hermon (Mt. Hermon), Cb, 4a
Babel (Babylon), Ec, 2d
Babylon, Db, 3a
Babylon (Babel), Ec, 2d
Babylon (Cairo), Bb, 3b
Babylonia, Fc, 9b
Bactra, Jb, 5b; Jb, 9b
Bactria, Id, 18
Bactria (Zariaspa), Jb, 9b
Baetica, Ae, 15
Baetis, F., Ae, 15
Bagacum, Cb, 15
Bagistana, Gd, 18
Baiae, Cc, 14b
Bairat, Bb, 18a
Baithan, Jf, 19
Bakarei, Jg, 19
Baleares, Df, 20
Bannaventa, Ed, 17
Bantia, Db, 13
Bar Hill, Ba, 17
Barathrum, Inset, 7b
Barbaria, Gg, 18
Barbarike, Ie, 18
Barcino, Cd, 10
Barduli, Ea, 13
Barga, Ca, 3a
Barium, Ea, 13
Barka, Cd, 16
Barnus, M., Cb, 6
Bashan, Dc, 4a
Bashan, Mts. of, Ce, 4c
Basilica Aemilia, Inset, 13b
Basilica Constantini, Inset, 13b
Basilica Iulia, Inset, 13b
Basilica Sempronia, Inset, 13a
Basilica Ulpia, Inset, 13b
Bastarnae, Id, 20
Bastarni M., Da, 16
Bastetani, Be, 15
Basti, Be, 15
Bastuli, Be, 15
Batanaea, Db, 4d
Batava, Ec, 15
Batavi, Cb, 15
Bath (Aqua Sulis), De, 17
Bauxanum, Fa, 12
Beeroth, Be, 4a
Beer-sheba, Af, 4a
Behistun, Fc, 5b
Beilan Pass, Db, 5b
Beirut, Cb, 3a
Belbina, De, 7
Belgae, De, 17
Belgae, Bb, 1
Belgica, Cc, 15
Bellunum, Ga, 12
Benacus, L., Eb, 12
Benares (Kasi), Cb, 18a
Beneventum, Ca, 13
Benjamin, Be, 4a
Benwell (Condercum), Inset, 17
Berea, Inset, Ca, 4f
Berenice (Aegyptus), Cd, 3a
Berenice (Arabia-Petraea), Jg, 11
Berenice (Euhesperiade), Cd, 16
Berga, Eb, 6
Bergomum, Db, 12
Bergula, Da, 7c
Beroe, Db, 16
Beroea (Macedonia), Cb, 16
Beroea (Syria), Fc, 16
Berrhoea, Db, 6
Berytus, Fd, 16
Bethany, Bd, 4d
Bethel (Luz), Be, 4a
Bethesda, Pool of, Inset, 4e
Beth-horon, Be, 4a
Bethlehem, Be, 4a
Bethsaida Julias, Cb, 4d
Beth-shean, Bd, 4a
Beth-shemish, Ae, 4a
Betriacum, Eb, 12
Bezabde, Eb, 9b
Bezer, Ce, 4a
Bezetha, Inset, 4e
Bhojas, Bb, 18a
Biainas, Eb, 2d
Bibracte, Cc, 15
Bibrax, Cc, 15
Bilbilis, Bd, 15
Bilitio, Da, 12
Birdoswald (Amboglanna), Inset, 17
Birrens (Blatobulgium), Ca, 17
Bisalate, Eb, 6
Bisanthe, Db, 7c
Bishri, Mt., Ca, 3a
Bit Yakin, Fc, 2d
Bithynia, Fc, 18; Je, 20
Bithynia-et-Pontus, Eb, 16
Bithynium, Eb, 16
Bitia, Be, 14a
Bituriges-Cubi, Cc, 15
Bituriges-Vivisci, Bc, 15
Blatobulgium (Birrens), Ca, 17
Boderia Aest., Inset, 17a
Bodetia, Dc, 12
Bodh Gaya, Cb, 18a
Bodotria Aest., Da, 17
Boebe, Dc, 6
Boebis, L., Dc, 6
Boeotia, Cb, 9a
Boeotians, Cb, 2b
Boghaz Keui (Hattusas), Cb, 2a
Boii, Fc, 12
Boius, M., Bb, 6
Bokhara, Id, 18
Bolan Pass, Jd, 9b
Bolbe, L., Eb, 6
Bolbitinic Mouth, Ba, 3b
Bolerium Pr., Af, 17
Bononia (Boulogne), Hf, 17
Bononia (Felsina), Fc, 12
Bononia (Gesoriacum), Cb, 15
Bononia (Moesia), Cb, 16
Borcovicium (Housesteads) Inset, 17
Boreale Pr., Inset, 17a
Borsippa, Db, 3a
Borysthenes, R., Jd, 20
Bosporus Cimmerius, Fa, 16
Bosporus Thracius, Fa, 7c
Bostra, Jf, 11
Bottais, Db, 6
Bovianum Undecumanorum, Ca, 13
Bovianum Vetus, Ca, 13
Bovillae, Ab, 14b
Bowness, Cb, 17
Bracara Augusta, Ad, 15
Bradanus, F., Eb, 13
Brancester (Branodunum) Gd, 17
Branodunum (Brancester), Gd, 17
Brauron, Ee, 7
Bravoniacum (Kirkby Thore), Db, 17
Bravonium, Dd, 17
Bremenium, Da, 17
Bremetennacum (Ribchester), Dc, 17
Bridgness, Ca, 17
Brigantes, Db, 17; Inset, 17a
Brigantium, Ac, 12
Brigantium (Hispania), Ad, 15
Brigantium (Rhaetia), Dc, 15
Brigetio, Ba, 16
Britain, Roman, 17
Britannia (Roman Diocese), Cc, 20
Brixellum, Ec, 12
Brixia, Eb, 12
Broad Wall, Inset, 4b
Brocavum (Brougham), Db, 17
Brough (Verterae), Db, 17
Brougham (Brocavum), Db, 17
Bructeri, Db, 15
Brundisium, Ge, 20
Brundulum, Gb, 12
Bruttii, Ed, 13
Bruttium, Ed, 13
Bryanium, Cb, 6
Bryges, Ca, 6
Bubastis (Pebeseth), Ba, 3b
Bucatium, Cd, 6
Bucephala, Kc, 9b
Buchetium, Bc, 6
Bulis, Dd, 7
Burdigala, Ce, 20
Burgh by Sands, Cb, 17
Burgundiones, Fd, 20
Burrium, De, 17
Busiris, Cc, 2a
Buthrotum, Bc, 6
Buto, Ba, 3b
Butuntum, Ea, 13
Buxentum, Db, 13
Buxton (Aquae), Ec, 17
Byblus, Dc, 9b
Byblus (Gebal), Bd, 4c
Byzantium, Ib, 5a; Fa, 9a
Byzantium (Constantinopolis), Ie, 20

Cabillonum, Cc, 15
Cabira, Fb, 16
Caburrum, Bc, 12
Cabyle, Db, 16
Cadusii, Fb, 9b
Caecina, Ed, 12
Caelia, Ea, 13
Caelimontana, Pa., Inset 11c
Caelimontium, Inset, 11d
Caer Flos, Cd, 17
Caer Gai, Cd, 17
Caer Sws, Cd, 17
Caere, Ge, 12
Caerleon (Isca), De, 17
Caesar Augusta, Ce, 20
Caesarea (Cappadocia), Kf, 20
Caesarea I. (Gallia), Bc, 15
Caesarea (Judaea), Ab, 4d; Ed, 16
Caesarea (Mauretania), Df, 20
Caesarea (Mazaca), Fc, 16
Caesarea Philippi, Ca, 4d
Caesariensis, Ce, 15
Caesarodunum, Cc, 15
Caesena, Gc, 12
Caetobriga, Ae, 15
Caicus, F., Eb, 2b
Caieta, Ba, 13
Calabria, Fb, 13
Calacte, Cd, 13
Calagurris, Bd, 15
Calauria, I., Ee, 7
Calcaria (Tadcaster), Ec, 17
Calchedon (Chalcedon), Ib, 5a
Calebites (Kenizzites), Af, 4a
Caledonia, Ab, 20
Caledonii, Inset, 17a
Cales (Campania), Ca, 13
Cales (Umbria), Gd, 12
Callatis, Db, 16
Calleva Atrebatum (Silchester), Fe, 17
Callinicum, Kf, 20
Callipolis, Fb, 13
Callirrhoe, Cd, 4d
Callonae, Fc, 9b
Calpe, Ca, 5b
Calpe, M., Ae, 15
Calvary, Inset, 4e
Calydnae, Ec, 2b
Calydon, Cd, 7
Calymnos, Ge, 8
Camarina, Fc, 5a
Cambodunum, Ec, 15
Camerinum, Hd, 12
Camirus, Ec, 2b
Campania, Cb, 13
Campus Agrippae, Inset, 11d
Campus Esquilinus, Inset, 11c
Campus Martius, Inset, 11c
Campus Vaticanus, Inset, 11c
Campus Viminalis, Inset, 11c
Camulodunum (Colchester), Ge, 17
Camuni, Eb, 12
Cana, Bb, 4d
Canaan, Dc, 2a
Canaanites, Af, Bd, 4a
Canastraeum Pr., Ec, 6
Cane, Gf, 18
Cannae, Ea, 13
Canopic Mouth, Ba, 3b
Canopus, Bc, 9b
Canovium, Cc, 17
Cantabri, Bd, 15
Canterbury (Durovernum), Ge, 17
Cantii, Ge, 17
Canusium, Ea, 13
Capena, Ge, 12
Capernaum, Cb, 4d
Capetani, Be, 10
Caphereus Pr., Fd, 7
Caphyae, De, 7
Capitol, Inset, 11d
Capitolinus, M., Insets, 13a, b
Capitolium, Insets, 13a, b
Cappadocia, Kf, 20
Capraria, Dd, 12
Capreae Ins., Cb, 13
Capsa, Df, 15
Capua, Ca, 13
Caraceni, Jf, 12
Carales, De, 15
Carana, Ke, 11
Carcer, Insets, 13a, b
Carchemish, Da, 4c
Cardamyle, Cc, 9a
Cardia, Cb, 7c
Cardiff, Ce, 17
Carduchi, Eb, 5b
Caria, Fc, 9a
Carians, Bb, 2a
Carinae, Inset, 11c
Carlisle (Luguvallium), Db, 17
Carmana, Hc, 5b
Carmania, Hc, 9b; He, 18
Carmarthen (Maridunum), Be,17
Carmel, Mt., Ac, 4a
Carmentalis, Pa, Inset, 11c
Carnarvon (Segontium), Bc, 17
Carni, Ga, 12; Dc, 18
Carnuntum, Ba, 16
Carolis, Ef, 20
Carpathos I., Hf, 8
Carpatus Mons, Hd, 20
Carpetani, Bd, 15
Carpis, Ee, 15
Carrawburgh (Procolitia), Inset, 17
Carrea Potentia, Bc, 12
Carrhae, Fc, 16; Ab, 18b
Carsioli, He, 12
Carsulae, Ge, 12
Carteia, Ae, 15
Cartenna, Ce, 15
Carthago, Ff, 20
Carthago Nova, Cf, 20
Caruanca, M., Ja, 12
Carusadius, M., Hb, 12
Carvoran (Magnae), Inset, 17
Caryae, De, 7
Carystus (Euboea), Fd, 7
Carystus (Laconia), De, 7
Caspian Gates, Gb, 9b
Caspii, Fa, 9b
Cassanitae, Ge, 18
Cassiope, Ac, 6
Castell Collen, Cd, 17
Casthanaea, Dc, 6
Castle Flemish, Be, 17
Castlecary, Ca, 17
Castlehill, Ba, 17
Castlesteads, Inset, 17
Castra Exploratorum, Ca, 17
Castra Praetoria, Inset, 11d
Castrense, A., Inset, 11d
Castrum Novum, He, 12
Castrum Truentinum, He, 12
Castulo, Be, 15
Casuentus, F., Eb, 13
Catana (Catane), De, 13
Cataractonium (Catterick Bridge), Eb, 17
Cathaei, Kc, 9b
Catterick Bridge (Cataractonium), Eb, 17
Catuvellauni, Fe, 17
Cauca, Bd, 15
Caucasus Mts., Fb, 16
Caudium, Ca, 13
Caulonia, Ed, 13
Causennae (Ancaster), Fd, 17
Cauvery, R., Jf, 19
Cayster, R., Hc, 8
Cayster Plain, Cb, 5b
Ceba, Cc, 12
Cebenna, M., Cd, 15
Cebrene, Cc, 7c
Cecryphalea, Ee, 7
Celaenae, Bb, 9b
Celeia, Ba, 16
Celenderis, Cb, 2d
Celetrum, Cb, 6
Cellae, Cb, 6
Celti, Da, 5a
Celtiberi, Bd, 15
Celtica, Cc, 15
Celtici, Ae, 15
Cemenelum, Bd, 12
Cenabum, Cc, 15
Cenaeum Pr., Cc, 8
Cenchreae, Ee, 7
Cenomani, Eb, 12
Centumcellae, Fe, 12
Centuripa, Ce, 13
Ceos, Fe, 7
Cephallenia Bd, 7; Cc, 16
Cephallenians, Bb, 2b
Cephalœdium, Be, 13
Cephisia, Ed, 7
Cephisus, Dd, 6
Ceramicus, Inset, 7b
Cerasus, Da, 5b
Cercinitis L., Eb, 6
Ceriadae, Inset, 7b
Cerinthus, Ed, 6
Cermalus, Insets, 13a, b
Cespius, M., Inset, 11c
Ceylon (Simkala), Fe, 18b
Ceylon (Tamraparni), Cd, 18a
Chaeronea, Dd, 6
Chalastra, Db, 6
Chalce, He, 8
Chalcedon, Ie, 20
Chalcedon (Calchedon), Ib, 5a Fa, 9a
Chalcidice, Ca, 9a

INDEX

Chalcis (Aetolia), Cd, 7
Chalcis (Epirus), Cc, 6
Chalcis (Euboea), Ed, 6
Chalcis, Syria, Fc, 16
Chaldaea, Ec, 2*d*
Chalybes, Da, 2*d*
Chalybon, Db, 9*b*
Chambal, R., Je, 19
Chang-an, Md, 19
Chang-Jeh, Md, 19
Charadra, Bc, 6
Charidemi Pr., Be, 15
Chatti, Cb, 18
Chauci, Db, 15
Chelonatus Pr., Ce, 7
Chephirah, Be, 4*a*
Chera, Jf, 19
Chera, Kingdom of, Ee, 18*b*
Cherethites, Af, 4*c*
Chersonesus (Thrace), Da, 9*a*
Chersonesus Cimbrica, Da, 10
Chersonesus Pr., Be, 14*a*
Chersonesus, Pr., Fd, 6
Chersonesus Taurica, Ea, 16
Cherusci, Db, 18
Chester (Deva), Dc, 17
Chesterford, Gd, 17
Chesterholm (Vindolanda), Inset, 17
Chester-le-Street, Eb, 17
Chesters (Cilurnum), Inset, 17
Chiang-Hsia, Nd, 19
Chiao Chow, Ne, 19
Chichester (Regnum), Ff, 17
Ching-chao, Md, 19
Ching-chow, Nd, 19
Ching Chow, Nd, 19
Chinnereth, Sea of, Cc, 4*a*
Chios, Fc, 8
Choaspes, R., Fc, 5*b*
Chola, Jf, 19
Chola, K. of, Bc, 18*a*; Ed, 18*b*
Chorasmia, Hc, 18
Chorasmii, Ha, 9*b*
Chorazin, Cb, 4*d*
Chryse, Eb, 2*b*
Chrysopolis, Ie, 20
Cibalae, Gd, 20
Cibyra, Dc, 1*b*
Cicones, Da, 2*b*
Cierium, Dc, 6
Cilicia, Jf, 20
Cilicia (Khilakku), Cb, 2*d*
Cilician Gates, Cb, 5*b*
Cilurnum (Chesters), Inset, 17
Cimbrica Chersonesus, Da, 15
Ciminius, L., Ge, 12
Cimmerians, Cb, 2*d*
Cimmerians (Gomer), Ea, 2*d*
Cimolos, Ff, 7
Cinaros, Ge, 8
Cingulum, Hd, 12
Circeii, Ba, 13
Circesium, Lf, 20
Circus Flaminius, Inset, 13*a*
Circus Maximus, Inset, 13*b*
Cirrha, Dd, 7
Cirta, Ef, 20
Cispadana, Ec, 12
Citerior, Hispania, Be, 15
Cithaeron M., Ed, 7
Citium (Cyprus), Ed, 16
Citium (Macedonia), Db, 6
City of Salt, Bf, 4*a*
Clanis, F., Ge, 12
Clanoventa (Ravenglass), Cb, 17
Classis, Gc, 12
Clastidium, Db, 12
Claterna, Fc, 12
Claudia, Aq., Inset, 11*d*
Clausentum, Ef, 17
Clavenna, Da, 12
Clazomenae, Ic; 5*a*, Gc, 8
Cleonae (Argolis), De, 7
Cleonae (Chalcidice), Fb, 6
Clepsydra, Inset, 7*a*
Clesis, Eb, 12
Cliternia, Kf, 12
Clitor, De, 7
Cloaca Maxima, Inset, 13*a*
Clota Aest, Ba, 17
Clunia, Bd, 15
Clupea, Ee, 15
Clusium, Fd, 12
Cnidus, Ic, 5*a*
Cnossus, Dc, 16
Cocala, Jd, 9*b*
Coccium (Wigan), Dc, 17
Coele, Inset, 7*b*
Coelesyria, Fd, 18
Colapis, F., Kb, 12
Colchester (Camulodunum), Ge, 17
Colchis, Kd, 11
Collina, Inset, 11*c*
Collina, Pa., Inset, 11*c*
Collis Hortorum, Inset, 11*c*
Collis Quirinalis, Inset, 11*c*
Collis Viminalis, Inset, 11*c*
Collytus, Inset, 7*b*
Colonia Agrippina, Ec, 20
Colophon, Eb, 9*a*
Colossae, Bb, 5*b*
Colosseum, Inset, 13*b*
Colossus Neronis, Inset, 13*b*
Columbarium Pr., Bd, 14
Columna Traiani, Inset, 13*b*
Columnae Herculis, Ae, 15
Comana (Bithynia), Fb, 16
Comana (Cappadocia), Fc, 16
Comitium, Insets, 13*a*, *b*
Commagene, Fc, 16
Compsa, Db, 13
Comum, Db, 12
Concordia (Venetia), Gb, 12
Condate, Bc, 15
Condercum (Benwell), Inset, 17
Coneta, Gb, 12
Confluentes, Db, 15
Conimbriga, Ad, 15
Consentia, Ec, 13
Consilinum, Db, 13
Constantinopolis (Byzantium), Ie, 20
Contestani, Be, 15
Contrebia, Bd, 15
Copae, Ed, 7
Copais, L., Ed, 7
Coptos (Kebtu), Cd, 3*b*
Cora, Aa, 13
Coracesium, Ec, 16
Corbridge (Corstopitum), Db, 17
Corcyra, Ac, 6
Corduba, Be, 15; Cf, 20
Corfinium, He, 12
Corinium, Inset, 17*a*
Corinium (Cirencester), Ee, 17
Corinth, De, 7
Corinthus, Ed, 18
Corioli, Ab, 14*b*
Coritani, Fc, 17
Corner Gate (Old Gate), Inset, 4*b*
Cornovii, Dd, 17
Cornus, Dd, 15
Corodamum Pr., Ie, 18
Corone, Cf, 7
Coronea, Dd, 7
Corsi, Bd, 14*a*
Corsica, Ce, 12
Corstopitum (Corbridge), Db, 17
Cortona, Gd, 12
Coryceum Pr., Gc, 8
Cos, He, 8
Cossaei, Fc, 9*b*
Cossura, I., Ee, 15
Costoboci, Da, 16
Cotiaeum, Dc, 16
Cotini, Dc, 18
Cotyora, Da, 5*b*
Cramond, Ca, 17
Cranii M., Cc, 6
Crannon, Dc, 6
Cratea, Eb, 16
Crathis, F., Ec, 13
Cremna, Ec, 16
Cremona, Eb, 12
Crenides, Fa, 6
Crestonia, Eb, 6
Creta, Hf, 20
Crete, Inset, 7*d*
Crexa I., Jc, 12
Crimisa Pr., Fc, 13
Crisa, Dd, 7
Criumetopon Pr., Aa, 7*d*
Crixia, Cc, 12
Crococalana, Fc, 17
Crocodilopolis-Arsinoe (Shedet), Bb, 3*b*
Crommyon, Ee, 7
Croton, Gc, 5*a*
Crypta, Inset, 11*d*
Ctesiphon, Kf, 11
Cularo, Dc, 15
Cullu, De, 15
Cumae, Fb, 5*a*
Cunaxa, Ec, 5*b*
Cunetio, Ee, 17
Cupra Maritima, Hd, 12
Cures, Ge, 12
Curia, Inset, 13*b*
Curia (Rhaetia), Dc, 15
Curia Hostilia, Inset, 13*a*
Curia Iulia, Inset, 11*d*
Curicta I., Jb, 12
Curium, Jd, 5*a*
Cusae (Gosu), Bc, 3*b*
Cutch, Ie, 19
Cutha, Ec, 2*d*
Cuttiae, Cb, 12
Cyclades, Ed, 8
Cydathenæum, Inset, 7*b*
Cydonia, Cc, 16
Cyllene, Cd, 7
Cyllene M., De, 7
Cyme, Aeolis, Gc, 8
Cyme, Euboea, Fd, 6
Cynaetes, Ae, 15
Cynaetha, Dd, 7
Cynopolis, Bb, 3*b*
Cynoscephalae, Dc, 6
Cynossema, Ea, 9*a*
Cynuria, De, 7
Cynus, Ed, 6
Cyparissiae, Ce, 7
Cypas, Cb, 7*c*
Cyprus, Ec, 16
Cypsela, Cb, 7*c*
Cyrenaica, Ed, 18
Cyrenaica-Creta, Cd, 16
Cyrene, Hg, 20
Cyropolis, Jb, 5*b*
Cyrrhus, Db, 6
Cyrus, R, Fa, 2*d*; Ld, 11
Cythera, I., Df, 7
Cythnos, Fe, 7
Cytinium, Dd, 6
Cyzicus, Ha, 8

DACIA, Ca, 16
Dacia, Diocese of, He, 20
Dadicae, Kb, 5*b*
Dahae, Hb, 9*b*
Daix, R., Hb, 18
Dalmatia, Ge, 20
Damascus, Da; 4*a*
Damnonii, Inset, 17*a*
Dan, Bd, 4*c*
Dan (Tribe), Ae, Cb, 4*a*
Danubius (Ister), F., Db, 16
Danum (Doncaster), Ec, 17
Daphnae, Cc, 5*b*
Dardani, Aa, 9*b*
Dardanians, Eb, 2*b*
Dardanus, Cb, 7*c*
Daritae, Gb, 5*b*
Dascylium, Cb, 5*b*
Dascylium, Eb, 7*c*
Dassaretae, Bb, 6
Datum, Hb, 5*a*
Davaka, Kingdom of, Fc, 18*b*
David's House, Inset, 4*b*
Debir (Kirjath Sepher), Af, 4*a*
Decapolis, Cb, 4*d*
Decelea, Cb, 9*a*
Delcus, Ea, 7*c*
Delium, Cb, 9*a*
Delos, Dc, 9*a*
Delphi, Hc, 5*a*
Delphi (Indraprastha), Ec, 18*b*
Delphinium, Gc, 8
Demetae, Be, 17
Demetrias, Dc, 6
Derbe, Eb, 4*f*
Der ez Zor, Da, 3*a*
Derrhis Pr., Fc, 6
Dertona, Cc, 12
Dertosa, Cd, 15
Deserta Libyca, Hg, 11
Dessinus, Ie, 11
Deva (Chester), Dc, 17
Devagiri, Ed, 18*b*
Devarashtra, Ed, 18*b*
Dhauli, Cc, 18*a*
Dia, Ca, 7*d*
Dialas, R., Fc, 5*b*
Dianium, Hispania, Ce, 15
Dianium, Italy, Fe, 12
Dicaea, Bb, 7*c*
Dicte M., Ca, 7*d*
Didyme, Cd, 13
Diogenium, Inset, 7*b*
Diomea, Inset, 7*b*
Dion, Db, 4*d*
Dioscoridis I., Hf, 18
Dioscurias, Lb, 5*a*
Dioscurias Pr., Fd, 13
Diospolis Parva, Cc, 3*b*
Dipaea, De, 7
Dipylum, Inset. 7*b*
Dium (Chalcidice), Fb, 6
Dium (Euboea), Dd, 6
Dium (Macedonia), Db, 6
Divodurum, Dc, 15
Divona, Cd, 15
Doberus, Da, 6
Dobuni, De, 17
Dodona, Bc, 6
Doliche, Db, 6
Dolopes, Cc, 6
Dolopes, Is., Ec, 6
Domus Augustana, Inset, 13*b*
Domus Caligulae, Inset, 13*b*
Domus Flaviana, Inset, 13*b*
Domus Liviae, Inset, 13*b*
Domus Septimii Severi, Inset, 13*b*
Domus Tiberiana, Inset, 13*b*
Doncaster (Danum), Ec, 17
Dor, Ac, 4*a*
Dorchester (Durnovaria), Df, 17
Doris, Dd, 6
Doris, He, 8
Doriscus, Ba, 5*b*
Dorylaeum, Ec, 16
Dothan, Be, 4*c*
Drabescus, Fa, 6
Drangiana, Id, 18
Drapsaca, Jb, 9*b*
Dravus, F., Ba, 16
Drepanum (Phrygia), Fb, 7*c*
Drepanum (Sicilia), Ad, 13
Drepanum Pr., Cd, 7
Drinius, F., Bb, 16
Droi, Ea, 6
Drubetae, Cb, 16
Drumburgh, Inset, 17
Druzipara, Da, 7*c*
Dryopes, Cc, 6
Dubrae, He, 17
Du-kau (Antaeopolis), Bc, 3*b*
Dulichium, Bb, 2*b*
Duma, Dc, 2*d*
Dumnonii, Bf, 17
Dur Kurigalzu, Ec, 2*a*
Dur Shaarukin, Eb, 2*d*
Duranius, F., Cd, 15
Duria Major, F., Bb, 12
Duria Minor, F., Bb, 12
Durius, F., Ad, 15
Durnovaria(Dorchester), Df, 17
Durobrivae, Fd, 17
Durobrivae (Rochester), Ge, 17
Durocobrivae, Fe, 17
Durocortorum, Cc, 15
Durostorum, Db, 16
Durotriges, Df, 17
Durovernum (Canterbury), Ge, 17
Dymae, Cb, 7*c*
Dyme, Cd, 7
Dyrrhachium, He, 20
Dyrta Kb, 9*b*
Dystus, Fd, 7

EAST, DIOCESE OF THE (Orientis), Kg, 20
East, Prefecture of the, Jg, 20
East Roman Empire, If, 20
Ebal, Mt., Bd, 4*a*
Ebchester (Vindomora), Inset, 17
Eburacum (York), Eb, 17
Ebusus, Ce, 15
Ecbatana, Fc, 5*b*; Gd, 18
Ecbatana (Achmetha), Fc, 2*d*
Ecdippa, Ba, 4*d*
Echedorus, F., Db, 6
Echinades Ins., Cd, 7
Echinus, Dd, 6
Ecnomus Pr., Be, 13
Edessa (Macedonia), Cb, 16
Edessa (Syria), Fc, 16
Edetani, Bd, 15
Edinburgh, Ca, 17
Edom, Bg, 4*c*
Edomites, Bf, 4*a*
Edones, Ea, 6
Edrum, Eb, 12
Eglon, Ae, 4*a*
Egypt, Bc, 3
Egypt, Diocese of (Ægyptus), Ih, 20
Egypt (Musri, Mizraim, Kush), Cd, 2*d*
Eileithyiapolis, Bc, 3*a*
Eion, Eb, 6
Eira, Ce, 7
Eium, Ca, 9*a*
Ekron, Ae, 4*a*
Elaea, Aeolis, Hc, 8
Elaea, Thesprotia, Bc, 6
Elaeus, Ba, 9*b*
Elam, Eb, 3*a*
Elatea, Dd, 6
Elath, Ah, 4*c*
Elburz, Cb, 18*b*
Elea, Db, 13
Elephantine I., Bd, 3*a*
Eleusinium, Inset, 7*a*
Eleusis, Ed, 7
Eleutherae, Ed, 7
Eleutherna, Ba, 7*d*
Eleutherus, F., Cb, 3*a*
Elimberrum, Cd, 15
Elimea, Cb, 6
Elis, Ce, 7
Ellipi, Fc, 2*d*
Elymi, Ae, 13
Emathia, Da, 6
Emerita Augusta, Bd, 18
Emmaus, Ad, 4*d*
Emona, Ja, 12
Emporiae, Db, 5*a*
Emporium, Inset, 11*c*
Emporium Segestanorum, Ad, 13
En Mont (Hermonthis), Cd, 3*b*
Endidae, Fa, 12
Endor, Bc, 4*a*
Enet (Tentyra), Cc, 3*b*
Engannim, Bd, 4*a*
Entella, Be, 13
Eordaei, Cb, 6
Eordaicus, F., Bb, 6
Epeans, Bb, 2*b*
Ephesus, Hd, 8
Ephraim, Bd, 4*a*
Ephraim, Mt., Bd, 4*a*
Ephyra, Bc, 6
Epidamnus, Gb, 5*a*
Epidaurus (Argolis), Ee, 7
Epidaurus (Illyricum), Bb, 16
Epidaurus Limera, Df, 7
Epidium Pr., Aa, 17
Epiphania, Fc, 16
Epirus, Bc, 6
Eporedia, Bb, 12
Erandapalla, Ec, 18*b*
Erech, Eb, 3*a*
Erechtheum, Inset, 7*a*
Eresus, Fb, 8
Eretria (Euboea), Ed, 7
Eretria (Phthiotis), Dc, 6
Ergines, Ca, 7*c*
Eridu, Eb, 3*a*
Erineus, Dd, 6
Eriza, Fc, 16
Ermine Street, Fd, 17
Erymanthus, F., Ce, 7
Erymanthus, M., Ce, 7
Erythrae, Eb, 9*a*
Erythraeum Mare, Gd, 5*b*
Eryx, Ad, 13
Esdraelon, Plain of, Bb, 4*d*
Esquiliae, Inset, 11*d*
Esquilina, Inset, 11*c*
Esquilina, Pa., Inset, 11*c*
Etruria, Fd, 12
Etrusci (Tusci), Bb, 14*c*
Etymander, R., Ic, 5*b*
Euboea, Db, 9*a*
Euganei, Eb, 12
Euhesperidae (Berenice), Cd, 16
Eulaeus, F., Gc, 5*b*
Eupatoria, Fb, 16
Euphrates, R., Db, 3; Gd, 18
Euripus, Dc, 8
Europa, Bb, 1
Europus, Da, 6
Eurotas, F., De, 7
Eurytanes, Cd, 6
Eutaea, De, 7
Euthane, He, 8
Exeter (Isca Dumnoniorum), Cf, 17
Ezion Geber, Bh, 4*c*

FABRATERIA, Ba, 13
Faesulae, Fd, 12
Fair Havens, Cc, 4*f*
Faleria, Hd, 12
Falerii, Ge, 12
Fanum, Hd, 12
Faventia, Fc, 12
Felsina, Fc, 12
Feltria, Fa, 12
Ferentinum, Ba, 13
Fidenae, Gf, 12
Fidentia, Ec, 12
Fifth Cataract of Nile, Be, 3
Firmum Hd, 12

First Cataract of Nile, Bd, 3
Fiscellus, M., He, 12
Flaminia, Pa., Inset, 11d
Flanona, Jb, 12
Flaviobriga, Bd, 15
Flavium A. (Colosseum), Inset, 11d
Flevo L., Db, 15
Florentia, Fd, 12
Florentiola, Dc, 12
Flumen Senus, Inset, 17a
Flumen Vidua, Inset, 17a
Flumentana, Pa., Inset, 11c
Folkestone, He, 17
Fontinalis, Pa., Inset, 11c
Forest of Arden, Ed, 17
Forest of Dean, Dc, 17
Formiae, Bb, 14b
Forum Appii, Aa, 4f
Forum Augusti, Inset, 13b
Forum Boarium, Inset, 13b
Forum Cornelii, Fc, 12
Forum Fulvii, Cb, 12
Forum Germanorum, Bc, 12
Forum Holitorium, Inset, 13a
Forum Iulii, Dd, 15
Forum Iulium (Roma), Inset, 13b
Forum Iulium (Venetia), Ha, 12
Forum Livii, Gc, 12
Forum Nervae, Inset, 13b
Forum Pacis, Inset, 13b
Forum Popilii (Cispadana), Gc, 12
Forum Popilii (Lucania), Db, 13
Forum Romanum, Inset, 13b
Forum Sempronii, Gd., 12
Forum Traiani, Inset, 13b
Forum Traiani, Sardinia, Be, 14a
Forum Vibii, Bc, 12
Fosse Way, Ed, 17
Fourth Cataract of Nile, Be, 3a
Franci, Ec, 20
Fregellae, Ba, 13
Fregenae, Gf, 12
Frentini, Je, 12
Frento, F., Kf, 12
Fretum Gaditanum, Ae, 15
Fretum Gallicum, Cb, 15
Fretum Gallicum (Corsica), Dd, 15
Frisii, Ec, 20
Fucinus, L., Hf, 12
Fulaeus, F., Eb, 3a
Fulginium, Ge, 12
Fundi, Ba, 13

GABAEUM Pr., Bc, 15
Gad (Tribe), Cd, Ce, 4a
Gadara, Cb, 4d
Gades, Bf, 20
Gaetuli, Bc, 1
Galatia, Jf, 20
Galilee, Bb, 4d
Galilee, Sea of, Cb, 4a
Gallaecia, Ad, 15
Gallia, Dd, 20
Gallia Cisalpina, Eb, 12
Gambalu, Fc, 2d
Gandaria, Kc, 5b
Gandhara, Jd, 19
Gandhara, Kingdom of, Eb, 18b
Ganges, R., Je, 19
Gangra, Eb, 16
Ganos, Db, 7c
Garganum Pr., Ea, 13
Garganus, M., Da, 13
Gariannonum, Hd, 17
Garsaura, Ec, 16
Garumna, F., Bd, 15
Gath, Ae, 4a
Gaugamela, Eb, 9b
Gaul (Gallia), Diocese of, Dd, 20
Gaul (Gallia), Prefecture of, Dd, 20
Gaulanitis, Cb, 4d
Gaya, Fc, 18b
Gaza, Ae, 4a
Gazaca, Gd, 18
Geba, Be, 4a
Gebal (Byblus), Bd, 4c
Gedrosia, Ie, 18
Gela, Ce, 13
Gelas, F., Ce, 13
Gellygaer, Ce, 17
Gem Aton, Bd, 3a
Genath (Gate Genath), Inset, 4e
Geneva, Dc, 15
Genua, Cc, 12
Genusium, Eb, 13
Gepidae, Hd, 20
Geraestus Pr., Fe, 7
Gerania, M., Cc, 8
Gerasa, Cc, 4d
Gergesa, Cb, 4d
Gergovia, Cc, 15
Gerizim, Mt., Bd, 4a
Germania, Eb, 15
Germania Inferior, Db, 15
Germania Superior, Dc, 15
Geronthrae, Df, 7
Gerrha, He, 18
Gerrhaei, Ge, 18
Gerunda, Cd, 15
Gerunium, Da, 13
Geshuri, Cc, 4a
Gesoriacum (Bononia), Cb, 15
Getae, Ba, 9b
Gezer, Ae, 4a
Ghazni, Jc, 9b
Gibbethon, Ae, 4a
Gibeon, Be, 4a
Gigonus, Eb, 6
Gihon Sinnor, Inset, 4b
Gilboa, Mt., Bd, 4a
Gilead, Cd, 4a
Gilgal, Ce, 4a
Ginaea, Bc, 4d
Gionar Hill, Bb, 18a
Gizeh, Cc, 2a
Glevum (Gloucester), De, 17
Gloucester (Glevum), De, 17
Gnathia, Fb, 13
Gobannium (Abergavenny), Ce, 17
Godavari, R., Jf, 19
Golan Cc, 4a ,
Golden Gate(Jerusalem),Inset,4e
Gomer (Cimmerians), Ea, 2d
Gomphi, Cc, 6
Gonnus, Dc, 6
Gorditanum Pr., Bd, 14
Gordium, Ec, 16
Gortyna, Id, 5a
Gortys, De, 7
Goshen (Egypt), Ba, 3b
Gosu (Cusae), Bc, 3b
Gozan (Guzana), Eb, 2d
Graecia, Ab, 5b
Granicus, Ba, 9b
Granicus, F., Db, 7c
Graviscae, Fe, 12
Great Chesters (Aesica), Inset, 17
Great Sea, The, Ac, 4a
Greece, 7
Greece (Achaea), Cb, 4,
Grumentum Db, 13
Grumum, Eb, 13
Gryneium, Eb, 9a
Gujarat, Ec, 18b
Gulashkird, Hd, 9b
Gurgum, Db, 2d
Guttones, Db, 18
Guzana (Gozan), Eb, 2d
Gwalior, Ec, 18
Gymnias, Da, 5b
Gytheum, Df, 7

HABIRU (Shasu), Cb, 3a
Habitancum, Da, 17
Hadrianopolis, Db, 16; Ie, 20
Hadrumetum, Ee, 15
Haemus, M., Ba, 9b
Hagia Triada, Bc, 2a
Halap (Aleppo), Ca, 3a
Haliacmon, F., Db, 6
Haliartus, Ed, 7
Halicarnassus, Bb, 5b; Ee, 9a
Halicyae, Ae, 13
Halieis, Ee, 7
Halton (Hunnum), Ea, 17
Halus, Dc, 6
Halycus, F., Be, 13
Halys, R., Eb, 16
Hamath, Cb, 4c
Han Dominions, Nd, 19
Han-chung, Md, 19
Hanigalbat, Ca, 3a
Hardknot, Cb, 17
Harmozia. He, 18
Harosheth, Bc, 4a
Harran, Ca, 3a
Hasta, Baetica, Ae, 15
Hasta, Liguria, Cc, 12
Hatra, Gd, 18
Hatria (Picenum), Je, 12
Hatria (Venetia), Gb, 12
Hatti (Hittites), Cb, Db, 2d
Hattusas (Boghaz Keui), Cb, 2a
Hazor, Bd, 4c
Hebron (Kirjath Arba), Be, 4a
Hebrus, F., Db, 16
Hecatompylos, Gg, 9b
Helena (Graecia), Fe, 7
Helice, Dd, 7
Helicon M., Dd, 7
Heliopolis (On), Ba, 3b
Hellas, Ab, 9b
Hellespontus, If, 20
Helorus, Df, 13
Helos, Df, 7
Helvetii, Dc, 15
Hemesa, Fd, 16
Henen-seten (Heracleopolis magna), Bb, 3b
Henna, Ce, 13
Hephaestia, Bc, 7c
Heraclea, Caria, Hd, 8
Heraclea Chersonesus, Eb, 16
Heraclea (Lucania), Eb, 13
Heraclea Lyncestis, Ca, 6
Heraclea (Malis), Dd, 6
Heraclea Minoa, Be, 13
Heraclea Pontica, Eb, 16
Heracleopolis magna (Henen-seten), Bb, 3b
Heracleum, Db, 6
Heracleum (Theseum), Inset, 7b
Heracleum Pr., Ee, 13
Heraea, Ce, 7
Heraei M., Ce, 13
Heraeum, Pr., Dd, 7
Herat, see Alexandria
Herculaneum, Cb, 13
Herculia, Ba, 16
Herculis Pr., Be, 17
Herdoniae, Da, 13
Hermeius Smyrnaeos, Gc, 8
Hermione, Ee, 7
Hermon, Mt., Cb, 4a
Hermonthis (En Mont), Cd, 3b
Hermopolis Magna (Hmunu), Bc, 3b
Hermunduri, Eb, 15
Hermupolis, Ig, 11
Hermus, F., Dc, 16
Hernici, Ba, 13
Herod Agrippa, Kingdom of, Fc, 4f
Herod's Palace, Inset, 4e
Herod's Temple, Inset, 4e
Herodium, Bd, 4d
Heruli, Jd, 20
Heshbon, Ce, 4a
Hestiaeotis, Cc, 6
Hibernia, Bc, 20
Hiddekel (Tigris), F., Ec, 2d
Hiera, Ad, 13
Hierapolis, Kf, 20
Hierapytna, Ca, 7d
Hierasus, F., Da, 16
Hieropolis, Fc, 16
Hierosolyma, Fd, 18
Hierosolyma (Jerusalem), Dc, 5b
High Street, Db, 17
Himalaya Mts., Ba, 18a
Himera, Fc, 5a
Himera, F., Ce, 13
Hindu, Kush, Ba, 18a
Hinnom (Gehenna), Valley of, Insets, 4e, 4b
Hippicus Tower, Inset, 4e
Hippo, Ef, 20
Hippo Diarrhytus, Ec, 5a
Hippo Regius, Ec, 5a
Hippo Zarytus, De, 15
Hippodrome, Inset, 13b
Hipponium, Ed, 13
Hipponon, Bb, 3b
Hippos, Cb, 4d
Hirpini, Ca, 13
Hispalis, Ae, 15
Hispania, Ce, 20
Hispellum, Gd, 12
Histiaea, Ed, 6
Histonium, Je, 12
Hit, Bb, 18b
Hittites (Hatti), Cb, Db, 2d
Hittites (Hatti), Ca, 3a
Hittites (Kalti), Cb, 4c
Hmunu (Hermopolis Magna) Bc, 3b
Holyhead, Bc, 17
Homolium, Dc, 6
Honan, Nd, 19
Horologium, Inset, 7b
Horta, Ge, 12
Horti, Inset, 7b
Hostilia, Fb, 12
Housesteads (Borcovicium), Inset, 17
Hsu Chow, Nd, 19
Huai, R., Od, 19
Hui-hi, Od, 19
Hunni, Db, 1
Hunnum (Halton), Ea, 17
Hurmunduri, Db, 18
Hyccara, Bd, 13
Hydaspes, F., Kc, 9b
Hydrea, Ee, 7
Hydronte, Gb, 13
Hydruntum, Gb, 13
Hymettus, M., Ee, 7
Hypanis, F., Ea, 16
Hypothebae (Thebes), Cb, 2b
Hypanis, F., Fa, 16
Hypsas, F., Ae, 13
Hypsele, Bc, 3b
Hyrcania, Hd, 18
Hyrcanium (M. Caspium), Db, 1
Hysiae, De, 7

IADER (Illyricum), Bb, 16
Ialysus, Fc, 9a
Iambia, Fe, 18
Ianiculum Arx, Inset, 11
Iapygia, Cb, 14c
Iasa, Hd, 8
Iasus, Ec, 9a
Iaxartes, F., Eb, 1
Iazyges, Ec, 18
Iberia, Cc, 5a
Iberia (Caucasus), Kd, 11
Iberus, R., Ce, 20
Ibleam, Bd, 4a
Icaria, Gd, 8
Iceni, Gd, 17
Ichthys Pr., Ce, 7
Icknield Wat, Gd, 17
Iconium, Ec, 16
Icosium, Ce. 15
Ictis, Ab, 15
Icus, Ec, 6
Ida, M., Ba, 7d
Ida, Mt. (Troy), Eb, 2b
Idomene, Cc, 6
Idumaea, Ae, 4d
Igilgili, De, 15
Igilium, Ee, 12
Iguvium, Gd, 12
Ilchester, De, 17
Ilerda, Cd, 15
Ilici, Be, 15
Ilissus, Inset, 7b
Ilium, Cc, 7c
Ilium (Troy), Bb, 2a
Ilkley (Olicana), Ec, 17
Illergetes, Cd, 15
Illubri, Cb, 2d
Illyra, Ba, 6
Illyria, Diocese of, Ge, 20
Illyria, Prefecture of, Hf, 20
Illyricum, Bb, 16; Gd, 20
Ilos, Inset, 2c
Ilva, Fb, 5a
Imaus Mons, Ec, 1; Kc, 9b
Imbros, Fa, 8
Imperial Fora, Inset, 13b
India, Fc, 1
Indoscythia, Ec, 1
Indraprastha (Delhi), Ec, 18b
Indus, R., Ie, 19
Industria, Cb, 12
Inessa, Ce, 13
Ingira, Cb, 2d
Insubres, Db, 12
Interacrea, He, 12
Interamna (Etruria), Ge, 12
Interamna (Latium), Ba, 13
Interamna (Picenum), He, 12
Interamnium, Ec, 13
Intimilii, Bd, 12
Inveravon, Ca, 17
Inveresk, Da, 17
Iol Cæsarea, Ce, 15
Iolcus, Dc, 6
Iomnium, Ce, 15
Ionia, Gc, 8
Ioppe, Ed, 16
Ios I., Fe, 8
Ipsus, Bb, 9c
Irchester, Fd, 17
Iria, Dc, 12
Iria Flavia, Ad, 15
Irina Palus, Ke, 9b
Is, Ec, 9b
Isaura, Ec, 16
Isauria, Jf, 20
Isca (Caerleon), De, 17
Isca Dumnoniorum (Exeter), Cf, 17
Isca Silurum, Bb, 15
Iseum, Inset, 11d
Isin, Eb, 3a
Isis et Serapis, Inset, 11d
Israel, Dc, 2d
Israel, Kingdom of, Be, 4c
Issachar, Bc, 4a
Issus, Db, 9b
Istakr (Persepolis), Cb, 18b
Ister (Danubius), F., Hb, 5a
Istone, M., Ac, 6
Istri, Ba, 14c
Istria, Hb, 12
Istrus, Ib, 5a
Isurium, Eb, 17
Italia, Ed, 10
Italia, Diocese of, Fe, 20
Italica, Ae, 15
Italy, Ancient, 12-13
Italy, Prefecture of, Fe, 20
Itanus, Da, 7d
Ithaca, Bd, 7
Ithome, Cc, 6
Ithome, M., Ce, 7
Ituna Aest., Cb, 17
Ituraea, Ca, 4d
Iulia, Aq., Inset, 11
Iuliobona, Cc, 15
Iuliobriga, Bd, 15
Iuliomagus, Bc, 15
Iulium Carnicum, Ha, 12
Iunonis Reginae, Templum, Inset, 11
Iuvanum (Samnium), Jf, 12
Iuvavum, Ec, 15
Iverni, Inset, 17a

JABBOK, R., Cd, 4a
Jabesh Gilead, Be, 4c
Jalandhar, Eb, 18b
Jamnia, Ad, 4d
Japho (Joppa), Ad, 4a
Jaugada, Cc, 18a
Jaxartes, R., Ic, 18
Jebus (Jerusalem), Be, 4a
Jerameelites, Af, 4c
Jericho, Be, 4a
Jerusalem, Jg, 4b, 4e, 20
Jerusalem (Hierosolyma), Dc, 5b
Jerusalem (Jebus), Bf, 4c
Jeshimon, Be, 4a
Jezreel, Bc, 4a
Jezreel, Valley of, Bc, 4a
Joppa (Japho), Ad, 4a
Jordan, R., Cb, 3a; Cd, 4a
Judæa, Bd, 4a
Judæa, Wilderness of, Bd, 4d
Judah, Be, 4d
Judah, Kingdom of, Bf, 4c
Judgement, House of, Inset, 4b
Jumna, R., Je, 19
Junagarh, Ec, 18b
Jupiter Ammonium, Bd, 5b
Juti, Eb, 20

KABUL, Id, 19
Kadesh, Cb, 3a
Kadesh Barnea, Ag, 4c
Kalakh, Da, 3a
Kalinga, K. of, Cc, 18a
Kallikolone, Inset, 2c
Kalsi, Ba, 18a
Kalti (Hittites), Da, 4c
Kamarapura, Kingdom of, Gc, 18b
Kambojas, Ca, 18a
Kanatha, Db, 4d
Kanchi, Ed, 18b
Kanesh, Db, 2a
Kaplavasti, Cb, 18a
Karachi (Alexandria Portus), Je, 9b
Kara-shahr, Kc, 19
Karkar, Db, 2d
Karnak Temples, Cd, 3b
Kartripura, K. of, Eb, 18b
Kashgar, Jd, 19
Kashiari, Mt., Da, 3a
Kashkai, Db, 2d
Kashmir, Ba, 18a
Kasi (Benares), Cb, 18a
Katna, Da, 3a
Kaviripaddanam, Kf, 19
Ke Chow, Nd, 19
Kebtu (Coptos), Cd, 3b
Kedah (Kidri), Dc, 2d
Kedesh, Bd, 4c
Kedesh, Bb, 4a
Kenath, Dc, 4a

Kenites, Bf, 4*a*
Kenizzites (Calebites), Af, 4*a*
Kera, Eb, 2*d*
Keralaputra, K. of, Bc, 18*a*
Khabur, F., Da, 3*a*
Khesout (Xois), Ba, 3*b*
Khidalu, Ec, 2*d*
Khilakku (Cilicia), Cb, 2*d*
Khojent (Alexandria Eschata), Ja, 9*b*
Khotan, Kd, 19
Khubushkia, Eb, 2*d*
Khyber P., Kc, 9*b*
Kidri (Kedah), Dc, 2*d*
Kidron, R., Bd, 4*d*
Kidron, Val. of, Insets, 4*e*, 4*b*
Kilif (Alexandria Oxiana), Jb, 9*b*
Kir-hiraseth, Cf, 4*a*
Kirjath Arba (Hebron), Be, 4*a*
Kirjath-jearim, Be, 4*a*
Kirjath Sepher (Debir), Af, 4*a*
Kirkby Thore (Bravoniacum), Db, 17
Kish, Db, 3*a*
Kishon, R., Bc, 4*a*
Kistna, R., Jf, 19
Kizzuwatna, Ca, 3*a*
Kode, Cb, 3*a*
Konkan, S., Jf, 19
Korkai, Jg, 19
Kosala, K. of, Bb, 18*a*
Kottura, Fd, 18*b*
Kuang Han, Md, 19
Kuang-ling, Nd, 19
Kuang-Yang, Nd, 19
Kucha, Kc, 19
Kudal, Jg, 19
Kumani, Ca, 3*a*
Kummeh, Bd, 3*a*
Kummukh, Ca, 3*a*
Kurti, Da, 3*a*
Kush, Bd, 3*a*
Kushan Dominions, Id, 18
Kusinagara, K. of, Cb, 18*a*
Kuti, Da, 3*a*

LABEATIS, L., Bb, 16
Labyrinth, Bb, 3*b*
Lacedaemon (Sparta), De, 7
Lacedaemonia, Cc, 9*a*
Lachish, Ae, 4*a*
Lacinium Pr., Fc, 13
Laconia, Df, 7
Lactodorum, Ed, 17
Ladon, F., Ce, 7
Laevi, Cb, 12
Lagash, Eb, 3*a*
Laish (Dan), Cb, 4*a*
Lalita Patan, Cb, 18*a*
Lambaesis, De, 10
Lamia, Dd, 6
Laminium, Be, 15
Lampsacus, Ba, 2*d*; Cb, 7*c*
Lancaster, Db, 17
Langobardi, Fc, 20
Lanuvium, Aa, 13
Laodicea, Dc, 16
Laodicea (Syria), Fc, 16
Lappa, Ba, 7*d*
Larinum, Ca, 13
Larissa, Assyria, Eb, 5*b*
Larissa, Dardanians, Eb, 2*b*
Larissa, Thessalia, Dc, 6
Larissa Cremaste, Dd, 6
Larius, L., Da, 12
Larsa, Eb, 3*a*
Larymna, Ed, 6
Las, Df, 7
Lasea, Db, 4*f*
Lasium, Ce, 7
Latina, Pa., Inset, 11*d*
Latini, Aa, 13
Latium, Aa, 13
Latopolis, Cd, 3*b*
Laumellum, Cb, 12
Laurentum, Gf, 12
Lauriacum, Ec, 15
Laurium M., Ee, 7
Lauriya Araraj, Cb, 18*a*
Laus, Dc, 13
Laus Pompeia, Db, 12
Lavatrae, Eb, 17
Lebadea, Dd, 7
Lebanon, Ho. of, Inset, 4*b*
Lebanon, Mts., Cb, 3*a*
Lebedus, Gc, 8
Lebinthus, I., Gd, 8
Lechaeum, De, 7
Legiolium, Ec, 17
Leicester (Ratae), Ed, 17
Lemanus, L., Dc, 15
Lemnos, Bc, 7*c*
Leontes, R., Ba, 4*d*
Leontini, Ce, 13
Leontium, Cd, 7
Lepontii, Ca, 12
Lepreum, Ce, 7
Leptis Magna, Ef, 10
Leptis Minor, Ee, 10; Ee, 15
Leros I., Gd, 8
Lesbos, Gb, 8
Letocetum, Ed, 17
Letopolis, Ba, 3*b*
Leuca, M., Aa, 7*d*
Leucae, Df, 7
Leucae Is., Db, 7*d*
Leucas, Bd, 6
Leucate Pr., Bd, 6
Leuce, Gc, 13
Leuce acte, Fe, 7
Leucimma Pr., Ab, 9*a*
Leucopetra Pr., De, 13
Leucos Limen, Bc, 3*a*
Leuctra, Boeotia, Ed, 7
Leuctra, Laconia, Ce, 8
Liang Chow, Md, 19
Liao-tung, Oc, 19
Libanus, M., Fd, 16
Libarna, Cc, 12
Libnah, Af, 4*c*
Liburnia, Bb, 16
Libya, Dd, 16
Libyan Des., Ab, 3*b*
Libyans, Bc, 2*a*
Liger, R., Cd, 20
Ligures, Eb, 5*a*
Ligures Bebiani, Ca, 13
Liguria, Bc, 12
Lilybaeum, Ae, 13
Limes, Dc, 15
Limnae, Inset, 7*b*
Limnaea, Cd, 6
Limonum, Cc, 15
Lincoln (Lindum), Fc, 17
Lindum (Lincoln), Fc, 17
Lindus, Fc, 2*b*
Lingones, Fc, 12
Lipara, Gc, 5*a*
Liparaeae Ins., Cd, 13
Liris, F., Ba, 13
Lissos Pr., Bb, 16
Lissus, Bb, 16
Liternum, Cb, 13
Littlechester, Ed, 17
Littus Saxonicum, Hd, 17
Lixus, Bc, 5*a*
Llandovery, Cd, 17
Llanio, Bd, 17
Locri (Magna Graecia), Gc, 5*a*
Locri, R., Cb, 2*b*
Locri Epizephyrii, Ed, 13
Locris (Epicnemidia), Dd, 6
Locris (Opuntia), Ed, 6
Locris Ozolis, Dd, 7
Lod, Ae, 4*a*
Logia Sinus, Ab, 17
Londinium, Ge, 17
Longaticum, Jb, 12
Lousonna, Aa, 12
Lower City, Inset, 4*e*
Lower Egypt, Ba, 3*b*
Loyang, Nd, 19
Luca, Ed, 12
Lucani, Cb, 14*c*
Lucania, Db, 13
Luceria, Da, 13
Lu-chiang, Nd, 19
Lucus Augusti, Ad, 15
Lugdunensis, Bc, 15
Lugdunum, Cc, 15
Lugdunum Batavorum, Cb, 15
Lugii, Fb, 15
Luguvallium (Carlisle), Db, 17
Luae, Mtes., Inset, 1
Luna, Ec, 12
Lung-Hsi, Md, 19
Lupiae, Gb, 13
Lusitani, Ae, 15
Lusitania, Ae, 15
Lutetia, Dd, 20
Luxor, Cd, 2*a*
Luz (Beth-el), Be, 4*a*
Lycaonia, Fd, 18
Lychnidus, Ba, 6
Lychnites, L., Ba, 6
Lychnitus, L., Ld, 11
Lycia, Ed, 18
Lycians, Bb, 2*a*
Lycopolis (Syout), Bc, 3*b*
Lyctus, Dd, 2*b*
Lydda, Ad, 4*d*
Lydia, If, 20
Lydians, Bb, 2*a*
Lympne (Portus Lemanis), He, 17
Lyncestis, Cb, 6
Lyrceus M., De, 7
Lyrnessus, Eb, 2*b*
Lysimacheia, Cb, 7*c*
Lysimachia, Acarnania, Cd, 6
Lysimachia, Thracia, Aa, 9
Lyttus, Ca, 7*d*

MACAE, He, 18
Macedonia, Cb, 6; Hf, 20
Macedonia, Diocese of, He, 20
Macestus, F., Eb, 7*c*
Machir (Manasseh), Dc, 4*a*
Macra, Dc, 12
Madaktu, Fc, 2*d*
Madraka, Eb, 18*b*
Madura, Ed, 18*b*
Maeander, F., Dc, 16
Maeatae, Ca, 17
Maegaeum, Cb, 4*f*
Maenalus, De, 7
Maeonians, Eb, 2*b*
Mæotis, L., Ka, 5*a*
Mæotis Palus, Kd, 20
Magadha, Kingdom of, Fc, 18*b*
Magna Graecia, Gc, 5*a*
Magnae, Dd, 17
Magnae (Carvoran), Inset, 17
Magnesia (Caria), Hd, 8
Magnesia (Graecia), Dc, 6
Magnesia (Lydia), Dc, 16
Magnus Portus (Portsmouth Harb.), Ef, 17
Magnus Sinus, Gd, 1
Maha Kosala, Fc, 18*b*
Mahanadi, R., Ke, 19
Mahanaim, Cd, 4*a*
Mahendragiri, Mt., Fd, 18*b*
Maior, I., Ce, 15
Malaca, Cc, 5*a*
Malatia (Melid), Db, 2*d*
Malaya, Ec, 18*b*
Malea Pr., Ef, 7
Malis, Dd, 6
Mallus, Kc, 5*a*
Malwa, Je, 19
Manasseh (Machir), Dc, Bd, 4*a*
Manchester (Mancunium), Dc, 17
Mancunium (Manchester), Dc, 17
Mandrae, Ec, 7*c*
Manduria, Fb, 13
Manju Patan, Ke, 19
Mannai, Fb, 2*d*
Mansera, Ba, 18*a*
Mantinea, Cc, 9*a*
Mantua, Eb, 12
Maracanda, Jb 9*b*
Marakanda, Jb, 5*b*
Marash, Ca, 3*a*
Marathon, Ed, 7
Marcelli, Th., Inset, 11*d*
Marcellum, Inset, 13*a*
Marcomanni, Fd, 20
Mardi, Fb, 9*b*
Mardin, Da, 3*a*
Mare Adriaticum, Ge, 20
Mare Ægaeum, If, 20
Mare Africum, Fc, 5*a*
Mare Australis, Inset, 1
Mare Balearicum, Dc, 5*a*
Mare Cantabricum, Bc, 18
Mare Caspium, Ne, 20
Mare Creticum, Ee, 8
Mare Cronium, Inset, 1
Mare Egyptum, Jd, 5*a*
Mare Erythraeum, Ec, 9*c*
Mare Etruscum, Bc, 14*c*
Mare Externum, Ac, 5*a*
Mare Gangeticus, Fd, 1
Mare Icarium, Gd, 8
Mare Internum, Dd, 18
Mare Ionium, Gf, 20
Mare Ligurum, Eb, 5*a*
Mare Myrtoum, Ef, 7
Mare Siculum, Gc, 5*a*
Mare Suevicum, Gb, 20
Mare Thracicum, Ec, 6
Mare Tyrrhenum, Ff, 20
Marea, Bc, 5*b*
Margiana, Id, 18
Margus, F., Margiana, Ib, 5*b*
Margus, F., Moesia, Gd, 10
Mari, Db, 2*a*
Mariana, De, 12
Maridunum (Carmarthen), Be, 17
Marisus, F., Ca, 16
Marmarica, Cd, 16
Maronea, Ib, 5*a*
Marrucini, Je, 12
Marruvium, Hf, 12
Marsi, Hf, 12
Maryport (Uxellodunum), Cb, 17
Massaga, Kc, 9*b*
Massagetae, Hc, 18
Massilia, Ee, 20
Mateola, Eb, 13
Mathura (Meerut), Ec, 18*b*
Matiana, L., Le, 11
Matianus, L., Fb, 2*d*
Mattieni, Eb, 5*b*
Mauretania, Df, 20
Mausoleum Augusti, Inset, 11*d*
Mausoleum Hadriani, Inset, 11*d*
Mazaca (Cæsarea), Fc, 16
Mazara, Ae, 13
Medeon, Cd, 6
Media, Gd, 18
Median Wall, Ec, 2*d*
Mediolanum, Db, 12
Mediolanum Santonum, Bc, 15
Medma, Dd, 13
Medus, F., Gc, 5*b*
Meerut (Mathura), Ec, 18*b*
Meerut (Mirath), Bb, 18*a*
Megalopolis, De, 7
Megara, Hc, 5*a*
Megara (Sicilia), Gc, 5*a*
Megara Hyblaea, De, 13
Megaris, Ed, 7
Megiddo, Bc, 4*a*
Melandra Castle, Ec, 17
Melazgert, Eb, 2*d*
Meliboea (Hestiaeotis), Cc, 6
Meliboea (Magnesia), Dc, 6
Melid (Malatia), Db, 2*d*
Melita, Inset, Ab, 4*f*
Melitaea, Dc, 6
Melite, Ff, 20
Melite, Db, 9*b*
Melitene, Fc, 16
Melli, Kc, 9*b*
Mellte, Inset, 7*b*
Melos, Ff, 7
Melpum, Db, 12
Memphis, Jh, 20
Memphis (Men-nofer), Bb, 3*b*
Memphis (Noph), Cd, 2*d*
Menaenum, Ce, 13
Menapii, Cb, 15
Mende, Hc, 5*a*; Ec, 6
Mendes, Ba, 3*b*
Menet Hufu (Speos Artemidos) Bc, 3*b*
Men-nofer (Memphis), Bb, 3*b*
Merinum, Ea, 13
Meroë, Cd, 1; Be, 3*a*
Merom, Waters of, Cb, 4*a*
Merv, Db, 18*b*
Mesambria, Bb, 7*c*
Mesembria, Ib, 5*a*; Db, 16
Mesheck (Mushki), Db, 2*d*
Mesopotamia, Eb, 9*b*
Messana, Gf, 20
Messana (Zancle), Dd, 13
Messapii, Fb, 13
Messene, Ce, 7
Messenia, Ce, 7
Meta Sudans, Inset, 13*b*
Metapontum, Eb, 13
Metaris, Aest, (The Wash), Gc, 17
Metaurus, F., Gd, 12
Metellinum, Ae, 15
Methana, Ee, 7
Methone (Macedonia), Db, 6
Methone (Messenia), Cf, 7
Methone (Thessalia), Ec, 6
Methydrium, De, 7
Methymna, Gb, 8
Metroni, Pa., Inset, 11*d*
Metropolis, Cd, 6
Mevania, Ge, 12
Michmash, Be, 4*a*
Middle Egypt, Bb, 3*b*
Midea, De, 7
Miletus, Hd, 8
Miletus (Creta), Dd, 2*b*
Milid, Ca, 3*a*
Min Yueh, Ne, 19
Minaei, Gf, 18
Mincius, F., Eb, 12
Minius, F., Ad, 15
Minnagara, Ie, 19
Minor I., Cd, 15
Minturnae, Ba, 13; Bb, 14*b*
Mirath (Meerut), Bb, 18*a*
Misenum Pr., Cb, 13
Mitanni, Ca, 3*a*
Mitylene, Gb, 8
Mizpeh, Be, 4*a*
Moab, Cf, 4*a*
Moabites, Cf, 4*a*
Modicia, Db, 12
Moeris, L., Bb, 3*b*
Moesia Inferior, Db, 16
Moesia Superior, Cb, 16
Moguntiacum, Ec, 20
Mohammerah (Alexandria), Fc, 9*b*
Mona, Bc, 17
Monapia, Bb, 17
Monitia, Dc, 12
Mons Albanus, Ab, 14*b*
Mons Apenninus, Ed, 10; Fd, 12
Mons Caelius, Inset, 11*c*
Mons Esquilinus, Inset, 11*d*
Mons Ianiculus, Inset, 11*d*
Mons Pincius, Inset, 11*d*
Mons Sacer, Ab, 14*b*
Montes Bastarnici, Hc, 10
Montes Serrorum, Ca, 16
Monumentum Philopappi, Inset, 7*b*
Mopsuestia, Db, 5*b*
Morgantia, Ce, 13
Mosa, F., Dc, 15
Moschi, Ea, 5*b*
Mosella, F., Db, 15
Motya, Ae, 13
Motyca, Cf, 13
Mugonia, Pa., Inset, 11*c*
Munda, Be, 15
Murattash, Da, 3*a*
Mursa, Gd, 20
Murus Aurelius, Inset, 11*d*
Murus Hadriani, Cb, 20
Murus Medius, Inset, 7*b*
Murus Phalericus, Inset, 7*b*
Murus Septentrionalis, Inset, 7*b*
Musarum Mons, Inset, 7*b*
Musasir, Eb, 2*d*
Mushki (Mesheck), Db. 2*d*
Musri, Ca, 3*a*
Mutina, Ec, 12
Muziris, Jf, 19
Mycale, M., Hd, 8
Mycalessus, Ed, 7
Mycenae, De, 7
Mygdonia, Db, 6
Mykonos, Fd, 8
Mylae, Dd, 13
Mylasa, Bb, 9*b*
Myndus, Hd, 8
Myos Hormos, Bc, 3*a*
Myra, Ec, 16
Myrcinus, Eb, 6
Myriandrus, Db, 5*b*
Myrina, Db, 9*a*
Mysia, Ic, 5*a*
Mysians, Bb, 2*a*
Mytilene, Eb, 9*a*

NABAITE (Nebaioth), Dc, 2*d*
Nabataeans, Cd, 4*d*
Nabataei, Fe, 18
Naevia, Pa., Inset, 15*c*
Naharin, Ca, 3*a*
Nain, Bb, 4*d*
Nairi, Da, 3*a*
Naissus, He, 20
Namri, Fb, 2*d*
Nandangarh, Cb, 18*a*
Napata, Be, 3*a*
Naphtali, Cc, 4*a*
Napoca, Ca, 16
Nar, F., Ge, 12
Narbada, R., Je, 19
Narbada (Normada), R., Bb, 18*a*
Narbo, De, 20
Narbo Martius, Cd, 15
Narbonensis, Cd, 15
Narmada (Narbada), R., Bb, 18*a*
Narnia. Ge, 12
Narona, Bb, 16
Nasamones, Cd, 16
Natron Lakes, Ba, 3*b*
Naucratis, Cc, 5*b*
Naulochus, Dd, 13
Naupactus, Cd, 6
Nauplia, De, 7
Nauportus, Jb, 12
Navalia, Inset, 11*d*
Navalis, Pa., Inset, 11*c*
Naxos, Euboea, Fd, 8
Naxos, Sicilia, Gc, 5*a*; Dc, 13

Naxuana, Le, 11
Nazareth, Bb, 4*d*
Neae, Fb, 8
Neaethus, F., Ec, 13
Neapolis, Be, 14*a*
Neapolis (Africa), Ee, 15
Neapolis (Apulia), Fb, 13
Neapolis, Campania, Cb, 13
Neapolis (Macedonia), Fb, 6
Neath (Nidum), Ce, 17
Nebaioth (Nabaite), Dc, 2*d*
Nebrodes Montes, Ce, 13
Nebut (Apollinopolis parva), Cd, 3*b*
Nedon, F., De, 7
Neetum, Cf, 13
Nemausus, Cd, 15
Nemea, De, 7
Nemetacum, Cb, 15
Nepal, Kingdom of, Fc, 18*b*
Nepete, Ge, 12
Nerium Pr., Ad, 15
Neronianus, Inset, 11*d*
Nersae, He, 12
Nervii, Cb, 15
Nesactium, Jc, 12
Nestus, F., Fa, 6
Newcastle (Pons Aelii), Inset, 17
Nicaea, Db, 16
Nicaea (Bactria), Jc, 9*b*
Nicaea (India), Kc, 9*b*
Nicaea (Liguria), Eb, 5*a*; Dd, 15
Nicephorium, Fc, 16
Nicomedia, Db, 16
Nicopolis (Armenia Minor), Fb, 16
Nicopolis (Epirus), Bd, 6
Nidum (Neath), Ce, 17
Nigir, R., Bd, 1
Nigliva, Cb, 18*a*
Nigritae, Ad, 1
Nile, R., Bc, 3*a*
Nile Delta, Ed, 16
Nilus, Ec, 4*f*
Nineveh, Da, 3*a*; Eb, 2*d*
Ningus, F., Hb, 12
Ninus, Lf, 20
Nippur, Eb, 3*a*
Nisaea, Ee, 7
Nishapur, Cb, 18*b*
Nisibis, Eb, 2*d*
Nisyros, I., He, 8
Nisyrus, Ec, 2*b*
Niy, Ca, 3*a*
No Ammon (Thebes), Cd, 3*b*
Nola, Cb, 13
Nomentum, Ge, 12
Nomentana Pa., Inset, 11*d*
Noph (Memphis), Cd, 2d
Nora, Be, 14*a*
Norba (Apulia), Fb, 13
Norba (Hispania), Ae, 15
Norba (Latium), Aa, 13
Noreia, Ec, 10
Noricum, Fd, 20
Northern Hiung-nu, Kc, 19
Notium, Ec, 9*a*
Nova Via, Insets, 13*a*, *b*
Novae, Ie, 20
Novae Athenae, Inset, 7*b*
Novantae, Bb, 17
Novantarum Pr., Inset, 17*a*
Novaria, Cb, 12
Noviodunum, Kb, 12
Noviomagus (Germania), Db, Dc, 15
Noviomagus (Lugdunensis), Cc, 15
Nubae, Cd, 1
Nubian Desert, Bd, 3*a*
Nuceria, Gd, 12
Nuceria Alfaterna, Cb, 13
Numana, Hd, 12
Numantia, Bd, 15
Numicius, F., Aa, 13
Numidia, De, 15
Nursia, He, 12
Nymphaeum Pr., Fb, 6
Nysa, Jc, 9*b*

OASIS MAGNA, Bd, 2*d*
Oasis Parva, Bd, 2*d*
Oasis Siwa (Ammonium), Bb, 2*d*
Oceanus Aethiopicus, Inset, 1
Oceanus Atlanticus, Ad, 20
Oceanus Britannicus, Bc, 18
Oceanus Germanicus, Db, 20
Oceanus Hibernicus, Bc, 17
Oceanus Indicus, Inset, I
Oceanus Occidentalis, Inset, I
Ocelum, Bb, 12
Ochus, F., Ib., 5*b*
Ocriculum, Ge, 12
Ocrinum Pr., Af, 17
Octapitarum Pr., Ae, 17
Octaviae, P., Inset, 11*d*
Octavii, P., Inset, 11*d*
Octodurum, Ba, 12
Octodurus, Dc, 15
Odessus, Db, 16
Odeum, Inset, 7*a*
Odomanti, Ea, 6
Odrysae, Ba, 9*b*
Oea, Ef, 10
Oeneon, Cd, 7
Oeniadae, Bb, 9*a*
Oenoe (Argolis), De, Ed, 7
Oenoe (Attica), Ed, 7
Oenoe (Elis), Ce, 7
Oenophyta, Ed, 7
Oenthea, Dd, 7
Oenussae, Is. Ionia, Gc, 8
Oenussae Ins., Messenia, Cf, 7
Oescus, Cb, 16
Oesyme, Fb, 6
Oeta, Dd, 6
Oeta, M., Dd, 6
Oglasa, Ee, 12
Olbia (Sardinia), Dd, 15
Olbia (Scythia), Ea, 16
Old Kilpatrick, Ba, 17
Olenus, Cd, 7
Olicana (Ilkley), Ec, 17
Olisippo, Ae, 15
Olives, Mt. of, Bd, 4*d*
Olizon, Ec, 6
Ollius, Eb, 12
Oloosson, Dc, 6
Olpae, Cd, 6
Olympieum, Inset, 7*b*
Olympia, Ce, 7
Olympus, Db, 6
Olynthus, Eb, 6
Omanitae, Hf, 18
Ombos, Bd, 3*a*
Omphis, Kingdom of, Kc, 9*b*
On (Heliopolis), Ba, 3*b*
Onchesmus, Bc, 6
Onchestus, F., Dc, 6
Onugnathos Pr., Df, 7
Ophel, Inset, 4*b*
Ophel, Wall of, Inset, 4*b*
Ophionenses, Cd, 6
Ophrah, Be, 4*a*
Ophrynium, Inset, 2*c*
Opis, Ec, 5*b*
Opis (Upi), Ec, 2*d*
Opitergium, Gb, 12
Oppius, M., Inset, 11*c*
Opus, Ed, 6
Opus, Pr., Dd, 7
Orcades, Inset, 17*a*
Orchoe, Fc, 9*b*
Orchomenus (Arcadia), De, 7
Orchomenus (Boeotia), Dd, 6
Ordovices, Cd, 17
Orestis, Cb, 6
Oreus, Cb, 9*a*
Oricus, Aa, 9*a*
Orneae, De, 7
Orontes, R., Cb, 4*c*
Oropus, Ed, 7
Ortona, Je, 12
Orumbovii, Db, 12
Osca, Bd, 15
Oscela, Ca, 12
Osci, Bb, 14*c*
Osii, Eb, 18
Osrhoene, Fc, 16
Ossa, M., Dc, 6
Osteodes, Ins., Bd, 13
Ostia, Gf, 12
Ostiensis, Pa., Inset, 11*d*
Ostrogothi, Id, 20
Otadini, Da, 17
Othona (Bradwell), Ge, 17
Othrys, M., Dd, 6
Ovilava, Ec, 15
Oxianus Lacus, Ea, 9*c*
Oxus, R., Ia, 9*b*
Oxydraces, Kc, 9*b*
Oxyrhynchus, Bb, 3*b*

PACHYNUS PR., Df, 13
Padan Aram, Db, 2*d*
Padmavati, Ec, 18*b*
Padus, F., Fb, 12
Paedagogium, Inset, 13*b*
Paeligni, He, 12
Paeones, Aa, 9*b*
Paeonia, Da, 6
Paeonians, Ca, 2*b*
Paestum, Cb, 13
Pagae, Ed, 7
Pagasae, Dc, 6
Paithan, Ed, 18*b*
Palaestina, Fd, 18
Palatinus, M., Inset, 13*b*
Palatium, Inset, 11*d*
Palatium Caesarum, Inset, 11*d*
Palestina, Cc, 5*b*
Palinuri Pr., Db, 13
Palla, Df, 12
Pallantia, Bd, 15
Pallantium, De, 7
Pallatina, Inset, 11*c*
Pallavas, Jf, 19
Pallene (Attica), Ed, 7
Pallene (Chalcidice), Eb, 6
Palma, Ce, 15
Palmyra, Kg, 20
Paludes Pomptinae, Ba, 13
Pamisus, F., Ce, 7
Pamphylia, If, 20
Panacton, Ed, 7
Panarus, F., Ec, 12
Pandateria, Bb, 13
Pandya, K. of, Bd, 18*a*
Pandosia, Bc, 6
Pangaeus, M., Fb, 6
Panjadada, Jd, 19
Pannonia (Interior), Ba, 16
Pannonia (Superior), Ba, 16
Panopolis (Shem), Bc, 3*b*
Panormus (Achaea), Cd, 7
Panormus (Phrygia), Db, 7*c*
Panormus (Sicilia), Bd, 13
Pantheon, Inset, 11*d*
Panticapaeum, Ka, 5*a*
Pantimathi, Fb, 5*b*
Paphlagonia, Je, 20
Paphlagonians, Ca, 2*d*
Paphos, Jd, 5*a*
Paraetacene, Jb, 9*b*
Paraetonium, Bc, 9*b*
Paran, Wilderness of, Ag, 4*c*
Parapanisadae, Jc, 9*b*
Parapanisus Mons, Jb, 5*b*
Parentium, Hb, 12
Paricanii, Jd, 5*b*
Parisii (Yorkshire), Fc, 17
Parium, Db, 7*c*
Parma, Ec, 12
Parnassus M., Dd, 6
Parnes M., Ed, 7
Parnon M., De, 7
Paropanisadai, Aa, 18*a*
Paros, Fd, 8
Parthenicum, Bd, 13
Parthenon, Inset, 7*a*
Parthia, Cb, 18*b*
Parthian Empire, Hd, 18
Parushapura, Jd, 19
Pasargadae, Gc, 5*b*
Pasitigris, F., Fc, 2*d*
Pataliputra, Cb, 18*a*
Patara, Dc, 16
Patavium, Fb, 12
Patmos I., Gd, 8
Patrae, Cd, 7
Pattala, Jd, 9*b*
Pauca, Cf, 12
Pausicae, Fb, 5*b*
Pautalia, Cb, 16
Pax Iulia, Ae, 15
Paxos, Bc, 6
Pebeseth (Bubastis), Ba, 3*b*
Pedasus, Eb, 2*b*
Pedone, Bc, 12
Pedum, Ab, 14*b*
Pelagonia, Ca, 6
Pelion M., Ec, 6
Pelium, Bb, 6
Pella (Macedonia), Db, 6
Pella (Palestina), Fd, 16; Cc, 4*d*
Pellene, Dd, 7
Peloponnesus, Hc, 5*a*
Pelorum Pr., Dd, 13
Pelso, L., Ba, 16
Peltae, Bb, 5*b*
Pelusic Mouth, Ca, 3*b*
Pelusium, Cc, 9*b*
Peneus, F., Cc, 6
Peneus, F., Ce, 7
Pennal, Cd, 17
Penneloci, Aa, 12
Pentapolis, Gf, 10
Pentri, Ca, 13
Penuel, Cd, 4*a*
Peparethus, Ec, 6
Peraea, Cd, 4*d*
Perga, Eb, 4*f*
Pergamos, Db, 4*f*
Pergamum, Dc, 16
Perge, Cb, 9*b*
Perinthus, Ba, 9*b*
Per-Ramses, Ca, 3*b*
Perrhaebi, Dc, 6
Persarum Regnum, Mg, 20
Persepolis, Gd, 5*b*
Persian Empire, 5*b*
Persian Gates, Gc, 9*b*
Persis, Gc, 5*b*; Cb, 18*b*
Perusia, Gd, 12
Pessinus, Jf, 20
Petelia, Fc, 13
Petra (Arabia), Fd, 16
Petra (Graecia), Db, 6
Petra (Sela), Bg, 4*c*
Petra (Sicilia), Ce, 13
Petrianae, Cb, 17
Peuce I., Ba, 9*b*
Pevensey (Anderida), Gf, 17
Phaeca, Cc, 6
Phaestus, Crete, Ba, 7*d*
Phaestus, Locris Ozolis, Dd, 7
Phalara, Dd, 6
Phalerum, Ee, 7
Phaloria, Cc, 6
Phanagoria, Fa, 16
Pharae (Achaea), Cd, 7
Pharae (Messenia), De, 7
Pharcadon, Dc, 6
Pharnacia, Fb, 16
Pharpar, R., Cd, 4*c*
Pharsalus, Dc, 6
Pharus I., Dd, 16
Phasaelis, Bc, 4*d*
Phaselis, Jc, 5*a*
Phasis, Gb, 16
Phatnitic Mouth, Ba, 3*b*
Pheneus, De, 7
Pherae, Dc, 6
Phigalia, Ce, 7
Phila, Dc, 6
Philace, Db, 6
Philadelphia (Asia), Db, 4*f*
Philadelphia (Palestine), Cd, 4*d*
Philippi, Aa, 9*b*
Philippi, P., Inset, 11*d*
Philippopolis, Cb, 16
Philistia, Ae, 4*a*
Philistines, Cc, 2*a*
Phinopolis, Ea, 7*c*
Phintias, Be, 13
Phlius, De, 7
Phocaea, Ic, 5*a*
Phocians, Cb, 2*b*
Phocis, Dd, 6
Phoenice, Bc, 6
Phoenicia, Fd, 18
Phoenicussa, Cd, 13
Pholegandros, Ff, 7
Phraaspa, Gd, 18
Phrygia, If, 20
Phrygians, Cb, 2*a*
Phthia, Cb, 2*b*
Phthiotis, Dc, 6
Phylace, Dc, 6
Phyle, Ed, 7
Picentes, Hd, 12
Picentia, Cb, 13
Picentini, Cb, 13
Picenum, Hd, 12
Picti, Cb, 20
Pictones, Bc, 15
Pillars of Hercules, Bc, 5*a*
Pinciana, Pa., Inset, 11*d*
Pindus, Mts., Cc, 6
Ping Chow, Md, 19
Pinna, He, 12
Piquentum, Jb, 12
Pir, Cc, 9*a*
Piraeus, Ee, 7
Piranum, Hb, 12
Piresiae, Dc, 6
Pisa (Graecia), Ce, 7
Pisae, Ed, 12
Pisanus Port, Ed, 12
Pisatis, Ce, 7
Pisaurum, Gd, 12
Piscina Publica, Inset, 11*d*
Pisgah, Mt., Ce, 4*a*
Pishtapura, Fd, 18*b*
Pisidia, Jf, 20
Pistoria, Ed, 12
Pithecusa Ins., Bb, 13
Pithom, Ba, 3*b*
Pitinum Pisaurense, Gd, 12
Pityus, Ke, 20
Pityusa, I., Ee, 7
Pityusae Ins., Ce, 15
Placentia, Db, 12
Planasia, Ee, 12
Plataea, Cb, 9*a*
Plavis, F., Ga, 12
Plemmyrium Pr., De, 13
Pleuron, Cd, 7
Plumbaria, Be, 14*a*
Pnyx, Inset, 7*b*
Poediculi, Eb, 13
Poeni, Bc, Ac, 14*c*
Poetovio, Gd, 20
Pola, Hc, 12
Polacticum Pr., Hc, 12
Polemon, K. of, Fb, 4*f*
Pollentia, Bc, 12
Polyaegus, Fc, 6
Polyrrhenia, Aa, 7*d*
Pompaelo, Bd, 15
Pompeia, P., Inset, 11*d*
Pompeii, Cb, 13
Pompeii, Th., Inset, 11*d*
Pompeiopolis (Paphlagonia), Eb, 16
Pompeiopolis (Soli), Ec, 16
Pons Aelii (Newcastle), Inset, 17
Pons Aemilius, Inset, 13*a*
Pons Aeni, Ec, 15
Pons Aureoli, Db, 12
Pons Cestius, Inset, 11*c*
Pons Fabricius, Inset, 11*c*
Pontes, Fe, 17
Pontiae Ins., Ab, 13
Pontus, Jf, 20
Pontus, Diocese of, If, 20
Pontus Euxinus, Je, 20
Populonia, Fb, 5*a*
Porolissum, Ca, 16
Porta Archarnica, Inset, 7*b*
Porta Capena, Inset, 11*d*
Porta Carmentalis, Inset, 13*a*
Porta Diomea, Inset, 7*b*
Porta Flumentana, Inset, 13*a*
Porta Hadriani, Inset, 7*b*
Porta Itonia, Inset, 7*b*
Porta Mugonia, Inset, 13*a*
Porta Piraeica, Inset, 7*b*
Porta Ratumena, Inset, 13*a*
Porta Romanula, Inset, 13*a*
Porticus Metelli, Inset, 13*a*
Porticus Octaviae, Inset, 13*b*
Portsmouth Harb. (Magnus Portus), Ef, 17
Portuensis, Pa., Inset, 11*d*
Portus Adurni, Ef, 17
Portus Aedro, Gb, 12
Portus Cale, Ad, 15
Portus Herculis Monoeci, Bd, 12
Portus Itius, Cb, 15
Portus Lemanis (Lympne), He, 17
Portus Magnus, Be, 15
Portus Mauritii, Cd, 12
Portus Namnetum, Bc, 15
Portus Veneris (Gallia), Cd, 15
Portus Veneris (Italia), Dc, 12
Porus, Kingdom of, Kc, 9*b*
Posidium, Pr., Chalcidice, Eb,
Posidium Pr. (Italia), Cb, 13
Posidium Pr. (Pallene), Ec, 6
Posidium Pr. (Phthiotis), Ec, 6
Posidonia (Paestum), Cb, 13
Potaissa, Ca, 16
Potentia (Lucania), Db, 13
Potentia (Picenum), Hd, 12
Potidaea, Ca, 9*a*
Praeneste, Gf, 12
Praenestina, Pa., Inset, 11*d*
Prarjuna, Ec, 18*b*
Prasiae (Attica), Fe, 7
Prasiae (Laconia), De, 7
Prayaga, Cb, 18*a*
Priapus, Db, 7*c*
Priene, Hd, 8
Prista, Db, 16
Privernum, Bb, 14*b*
Procolitia (Carrawburgh), Inset, 17
Proconnesus, Db, 7*c*
Prophthasia, Ic, 9*b*
Propontis, Ib, 5*a*
Propylaea, Inset, 7*a*
Provincia, Cd, 15
Prusa, Fb, 7*c*
Prytaneum, Inset, 7*a*
Psacum, Pr., Aa, 7*d*
Pselchis, Bd, 3*a*
Psophis, Ce, 7
Psyra, I., Fc, 8

Psyttalea, I., Ee, 7
Pteleum, Dc, 6
Pteria, Cb, 5b
Ptolemais (Pentapolis), Cd, 16
Ptolemais (Phoenicia), Bb, 4d
Ptolemais Hermiu, Ig, 11
Pura, Ie, 18
Puteoli, Cb, 13
Pydna, Ca, 9a
Pylae, Ec, 5b
Pylae Ciliciae, Ec, 16
Pylos, Bc, 9a
Pylus, Elis, Ce, 7
Pylus, see Pylos
Pyramids, Bb, 3b
Pyramus, F., Db, 5b
Pyrenaei Mtes., De, 20
Pyretus, R., Id, 20
Pyrgi, Ge, 12
Pyrrha, Gb, 8
Pythium, Db, 6
Pytho, Cb, 2b
Pyxus, Db, 13

Quadi, Gd, 20
Quadrata, Cb, 12
Querquetulana, Pa., Inset, 11c

Rabbath-ammon, Ce, 4a
Rakoti (Alexandria), Aa, 3b
Ramah, Asher, Bc, 4a
Ramah, Benjamin, Be, 4a
Ramoth Gilead, Dc, 4a
Rampurwa, Cb, 18a
Raphana, Db, 4d
Ratae (Leicester), Ed, 17
Ratiaria, Cb, 16
Ratumena, Pa., Inset, 11c
Ravenglass (Clanoventa), Cb, 17
Ravenna, Gc, 12
Reate, Ge, 12
Reculver (Regulbium), He, 17
Regia, Insets, 13a, b
Regillus, L., Ab, 14b
Regina, Ec, 15
Regma, He, 18
Regni, Ff, 17
Regnum (Chichester), Ff, 17
Regnum Bosporanum, Fa, 16
Regnum Parthorum, Ke, 11
Regulbium (Reculver), He, 17
Remi, Cc, 15
Renus, F., Fc, 12
Republican Forum, 13a
Rerigonius Sinus, Ba, 17
Resaena, Bb, 18b
Restan, Cb, 3a
Reuben, Ce, 4a
Rha, R., Md, 20
Rhacotis (Alexandria), Bc, 9b
Rhaeti, Ba, 14c
Rhaetia, Ed, 20
Rhagae, Hd, 18
Rhamnus, Fd, 7
Rheba, Fa, 7c
Rhegium (Bruttium), Dd, 13
Rhegium Lepidum, Ec, 12
Rhenea, Fd, 8
Rhenus, F , Ed, 20
Rhion (Asine), Cf, 7
Rhithymna, Ba, 7d
Rhium Pr., Cd, 7
Rhodanus, F., Cd, 15; Ee, 20
Rhodope, M, Fa, 6; Gd, 10
Rhodus, If, 20
Rhoeteum, Inset, 2c
Rhoeteum Pr., Inset, 2c
Rhotanus, F., De, 12
Rhypes, Dd, 7
Rhytium, Dd, 2b
Ribchester (Bremetennacum), Dc, 17
Riblah, Cc, 4c
Richborough (Rutupiae), He, 17
Ricina (Liguria), Dc, 12
Ricina (Picenum), Hd, 12
Rigomagus, Cb, 12
Ripuarii, Ec, 20
Robogdii, Inset, 17a
Robogdium Prom., Aa, 17
Rochester (Durobrivae), Ge, 17
Rockingham Forest, Fd, 17
Roma, Gf, 12
Roma Quadrata, Inset, 13a
Roman Britain, 17
Roman Empire, 10-11; 15; 16
Romanula, Pa., Inset, 11c
Rostra Nova, Inset, 13b
Rostra Vetera, Inset, 13a
Rotomagus, Cc, 15
Rough Castle, Ca, 17
Roxolæni, Fc, 18
Rubi, Ea, 13
Rubico, F., Gc, 12
Rudchester (Vindobala), Inset, 17
Rudiae, Gb, 13
Rugii, Fc, Hd, 20
Rummindei, Cb, 18a
Rupnath, Bb, 18a
Rusaddir, Be, 15
Rusellae, Fe, 12
Rusgonia, Ce, 15
Rutuli, Ab, 14b
Rutupiae (Richborough), He, 17
Ruvignium, Hb, 12
Ryknield Way, Ed, 17

Sabaei, Dd, 1
Sabatinus, L., Ge, 12
Sabini, Ge, 12
Sabrina Aest. (Severn), Ce, 17
Sabrina, F., Bb, 15
Sacae (Scythae), Kb, 5b
Sacra Via (Athens), Inset, 7a
Sacra Via (Roma), Inset, 13b
Sacrum Pr., Dd, 12
Saepta, Inset, 11c
Saepta Iulia, Inset, 13b
Saetabis, Be, 15
Saevo M., Ba, 1
Sagalassus, Cb, 9b
Sagartia, Hc, 5b
Sagrus, Je, 12
Saguntum, Cc, 5a
Sai (Sais), Ba, 3b
St. Albans (Verulamium), Fe, 17
Sais (Sai), Ba, 3b
Sais (Zau), Cc, 2d
Sakas, Je, 19
Salamis (Cyprus), Jc, 5a
Salamis (Graecia), Ee, 7
Salapia, Da, 13
Salaria, Pa., Inset, 11d
Salassi, Bb, 12
Salcah, Ce, 4c
Saldae, De, 15
Salernum, Cb, 13
Salii, Ec, 20
Salisbury (Sorbiodunum), Ee, 17
Sallentini, Fb, 13
Sallentinum Pr., Gc, 13
Salmantica, Ad, 15
Salonae, Bb, 16
Salt Sea, The, Bf, 4a
Salutaris, Pa., Inset, 11
Samal, Ca, 3a
Samaria, Bc, 4d
Samaria (Sebaste), Bc, 4d
Samarobriva, Cc, 15
Samatata, Kingdom of, Fc, 18b
Same, Bd, 7
Samnites, Bb, 14c
Samnium, Ca, 13
Samos, Gd, 8
Samos (Cephallenia), Bb, 2b
Samosata, Je, 11
Samothrace, Fa, 8
Sane, Eb, 6
Sangala, Kc, 9b
Sangarius, Eb, 16
Sanqualis, Pa., Inset, 11c
Santones, Bc, 15
Saradaush, Da, 3a
Sarangae, Ic, 5b
Sardes, Dc, 16
Sardinia-Corsica, Dd, 10
Sardis, Inset, Db, 4f
Sarmatia, Jc, 20
Sarmizegethusa, Ec, 18
Sarnia, Bc, 15
Sarpedon Pr., Cb, 7c
Sarsina, Gd, 12
Sarus, F., Db, 5b
Saspires Alardoii, Ea, 5b
Sassanid Kingdom, Cb, 18b
Satala, Fb, 16
Saticula, Ca, 13
Satiyaputra, K. of, Bc, 18a
Satricum, Aa, 13
Sattagydia, Jc, 5b
Saturnia, Fe, 12
Saurashtra, Je, 19
Savaria, Ba, 16
Savo, Cc, 12
Savus, F., Ba, 16
Saxones, Ec, 20
Saxum Tarpeium, Inset, 13a
Scalae Caci, Inset, 13a
Scallabis ,Ae, 15
Scamander, F., Cc, 7c
Scandia, Fa, 20
Scandiae Ins., Ea, 15
Scarbantia, Ba, 16
Scardona, Bb, 16
Scardus, M., Ba, 6
Scepsis, Cc, 7c
Sciathus, Ec, 6
Scillus, Bd, 8
Scione, Ec, 6
Scodra, Bb, 16
Scoti, Bc, 20
Scotus, Da, 8
Scupi, Cb, 16
Scylacium, Ed, 13
Scyllaeum, Dd, 13
Scyllaeum Pr. (Argolis), Ee, 7
Scyllaeum Pr. (Bruttium), Dd, 13
Scyros, Fd, 6
Scyrus, Db, 9a
Scythae (Sacae), Kb, 5b
Scythia, Jb, 19
Scythopolis, Bc, 4d
Sebaste (Samaria), Bc, 4d
Sebastea, Fc, 16
Sebinus, L., Eb, 12
Secia, F., Ec, 12
Second Cataract of Nile, Bd, 3
Secretarium, Inset, 13b
Sedunum, Ba, 12
Segedunum (Wallsend), Ea, 17
Segelocum, Fc, 17
Segesta (Liguria), Dc, 12
Segesta (Sicilia), Ae, 13
Segestanorum, Ad, 13
Segobriga, Be, 15
Segodunum, Cd, 15
Segontium (Carnarvon), Bc, 17
Segovia, Bd, 15
Segusio, Ab, 12
Seir, Cb, 3a
Sela (Petra), Bg, 4c
Seleucia, Ec, 16
Seleucia (Mesopotamia), Kf, 11
Seleucia (Syria), Fb, 4f
Selgovae, Ca, 17
Selinus (Cilicia), Ec, 16
Selinus (Sicilia), Ae, 13
Sellasia, De, 7
Selymbria, Ea, 7c
Semachonitis, L., Ca, 4d
Semneh, Bd, 3a
Sena Gallica, Hd, 12
Sena Iulia, Fd, 12
Senaculum, Inset, 13a
Sengara. Da, 3a
Senia, Aa, 16
Senones (Gallia), Cc, 15
Senones (Italia), Gd, 12
Sentinum, Gd, 12
Senzar, Ca, 3a
Sepharvaim (Sippar), Ec, 2d
Sepias Pr., Ec, 6
Sepphoris, Bb, 4d
Septimania, Pa., Inset, 11d
Sepulcrum C. Cestii, Inset, 11d
Sequana, R., Dd, 20
Sequani, Dc, 15
Serdica, Cb, 16
Serica, Gc, 1
Seriphos, Fe, 7
Sermyle, Eb, 6
Servitium, Ba, 16
Sessites, F., Cb, 12
Sestus, Ba, 5b
Seteia Aest., Cc, 17
Setia, Ba, 13
Severn (Sabrina Aest.), R., Ce, 17
Shahbazgarhu, Ba, 18a
Sharon, Plain of, Ac, 4d
Shasu (Habiru), Cb, 3a
Shechem, Bd, 4a
Shechem (Sychem), Bc, 4d
Shedet (Crocodilopolis-Arsinoë), Bb, 3b
Shel Gharraf, Eb, 3a
Shem (Panopolis), Bc, 3b
Shephelah, Ad, 4d
Sherwood Forest, Ec, 17
Shiloh, Bd, 4a
Shubari, Da, 3a
Shushan (Susa), Fc, 2d
Shuster, Bb, 18b
Sicani, Ae, 13
Sicca, De, 15
Sicelia, Inset, 7b
Sicilia, Be, 13; Ff, 20
Sicinos, I., Fe, 8
Siculi, Ce, 13
Sicyon, De, 7
Siddapura, Bc, 18a
Siddim, Vale of, Bf, 4a
Side, Bithynia et Pontus, Fb, 16
Side, Pamphylia, Jc., 5a
Sidon, Dc, 5b; Dc, 9b
Sidon (Zidon), Ba, 4d
Sidonians, see Zidonians
Siga, Be, 15
Sigeum, Ic, 5a
Sigeum Pr., Inset, 2c
Signia, Ba, 13
Sila M., Dd, 13
Silarius, F., Db, 13
Silchester (Calleva Atrebatum), Fe, 17
Siloam, Pool of, Inset, 4e
Silures, Ce, 17
Simeon, Af, 4a
Simkala (Ceylon), Fe, 18b
Simoeis, F., Inset, 2c
Simyra, Bc, 4c
Sinae, Gc, 1
Sinai, Mt., Bc, 3a
Sinai Pen., Bc, 3a
Sind, Ie, 19
Singara, Lf, 20
Singidunum, Cb, 16
Singus, Eb, 6
Sinope, Fb, 16
Sinuessa, Ba, 13
Sinus Acanthus, Eb, 6
Sinus Aelanites, Bc, 3a
Sinus Alcyonicus, Ed, 7
Sinus Ambracicus, Bd, 6
Sinus Arabicus, Cd, 3a
Sinus Argolicus, De, 7
Sinus Astacenus, Fb, 7c
Sinus Aualites, Gb, 18
Sinus Caystrius, Hd, 8
Sinus, Ceramicus, He, 8
Sinus Cianus, Fb, 7c
Sinus Corinthiacus, Dd, 7
Sinus Crisaeus, Dd, 7
Sinus Cumanus, Cb, 13
Sinus Cyparissius, Ce, 7
Sinus Didymi, Ca, 7d
Sinus Euboicus, Ed, 6
Sinus Flanaticus, Jb, 12
Sinus Heroopolites, Bc, 3a
Sinus Laconicus, Df, 7
Sinus Laus, Db, 13
Sinus Ligusticus, Dd, 15
Sinus Maliacus, Dd, 6
Sinus Messeniacus, Df, 7
Sinus Oxianus, Hc, 18
Sinus Paestanus, Cb, 13
Sinus Pagasaeus, Dc, 6
Sinus Persicus, Eb, 3a
Sinus Saronicus, Ee, 7
Sinus Scylaceus, Ed, 13
Sinus Singiticus, Eb, 6
Sinus Strymonicus, Eb, 6
Sinus Tarentinus, Fb, 13
Sinus Thermaicus, Db, 6
Sinus Thesproticus, Bc, 6
Sinus Toronaicus, Eb, 6
Siphae, Ed, 7
Siphnos, Ff, 7
Sipontum, Da, 13
Sippar, Ec, 5b
Sippar (Sepharviam), Ec, 2d
Siris, Eb, 13
Siris, F., Eb, 13
Sirmio, Eb, 12
Sirmium, Ge, 20
Siscia, Gd, 20
Sithonia, Eb, 6
Sitifis, De, 15
Sittace, Ec, 5b
Smyrna, Hc, 8
Smyrna Nova, Hc, 8
So-fang, Mc, 19
Sogdiana, Jb, 5b; Jb, 9b
Sogdiana, Ib, 9b
Soleb, Bd, 3a
Soli (Cilicia), Jc, 5a
Soli (Cyprus), Jc, 5a
Soli (Pompeiopolis), Ec, 16
Sollium, Bd, 6
Solomon's Palace, Inset, 4b
Soluntum, Bd, 13
Solus, Fc, 5a
Solygea, De, 7
Sopara, Bc, 18a
Sopianae, Ba, 16
Sora, Ba, 13
Soracte M., Ge, 12
Sorbiodunum (Salisbury), Ee, 17
Sorek, R., Ae, 4a
South Shields, Inset, 17b
Southern Hiung-nu, Mc, 19
Spain (Diocese of Hispania), Ce, 20
Spalauthra, Ec, 6
Sparta, De, 7
Spartolus, Ca, 9a
Speluncae, Ba, 13
Speos Artemidos (Menet Hufu), Bc, 3b
Spercheus, F., Dd, 6
Sphacteria, Bc, 9a
Spinae, Ee, 17
Spoletium, Ge, 12
Sravasti, Ke, 19
Srinagar, Ba, 18a
Stabiae, Cb, 13
Stadium (Athens), Inset, 7b
Stadium Domitiani, Inset, 11d
Stagira, Eb, 6
Stanwix, Inset, 17
Stenyclarus, De, 7
Stephen's Gate, Inset, 4e
Stoa Hadriani, Inset, 7b
Stoa of Eumenes, Inset, 7a
Stobi, Cb, 16
Stratonicaea, Eb, 6
Stratonice, Da, 8
Stratus, Cd, 6
Strongyle, Dd, 13
Strymon, F., Cb, 16
Stura, F., Bc, 12
Stymphalus, De, 7
Styra, Fd, 7
Suana, Fe, 12
Sublicius, Inset, 11d
Sublupatia, Eb, 13
Subura, Inset, 11c
Suburana, Inset, 11c
Sucro, F., Be, 15
Sudeti Mts., Eb, 15
Suessa Aurunca, Ba, 13
Suessa Pometia, Aa, 13
Suessula, Ca, 13
Suevi, Ed, 20
Suevi, Semnones, Db, 18
Sugambri, Db, 15
Suindinum, Cc, 15
Sulci, De, 15
Sumer, Eb, 3a
Sunium, Fe, 7
Sunium Pr., Fe, 7
Surashtra, Ec, 18b
Surrentum, Cb, 13
Susa, Fc, 5b
Susa (Shushan), Fc, 2d
Susia, Hb, 9b
Susiana, Fc, 5b; Gd, 18
Sutrium, Ge, 12
Sutu, Db, 3a
Syagros Pr., Hf, 18
Sybaris, Gc, 5a
Sybota, Bb, 9a
Sychem (Shechem), Bc, 4d
Syene, Ce, 5b
Symaethus, F., De, 13
Syme, Ec, 9a
Synnada, Ec, 16
Syout (Lycopolis), Bc, 3b
Syracusae, Gc, 5a; De, 13; Gf, 20
Syria, Dc, 9b
Syria Deserta, Gd, 18
Syrian Desert, Cb, 3a
Syrians (Aramaeans), Dc, 4c
Syrnos I., Ge, 8
Syros, Fe, 7
Syrtis Major, Gg, 20
Syrtis Minor, Fg, 20
Sze Chow, Nd, 19

Taanach, Bc, 4a
Tabal, Cb, 2d
Tabernae Argentariae, Inset, 13a
Tabernae Veteres, Inset, 13a
Tabor, Mt., Bc, 4a
Tabularium, Inset, 13b
Tadcaster (Calcaria), Ec, 17
Tadmor (Palmyra), Cb, 3a
Tadmor (Tamar), Ec, 4c
Taenarum Pr., Df, 7
Tagus, F., Ae, 15
Tai Yuan, Nd, 19
Taliata, Cb, 16
Talmis, Bd, 3a
Tamar (Tadmor), Ec, 4c
Tamesa, F., Bb, 15
Tamesa Aest., Inset, 17a
Tamralipti, Cb, 18a
Tamraparni (Ceylon), Cd, 18a
Tanager, F., Db, 13

Tanagra, Ed, 7
Tanais, Ka, 5a
Tanais, R., Db, 1
Tanarus, F., Cc, 12
Tanis (Zoan), Ba, 3b
Tanitic Mouth, Ca, 3b
Taphiae Ins., Bd, 6
Taprobane, Fd, 1
Tapti, R., Je, 19
Tapuritae, Gb, 9b
Taras, Fb, 13
Tarentum, Fb, 13
Tarnaiae, Aa, 12
Tarquinii, Fe, 12
Tarracina, Ba, 13
Tarraco, De, 20
Tarraconensis, Bd, 15
Tarsatica, Aa, 16
Tarshish (Tartessus), Bc, 5a
Tarsius, F., Dc, 7c
Tarsus, Cb, 5b
Tartessus (Tarshish), Bc, 5a
Tarus, F., Dc, 12
Tarvenna, Cb, 15
Tarvisium, Gb, 12
Tatta, L., Cb, 5b
Taulantii, Aa, 6
Taurianum Pr., Dd, 13
Taurica, Jd, 20
Taurini, Bc, 12
Tauromenium De, 13
Taurus, Jf, 20
Taurus, M., Ec, 16
Taurus Pr., De, 13
Tavium, Ec, 16
Taxila, Eb, 18b
Taygetus, M., De, 7
Teanum, Ca, 13
Teanum Apulum, Da, 13
Teate, Je, 12
Tecmon, Bc, 6
Tegea, De, 7
Tegianum, Db, 13
Tehenu, Ba, 3b
Teira, Hc, 8
Tekoa, Be, 4a
Telamon, Fe, 12
Telesia, Ca, 13
Tell-el-Amarna (Akhetaton), Bc, 3b
Telmessus, Dc, 16
Telos, Ec, 9a
Tempe, F., Dc, 6
Temple (Jerusalem), Inset, 4b
Templeborough, Ec, 17
Templum Antonini et Faustinae, Inset, 13b
Templum Apollinis, Inset, 13b
Templum Athene, Inset, 7a
Templum Augusti, Inset, 13b
Templum Castorum, Insets, 13a, b
Templum Concordiae, Insets, 13a, b
Templum Dianae, Inset, 11c
Templum Divi Romuli, Inset, 13b
Templum Divi Traiani, Inset, 13b
Templum Divorum, Inset, 13b
Templum Iani, Inset, 13a
Templum Iovis Capitolini, Insets, 13a, b
Templum Iovis Statoris, Insets, 13a, b
Templum Iovis Victoris, Insets, 13a, b
Templum Iunonis Lucinae, Inset, 11c
Templum Iunonis Monetae, Insets, 13a, b
Templum Martis Ultoris, Inset, 13b
Templum Minervae, Inset, 13b
Templum Pacis, Insets, 13b
Templum Quirini, Inset, 11c
Templum Romae et Augusti, Inset, 7a
Templum Sacrae Urbis, Inset, 13b
Templum Salutis, Inset, 11c
Templum Saturni, Inset, 13a
Templum Semonis Sanci, Inset, 11c
Templum Veneris et Romae, Inset, 13b
Templum Veneris Genetricis, Inset, 13b
Templum Vespasiani, Inset, 13b
Tempsa, Ed, 13
Tena Aest., Inset, 17a
Tenebrium Pr., Ce, 15
Tenedos, Gb, 8
Tenos, Fd, 8
Tentyra (Enet), Cc, 3b
Teos, Eb, 9a
Teredon, Fc, 9b
Tergeste, Hb, 12
Terina, Ec, 13
Teurnia, Ec, 15
Teuthrone, Df, 7
Teutones, Db, 15
Thaenae, Ef, 15
Thalaba, Ge, 18
Thapsacus, Db, 5b
Thapsacus (Tiphsah), Eb, 4c
Thapsus (Africa), Ee, 15; Ff, 20
Thapsus (Silicia), De, 13
Thara, Gb, 9b
Tharrus, Ec, 5a
Tharu, Ca, 3b
Thasos, Fb, 6
Theatrum Dionysi, Inset, 7a
Theatrum et Porticus Pompeii, Inset, 11
Theatrum Marcelli, Inset, 13b
Thebae, Achaea, Cc, 16
Thebae, Libya, Cc, 1; Ig, 11
Thebe, Eb, 2b
Thebes (Boeotia), Ed, 7
Thebes (Hypothebae), Cb, 2b
Thebes (No Ammon), Cd, 3b
Thebes (Phthiotis), Dc, 6
Thebez, Bd, 4a
Thelpusa, Ce, 7
Thera, Dc, 9a
Therma, Eb, 6
Thermae, Be, 13
Thermae Agrippae, Inset, 11d
Thermae Antoninianae, Inset, 11d
Thermae Constantini, Inset, 11d
Thermae Diocletiani, Inset, 11d
Thermae Neptuni, Inset, 11d
Thermae Neronianae, Inset, 11d
Thermae Quirini, Inset, 11d
Thermae Salurni, Inset, 11d
Thermae Selinuntiae, Be, 13
Thermae Solis, Inset, 11d
Thermae Traiani, Inset, 11d
Thermae Vestae, Inset, 11c
Thermessa, Cd, 13
Thermopylae, Dd, 6
Thermum, Cd, 6
Thespiae, Ed, 7
Thesprotia, Bc, 6
Thessalia, Dc, 6
Thessalonica, He, 20
Thessaly, see Thessalia
Theudoria, Cc, 6
Theveste, De, 15
Third Cataract of Nile, Be, 3a
Thisbe, Cb, 2b
Thoricus, Fe, 7
Thospitis, L., Eb, 5b
Thrace, see Thracia
Thracia, Fa, 6; Ie, 20
Thracia, Diocese of, Ie, 20
Three Taverns, Aa, 4f
Thronium, Cb, 9a
Throsmos, Inset, 2c
Thule, Inset, 17a
Thurii, Ec, 13
Thusdrus, Ee, 15
Thyateira, Hc, 8
Thyatira, Db, 4f
Thymbra, Inset, 2c
Thyrea, De, 7
Thyrrheum, Bd, 6
Thyrsus, F., Bd, 14a
Thyssus, Fb, 6
Tiberias, Bb, 4d
Tiberina, I., Inset, 11d
Tiberis, F., Gf, 12
Tibur, Gf, 12
Tiburtina, Pa., Inset, 11d
Ticinum, Db, 12
Ticinus, F., Cb, 12
Tifernum, Gd, 12
Tifernus, F., Kf, 12
Tigranocerta, Ke, 11
Tigris (Hiddekel), F., Ec, 2d
Tigris, R., Db, 3
Tigullia, Dc, 12
Til Barsip, Db, 2d
Tilaventus, F., Ga, 12
Tilgarimmu (Togarmah), Db, 2d
Tingis, Bd, 18
Tingitana, Bf, 15
Tingitania, Cg, 20
Tipasa, Ce, 15
Tiphsah (Thapsacus), Eb, 4c
Tipsah, Db, 2d
Tiryns, De, 7
Tisia, F., Ca, 16
Titulcia, Bd, 15
Tium, Eb, 16
Tob, Cc, 4a
Togarmah (Tilgarimmu), Db, 2d
Tolentinum, Hd, 12
Toletum, Bd, 15
Tolosa, De, 20
Tomen-y-mur, Cd, 17
Tomi, Hd, 11
Topra, Bb, 18a
Torone, Ec, 6
Tralles, Bb, 2d
Transpadana, Cb, 12
Trapezus, Ke, 20
Trans Tiberim, Inset, 11d
Trasimenus, L., Gd, 12
Treba, Hf, 12
Trebbia, F., Dc, 12
Trebula, Ge, 12
Treveri, Dc, 10
Triballi, Aa, 9c
Tricca, Cc, 6
Trichonius, L., Cd, 6
Tridentini, Fa, 12
Tridentum, Fa, 12
Trigemina, Pa., Inset, 11c
Trimontium, Da, 17
Trinovantes, Ge, 17
Triphylia, Ce, 7
Tripodes, Inset, 7a
Tripolis, Fg, 20
Tripolis (Phoenicia), Fd, 16
Tripolis (Pontus), Fb, 16
Tripolitana, Ef, 10
Tritaea, Cd, 7
Tritonis, L., Df, 10
Triturrita, Ed, 12
Troas, Db, 4f
Troesmis, Da, 16
Troezen, Ee, 7
Trojan Plain, Inset, 2c
Troy (Ilium), Bb, 2a
Tsang-Wu, Ne, 19
Tuder, Ge, 12
Tullianum, Insets, 13a, b
Tullum, Dc, 15
Tunes, Ee, 15
Tung-hai, Nd, 19
Tun-Huang, Ld, 19
Tuola, F., De, 12
Turdetani, Ae, 15
Turduli, Be, 15
Turushpa (Van), Eb, 2d
Tusci (Etrusci), Bb, 14c
Tusculum, Aa, 13
Tyana, Ba, 3a
Tymphaea, Cc, 6
Tymphe M., Cc, 6
Tymphrestus M., Cd, 6
Tyndaris, Cd, 13
Tyras, Ja, 5a
Tyras, R., Id, 20
Tyre, Bb, 4a; Kg, 20
Tyrrhenia, Fb, 5a
Tyrus, Fd, 18

UBI, Cb, 3a
Ugarit, Dc, 2a
Ujjain, Je, 19
Ulpiana, Cb, 16
Ulterior Hispania, Ad, 15
Umbria, Gd, 12
Umbri, Gd, 12
Umbro, F., Fe, 12
Upi (Opis), Ec, 2d
Upper City (Jerusalem), Inset, 4e
Upper Egypt, Bc, 3b
Ur, Eb, 3a
Uraipur, Bc, 18a
Uraiyu, Jf, 19
Urartu (Ararat), Eb, 2d
Urbs Salvia, Hd, 12
Urcinium, Ce, 12
Uria, Fb, 13
Urium, Da, 13
Uruk (Erech), Fc, 2d
Uselis, Be, 14a
Ustica, Bd, 13
Utica (Africa), Cf, 14; De, 15
Utii, Hd, 5b
Uxantis, Ac, 15
Uxellodunum (Maryport), Cb, 17
Uxii, Gc, 9b
Uzentum, Gc, 13

VACCAEI, Ad, 15
Vada, Ed, 12
Vada Sabatia, Cc, 12
Vadimonis, L., Ge, 12
Vagienni, Bc, 12
Vaisis, Eb, 2d
Valabhi, Ec, 18b
Valentia (Gallia), Cd, 15
Valentia (Hispania), Be, 15
Vallis Murcia, Inset, 11c
Vallis Quirini, Inset, 11c
Vallum Antonini, Ba, 17
Vallum Hadriani, Da, 17
Valvata, Ed, 12
Van (Turushpa), Eb, 2d
Vandali, Gc, 20
Vanga, Cb, 18a
Vapincum, Dd, 15
Vascones, Bd, 15
Vectis, Ef, 17
Veii, Ge, 12
Velabrum, Insets, 13a, b
Veldidena, Ec, 15
Veleia, Dc, 12
Velia, Inset, 13a
Velia (Elea), Db, 13
Velitrae, Aa, 13
Veltae, Eb, 18
Venafrum, Ca, 13
Venedae, Ib, 20
Veneris et Romae, Inset, 11d
Veneti (Gallia), Bc, 15
Veneti (Italia), Gb, 12; Ec, 15
Venetia, Fb, 12
Vengi, K. of, Fd, 18b
Vengipura, Fd, 18b
Venonae, Ed, 17
Venonetes, Da, 12
Venta, Inset, 17a
Venta Belgarum (Winchester), Ee, 17
Venta Icenorum, Hd, 17
Venta Silurum, De, 17
Venusia, Db, 13
Verbanus, L., Ca, 12
Vercellae, Cb, 12
Veretum, Gc, 13
Verlucio, De, 17
Vernemetum, Ed, 17
Verona, Fb, 12
Verterae (Brough), Db, 17
Vertones Oretani, Ad, 15
Verulamium (St. Albans), Fe, 17
Vesontio, Dc, 15
Vestini, He, 12
Vesunna, Cc, 15
Vesuvius, M., Cb, 13
Vetera, Db, 15
Vettona, Ge, 12
Vetulonia, Ee, 12
Via Aemilia, Ec, Gc, 12
Via Appia, Aa, Eb, 13
Via Asinaria, Inset, 11c
Via Aurelia, Ed, 12
Via Cassia, Fe, 12
Via Claudia Augusta, Gb, 12
Via Clodia, Fe, 12
Via Dolorosa, Inset, 4e
Via Domitia, Cd, 15
Via Flaminia, Gd, 12
Via Galaria, Inset, 11c
Via Iulia, Cc, 12
Via Lata, Inset, 11d
Via Latina, Ba, 13
Via Nomentana, Inset, 11c
Via Ostiensis, Inset, 11c
Via Popilia, Db, 13
Via Portuensis, Inset, 11c
Via Postumia, Fb, 12
Via Praenestina, Inset, 11c
Via Sacra (Athens), Inset, 7b
Via Sacra (Rome), Inset, 11c
Via Salaria, He, 12
Via Tiburtina, Inset, 11c
Via Triumphalis, Inset, 11c
Via Valeria (Italia), He, 12
Via Valeria (Sicilia), Ce, 13
Viadua, F., Fb, 10
Viadua, R., Gc, 20
Vibinum, Da, 13
Vicetia, Fb, 12
Vicus Iugarius, Insets, 13a, b
Vicus Longus, Inset, 11c
Vicus Patricius, Inset, 11c
Vicus Tuscus, Insets, 13a, b
Vienna (Gallia), Cc, 15
Vienna (Vienne), Dd, 20
Villa Publica, Inset, 11c
Viminacium, He, 20
Viminalis, Pa., Inset, 11c
Vindelicia, Ec, 15
Vindobala (Rudchester), Inset, 17
Vindobona, Ba, 16
Vindolanda (Chesterholm), Inset, 17
Vindomora (Ebchester), Inset, 17
Vinovia, Eb, 17
Vintium, Bd, 12
Virgin's Well, Inset, 4e
Virgo, Aq., Inset, 11d
Viroconium (Wroxeter), Dd, 17
Virodunum, Dc, 15
Virunum, Ec, 10
Visigothi, Hd, 20
Vistula, F., Gb, 10; Hc, 20
Visurgis, F., Db, 15
Vitricium, Bb, 12
Viviscus, Aa, 12
Volaterrae, Ed, 12
Volcanal, Inset, 13a
Volcei, Db, 13
Volsci, Bb, 14c; Ba, 13
Volsiniensis, L., Fe, 12
Volsinii (novus), Ge, 12
Volsinii (vetus), Ge, 12
Volturnum, Ba, 13
Volturnus, F., Ca, 13
Volubilis, Af, 10
Vomanus, F., Je, 12
Vosegus, M., Dc, 15
Vulci, Fe, 12

WADI TUMILAT, Ba, 3b
Walls (Jerusalem), Inset, 4e
Wallsend (Segedunum), Ea, 17
Walton Castle, He, 17
Warrington, Dc, 17
Wash, The (Metaris Aest.), Gc, 17
Watling Street, Dd, 17
Western Satraps, Ec, 18b
Wigan (Coccium), Dc, 17
Winchester (Venta Belgarum), Ee, 17
World (Ancient), 1
World (Eratosthenes), 1b
World (Ptolemy), 1a
World (Herodotus), 1a
World (Strabo), 1c
Wroxeter (Viroconium), Dd, 17
Wuchun, Nd, 19
Wu-Wei, Md, 19

XANTHUS, Bb, 9b
Xerxes Canal, Eb, 6
Xois (Khesout), Ba, 3b
Xyniae, Dc, 6

Y GAER, Cd, 17
Yamutbul, Fc, 2d
Yandheya, Ec, 18b
Yang Chow, Ne, 19
Yangtze R., Od, 19
Yarkand, Jd, 19
Yarmuk, R., Cc, 4a
Yavanas, Id, 18
Yenoam, Cb, 3a
Yih Chow, Md, 19
Ying-chuan, Nd, 19
York (Eburacum), Eb, 17
Yu Chow, Nd, 19
Yu-chang, Ne, 19
Yueh-Sui, Me, 19
Yun Chow, Nd, 19
Yun-chung, Nc, 19

ZACYNTHUS, Hc, 5a
Zadadrus, F., Kc, 9b
Zadracarta, Gb, 9b
Zagros Mts., see Zagrus Mons.
Zagrus Mons, Fc, 5b
Zahi, Cb, 3a
Zaitha, Bb, 18b
Zakaray, Ac, 4a
Zama Regia, De, 15
Zamua, Fb, 2d
Zancle (Messana), Dd, 13
Zarax, Ef, 7
Zariaspa, Ib, 9b
Zariaspa (Bactria), Jb, 9b
Zau (Sais), Cc, 2d
Zebulun, Bc, 4a
Zela, Fb, 16
Zeleia, Db, 7c
Zephyrium Pr., Ed, 13
Zeugma, Fc, 16
Zidon (Sidon), Ba, 4a
Zidonians, Bb, 4a
Ziklag, Af, 4a
Zikurtu, Fb, 2d
Zilis, Ae, 15
Zoan (Tanis), Ba, 3b
Zobah, Cc, 4c

PRINTED IN GREAT BRITAIN BY GEORGE PHILIP AND SON, LIMITED, LONDON

MUIR'S HISTORICAL ATLAS

MEDIEVAL & MODERN

PREFACE

FIFTY YEARS afford a searching test of the qualities of any work designed to satisfy the needs of many thousands of teachers and students in universities and in the higher classes of schools and colleges, especially when the book is planned on a scale which, despite the utmost economy in production, necessarily implies a fairly substantial price. The present editors of Ramsay Muir's *Historical Atlas: Mediaeval and Modern*, may fairly claim that the work which they are now partly refashioning has triumphantly stood that test, amply justifying the pride which Ramsay Muir and George Philip felt in their original edition of it. The *Atlas* has now run through eight editions and many reprints, and has so fully satisfied the need which brought it into being that it still has no serious rival in the British market over its own range and at a comparable price. It is no exaggeration to say that the Ramsay Muir historical atlases, pioneer works at their first appearances, demonstrating for the first time how a modern study of historical geography might illuminate so much of the study of history, played a decisive part in establishing historical geography as an integral part of the study and teaching of history in Britain. In so doing they did much to shape the new canon of our present method of teaching historical geography, especially by their demonstration of the physical basis of the subject, and also by their systematic conventions for representing historical data on coloured maps in such a way as to facilitate comparison between successive maps over long periods of time. To attempt now to recast a work which has not only thoroughly established itself in our educational provision, but has actually helped to shape our thinking and teaching of history, is no light responsibility.

Yet, after fifty years, reshaping there must be: in 1927, after only sixteen years, Ramsay Muir and George Philip themselves drastically refashioned this *Atlas* for its sixth edition. Muir never claimed that the *Atlas* was in any sense a work of original research, save where, as on British India, his own special knowledge enabled him at one or two points to make it so; the present editors can claim no more for this ninth edition. To make an atlas of this kind a work of original research would entail employing a specialist to design each separate map: this work aspires only to render in map form the conclusions of the best modern authorities readily available to the editors at the time when their work of revision was in process. But even this entails change. There are always errors and omissions to be rectified: the inevitable slow accretion of too many names on the successive editions of certain maps requires periodic pruning: the appearance of new and authoritative books, whether monographs, standard histories or works of reference, and even of new maps and atlases, inevitably necessitates change if the work is to be kept up to date. Most of all, we must keep pace with History itself. The last thirty years have not only seen rapid and tremendous changes in the political maps of the more familiar parts of the world, but have also forced on our attention regions virtually ignored in common history teaching until today. So we have been compelled to make great changes in this standard instrument of teaching history, some of them changes which we adopted grudgingly, others which we know the original editors would themselves have wished to see.

Inflation and rising costs have imposed sharp limits on us. Seeking to keep the price of the *Atlas* within the reach of those for whom it was first designed, we can in fact claim that, allowing for the changes in money value, the *Atlas*, at its present price, is no dearer than it was in 1911. But this has been achieved only by sharp cuts. The stimulating letterpress introduction of the first edition disappeared in 1952. Now one or two familiar maps have been dropped, and a few others reduced from double to single-page size, though we venture to think that the practical value of the *Atlas* to students has not materially suffered thereby. All this, with other rearrangements designed to save space without sacrificing content, has been done to make room for ten totally new plates illustrating world history since 1926, and especially recording the course of the shattering upheavals wrought in the world in that quarter-century of wars and revolutions. The result has been drastically to change the geographical and the chronological balance of the *Atlas*, shifting it much nearer our own contemporary age, and also away from our former European preoccupations.

Even so, the present edition tells as much as did any earlier edition of the *Atlas* of the history of the world before 1926—in fact, considerably more. New maps show the Norman conquest of S. Italy and Sicily, the rise of the house of Luxemburg, the rise of the house of Burgundy, the decline of the Ottoman Empire, Russian expansion in Turkestan, and the south-eastern United States during the Civil War. Many more maps have been redesigned to make them more informative, not merely by adding new names, but also by employing new technical processes of colour-printing to make them tell a more detailed story of the stages of development in many lands and at many periods. In particular several maps of the more familiar parts of the world—Western and Central Europe, France, Germany, Italy, England and Wales, Scotland, Ireland, North America, South America, South Africa—have been coloured politically in the present edition, whereas in earlier editions they had a basis of physical colouring. Lest this be thought a retreat from one of Ramsay Muir's basic principles in designing the original *Atlas*, the editors assert that in this respect Muir's teaching has by now succeeded so completely that, at a time when modern schools everywhere are teaching physical geography and providing their pupils handsomely with atlases of physical geography, it is no longer necessary to provide physically-coloured maps in a historical atlas except where the subject-matter of the map especially requires a physical basis for its understanding. This change, we think, fully justified by present circumstances, has enabled us to add greatly to the historical content of the present edition. In re-designing these maps and in reviewing the content of many others, thousands of entries have been made: in many maps new place-names have been added, new boundaries shown, in some overcrowded maps the amount of lettering has been reduced. The aim has been throughout to make the *Atlas* an efficient work of reference for the teachers and students, furnishing without overcrowding all the information which they could reasonably expect to find for any but the most specialised and detailed work. Revision of this kind is a never-ending process, and will continue to be recorded in future reprints and editions. The editors owe much to the helpful criticism of users who have reported omissions and errors or who have made other suggestions for improvement; these, whenever advisable, have been incorporated. Further suggestions and criticisms will be welcomed as hitherto, for no work of this kind can hope to attain perfection.

It remains to acknowledge our greatest debts. First of all to Ramsay Muir and George Philip, whose original design we inherited and have tried to preserve as far as we could in greatly changed conditions. The memory of their friendly guidance is a valued inspiration to one of the present editors, who was a pupil of the one and a junior colleague of the other of the makers of this *Atlas*. Then to the late Mr. George Goodall, editor of the seventh edition and joint editor of the eighth, who played a large part in planning some of the changes embodied in the present version—a steady counsellor and shrewd guide whose knowledge and practical experience were always freely given, and who understood the limits of the possible.

R. F. Treharne.

H. Fullard.

CONTENTS

1 The Realms of Civilisation c.200 a.d. 1 : 50m.

2 Europe on the Eve of the Barbarian Invasions c.395 a.d. 1 : 25m.
- A *Europe* c.476 a.d. 1 : 40m.

3a Roman Britain 1 : 3m.
- B *Britain according to Ptolemy*
- C *Hadrian's Wall* 1 : 1½m.

4a Europe c.526 a.d. 1 : 25m.
- B *Europe* c.600 a.d. 1 : 25m.

5 Italy c.600 a.d. 1 : 5m.
- A *Rome in the Middle Ages* 1 : 100,000
- B *Papal Lands* c.800 a.d. 1 : 8m.

6 The Conquests of Islam 1 : 30m.
- A *Iraq, Syria and Mesopotamia* 1 : 15m.
- B *The Disintegration of Islam* 1 : 70m.

7a The Teutonic Invaders of Britain 1 : 8m.
- B *England under Offa and Egbert* 1 : 6m.
- C *The Treaty of* 886 *and the Reconquest of the Danelaw* 1 : 6m.

8 Europe in the Age of Charlemagne 1 : 20m.
- A *The Partitions of Verdun* 843 *and Mersen* 870 1 : 20m.
- B *The Frankish Empire before Charlemagne* 1 : 20m.
- C *Races of Western and Central Europe* c.800 1 : 40m.

9 Europe c.900 a.d. 1 : 20m.

10 Germany about the year 962 a.d. 1 : 5m.

11 France and Burgundy about the year 1032 a.d. 1 : 5m.

12 England and her Viking Invaders 1 : 8m.

13 England according to the Domesday Survey 1086 1 : 2½m.

14 Scotland c.500–c.1200 a.d. 1 : 2m.
- A *Ecclesiastical Scotland* c.1500 1 : 8m.

15 Ireland before the English Invasion 1 : 2m.
- A *Ecclesiastical Ireland* c.1500 1 : 8m.

16 Europe at the time of the First Crusade c.1100 a.d. 1 : 20m.
- A *Advance and Divisions of Christianity to* c.1096 1 : 60m.

17 The Angevin Empire and the Kingdom of France 1 : 6m.
- A *Growth of the French Monarchy from Philip Augustus to the Hundred Years' War* 1 : 10m.

18a Second and Third Crusades 1 : 20m.
- B *Fourth and later Crusades* 1 : 20m.
- C *Christian States in Syria* c.1100 1 : 5m.
- D *Jerusalem during the Crusades* 1 : 25,000
- E *Constantinople* 1 : 200,000

19 Eastern Europe c.1250 1 : 15m.

20-21 Western and Central Europe in the Early Thirteenth Century 1 : 6m.
- A *Rise of the Norman Kingdom of Italy and Sicily* 1 : 6⅓m.
- B *Germany under Frederick Barbarossa* 1 : 12m.

22 Western and Central Europe c.1500: Ecclesiastical Provinces and Mediæval Universities 1 : 10m.
- A *Suburbicarian District of Rome* 1 : 5m.

23a Italy in the xi Century 1 : 10m.
- B *Italy in the XII and XIII Centuries* 1 : 8m.
- C *Iberian Peninsula: the Reconquest* 1037–1270 1 : 10m.
- D *Iberian Peninsula* 1270–1492 1 : 10m.

24 Europe c.1360 1 : 20m.

25 Asia under the Mongols 1 : 45m.

26 The Baltic Lands and the Hanseatic League in the xiv, xv and xvi Centuries 1 : 10m.

27 Mediæval England and Wales c.1399 1 : 2½m.
- A *London* 1 : 75,000

28a Wales and the Marches in the xiii Century 1 : 2½m.
- B *The Scottish Borders* 1 :2½m.
- C *France at the Peace of Bretigny* 1360 1 : 9m.
- D *France in* 1429 1 : 9m.

29a The Alpine Barrier and the Neighbouring Battlefields 1 : 5m.
- B *Growth of the Swiss Confederation* 1 : 2m.

30-31 Western and Central Europe in the later Fifteenth Century 1 : 6m.
- A *Rise of the House of Burgundy* 1 : 6½m.
- B *Rise of the House of Luxemburg* 1 : 10m.

32a Italy during the Renaissance 1 : 5m.
- B *Italy in the XVII and XVIII Centuries* 1 : 10m.
- C *Italy in the XIX and XX Centuries* 1 : 10m.
- D *Growth of Venice* 1 : 5m.
- E *Growth of Florence* 1 : 5m.

CONTENTS

33A GROWTH OF THE OTTOMAN EMPIRE 1 : 20M.
B *Algiers* 1 : 30M.
C *Growth of the Habsburg Dominions to* 1914 1 : 10M.

34 EUROPE IN 1519 1 : 15M.

35 THE WORLD IN 1490 1 : 165M.
A *The World according to Ptolemy* : 150
B *The World according to Edrisi* : 1154
C *The World according to Fra Mauro* : 1459

36 ECCLESIASTICAL ENGLAND TO THE TIME OF HENRY VIII 1 : 3M.
A *English Dioceses in the Anglo-Saxon Period* c.800 1 : 9M.

37A SCOTLAND IN THE XVI AND XVII CENTURIES 1 : 3M.
B *Ireland before the Tudor Conquest* 1 : 3M.
C *The English Plantation of Ireland* 1 : 8M.

38-39 WESTERN AND CENTRAL EUROPE 1555–1648 1 : 6M.
A *Religions of Central Europe* c.1618 1 : 18M.
B *Alsace-Lorraine during the Thirty Years' War* 1 : 3M.
C *Ernestine and Albertine Lands in Saxony* 1 : 3½M.

40A THE WORLD AT THE TREATY OF SARAGOSSA 1529 1 : 165M.
B *The World according to Behaim* 1492
C *The World according to Schöner* 1523

41A PORTUGUESE TRADE EMPIRE IN THE FAR EAST c.1580 1 : 50M.
B *South America* c.1650 1 : 50M.

42 THE WORLD 1588–1650 1 : 165M.
A *The World according to Mercator* 1587
B *Australia according to Tasman* 1643

43A WEST INDIES AND CENTRAL AMERICA 1 : 25M.
B *Political Distribution in* 1650 1 : 50M.
C *Political Distribution in* 1763 1 : 50M.
D *Political Distribution in* 1855 1 : 50M.

44 EXPLORATION OF NORTH AMERICA 1 : 35M.

45A EARLY COLONISATION OF NORTH AMERICA 1607–1689 1 : 10M.
B *New England and the Middle Colonies* 1620–1650 1 : 5M.

46A THE NETHERLANDS IN THE XVII CENTURY 1 : 2½M.
B *Campaign of Waterloo* 1 : 1M.
C *The Netherlands: Political Distribution in the later Middle Ages* 1 : 5M.

47 EUROPE AFTER THE PEACE OF WESTPHALIA 1648 1 : 15M.

48A ENGLAND DURING THE CIVIL WAR 1642–43 1 : 4M.
B *England during the Civil War* 1644–45 1 : 4M.

49A SCOTLAND SINCE THE RESTORATION 1 : 3M.
B *Ireland since the XVII Century* 1 : 3M.
C *The Cromwellian Settlement in Ireland* 1 : 8M

50 CENTRAL AND EASTERN EUROPE IN 1667 1 : 12M.

51 CENTRAL AND EASTERN EUROPE IN 1795 1 : 12M.

52 THE WORLD AT THE TREATIES OF UTRECHT 1713–15 1 : 165M.
A *India at the beginning of the XVII Century* 1 : 30M.
B *Gilolo and Ternate* 1 : 2½M.
C *The Moluccas or Spice Islands* 1 : 20M.

53 FRANCE AND WESTERN GERMANY 1660–1789 1 : 6M.
A *Paris at the time of the French Revolution* 1 : 50,000

54 EUROPE IN 1740 1 : 15M.

55A THE NARROW SEAS 1 : 6M.
B *The North Atlantic* 1 : 60M.

56 NORTH AMERICA 1689–1783 1 : 10M.
A *Quebec* 1 : 250,000
B *Boston* 1 : 1M.

57 NORTH AMERICA IN THE ERA OF CONFLICT 1750–1783 1 : 5M.
A *West and South* 1778–1781 1 : 20M.
B *New York*

58 THE WORLD AT THE TREATY OF PARIS 1763 1 : 165M.
A *The World according to Homan* 1716
B *The World according to D'Anville* 1772

59A INDIA IN THE TIME OF CLIVE AND WARREN HASTINGS 1 : 20M.
B *Calcutta* 1 : 10M.
C *India in* 1805 1 : 20M.
D *Madras* 1 : 10M.

60A THE GROWTH OF BRANDENBURG-PRUSSIA 1 : 6M.
B *The Growth of Prussia* 1 : 6M.

61 GROWTH OF THE RUSSIAN EMPIRE IN EUROPE UP TO 1914 1 : 20M.
A *Partitions of Poland* 1 : 15M.
B *Russian Expansion in Turkestan* 1855–1895 1 : 21¼M.

62 EUROPE UNDER NAPOLEON 1810 1 : 15M.

63 THE IBERIAN PENINSULA AT THE TIME OF THE PENINSULAR WAR 1 : 5M.
A *Strait of Gibraltar* 1 : 2½M.
B *The Lines of Torres Vedras* 1 : 1M.

CLASSIFIED LIST OF MAPS AND SUBJECTS

A

ABBASID Caliphate, 8, 9
Abbasids, Disintegration of Islam under the, 6B
Aden Protectorate, 93
Afghan Supremacy, 59A
Afghanistan, 61B, 74, 92
Africa, 1923, 96C
Africa, 1961, 94, 96D
Africa, Partition and Exploration of, 80A
Ahmadnagar, 52A
Alaska, 71A, 75
Alaska Boundary Dispute, 71B
Alban, Kingdom of, 14
Albania, 78, 82, 84, 85, 88, 89
Albertine Lands in Saxony, 39C
Albigensian Crusade, 20
Albuquerque, Track of, 40
Algeria, 24, 80A, 96C, 96D
Almohad Empire, 18
Alpine Barrier and the Neighbouring Battlefields, 29A
Alsace-Lorraine during the Thirty Years' War, 39B
Anatolia, 33A
Angevin Empire, 17
Anglo-Egyptian Sudan, 80A, 96C
Angola, 80A, 96C, 96D
Annam, 74
Antarctic Exploration, 69C
Antarctica, 95
Antioch, Principality of, 18C
Apulia and Calabria, Duchy of, 21A
Aquitaine, Duchy of, 17
Arab League States, 93, 94-95
Arabia, 1, 6, 25, 41A, 96C
Aragon, 24
Aragon, Kingdom of, 23C, 23D
Archbishoprics in the Baltic Lands, 26
Archbishoprics in England at the Domesday Survey, 13
Archbishoprics in France and Burgundy, 1032 A.D., 11
Archbishoprics in Western and Central Europe in the later 15th century, 30-31
Archiepiscopal Provinces in Western and Central Europe, c.1500, 22
Archiepiscopal Sees in England to the time of Henry VIII, 36
Archiepiscopal Sees in Ireland c.1500, 15A
Archiepiscopal Sees in Scotland c.1500, 14A
Archiepiscopal Sees in Western and Central Europe c.1500, 22
Arctic Exploration, 69B
Argentina, 68
Arles, Kingdom of, 20
Armenia, Kingdom of, 19
Ascanians, Lands held by the, 21B
Asia, 94
Asia, Eastern, 1945–61, 91
Asia, European Influence and Russian Expansion in, 74
Asia under the Mongols, 25
Asia Minor, 86C
Asiatic Fronts in the Great War, 86C
Asoka Empire, 1
Assam, 74
Atlanta and Chattanooga Campaigns, 72A
Australasia, Exploration and Settlement of, 77
Australia, 75, 95
Australia, Commonwealth of, 77
Australia according to Tasman, 42B
Austria, 50, 65A, 84, 85, 87, 88, 89
Austria-Hungary, 82
Austrian Empire, 64, 65B
Austrian Netherlands, 55A
Aversa, County of, 21A
Ayubites, Empire of the, 18B

B

BACHAN, 52C
Bahama Islands, 43A
Balkan Peninsula 1800–1914, 78
Balkan Peninsula, Slavonic and Bulgarian Powers in, 78A
Baltic Lands and the Hanseatic League, 26
Baluchistan, 74
Barcelona, County of, 11, 23C
Bartholemew Diaz, Track of, 35
Basutoland, 80A, 81B, 96C, 96D
Batavian Republic, 51
Bavaria, 10
Bechuanaland, 96C, 96D
Bechuanaland Protectorate, 80A
Belgian Congo, 80A, 96C
Belgium, 82, 83A, 84, 85, 87, 88, 89
Benevento, D. of, 23A
Bengal, 59A, 59C, 73, 74
Bengal, Partition of, 73A
Berlin, World after the Congress of, 76
Bhonsla's Lands, 73
Bhutan, 73, 74, 91, 92
Bihar and Orissa, 73
Bijapur, 52A
Bishoprics in the Baltic Lands, 26

Bishoprics in England at the Domesday Survey, 13
Bishoprics in England to the time of Henry VIII, 36
Bishoprics in France and Burgundy 1032 A.D., 11
Bishoprics in Ireland, 1150, 15
Bishoprics in Western and Central Europe in the later 15th century, 30–31
Bohemia, 10
Bohemia, Kingdom of, 31, 39
Bohemia and Luxemburg, Lands of the House of, 24
Bohemia-Moravia, Prot. of, 87
Bolivia, 68, 68A
Bosnia, 78, 79
Boston, 56B
Bourbon Lands, 34, 54
Brandenburg, 34
Brandenburg-Prussia, 47, 50, 54
Brandenburg-Prussia, Growth of, 60A
Brazil, 41B, 68
Britain according to Ptolemy, 3B
Britain, Roman, 3A
Britain, Teutonic Invaders of, 7A
British Columbia, 75
British Guiana Boundary, 68B
British Honduras, 75
British Isles, 88
British North America, Growth of, 70–71
British North Borneo, 74, 75, 90
British Somaliland, 80A
Brittany, County of, 11
Brunei, 74, 75, 90, 91
Bulgaria, 24, 78, 79, 82, 84, 85, 88, 89
Bulgaria, Kingdom of, 9, 19
Bulgarian Kingdom, 18B
Bulgarian Powers in the Balkan Peninsula, 78A
Burgundian Kingdom, 4A
Burgundy, Kingdom of, 11, 16
Burgundy, Lands of the House of, 30–31
Burgundy, Rise of the House of, 31A
Burma, 73, 90, 91, 92
Byzantine Territory in Italy c.1000, 23A

C

CABOT, Track of, 40
Cabral, Track of, 40
Calabria and Apulia, Duchy of, 21A
Calcutta, 59B
Caledonia, Pictish Kingdom of, 14
Calmar, Lands of the Union of, 34
Cambodia, 74, 91
Cameroon, 96D
Cameroons, 96C
Canada, 56, 69A, 75
Cape of Good Hope, 80A, 81A
Capua, Duchy of, 23A
Capua, Principality of, 21A
Carinthia, 10
Carolina, 67A
Carolingian Empire, 8
Carnatic, 59A, 59C, 59D
Carpini's Route, 25
Castile, Kingdom of, 23C, 23D, 24
Cathay, 25, 35
Central Africa, 96D
Central America, 43A, 94
Central America in 1650, 43B
Central America in 1763, 43C
Central America in 1855, 43D
Central Europe in 1939, 87
Central Europe, Religions of, 39A
Central Provinces, 74
Central and Eastern Europe in 1667, 50
Central and Eastern Europe in 1795, 51
Cephalonia, County of, 24
Ceylon, 52A, 59A, 59C, 73, 92
Chad, 96D
Charles, Kingdom of, 8A
Chile, 41B, 68
China, 41A, 74, 75, 90
China, Great Wall of, 1
Chinese Republic, 91
Christian States in Syria c.1100, 18C
Christianity, Advance and Divisions of, to c.1096, 16A
Church, States of the, 30–31, 32A
Church Lands, 19, 20, 24, 26, 30–31, 34, 38–39, 47, 50, 51, 53, 54
Cilicia, 18C
Cinque Ports, 27
Civil War, England during the, 48
Civil War, South Eastern United States during the, 72
Cochin China, 74
Colombia, 68, 68A, 75
Columbus, Track of, 40
Commonwealth Countries, 94–95
Communist Bloc, 94–95
Congo, 96D
Congo (former French), 96D
Constantinople, 18E
Cook's Voyages, 58
Cordova, Enirate of, 6, 8, 9
Cossack Penetration, Lines of, 42
Costa Rica, 75
Crete, 78
Crusades, 16, 18
Cuba, 43A, 43B, 43C, 43D, 75

Cyprus, 93
Cyprus, Kingdom of, 18A
Czechoslovakia, 84, 85, 89

D

DAHOMEY, 96B, 96D
Dalmatia, 34
Dalriada, Scottish Kingdom of, 14
Dampiers' Voyages, Track of, 52
Danelaw, Reconquest of the, 7C
Danish Towns in Ireland, 15
Dardanelles, 86D
Delhi, Sultanate of, 25
Denmark, 9, 12, 24, 26, 34, 47, 50, 51, 62, 64, 82, 84, 85, 87, 88, 89
Denmark and Norway, 54
Djagatai Empire, 25
Domesday Survey, England according to the, 13
Dominican Republic, 75
Drake's Voyage, Track of, 42
Dutch East Indies, 74, 75, 90

E

EAST Anglia, 12
East Pakistan, 91, 92
East Roman Empire, 2, 6, 8, 9
East Roman Empire, Themes of the, 9
Eastern Asia 1945–1961, 91
Eastern Association, 48A
Eastern Campaigns of the American Civil War, 72B
Eastern Empire, 16, 24
Eastern Europe, 19
Ecclesiastical England to the time of Henry VIII, 36
Ecclesiastical Fiefs in France and Burgundy 1032 A.D., 11
Ecclesiastical Provinces in Western and Central Europe c.1500, 22
Ecuador, 68, 68A, 75
Egypt, 79, 80A, 93, 96C, 96D
Egypt and the Nile Valley, 80B
Eire, 49B
El Cid, Dominion of, 23C
England, 24, 34, 47, 54, 55A, 62
England during the Civil War, 48
England according to the Domesday Survey 1086, 13
England, Ecclesiastical to the time of Henry VIII, 36
England under Edward the Confessor, 12
England before the Industrial Revolution c.1701, 66A
England after the Industrial Revolution 1911, 66B
England under Offa and Egbert, 7B
England, Treaty of 886 and Reconquest of the Danelaw, 7C
England and her Viking Invaders, 12
England and Wales, Mediæval c.1399, 27
English Dioceses in the Anglo-Saxon Period, 36A
Episcopal Sees in England to the time of Henry VIII, 36
Episcopal Sees in Ireland c.1500, 15A
Episcopal Sees in Scotland 500–1200 A.D., 14
Episcopal Sees in Scotland c.1500, 14A
Episcopal Sees in Western and Central Europe c.1500, 22
Er Riff, 88
Eritrea, 80A, 80B, 93, 96C, 96D
Estonia, 84, 85, 87, 88, 89
Ethiopia, 80A, 96C, 96D
Europe c.476 A.D., 2
Europe c.526 A.D., 4
Europe c.600 A.D., 4
Europe c.768–814, 8
Europe c.900, 9
Europe c.1100, 16
Europe c.1360, 24
Europe 1519, 34
Europe 1648, 47
Europe 1740, 54
Europe 1810, 62
Europe 1815, 64
Europe 1923, 84
Europe 1942, 88
Europe 1961, 89
Europe, Linguistic Divisions, 85
Europe, Races of Western and Central, c.800, 8C
Exploration of Africa, 80
Exploration of the Antarctic, 69C
Exploration of the Arctic, 69B
Exploration of Australasia, 77
Exploration of North America, 44

F

FEDERATED Malay States, 74
Ferrara, D. of, 32A
Fiji Is., 75C
Finland, 84, 85, 88, 89
Flanders, County of, 11
Florence, Growth of, 32E
Florence, Republic of, 30–31, 32A
Formosa, 91
France, 34, 47, 54, 64, 82, 84, 85, 88, 89
France c.1032 A.D., 11
France in 1429, 28D
France, Kingdom of, 12, 16, 17, 20–21, 24, 38
France at the Peace of Bretigny, 28C
France and Western Germany 1660–1789, 53
Franco-German War, 76A
Franconia, 10

Frankish Empire, 6, 8
Frankish Empire before Charlemagne, 8B
Frankish Kingdom, 4A, 4B, 7A
French Appanages, 20, 30
French Community, 94–95
French Empire, 62
French Equatorial Africa, 80A, 96C
French Indo-China, 75, 90
French Monarchy, Growth of the, 17A
French Royal Domain, 11, 16, 17, 20, 24, 30, 38
French Somaliland, 80A
French West Africa, 80A, 96C

G

GABON, 96D
Galloway, Pictish Sub-Kingdom of, 14
Gambia, 80A, 96B, 96C, 96D
Gascony, Duchy of, 11, 17
Genoa, Republic of, 30, 32A, 38
Genoese Dominions, 19
German Confederation, 64, 65C
German East Africa, 80A
German Empire, 82
German Empire 1871, 65E
German South-West Africa, 80A, 81A
German Zollverein, Growth of the, 65D
Germany, 84, 85, 87, 88, 89
Germany c.962 A.D., 10
Germany, Kingdom of, 16, 20–21, 21B
Germany under Frederick Barbarossa, 21B
Germany, Reconstruction of, by Napoleon 1803, 65A
Germany, Reconstruction of, by Napoleon 1807, 65B
Ghana, 96B, 96D
Gibraltar, 63
Gilolo and Ternate, 52B
Golconda, 52A
Gold Coast, 80A, 96C
Golden Horde, Khanate of the, 19, 24, 25
Granada, Kingdom of, 23C, 23D
Greater Antilles, 43A, 43C
Greece, 78, 79, 82, 84, 85, 88, 89, 93
Guatemala, 75
Guiana, 41B, 55B, 68, 68B, 75
Guienne, Duchy of, 11
Guinea, 96B, 96D
Gwynedd, Principality of, 28

H

HABSBURG Dominions, Growth of the, 33C
Habsburgs, Lands of the, 24, 30–31, 34, 38–39, 53
Hadhramaut, 74
Hadrian's Wall, 3C
Haiti, 75
Han Dominions, 1
Hanseatic League, 26
Hawaii, 75D
Hindustan, 40A
Hispaniola, 43A, 43B
Hohenzollern, Lands of the House of, 30–31, 38–39, 50, 53
Holland, 82, 84, 85
Holy Roman Empire, 16, 20–21, 24, 30–31, 34, 38–39, 54, 65
Honduras, 75
Hungary, 16, 19, 24, 34, 47, 51, 54, 79, 84, 85, 87, 88, 89
Hungary, Imperial, 39
Huguenot Centres in France, 38
Hyderabad, 74

I

IBERIAN Peninsula 1037–1270, 23C
Iberian Peninsula 1270–1492, 23D
Iberian Peninsula at the time of the Peninsular War, 63
Iceland, 88, 89
Iconium, Kingdom of, 18A
Ifni, 96C, 96D
Ilkhan Empire, 25
Imperial Free Cities, 53
Imperial Hungary, 39
India, 35, 74
India in 1805, 59C
India in 1858, 73
India at the beginning of the XVII century, 52A
India in the time of Clive and Warren Hastings, 59A
India, Pakistan, Burma and Ceylon 1961, 92
Indies, 42
Indonesia, 91
Industrial Revolution, England before and after the, 66
Iraq, 6A, 88, 89, 93
Ireland, 24, 34, 47, 54, 62, 89
Ireland since the XVII century, 49B
Ireland, the Cromwellian Settlement in, 49B
Ireland, Ecclesiastical c.1500, 15A
Ireland before the English Invasion, 15
Ireland before the Tudor Conquest, 37B
Islam, Conquests of, 6
Islam, Disintegration under the Abbasids, 6B
Israel, 89, 93
Italian East Africa 1936–41, 96A
Italian Front in the Great War, 86B
Italian Somaliland, 80A, 96C
Italy, 82, 84, 85, 88, 89
Italy, Kingdom of, 9, 16, 20–21, 62
Italy c.600 A.D., 5
Italy in the XI century, 23A

Italy in the XII and XIII centuries, 23B
Italy in the XVII and XVIII centuries, 32B
Italy in the XIX and XX centuries, 32C
Italy during the Renaissance, 32A
Italy and Sicily, Rise of the Norman Kingdom of, 21A
Ivory Coast, 96B, 96D

J

JACKSON'S Campaign, 71F
Jagellons, Lands of the, 26, 31
Jalayas, Dominions of the, 24
Jammu and Kashmir, 92
Japan, 74, 90, 91
Japanese Empire, 75
Japanese Expansion 1928–42, 90
Jerusalem, Kingdom of, 18C
Jerusalem during the Crusades, 18D
Jordan, 89, 93
Joscelin, Lordship of, 18C

K

KAMERUN, 80A
Kashmir, 73, 74
Kenya, 96C, 96D
Khazar Empire, 9
Khmer Empire, 25
Korea, 74, 75, 90, 91
Kublai Khan, Empire of, 25
Kushan Dominions, 1
Kuwait, 93

L

LAOS, 74, 91
Latin Empire, 19
Latvia, 84, 85, 87, 88, 89
Lebanon, 89, 93
Leon, Kingdom of, 9, 23C
Leon and Castile, Kingdom of, 16, 23C
Lesser Antilles, 43A, 43C
Liberia, 80A, 96B, 96C, 96D
Libya, 80A, 96C, 96D
Lithuania, 24, 84, 85, 87, 88, 89
Lombard Duchies, 23A
Lombard Kingdom, 5
Lombard Territories, 5
Lombardy, Kingdom of, 23A
London, 27
Lothar, Kingdom of, 8A
Lotharingia, 10
Louis, Kingdom of, 8A
Louisiana, 56
Lucca, Republic of, 30, 32A
Luxembourg, 89
Luxemburg, Rise of the House of, 31A

M

MADAGASCAR, 80A
Madras, 59D
Magellan, Track of, 40
Majapahit, 40A
Majorca, Kingdom of, 23D
Malay Peninsula, 75
Malaya, 90, 91
Mali, 96D
Mameluke Sultans, 24
Manchukuo, 90
Manchuria, 74, 75, 90
Marco Polo's Routes, 25, 35
Matilda, Lands of Countess, 23B
Mauritania, 96D
Mercia, 12
Mersen, Treaty of, 8A, 9
Mesopotamia, 6A
Mexico, 43A, 43B, 43C, 43D, 75
Mien, 25
Milan, Duchy of, 30, 32A, 38
Modena, Duchy of, 32A, 38
Mogul Empire, 41A, 52A
Mohammed Abtin, Dominions of, 24
Moluccas, 52C
Monasteries in England at the Domesday Survey, 13
Monasteries in England to the time of Henry VIII, 36
Monasteries in Ireland c.1150, 15
Monasteries in Scotland c.500–1200 A.D., 14
Monasteries in Western and Central Europe c.1500, 22
Mongol Il-Khans, Empire of the, 19
Mongolia, 74, 75, 90, 91
Montenegro, 78, 82
Moravian Empire, 9
Morocco, 24, 64, 80A, 96C, 96D
Mozambique, 80A, 96C, 96D
Mysore, 59A, 59C, 73, 74

N

NAPLES, Kingdom of, 24, 32A, 62
Naples and Sicily, Kingdom of, 23B
Narrow Seas, 55A
Natal, 80A
Natal and Zululand, 81D
Navarre, Kingdom of, 11, 23C, 30
Near and Middle East, 1939–1961, 93
Nelson's Track, 55B
Nepal, 73, 74, 91, 92
Netherlands, 53, 64, 87, 88, 89

Netherlands in the XVII century, 46A
Netherlands, Political Distribution in the Later Middle Ages, 46C
New England, 67A
New England and the Middle Colonies 1620–1650, 45B
New Guinea, Territory of, 77
New Holland, 42B
New York, 57B
New Zealand, 75, 77, 77A
Newfoundland, 45A
Niagara Frontier, 71D
Nicaea, Empire of, 18B, 19
Nicaragua, 75
Niger, 96D
Nigeria, 80A, 96B, 96C, 96D
Nigritia, 58
Nizam's Dominions, 59A, 59C, 73
Norman Kingdom of Italy and Sicily, 18A, 21A
Normandy, 12
Normandy, Duchy of, 11, 17
North America 1689–1783, 56
North America 1750–1783, 57
North America, Growth of British, 70–71
North America, Early Colonisation of, 45A
North America, English Crown Grants, 67A
North America, Exploration of, 44
North Atlantic, 55B
North Atlantic Treaty Organisation, 94–95
North Borneo, 91
North East Boundary Dispute, 71E
North East New Guinea, 75
North West Provinces, 73
Northern Ireland, 49B
Northern Rhodesia, 80A, 96C, 96D
Northumbria, 12
Norway, 12, 24, 34, 82, 84, 85, 88, 89
Norway, Kingdom of, 9, 26
Novgorod, Republic of, 19
Nyasaland, 80A, 96C, 96D

O

ODOACER, Kingdom of, 2
Oman, 74, 93
Orange Free State, 80A, 81B
Orange River Colony, 81A
Orange River Sovereignty, 81B
Organisation of American States, 94–95
Ostrogothic Kingdom, 4
Ottoman Empire, 34, 39, 47, 50, 51, 54, 64, 74, 82
Ottoman Empire, Decline of the, 79
Ottoman Empire, Growth of the, 33A
Oudh, 59A, 59C, 62, 73

P

PACIFIC, Partition of the, 75
Pakistan, 92
Palestine, 6A, 88
Panama, 68, 75
Papal Lands c.800 A.D., 5B
Papal States, 24, 32B, 32C, 34, 39, 47
Papal States in XV century and early XVI century, 32A
Papal Territory in Italy c.1000, 23A
Papal Territory in Italy in the XII and XIII centuries, 23B
Papua, Territory of, 77
Paraguay, 68
Paris at the time of the French Revolution, 53A
Paris, World at the Treaty of, 58
Parma, Duchy of, 38
Parthian Empire, 1
Persia, 6, 41A, 74, 93
Peru, 68, 68A
Peru, Lower, 41B
Peru, Upper, 41B
Peru, Vice-Royalty of, 41B, 42
Philippine Islands, 74, 75, 90
Philippines, 75E, 91
Piedmont, Principality of, 38
Poland, 16, 34, 47, 50, 54, 74, 84, 85, 87, 88, 89
Poland, Kingdom of, 19, 21, 24, 31, 39
Poland, Partitions of, 61A
Polygars, 52A
Portugal, 24, 34, 47, 54, 62, 63, 82, 84, 85, 88, 89
Portugal, County of, 23C
Portugal, Kingdom of, 23D
Portuguese Guinea, 80A, 96B, 96C, 96D
Portuguese Trade Empire in the Far East c.1580, 41A
Prussia, 51, 62, 64, 65A, 65B, 65C, 65E
Prussia, Growth of, 60B
Prussia, Kingdom of, 65D
Punjab, 73, 74

Q

QATAR, 93
Quebec, 56A

R

RAJPUTANA, 59A, 59C, 73, 74
Rhine, Confederation of the, 62, 65
Rio de Oro, 80A, 96C
Roman Dioceses, 2
Roman Empire, 1, 2, 4A, 4B
Roman Prefectures, 2
Rome in the Middle Ages, 5A
Rome, Suburbicarian District of, 22A
Rubruquis' Route, 25

Rum, Kingdom of, 18A
Rumania, 78, 79, 82, 84, 85, 87, 88, 89
Rus, Kingdom of, 16
Russia, 34, 47, 54, 64, 74, 82
Russian Empire, 62, 74
Russian Empire in Europe, Growth of the, 61
Russian Expansion in Turkestan, 61B
Russian States, 24
Russo-Japanese War, 76B

S

SALADIN and the Ayubites, Empire of, 18A
Salerno, Duchy of, 23A
Salerno, Principality of, 21A
Salonica Front in the Great War, 86A
Salvador, 75
Samoa, 75B
Saracen Lands in the Iberian Peninsula, 23C
Saracen Territory in Italy c.1000, 23A
Sarawak, 74, 75, 90, 91
Sardinia, Kingdom of, 32B, 32C, 51, 62
Saudi-Arabia, 93, 96D
Savoy, Duchy of, 30, 32A
Savoy, Lands of the Counts of, 23B
Saxony, 10
Saxony, Ernestine and Albertine Lands in, 39C
Schleswig-Holstein 1864, 65F
Scotland, 12, 24, 34, 47, 54, 62
Scotland c.500–c.1200 A.D., 14
Scotland in the XVI and XVII centuries, 37A
Scotland Ecclesiastical c.1500, 14
Scotland since the Restoration, 49A
Scottish Borders, 28B
Seljuk Empire, 16
Seljuk Empire of Rum or Iconium, 18B
Seljuk Kingdom of Rum or Iconium, 19
Seljuk Turkish Amirates, 19
Senegal, 96D
Sequeira, Track of, 40
Serbia, 78, 79, 82
Siam, 74, 75, 90, 91
Siberia, 74
Sibir, Khanate of, 25
Sicily, County of, 21A
Sicily, Kingdom of, 19, 23B, 24, 62
Sicily and Italy, Rise of the Norman Kingdom of, 21A
Siena, Republic of, 30–31, 32A
Sierra Leone, 80A
Sikkim, 29, 91
Sind, 73, 74
Singapore, 75A
Sinkiang, 74, 75
Slovakia, 87
Somali Republic, 96D
Song Empire, 25
South Africa, Republic of, 96D
South Africa, Union of, 80A, 96C
South Africa before and after the Great Trek, 81B
South Africa showing Growth of British Power, 81A
South African Republic, 81B
South America c.1650, 41B
South America in the XIX and XX centuries, 68
South America, North West, 68A
South East Asia Collective Defence Treaty, 94–95
South Eastern United States during the Civil War, 72
South West Africa, 96C, 96D
Southern Rhodesia, 80A, 96C, 96D
Spain, 34, 47, 54, 62, 63, 64, 82, 84, 88, 89
Spanish Guinea, 80A, 96C, 96D
Spanish Morocco, 96C
Spanish Netherlands, 38
Spanish Sahara, 96D
Spice Islands, 52C
Staufen, Demesne Lands held by the House of, 21B
Staufen, Duchies held by the House of, 21B
Stephen Dushan, Dominions of, 24
Stephen Dushan, Empire of, 24
Strathclyde, British Kingdom of, 14
Sudan, 96D
Swabia, 10
Swaziland, 80A, 96C, 96D
Sweden, 9, 24, 26, 34, 47, 50, 51, 54, 62, 82, 84, 85, 88, 89
Sweden and Norway, 64
Swiss Confederation, 30, 34, 38, 50, 51
Swiss Confederation, Growth of the, 29B
Switzerland, 47, 54, 64, 82, 84, 85, 87, 88, 89
Syria, 6A, 88, 89, 93
Syria c.1100, Christian States in, 18C

T

TAMURLANE, Empire of, 25
Tanganyika, 96C, 96D
Tasman's Voyages, Track of, 42
Ternate, 52B, 52C
Themes of the East Roman Empire, 9
Tibet, 73, 74, 91, 92
Tidor, 52C
Timur, Empire of, 25
Togo, 80A, 96B, 96D
Togoland, 96C
Tongking, 74, 75
Torres Vedras, Lines of, 63B
Trade Routes in Asia in the Middle Ages, 25

Trade Routes of the Baltic Lands and the Hanseatic League, 26
Trade Routes of the Portuguese Trade Empire in the Far East c.1580, 41
Transjordan, 88
Transvaal, 80A, 81A
Trebizond, Empire of, 19
Tripoli, 24
Trucial Oman, 93
Tunis, 24, 80A
Tunisia, 88, 89, 96C, 96D
Turkestan, 74
Turkestan, Russian Expansion in, 61B
Turkey, 82, 84, 85, 86, 88, 89, 93
Tuscany, 23B
Tuscany, Duchy of, 23A
Tuscany, Grand Duchy of, 32B, 32C, 38–39
Two Sicilies, Kingdom of the, 18B, 32B, 32C, 50, 51, 54, 64

U

UGANDA, 96C, 96D
Ukraine, 74
Union of South Africa, 80A, 96C
Union of Soviet Socialist Republics, 75, 84, 85, 87, 88, 89
United Kingdom, 55B, 64, 82, 84, 89
United Provinces, 46, 47, 50, 54, 55A
United Provinces, Republic of, 38
United States, 55B, 75, 76
United States 1783–1803, 67B
United States 1803–1830, 67C
United States, Growth of the, 70–71
United States Slavery and Emancipation, 67D
Universities, Mediæval, in Western and Central Europe c.1500, 22
Upper Burma, 74
Uruguay, 68
Utrecht, World at the Treaties of, 52

V

VANDAL Kingdom, 2A, 4A
Vasco da Gama, Track of, 40
Venetian Territories in the XII century, 23B
Venezuela, 41B, 68, 68A, 74
Venice, 54
Venice, Growth of, 32D
Venice, Republic of, 30–31, 32A, 32B, 38–39, 47, 50, 51
Venice, Territories of the Signoria of, 19
Verdun, Treaty of, 8A
Vicksburg Campaigns in the American Civil War, 72C
Vienna, Europe after the Congress of, 64
Vietnam, 91
Villeneuve's Track, 55B
Virginia, 67A
Visigothic Kingdom, 2A, 4A
Volta, 96B, 96D

W

WALES, 34, 47, 54, 62
Wales, Principality of, 27
Wales and the Marches, 28A
Warsaw, Grand-Duchy of, 62
Waterloo, Campaign of, 46B
Welf, Demesne Lands held by the House of, 21B
Welf, Duchies held by the House of, 21B
Wessex, 12
West Africa to 1914, 81C
West Africa 1961, 96B
West Indies, 55B
West Indies and Central America, 43A
West Indies and Central America 1650, 43B
West Indies and Central America 1763, 43C
West Indies and Central America 1855, 43D
West Pakistan, 92
West Roman Empire, 2
Western Front in the Great War, 83A and B
Western Germany 1660–1789, 53
Western Samoa, 75B
Western and Central Europe in the early XIII century, 20–1
Western and Central Europe c.1500, 22
Western and Central Europe in the later XV century, 30–31
Western and Central Europe 1555–1648, 38–39
Westphalia, Europe after the Peace of, 47
Wettin, Lands of the House of, 30–31, 38–39
Wittelsbach, Lands of the House of, 30–31, 38–39
World 1490, 35
World 1588–1650, 42
World 1713–15, 52
World 1763, 58
World 1830, 69
World 1878, 76
World 1914, 83
World 1919–1927, 86
World 1961, 94–95
World according to Behaim, 40B
World according to D'Anville, 58B
World according to Edrisi, 35B
World according to Fra Mauro, 35C
World according to Homan, 58A
World according to Mercator, 42A
World according to Ptolemy, 35A
World according to Saragossa, 40A
World according to Schöner, 40C

Y

YEMEN, 93
Yugoslavia, 84, 85, 88, 89

Z

ZIPANGU, 25
Zululand, 81D

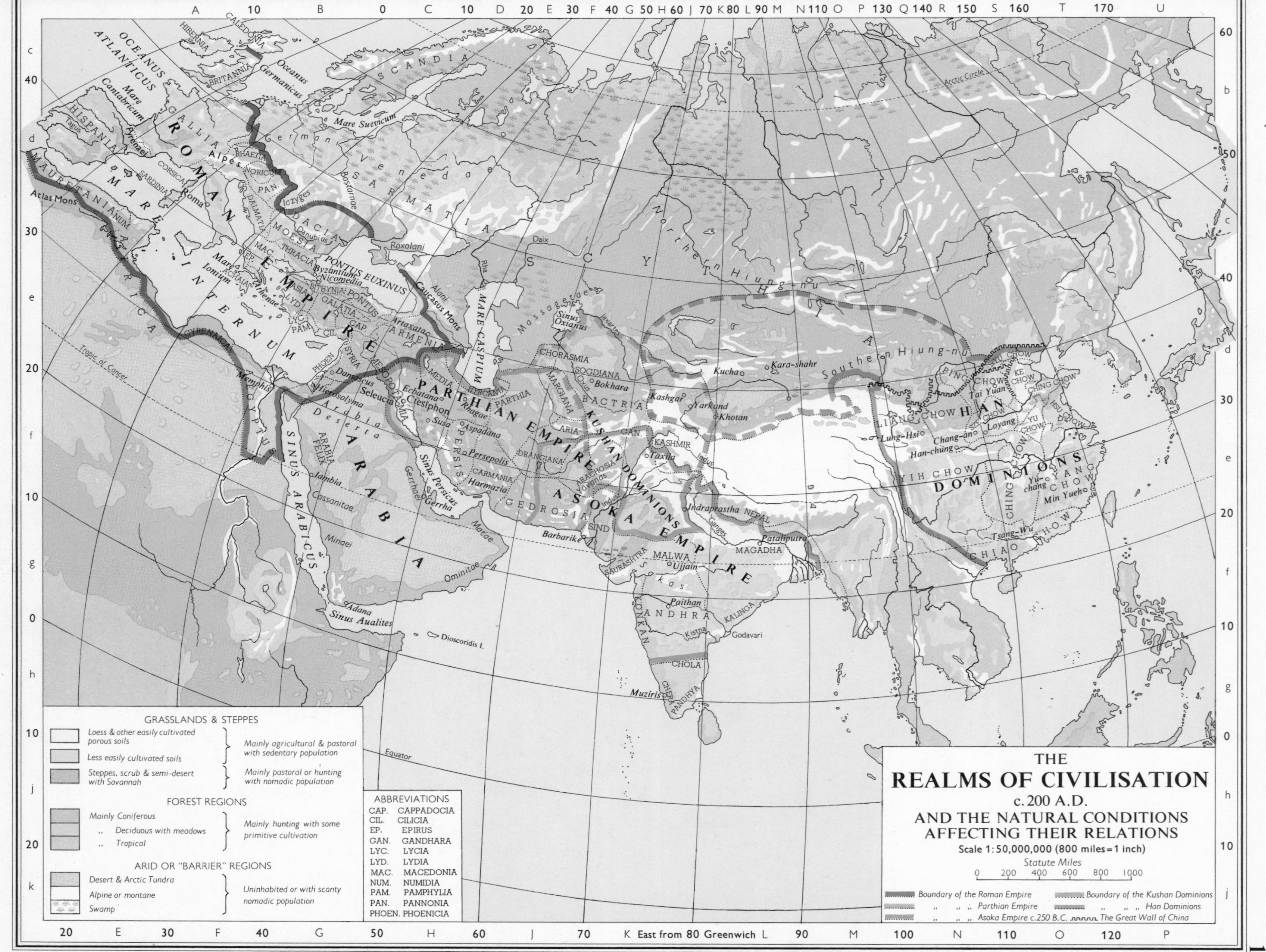
THE
REALMS OF CIVILISATION
c. 200 A.D.
AND THE NATURAL CONDITIONS
AFFECTING THEIR RELATIONS
Scale 1:50,000,000 (800 miles = 1 inch)
Statute Miles
0 200 400 600 800 1000
Boundary of the Roman Empire
,, ,, ,, Parthian Empire
,, ,, ,, Asoka Empire c.250 B.C.
Boundary of the Kushan Dominions
,, ,, ,, Han Dominions
The Great Wall of China
GRASSLANDS & STEPPES
Loess & other easily cultivated porous soils
Less easily cultivated soils
Mainly agricultural & pastoral with sedentary population
Steppes, scrub & semi-desert with Savannah
Mainly pastoral or hunting with nomadic population
FOREST REGIONS
Mainly Coniferous
,, Deciduous with meadows
,, Tropical
Mainly hunting with some primitive cultivation
ARID OR "BARRIER" REGIONS
Desert & Arctic Tundra
Alpine or montane
Swamp
Uninhabited or with scanty nomadic population
ABBREVIATIONS
CAP. CAPPADOCIA
CIL. CILICIA
EP. EPIRUS
GAN. GANDHARA
LYC. LYCIA
LYD. LYDIA
MAC. MACEDONIA
NUM. NUMIDIA
PAM. PAMPHYLIA
PAN. PANNONIA
PHOEN. PHOENICIA
East from 80 Greenwich
ROMAN EMPIRE
MARE INTERNUM
PARTHIAN EMPIRE
KUSHAN DOMINIONS
ASOKA EMPIRE
HAN DOMINIONS
ARABIA
SARMATIA
SCYTHIA
OCEANUS ATLANTICUS
Mare Cantabricum
Oceanus Germanicus
Mare Suevicum
SCANDIA
PONTUS EUXINUS
MARE CASPIUM
Sinus Persicus
SINUS ARABICUS
Sinus Aualites
Arctic Circle
Tropic of Cancer
Equator
Northern Hiung-nu
Southern Hiung-nu
AFRICA
AEGYPTUS
HISPANIA
GALLIA
BRITANNIA
CALEDONIA
HIBERNIA
Roma
Byzantium
Nicomedia
Damascus
Hierosolyma
Seleucia
Ctesiphon
Ecbatana
Persepolis
Bokhara
Kashgar
Yarkand
Khotan
Kucha
Kara-shahr
Taxila
Indraprastha
Pataliputra
Ujjain
Paithan
Muziris
Tai Yuan
Loyang
Chang-an
Han-chung
Lung-Hsi
Min Yueh
Tsang-Wu
COPYRIGHT, GEORGE PHILIP & SON, LTD.

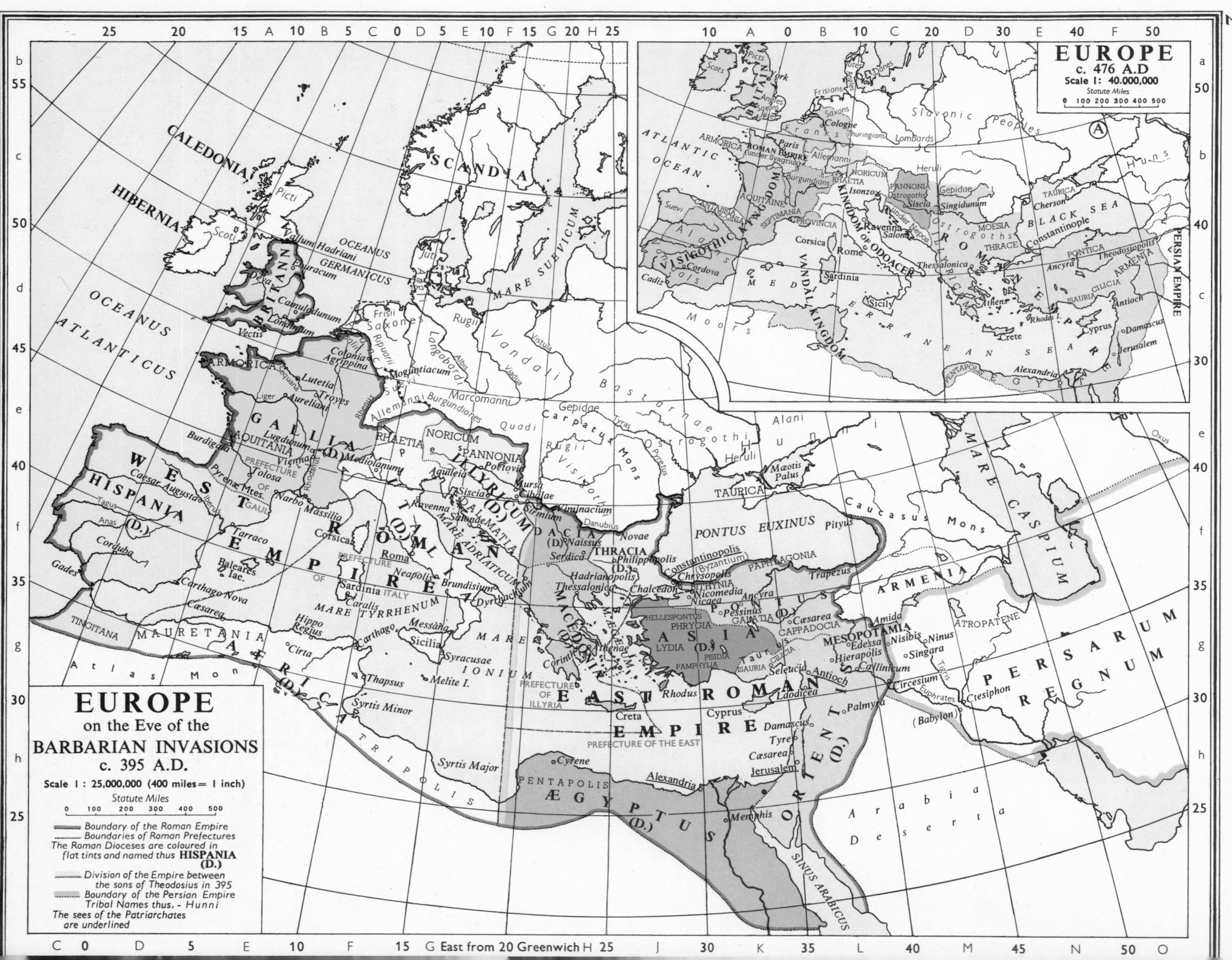
EUROPE
on the Eve of the
BARBARIAN INVASIONS
c. 395 A.D.
Scale 1 : 25,000,000 (400 miles = 1 inch)
Statute Miles
0 100 200 300 400 500
Boundary of the Roman Empire
Boundaries of Roman Prefectures
The Roman Dioceses are coloured in flat tints and named thus HISPANIA (D.)
Division of the Empire between the sons of Theodosius in 395
Boundary of the Persian Empire
Tribal Names thus. - Hunni
The sees of the Patriarchates are underlined
EUROPE
c. 476 A.D
Scale 1: 40.000,000
Statute Miles
0 100 200 300 400 500
East from 20 Greenwich

ROMAN BRITAIN
Scale 1:3,000,000 (48 miles = 1 inch)
Statute Miles
0 10 20 30 40 50
Roman Roads thus
Tribal names REGNI
Modern names within brackets
Forests
Marshes
Roman permanent forts
" civil sites
Signal Stations
Highlands over 3000 feet
" from 1200-3000 feet
Uplands " 600-1200 "
Lowlands " 300- 600 "
" " 0- 300 "
BRITAIN according to PTOLEMY
HADRIAN'S WALL
Scale 1:1,500,000 (24 miles = 1 inch)
West from Greenwich
OCEANUS HIBERNICUS
HIBERNIA
Litus Saxonicum

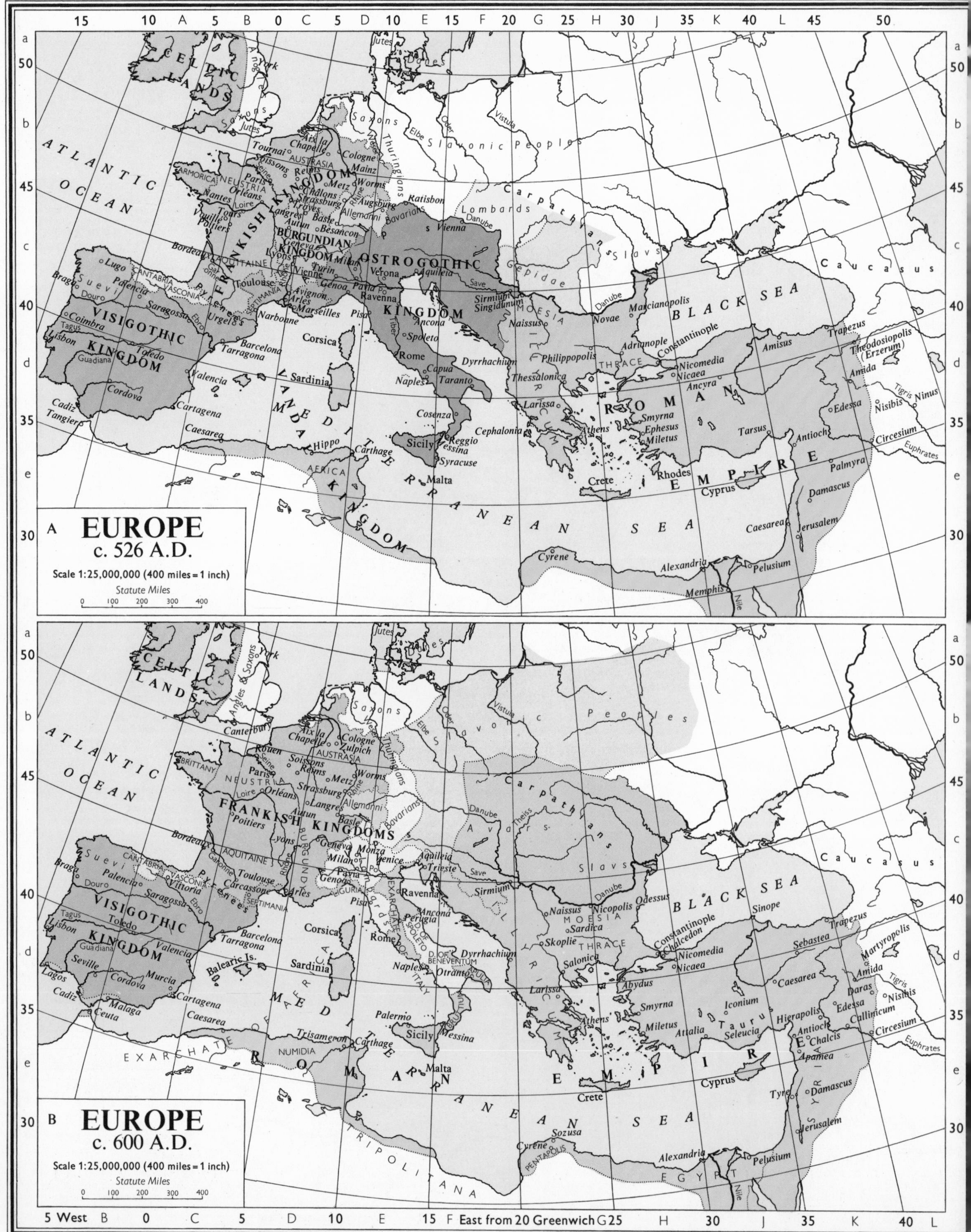
A EUROPE
c. 526 A.D.
Scale 1:25,000,000 (400 miles = 1 inch)
Statute Miles
0 100 200 300 400
B EUROPE
c. 600 A.D.
Scale 1:25,000,000 (400 miles = 1 inch)
Statute Miles
0 100 200 300 400
ATLANTIC OCEAN
CELTIC LANDS
FRANKISH KINGDOM
BURGUNDIAN KINGDOM
OSTROGOTHIC KINGDOM
VISIGOTHIC KINGDOM
VANDAL KINGDOM
ROMAN EMPIRE
MEDITERRANEAN SEA
BLACK SEA
Slavonic Peoples
Carpathians
Caucasus
Saxons
Jutes
Danes
Thuringians
Lombards
Bavarians
Allemanni
Gepidae
Slavs
Suevi
AUSTRASIA
NEUSTRIA
ARMORICA
AQUITAINE
CANTABRIA
VASCONIA
SEPTIMANIA
MOESIA
THRACE
ILLYRICUM
AFRICA
Corsica
Sardinia
Sicily
Malta
Crete
Cyprus
Rhodes
Rome
Ravenna
Constantinople
Alexandria
Jerusalem
Damascus
Antioch
Carthage
FRANKISH KINGDOMS
Anglo Saxons
BRITTANY
Avars
EXARCHATE OF AFRICA
NUMIDIA
TRIPOLITANA
PENTAPOLIS
EGYPT
SYRIA
Taurus
Balearic Is.
DUCHY OF SPOLETO
DUCHY OF BENEVENTUM
APULIA
CALABRIA
BRUTTIUM
LIGURIA
Lombards
5 West
East from 20 Greenwich

ITALY
c. A.D. 600
Scale 1:5,000,000 (80 miles=1 inch)
Statute Miles
0
50
100
Lombard Territories
Other lands owed a real or nominal allegiance to the Eastern Empire
Over 3000 feet
1200-3000 ,,
600-1200 ,,
0- 600 ,,
PAPAL LANDS
c. A.D. 800
Scale 1:8,000,000
Statute Miles
Papal Lands
Before A.D. 754
754-774
774-814
Ferrara
Cabellum
Comiaclum
Bononia
Ravenna
Faventia
Cesenae
Ariminum
Pisaurum
Fanum
Urbinum
Senogalliae
Aesium
Ancona
Humana
Auximum
Castrum Felicitatis
Eugubium
Perusia
Populonium
Balneum Regis
Spoletum
Rosellae
Suana
Tuscana
Ameria
Narnia
Horta
Biterum
Sutrium
SABINENSIS
Roma
Sora
Arpinum
Arces
Ceccanum
Aquinum
Theanum
Capua
ROME
in the Middle Ages
Scale 1:100,000
Statute Miles
Vatican
S. Peter's
Leonine City
Castle of S. Angelo
S. Lorenzo in Lucina
S. Susanna
S. Silvestro
Baths of Diocletian
S. Lorenzo Fuori le Mura
S. Agostino
S. Lorenzo in Damaso
Pantheon
S. Maria Maggiore
Cancelleria
S. Agata
S. Prassede
Capitol
S. Pietro
Baths of Titus
S. Clemente
S. Maria in Trastevere
House of Rienzi
Colosseum
S. Croce
Lateran
Trans Tiberis
Palatine
S. Cecilia
S. Sabina
Quattro Coronati
S. Stefano
Aventine
S. Prisca
S. Sisto
S. Balbina
Baths of Carasalla
S. Cesareo
Tiber
Brenner P.
Chur
St. Gotthard P.
Bernardino P.
Chiavenna
Val Tellina
Bellinzona
Sion
Bozen
FRIULI
Drave
Save
Trent
Feltre
Belluno
L. Como
Aosta
Little St. Bernard P.
Mt. Cenis P.
Maggiore
Como
Bergamo
Monza
Milan
Novara
Brescia
Verona
Vicenza
Treviso
Aquileia
Trieste
PANNONIA
Padua
Venice
Istria
VENETIA
Vercelli
Pavia
Cremona
Mantua
Turin
Susa
Asti
Alba
Tortona
Piacenza
Parma
Reggio
Modena
Ferrara
Comacchio
Bologna
EXARCHATE
Ravenna
Pola
Genoa
Savona
Gulf of Genoa
Ventimiglia
Nice
Faenza
Rimini
Pesaro
Zara
DALMATIA
Lucca
Florence
Faesulae
Pisa
Arno
Urbino
PENTAPOLIS
Ancona
Osimo
Fermo
Spalato
TUSCANY
Siena
Taginae
Perugia
Camerino
Assisi
Chiusi
Nursia
Spoleto
Ascoli
Piombino
Elba
Orvieto
Todi
UMBRIA
DUCHY OF SPOLETO
Reate
Chieti
Viterbo
Sutrium
CORSICA
Aleria
Ajaccio
(to Exarchate of Africa)
Civita Vecchia
Rome
Ostia
ADRIATIC SEA
Mt. Gargano
Lucera
Sipontum
Mte. Cassino
DUCHY OF BENEVENTUM
APULIA
Canusium
Bari
Terracina
Gaeta
Capua
CAMPANIA
Benevento
Garigliano
Naples
Salerno
Sorrento
Capri
Amalfi
Paestum
Brindisi
Tarentum
CALABRIA
Lecce
Otranto
Torres
SARDINIA
Galtelli
TYRRHENIAN SEA
BASILICATA
Cosenza
Cortona
BRUTTIUM
Squillace
Lipari Is.
Locri
Messina
Reggio
Palermo
Trapani
Lilybaeum
SICILY
Taormina
Mt. Etna
Trocala
Catana
Leontini
Girgenti
Syracuse
East from Greenwich

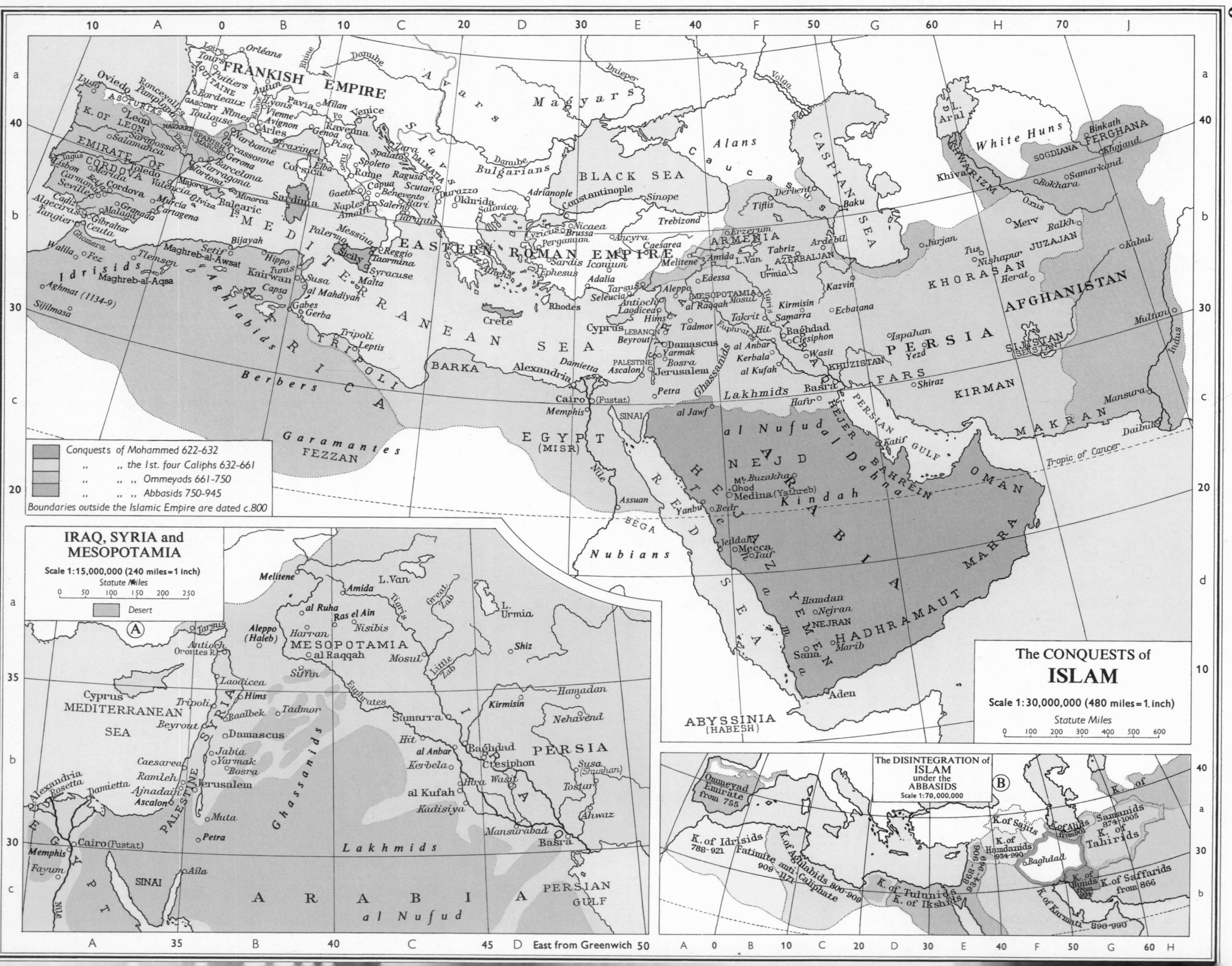
The CONQUESTS of
ISLAM
Scale 1:30,000,000 (480 miles=1 inch)
Statute Miles
0 100 200 300 400 500 600
Conquests of Mohammed 622-632
" " the 1st. four Caliphs 632-661
" " " Ommeyads 661-750
" " " Abbasids 750-945
Boundaries outside the Islamic Empire are dated c.800
IRAQ, SYRIA and
MESOPOTAMIA
Scale 1:15,000,000 (240 miles=1 inch)
Statute Miles
0 50 100 150 200 250
Desert
A
The DISINTEGRATION of
ISLAM
under the
ABBASIDS
Scale 1:70,000,000
B
East from Greenwich
FRANKISH EMPIRE
EMIRATE OF CORDOVA
EASTERN ROMAN EMPIRE
MEDITERRANEAN SEA
BLACK SEA
CASPIAN SEA
PERSIA
ARABIA
AFRICA
EGYPT (MISR)
ABYSSINIA (HABESH)
AFGHANISTAN
KHORASAN
RED SEA
PERSIAN GULF
Tropic of Cancer
MESOPOTAMIA
Ommeyad Emirate from 755
K. of Idrisids 788-921
Fatimite anti Caliphate 909-1171
K. of Aghlabids 800-909
K. of Tulunids
K. of Ikshids
K. of Saffarids from 866
K. of Karmat 890-990

THE TEUTONIC INVADERS of BRITAIN in the 5th and 6th Centuries
Scale 1:8,000,000 (130 miles = 1 inch)
Statute Miles
0 50 100 150
Approximate extent of English Settlements c.500
Conquests by 600
Conquests by 660
Conquests by 800
Principal Roman Roads
Jutes (Hypothetical)
Saxons
Angles
Movements on the continent before 400 A.D.
Saxons, Angles, Frisians in 5th and 6th Centuries
West from A Greenwich 8
East from E Greenwich 8
NEUSTRIA
FRANKISH KINGDOM
AUSTRASIA
SALIAN FRANKS
ALAMANNI
BRITTANY
FRISIANS
SAXONS
THURINGIANS
JUTES
DANES
ENGLAND under OFFA and EGBERT
Scale 1:6,000,000 (96 miles = 1 inch)
Statute Miles
0 20 40 60 80 100
Limits of direct rule of Offa, c.796
Limits of effective overlordship of Offa
Limits of direct rule of Egbert, 829
Limits of effective overlordship of Egbert
The TREATY of 886 and the RECONQUEST of the DANELAW
Scale 1:6,000,000 (96 miles = 1 inch)
Statute Miles
0 20 40 60 80 100
Wessex at Alfred's accession
English Mercia by the Treaty of 886
Other English lands
Guthrum's kingdom
Other Danish lands
Norwegian settlements c.900-925
Stages of the English reconquest (with dates)
The Five Boroughs are underlined
IRISH SEA
NORTH SEA
ENGLISH CHANNEL
4 West from B Greenwich 2

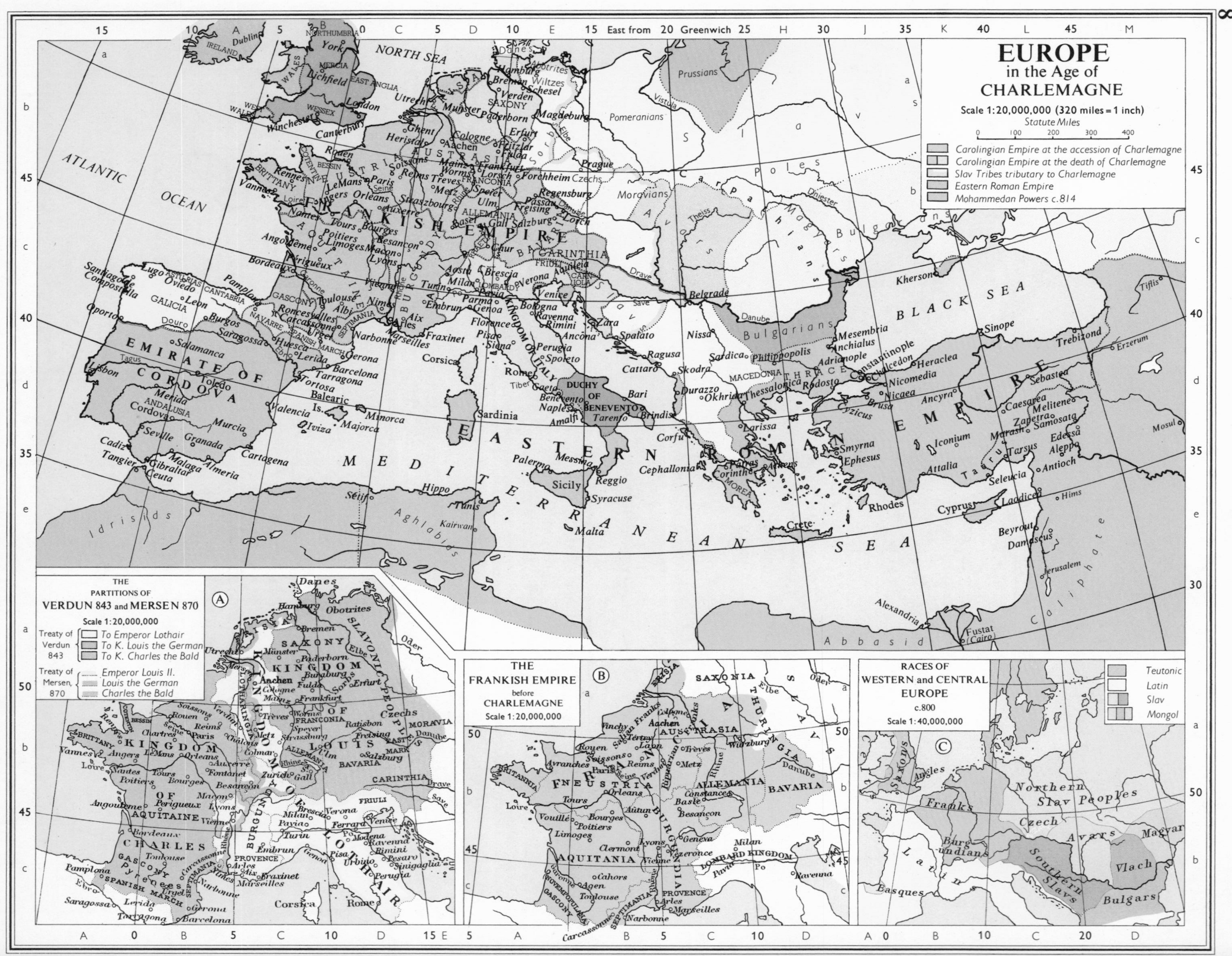
EUROPE
in the Age of
CHARLEMAGNE
Scale 1:20,000,000 (320 miles = 1 inch)
Statute Miles
0 100 200 300 400
Carolingian Empire at the accession of Charlemagne
Carolingian Empire at the death of Charlemagne
Slav Tribes tributary to Charlemagne
Eastern Roman Empire
Mohammedan Powers c.814
East from Greenwich
NORTH SEA
ATLANTIC OCEAN
FRANKISH EMPIRE
EMIRATE OF CORDOVA
KINGDOM OF ITALY
DUCHY OF BENEVENTO
BLACK SEA
EASTERN ROMAN EMPIRE
MEDITERRANEAN SEA
Bulgarians
Abbasid Caliphate
Aghlabids
Idrisids
THE
PARTITIONS OF
VERDUN 843 and MERSEN 870
Scale 1:20,000,000
Treaty of Verdun 843
To Emperor Lothair
To K. Louis the German
To K. Charles the Bald
Treaty of Mersen, 870
Emperor Louis II.
Louis the German
Charles the Bald
KINGDOM OF LOUIS
KINGDOM OF LOTHAIR
KINGDOM OF CHARLES
THE
FRANKISH EMPIRE
before
CHARLEMAGNE
Scale 1:20,000,000
RACES OF
WESTERN and CENTRAL
EUROPE
c.800
Scale 1:40,000,000
Teutonic
Latin
Slav
Mongol

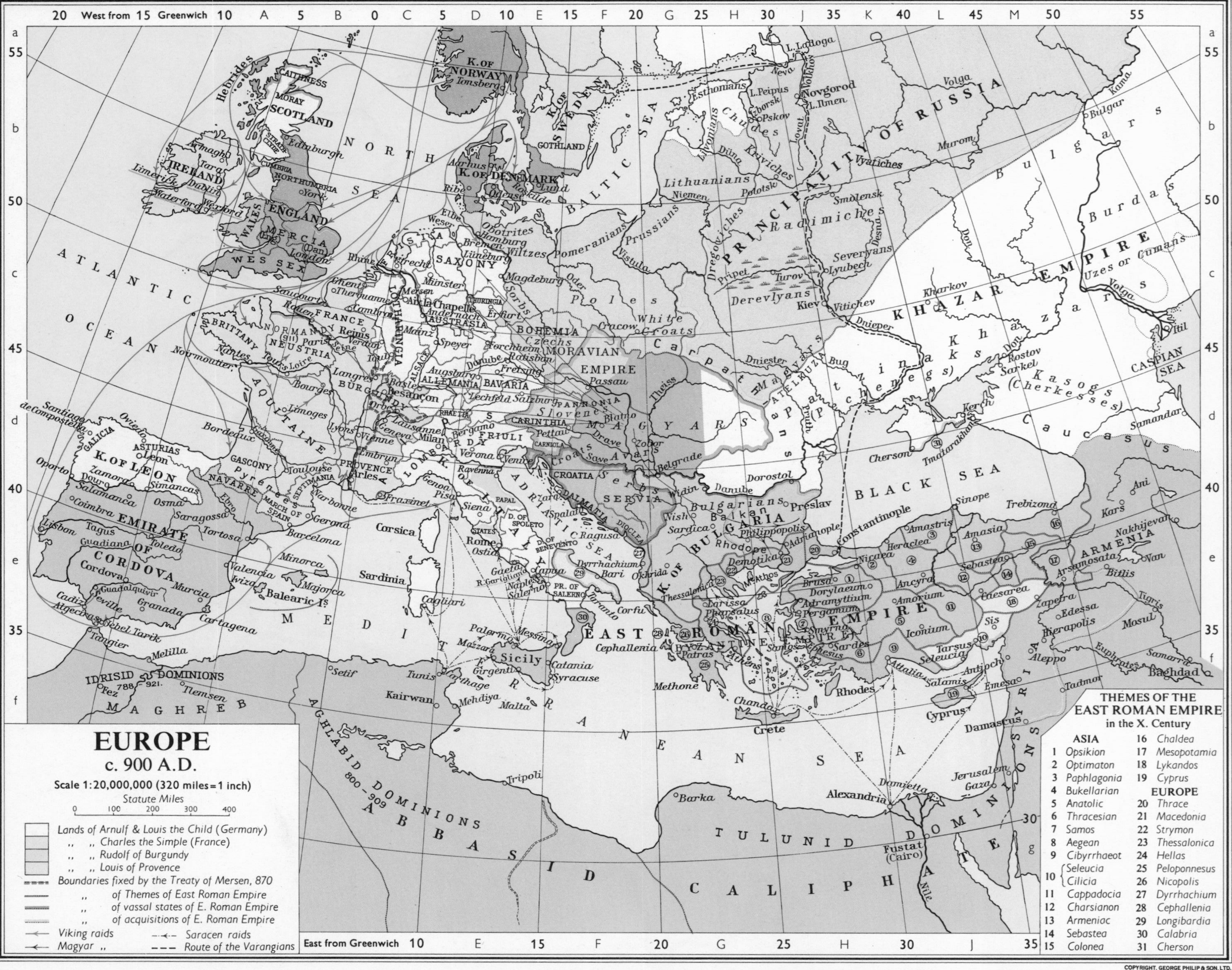
EUROPE
c. 900 A.D.
Scale 1:20,000,000 (320 miles=1 inch)
Statute Miles
0 100 200 300 400
Lands of Arnulf & Louis the Child (Germany)
,, ,, Charles the Simple (France)
,, ,, Rudolf of Burgundy
,, ,, Louis of Provence
Boundaries fixed by the Treaty of Mersen, 870
,, of Themes of East Roman Empire
,, of vassal states of E. Roman Empire
,, of acquisitions of E. Roman Empire
Viking raids
Magyar ,,
Saracen raids
Route of the Varangians
THEMES OF THE EAST ROMAN EMPIRE in the X. Century
ASIA
1 Opsikion
2 Optimaton
3 Paphlagonia
4 Bukellarian
5 Anatolic
6 Thracesian
7 Samos
8 Aegean
9 Cibyrrhaeot
10 Seleucia
Cilicia
11 Cappadocia
12 Charsianon
13 Armeniac
14 Sebastea
15 Colonea
16 Chaldea
17 Mesopotamia
18 Lykandos
19 Cyprus
EUROPE
20 Thrace
21 Macedonia
22 Strymon
23 Thessalonica
24 Hellas
25 Peloponnesus
26 Nicopolis
27 Dyrrhachium
28 Cephallenia
29 Longibardia
30 Calabria
31 Cherson
West from 15 Greenwich
East from Greenwich

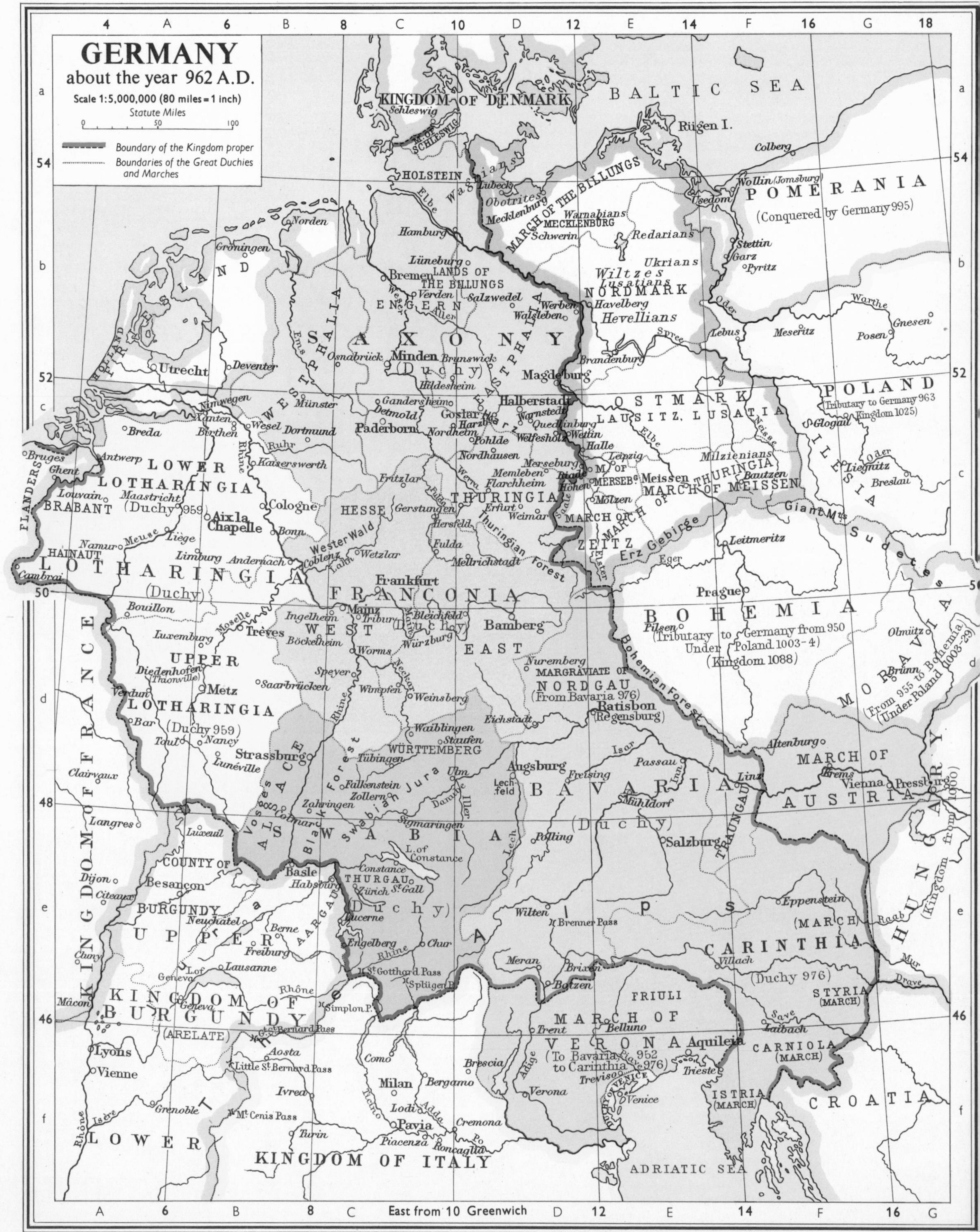

GERMANY
about the year 962 A.D.
Scale 1:5,000,000 (80 miles = 1 inch)
Statute Miles
0
50
100
Boundary of the Kingdom proper
Boundaries of the Great Duchies and Marches
KINGDOM OF DENMARK
Schleswig
M. OF SCHLESWIG
BALTIC SEA
Rügen I.
Colberg
HOLSTEIN
Lubeck
Obotrites
Mecklenburg
MARCH OF THE BILLUNGS
Warnabians
MECKLENBURG
Schwerin
Redarians
Wollin (Jomsburg)
Usedom
POMERANIA
(Conquered by Germany 995)
Stettin
Garz
Pyritz
Ukrians
Wiltzes
Lusatians
NORDMARK
Havelberg
Hevellians
Werben
Walsleben
Oder
Warthe
Meseritz
Posen
Gnesen
Lebus
Spree
Brandenburg
Magdeburg
Norden
Hamburg
Elbe
Lüneburg
Bremen
LANDS OF THE BILLUNGS
Verden
Salzwedel
ENGERN
Groningen
FRIESLAND
HOLLAND
Utrecht
Deventer
WESTPHALIA
Ems
Osnabrück
Minden
SAXONY
(Duchy)
Brunswick
Hildesheim
EASTPHALIA
Halberstadt
POLAND
(Tributary to Germany 963
Kingdom 1025)
OSTMARK
LAUSITZ, LUSATIA
Glogau
SILESIA
Liegnitz
Breslau
Neisse
Nimwegen
Xanten
Birthen
Wesel
Dortmund
Münster
Gandersheim
Detmold
Paderborn
Goslar
Harz
Nordheim
Pöhlde
Wernstedt
Quedlinburg
Welfesholz
Wettin
Halle
Leipzig
M. OF MERSEBG
Meissen
Milzienians
MARCH OF THURINGIA
MARCH OF MEISSEN
Bautzen
Breda
Bruges
Ghent
Antwerp
FLANDERS
LOWER LOTHARINGIA
Louvain
Maastricht
(Duchy 959)
BRABANT
Aix la Chapelle
Cologne
Ruhr
Kaiserswerth
Nordhausen
Memleben
Flarchheim
Merseburg
Riade
Hohen
Mölzen
Fritzlar
HESSE
Gerstungen
THURINGIA
Erfurt
Weimar
Saale
MARCH OF ZEITZ
ZEITZ
Erz Gebirge
Giant Mts
Sudetes
Leitmeritz
Eger
Namur
Meuse
Liège
Bonn
Wester Wald
Hersfeld
Fulda
Thuringian Forest
HAINAUT
Cambrai
LOTHARINGIA
(Duchy)
Limburg
Andernach
Coblenz
Wetzlar
Lahn
Mellrichstadt
Frankfurt
FRANCONIA
Prague
BOHEMIA
Pilsen
(Tributary to Germany from 950
Under Poland 1003-4)
(Kingdom 1088)
Olmütz
Bouillon
Moselle
Mainz
Tribur
Bleichfeld
Ingelheim
WEST
(Duchy)
Bamberg
EAST
Luxemburg
Trèves
Böckelheim
Worms
Würzburg
Main
UPPER LOTHARINGIA
Diedenhofen (Thionville)
Metz
Saarbrücken
Speyer
Neckar
Nuremberg
MARGRAVIATE OF NORDGAU
(From Bavaria 976)
Bohemian Forest
MORAVIA
Brünn
(From 955 to Bohemia)
(1003-29 Under Poland)
Verdun
Bar
(Duchy 959)
Toul
Nancy
Wimpfen
Weinsberg
Rhine
Ratisbon
(Regensburg)
Eichstadt
Waiblingen
Staufen
WÜRTTEMBERG
Strassburg
Lunéville
ALSACE
Vosges
Black Forest
Tübingen
Swabian Jura
Ulm
Augsburg
Isar
Passau
Inn
Linz
Altenburg
MARCH OF AUSTRIA
Krems
Vienna
Pressburg
Clairvaux
Falkenstein
Zollern
Zähringen
Colmar
Danube
Iller
Lech feld
Freising
BAVARIA
(Duchy)
Mühldorf
TRAUNGAU
HUNGARY
(Kingdom from 1000)
Langres
Luxeuil
SWABIA
Sigmaringen
Lech
Polling
Salzburg
L. of Constance
COUNTY OF BURGUNDY
Dijon
Citeaux
Besançon
Basle
Habsburg
Constance
THURGAU
Zürich
St. Gall
(Duchy)
AARGAU
ALPS
Eppenstein
(MARCH)
Raab
Wilten
Brenner Pass
Neuchâtel
Berne
UPPER
Lucerne
Freiburg
Engelberg
Chur
Rhine
CARINTHIA
Villach
(Duchy 976)
Mur
Drave
STYRIA (MARCH)
Cluny
L. of Geneva
Lausanne
St. Gotthard Pass
Splügen P.
Meran
Brixen
Botzen
FRIULI
Mâcon
KINGDOM OF BURGUNDY
(ARELATE)
Geneva
Rhône
Simplon P.
Gt. St. Bernard Pass
MARCH OF VERONA
Trent
Belluno
Save
Laibach
Aquileia
(To Bavaria 952
to Carinthia 976)
CARNIOLA (MARCH)
KINGDOM OF FRANCE
Lyons
Vienne
Aosta
Little St. Bernard Pass
Como
Brescia
Adige
Piave
Treviso
DUCHY OF VENICE
Venice
Trieste
Milan
Bergamo
Verona
ISTRIA (MARCH)
CROATIA
Ivrea
Grenoble
Isère
Mt. Cenis Pass
Lodi
Adda
Ticino
Pavia
Cremona
LOWER
Turin
Piacenza
Roncaglia
Po
KINGDOM OF ITALY
ADRIATIC SEA
East from 10 Greenwich

FRANCE &
BURGUNDY
showing
the Feudal Lordships
about the year 1032 A.D.
Scale 1:5,000,000 (80 miles = 1 inch)
Statute Miles
0
50
100
Archbishopric
Bishopric
(D) Duchy
(C) County
(V) Viscounty
(S) Seigneurie
(M) Marquisate
Boundary of France
,, of Royal Domain
,, of Burgundy
,, of Ecclesiastical Fiefs
East from 4 Greenwich
NORTH SEA
ENGLISH CHANNEL
BAY OF BISCAY
MEDITERRANEAN SEA
COUNTY OF FLANDERS
DUCHY OF LOTHARINGIA
KINGDOM OF GERMANY
D. OF NORMANDY
COUNTY OF BRITTANY
C. OF MAINE
CHAMPAGNE
C. OF TROYES
C. OF BLOIS
C. OF NANTES
TOURAINE
C. OF POITOU
C. OF BOURBON
(BURGUNDY)
COUNTY OF NEVERS
D. OF BURGUNDY
UPPER BURGUNDY
(REGNUM JURENSE)
KINGDOM OF BURGUNDY
(ARELATE)
LOWER BURGUNDY
(REGNUM PROVINCIAE)
(to 933)
C. OF PROVENCE
DUCHY OF GUIENNE
(AQUITAINE)
C. OF ANGOULEME
V. OF LIMOUSIN
C. OF PERIGORD
C. OF LA MARCHE
C. OF AUVERGNE
C. OF ROUERGUE
C. OF TOULOUSE
D. OF GASCONY
K. OF NAVARRE
COUNTY OF BARCELONA
(SPANISH MARCH)
ITALY
London
Paris
Orléans
Tours
Bordeaux
Toulouse
Lyons
Vienne
Arles
Marseilles
Barcelona
Dijon
Rouen
Reims
Chartres
Poitiers
Limoges
Nantes
Angers
Bourges
Clermont
Narbonne
Montpellier
Avignon
Besançon
Geneva
Lausanne
Metz
Toul
Verdun
Trèves
Mainz
Cologne
Liège
Brussels
Antwerp
Ghent
Bruges
Utrecht
Munster
Paderborn
Worms
Speyer
Strassburg
Basle
Habsburg
Aosta
Turin
Nice
Toulon
Pamplona
Tudela
Saragossa
Lerida
Vich
Gerona
Urgel
Perpignan
Elne

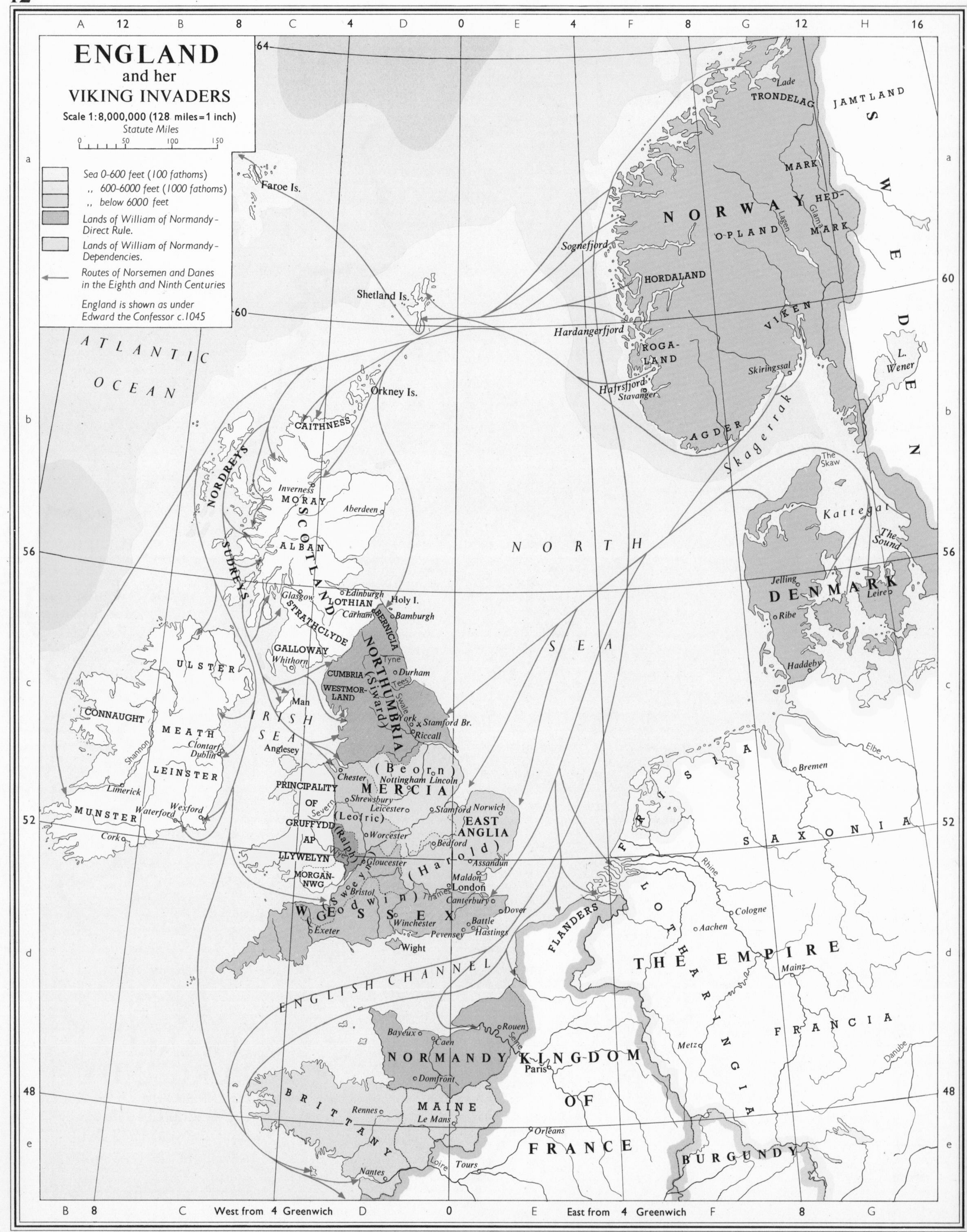
ENGLAND
and her
VIKING INVADERS
Scale 1:8,000,000 (128 miles=1 inch)
Statute Miles
0 50 100 150
Sea 0-600 feet (100 fathoms)
,, 600-6000 feet (1000 fathoms)
,, below 6000 feet
Lands of William of Normandy - Direct Rule.
Lands of William of Normandy - Dependencies.
Routes of Norsemen and Danes in the Eighth and Ninth Centuries
England is shown as under Edward the Confessor c.1045
ATLANTIC OCEAN
Faroe Is.
Shetland Is.
Orkney Is.
NORTH SEA
NORWAY
TRONDELAG
Lade
JAMTLAND
MARK
HED-MARK
OPLAND
Lagen
Glama
Sognefjord
HORDALAND
Hardangerfjord
ROGA-LAND
Hafrsfjord
Stavanger
VIKEN
Skiringssal
AGDER
Skagerrak
SWEDEN
L. Wener
The Skaw
Kattegat
The Sound
DENMARK
Jelling
Leire
Ribe
Haddeby
CAITHNESS
NORDREYS
SUDREYS
Inverness
MORAY
Aberdeen
SCOTLAND
ALBAN
Edinburgh
LOTHIAN
Glasgow
Carham
STRATHCLYDE
Holy I.
Bamburgh
BERNICIA
GALLOWAY
Whithorn
CUMBRIA
WESTMOR-LAND
NORTHUMBRIA (Siward)
Tyne
Durham
Tees
Swale
York
Stamford Br.
Riccall
Man
IRISH SEA
Anglesey
ULSTER
CONNAUGHT
MEATH
Clontarf
Dublin
Shannon
LEINSTER
Limerick
MUNSTER
Waterford
Wexford
Cork
PRINCIPALITY OF GRUFFYDD AP LLYWELYN
MORGAN-NWG
Chester
(Beorn)
Nottingham
Lincoln
MERCIA
Shrewsbury
Leicester
Severn
(Leofric)
(Ralph)
Worcester
Wye
Stamford
Norwich
EAST ANGLIA
Bedford
(Harold)
Gloucester
Assandun
Maldon
London
Thames
Bristol
(Sweyn)
(Godwin)
Canterbury
Dover
WESSEX
Exeter
Winchester
Battle
Hastings
Pevensey
Wight
ENGLISH CHANNEL
FLANDERS
FRISIA
Bremen
Elbe
SAXONIA
Rhine
Cologne
Aachen
LOTHARINGIA
THE EMPIRE
Mainz
FRANCIA
Metz
Danube
Rouen
Seine
Bayeux
Caen
NORMANDY
KINGDOM OF FRANCE
Paris
Domfront
BRITTANY
Rennes
MAINE
Le Mans
Orleans
Nantes
Loire
Tours
BURGUNDY
West from Greenwich
East from Greenwich

ENGLAND
according to the
DOMESDAY SURVEY
1086
Scale 1:2,500,000 (40 miles = 1 inch)
Statute Miles
0 5 10 20 30 40 50
For modern spelling of Domesday names see Index
English Shires
Welsh Principalities
Palatine earldoms surviving in 1086
Forfeited palatinate of Hereford
Burgi and Civitates surveyed in Domesday Book are shown thus Eboracum others thus Lundonia
Burgi and Civitates on the royal domain.
Burgi and Civitates on mediate fiefs.
Burgi and Civitates not named in Domesday Book.
Royal castles named in Domesday Book.
Royal castles not named in Domesday Book.
Private castles named in Domesday Book.
Private castles not named in Domesday Book.
Archbishopric
Bishopric
Collegiate foundations
Monastic foundations.
Berewic
Lindisfarna
Is. Farnea
Bebbanburh
Alnwick
Redesdale
Morpeth
S.C.L.
Bellingtun
Munekeceastre
Tinemuthe
Gyrwe
Weremuthe
Bewcastle
Werc
Hagustalham (Hexesham)
Gatesheved
Alston
Cuncacestre
Dunholm
Carleo
NORTHYMBRALAND
CUMBRIA
S.Cuthberhtes-Land
Bowes
Brough
Appleby
Derlington
Sedberuie
Witebi
Ghillinges
C. Alani
Iarum
Clyveland
Catric
Alvertune
Nor-Treding
Elmeslae
Tresch
Pickeringham
Muncaster
Bodele
Futhernesse
Is. de Man
Cherchebi
Daltune
EVRVICSCIRE
Bretlinton
Ripun
Chenaresburg
Stanfordbrycge
Loncastre
Crave
Eboracum
Skipsea
Sciptone
Evrvic
Poclinton
Fulford
E. Treding
Helderness
Agemundreness
Prestune
Scireburne
Selebi
Beverlie
Hovedene
Wes-Treding
Ripa
Peneverdant
Wachefeld
Tateshale
INTER RIPAM ET MERSHAM
Fornbi
Mamecastre
Westderbei
Mersha
Coningesburg
Dadisleia
Wes-Treding
Nor-Treding
Grimesbi
Gainesburg
Ludes
LINCOLESCIRE
Stau
Blida
Lincolia
Sud-Treding
N.T.
Bolinbroc
Mon
Aberlleiniog
Deganwy
Roelant
Llanelwy
Tegeingl
Rhos
Bangor
Caer Segont
Heletune
Doneham
Frotesham
CESTRESCIRE
Cestre
Cinbretune
Offa's
Pecfers
Bolsover
Hawarden
DERBYSCIRE
Sudwelle
SNOTINGHAMSCIRE
Newerche
Grantham
Chetsteven
Holland
GWYNEDD
Rhufoniog
Ial
Depenbech
Maelor
Actune
Wich
Bangor
Snotingeham
Derby
Belvedoir
Folchinge-ham
Spallinge
Edeyrnion
Cynllaith
Oswestry
Meresberie
Luvre
Toteberie
STADFORDSCIRE
Burtone
Medeltune
Wella
St. Benedictus de Holme
Gernemutha
Acra
Norwic
Stadford
Penkridge
Licefelle
LEDECESTRESCIRE
Stanford
Wisbeche
Roteland (to Snotingham)
Ledecestre
Meirionydd
POWYS
Sciropesberie
SCIROPESCIRE
Caus
Chirbury
Montgomery
Wenloch
Tamworde
Torni
Burg
Ramesyg
HUNTEDUNSCIRE
GRENTEBRIGESCIRE
NORDFULC
Tettenhall
Dudelei
Rochingeham
Elyg
Tetford
Beccles
Cydewain
Stantune
Quatford
Coventreu
NORTHANTONESCIRE
Huntedun
Wiceford
Eia
Llanbadarn Fawr
Arwystli
Ceri
Lentewrde
Ludlow
WARWICSCIRE
S. Ives
Yxninga
S. Edmundi
Dunewic
Maelienydd
Aymetone
WIRECESTRESCIRE
Wiche
Warwic
Grentebrige
SUDFULC
Wigemor
Castr. Ricardi
Leofminstre
Wirecestre
Wedone
Northantone
Bedeforde
Clara
Orford
Raddenore
Herdeslege
Persore
Elnestow
Gipewiz
Ceredigion
Cardigan
Buellt
Elfael
HEREFORDSCIRE
Clifford
Hereford
Malferna
Evesham
BEDEFORDSCIRE
Escewelle
Waledana
Sudberie
DEHEUBARTH
Ewias
Teodekesberie
Bochingeham
Haingeham
Mynyw
Dyfed
Dinevor
Arcenefeld
Dene
Wincelcumbe
OXENEFORDSCIRE
HERTEFORDSCIRE
Colecestra
Brycheiniog
Monemude
Glowecestre
Berchamstede
Hertforde
EXSESSA
Merse
GWENT
Foresta
GLOWECESTRESCIRE
Nesse
Eglesham
Oxeneford
BOCHINGEHAMSCIRE
Va.S.Albani
Malduna
Penbroc
Cirencestre
Berchelai
Abbendone
Waltham
Rageneia
Caerleon
Striguil
Crichelade
Walingeford
Wicumbe
MIDELSEXE
MORGANNWG
BERROCHESCIRE
Lundonia
Barking
Llandaf
Caerdydd
Malmesberie
Westmonasterium
Cauna
Merleberge
Redinges
Stanes
Deptford
Seseltre
Bristou
Bade
Bradeford
Bedvinde
Sudwerca
Rouecestre
Banwelle
Certesyg
Cantuaria
Sandwic
Alseberge
WILTESCIRE
Basinges
SUDRIE
Gildeford
Forewic
Welle
Glastingeberie
Guerminstre
Ambresberie
HANTESCIRE
Goldelminge
CHENTH
Tonebridge
Dovere
Piltune
Portloc
Torre
Briwetone
Wiltunie
Folkestone
Barnestable
SUMORSETE
Andredsweald
Heda
Tantone
Lanporth
Sarisberie
Sceptesberie
Wintonia
Romenel
Baentone
Adelingi
Givelcestre
Mileburne
Romesey
Hantune
Rye
Montagud
Scireburne
Rincoede
SUDSEXE
Ecclesia de Labatailge
Staýninges
Lawes
Ferle
Hastinges
Cerneli
Creneburne
Porcestre
Cicestre
DEVENESCIRE
DORSETE
Winburne
Nova Foresta
Brembre
Borne
Pevenesel
Ochementone
Exonia
Bridport
Tvinam
Harundel
Dorcestre
Alwinestune
Tintagel
Lideforde
Lym
Warham
Is. de Wiht
Dunhevet
Lanstavetone
Powderham
Abedesberie
Warham (Corfe)
Tavestoche
S.Neotus
Bucfestre
Beri
Tremetone
Totenais
S.Carentochus
S.Pieranus
S.Germanus
Plintone
CORNVALGE
S.Probus
Combie
S.Achebrannus
S.Michael
S.Berriane
West from 3 Greenwich
A B C D E F G H
5 4 3 2 1 0 1
a b c d e f
55 54 53 52 51

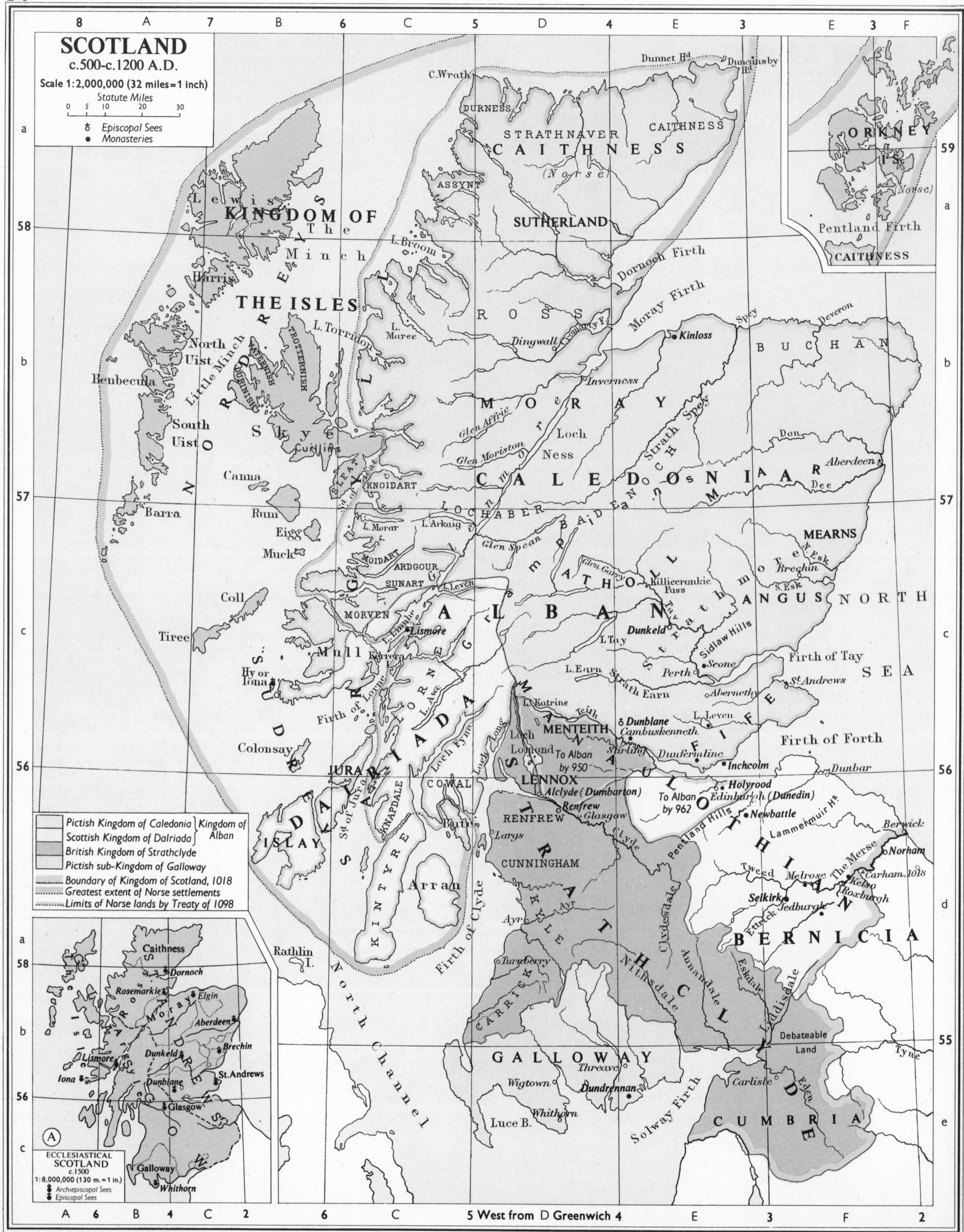
SCOTLAND
c.500-c.1200 A.D.
Scale 1:2,000,000 (32 miles=1 inch)
Statute Miles
0 5 10 20 30
Episcopal Sees
Monasteries
Pictish Kingdom of Caledonia
Scottish Kingdom of Dalriada
Kingdom of Alban
British Kingdom of Strathclyde
Pictish sub-Kingdom of Galloway
Boundary of Kingdom of Scotland, 1018
Greatest extent of Norse settlements
Limits of Norse lands by Treaty of 1098
KINGDOM OF THE ISLES
NORDREYS
SUDREYS
CAITHNESS
(Norse)
STRATHNAVER
DURNESS
ASSYNT
SUTHERLAND
ROSS
MORAY
CALEDONIA
BUCHAN
MEARNS
ANGUS
ATHOLL
ALBAN
MENTEITH
LENNOX
To Alban by 950
To Alban by 962
LOTHIAN
FIFE
DALRIADA
LORN
COWAL
KNAPDALE
KINTYRE
STRATHCLYDE
RENFREW
CUNNINGHAM
KYLE
CARRICK
GALLOWAY
BERNICIA
CUMBRIA
Debateable Land
KNOIDART
LOCHABER
MOIDART
ARDGOUR
SUNART
MORVEN
Lewis
Harris
North Uist
Benbecula
South Uist
Barra
Skye
Cuillins
Canna
Rum
Eigg
Muck
Coll
Tiree
Mull
Kerrera
Hy or Iona
Lismore
Colonsay
JURA
ISLAY
Arran
Bute
Rathlin I.
The Minch
Little Minch
L. Torridon
L. Maree
L. Broom
L. Morar
L. Arkaig
L. Leven
L. Linnhe
Firth of Lorne
Sd. of Jura
L. Awe
Loch Fyne
Loch Long
Loch Lomond
L. Katrine
L. Tay
L. Earn
L. Leven
Loch Ness
Glen Affric
Glen Moriston
Glen Spean
Glen Garry
Glen More
Strath Spey
Strath Earn
Strathmore
Killiecrankie Pass
Sidlaw Hills
Mounth
Lammermuir Hs.
Pentland Hills
The Merse
C. Wrath
Dunnet Hd.
Duncansby Hd.
Dornoch Firth
Moray Firth
Cromarty F.
Dingwall
Kinloss
Inverness
Spey
Deveron
Don
Dee
Aberdeen
N. Esk
S. Esk
Brechin
Tay
Dunkeld
Scone
Perth
Abernethy
St. Andrews
Firth of Tay
NORTH SEA
Teith
Dunblane
Cambuskenneth
Stirling
Dunfermline
Inchcolm
Firth of Forth
Dunbar
Holyrood
Edinburgh (Dunedin)
Newbattle
Berwick
Norham
Carham, 1018
Kelso
Roxburgh
Melrose
Tweed
Selkirk
Jedburgh
Ettrick
Alclyde (Dumbarton)
Renfrew
Glasgow
Clyde
Largs
Ayr
Firth of Clyde
Clydesdale
Annandale
Nithsdale
Eskdale
Liddisdale
Turnberry
North Channel
Threave
Dundrennan
Wigtown
Whithorn
Luce B.
Solway Firth
Carlisle
Eden
Tyne
ORKNEY IS.
(Norse)
Pentland Firth
CAITHNESS
ECCLESIASTICAL SCOTLAND c.1500
1:8,000,000 (130 m.=1 in.)
Archiepiscopal Sees
Episcopal Sees
Caithness
Dornoch
Rosemarkie
Ross
Moray
Elgin
Aberdeen
Brechin
Dunkeld
St. Andrews
Lismore
Iona
The Isles
Argyll
Dunblane
Glasgow
Galloway
Whithorn
5 West from Greenwich 4

IRELAND
before the
ENGLISH INVASION
Scale 1:2,000,000 (32 miles=1 inch)
Statute Miles
0 10 20 30 40
Bishoprics existing in 1150
Monasteries
Anglo-Norman Castles erected during reign of Henry II
Irish Clans thus: O'Dowd
Danish Towns underlined in Red
Over 3000 feet
1200-3000 „
600-1200 „
0- 600 „
ECCLESIASTICAL
IRELAND
c.1500
1:8,000,000 (130m=1 in.)
Archiepiscopal Sees
Episcopal Sees
A
Derry
Connor
Raphoe
Ardstraw
Dromore
Clogher
Killala
Armagh
Down patrick
Achonry
Mayo
Elphin
Roscommon
Ardagh
Tuam
Trim
Enaghdune
Clonmacnoise
Dublin
Kilmacduagh
Clonfert
Kildare
Kilfenora
Killaloe
DUBLIN
Leighlin
Limerick
Ferns
Emly
Kilkenny
Ardfert
Cashel
CASHEL
Lismore
Waterford
Aghadoe
Cork
Cloyne
Ross
Malin Hd
Rathlin I.
L. Swilly
Tory I.
Errigal
TYR CONNELL
TYR OWEN
L. Foyle
DALRIADA
Trostan
Scots
Antrim
North Channel
Aran I.
Derry
Raphoe
Sperrin Mts
Finn
ULADH
(ULTONIA, ULSTER)
Connor
Bluestack
Slieve League
O'Neill
Lough Neagh
Bann
Main
L. Erne
Clogher
Blackwater
Armagh
Down
Mourne Mts
BREFFNY
O'Rourke
OIRGHIALLA
(URIEL)
O'Carroll
Killala
O'Dowd
Ox Mts
Achonry
L. Allen
Nephin
L. Conn
Achill I.
Elphin
O'Connor
O'Reilly
L. Gowna
Clew B.
Mayo
Croagh Patrick
CONNACHT
L. Sheelin
Kells
Muilrea
L. Mask
Robe
ANNALY
Granard
MIDHE
(MEATH)
O'Neill
Duleek
Skreen
Tara
Trim
Boyne
Roscommon
Ardagh
Inny
Twelve Pins
Tuam
L. Corrib
Clare
Suck
O'Kelly
L. Ree
IRISH SEA
O'Flaherty
Athlone
Clonard
Castlejordan
Howth Hd
Dublin
Enaghdun
Brosna
Clonmacnoise
Bog of Allen
Liffey
Kippure
O'Shaughnessy
Clonfert
OFFALY
Kildare
O'Dempsey
Shannon
Birr
Slieve Bloom
Narragh
Glendalough
Wicklow
Wicklow Hd
Aran Is
Kilmacduagh
Athy
Lugnaquillia
L. Derg
Wicklow Mts
Kilfenora
Timahoe
O'Toole
Barrow
LAIGHIN
(LEINSTER)
Arklow
Avoca
Carlow
THOMOND
Killaloe
O'Brien
ORMOND
Leighlin
Fergus
Inis Cathy
Limerick
Nore
Black Cas
Slaney
Kilkenny
Loop Hd
Ferns
Golden Vale
Mac Murrough
R. Shannon
Cashel
Enniscorthy
OSSORY
MacGillipatrick
Emly
MUMHA
Galty Mts
Suir
Ardfinnan
Comeragh Mts
Wexford
Ardfert
Brandon Hill
(MOMONIA, MUNSTER)
Knockmealdown Mts
Waterford
DECIES
Carnsore Pt
Bannow B.
Dunmore Hd
Blackwater
Aghadoe
Lismore
Dingle B.
Boggerah Mts
Lakes of Killarney
Mc Carthy
Macgillicuddys Reeks
Carrantuohill
DESMOND
Cork
Lee
Cloyne
Kenmare R.
Bandon
Bere I.
Bantry B.
Ross
Old Head of Kinsale
Mizen Hd
C. Clear
ATLANTIC OCEAN
A 10 B 9 West from C Greenwich 8 D 7 E 6 F
54
53
52
55

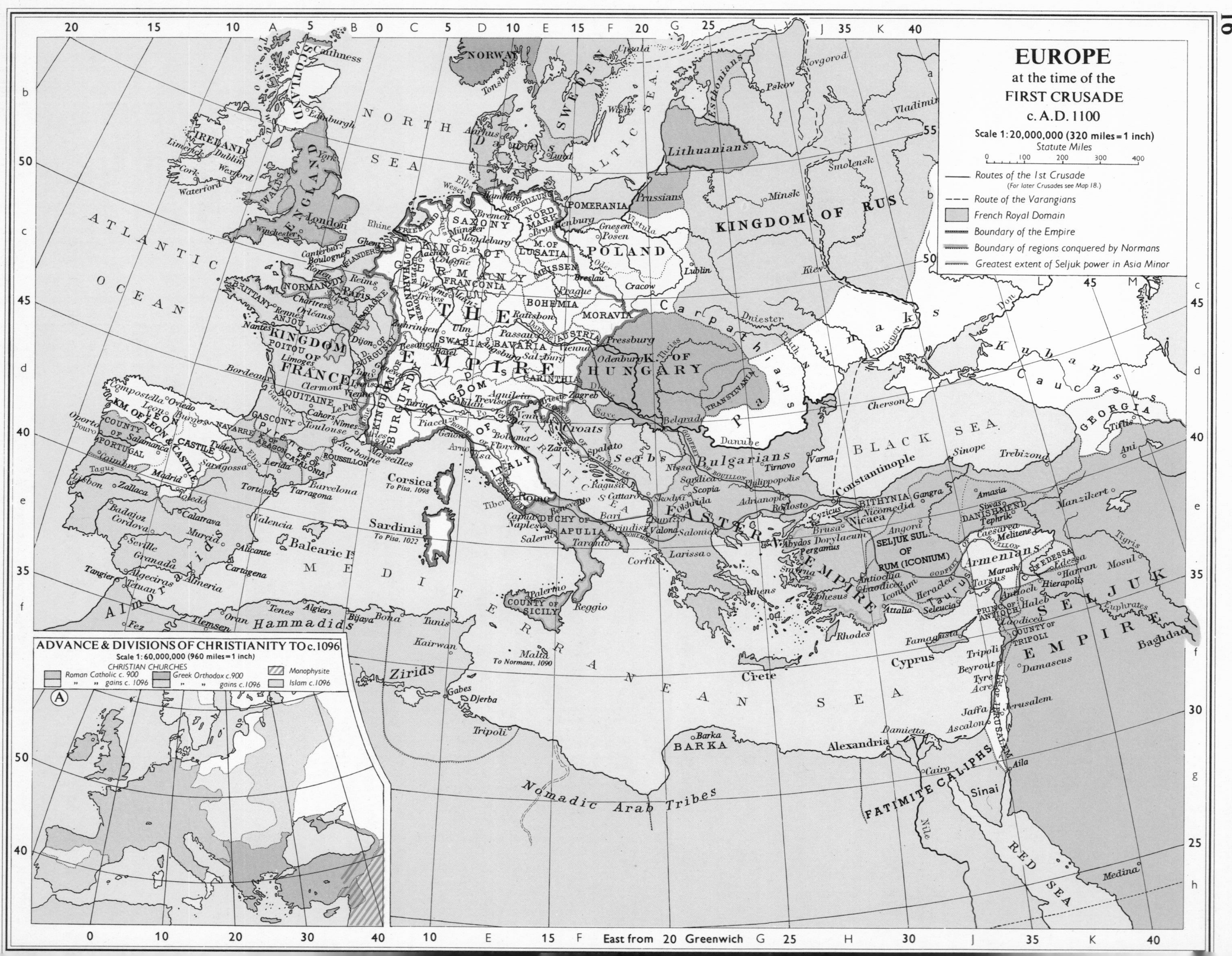
EUROPE
at the time of the
FIRST CRUSADE
c. A.D. 1100
Scale 1:20,000,000 (320 miles=1 inch)
Statute Miles
0 100 200 300 400
Routes of the 1st Crusade
(For later Crusades see Map 18.)
Route of the Varangians
French Royal Domain
Boundary of the Empire
Boundary of regions conquered by Normans
Greatest extent of Seljuk power in Asia Minor
East from 20 Greenwich
ADVANCE & DIVISIONS OF CHRISTIANITY TO c.1096
Scale 1:60,000,000 (960 miles=1 inch)
CHRISTIAN CHURCHES
Roman Catholic c. 900
" " gains c. 1096
Greek Orthodox c.900
" " gains c.1096
Monophysite
Islam c.1096
A
KINGDOM OF RUS
K. OF HUNGARY
KINGDOM OF FRANCE
POLAND
THE EMPIRE
EASTERN EMPIRE
SELJUK EMPIRE
SELJUK SUL. OF RUM (ICONIUM)
FATIMITE CALIPHS
KINGDOM OF JERUSALEM
ATLANTIC OCEAN
NORTH SEA
BALTIC SEA
BLACK SEA
MEDITERRANEAN SEA
RED SEA
Nomadic Arab Tribes

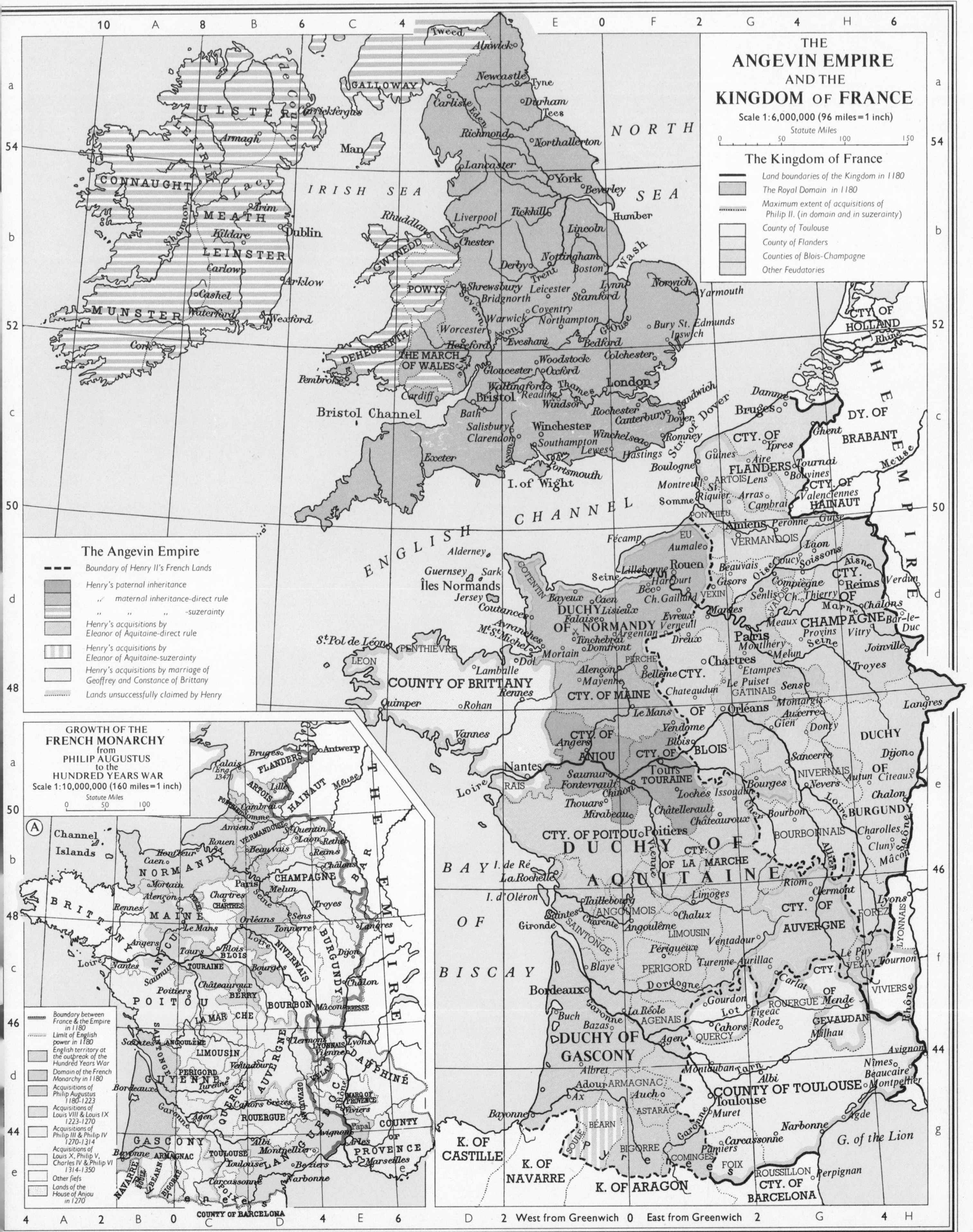
THE ANGEVIN EMPIRE AND THE KINGDOM OF FRANCE
Scale 1:6,000,000 (96 miles=1 inch)
Statute Miles
0 50 100 150
The Kingdom of France
Land boundaries of the Kingdom in 1180
The Royal Domain in 1180
Maximum extent of acquisitions of Philip II. (in domain and in suzerainty)
County of Toulouse
County of Flanders
Counties of Blois-Champagne
Other Feudatories
The Angevin Empire
Boundary of Henry II's French Lands
Henry's paternal inheritance
" maternal inheritance-direct rule
" " -suzeraintyy
Henry's acquisitions by Eleanor of Aquitaine-direct rule
Henry's acquisitions by Eleanor of Aquitaine-suzerainty
Henry's acquisitions by marriage of Geoffrey and Constance of Brittany
Lands unsuccessfully claimed by Henry
GROWTH OF THE FRENCH MONARCHY from PHILIP AUGUSTUS to the HUNDRED YEARS WAR
Scale 1:10,000,000 (160 miles=1 inch)
Statute Miles
0 50 100
Boundary between France & the Empire in 1180
Limit of English power in 1180
English territory at the outbreak of the Hundred Years War
Domain of the French Monarchy in 1180
Acquisitions of Philip Augustus 1180-1223
Acquisitions of Louis VIII & Louis IX 1223-1270
Acquisitions of Philip III & Philip IV 1270-1314
Acquisitions of Louis X, Philip V, Charles IV & Philip VI 1314-1350
Other fiefs
Lands of the House of Anjou in 1270
NORTH SEA
IRISH SEA
ENGLISH CHANNEL
BAY OF BISCAY
G. of the Lion
Bristol Channel
ULSTER
CONNAUGHT
MEATH
LEINSTER
MUNSTER
GALLOWAY
GWYNEDD
POWYS
DEHEUBARTH
THE MARCH OF WALES
Dublin
London
Îles Normands
COUNTY OF BRITTANY
DUCHY OF NORMANDY
CTY. OF MAINE
CTY. OF ANJOU
CTY. OF BLOIS
TOURAINE
CTY. OF POITOU
DUCHY OF AQUITAINE
CTY. OF LA MARCHE
DUCHY OF GASCONY
COUNTY OF TOULOUSE
CTY. OF AUVERGNE
CTY. OF CHAMPAGNE
DUCHY OF BURGUNDY
FLANDERS
CTY. OF HAINAUT
DY. OF BRABANT
CTY. OF HOLLAND
THE EMPIRE
Paris
K. OF CASTILLE
K. OF NAVARRE
K. OF ARAGON
CTY. OF BARCELONA
West from Greenwich
East from Greenwich

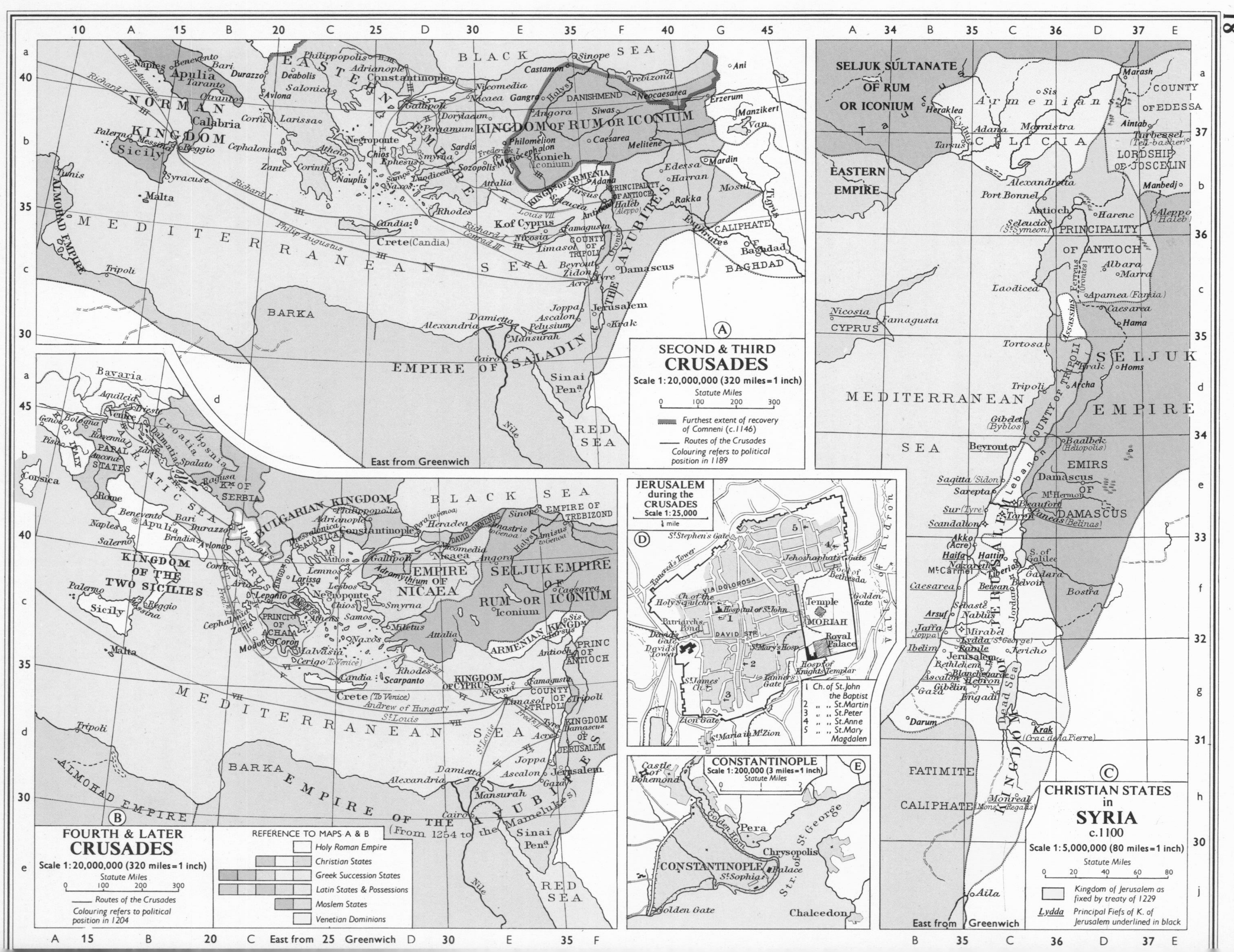
SECOND & THIRD CRUSADES
Scale 1:20,000,000 (320 miles=1 inch)
Statute Miles
0 100 200 300
Furthest extent of recovery of Comneni (c.1146)
Routes of the Crusades
Colouring refers to political position in 1189
East from Greenwich
FOURTH & LATER CRUSADES
Scale 1:20,000,000 (320 miles=1 inch)
Statute Miles
0 100 200 300
Routes of the Crusades
Colouring refers to political position in 1204
REFERENCE TO MAPS A & B
Holy Roman Empire
Christian States
Greek Succession States
Latin States & Possessions
Moslem States
Venetian Dominions
East from Greenwich
JERUSALEM during the CRUSADES
Scale 1:25,000
¼ mile
1 Ch. of St. John the Baptist
2 „ „ St. Martin
3 „ „ St. Peter
4 „ „ St. Anne
5 „ „ St. Mary Magdalen
CONSTANTINOPLE
Scale 1:200,000 (3 miles=1 inch)
Statute Miles
CHRISTIAN STATES in SYRIA c.1100
Scale 1:5,000,000 (80 miles=1 inch)
Statute Miles
0 20 40 60 80
Kingdom of Jerusalem as fixed by treaty of 1229
Lydda Principal Fiefs of K. of Jerusalem underlined in black
East from Greenwich

EASTERN EUROPE
c. 1250
Scale 1:15,000,000 (240 miles=1 inch)
Statute Miles
0 50 100 150 200 250 300 350
Latin Empire
Latin States dependent on the Empire
Greek "Empires"
Church Lands
Territories of the Signoria of Venice
" seized by leading Venetian families
Genoese Dominions
Mongol Conquests (Il-Khans)
Seljuk Turkish Amirates
East from 20 Greenwich
K. OF SWEDEN
Finnish Peoples
REPUBLIC OF NOVGOROD
RUSSIA
Votyaks
Viatka (to Novgorod)
BALTIC SEA
ESTHONIA
INGRIA
TEUTONIC KNIGHTS
LIVONIA
KURLAND
SAMOGITIA
GRAND DUCHY OF LITHUANIA
TEUT. PRUSSIA
POMERELIA
TVER
SUZDAL
SMOLENSK
GREAT BULGARIA
MUROM-RIAZAN
CHERNIGOV
SEVERSKI
UKRAINE
KIEV
KHANATE OF THE GOLDEN HORDE
Cumans
Polovtsi
HOLY ROMAN EMPIRE
K. OF POLAND
SILESIA
BOHEMIA
AUSTRIA
GALICIA
K. OF HUNGARY
TRANSYLVANIA
CROATIA
DALMATIA
BOSNIA
Vlachs
K. OF SERVIA
K. OF BULGARIA
PAPAL STATES
ADRIATIC SEA
KINGDOM OF SICILY
DESPOTATE OF EPIRUS
EMPIRE OF SALONICA
EMPIRE OF NICAEA
PR. OF ACHAIA
MEDITERRANEAN SEA
Crete
K. OF CYPRUS
BLACK SEA
S. of Azov
Crimea
Kaffa (Genoese ?1280)
Soldaia (Venetian ?1285)
Cembala (Genoese 1380)
Alans
Caucasus
Lesgians
GEORGIA
LAZICA
IBERIA
EMP. OF TREBIZOND
AMIRATE OF KIZIL AHMADLI
SELJUK KINGDOM OF RUM OR ICONIUM
ARMENIA
AMIRATE OF KARAMAN
GERMIYAN
HAMID
MENTESHE
AYDIN
AMIRATE OF TEKKE
K. OF ARMENIA
PR. OF ANTIOCH
EMPIRE OF THE MONGOL IL-KHANS
KHORASAN
CASPIAN SEA
Elburz
Constantinople (reconquered 1261)
Kiev
Novgorod
Vladimir
Moscow
Sarai
Astrakhan
Trebizond
Sinope
Iconium
Nicaea
Rome
Venice
Naples
Tabriz
Hamadan (Ecbatana)
Volga
Don
Dnieper
Dniester
Danube
Vistula
Ural
Emba

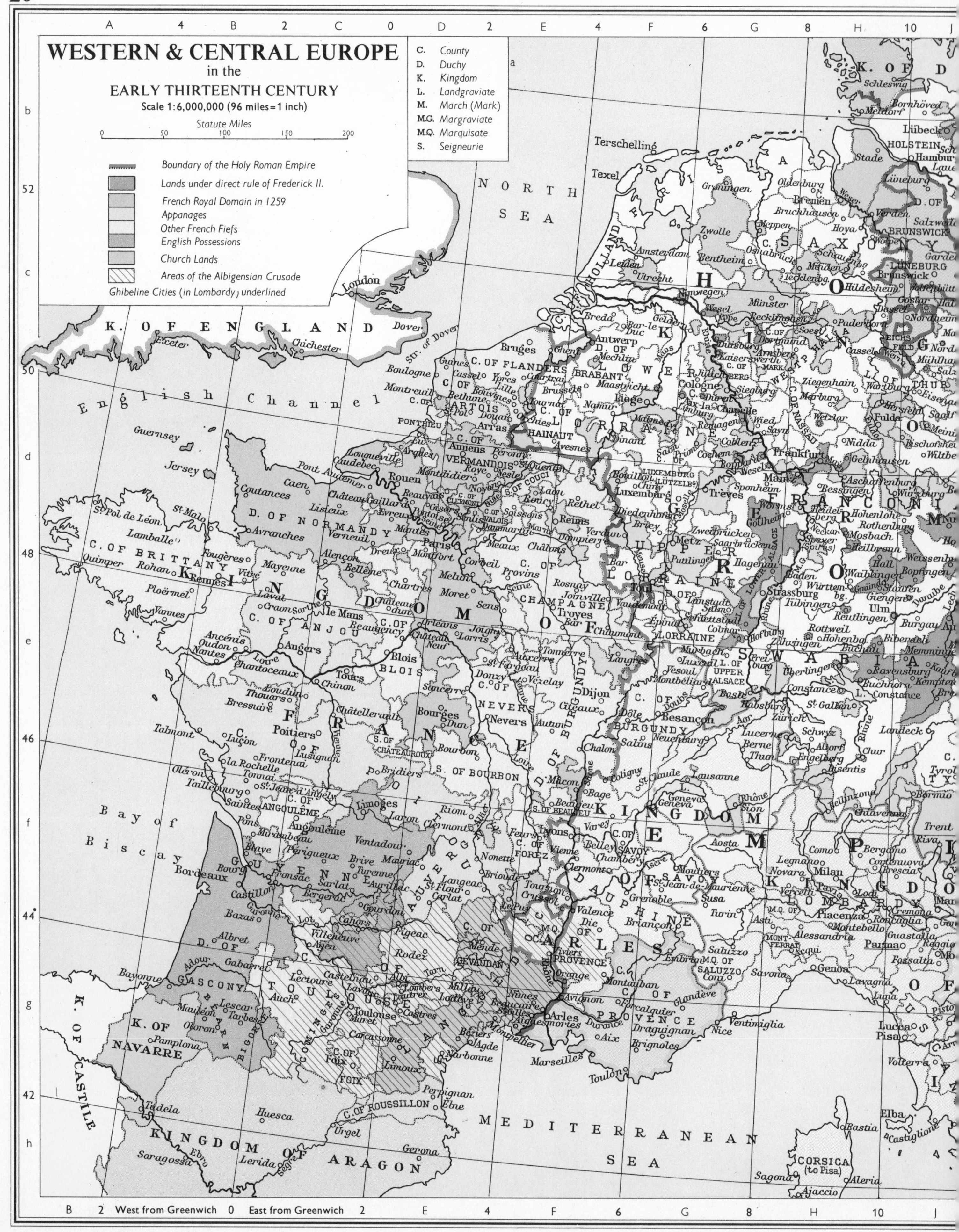
WESTERN & CENTRAL EUROPE
in the
EARLY THIRTEENTH CENTURY
Scale 1:6,000,000 (96 miles=1 inch)
Statute Miles
0 50 100 150 200
Boundary of the Holy Roman Empire
Lands under direct rule of Frederick II.
French Royal Domain in 1259
Appanages
Other French Fiefs
English Possessions
Church Lands
Areas of the Albigensian Crusade
Ghibeline Cities (in Lombardy) underlined
C. County
D. Duchy
K. Kingdom
L. Landgraviate
M. March (Mark)
M.G. Margraviate
M.Q. Marquisate
S. Seigneurie
NORTH SEA
English Channel
Bay of Biscay
MEDITERRANEAN SEA
K. OF ENGLAND
London
Dover
Chichester
Exeter
Str. of Dover
Guernsey
Jersey
KINGDOM OF FRANCE
D. OF NORMANDY
C. OF BRITTANY
C. OF ANJOU
C. OF FLANDERS
ARTOIS
PONTHIEU
VERMANDOIS
CHAMPAGNE
BLOIS
S. OF BOURBON
C. OF ANGOULÊME
C. OF FOREZ
GEVAUDAN
C. OF TOULOUSE
C. OF FOIX
C. OF ROUSSILLON
GASCONY
BEARN
BIGORRE
K. OF NAVARRE
K. OF CASTILE
KINGDOM OF ARAGON
D. OF BURGUNDY
C. OF BURGUNDY
KINGDOM OF ARLES
DAUPHINÉ
PROVENCE
C. OF PROVENCE
C. OF SAVOY
M.Q. OF SALUZZO
LOMBARDY
KINGDOM OF ITALY
LOWER LORRAINE
UPPER LORRAINE
LORRAINE
BRABANT
C. OF HAINAUT
HOLLAND
FRISIA
SAXONY
WESTPHALIA
FRANCONIA
SWABIA
L. OF UPPER ALSACE
LUXEMBURG
HOLSTEIN
LUNEBURG
BRUNSWICK
Paris
Rouen
Caen
Orléans
Tours
Poitiers
Bordeaux
Toulouse
Carcassonne
Narbonne
Montpellier
Avignon
Arles
Marseilles
Toulon
Nice
Lyons
Dijon
Besançon
Reims
Metz
Verdun
Toul
Strassburg
Cologne
Aix-la-Chapelle
Liège
Mainz
Worms
Frankfurt
Treves
Ghent
Bruges
Antwerp
Utrecht
Amsterdam
Milan
Genoa
Turin
Pavia
Piacenza
Parma
Cremona
Lucca
Pisa
Trent
Zürich
Constance
Basle
Saragossa
Lerida
Huesca
Gerona
Perpignan
Pamplona
Tudela
CORSICA (to Pisa)
Bastia
Ajaccio
Elba
Terschelling
Texel
Lübeck
Hamburg
Schleswig
West from Greenwich
East from Greenwich

Rise of the
NORMAN KINGDOM
of
ITALY & SICILY
Scale 1:6,300,000 (100 miles=1 inch)
Statute Miles
Note: Dates indicate Norman Conquest
Duchy of Apulia and Calabria c. 1085
County of Sicily by 1091
Principality of Salerno by 1077
County of Aversa by 1029
Principality of Capua by 1060 (including County of Aversa)
Papal Territories (including Benevento)
N. Frontier of Kingdom under Roger II.
ABRUZZI
CAMPAGNA
PR. OF CAPUA
MOLISE
CAPITANATA
PR. OF BENEVENTO
APULIA
PRINCIPATO
SALERNO
BASILICATA
CALABRIA
Malta (1091)
GERMANY
under
FREDERICK BARBAROSSA
Scale 1:12,000,000 (192 miles=1 inch)
Statute Miles
Limits of the Empire at the accession of Frederick Barbarossa 1152
Duchies held by the House of Staufen before 1176
Demesne lands of the House of Staufen before 1176
Duchies held by the House of Welf before 1176
Demesne lands of the House of Welf before 1176
Lands held by the Ascanians
DENMARK
BALTIC SEA
PRUSSIA
POMERANIA
MARCH OF BRANDENBURG
DUCHY OF SAXONY
KINGDOM OF POLAND
SILESIA
KINGDOM OF GERMANY
BOHEMIA
MARCH OF MORAVIA
FRANCONIA
DUCHY OF UPPER LOTHARINGIA (Lorraine)
D. OF SWABIA
DUCHY OF BAVARIA
DUCHY OF AUSTRIA
DUCHY OF STYRIA
D. OF CARINTHIA
KINGDOM OF HUNGARY
KINGDOM OF BURGUNDY OR ARLES
KINGDOM OF ITALY
KINGDOM OF FRANCE
ADRIATIC SEA
Gulf of Genoa
D. OF POMERANIA
KINGDOM OF POLAND
M. OF LAUSITZ
D. OF SILESIA
K. OF BOHEMIA
M. OF MORAVIA
D. OF AUSTRIA
D. OF STYRIA
CARINTHIA
D. OF CARNIOLA
KINGDOM OF HUNGARY
CROATIA
BOSNIA
ADRIATIC SEA
K. OF THE TWO SICILIES
M. OF ANCONA
SPOLETO
East from Greenwich

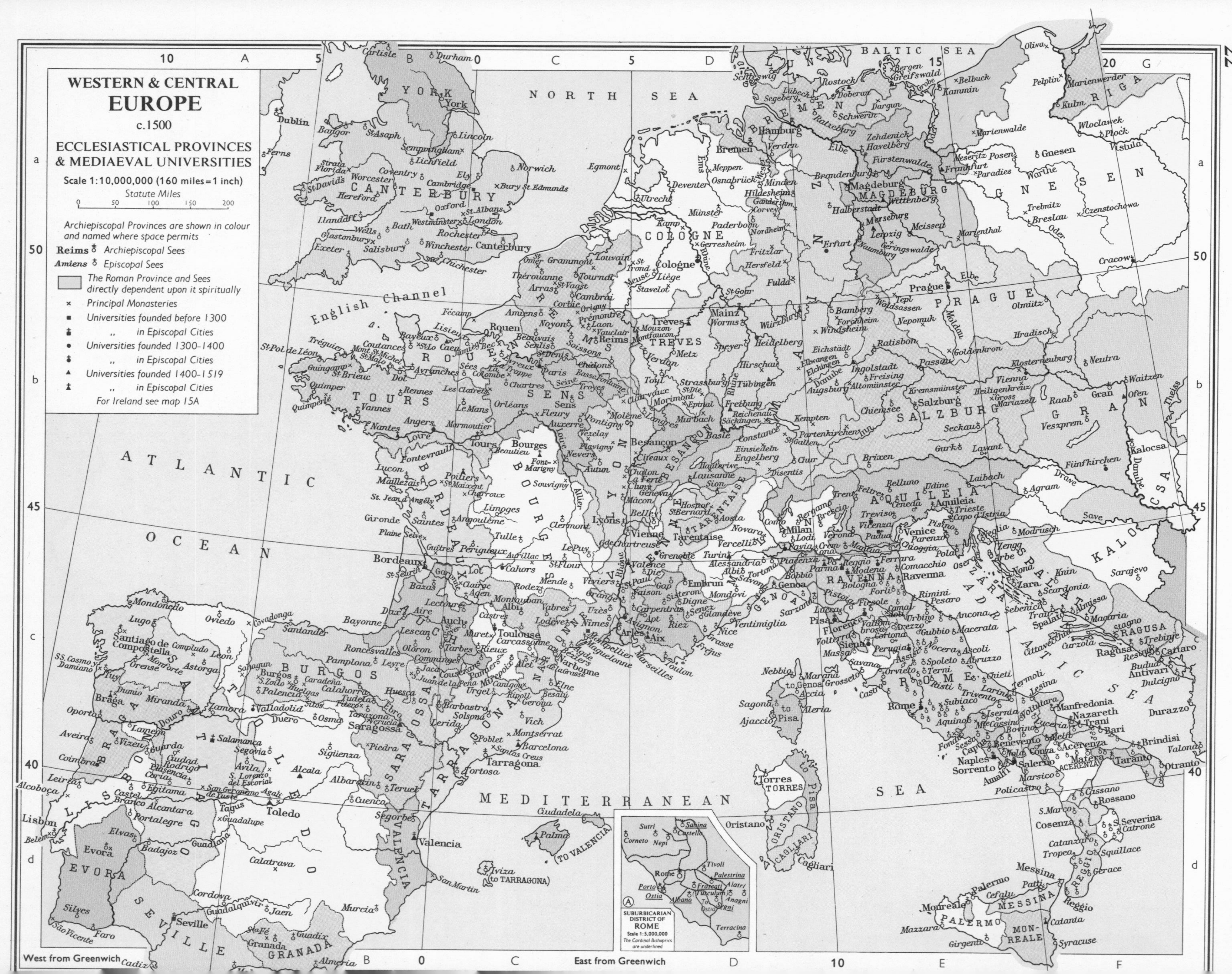

WESTERN & CENTRAL
EUROPE
c.1500
ECCLESIASTICAL PROVINCES
& MEDIAEVAL UNIVERSITIES
Scale 1:10,000,000 (160 miles=1 inch)
Statute Miles
0 50 100 150 200
Archiepiscopal Provinces are shown in colour and named where space permits
Reims Archiepiscopal Sees
Amiens Episcopal Sees
The Roman Province and Sees directly dependent upon it spiritually
Principal Monasteries
Universities founded before 1300
,, in Episcopal Cities
Universities founded 1300-1400
,, in Episcopal Cities
Universities founded 1400-1519
,, in Episcopal Cities
For Ireland see map 15A
NORTH SEA
BALTIC SEA
ATLANTIC OCEAN
MEDITERRANEAN SEA
ADRIATIC SEA
English Channel
SUBURBICARIAN DISTRICT OF ROME
Scale 1:5,000,000
The Cardinal Bishoprics are underlined
West from Greenwich
East from Greenwich

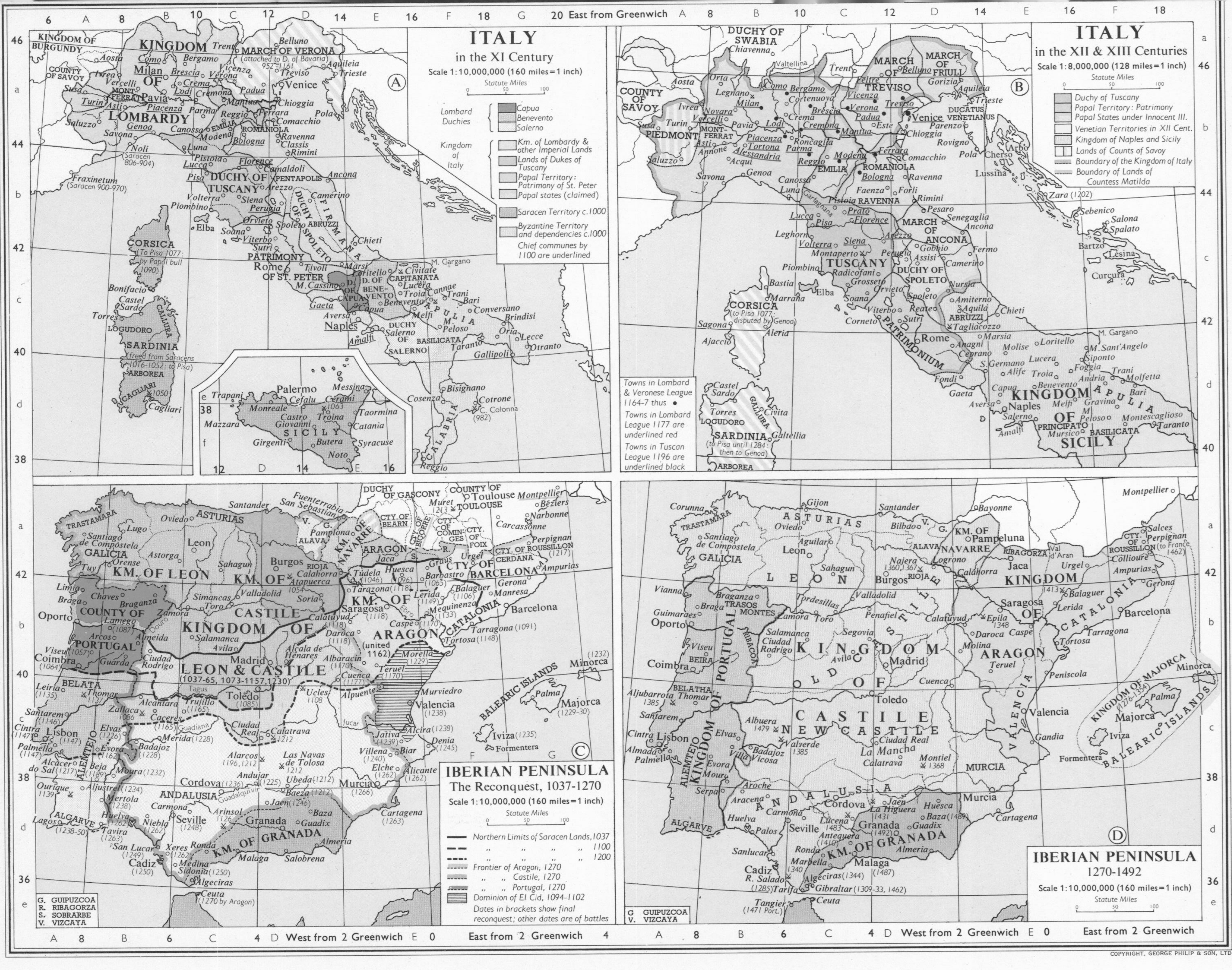

ITALY
in the XI Century
Scale 1:10,000,000 (160 miles=1 inch)
Statute Miles
Lombard Duchies
Capua
Benevento
Salerno
Kingdom of Italy
Km. of Lombardy & other Imperial Lands
Lands of Dukes of Tuscany
Papal Territory: Patrimony of St. Peter
Papal states (claimed)
Saracen Territory c.1000
Byzantine Territory and dependencies c.1000
Chief communes by 1100 are underlined
ITALY
in the XII & XIII Centuries
Scale 1:8,000,000 (128 miles=1 inch)
Statute Miles
Duchy of Tuscany
Papal Territory: Patrimony
Papal States under Innocent III.
Venetian Territories in XII Cent.
Kingdom of Naples and Sicily
Lands of Counts of Savoy
Boundary of the Kingdom of Italy
Boundary of Lands of Countess Matilda
Towns in Lombard & Veronese League 1164-7 thus ●
Towns in Lombard League 1177 are underlined red
Towns in Tuscan League 1196 are underlined black
IBERIAN PENINSULA
The Reconquest, 1037-1270
Scale 1:10,000,000 (160 miles=1 inch)
Statute Miles
Northern Limits of Saracen Lands, 1037
" " " " 1100
" " " " 1200
Frontier of Aragon, 1270
" " Castile, 1270
" " Portugal, 1270
Dominion of El Cid, 1094-1102
Dates in brackets show final reconquest; other dates are of battles
G. GUIPUZCOA
R. RIBAGORZA
S. SOBRARBE
V. VIZCAYA
IBERIAN PENINSULA
1270-1492
Scale 1:10,000,000 (160 miles=1 inch)
Statute Miles
G GUIPUZCOA
V. VIZCAYA
COPYRIGHT, GEORGE PHILIP & SON, LTD.

EUROPE
c. 1360
Scale 1: 20,000,000 (320 miles = 1 inch)
Statute Miles
0 100 200 300 400
Boundary of the Holy Roman Empire
a Lands of the Habsburgs
b ,, ,, House of Bohemia and Luxemburg
c Eastern Empire
Dominions of Edward III in 1360
French Royal Domain
Church Lands
Boundary of Dominions of Stephen Dushan (1331-55)
West from 5 Greenwich
East from 20 Greenwich
ATLANTIC OCEAN
NORTH SEA
BALTIC SEA
BLACK SEA
MEDITERRANEAN SEA
SCOTLAND
IRELAND
NORWAY
SWEDEN
FINLAND
DENMARK
GOTHLAND
KINGDOM OF FRANCE
BRITTANY
DUCHY OF AQUITAINE
PORTUGAL
KINGDOM OF CASTILE
ARAGON
NAVARRE
GRANADA
HOLY ROMAN EMPIRE
BRANDENBURG
POMERANIA
BOHEMIA
SILESIA
MORAVIA
BAVARIA
AUSTRIA
TYROL
STYRIA
CARINTHIA
PROVENCE
PAPAL STATES
KINGDOM OF NAPLES
KINGDOM OF SICILY
TEUTONIC KNIGHTS
LIVONIA
ESTHONIA
SAMOGITIA
LITHUANIA
PODLESIA
VOLHYNIA
PODOLIA
UKRAINE
KINGDOM OF POLAND
HUNGARY
TRANSYLVANIA
MOLDAVIA
WALLACHIA (To Hungary 1368)
CROATIA
BOSNIA
SERVIAN EMP. OF STEPHEN DUSHAN (1331-55)
BULGARIA
ALBANIAN PRINCES
E. EMPIRE
LATIN STATES
PR OF ACHAIA
COUNTY OF CEPHALONIA
RUSSIAN STATES
PRINCIPALITY OF MOSCOW
KHANATE OF THE GOLDEN HORDE (Mongols)
Ottoman Turks
Seljuk Turks (Eight Emirates)
EMPIRE OF TREBIZOND
GEORGIA
DOMS OF MOHAMMED ABTIN
DOMINIONS OF THE JALAYAS
Kara Kuyunli
Turkomans
KINGDOM OF CYPRUS
MAMELUKE SULTANS
BARKA
MOROCCO (MARINIDS) 1269-1470
ALGERIA (ZIYANIDS 1235-1393)
TUNIS (HAFSIDS)
TRIPOLI 1228-1534

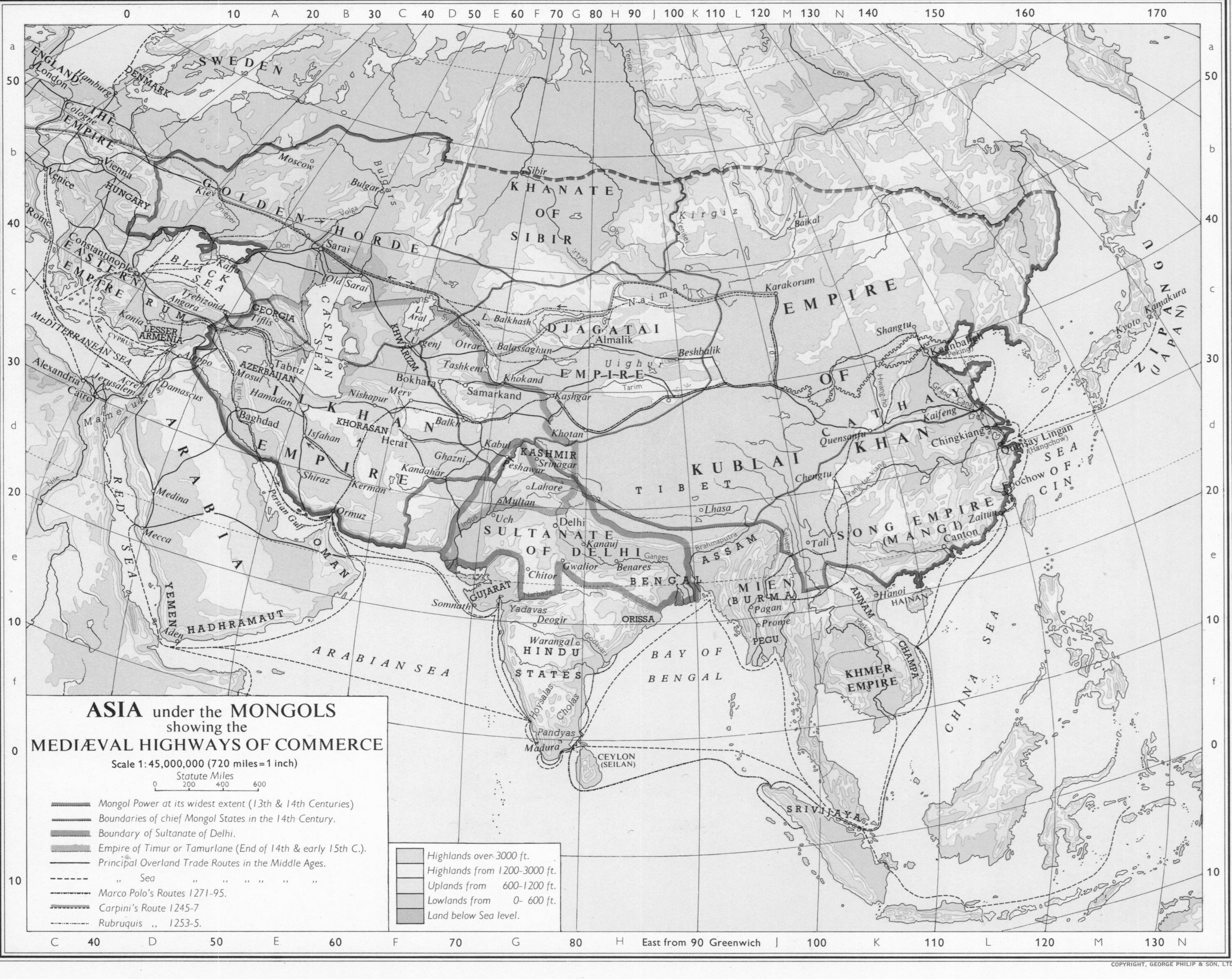
ASIA under the MONGOLS
showing the
MEDIÆVAL HIGHWAYS OF COMMERCE
Scale 1:45,000,000 (720 miles=1 inch)
Statute Miles
0 200 400 600
Mongol Power at its widest extent (13th & 14th Centuries)
Boundaries of chief Mongol States in the 14th Century.
Boundary of Sultanate of Delhi.
Empire of Timur or Tamurlane (End of 14th & early 15th C.).
Principal Overland Trade Routes in the Middle Ages.
" Sea " " " " " "
Marco Polo's Routes 1271-95.
Carpini's Route 1245-7
Rubruquis " 1253-5.
Highlands over 3000 ft.
Highlands from 1200-3000 ft.
Uplands from 600-1200 ft.
Lowlands from 0- 600 ft.
Land below Sea level.
East from 90 Greenwich
SWEDEN
DENMARK
ENGLAND
London
Hamburg
Cologne
THE EMPIRE
Vienna
Venice
HUNGARY
Rome
Constantinople
EASTERN EMPIRE
GOLDEN HORDE
Kiev
Dnieper
Moscow
Bulgars
Bulgar
Volga
Don
Sarai
Old Sarai
BLACK SEA
Kaffa
Trebizond
Angora
RUM
Konia
LESSER ARMENIA
CYPRUS
MEDITERRANEAN SEA
Alexandria
Cairo
Jerusalem
Acre
Damascus
Aleppo
Mameluks
Nile
GEORGIA
Tiflis
AZERBAIJAN
Tabriz
Mosul
Hamadan
Tigris
Baghdad
CASPIAN SEA
ILKHAN EMPIRE
Isfahan
KHORASAN
Herat
Nishapur
Merv
Shiraz
Kerman
Ormuz
Persian Gulf
KHWARIZM
Urgenj
Bokhara
Aral
Samarkand
Tashkent
Otrar
L. Balkhash
Balassaghun
Khokand
Kashgar
DJAGATAI
Almalik
Uighur EMPIRE
Beshbalik
Tarim
Naiman
Balkh
Kabul
Ghazni
Kandahar
KHANATE OF SIBIR
Sibir
Irtysh
Ob
Yenisei
Kirgiz
Baikal
Lena
Amur
Karakorum
EMPIRE OF KUBLAI KHAN
Shangtu
Kambaligh
(Peking)
Hwang-ho
Grand Canal
Kaifeng
CATHAY
Quensanfu
Chingkiang
Quinsay Lingan
(Hangchow)
Foochow
SEA OF CIN
Zaitun
Canton
SONG EMPIRE
(MANGI)
Chengtu
Yang-tse-kiang
Tali
TIBET
Lhasa
Khotan
KASHMIR
Srinagar
Peshawar
Lahore
Multan
Uch
Indus
SULTANATE OF DELHI
Delhi
Kanauj
Gwalior
Benares
Ganges
Chitor
BENGAL
Brahmaputra
ASSAM
MIEN
(BURMA)
Salween
Pagan
Prome
PEGU
GUJARAT
Narbada
Somnath
Yadavas
Deogir
ORISSA
Warangal
Godavari
HINDU STATES
Hoysalas
Cholas
Pandyas
Madura
CEYLON
(SEILAN)
BAY OF BENGAL
ARABIAN SEA
ARABIA
Medina
Mecca
RED SEA
YEMEN
Aden
HADHRAMAUT
OMAN
ANNAM
Hanoi
HAINAN
Mekong
CHAMPA
KHMER EMPIRE
SRIVIJAYA
CHINA SEA
ZIPANGU
(JAPAN)
Kyoto
Kamakura

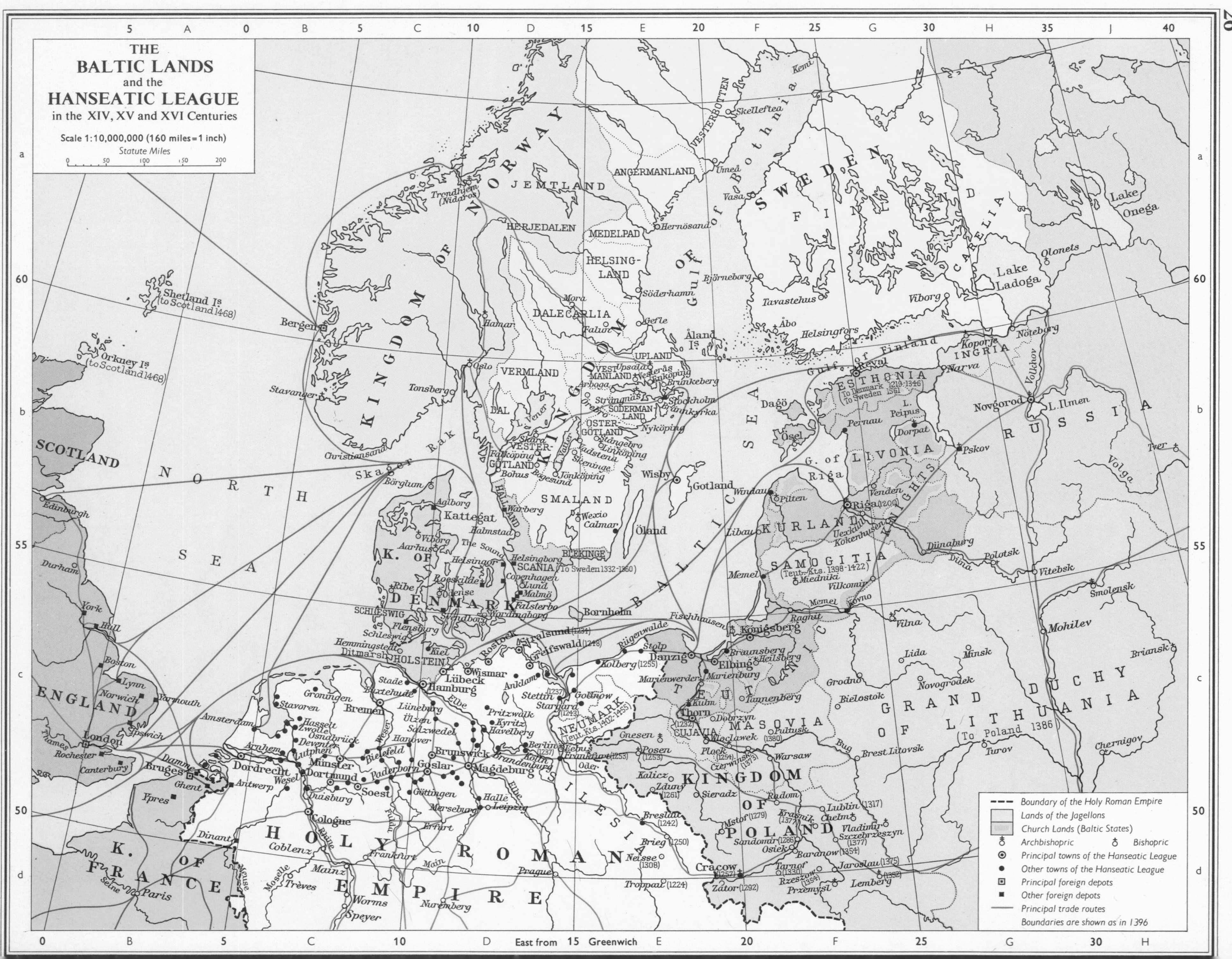
THE
BALTIC LANDS
and the
HANSEATIC LEAGUE
in the XIV, XV and XVI Centuries
Scale 1:10,000,000 (160 miles=1 inch)
Statute Miles
0 50 100 150 200
Boundary of the Holy Roman Empire
Lands of the Jagellons
Church Lands (Baltic States)
Archbishopric
Bishopric
Principal towns of the Hanseatic League
Other towns of the Hanseatic League
Principal foreign depots
Other foreign depots
Principal trade routes
Boundaries are shown as in 1396
East from 15 Greenwich
KINGDOM OF NORWAY
KINGDOM OF SWEDEN
FINLAND
CARELIA
INGRIA
ESTHONIA
(To Denmark 1219-1346)
(To Sweden 1561)
LIVONIA
KURLAND
SAMOGITIA
(Teut. Kts. 1398-1422)
RUSSIA
GRAND DUCHY OF LITHUANIA
(To Poland 1386)
KINGDOM OF POLAND
MASOVIA
CUJAVIA
TEUTONIC
KNIGHTS
K. OF DENMARK
HOLY ROMAN EMPIRE
SILESIA
NEUMARK
(Teut. Kts. 1402-1455)
K. OF FRANCE
ENGLAND
SCOTLAND
NORTH SEA
BALTIC SEA
Gulf of Bothnia
Gulf of Finland
G. of Riga
Skager Rak
Kattegat
The Sound
Shetland Is (to Scotland 1468)
Orkney Is (to Scotland 1468)
Lake Ladoga
Lake Onega
L. Ilmen
L. Peipus
JEMTLAND
HERJEDALEN
ANGERMANLAND
MEDELPAD
HELSING-LAND
DALECARLIA
VERMLAND
UPLAND
VEST-MANLAND
SODERMAN-LAND
OSTER-GOTLAND
VESTER-GOTLAND
DAL
SMALAND
HALLAND
SCANIA (To Sweden 1332-1360)
BLEKINGE
VESTERBOTTEN
SCHLESWIG
HOLSTEIN
Ditmarsh
Gotland
Öland
Bornholm
Dagö
Ösel
Åland Is
Bergen
Stavanger
Tonsberg
Oslo
Hamar
Trondhjem (Nidaros)
Christiansand
Börglum
Stockholm
Upsala
Visby
Calmar
Wexio
Novgorod
Pskov
Dorpat
Pernau
Reval
Narva
Riga (1200)
Königsberg
Danzig
Elbing
Thorn
Lübeck
Hamburg
Bremen
Cologne
Magdeburg
Brunswick
Cracow
Warsaw
Vilna
Kovno
London
Bruges
Antwerp
Paris
Prague
Elbe
Oder
Volga
Rhine

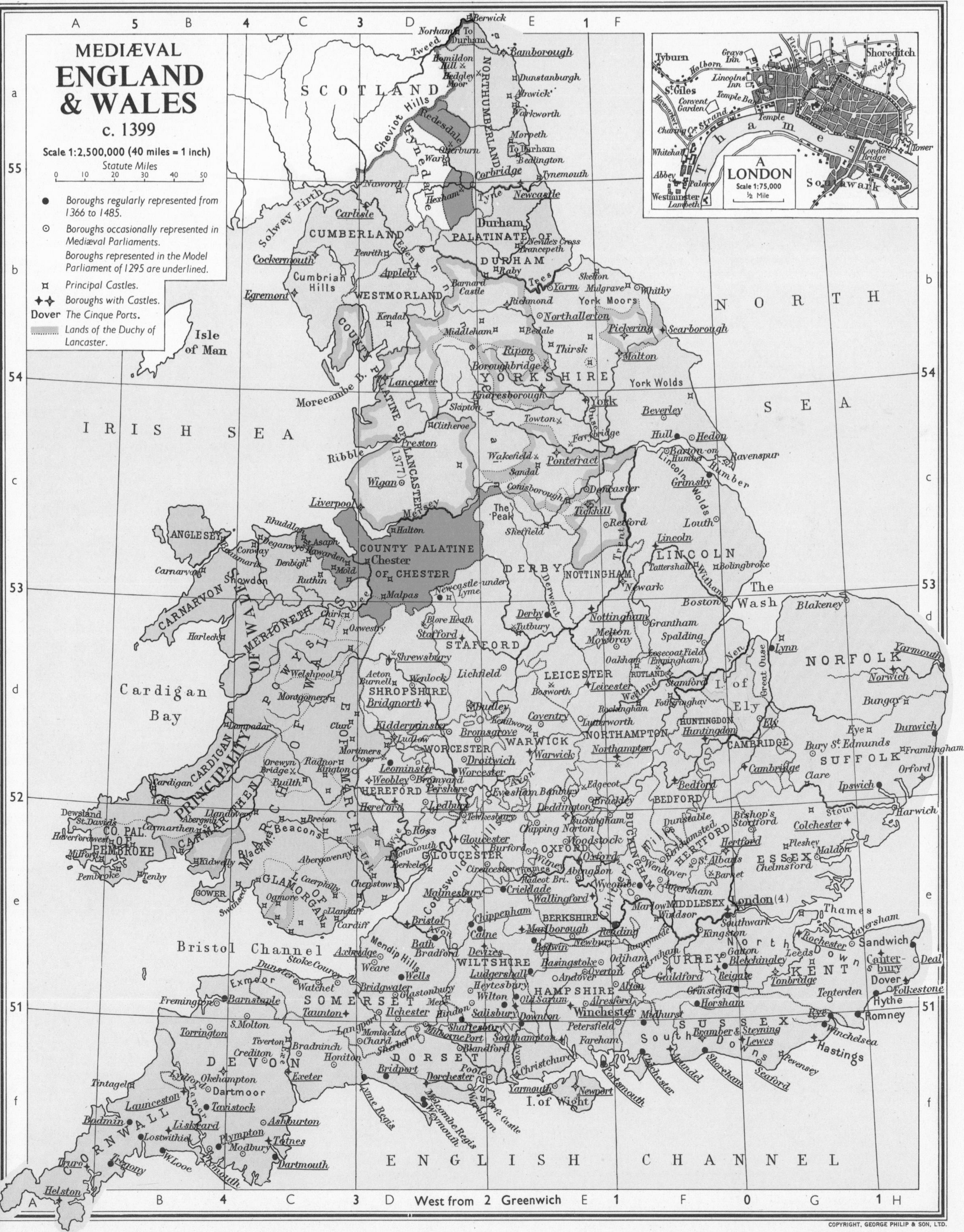
MEDIÆVAL
ENGLAND & WALES
c. 1399
Scale 1:2,500,000 (40 miles = 1 inch)
Statute Miles
0 10 20 30 40 50
Boroughs regularly represented from 1366 to 1485.
Boroughs occasionally represented in Mediæval Parliaments.
Boroughs represented in the Model Parliament of 1295 are underlined.
Principal Castles.
Boroughs with Castles.
Dover The Cinque Ports.
Lands of the Duchy of Lancaster.
A LONDON
Scale 1:75,000
½ Mile
Tyburn
Holborn
Grays Inn
Lincolns Inn
Fleet
Shoreditch
Moorfields
St. Giles
Covent Garden
Temple Bar
Strand
Temple
Charing Cr.
Whitehall
Abbey
Palace
Westminster
Lambeth
Thames
London Bridge
Tower
Southwark
SCOTLAND
Berwick
Norham
Tweed
To Durham
Homildon Hill
Hedgley Moor
Cheviot Hills
Redesdale
Tynedale
NORTHUMBERLAND
Bamborough
Dunstanburgh
Alnwick
Warkworth
Morpeth
To Durham
Bedlington
Otterburn
Wark
Tynemouth
Corbridge
Hexham
Tyne
Newcastle
Naworth
Solway Firth
Carlisle
CUMBERLAND
Penrith
Pennine
Eden
Cockermouth
Appleby
Cumbrian Hills
Egremont
WESTMORLAND
Kendal
Durham
PALATINATE OF DURHAM
Neville's Cross
Brancepeth
Raby
Tees
Barnard Castle
Yarm
Skelton
Mulgrave
Whitby
York Moors
Richmond
Northallerton
Pickering
Scarborough
Middleham
Bedale
Thirsk
Ripon
Malton
Isle of Man
COUNTY PALATINE OF LANCASTER (1377)
Lancaster
Morecambe B.
Boroughbridge
YORKSHIRE
York Wolds
Knaresborough
York
Skipton
Ouse
Beverley
Clitheroe
Towton
Hull
Hedon
Ferrybridge
Preston
Ribble
Barton-on-Humber
Ravenspur
Wakefield
Pontefract
Humber
Sandal
Lincoln Wolds
Wigan
Grimsby
Conisborough
Doncaster
Tickhill
Liverpool
Mersey
The Peak
Sheffield
Retford
Louth
Halton
IRISH SEA
NORTH SEA
ANGLESEY
Rhuddlan
St. Asaph
Degannwy
Hawarden
Conway
Beaumaris
Denbigh
Mold
Carnarvon
Snowdon
Ruthin
COUNTY PALATINE Chester OF CHESTER
Malpas
Newcastle-under-Lyme
DERBY
Derwent
NOTTINGHAM
Trent
Lincoln
LINCOLN
Tattershall
Bolingbroke
Witham
Newark
Boston
The Wash
Blakeney
CARNARVON
MERIONETH
PRINCIPALITY OF WALES
Harlech
Chirk
Oswestry
Dee
Blore Heath
Stafford
STAFFORD
Derby
Tutbury
Nottingham
Melton Mowbray
Grantham
Spalding
Losecoat Field (Empingham)
Oakham
RUTLAND
Lynn
NORFOLK
Yarmouth
Norwich
Shrewsbury
Lichfield
LEICESTER
Leicester
Bosworth
Welland
Stamford
Nen
I. of Ely
Great Ouse
Welshpool
Acton Burnell
Wenlock
SHROPSHIRE
Bridgnorth
Montgomery
POWYS
Cardigan Bay
Dudley
Kenilworth
Coventry
Rockingham
Fotheringhay
Bungay
Kidderminster
Ludlow
Bromsgrove
Lutterworth
NORTHAMPTON
HUNTINGDON
Huntingdon
Ely
Eye
Dunwich
Framlingham
Lampadar
Clun
Mortimers Cross
WORCESTER
Droitwich
WARWICK
Warwick
Northampton
CAMBRIDGE
Cambridge
Bury St. Edmunds
SUFFOLK
Orford
CARDIGAN
Orewyn Bridge
Radnor
Knighton
Leominster
Builth
Worcester
Avon
Bedford
Clare
Ipswich
Weobley
Bromyard
Pershore
Evesham
Banbury
Edgecot
HEREFORD
Cardigan
Tefi
Llandovery
Abergwili
Carmarthen
CARMARTHEN
Hereford
Ledbury
Deddington
Brackley
BEDFORD
Dewsland
St. Davids
Haverfordwest
CO. PAL. OF PEMBROKE
Milford
Pembroke
Tenby
Kidwelly
Brecon
Beacons
Black Mts.
MARCH OF WALES
Wye
Ross
Tewkesbury
Cotswold Hills
Chipping Norton
Buckingham
BUCKINGHAM
Dunstable
Berkhamsted
HERTFORD
Bishop's Stortford
Hertford
Stour
Colchester
Harwich
Abergavenny
Usk
Monmouth
Gloucester
GLOUCESTER
Berkeley
Burford
OXFORD
Woodstock
Witney
Cirencester
Oxford
Thames
Radcot Bri.
Abingdon
Wendover
St. Albans
Barnet
ESSEX
Chelmsford
Pleshey
Maldon
GOWER
Swansea
GLAMORGAN
Caerphilly
Ogmore
Chepstow
Malmesbury
Cricklade
Wallingford
Wycombe
Chiltern Hills
Amersham
MIDDLESEX
London (4)
Marlow
Windsor
Llandaff
Cardiff
Bristol
Chippenham
BERKSHIRE
Calne
Marlborough
Reading
Southwark
Kingston
Runnymede
Thames
Faversham
Rochester
Sandwich
Bristol Channel
Axbridge
Mendip Hills
Bath
Bradford
Devizes
Bedwin
Newbury
Farnham
Gatton
Bletchingley
SURREY
North Downs
KENT
Canterbury
Deal
Leeds
Dunster
Stoke Courcy
Weare
Wells
WILTSHIRE
Basingstoke
Odiham
Watchet
Exmoor
Bridgwater
Glastonbury
Ludgershall
Heytesbury
Andover
Overton
Alton
Guildford
Reigate
Tonbridge
Dover
Folkestone
Fremington
Barnstaple
SOMERSET
Mere
Wilton
Old Sarum
HAMPSHIRE
Alresford
Grinstead
Horsham
Tenterden
Hythe
Taunton
Ilchester
Hindon
Salisbury
Downton
Winchester
Midhurst
Rye
Romney
Torrington
S. Molton
Langport
Montacute
Chard
Shaftesbury
Milborne Port
Petersfield
SUSSEX
Bramber & Steyning
Winchelsea
Tiverton
Crediton
Bradninch
Exe
Sherborne
DORSET
Blandford
Southampton
Fareham
South Downs
Lewes
Hastings
DEVON
Honiton
Bridport
Poole
Christchurch
Chichester
Arundel
Shoreham
Pevensey
Seaford
Exeter
Dorchester
Yarmouth
Newport
Portsmouth
Tintagel
Lydford
Okehampton
Dartmoor
Lyme Regis
Melcombe Regis
Weymouth
Wareham
Corfe Castle
I. of Wight
Launceston
Tamar
Tavistock
Bodmin
CORNWALL
Liskeard
Ashburton
Lostwithiel
Plympton
Modbury
Totnes
Truro
Tregony
W. Looe
Plymouth
Dartmouth
Helston
ENGLISH CHANNEL
West from 2 Greenwich
A B C D E F G H
a b c d e f
55 54 53 52 51
5 4 3 2 1 0 1

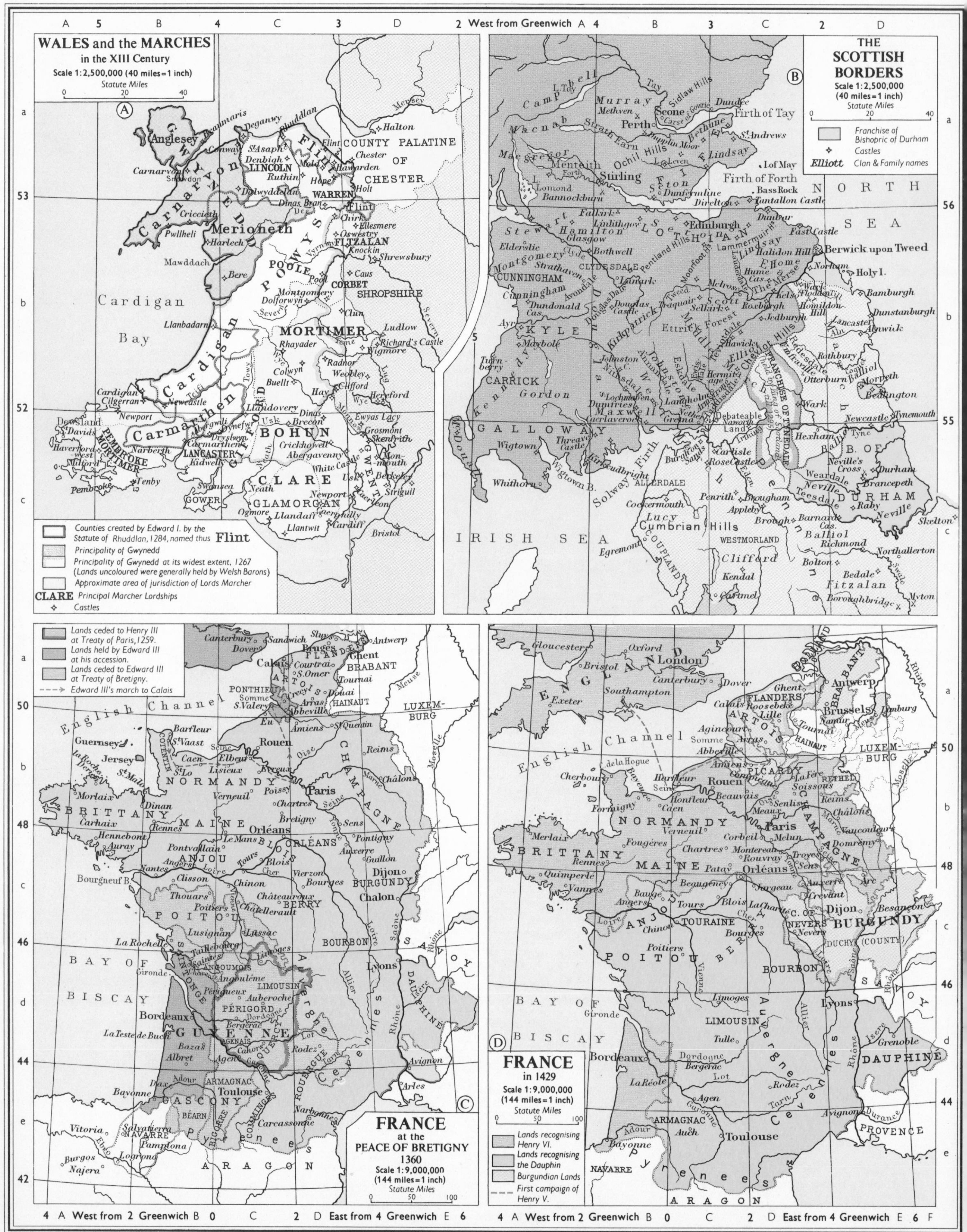
WALES and the MARCHES
in the XIII Century
Scale 1:2,500,000 (40 miles=1 inch)
Statute Miles
Counties created by Edward I. by the Statute of Rhuddlan, 1284, named thus Flint
Principality of Gwynedd
Principality of Gwynedd at its widest extent, 1267 (Lands uncoloured were generally held by Welsh Barons)
Approximate area of jurisdiction of Lords Marcher
CLARE Principal Marcher Lordships
Castles
THE SCOTTISH BORDERS
Scale 1:2,500,000
(40 miles=1 inch)
Statute Miles
Franchise of Bishopric of Durham
Castles
Elliott Clan & Family names
Lands ceded to Henry III at Treaty of Paris, 1259.
Lands held by Edward III at his accession.
Lands ceded to Edward III at Treaty of Bretigny.
Edward III's march to Calais
FRANCE
at the
PEACE OF BRETIGNY
1360
Scale 1:9,000,000
(144 miles=1 inch)
Statute Miles
FRANCE
in 1429
Scale 1:9,000,000
(144 miles=1 inch)
Statute Miles
Lands recognising Henry VI.
Lands recognising the Dauphin
Burgundian Lands
First campaign of Henry V.
West from Greenwich
East from Greenwich

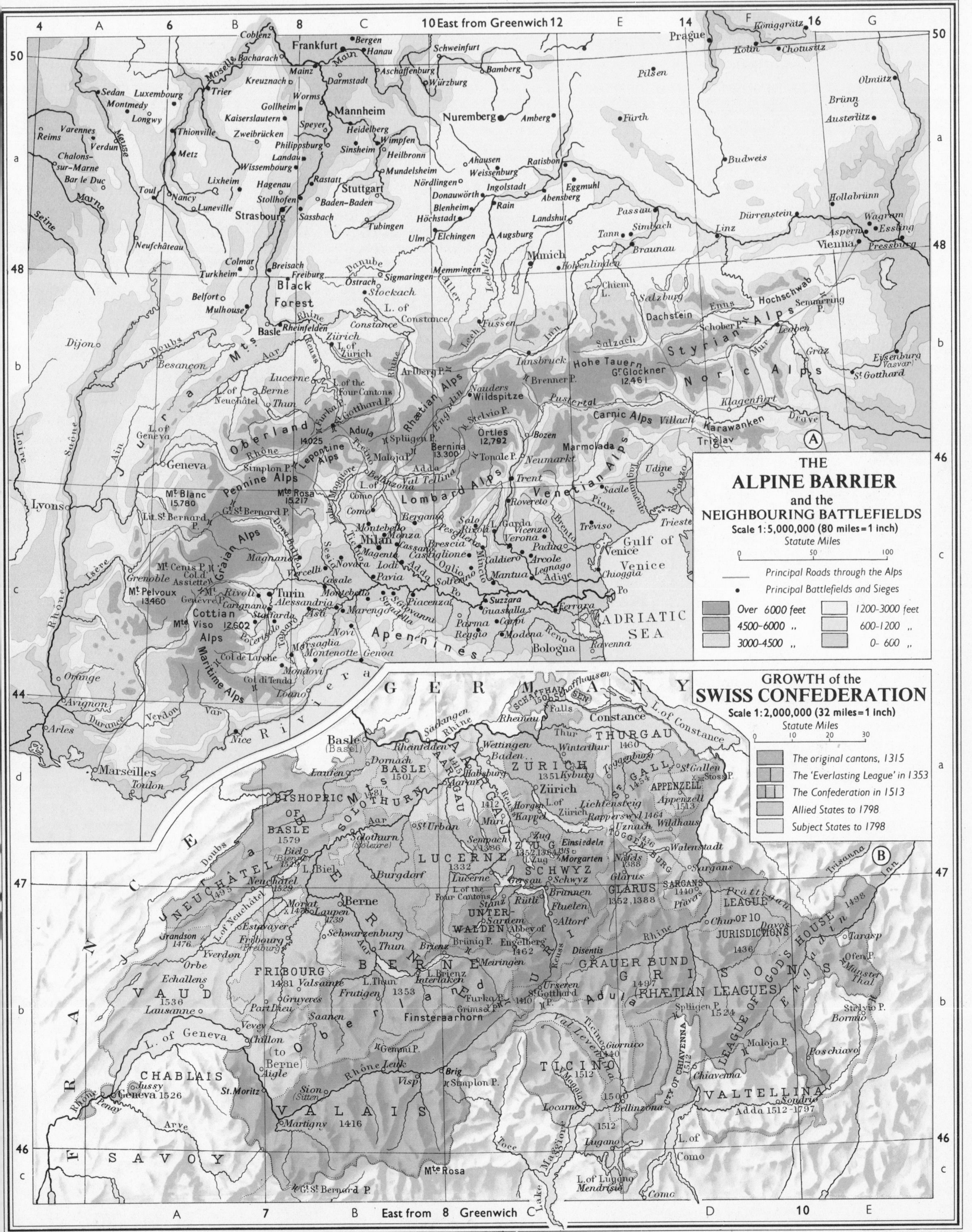
THE
ALPINE BARRIER
and the
NEIGHBOURING BATTLEFIELDS
Scale 1:5,000,000 (80 miles=1 inch)
Statute Miles
Principal Roads through the Alps
Principal Battlefields and Sieges
Over 6000 feet
4500-6000 ,,
3000-4500 ,,
1200-3000 feet
600-1200 ,,
0- 600 ,,
GROWTH of the
SWISS CONFEDERATION
Scale 1:2,000,000 (32 miles=1 inch)
Statute Miles
The original cantons, 1315
The 'Everlasting League' in 1353
The Confederation in 1513
Allied States to 1798
Subject States to 1798
10 East from Greenwich 12
East from 8 Greenwich

WESTERN & CENTRAL EUROPE
in the
LATER FIFTEENTH CENTURY
Scale 1:6,000,000 (96 miles 1 inch)
Statute Miles
0 50 100 150 200
Boundary of the Holy Roman Empire 1477
Boundaries of Electoral States within the Empire
Church Lands
Lands of the House of Hohenzollern
,, ,, ,, ,, ,, Wittelsbach (Palatinate Branch)
,, ,, ,, ,, ,, ,, (Bavarian ,,)
,, ,, ,, ,, ,, Wettin
,, ,, ,, ,, ,, Habsburg
,, ,, ,, ,, ,, Burgundy
Free Cantons of the Swiss Confederation
Allied ,, ,, ,, ,, ,,
Imperial Free Cities
French Royal Domain 1461
Appanages
Other French Fiefs
AB Archbishopric
B. Bishopric
BUR. Burgraviate
C. County
D. Duchy
EL. Electorate
K. Kingdom
L. Landgraviate
M. Margraviate or Marquisate
PR. Principality
R. Republic
S. Seigneurie
V. Viscounty
NORTH SEA
K. OF ENGLAND
English Channel
Bay of Biscay
MEDITERRANEAN SEA
C. OF FLANDERS
DUCHY OF BRABANT
C. OF ARTOIS
NORMANDY
PICARDY
DUCHY OF BRITTANY (to France 1491)
ANJOU
MAINE
TOURAINE
POITOU
GUYENNE
LANGUEDOC
CHAMPAGNE
D. OF BURGUNDY
FRANCHE COMTÉ
D. OF BOURBON
AUVERGNE
DAUPHINÉ
PROVENCE
DUCHY OF SAVOY
PIEDMONT
DUCHY OF MILAN
REPUBLIC OF GENOA
THE SWISS CONFEDERATION
DUCHY OF LUXEMBURG
LORRAINE
K. OF NAVARRE
KINGDOM OF ARAGON
K. OF CASTILE
CORSICA (to Genoa 1367)
D. OF HOLSTEIN
D. OF SCHLESWIG
DUCHY OF BRUNSWICK LÜNEBURG
D. OF GELDERLAND
Paris
Rouen
Orleans
Bordeaux
Lyons
Marseilles
Toulouse
Dijon
Nantes
Rennes
Brussels
Antwerp
Bruges
Ghent
Cologne
Mainz
Frankfurt
Strassburg
Basle
Berne
Geneva
Turin
Milan
Genoa
Bremen
Hamburg
Lübeck
Augsburg
Ulm
Avignon
Lisbon
West from Greenwich
East from Greenwich

RISE OF THE HOUSE of BURGUNDY
Scale 1:6,500,000
(104 miles=1 inch)
Statute Miles
Eastern frontier of K. of France
Duchy of Burgundy 1363
Inheritance of Margaret, Ctss. of Flanders
Lands of Philip the Bold 1363-1404
Acquisitions of John the Fearless 1404-1419
Acquisitions of Philip the Good 1419-1467
Acquisitions of Charles the Bold 1467-1477
Lands of junior branch of House of Burgundy in 1467
Bishoprics
RISE OF THE HOUSE of LUXEMBURG
Scale 1:10,000,000
(160 miles=1 inch)
Statute Miles
Duchy of Luxemburg
Lands of King John in 1310
Subsequent gains by King John
Gains of Charles IV.
Possessions of Wenzel, D. of Luxemburg (1354-1383)
Gains of Emperor Sigismund
Dates indicate acquisition by House of Luxemburg
Frontier of the Empire
KINGDOM OF POLAND
LANDS OF THE JAGELLONS
TEUTONIC KNIGHTS
DUCHY OF SILESIA
KINGDOM OF BOHEMIA
M. OF MORAVIA
ARCHDUCHY OF AUSTRIA
DUCHY OF STYRIA
CARINTHIA
D. OF CARNIOLA
KINGDOM OF HUNGARY
OTTOMAN EMPIRE
BOSNIA
DALMATIA
HERZEGOVINA
CROATIA
ADRIATIC SEA
K. OF NAPLES
KINGDOM OF FRANCE
DUCHY OF BURGUNDY
DUCHY OF LUXEMBURG
THE EMPIRE
KM. OF DENMARK
KM. OF POLAND
KM. OF BOHEMIA
KM. OF HUNGARY
KM. OF FRANCE
AUSTRIA
BAVARIA
TYROL

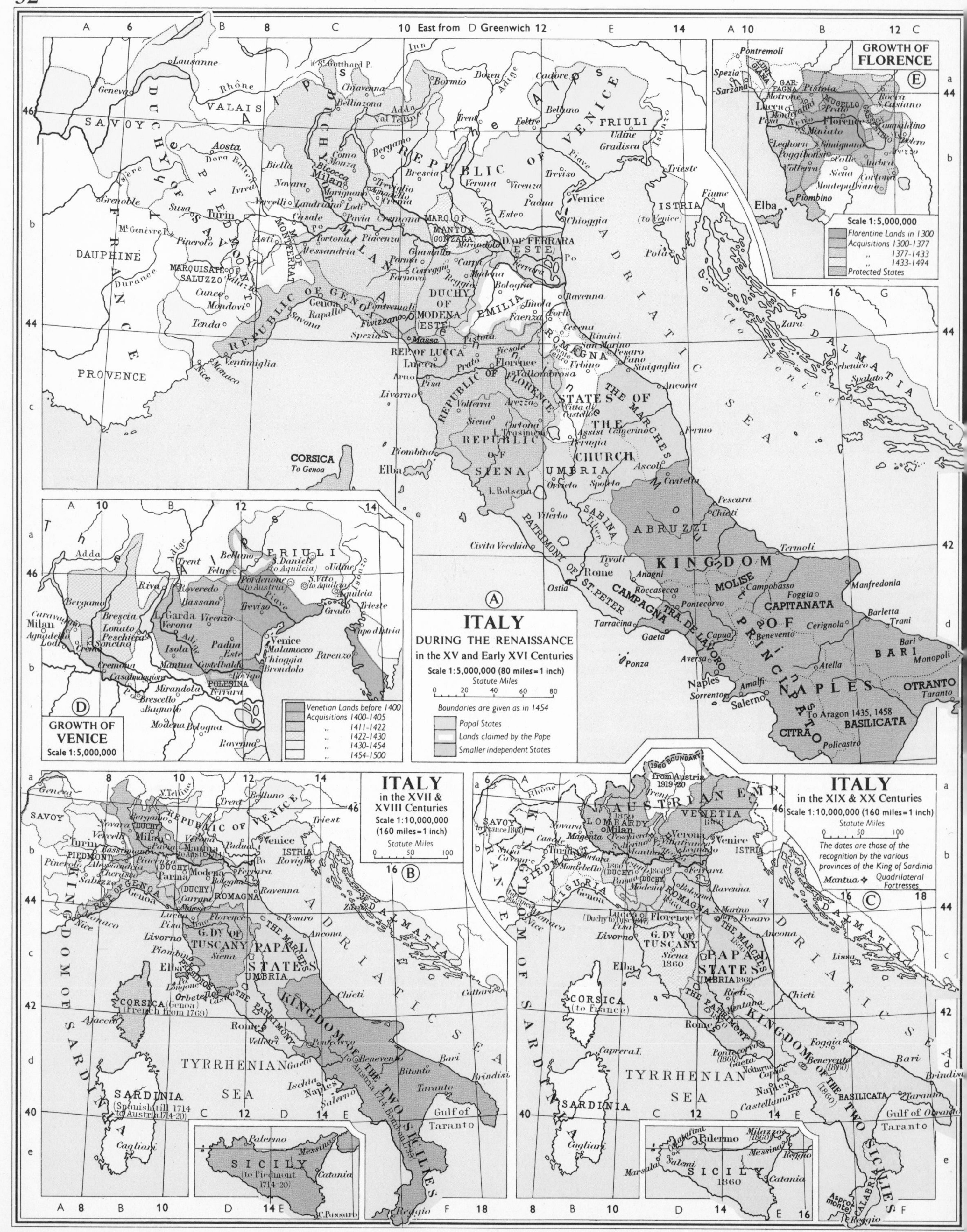
ITALY
DURING THE RENAISSANCE
in the XV and Early XVI Centuries
Scale 1:5,000,000 (80 miles=1 inch)
Statute Miles
0 20 40 60 80
Boundaries are given as in 1454
Papal States
Lands claimed by the Pope
Smaller independent States
A
10 East from D Greenwich 12
DUCHY OF SAVOY
DAUPHINÉ
PROVENCE
FRANCE
VALAIS
The ALPS
DUCHY OF MILAN
REPUBLIC OF VENICE
FRIULI
MARQ OF MANTUA GONZAGA
D. OF FERRARA ESTE
MARQUISATE OF SALUZZO
M. OF MONTFERRAT
REPUBLIC OF GENOA
DUCHY OF MODENA ESTE
REP. OF LUCCA
REPUBLIC OF FLORENCE
REPUBLIC OF SIENA
EMILIA
ROMAGNA
STATES OF THE CHURCH
THE MARCHES
UMBRIA
SABINA
PATRIMONY OF ST. PETER
CAMPAGNA
ABRUZZI
KINGDOM OF NAPLES
MOLISE
CAPITANATA
TRA. DE LAVORO
PRINCIPATO CITRA
BASILICATA
BARI
OTRANTO
To Aragon 1435, 1458
ADRIATIC SEA
DALMATIA
ISTRIA
CORSICA
To Genoa
Elba
GROWTH OF FLORENCE
E
Scale 1:5,000,000
Florentine Lands in 1300
Acquisitions 1300-1377
1377-1433
1433-1494
Protected States
GROWTH OF VENICE
D
Scale 1:5,000,000
Venetian Lands before 1400
Acquisitions 1400-1405
1411-1422
1422-1430
1430-1454
1454-1500
ITALY
in the XVII & XVIII Centuries
Scale 1:10,000,000
(160 miles=1 inch)
Statute Miles
0 50 100
B
KINGDOM OF SARDINIA
REP. OF GENOA
REPUBLIC OF VENICE
G. DY OF TUSCANY
PAPAL STATES
KINGDOM OF THE TWO SICILIES
TYRRHENIAN SEA
SARDINIA
(Spanish till 1714 to Austria 1714-20)
CORSICA (Genoa)
(French from 1769)
SICILY
(to Piedmont 1714-20)
to Austria 1714, Bourbon 1735
Gulf of Taranto
ITALY
in the XIX & XX Centuries
Scale 1:10,000,000 (160 miles=1 inch)
Statute Miles
0 50 100
The dates are those of the recognition by the various provinces of the King of Sardinia
Mantua ✣ Quadrilateral Fortresses
C
1960 BOUNDARY
from Austria 1919-20
AUSTRIAN EMP.
LOMBARDY
VENETIA
KINGDOM OF SARDINIA
LIGURIA
G. DY OF TUSCANY
PAPAL STATES
KINGDOM OF THE TWO SICILIES
CORSICA
(to France)
SARDINIA
SICILY
1860
TYRRHENIAN SEA
ADRIATIC SEA
DALMATIA
Gulf of Otranto
Gulf of Taranto

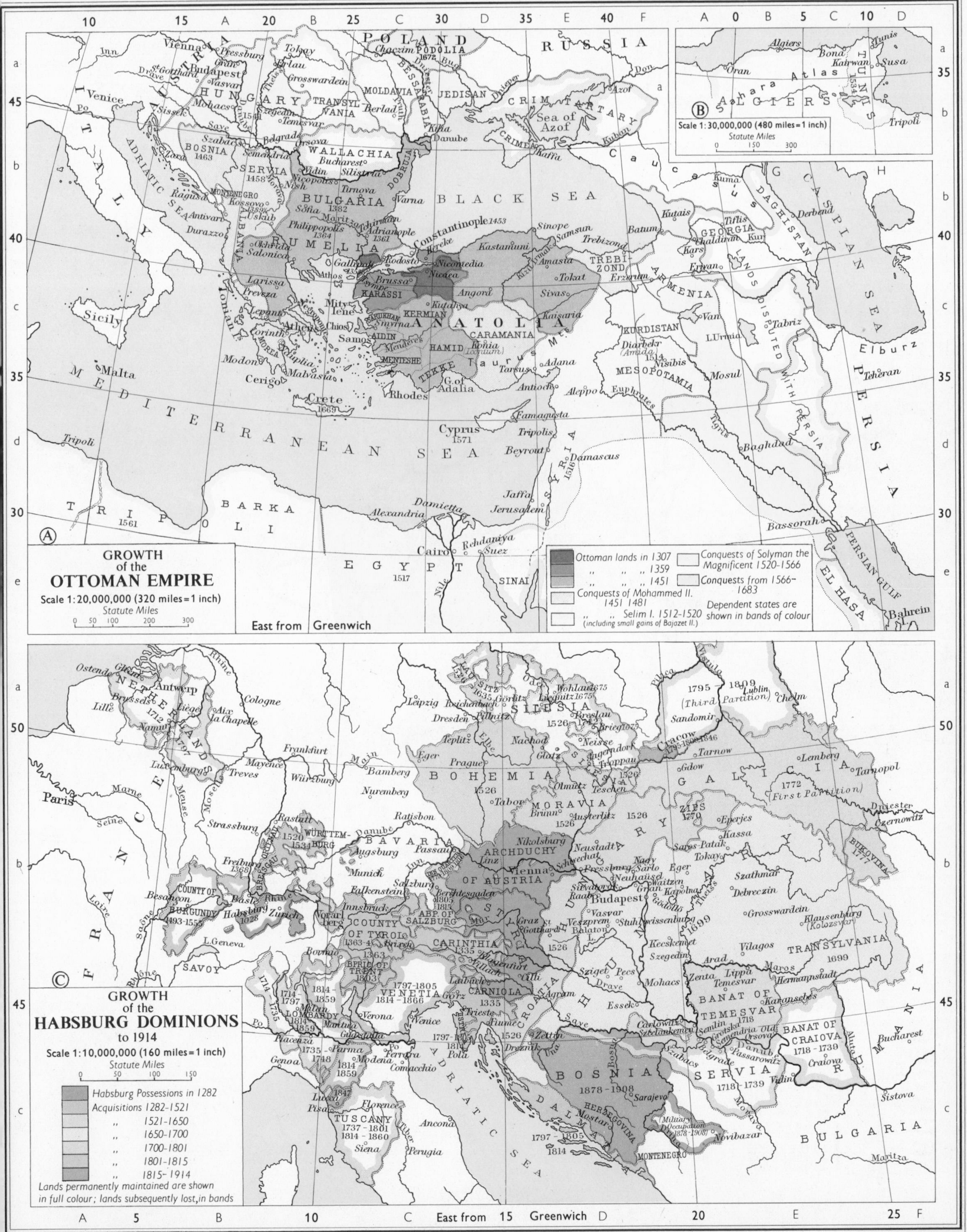
GROWTH
of the
OTTOMAN EMPIRE
Scale 1:20,000,000 (320 miles = 1 inch)
Statute Miles
0 50 100 200 300
East from Greenwich
Ottoman lands in 1307
„ „ „ 1359
„ „ „ 1451
Conquests of Mohammed II. 1451 1481
„ „ Selim I. 1512-1520 (including small gains of Bajazet II.)
Conquests of Solyman the Magnificent 1520-1566
Conquests from 1566-1683
Dependent states are shown in bands of colour
Scale 1:30,000,000 (480 miles = 1 inch)
Statute Miles
0 150 300
GROWTH
of the
HABSBURG DOMINIONS
to 1914
Scale 1:10,000,000 (160 miles = 1 inch)
Statute Miles
0 50 100 150
Habsburg Possessions in 1282
Acquisitions 1282-1521
„ 1521-1650
„ 1650-1700
„ 1700-1801
„ 1801-1815
„ 1815-1914
Lands permanently maintained are shown in full colour; lands subsequently lost, in bands
East from 15 Greenwich

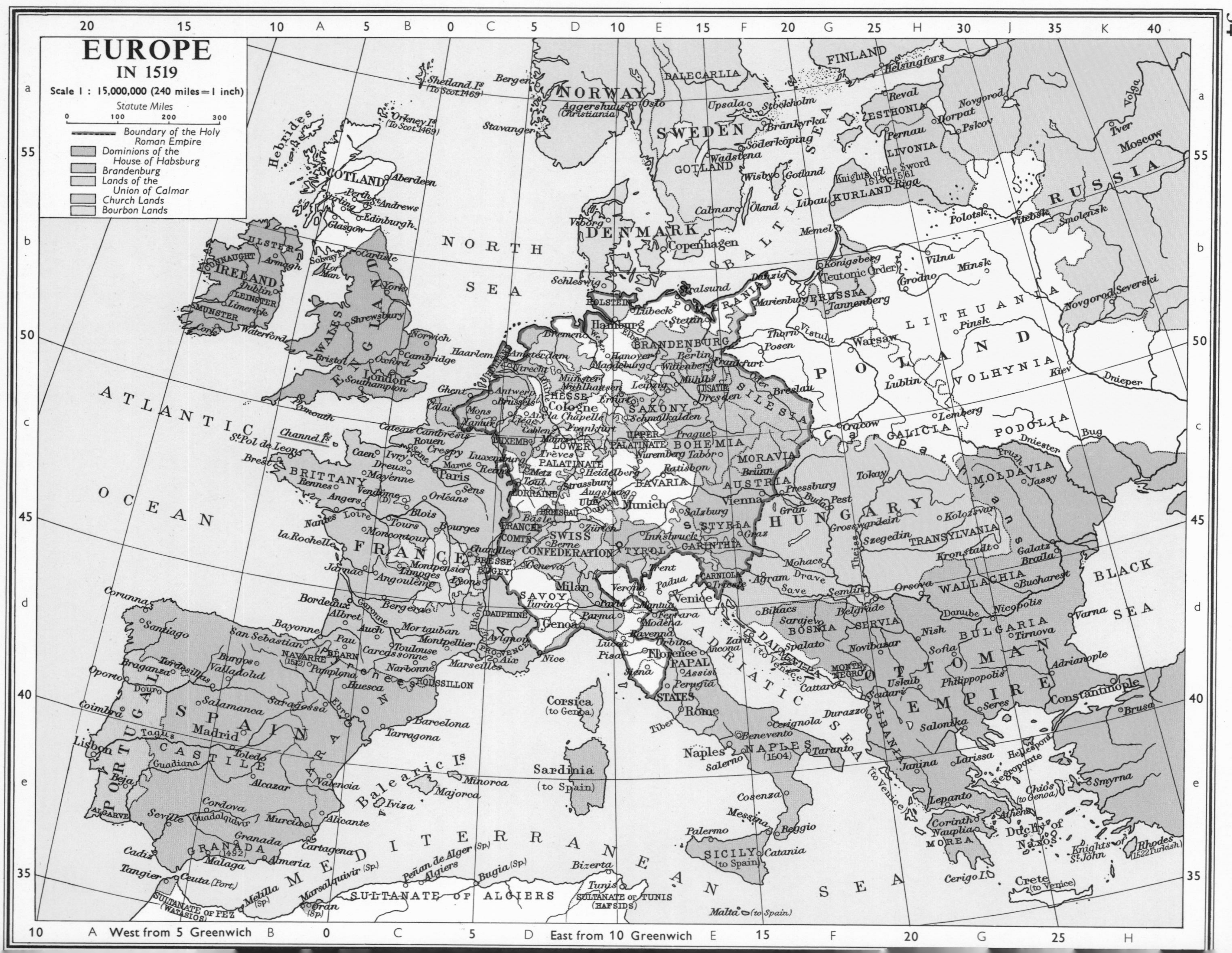
EUROPE
IN 1519
Scale 1 : 15,000,000 (240 miles = 1 inch)
Statute Miles
0 100 200 300
Boundary of the Holy Roman Empire
Dominions of the House of Habsburg
Brandenburg
Lands of the Union of Calmar
Church Lands
Bourbon Lands
West from 5 Greenwich
East from 10 Greenwich
ATLANTIC
OCEAN
NORTH
SEA
BALTIC SEA
BLACK SEA
ADRIATIC SEA
MEDITERRANEAN SEA
NORWAY
SWEDEN
DENMARK
FINLAND
DALECARLIA
GOTLAND
ESTHONIA
LIVONIA
KURLAND
Knights of the Sword 1515-1561
RUSSIA
Moscow
Tver
Novgorod
Pskov
Dorpat
Smolensk
Novgorod Severski
Vitebsk
Polotsk
LITHUANIA
POLAND
VOLHYNIA
PODOLIA
GALICIA
Warsaw
Vilna
Minsk
Grodno
Pinsk
Lublin
Kiev
Dnieper
Cracow
Lemberg
PRUSSIA
Teutonic Order
Königsberg
Tannenberg
Marienburg
Danzig
Memel
Thorn
Posen
Vistula
POMERANIA
Stralsund
Stettin
HOLSTEIN
Lübeck
Hamburg
Bremen
BRANDENBURG
Berlin
Frankfurt
Wittenberg
Hanover
Magdeburg
SAXONY
LUSATIA
Dresden
Leipzig
Erfurt
Schmalkalden
SILESIA
Breslau
BOHEMIA
Prague
Tabor
MORAVIA
Brünn
HESSE
Münster
Mühlhausen
Cologne
Aix la Chapelle
Frankfurt
Coblenz
LOWER PALATINATE
UPPER PALATINATE
Treves
Heidelberg
Nuremberg
Ratisbon
BAVARIA
Augsburg
Ulm
Munich
Danube
AUSTRIA
Vienna
Pressburg
Salzburg
STYRIA
Graz
CARINTHIA
CARNIOLA
Trieste
TYROL
Innsbruck
Trent
SWISS CONFEDERATION
Zürich
Berne
Basle
Geneva
BREISGAU
FRANCHE COMTÉ
LORRAINE
Metz
Toul
Strassburg
LUXEMBURG
Luxemburg
Antwerp
Brussels
Ghent
Mons
Namur
Liége
Amsterdam
Utrecht
Haarlem
Calais
Cateau Cambrésis
Rouen
Crespy
Ivry
Caen
Dreux
Paris
Sens
Marne
Rheims
Mayenne
Vendôme
Orléans
Blois
Tours
Bourges
Moncontour
BRITTANY
Rennes
Brest
St. Pol de Leon
Channel Is.
Angers
Nantes
Loire
la Rochelle
FRANCE
Jarnac
Angoulême
Limoges
Montpensier
Lyons
Charolles
BRESSE
BUGEY
DAUPHINÉ
Bordeaux
Garonne
Bergerac
Albret
Auch
Montauban
Toulouse
Montpellier
Carcassonne
Avignon
PROVENCE
Aix
Marseilles
Narbonne
ROUSSILLON
Bayonne
Pau
BEARN
NAVARRE (1512)
Pamplona
Rhône
SAVOY
Turin
Nice
Milan
Genoa
Parma
Verona
Padua
Venice
Mantua
Ferrara
Modena
Ravenna
Urbino
Lucca
Pisa
Florence
Siena
Ancona
Assisi
Perugia
PAPAL STATES
Rome
Tiber
Naples
Salerno
Benevento
Cerignola
NAPLES (1504)
Taranto
Cosenza
Messina
Reggio
Palermo
SICILY (to Spain)
Catania
Malta (to Spain)
Corsica (to Genoa)
Sardinia (to Spain)
HUNGARY
Buda
Pest
Gran
Tokay
Grosswardein
Szegedin
Kolozsvar
TRANSYLVANIA
Kronstadt
Theiss
Mohacs
Drave
Save
Agram
Semlin
Belgrade
Orsova
WALLACHIA
Bucharest
MOLDAVIA
Jassy
Pruth
Dniester
Bug
Galatz
Braila
Nicopolis
Varna
BULGARIA
Tirnova
Nish
Sofia
Adrianople
Constantinople
Brusa
Philippopolis
Seres
Salonika
SERVIA
Novibazar
BOSNIA
Sarajevo
Bihacs
Spalato
Zara
DALMATIA (to Venice)
Cattaro
MONTENEGRO
Scutari
Uskub
Durazzo
ALBANIA
OTTOMAN EMPIRE
Janina
Larissa
Lepanto
Corinth
Nauplia
MOREA
Athens
Negropont
Hellespont
Chios (to Genoa)
Smyrna
Duchy of Naxos
Knights of St. John
Rhodes (1522 Turkish)
Crete (to Venice)
Cerigo I.
SCOTLAND
Aberdeen
Perth
St. Andrews
Stirling
Edinburgh
Glasgow
Hebrides
Orkney Is. (To Scot. 1469)
Shetland Is. (To Scot. 1469)
Solway
I. of Man
Carlisle
York
ENGLAND
WALES
Shrewsbury
Norwich
Cambridge
Oxford
Bristol
London
Southampton
Plymouth
IRELAND
ULSTER
CONNAUGHT
LEINSTER
MUNSTER
Armagh
Dublin
Limerick
Cork
Waterford
Bergen
Stavanger
Aggershuus (Christiania)
Oslo
Upsala
Stockholm
Bränkyrka
Söderköping
Wadstena
Wisby
Gotland
Calmar
Öland
Libau
Riga
Reval
Pernau
Helsingfors
Viborg
Copenhagen
Schleswig
PORTUGAL
Oporto
Coimbra
Lisbon
Beja
ALGARVE
Braganza
Douro
Tagus
Guadiana
SPAIN
CASTILE
ARAGON
Corunna
Santiago
San Sebastian
Burgos
Tordesillas
Valladolid
Salamanca
Saragossa
Ebro
Huesca
Barcelona
Tarragona
Madrid
Toledo
Alcazar
Valencia
Cordova
Guadalquivir
Seville
Murcia
Alicante
Cadiz
Granada
GRANADA (1492)
Malaga
Almeria
Cartagena
Balearic Is.
Minorca
Majorca
Iviza
Tangier
Ceuta (Port.)
Melilla (Sp.)
Marsalquivir (Sp.)
Oran (Sp.)
SULTANATE OF FEZ (WATASIDS)
Peñon de Alger (Sp.)
Algiers
Bugia (Sp.)
SULTANATE OF ALGIERS
Bizerta
Tunis
SULTANATE OF TUNIS (HAFSIDS)

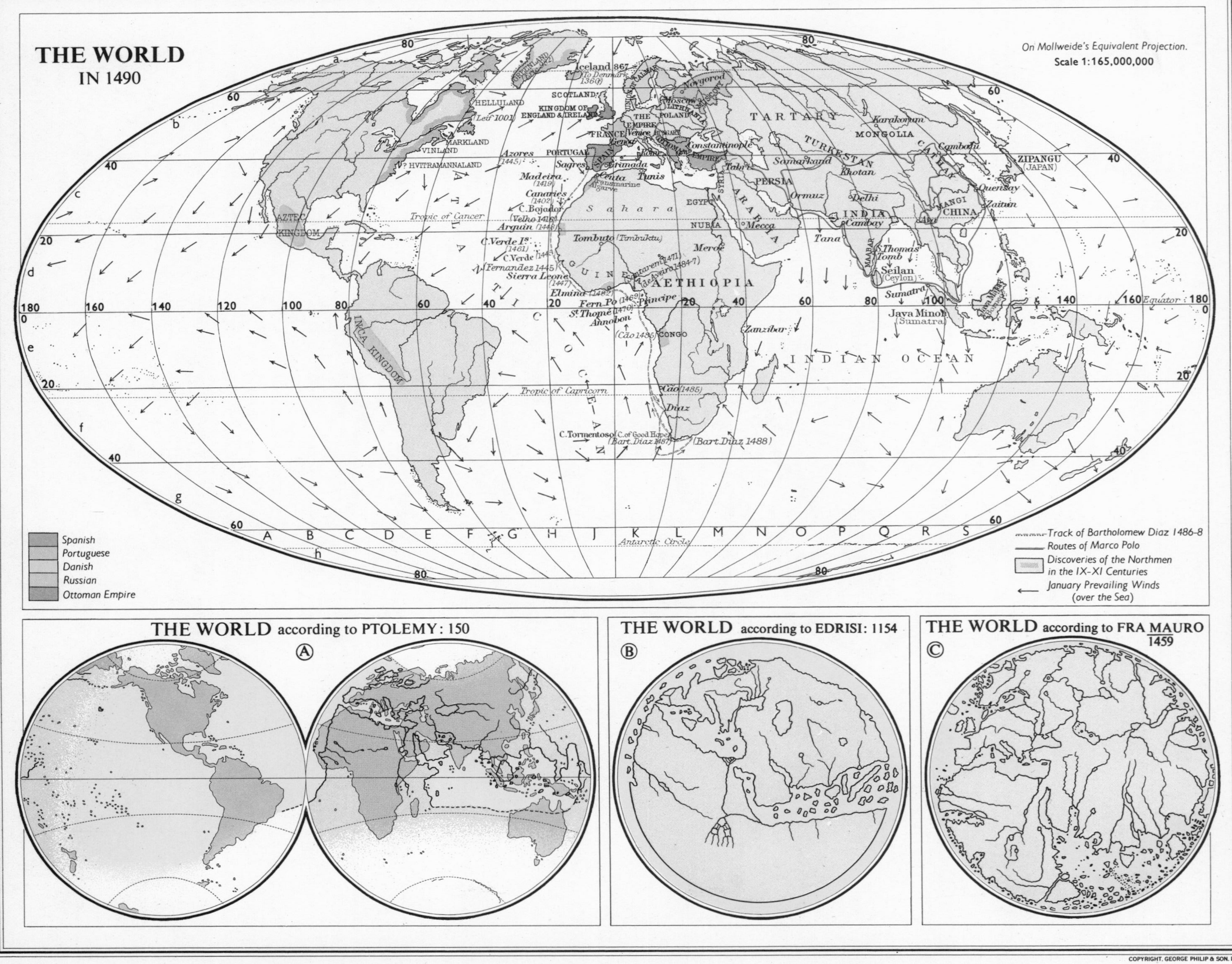
THE WORLD
IN 1490
On Mollweide's Equivalent Projection.
Scale 1:165,000,000
Spanish
Portuguese
Danish
Russian
Ottoman Empire
Track of Bartholomew Diaz 1486-8
Routes of Marco Polo
Discoveries of the Northmen in the IX-XI Centuries
January Prevailing Winds (over the Sea)
Iceland 867
SCOTLAND
KINGDOM OF ENGLAND & IRELAND
HELLULAND
Leif 1001
MARKLAND
VINLAND
? HVITRAMANNALAND
Azores (1445)
PORTUGAL
Sagres
SPAIN
FRANCE
THE EMPIRE
POLAND
Venice
HUNGARY
Genoa
Rome
Constantinople
Granada
Ceuta
Tunis
Madeira (1419)
Canaries (1402)
C. Bojador
Arguin
C. Verde Is.
Sierra Leone
Elmina
Fern. Po
St. Thomé
Annobon
Principe
CONGO
Zanzibar
C. Tormentoso
C. of Good Hope
(Bart. Diaz 1487)
(Bart. Diaz 1488)
Diaz
Tombuto (Timbuktu)
Sahara
GUINEA
AETHIOPIA
EGYPT
NUBIA
Meroe
ARABIA
Mecca
SYRIA
Tabriz
PERSIA
Ormuz
TARTARY
TURKESTAN
Samarkand
Khotan
Karakorum
MONGOLIA
CATHAY
Cambalu
ZIPANGU (JAPAN)
Quensay
Zaitun
MANGI
CHINA
Delhi
INDIA
Cambay
Tana
MAABAR
S. Thomas' Tomb
Seilan (Ceylon)
Sumatra
Java Minor (Sumatra)
INDIAN OCEAN
ATLANTIC OCEAN
AZTEC KINGDOM
INCA KINGDOM
Tropic of Cancer
Tropic of Capricorn
Equator
Antarctic Circle
A B C D E F G H J K L M N O P Q R S
THE WORLD according to PTOLEMY: 150
A
THE WORLD according to EDRISI: 1154
B
THE WORLD according to FRA MAURO 1459
C

ECCLESIASTICAL
ENGLAND
to the time of
HENRY VIII
Scale 1:3,000,000 (48 miles = 1 inch)
Statute Miles
0 10 20 30 40 50
The boundaries of Old Bishoprics in 1291 are shown in colours and named thus DURHAM
The boundaries of New Bishoprics (created by Henry VIII) are shown by broad red lines and named thus Chester
Dates of foundations of Dioceses thus 625
Boundary between Provinces of Canterbury and York
Archi-Episcopal Sees York
Episcopal Sees Ely
Parliamentary Abbeys represented in the House of Lords
Greater Monasteries, dissolved 1538-40
Other Monasteries
In many towns there were several Monastic Houses. The figure placed after the name represents the number.
ENGLISH DIOCESES
in the Anglo-Saxon Period
c.800
Scale 1:9,000,000 (150 miles = 1 inch)
Statute Miles
West from Greenwich
East from Greenwich
IRISH SEA
ENGLISH CHANNEL
Bristol Channel
Cardigan Bay
North Channel

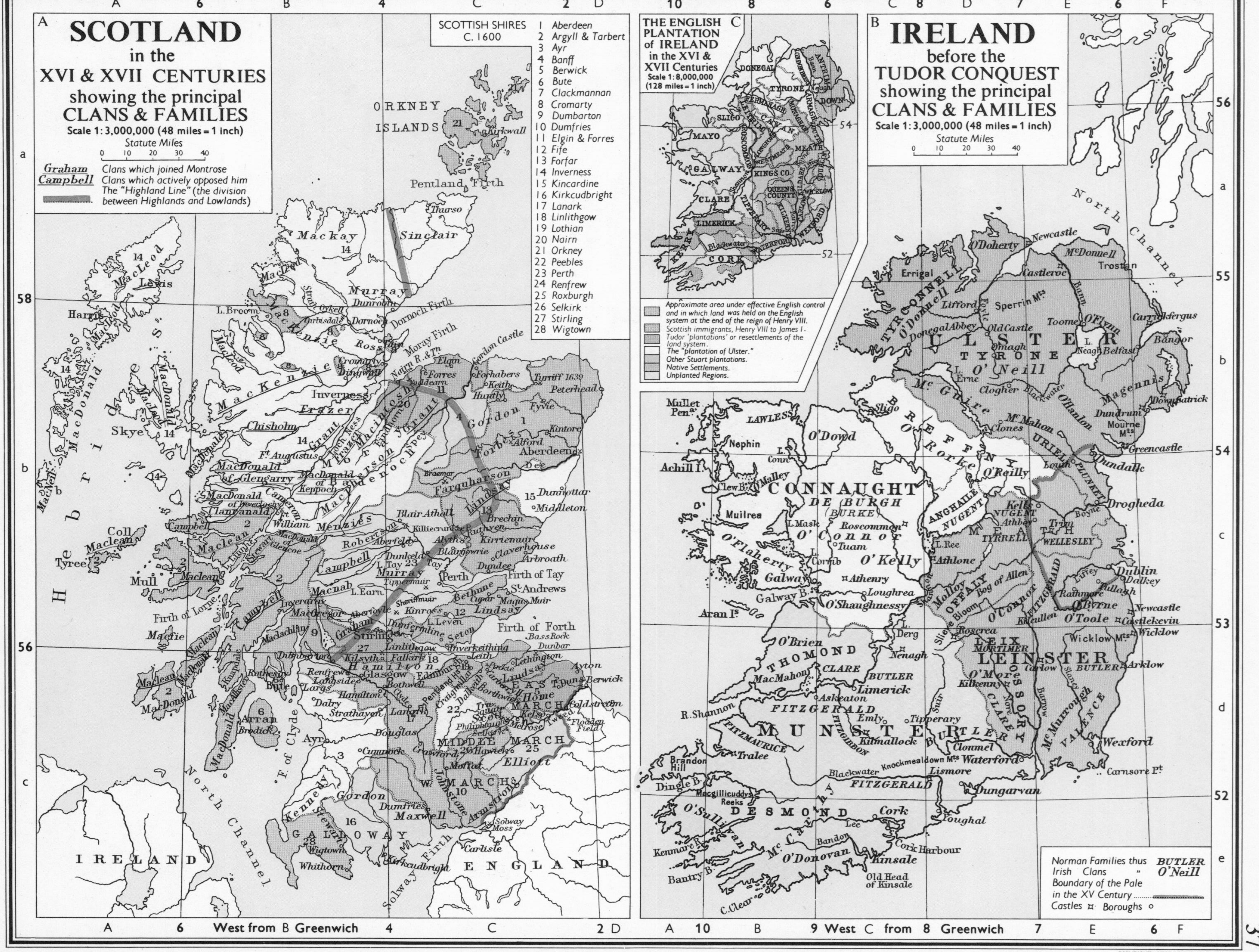

SCOTLAND in the XVI & XVII CENTURIES showing the principal CLANS & FAMILIES
Scale 1: 3,000,000 (48 miles = 1 inch)
Statute Miles
Graham — Clans which joined Montrose
Campbell — Clans which actively opposed him
The "Highland Line" (the division between Highlands and Lowlands)
SCOTTISH SHIRES C. 1600
1 Aberdeen
2 Argyll & Tarbert
3 Ayr
4 Banff
5 Berwick
6 Bute
7 Clackmannan
8 Cromarty
9 Dumbarton
10 Dumfries
11 Elgin & Forres
12 Fife
13 Forfar
14 Inverness
15 Kincardine
16 Kirkcudbright
17 Lanark
18 Linlithgow
19 Lothian
20 Nairn
21 Orkney
22 Peebles
23 Perth
24 Renfrew
25 Roxburgh
26 Selkirk
27 Stirling
28 Wigtown
THE ENGLISH PLANTATION of IRELAND in the XVI & XVII Centuries
Scale 1: 8,000,000 (128 miles = 1 inch)
Approximate area under effective English control and in which land was held on the English system at the end of the reign of Henry VIII.
Scottish immigrants, Henry VIII to James I.
Tudor 'plantations' or resettlements of the land system.
The "plantation of Ulster."
Other Stuart plantations.
Native Settlements.
Unplanted Regions.
IRELAND before the TUDOR CONQUEST showing the principal CLANS & FAMILIES
Scale 1: 3,000,000 (48 miles = 1 inch)
Statute Miles
Norman Families thus BUTLER
Irish Clans " O'Neill
Boundary of the Pale in the XV Century
Castles ⌑ Boroughs ○
West from B Greenwich
9 West C from 8 Greenwich

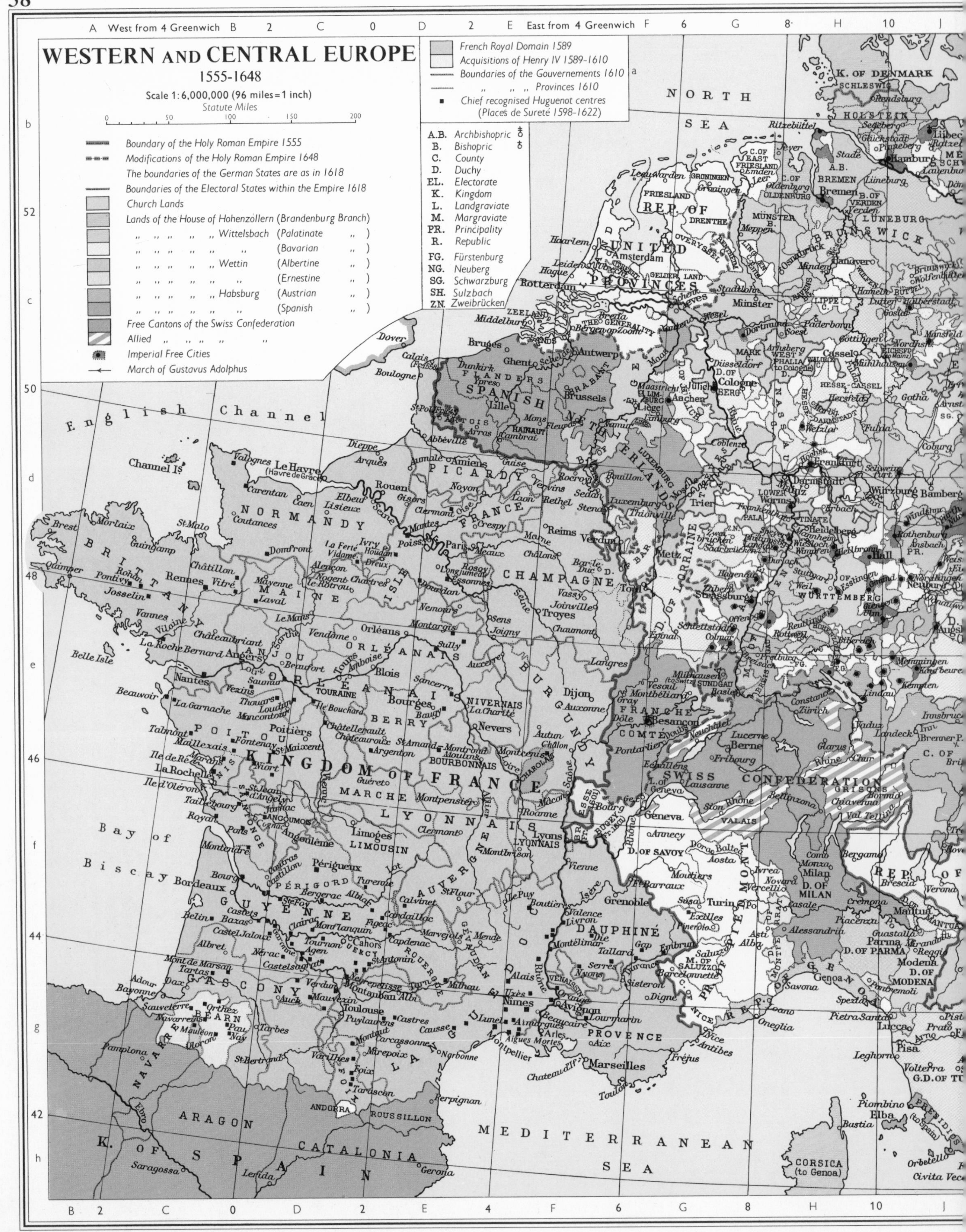
WESTERN AND CENTRAL EUROPE
1555-1648
Scale 1:6,000,000 (96 miles=1 inch)
Statute Miles
0 50 100 150 200
Boundary of the Holy Roman Empire 1555
Modifications of the Holy Roman Empire 1648
The boundaries of the German States are as in 1618
Boundaries of the Electoral States within the Empire 1618
Church Lands
Lands of the House of Hohenzollern (Brandenburg Branch)
" " " " " Wittelsbach (Palatinate ")
" " " " " " (Bavarian ")
" " " " " Wettin (Albertine ")
" " " " " " (Ernestine ")
" " " " " Habsburg (Austrian ")
" " " " " " (Spanish ")
Free Cantons of the Swiss Confederation
Allied " " " " "
Imperial Free Cities
March of Gustavus Adolphus
French Royal Domain 1589
Acquisitions of Henry IV 1589-1610
Boundaries of the Gouvernements 1610
" " " Provinces 1610
Chief recognised Huguenot centres
(Places de Sureté 1598-1622)
A.B. Archbishopric
B. Bishopric
C. County
D. Duchy
EL. Electorate
K. Kingdom
L. Landgraviate
M. Margraviate
PR. Principality
R. Republic
FG. Fürstenburg
NG. Neuberg
SG. Schwarzburg
SH. Sulzbach
ZN. Zweibrücken
West from 4 Greenwich
East from 4 Greenwich
NORTH SEA
English Channel
Bay of Biscay
MEDITERRANEAN SEA
KINGDOM OF FRANCE
SPANISH NETHERLANDS
UNITED PROVINCES
SWISS CONFEDERATION
K. OF SPAIN
ARAGON
CATALONIA
NORMANDY
BRITTANY
PICARDY
CHAMPAGNE
BURGUNDY
DAUPHINÉ
PROVENCE
LANGUEDOC
GUYENNE
GASCONY
POITOU
LYONNAIS
Paris
Lyons
Marseilles
Bordeaux
Toulouse
Geneva
Brussels
Antwerp
Amsterdam
Hamburg
Milan
CORSICA (to Genoa)

K. OF POLAND
GREAT POLAND
CUJAVIA
MAZOVIA
LITTLE POLAND
EAST PRUSSIA
WEST PRUSSIA
ERMELAND
LITH. G.D. OF LITHUANIA
D. OF POMERANIA
BRANDENBURG
SAXONY
D. OF SILESIA
LAUSITZ
K. OF BOHEMIA
M. OF MORAVIA
HUNGARY
A.D. OF AUSTRIA
D. OF STYRIA
D. OF CARINTHIA
D. OF CARNIOLA
C. OF GÖRZ
ISTRIA (to Venice)
CROATIA
SLAVONIA
IMPERIAL HUNGARY
TURKISH HUNGARY
OTTOMAN EMPIRE
BOSNIA
HERZEGOVINA
DALMATIA (to Venice)
MONTENEGRO
ADRIATIC SEA
PAPAL STATES
SAN MARINO
K. OF NAPLES
Königsberg
Danzig
Thorn
Warsaw
Cracow
Kalisz
Radom
Berlin
Frankfurt
Stettin
Breslau
Dresden
Prague
Olmütz
Brünn
Vienna
Pressburg
Graz
Buda
Pest
Gran
Raab
Szegedin
Mohacs
Agram
Laibach
Trieste
Zara
Spalato
Sarajevo
Mostar
Ragusa
Ancona
Rimini
Salzburg
Linz
Passau
RELIGIONS of CENTRAL EUROPE c.1618
Scale 1:18,000,000
Catholic
Lutheran
Calvinist
Protestant towns in Catholic surroundings
A
ALSACE-LORRAINE during the THIRTY YEARS WAR
Scale 1:3,000,000
Statute Miles
B
SPANISH NETHERLANDS
KINGDOM OF FRANCE
HOLY ROMAN EMPIRE
FRANCHE COMTÉ
MARGRAVIATE OF BADEN
SUNDGAU
Luxemburg
Trèves
Metz
Toul
Verdun
Nancy
Strassburg
Colmar
Mülhausen
Basle
Freiburg
Speyer
Church Lands
Habsburg Lands
Territory of Imperial Cities
Lands of Imperial Knights
Imperial Villages
Imperial Cities
Towns of the Alsatian League are underlined
ERNESTINE AND ALBERTINE LANDS IN SAXONY
Scale 1:3,500,000
Statute Miles
C
Albertine before 1547
Acquired by Albertine line from Ernestine line 1547 & 1554
Ernestine after 1554
Brandenburg
Electorate
Lausitz
Meissen
Thuringia
Reuss
Vogtland
Bohemia
Wittenberg
Leipzig
Dresden
Erfurt
Weimar
Jena
Gotha
Eisenach
Coburg
Magdeburg
COPYRIGHT, GEORGE PHILIP & SON, LTD.

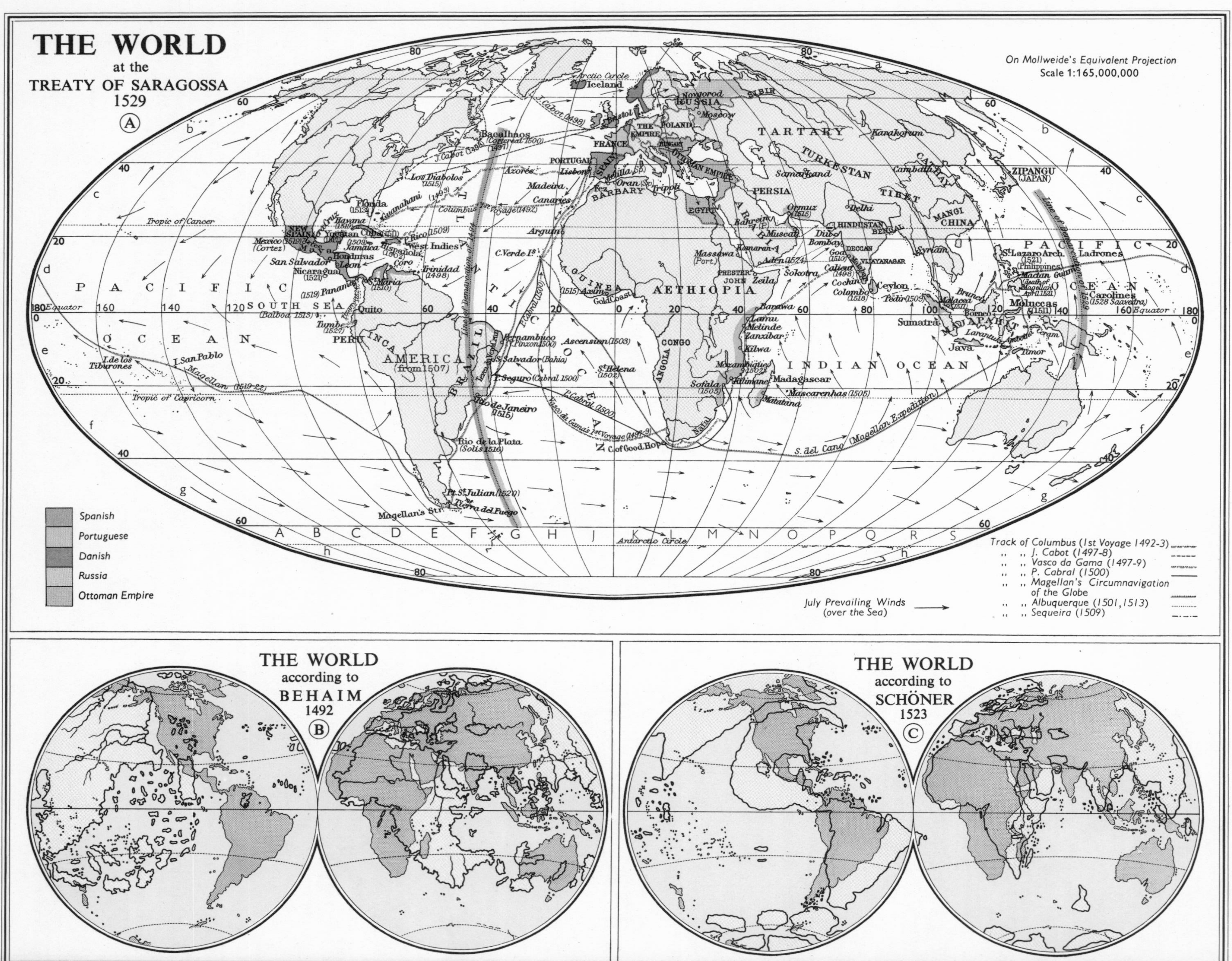
THE WORLD
at the
TREATY OF SARAGOSSA
1529
(A)
On Mollweide's Equivalent Projection
Scale 1:165,000,000
Spanish
Portuguese
Danish
Russia
Ottoman Empire
Track of Columbus (1st Voyage 1492-3)
,, ,, J. Cabot (1497-8)
,, ,, Vasco da Gama (1497-9)
,, ,, P. Cabral (1500)
,, ,, Magellan's Circumnavigation of the Globe
,, ,, Albuquerque (1501, 1513)
,, ,, Sequeira (1509)
July Prevailing Winds (over the Sea)
Arctic Circle
Iceland
Tropic of Cancer
Equator
Tropic of Capricorn
Antarctic Circle
PACIFIC OCEAN
ATLANTIC OCEAN
INDIAN OCEAN
SOUTH SEA
TARTARY
TURKESTAN
CATHAY
TIBET
PERSIA
ARABIA
AETHIOPIA
BARBARY
GUINEA
CONGO
ANGOLA
BRAZIL
AMERICA (from 1507)
PERU
INCA
NEW SPAIN
RUSSIA
POLAND
FRANCE
SPAIN
PORTUGAL
EGYPT
OTTOMAN EMPIRE
HINDUSTAN
BENGAL
MANGI
CHINA
ZIPANGU (JAPAN)
Line of Demarcation of 1494
Line of Demarcation of 1529
Magellan (1519-22)
Magellan's Str.
S. del Cano (Magellan Expedition)
Novgorod
Moscow
Karakorum
Samarkand
Ormuz (1515)
Delhi
Muscat
Diu
Bombay
Goa (1510)
Calicut (1498)
Cochin
Colombo (1518)
Ceylon
Sumatra
Malacca (1511)
Borneo
Java
Timor
Moluccas (1511)
Ladrones
Carolines (1528 Saavedra)
Madagascar
Mascarenhas (1505)
Sofala (1505)
Kilwa
Zanzibar
Melinde
Mozambique
Natal
C. of Good Hope
St. Helena (1502)
Ascension (1503)
Gold Coast
C. Verde Is.
Arguin
Canaries
Madeira
Azores
Lisbon
Bacalhaos
J. Cabot (1498)
Los Diabolos (1515)
West Indies
Trinidad (1498)
Florida (1513)
Havana
Mexico (Cortez)
San Salvador
Nicaragua (1521)
Honduras
Jamaica
Panama
Quito
Tumbe (1527)
Pernambuco
S. Salvador (Bahia)
Rio de Janeiro (1515)
Rio de la Plata (Solis 1516)
Pt. St. Julian (1520)
Tierra del Fuego
I. San Pablo
I. de los Tiburones
Massawa (Port.)
Zeila
Aden (1524)
Sokotra
Barawa
Syriam
Bruneo
Philippines
St. Lazaro Arch. (1521)
THE WORLD
according to
BEHAIM
1492
(B)
THE WORLD
according to
SCHÖNER
1523
(C)

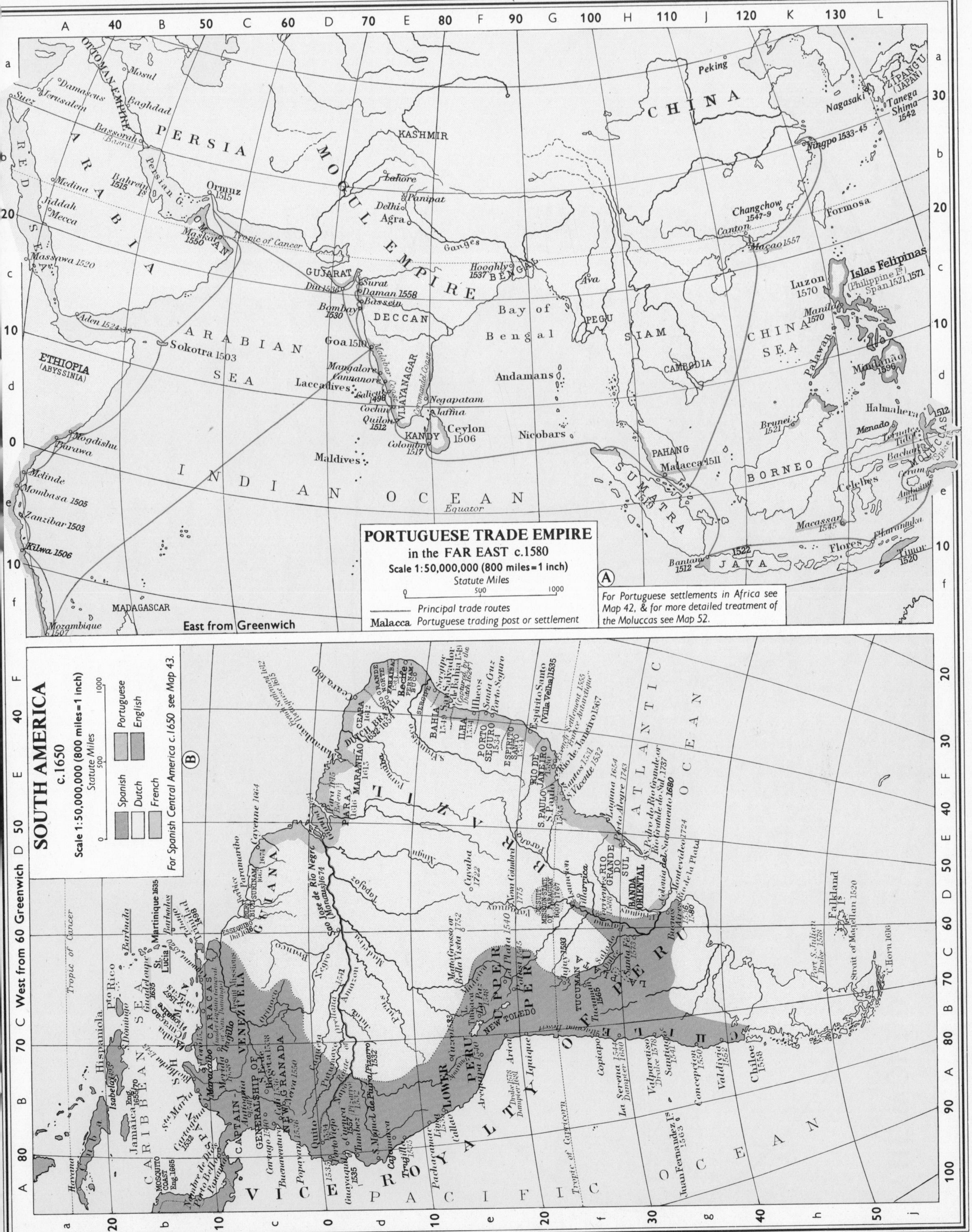
PORTUGUESE TRADE EMPIRE
in the FAR EAST c.1580
Scale 1:50,000,000 (800 miles=1 inch)
Statute Miles
0 500 1000
Principal trade routes
Malacca Portuguese trading post or settlement
For Portuguese settlements in Africa see Map 42, & for more detailed treatment of the Moluccas see Map 52.
East from Greenwich
A
PERSIA
ARABIA
MOGUL EMPIRE
CHINA
ARABIAN SEA
INDIAN OCEAN
Bay of Bengal
CHINA SEA
Equator
Tropic of Cancer
ETHIOPIA (ABYSSINIA)
MADAGASCAR
Ormuz 1515
Goa 1510
Diu 1536
Daman 1558
Bassein
Bombay 1530
Ceylon 1506
Colombo 1517
Malacca 1511
Maçao 1557
Ningpo 1533-45
Nagasaki
Tanega Shima 1642
Islas Felipinas (Philippine Is) Span.1521,1571
Mozambique 1507
Kilwa 1506
Zanzibar 1503
Mombasa 1505
Melinde
Sokotra 1503
Aden 1524-38
Massawa 1520
Timor 1520
Bantam 1512
SOUTH AMERICA
c.1650
Scale 1:50,000,000 (800 miles=1 inch)
Statute Miles
0 500 1000
Spanish
Portuguese
Dutch
English
French
For Spanish Central America c.1650 see Map 43.
B
West from 60 Greenwich
VICEROYALTY OF PERU
VICEROYALTY OF LA PLATA
BRAZIL
GUIANA
CARIBBEAN SEA
ATLANTIC OCEAN
PACIFIC OCEAN
Tropic of Capricorn
Tropic of Cancer

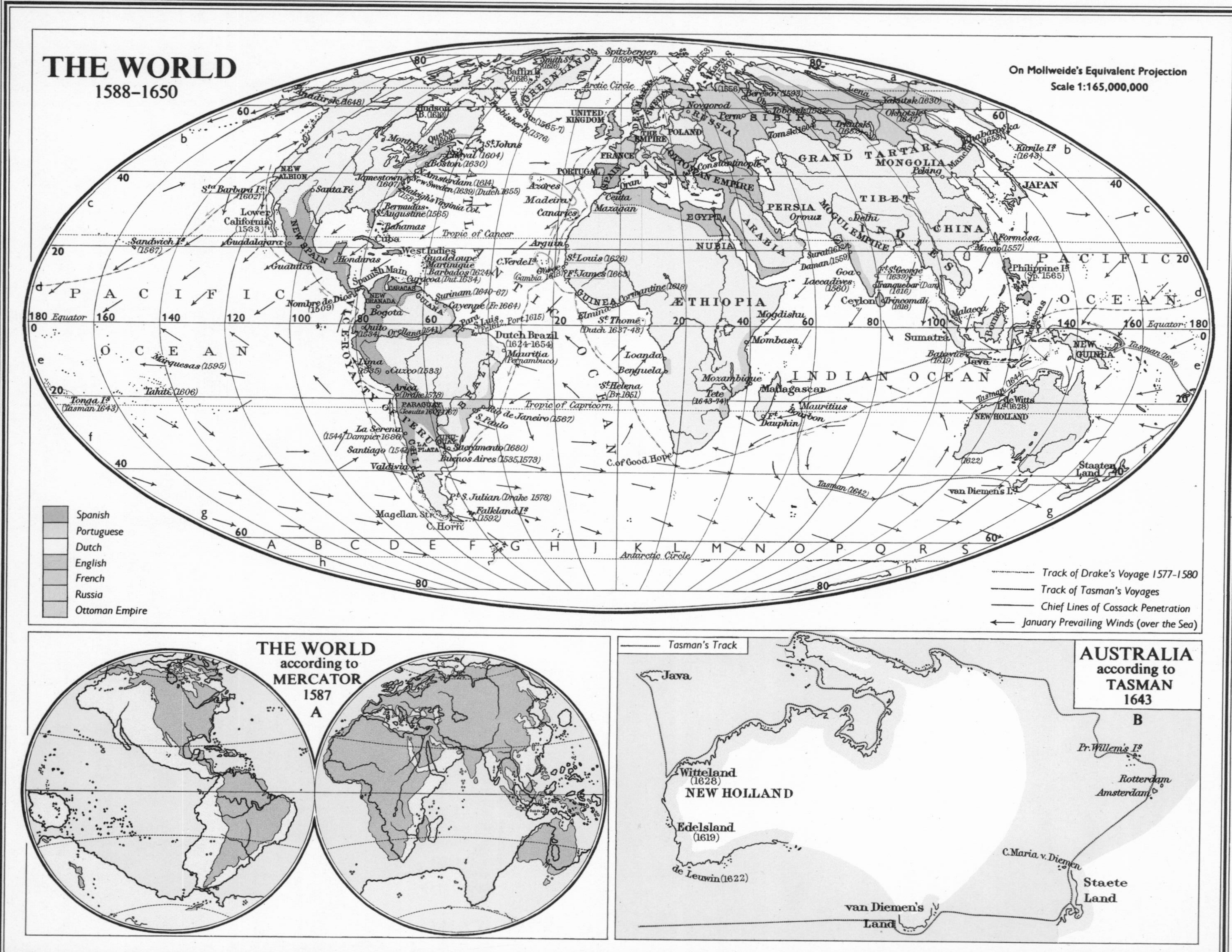
THE WORLD
1588–1650
On Mollweide's Equivalent Projection
Scale 1:165,000,000
Spanish
Portuguese
Dutch
English
French
Russia
Ottoman Empire
Track of Drake's Voyage 1577–1580
Track of Tasman's Voyages
Chief Lines of Cossack Penetration
January Prevailing Winds (over the Sea)
PACIFIC OCEAN
INDIAN OCEAN
NEW SPAIN
NEW ALBION
GREENLAND
UNITED KINGDOM
FRANCE
PORTUGAL
SPAIN
POLAND
RUSSIA
SIBIR
GRAND TARTARY
MONGOLIA
CHINA
TIBET
JAPAN
PERSIA
ARABIA
EGYPT
NUBIA
ÆTHIOPIA
GUINEA
OTTOMAN EMPIRE
MOGUL EMPIRE
INDIES
NEW GUINEA
NEW HOLLAND
Tropic of Cancer
Tropic of Capricorn
Equator
Arctic Circle
Antarctic Circle
C. of Good Hope
Magellan Str.
C. Horn
Dutch Brazil (1624–1654)
THE WORLD
according to
MERCATOR
1587
A
AUSTRALIA
according to
TASMAN
1643
B
Tasman's Track
Java
Witteland (1628)
NEW HOLLAND
Edelsland (1619)
de Leuwin (1622)
van Diemen's Land
C. Maria v. Diemen
Staete Land
Pr. Willem's Iˢ
Rotterdam
Amsterdam

A WEST INDIES AND CENTRAL AMERICA
showing the Dates of the Principal EUROPEAN SETTLEMENTS
Scale 1:25,000,000 (400 miles = 1 inch)
Statute Miles
0 100 200 300 400 500
Highlands over 3000 feet
" from 1200-3000 feet
Uplands " 600-1200 "
Lowlands " 0- 600 "
Mexican Silver Mines
West from 80 Greenwich
ATLANTIC OCEAN
GULF OF MEXICO
CARIBBEAN SEA
B POLITICAL DISTRIBUTION in 1650
C POLITICAL DISTRIBUTION in 1763
D POLITICAL DISTRIBUTION in 1855
Reference to the Three Inset Maps
Scale 1:50,000,000 (800 miles = 1 in.)
Spanish Territory effectively settled or controlled.
Spanish Territory claimed
British
French
Dutch
Danish & Swedish
Independent
United States

EXPLORATION OF
NORTH AMERICA
Scale 1: 35,000,000 (560 miles = 1 inch)
Statute Miles
0 200 400 600
EXPLORERS
Spanish
Ponce de Leon 1513
de Vaca 1528-36
de Soto 1539-42
Coronado 1540-42
Oñate 1598-1601, 1604
British
Hudson 1610-11
Baffin 1616
Foxe 1631
Hearne 1770-71
Cook 1778
Mackenzie 1789-93
Vancouver 1792-94
Ross 1829-32
Franklin 1845
French
Cartier 1534
Cartier 1535
Champlain 1603-15
Jolliet & Marquette 1673
La Salle 1679-81
La Vérendrye 1731-43
American
Lewis & Clark 1804-06
Pike 1806-07
Smith 1826-29
Frémont 1843-45
Others
Sverdrup 1898-1902
Stefansson 1913-18
ARCTIC OCEAN
Beaufort Bay
Greenland
Axel Heiberg I.
Ellesmere I.
Sverdrup Is.
Melville I.
Lancaster Sd.
Baffin Bay
Banks I.
Pr. of Wales I.
N. Somerset
Victoria I.
Boothia Pen.
Baffin Island
Davis Strait
Arctic Circle
Melville Pen.
Cumberland Sd.
Frobisher B.
Southampton I.
Hudson Str.
Ungava B.
Mackenzie
Ft. Simpson
Gt. Slave L.
Dubawnt L.
HUDSON BAY CO. TERRITORY
Labrador
Belle Isle
Newfoundland
C. Bonavista
C. Race
Ft. Chipewyan
Peace
Athabasca L.
Hudson Bay
Churchill
Port Nelson
York Factory
Nelson
Queen Charlotte Is.
Ft. George
James B.
Anticosti I.
C. Breton I.
Pr. Edward I.
Cumberland House
Yellowhead P.
Kicking Horse P.
Fraser
Vancouver I.
Ft. Victoria
L. Winnipeg
Ft. Maurepas
Ft. Dauphin
Crows Nest P.
Columbia
Ft. La Reine
Grand Portage
L. Superior
Sault Ste. Marie
Ottawa
Quebec (Stadacona)
Montreal (Hochelaga)
L. Champlain
Mandan Village
Ft. Vancouver
Snake
Ft. Boise
Ft. Hall
Gt. Salt L.
South P.
N. Platte
Utah L.
Wisconsin
L. Michigan
Huron
Georgian B.
L. Ontario
L. Oneida
Erie
Missouri
Illinois
St. Louis
ATLANTIC OCEAN
Sacramento
Kansas
Qivira
Las Vegas
Colorado
Pueblo
Arkansas
Santa Fé
San Diego
Gila
Llano Estacado
Mississippi
Alabama
St. Augustine
El Paso
Pecos
Tampa B.
Rio Grande
S. Antonio B.
Tropic of Cancer
Chihuahua
Sinaloa
Gulf of Mexico
Compostela
Caribbean Sea
PACIFIC OCEAN
ROCKY MOUNTAINS
West from Greenwich

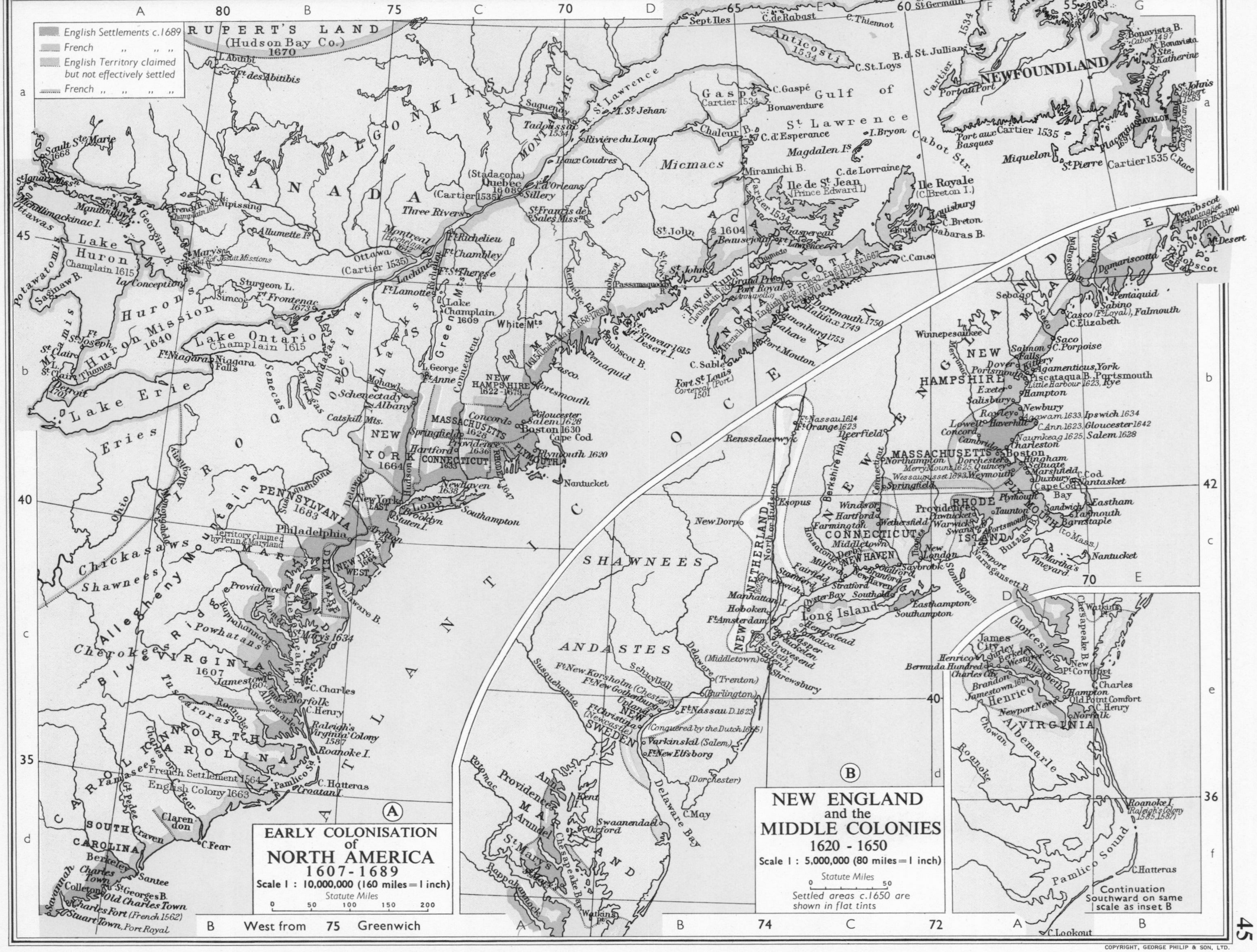

EARLY COLONISATION of NORTH AMERICA 1607-1689
Scale 1 : 10,000,000 (160 miles = 1 inch)
Statute Miles 0 50 100 150 200
West from 75 Greenwich
English Settlements c.1689
French " " "
English Territory claimed but not effectively settled
French " " " "
NEW ENGLAND and the MIDDLE COLONIES 1620 - 1650
Scale 1 : 5,000,000 (80 miles = 1 inch)
Statute Miles 0 50
Settled areas c.1650 are shown in flat tints
Continuation Southward on same scale as inset B
RUPERT'S LAND (Hudson Bay Co.) 1670
CANADA
ALGONKINS
MONTAGNAIS
NEWFOUNDLAND
Gulf of St Lawrence
Anticosti 1534
ACADIA
NOVA SCOTIA
Micmacs
Lake Huron
Lake Ontario
Lake Erie
Hurons
Huron Mission 1640
IROQUOIS
Senecas
Eries
NEW YORK 1664
PENNSYLVANIA 1683
MASSACHUSETTS 1628
CONNECTICUT 1633
NEW HAMPSHIRE 1622-1679
MAINE
DELAWARE
NEW JERSEY
MARYLAND
VIRGINIA 1607
NORTH CAROLINA
SOUTH CAROLINA
Allegheny Mountains
Blue Ridge
Chickasaws
Shawnees
Cherokees
Tuscaroras
ATLANTIC OCEAN
NEW NETHERLAND
NEW SWEDEN
ANDASTES
SHAWNEES
NEW ENGLAND
RHODE ISLAND
PLYMOUTH
NEW HAVEN
Long Island
Delaware Bay
Chesapeake B.
Pamlico Sound
Quebec 1608
Montreal
Boston 1630
Philadelphia
Jamestown 1607

THE NETHERLANDS
POLITICAL DISTRIBUTION
in the later
MIDDLE AGES
Scale 1:5,000,000 (80 miles=1 inch)
Statute Miles
0 40 80
Boundary of the Empire
C
FRIESLAND
HOLLAND
BPRIC OF UTRECHT
COUNTY OF GUELDERS
BP OF UTRECHT
TECKLENBURG
MÜNSTER
BISHOPRIC
BARONY OF BREDA
DUCHY OF BRABANT
C. OF CLEVE
C. OF MARK
ARCHBPRIC OF COLOGNE
DUCHY OF BERG
COUNTY OF FLANDERS
COUNTY OF LIMBURG
DUCHY OF JULIERS
COUNTY OF HAINAUT
COUNTY OF NAMUR
BPRIC OF CAMBRAI
DUCHY OF LUXEMBURG
ARCHBISHOPRIC OF TREVES
FRANCE
THE NETHERLANDS
IN THE XVII. CENTURY
showing also the
PRINCIPAL BATTLEFIELDS
Scale 1:2,500,000 (40 miles=1 inch)
Statute Miles
0 25 50
Spanish Territory
The United Provinces
French Acquisitions
Barrier Fortresses
A
Terschelling
Ameland
Vlieland
Texel
Helder
EAST FRIESLAND
Emden
GRONINGEN
Groningen
Leeuwarden
FRIESLAND
DRENTHE
Coevorden
ZUIDER ZEE
HOLLAND
Amsterdam
Haarlem
Leyden
The Hague
Delft
Rotterdam
Utrecht
UTRECHT
GELDERLAND
OVERYSSEL
Zwolle
Deventer
Zutphen
Arnhem
Nimwegen
BENTHEIM
CLEVE
Cleve
Wesel
Duisburg
ZEELAND
Walcheren
Middelburg
Flushing
THE GENERALITY LANDS
Breda
Bergen op Zoom
Antwerp
Mechlin
Bruges
Ghent
Ostend
Dunkirk
Gravelines
Calais
Boulogne
FLANDERS
Ypres
Lille
Tournai
ARTOIS
Arras
Douai
Cambrai
CAMBRESIS
HAINAUT
Mons
Valenciennes
Malplaquet
BRABANT
Brussels
Waterloo
Louvain
Namur
Charleroi
BISHOPRIC OF LIÈGE
Liège
Maestricht
JÜLICH
Aix-la-Chapelle
Cologne
Düsseldorf
BERG
LIMBURG
LUXEMBURG
Luxemburg
Sedan
Treves
Metz
Verdun
Nancy
FRANCE
ENGLAND
Meuse
Rhine
Moselle
CAMPAIGN OF WATERLOO
Scale 1:1,000,000
Statute Miles
0 5 10
Main Roads
Fortresses
B
Brussels
Louvain
Waterloo
Mt. St. Jean
La Haye Sainte
Wavre
La Belle Alliance
Plancenoit
Genappe
Nivelles
Quatre Bras
Ligny
Fleurus
Gembloux
Namur
Mons
Charleroi
Binche
Soignies
to Liege
East from Greenwich

EUROPE
after the
PEACE OF WESTPHALIA
1648
Scale 1: 15,000,000 (240 miles=1 inch)
Statute Miles
0 100 200 300
Spanish Dominions
Austrian Dominions
Brandenburg-Prussia
Swedish Dominions
Church Lands
Boundary of the Empire
West from 5 Greenwich
East from 10 Greenwich
ATLANTIC OCEAN
NORTH SEA
BALTIC SEA
MEDITERRANEAN SEA
BLACK SEA
ADRIATIC SEA
IRELAND
SCOTLAND
ENGLAND
WALES
NORWAY
DENMARK
SWEDEN
GOTHLAND
HALLAND
SCANIA
BLEKINGE (to Sw. 1658)
(to Sweden 1658-60)
FINLAND
CARELIA
INGRIA
ESTHONIA
LIVONIA
KURLAND
RUSSIA
LITHUANIA
PODLESIA
POLAND
VOLHYNIA
PODOLIA
GALICIA
LITTLE POLAND
GREAT POLAND
EAST PRUSSIA
WEST PRUSSIA
E. POMERANIA
MECKLENBURG
BRANDENBURG
HANOVER
HESSE
ELECTORATE OF SAXONY
SAXON STATES
SILESIA
BOHEMIA
MORAVIA
UPP. PALATINATE
BAVARIA
AUSTRIA
STYRIA
CARINTHIA
CARNIOLA
TYROL
SWITZERLAND
UNITED PROVS.
SPAN. NETHERLANDS
LORRAINE
FRANCHE COMTÉ (Sp.)
FRANCE
LANGUEDOC
SAVOY
PIEDMONT
REP. OF VENICE
TUSCANY
PAPAL STATES
KINGDOM OF THE TWO SICILIES (to Spain)
Corsica (to Genoa)
Sardinia (to Spain)
Sicily
Malta (Knights of St. John)
SPAIN
PORTUGAL
NAVARRE
ARAGON
CATALONIA
ROUSSILLON
Balearic Isles
HUNGARY
TRANSYLVANIA
MOLDAVIA
WALLACHIA
JEDISAN
BESSARABIA
DOBRUJA
OTTOMAN EMPIRE
SLAVONIA
CROATIA
BOSNIA
SERVIA
MONTENEGRO
ALBANIA
BULGARIA
RUMELIA
GREECE
MOREA
Ionian Is. (to Venice)
Crete (to Venice)
PASHALIK OF ALGERIA
P. OF TUNIS
Moscow
Stockholm
Copenhagen
Amsterdam
London
Paris
Berlin
Vienna
Prague
Warsaw
Cracow
Kiev
Madrid
Lisbon
Rome
Naples
Venice
Milan
Florence
Genoa
Constantinople
Pest
Buda
Belgrade
Budapest

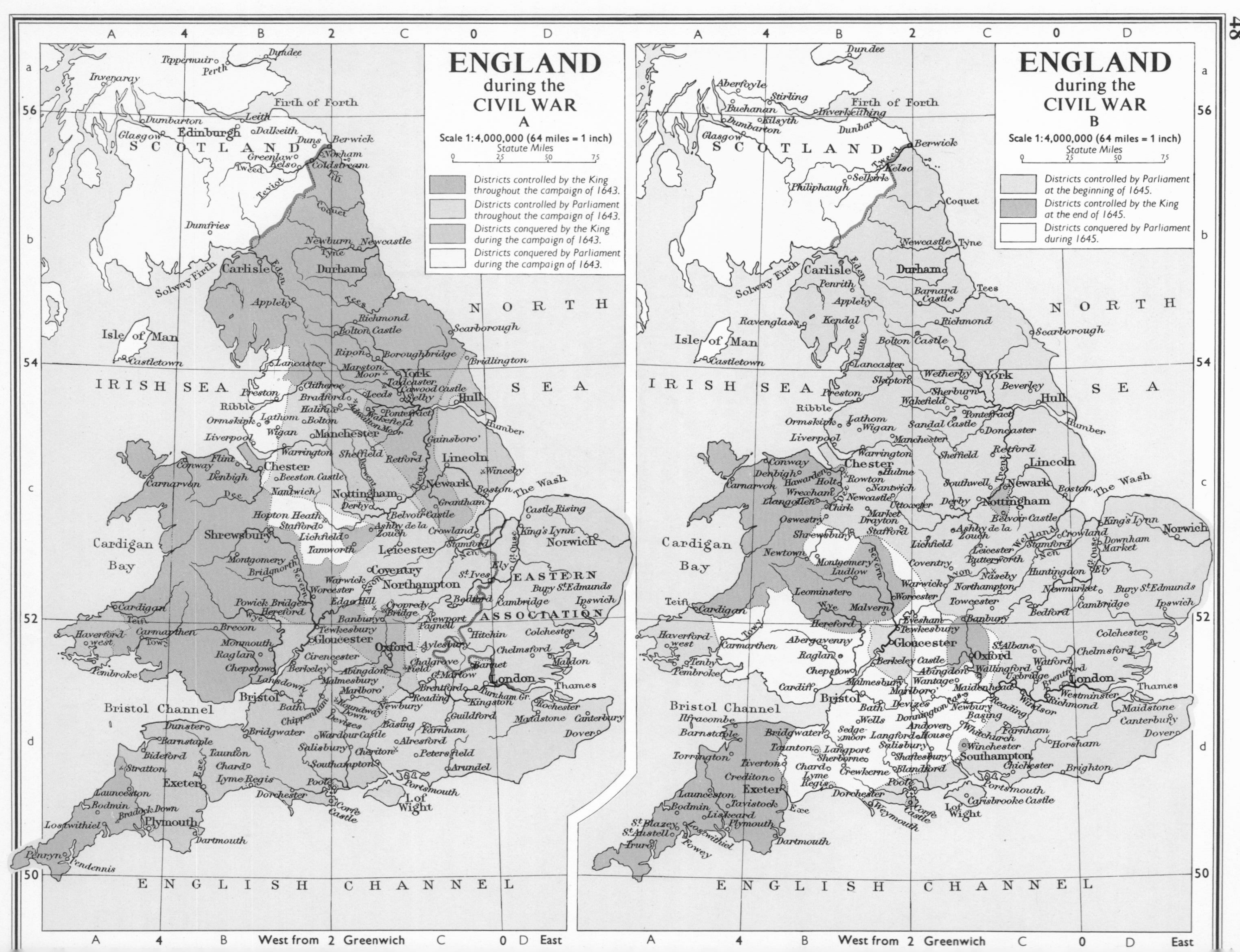
ENGLAND
during the
CIVIL WAR
A
Scale 1:4,000,000 (64 miles = 1 inch)
Statute Miles
0 25 50 75
Districts controlled by the King throughout the campaign of 1643.
Districts controlled by Parliament throughout the campaign of 1643.
Districts conquered by the King during the campaign of 1643.
Districts conquered by Parliament during the campaign of 1643.
ENGLAND
during the
CIVIL WAR
B
Scale 1:4,000,000 (64 miles = 1 inch)
Statute Miles
0 25 50 75
Districts controlled by Parliament at the beginning of 1645.
Districts controlled by the King at the end of 1645.
Districts conquered by Parliament during 1645.
SCOTLAND
NORTH SEA
IRISH SEA
ENGLISH CHANNEL
Bristol Channel
Cardigan Bay
EASTERN ASSOCIATION
West from 2 Greenwich
East

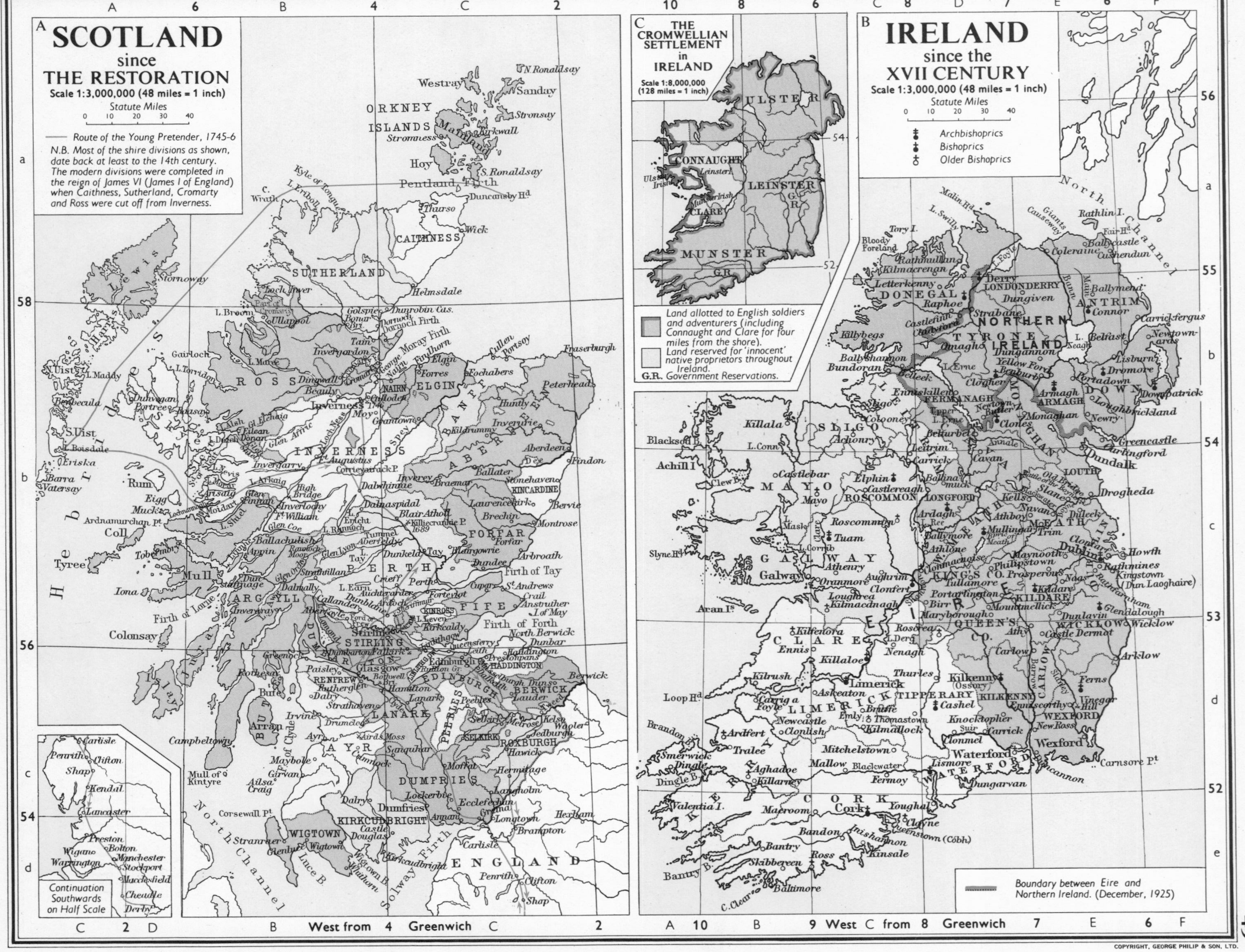
A SCOTLAND since THE RESTORATION
Scale 1:3,000,000 (48 miles = 1 inch)
Statute Miles
0 10 20 30 40
Route of the Young Pretender, 1745-6
N.B. Most of the shire divisions as shown, date back at least to the 14th century. The modern divisions were completed in the reign of James VI (James I of England) when Caithness, Sutherland, Cromarty and Ross were cut off from Inverness.
Continuation Southwards on Half Scale
West from 4 Greenwich
C THE CROMWELLIAN SETTLEMENT in IRELAND
Scale 1:8,000,000 (128 miles = 1 inch)
Land allotted to English soldiers and adventurers (including Connaught and Clare for four miles from the shore).
Land reserved for 'innocent' native proprietors throughout Ireland.
G.R. Government Reservations.
B IRELAND since the XVII CENTURY
Scale 1:3,000,000 (48 miles = 1 inch)
Statute Miles
0 10 20 30 40
Archbishoprics
Bishoprics
Older Bishoprics
Boundary between Eire and Northern Ireland. (December, 1925)
9 West C from 8 Greenwich

CENTRAL & EASTERN EUROPE in 1667

Scale 1:12,000,000 (192 miles=1 inch)

Statute Miles

0 50 100 200 300

- Austrian Dominions
- Spanish Dominions
- Hohenzollern Dominions (Brandenburg-Prussia)
- Swedish Dominions
- Church Lands
- Boundary of the Empire

CRETE (To Venice 1212 Turk. 1669) On same scale

CENTRAL & EASTERN EUROPE in 1795

Scale 1:12,000,000 (192 miles = 1 inch)

Statute Miles

Austrian Dominions
Kingdom of Prussia
Swedish Dominions
Church Lands
Boundary of the Empire

CRETE (Turkish 1669) On same scale

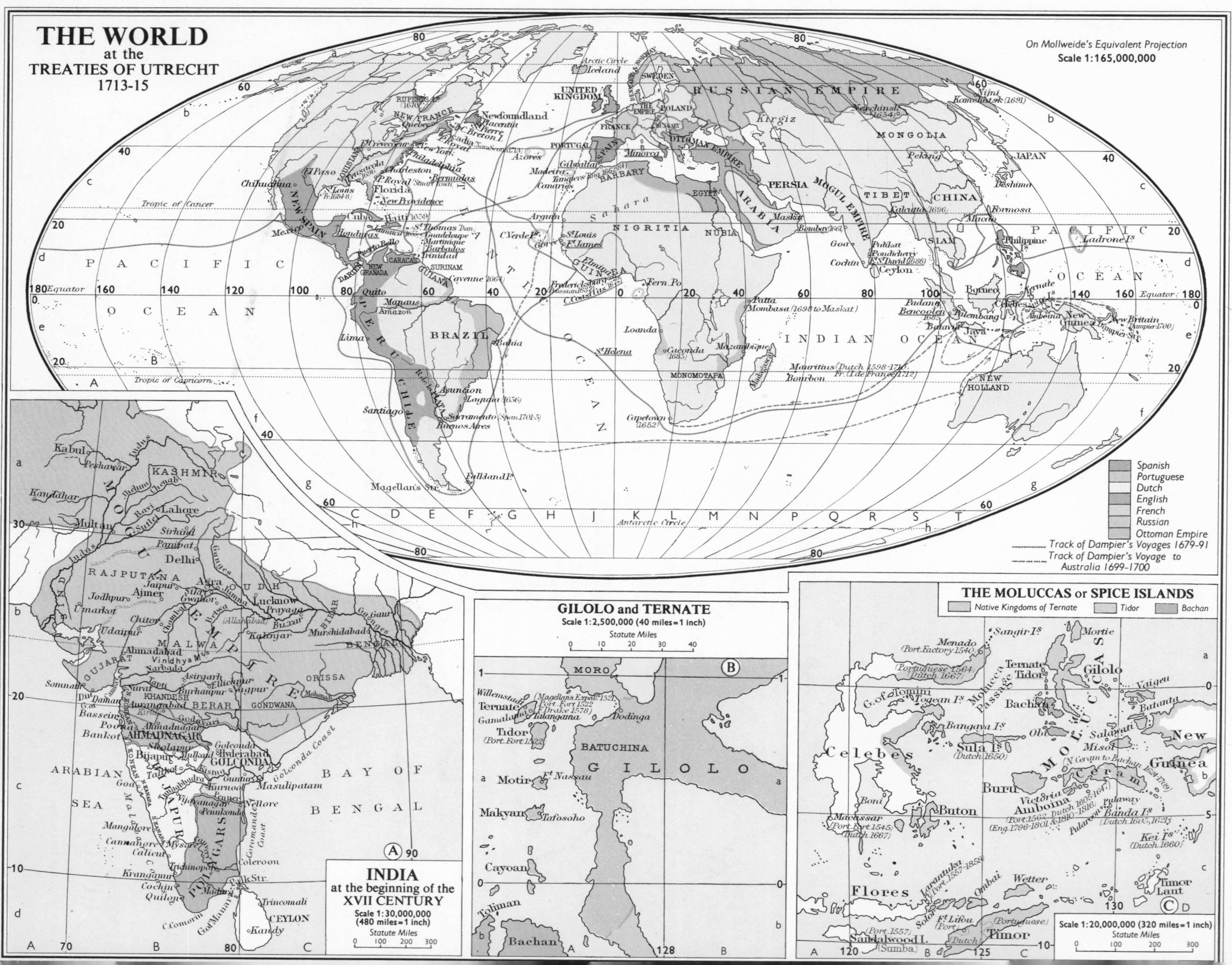
THE WORLD
at the
TREATIES OF UTRECHT
1713-15
On Mollweide's Equivalent Projection
Scale 1:165,000,000
Spanish
Portuguese
Dutch
English
French
Russian
Ottoman Empire
Track of Dampier's Voyages 1679-91
Track of Dampier's Voyage to Australia 1699-1700
RUSSIAN EMPIRE
MONGOLIA
CHINA
TIBET
JAPAN
PERSIA
MOGUL EMPIRE
ARABIA
OTTOMAN EMPIRE
NIGRITIA
NUBIA
BRAZIL
PERU
CHILE
NEW SPAIN
NEW FRANCE
NEW HOLLAND
PACIFIC OCEAN
INDIAN OCEAN
ATLANTIC OCEAN
INDIA
at the beginning of the
XVII CENTURY
Scale 1:30,000,000
(480 miles=1 inch)
Statute Miles
BAY OF BENGAL
ARABIAN SEA
GILOLO and TERNATE
Scale 1:2,500,000 (40 miles=1 inch)
Statute Miles
THE MOLUCCAS or SPICE ISLANDS
Native Kingdoms of Ternate
Tidor
Bachan
Scale 1:20,000,000 (320 miles=1 inch)
Statute Miles

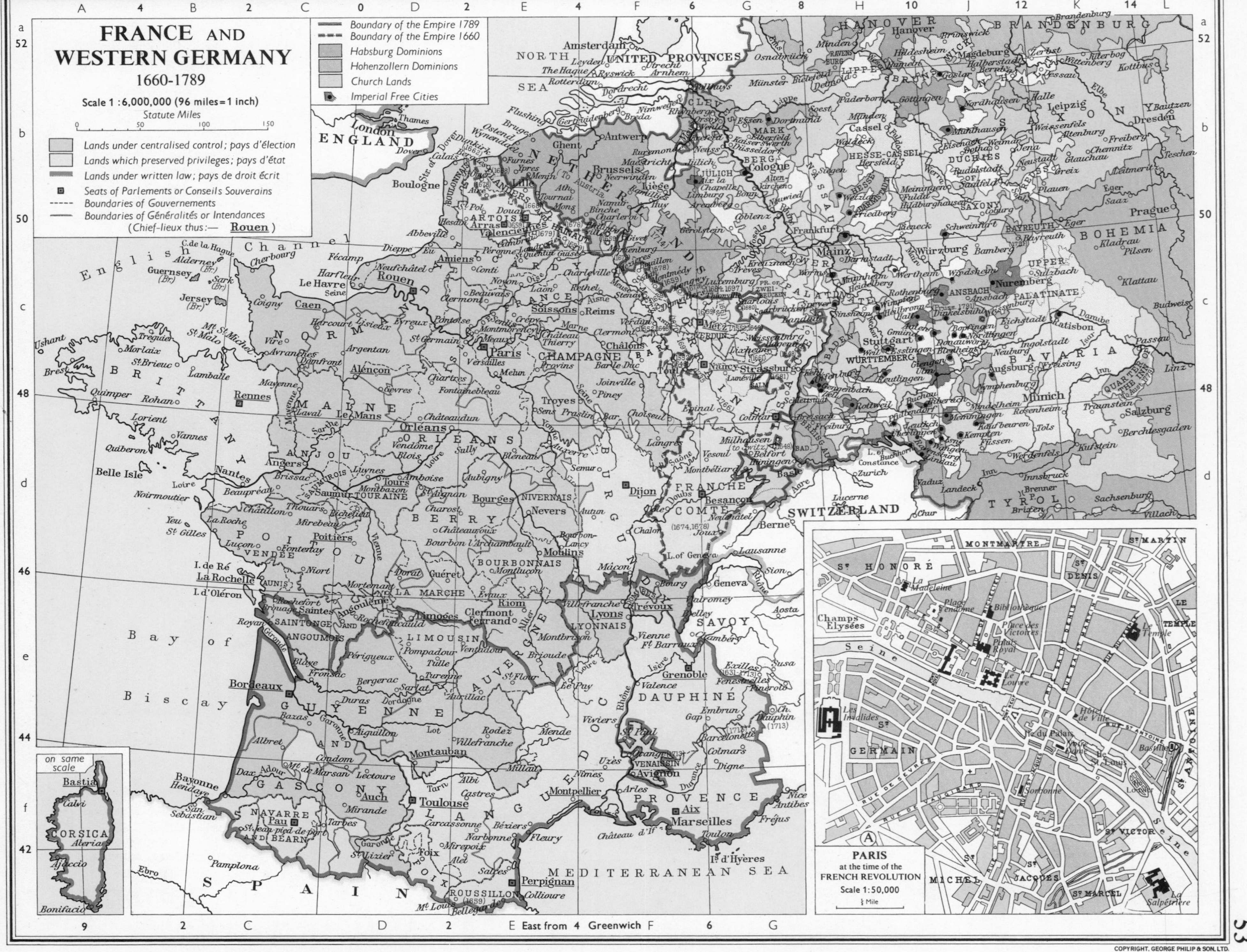

FRANCE AND WESTERN GERMANY
1660-1789
Scale 1 : 6,000,000 (96 miles = 1 inch)
Statute Miles
0 50 100 150
Lands under centralised control; pays d'élection
Lands which preserved privileges; pays d'état
Lands under written law; pays de droit écrit
Seats of Parlements or Conseils Souverains
Boundaries of Gouvernements
Boundaries of Généralités or Intendances
(Chief-lieux thus:— Rouen)
Boundary of the Empire 1789
Boundary of the Empire 1660
Habsburg Dominions
Hohenzollern Dominions
Church Lands
Imperial Free Cities
PARIS
at the time of the
FRENCH REVOLUTION
Scale 1:50,000
on same scale
CORSICA
East from 4 Greenwich

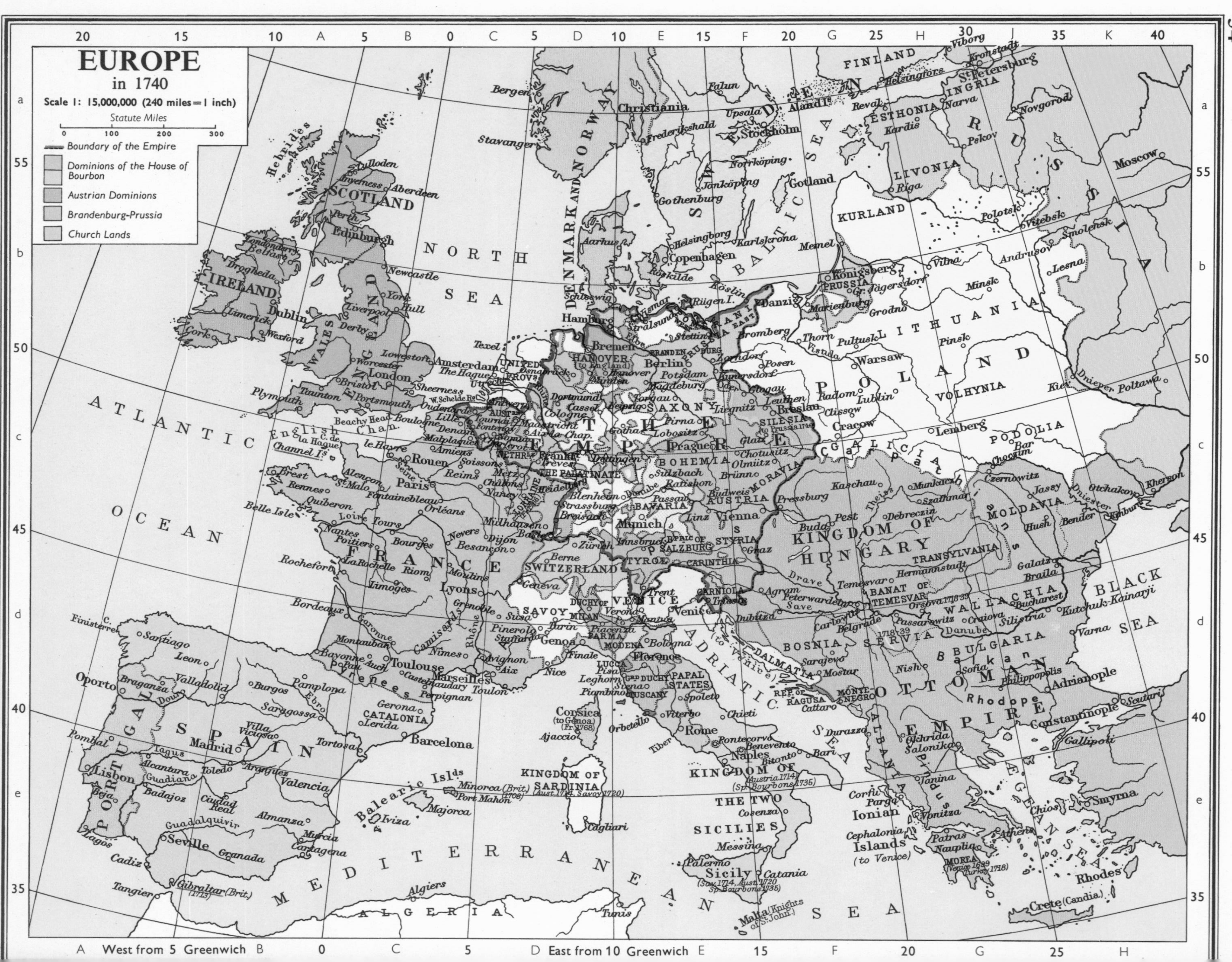

EUROPE
in 1740
Scale 1: 15,000,000 (240 miles = 1 inch)
Statute Miles
0 100 200 300
Boundary of the Empire
Dominions of the House of Bourbon
Austrian Dominions
Brandenburg-Prussia
Church Lands
ATLANTIC OCEAN
NORTH SEA
BALTIC SEA
BLACK SEA
MEDITERRANEAN SEA
ADRIATIC SEA
AEGEAN SEA
West from 5 Greenwich
East from 10 Greenwich

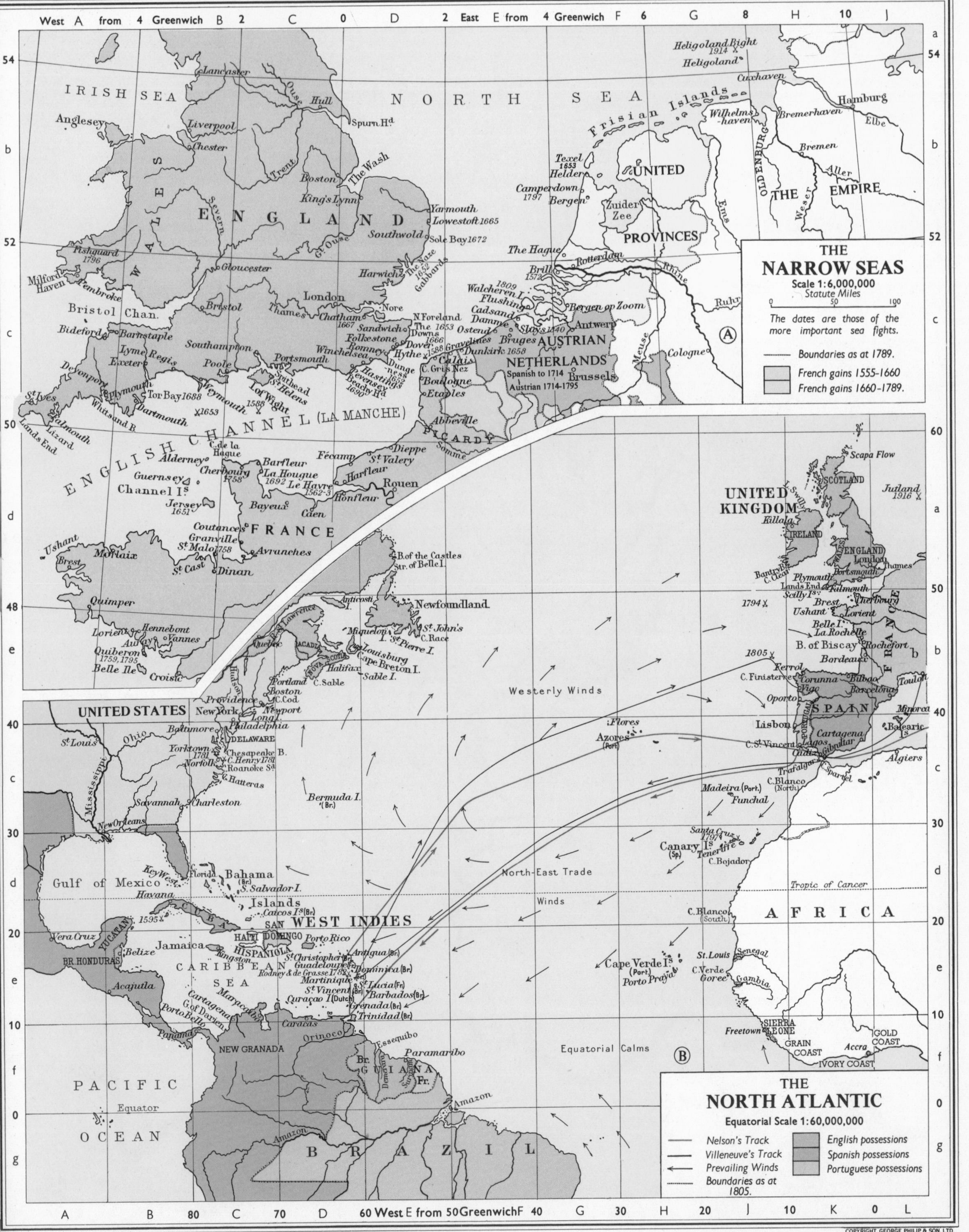
THE
NARROW SEAS
Scale 1:6,000,000
Statute Miles
The dates are those of the more important sea fights.
Boundaries as at 1789.
French gains 1555-1660
French gains 1660-1789.
A
IRISH SEA
NORTH SEA
ENGLISH CHANNEL (LA MANCHE)
ENGLAND
WALES
FRANCE
UNITED PROVINCES
AUSTRIAN NETHERLANDS
THE EMPIRE
THE
NORTH ATLANTIC
Equatorial Scale 1:60,000,000
Nelson's Track
Villeneuve's Track
Prevailing Winds
Boundaries as at 1805.
English possessions
Spanish possessions
Portuguese possessions
B
UNITED STATES
UNITED KINGDOM
SPAIN
AFRICA
BRAZIL
WEST INDIES
CARIBBEAN SEA
Gulf of Mexico
PACIFIC OCEAN
Westerly Winds
North-East Trade Winds
Equatorial Calms
Tropic of Cancer
Equator

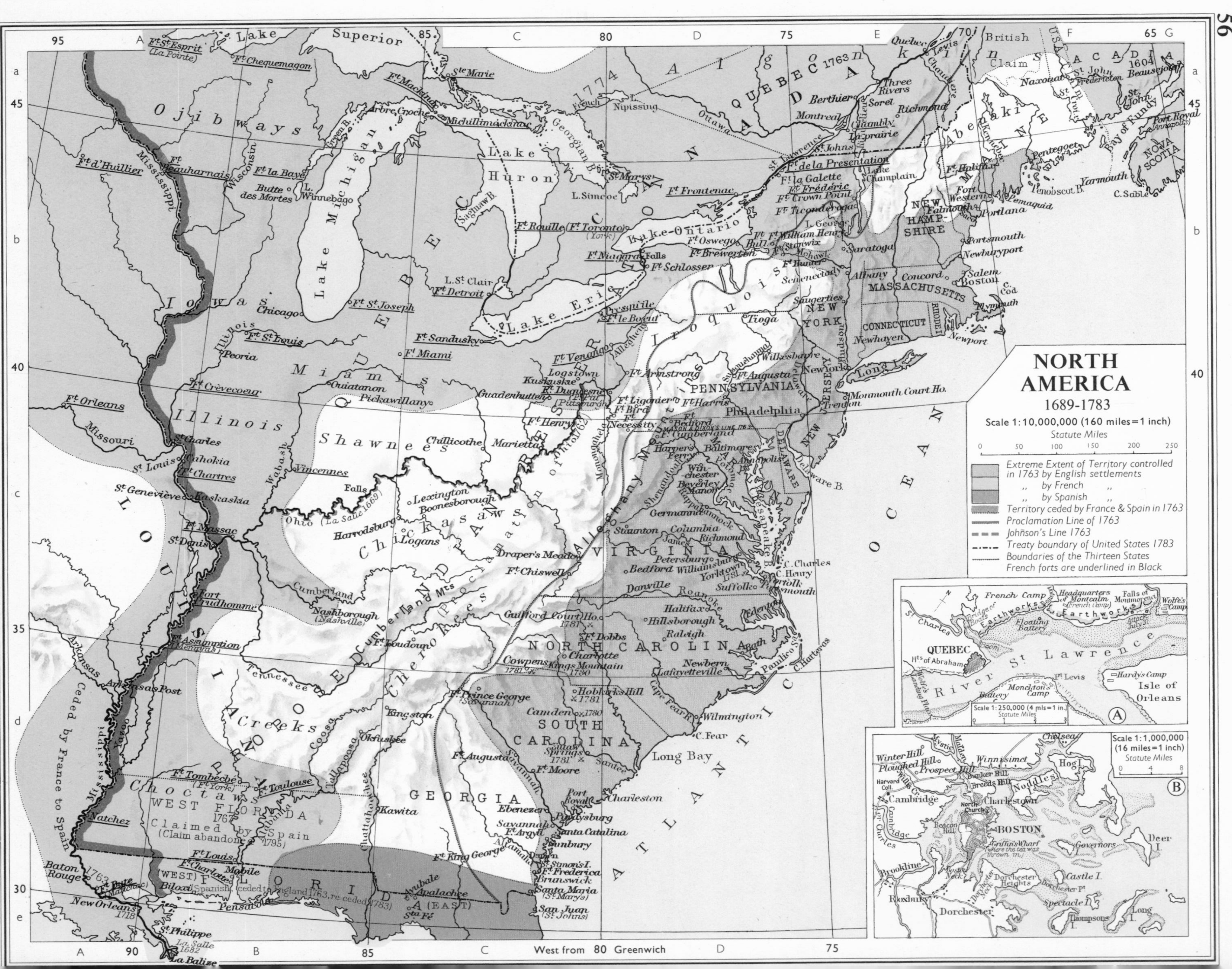
NORTH AMERICA
1689-1783
Scale 1:10,000,000 (160 miles=1 inch)
Statute Miles
0 50 100 150 200 250
Extreme Extent of Territory controlled in 1763 by English settlements
,, by French ,,
,, by Spanish ,,
Territory ceded by France & Spain in 1763
Proclamation Line of 1763
Johnson's Line 1763
Treaty boundary of United States 1783
Boundaries of the Thirteen States
French forts are underlined in Black
Scale 1:250,000 (4 mls=1 in.)
Statute Miles
QUEBEC
Hts of Abraham
French Camp
Headquarters of Montcalm (French camp)
Falls of Montmorency
Wolfe's Camp
Earthworks
Floating Battery
Attack July 31
St Charles
Wolfe's Landing Place
River St Lawrence
Pt Levis
Monckton's Camp
Battery
Hardy's Camp
Isle of Orleans
A
Scale 1:1,000,000 (16 miles=1 inch)
Statute Miles
0 4 8
B
Winter Hill
Ploughed Hill
Prospect Hill
Winnisimet
Chelsea
Mystic
Hog I.
Harvard Coll.
Cambridge
Bunker Hill
Breeds Hill
Noddles I.
Charlestown
North Church
Beacon Hill
BOSTON
Griffin's Wharf (where the tea was thrown in)
Governors I.
Deer I.
Brookline
Roxbury
Dorchester Heights
Dorchester Neck
Dorchester Pt
Castle I.
Spectacle I.
Dorchester
Thompsons I.
Long I.
95
90
85
80
75
70
65
West from 80 Greenwich
45
40
35
30
A
B
C
D
E
F
G
a
b
c
d
e
Lake Superior
Lake Michigan
Lake Huron
Georgian B.
Lake Erie
Lake Ontario
L. Simcoe
L. Nipissing
L. Winnebago
Saginaw B.
Green B.
Lake Champlain
Long I.
British Claim
U.S.A.
QUEBEC 1763
QUEBEC 1774
CANADA
ACADIA 1604
NOVA SCOTIA
Bay of Fundy
Abenaki
MAINE
NEW HAMPSHIRE
MASSACHUSETTS
RHODE I.
CONNECTICUT
NEW YORK
NEW JERSEY
PENNSYLVANIA
DELAWARE
MARYLAND
VIRGINIA
NORTH CAROLINA
SOUTH CAROLINA
GEORGIA
WEST FLORIDA 1767
Claimed by Spain (Claim abandoned 1795)
FLORIDA (WEST) (Spanish, ceded to England 1763, re-ceded 1783)
FLORIDA (EAST)
LOUISIANA
Ceded by France to Spain
INDIAN RESERVATION (Proclamation of 1763)
Ojibways
Iowas
Illinois
Miamis
Shawnees
Chickasaws
Cherokees
Creeks
Choctaws
Iroquois
ATLANTIC OCEAN
Quebec
Levis
Three Rivers
Sorel
Richmond
Berthier
Montreal
Chambly
Laprairie
St Johns
Ft de la Presentation
Ft la Galette
Ft Frédéric
Ft Crown Point
Ft Ticonderoga
L. George
Ft William Henry
Ft Bull
Ft Stanwix
Ft Oswego
Ft Brewerton
Ft Hunter
Schenectady
Saratoga
Albany
Saugerties
Tioga
Hudson
Mohawk
Ft Frontenac
Ft Niagara
Falls
Ft Schlosser
Ft Rouillé (Ft Toronto) (York)
Ft Ste Marys
St Lawrence
Ottawa
Nipissing
Ste Marie
Ft Michillimackinac
Ft Mackinac
Arbre Croche
Ft Chequemagon
Ft St Esprit (La Pointe)
Ft d'Huillier
Ft Beauharnais
Ft la Baye
Butte des Mortes
Wisconsin
Mississippi
Chicago
Ft St Joseph
Ft Detroit
L. St Clair
Ft Sandusky
Ft Miami
Ft St Louis
Illinois
Peoria
Ft Crèvecoeur
Ft Orleans
Missouri
St Charles
St Louis
Cahokia
Ft Chartres
St Geneviève
Kaskaskia
Ft Massac
St Denis
Fort Prudhomme
Ft Assumption (Memphis)
Arkansas
Arkansas Post
Yazoo
Natchez
Baton Rouge 1763
Ft Bute (Manchac)
New Orleans 1718
St Philippe
La Salle 1682
La Balize
Biloxi
Ft Charlotte
Mobile
Ft Louis
Pensacola
Ft Tombecbé (Ft York)
Ft Toulouse
Alabama
Tallapoosa
Coosa
Okfuskee
Kawita
Chattahoochee
Apalachee
Aucilla
St Marks
Sta Fé
San Juan (St Johns)
Santa Maria (St Marys)
Brunswick
Ft Frederica
St Simon's I.
Darien
Sunbury
Santa Catalina
Ft Argyll
Savannah
Purysburg
Ebenezer
Port Royal
Charleston
Ft King George
Altamaha
Ft Augusta
Ft Moore
Savannah
Santee
Camden 1780
Eutaw Springs 1781
Hobkirks Hill 1781
Cowpens 1781
Kings Mountain 1780
Ft Prince George (Savannah)
Charlotte
Ft Dobbs
Guilford Court Ho. 1781
Hillsborough
Halifax
Raleigh
Newbern
Lafayetteville
Cape Fear R.
Wilmington
C. Fear
Long Bay
Pamlico S.
Bath
Edenton
C. Hatteras
Roanoke
Danville
Bedford
Petersburg
Williamsburg
Yorktown 1781
Suffolk
Norfolk
Portsmouth
C. Henry
C. Charles
Chesapeake B.
Staunton
Germanna
Columbia
James
Richmond
Rappahannock
Shenandoah
Winchester
Beverley Manor
Harpers Ferry
Potomac
Baltimore
Annapolis
Delaware B.
Philadelphia
Trenton
Monmouth Court Ho.
New York
Newhaven
Newport
Plymouth
Boston
Salem
Cape Cod
Concord
Newburyport
Portsmouth
Portland
Falmouth
Fort Western
Pemaquid
Kennebec
Ft Halifax
Penobscot B.
Pentegoet
Yarmouth
C. Sable
Port Royal (Annapolis)
St John
Beausejour
Fredericton
Naxouat
St Croix
Chaudière
Wilkesbarre
Ft Augusta
Susquehanna
Ft Harris
Ft Bedford
Ft Cumberland
Mason & Dixon's Line 1763
Ft Ligonier
Ft Bird
Ft Necessity
Ft Pitt (Pittsburgh)
Ft Duquesne
Monongahela
Ft Armstrong
Allegheny
Ft Venango
Presqu'ile
Ft le Boeuf
Logstown
Kuskuskie
Guadenhutten
Ft Henry
Marietta
Chillicothe
Pickawillany
Ouiatanon
Wabash
Vincennes
Falls
Ohio (La Salle 1669)
Lexington
Boonesborough
Harrodsburg
Logans
Draper's Meadow
Ft Chiswell
Allegheny Mts
Cumberland Mts
Cumberland
Nashborough (Nashville)
Ft Loudoun
Tennessee
Kingston

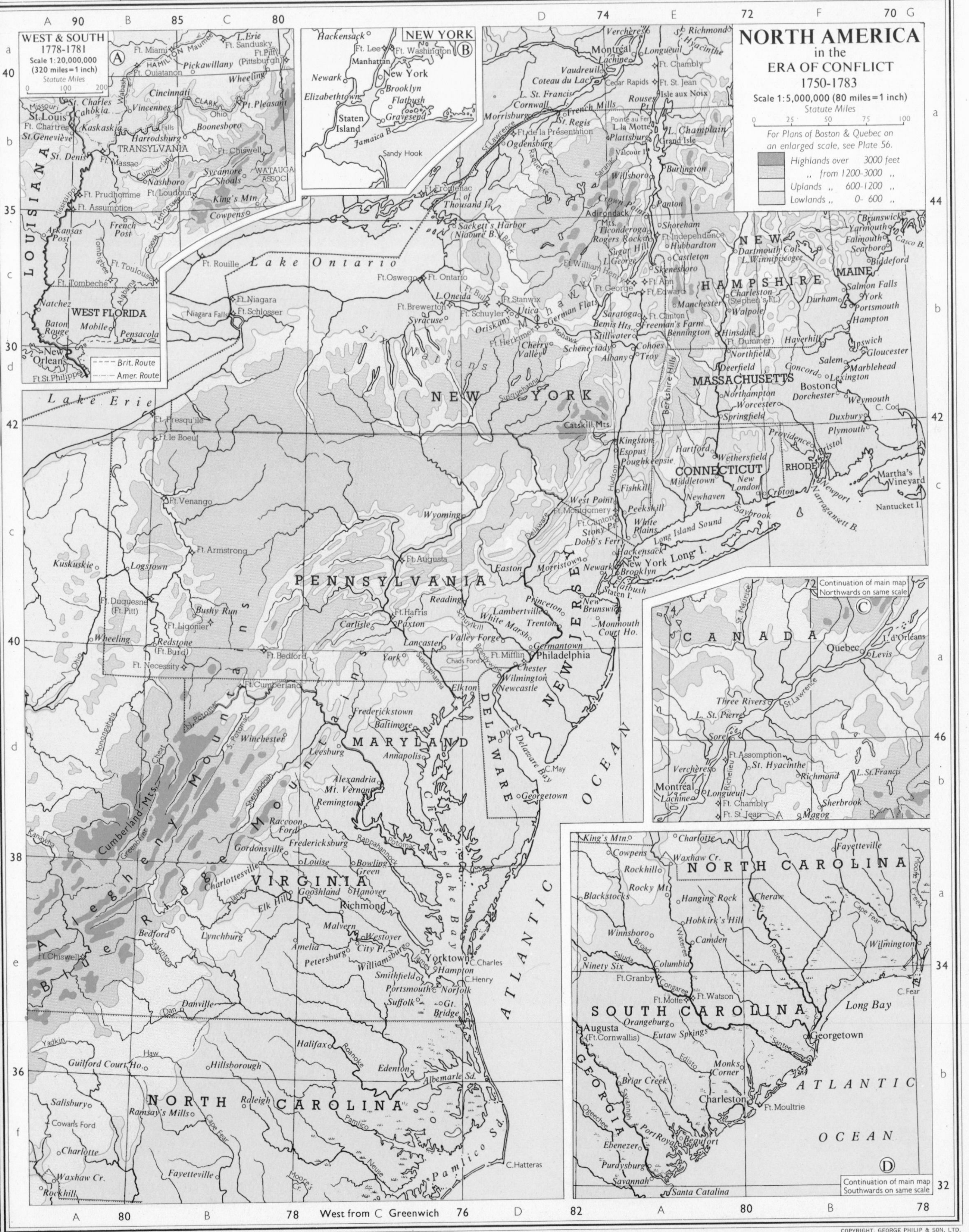
NORTH AMERICA
in the
ERA OF CONFLICT
1750-1783
Scale 1:5,000,000 (80 miles = 1 inch)
Statute Miles
0 25 50 75 100
For Plans of Boston & Quebec on an enlarged scale, see Plate 56.
Highlands over 3000 feet
,, from 1200-3000 ,,
Uplands ,, 600-1200 ,,
Lowlands ,, 0- 600 ,,
WEST & SOUTH
1778-1781
Scale 1:20,000,000
(320 miles = 1 inch)
Statute Miles
0 100 200
A
Brit. Route
Amer. Route
LOUISIANA
TRANSYLVANIA
WEST FLORIDA
St. Louis
Kaskaskia
Vincennes
Cincinnati
Pittsburgh
New Orleans
Natchez
Mobile
Pensacola
Baton Rouge
NEW YORK
B
Hackensack
Manhattan
New York
Brooklyn
Flatbush
Gravesend
Newark
Elizabethtown
Staten Island
Jamaica B.
Sandy Hook
Lake Ontario
Lake Erie
NEW YORK
PENNSYLVANIA
MARYLAND
DELAWARE
NEW JERSEY
VIRGINIA
NORTH CAROLINA
NEW HAMPSHIRE
MAINE
MASSACHUSETTS
CONNECTICUT
RHODE I.
ATLANTIC OCEAN
Six Nations
Mohawks
Allegheny Mountains
Blue Ridge Mountains
Cumberland Mts.
Catskill Mts.
Adirondack Mts.
Montreal
Lachine
L. Champlain
Ticonderoga
Crown Pt.
Saratoga
Albany
Schenectady
Ft. Niagara
Ft. Oswego
Ft. Duquesne (Ft. Pitt)
Philadelphia
Germantown
Valley Forge
Trenton
Princeton
Baltimore
Annapolis
Alexandria
Mt. Vernon
Richmond
Yorktown
Williamsburg
Norfolk
Boston
Lexington
Concord
Providence
Newport
Hartford
New London
Long Island Sound
Chesapeake Bay
Delaware Bay
Albemarle Sd.
Pamlico Sd.
C. Hatteras
C. Charles
C. Henry
C. May
C. Cod
Nantucket I.
Martha's Vineyard
Continuation of main map Northwards on same scale
C
CANADA
Quebec
Levis
Three Rivers
L. St. Pierre
St. Lawrence
Sorel
St. Hyacinthe
Richmond
Sherbrook
Continuation of main map Southwards on same scale
D
NORTH CAROLINA
SOUTH CAROLINA
GEORGIA
Charlotte
King's Mtn.
Cowpens
Camden
Hobkirk's Hill
Columbia
Ninety Six
Eutaw Springs
Charleston
Ft. Moultrie
Beaufort
Savannah
Augusta (Ft. Cornwallis)
Georgetown
Wilmington
Fayetteville
Long Bay
C. Fear
ATLANTIC OCEAN
West from Greenwich

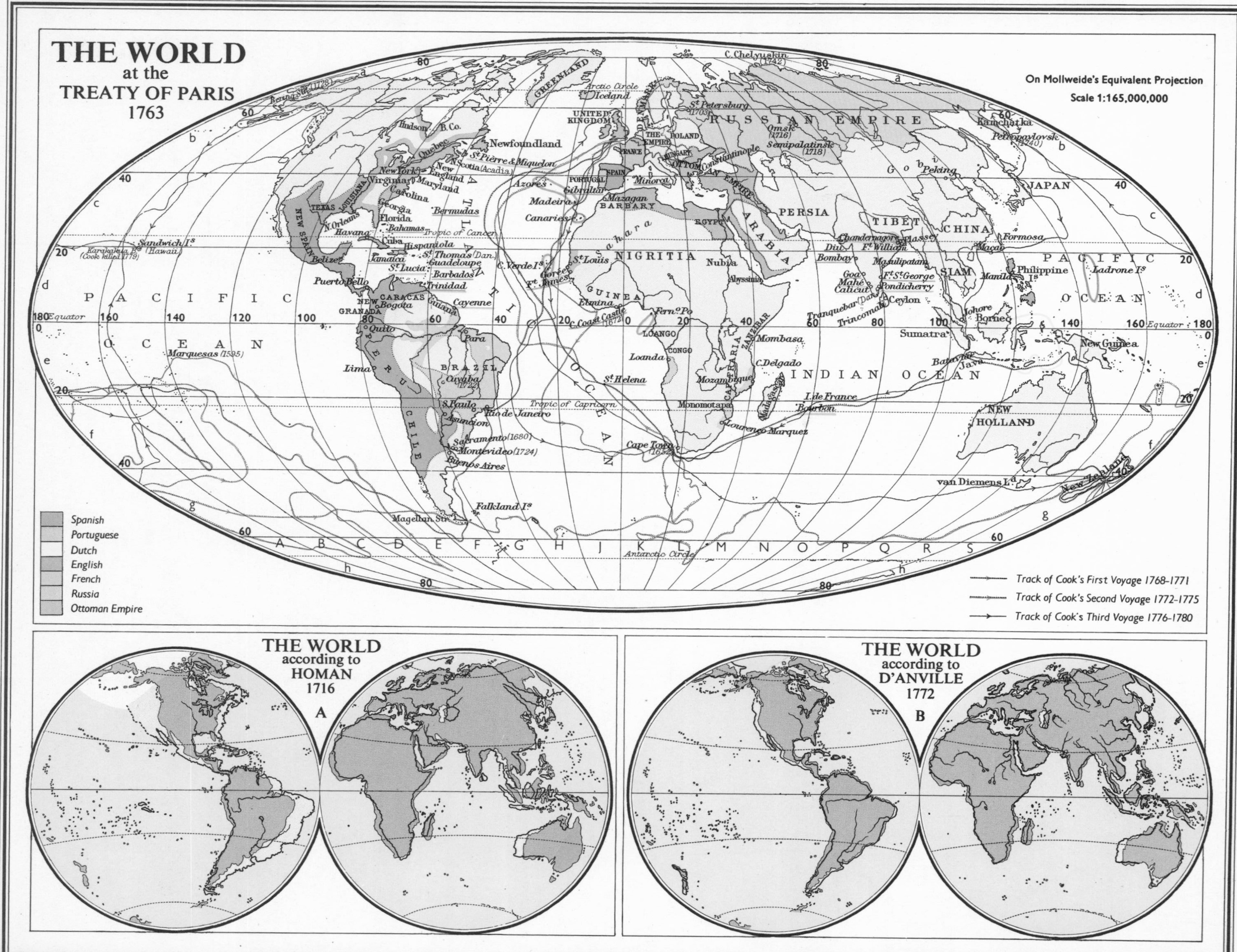
THE WORLD
at the
TREATY OF PARIS
1763
On Mollweide's Equivalent Projection
Scale 1:165,000,000
Spanish
Portuguese
Dutch
English
French
Russia
Ottoman Empire
Track of Cook's First Voyage 1768-1771
Track of Cook's Second Voyage 1772-1775
Track of Cook's Third Voyage 1776-1780
PACIFIC OCEAN
ATLANTIC OCEAN
INDIAN OCEAN
GREENLAND
Arctic Circle
Iceland
UNITED KINGDOM
DENMARK
St Petersburg (1703)
RUSSIAN EMPIRE
C. Chelyuskin (1742)
Omsk (1716)
Semipalatinsk (1718)
Kamchatka
Petropavlovsk (1740)
Gobi
Peking
JAPAN
TIBET
CHINA
Formosa
Macao
Philippine Is
Ladrone Is
Manila
SIAM
PERSIA
ARABIA
EGYPT
Nubia
Abyssinia
NIGRITIA
Sahara
GUINEA
Elmina
C. Coast Castle (1672)
Fern. Po
LOANGO
CONGO
Loanda
St Helena
Monomotapa
Mozambique
CAFFRARIA
ZANZIBAR
Mombasa
C. Delgado
Madagascar
I. de France
Bourbon
Lourenço Marquez
Cape Town (1652)
Bombay
Goa
Mahé
Calicut
Masulipatam
Ft St George
Pondicherry
Ceylon
Tranquebar (Dan.)
Trincomali
Plassey
Chandernagore
Ft William
Diu
Sumatra
Johore
Borneo
Batavia
Java
New Guinea
NEW HOLLAND
van Diemens Ld
New Zealand
Hudson B. Co.
Quebec
Newfoundland
St Pierre & Miquelon
N. Scotia (Acadia)
New York
New England
Virginia
Maryland
Carolina
Georgia
Florida
LOUISIANA
TEXAS
N. Orleans
NEW SPAIN
Bahamas
Bermudas
Tropic of Cancer
Havana
Cuba
Hispaniola
Jamaica
St Thomas (Dan.)
Guadeloupe
St Lucia
Barbados
Trinidad
Belize
Puerto Bello
CARACAS
NEW GRANADA
Bogota
Guiana
Cayenne
Quito
PERU
Lima
Para
BRAZIL
Cuyaba (1722)
S. Paulo
Rio de Janeiro
Asuncion
Sacramento (1680)
Montevideo (1724)
Buenos Aires
CHILE
Falkland Is
Magellan St.
Tropic of Capricorn
Antarctic Circle
Azores
Madeira
Canaries
C. Verde Is
Gorée
Ft James
St Louis
PORTUGAL
SPAIN
Gibraltar
Minorca
Mazagan
BARBARY
FRANCE
THE EMPIRE
POLAND
HUNGARY
OTTOMAN EMPIRE
Constantinople
Sandwich Is (Hawaii)
Karakakua B. (Cook killed 1779)
Bering St. (1728)
Marquesas (1595)
Equator
THE WORLD
according to
HOMAN
1716
A
THE WORLD
according to
D'ANVILLE
1772
B

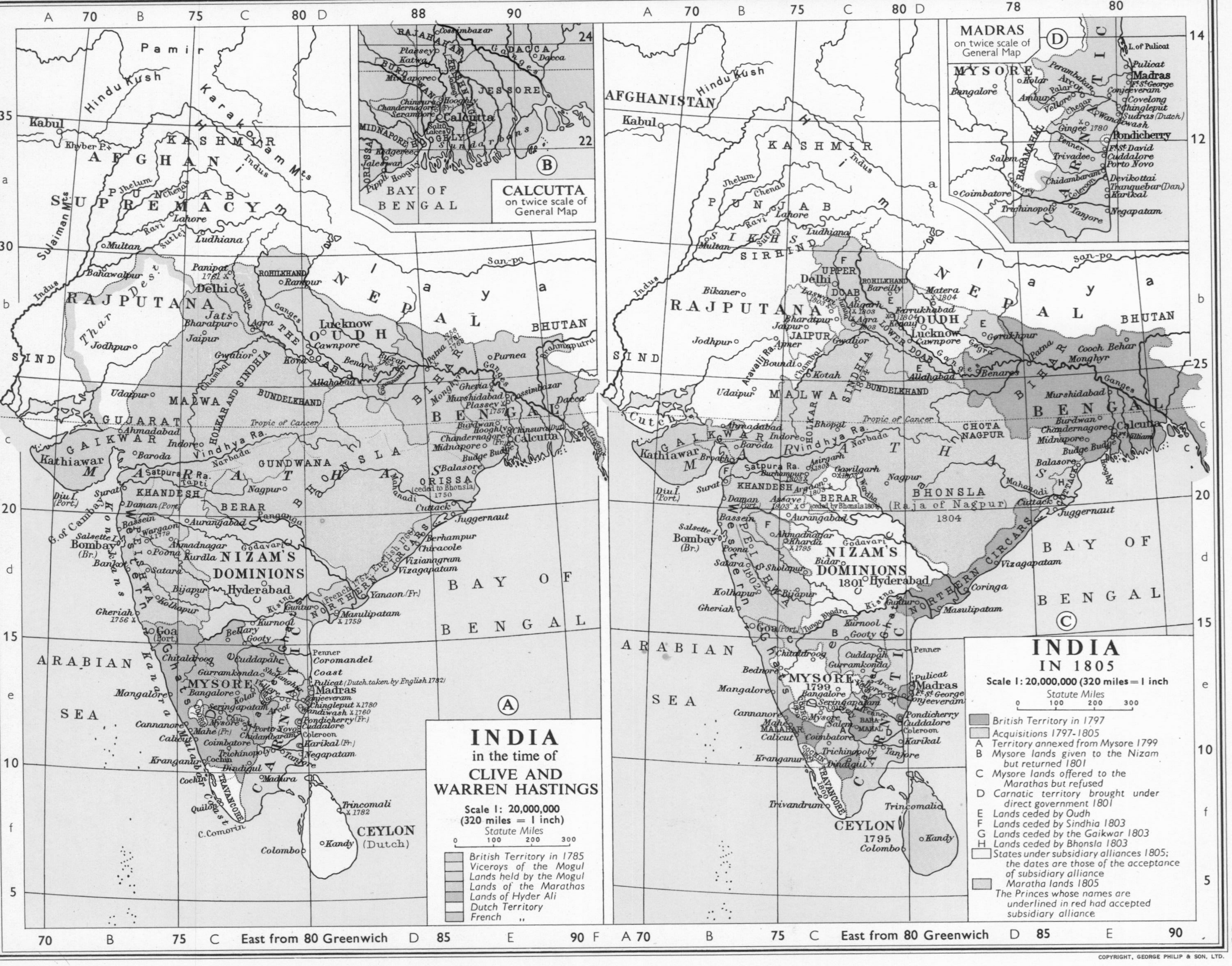
INDIA
in the time of
CLIVE AND
WARREN HASTINGS
Scale 1: 20,000,000
(320 miles = 1 inch)
Statute Miles
0 100 200 300
British Territory in 1785
Viceroys of the Mogul
Lands held by the Mogul
Lands of the Marathas
Lands of Hyder Ali
Dutch Territory
French ,,
A
CALCUTTA
on twice scale of
General Map
B
INDIA
IN 1805
Scale 1: 20,000,000 (320 miles = 1 inch
Statute Miles
0 100 200 300
British Territory in 1797
Acquisitions 1797-1805
A Territory annexed from Mysore 1799
B Mysore lands given to the Nizam but returned 1801
C Mysore lands offered to the Marathas but refused
D Carnatic territory brought under direct government 1801
E Lands ceded by Oudh
F Lands ceded by Sindhia 1803
G Lands ceded by the Gaikwar 1803
H Lands ceded by Bhonsla 1803
States under subsidiary alliances 1805; the dates are those of the acceptance of subsidiary alliance
Maratha lands 1805
The Princes whose names are underlined in red had accepted subsidiary alliance
C
MADRAS
on twice scale of
General Map
D
East from 80 Greenwich
East from 80 Greenwich

THE GROWTH OF
BRANDENBURG-PRUSSIA
Scale 1: 6,000,000 (96 miles=1 inch)
Statute Miles
0 25 50 75 100
Brandenburg at death of Frederick I. 1440
Acquisitions 1440-1608
Acquisitions 1608-1624
Acquisitions under the Great Elector, 1640-1688
Acquisitions under Frederick III, (I. of Prussia) 1689-1713 & Frederick William I., 1713-1740
Acquisitions under Frederick the Great 1740-1786
Acquisitions under Frederick William II., 1786-1797
Second Partition of Poland
Third Partition of Poland
Acquisitions under Frederick William III., 1797-1807
NORTH SEA
BALTIC SEA
SCHLESWIG
HOLSTEIN
MECKLENBURG
EAST PRUSSIA
WEST PRUSSIA
NEW EAST PRUSSIA
SOUTH PRUSSIA
NEUMARK
EASTERN POMERANIA
W. POMERANIA
PRIEGNITZ
UKERMARK
ALTMARK
MITTELMARK
MAGDEBURG
SAXONY
SILESIA
NEW SILESIA
BOHEMIA
AUSTRIA
BAVARIA
ANSBACH
BAYREUTH
Berlin
Danzig
Königsberg
Warsaw
Breslau
Prague
Hamburg
Hanover
Cologne
Stettin

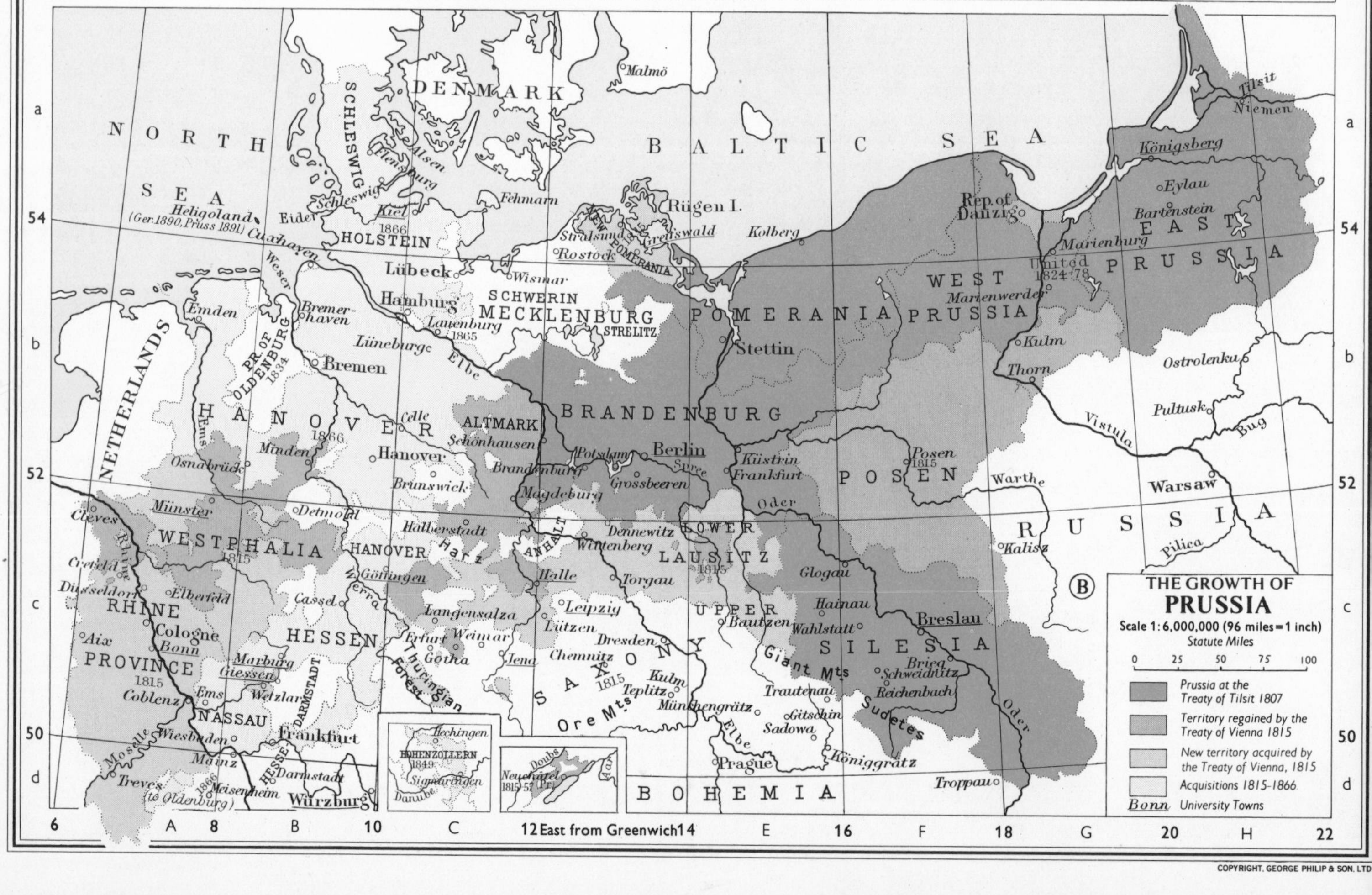
THE GROWTH OF
PRUSSIA
Scale 1: 6,000,000 (96 miles=1 inch)
Statute Miles
0 25 50 75 100
Prussia at the Treaty of Tilsit 1807
Territory regained by the Treaty of Vienna 1815
New territory acquired by the Treaty of Vienna, 1815
Acquisitions 1815-1866
Bonn University Towns
East from Greenwich
NORTH SEA
BALTIC SEA
DENMARK
NETHERLANDS
HANOVER
WESTPHALIA
RHINE PROVINCE
HESSEN
NASSAU
SAXONY
BRANDENBURG
POMERANIA
WEST PRUSSIA
EAST PRUSSIA
POSEN
SILESIA
RUSSIA
BOHEMIA
Berlin
Königsberg
Warsaw
Breslau
Prague
Cologne
Frankfurt

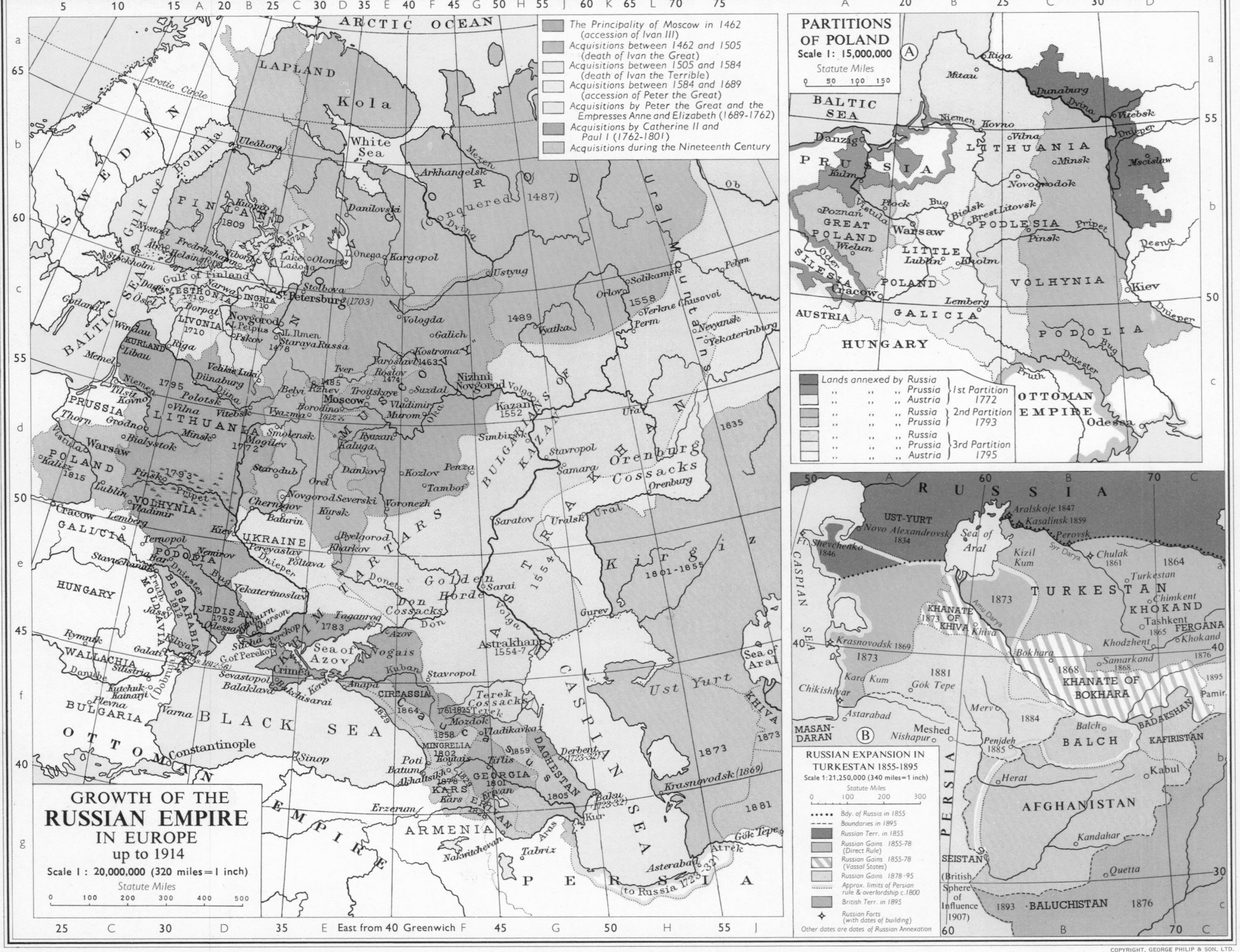
GROWTH OF THE RUSSIAN EMPIRE IN EUROPE up to 1914
Scale 1 : 20,000,000 (320 miles = 1 inch)
Statute Miles
The Principality of Moscow in 1462 (accession of Ivan III)
Acquisitions between 1462 and 1505 (death of Ivan the Great)
Acquisitions between 1505 and 1584 (death of Ivan the Terrible)
Acquisitions between 1584 and 1689 (accession of Peter the Great)
Acquisitions by Peter the Great and the Empresses Anne and Elizabeth (1689-1762)
Acquisitions by Catherine II and Paul I (1762-1801)
Acquisitions during the Nineteenth Century
East from 40 Greenwich
PARTITIONS OF POLAND
Scale 1: 15,000,000
Lands annexed by Russia, Prussia, Austria — 1st Partition 1772
Russia, Prussia — 2nd Partition 1793
Russia, Prussia, Austria — 3rd Partition 1795
RUSSIAN EXPANSION IN TURKESTAN 1855-1895
Scale 1:21,250,000 (340 miles=1 inch)
Bdy. of Russia in 1855
Boundaries in 1895
Russian Terr. in 1855
Russian Gains 1855-78 (Direct Rule)
Russian Gains 1855-78 (Vassal States)
Russian Gains 1878-95
Approx. limits of Persian rule & overlordship c.1800
British Terr. in 1895
Russian Forts (with dates of building)
Other dates are dates of Russian Annexation
COPYRIGHT, GEORGE PHILIP & SON, LTD.

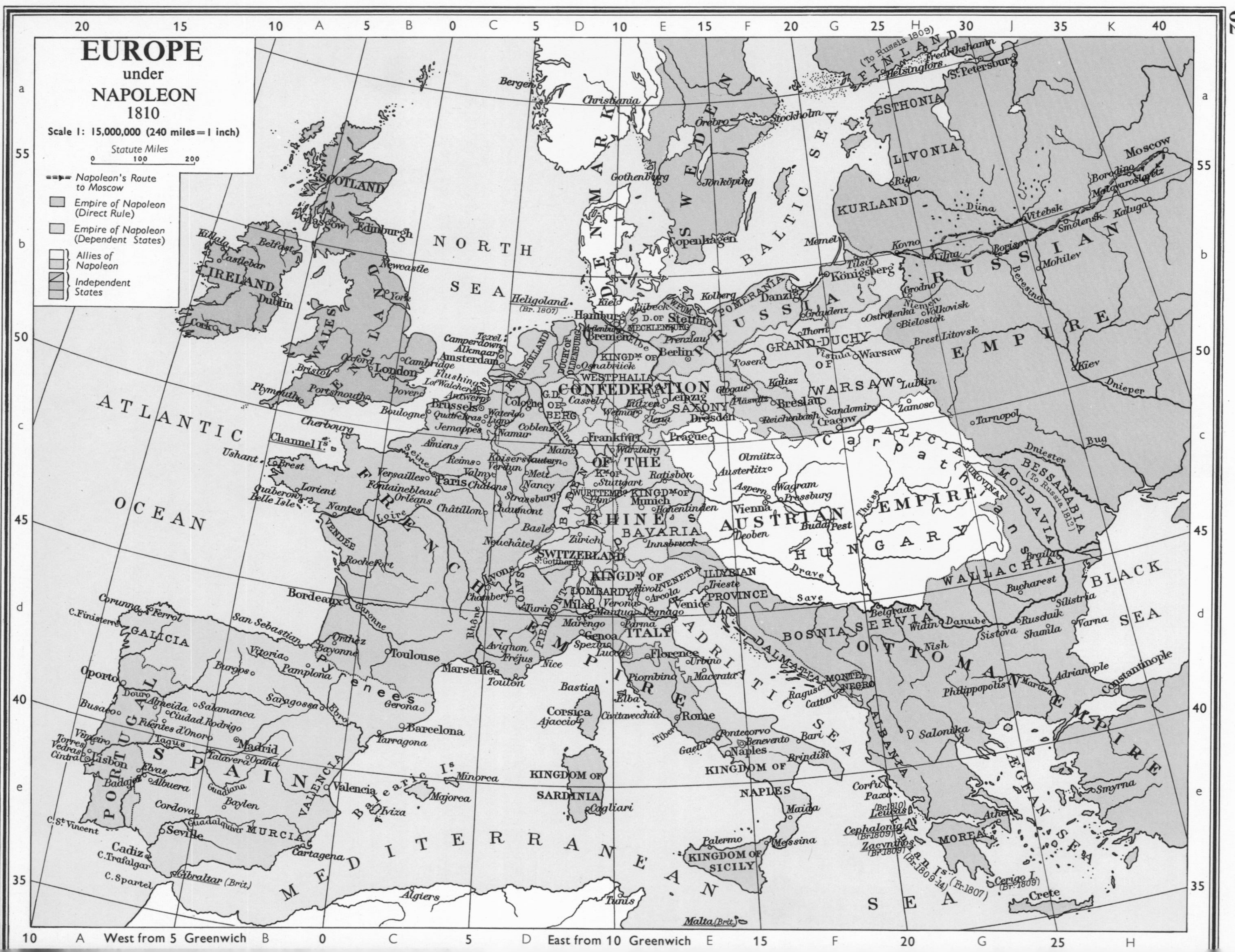
EUROPE
under
NAPOLEON
1810
Scale 1: 15,000,000 (240 miles = 1 inch)
Statute Miles
0 100 200
Napoleon's Route to Moscow
Empire of Napoleon (Direct Rule)
Empire of Napoleon (Dependent States)
Allies of Napoleon
Independent States
West from 5 Greenwich
East from 10 Greenwich
ATLANTIC OCEAN
NORTH SEA
BALTIC SEA
MEDITERRANEAN SEA
ADRIATIC SEA
BLACK SEA
ÆGEAN SEA
FRENCH EMPIRE
SPAIN
PORTUGAL
ENGLAND
WALES
SCOTLAND
IRELAND
DENMARK
SWEDEN
RUSSIAN EMPIRE
PRUSSIA
GRAND-DUCHY OF WARSAW
CONFEDERATION OF THE RHINE
AUSTRIAN EMPIRE
HUNGARY
OTTOMAN EMPIRE
KINGDOM OF ITALY
KINGDOM OF NAPLES
KINGDOM OF SICILY
KINGDOM OF SARDINIA
SWITZERLAND
ILLYRIAN PROVINCE
BAVARIA
SAXONY
KINGDM OF WESTPHALIA
FINLAND (To Russia 1809)
ESTHONIA
LIVONIA
KURLAND
BESSARABIA (To Russia 1812)
MOLDAVIA
WALLACHIA
SERVIA
BOSNIA
ALBANIA
DALMATIA
MORES
MOREA
GALICIA
VALENCIA
MURCIA
Moscow
Borodino
Smolensk
Vitebsk
Mohilev
Beresina
Vilna
Kovno
Grodno
Warsaw
Königsberg
Danzig
Berlin
Hamburg
Dresden
Leipzig
Prague
Vienna
Wagram
Austerlitz
Munich
Paris
Brussels
Waterloo
Amsterdam
London
Edinburgh
Dublin
Madrid
Lisbon
Cadiz
C. Trafalgar
Gibraltar (Brit.)
Barcelona
Toulouse
Bordeaux
Marseilles
Toulon
Genoa
Milan
Venice
Rome
Naples
Palermo
Malta (Brit.)
Corsica
Ajaccio
Cagliari
Tunis
Algiers
Constantinople
Adrianople
Salonika
Athens
Smyrna
Crete
Heligoland (Br. 1807)
Channel Is.
Stockholm
Copenhagen
Christiania
St. Petersburg
Riga
Kiev
Bucharest
Belgrade
Buda Pest
Pressburg
Dnieper
Dniester
Danube
Rhine
Ebro
Loire
Seine

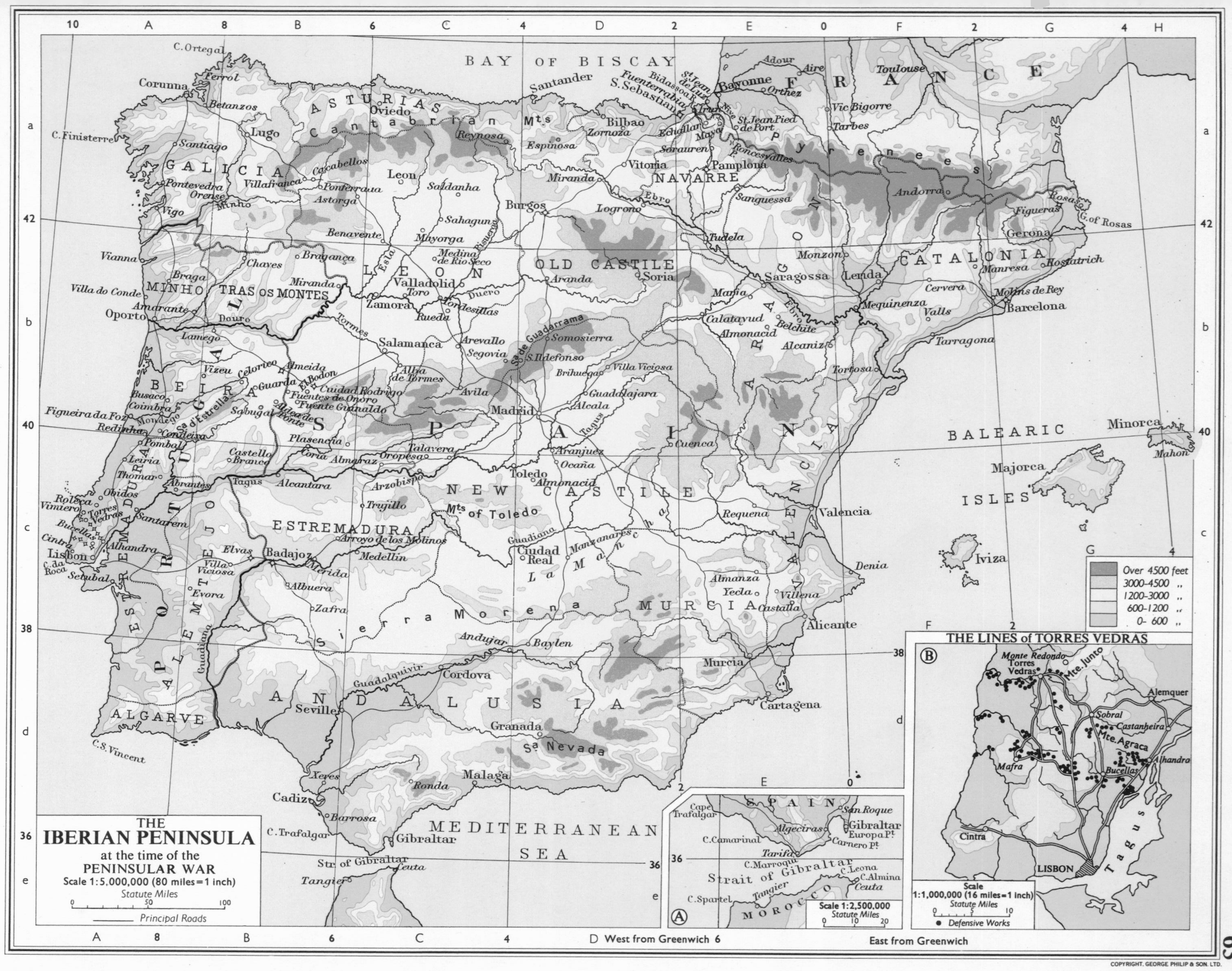

THE IBERIAN PENINSULA
at the time of the
PENINSULAR WAR
Scale 1:5,000,000 (80 miles=1 inch)
Statute Miles
Principal Roads
BAY OF BISCAY
MEDITERRANEAN SEA
BALEARIC ISLES
FRANCE
SPAIN
PORTUGAL
GALICIA
ASTURIAS
LEON
OLD CASTILE
NEW CASTILE
NAVARRE
ARAGON
CATALONIA
VALENCIA
MURCIA
ANDALUSIA
ESTREMADURA
ALEMTEJO
ALGARVE
MINHO
TRAS OS MONTES
BEIRA
Cantabrian Mts
Pyrenees
Sierra Morena
La Mancha
Mts of Toledo
Sa de Guadarrama
Sa Nevada
Sa d'Estrella
Madrid
Lisbon
Oporto
Salamanca
Valladolid
Burgos
Saragossa
Barcelona
Valencia
Cordova
Seville
Cadiz
Granada
Malaga
Gibraltar
Badajoz
Ciudad Rodrigo
Talavera
Vitoria
Pamplona
Coruna
Santander
Over 4500 feet
3000-4500
1200-3000
600-1200
0- 600
West from Greenwich
East from Greenwich
A
Cape Trafalgar
Strait of Gibraltar
MOROCCO
Scale 1:2,500,000
B
THE LINES of TORRES VEDRAS
Monte Redondo
Torres Vedras
Mte. Junto
Alemquer
Sobral
Castanheira
Mte. Agraca
Alhandra
Bucellas
Mafra
Cintra
LISBON
Tagus
Scale 1:1,000,000 (16 miles=1 inch)
Statute Miles
Defensive Works

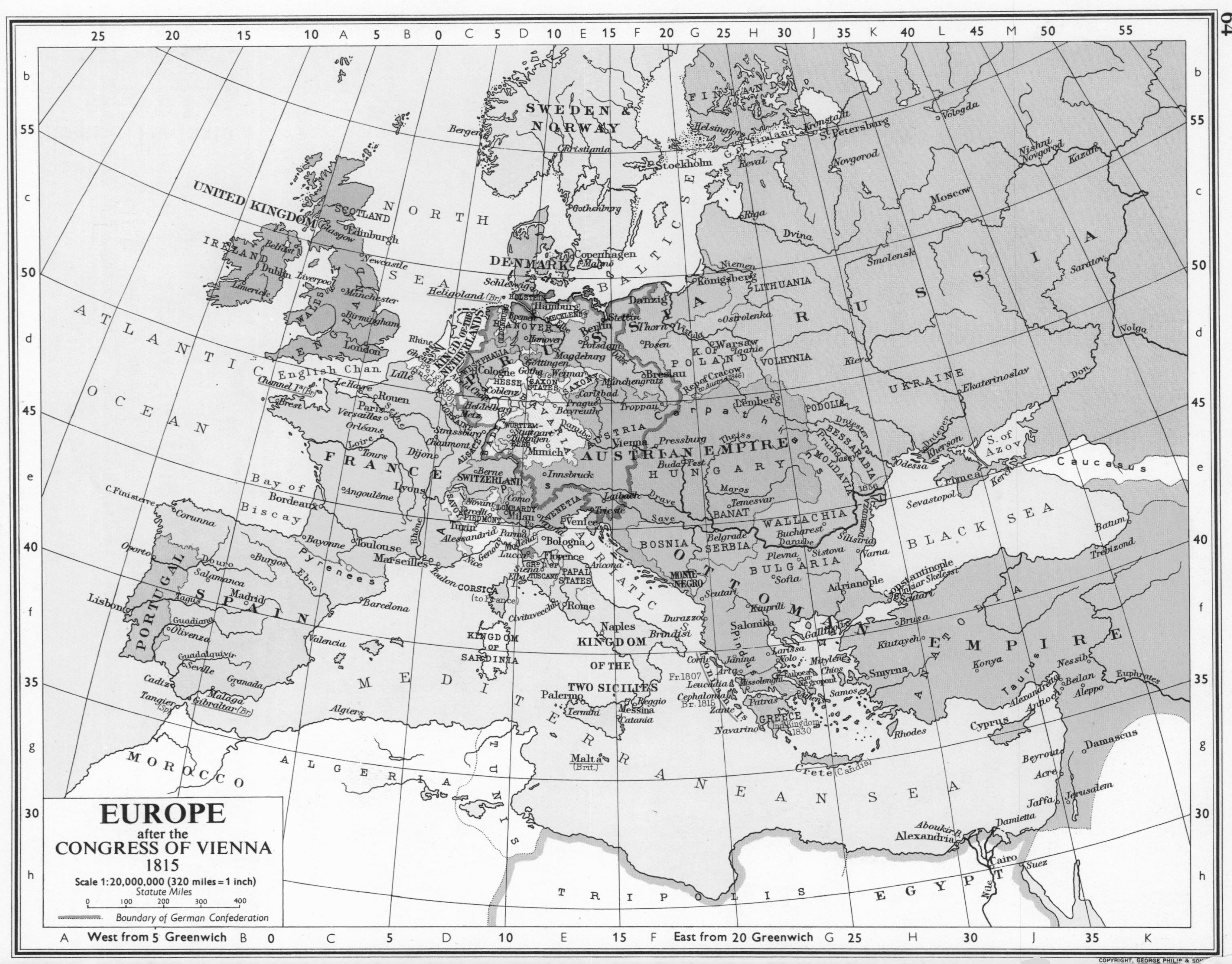
EUROPE
after the
CONGRESS OF VIENNA
1815
Scale 1:20,000,000 (320 miles = 1 inch)
Statute Miles
0 100 200 300 400
Boundary of German Confederation
West from 5 Greenwich
East from 20 Greenwich
UNITED KINGDOM
SCOTLAND
IRELAND
ENGLAND
WALES
NORTH SEA
ATLANTIC OCEAN
English Chan.
Bay of Biscay
FRANCE
SPAIN
PORTUGAL
SWEDEN & NORWAY
DENMARK
BALTIC SEA
KINGD. OF THE NETHERLANDS
PRUSSIA
HANOVER
HESSE
SAXONY
SWITZERLAND
AUSTRIAN EMPIRE
HUNGARY
K. OF POLAND
RUSSIA
LITHUANIA
VOLHYNIA
PODOLIA
UKRAINE
BESSARABIA
MOLDAVIA
WALLACHIA
BANAT
BOSNIA
SERBIA
BULGARIA
OTTOMAN EMPIRE
ANATOLIA
BLACK SEA
S. of Azov
Caucasus
KINGDOM OF SARDINIA
KINGDOM OF THE TWO SICILIES
PAPAL STATES
VENETIA
PIEDMONT
ADRIATIC
MEDITERRANEAN SEA
MOROCCO
ALGERIA
TUNIS
TRIPOLIS
EGYPT
GREECE
Indt. Kingdom 1830
Malta (Brit.)
Gibraltar (Br.)
Heligoland (Br.)
Channel Is. (Br.)
CORSICA (to France)
Crete (Candia)
Cyprus
Rep. of Cracow (to Austria 1846)
Fr. 1807
Br. 1815
London
Paris
Madrid
Lisbon
Berlin
Vienna
Warsaw
Moscow
St. Petersburg
Constantinople
Rome
Naples
Stockholm
Copenhagen
Cairo
Alexandria
Damascus
Jerusalem

1803 (A)
1807 (B)
A & B
RECONSTRUCTION OF GERMANY BY NAPOLEON
Scale 1:10,000,000 (160 miles=1 inch)
Statute Miles
0 50 100 150 200 250
Boundary of the Holy Roman Empire 1803
„ „ „ Rhine Confederation 1807
For Germany 1789 see Map 53, & for Germany 1795 see Map 51.
THE GERMAN CONFEDERATION
Scale 1:12,000,000 (192 miles=1 inch)
Statute Miles
0 50 100 150
Boundary of the Confederation
Kingdom of Prussia
Austrian Empire
(C)
15 East from C Greenwich
GROWTH OF THE GERMAN ZOLLVEREIN
Scale 1:12,000,000 (192 miles=1 inch)
0 50 100 150 Statute Miles
(D)
Prussian Customs Union 1819
Accessions to Prussian Customs Union 1819-31
Accessions to Prussian Customs Union 1831-37
Accessions to German Customs Union 1837-57
Accessions to German Customs Union 1857-71
Boundary of Bavaria-Württemberg Customs Union 1828-31
Boundary of Central German Customs Union 1828
Free Harbours
GERMAN EMPIRE 1871
Scale 1:20,000,000
Statute Miles
0 100 200
(E)
SCHLESWIG-HOLSTEIN 1864
Scale 1:5,000,000
Statute Miles
0 10 20 30
(F)

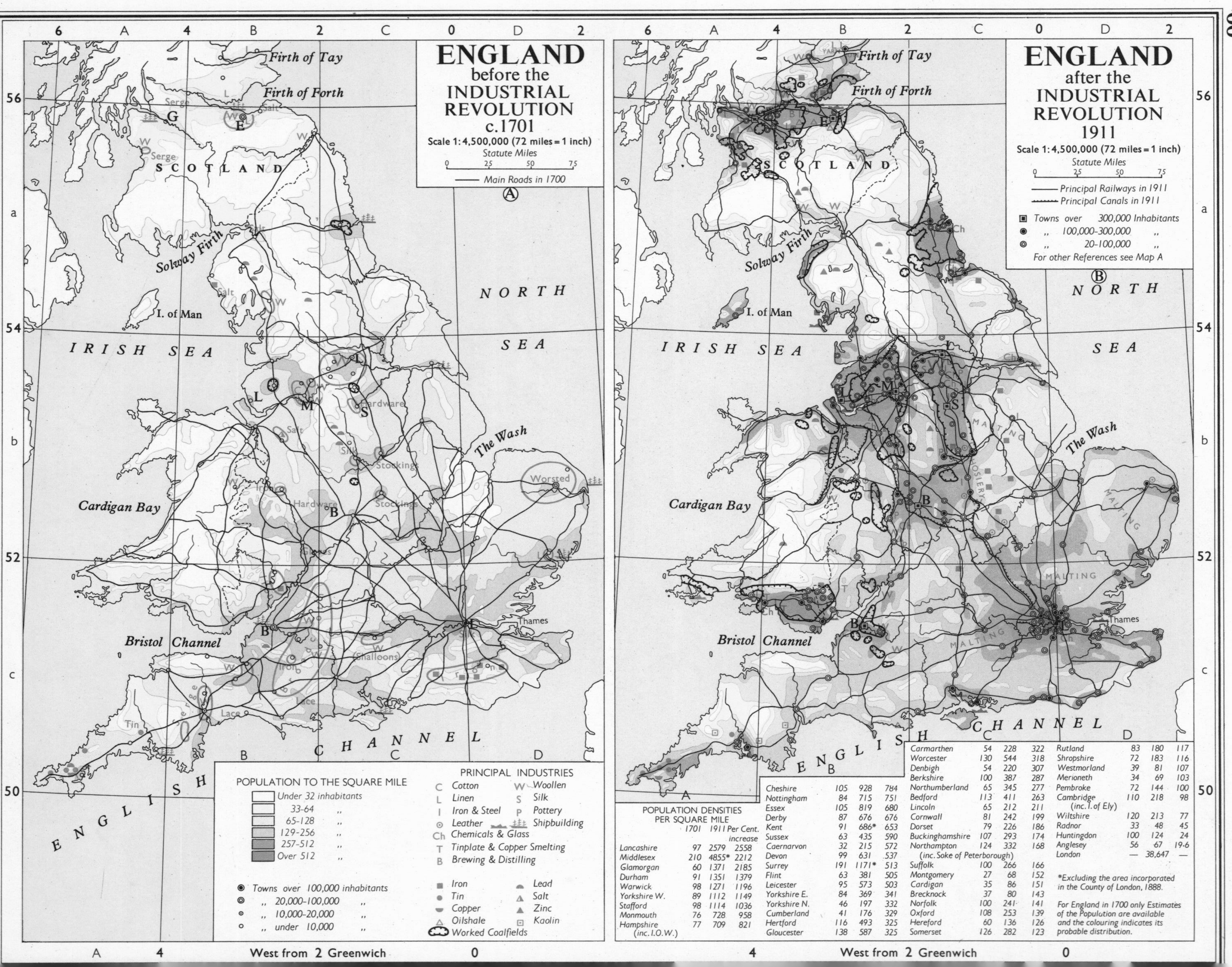

POPULATION DENSITIES PER SQUARE MILE

	1701	1911	Per Cent. increase
Lancashire	97	2579	2558
Middlesex	210	4855*	2212
Glamorgan	60	1371	2185
Durham	91	1351	1379
Warwick	98	1271	1196
Yorkshire W.	89	1112	1149
Stafford	98	1114	1036
Monmouth	76	728	958
Hampshire (inc. I.O.W.)	77	709	821
Cheshire	105	928	784
Nottingham	84	715	751
Essex	105	819	680
Derby	87	676	676
Kent	91	686*	653
Sussex	63	435	590
Caernarvon	32	215	572
Devon	99	631	537
Surrey	191	1171*	513
Flint	63	381	505
Leicester	95	573	503
Yorkshire E.	84	369	341
Yorkshire N.	46	197	332
Cumberland	41	176	329
Hertford	116	493	325
Gloucester	138	587	325
Carmarthen	54	228	322
Worcester	130	544	318
Denbigh	54	220	307
Berkshire	100	387	287
Northumberland	65	345	277
Bedford	113	411	263
Lincoln	65	212	211
Cornwall	81	242	199
Dorset	79	226	186
Buckinghamshire	107	293	174
Northampton (inc. Soke of Peterborough)	124	332	168
Suffolk	100	266	166
Montgomery	27	68	152
Cardigan	35	86	151
Brecknock	37	80	143
Norfolk	100	241	141
Oxford	108	253	139
Hereford	60	136	126
Somerset	126	282	123
Rutland	83	180	117
Shropshire	72	183	116
Westmorland	39	81	107
Merioneth	34	69	103
Pembroke	72	144	100
Cambridge (inc. I. of Ely)	110	218	98
Wiltshire	120	213	77
Radnor	33	48	45
Huntingdon	100	124	24
Anglesey	56	67	19·6
London	—	38,647	—

*Excluding the area incorporated in the County of London, 1888.

For England in 1700 only Estimates of the Population are available and the colouring indicates its probable distribution.

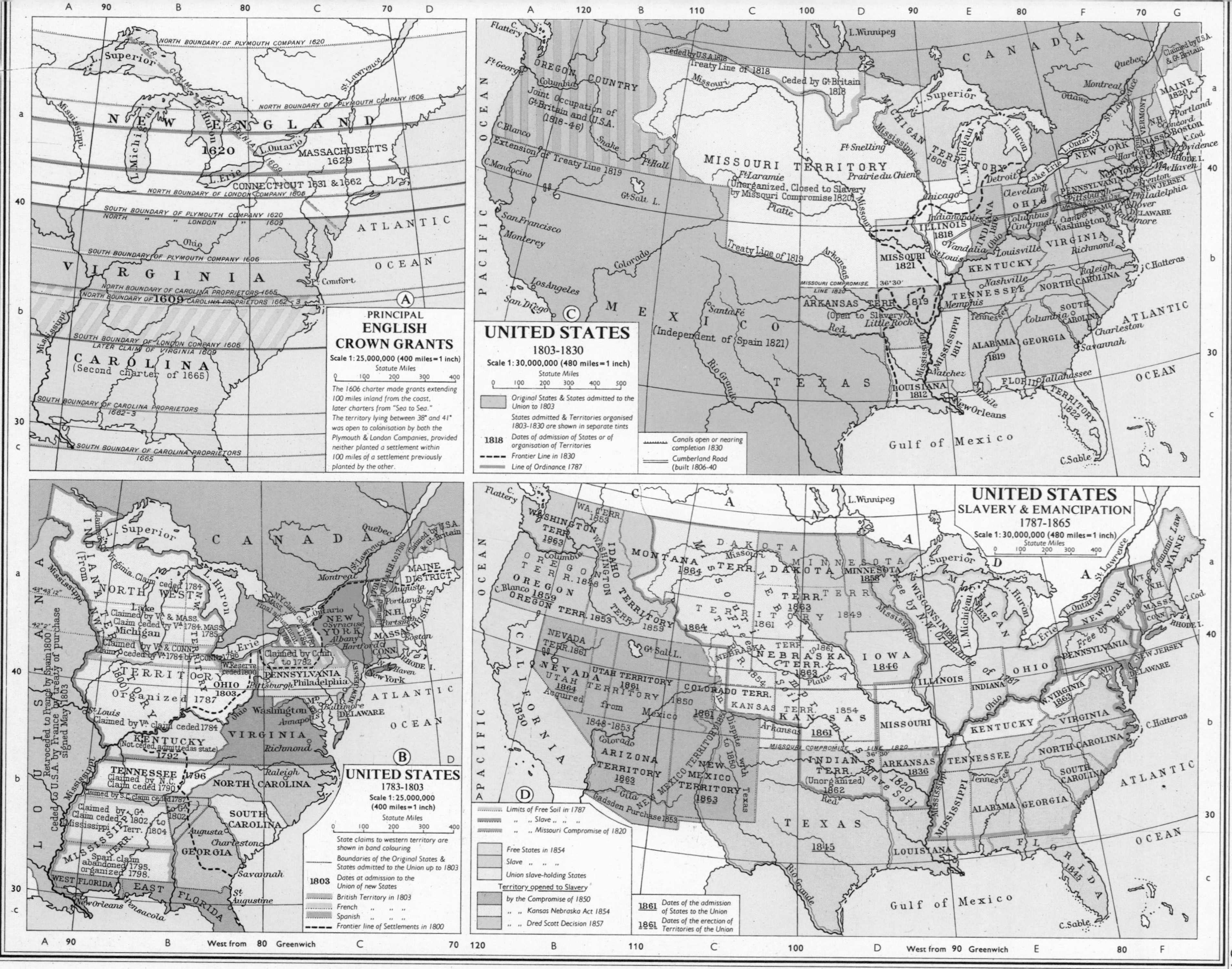
A
PRINCIPAL
ENGLISH
CROWN GRANTS
Scale 1: 25,000,000 (400 miles=1 inch)
Statute Miles
0 100 200 300 400
The 1606 charter made grants extending 100 miles inland from the coast, later charters from "Sea to Sea." The territory lying between 38° and 41° was open to colonisation by both the Plymouth & London Companies, provided neither planted a settlement within 100 miles of a settlement previously planted by the other.
NORTH BOUNDARY OF PLYMOUTH COMPANY 1620
NORTH BOUNDARY OF PLYMOUTH COMPANY 1606
NEW ENGLAND
1620
MASSACHUSETTS 1629
CONNECTICUT 1631 & 1662
NORTH BOUNDARY OF LONDON COMPANY 1606
SOUTH BOUNDARY OF PLYMOUTH COMPANY 1620
SOUTH BOUNDARY OF PLYMOUTH COMPANY 1606
VIRGINIA
NORTH BOUNDARY OF CAROLINA PROPRIETORS 1665
NORTH BOUNDARY OF 1609 CAROLINA PROPRIETORS 1662-3
SOUTH BOUNDARY OF LONDON COMPANY 1606
LATER CLAIM OF VIRGINIA 1609
CAROLINA
(Second charter of 1665)
SOUTH BOUNDARY OF CAROLINA PROPRIETORS 1662-3
SOUTH BOUNDARY OF CAROLINA PROPRIETORS 1665
ATLANTIC
OCEAN
Pt. Comfort
C
UNITED STATES
1803-1830
Scale 1: 30,000,000 (480 miles=1 inch)
Statute Miles
0 100 200 300 400 500
Original States & States admitted to the Union to 1803
States admitted & Territories organised 1803-1830 are shown in separate tints
1818 Dates of admission of States or of organisation of Territories
Frontier Line in 1830
Line of Ordinance 1787
Canals open or nearing completion 1830
Cumberland Road (built 1806-40
CANADA
OREGON COUNTRY
Joint Occupation of Gt. Britain and U.S.A. (1818-46)
Ceded by U.S.A. 1818
Treaty Line of 1818
Ceded by Gt. Britain 1818
Extension of Treaty Line 1819
MISSOURI TERRITORY
Unorganized, Closed to Slavery by Missouri Compromise 1820
MICHIGAN TERRITORY 1805
Treaty Line of 1819
MISSOURI COMPROMISE LINE 1820
36°30'
ARKANSAS TERR. 1819
(Open to Slavery)
MEXICO
(Independent of Spain 1821)
TEXAS
MISSOURI 1821
ILLINOIS 1818
INDIANA 1816
OHIO
KENTUCKY
TENNESSEE
MISSISSIPPI 1817
ALABAMA 1819
LOUISIANA 1812
FLORIDA TERRITORY 1822
GEORGIA
SOUTH CAROLINA
NORTH CAROLINA
VIRGINIA
PENNSYLVANIA
NEW YORK
VERMONT
MAINE 1820
Claimed by U.S.A. & Gt. Britain
PACIFIC
OCEAN
ATLANTIC
OCEAN
Gulf of Mexico
B
UNITED STATES
1783-1803
Scale 1: 25,000,000
(400 miles=1 inch)
Statute Miles
0 100 200 300 400
State claims to western territory are shown in band colouring
Boundaries of the Original States & States admitted to the Union up to 1803
1803 Dates at admission to the Union of new States
British Territory in 1803
French
Spanish
Frontier line of Settlements in 1800
CANADA
LOUISIANA
Retroceded to France by Spain 1800
Ceded to U.S.A. by France by treaty of purchase signed May 1803
INDIANA (From N.W.T.)
NORTH WEST TERRITORY
Organized 1787
OHIO 1803
KENTUCKY (Not ceded, admitted as state) 1792
TENNESSEE 1796
Claimed by N.C. Claim ceded 1790
MISSISSIPPI TERR.
Span. claim abandoned 1795, organized 1798.
WEST FLORIDA
EAST FLORIDA
GEORGIA
SOUTH CAROLINA
NORTH CAROLINA
VIRGINIA
PENNSYLVANIA
NEW YORK
MAINE DISTRICT
ATLANTIC
OCEAN
D
UNITED STATES
SLAVERY & EMANCIPATION
1787-1865
Scale 1: 30,000,000 (480 miles=1 inch)
Statute Miles
0 100 200 300 400
Limits of Free Soil in 1787
" Slave " "
" " Missouri Compromise of 1820
Free States in 1854
Slave " "
Union slave-holding States
Territory opened to Slavery
by the Compromise of 1850
" " Kansas Nebraska Act 1854
" " Dred Scott Decision 1857
1861 Dates of the admission of States to the Union
1861 Dates of the erection of Territories of the Union
WASHINGTON TERR. 1853
IDAHO TERRITORY
MONTANA TERR. 1864
DAKOTA TERR. 1861
MINNESOTA 1858
OREGON 1859
NEVADA 1864
UTAH TERRITORY 1861
CALIFORNIA 1850
COLORADO TERR. 1861
NEBRASKA TERR. 1854
KANSAS 1861
IOWA 1846
WISCONSIN 1848
MICHIGAN 1837
Free by N.W. Ordinance of 1787
ARIZONA TERRITORY 1863
NEW MEXICO TERRITORY 1863
Gadsden Purchase 1853
INDIAN TERR. (Unorganized) 1862
TEXAS 1845
FLORIDA 1845
W. VIRGINIA 1863
Free by operation of Economic Law
Gulf of Mexico
West from 80 Greenwich
West from 90 Greenwich

SOUTH AMERICA
in the
XIX & XX CENTURIES
Scale 1:30,000,000 (480 miles=1 inch)
Statute Miles
0 200 400 600
Approximate Boundaries of States in 1830
Boundaries subsequently & finally adjusted
Boundary of Greater Colombia, 1819-30
Boundary of Federation of Bolivia & Peru 1835-39
West from 50 Greenwich
PACIFIC OCEAN
COLOMBIA
1831 Republic of New Granada
1858 Granadine Confederation
1861 U.S. of New Granada
1863 U.S. of Colombia
1886 Republic of Colombia
VENEZUELA
ECUADOR
1830
PERU
BOLIVIA
BRAZIL
Independent Empire 1822
United States of Brazil 1889
CHILE
1810-18
ARGENTINA
Indep. 1810. 1810-17 United Provinces of La Plata
1825 Argentine Confederation 1853 Argentine Rep.
PARAGUAY
1811
URUGUAY
CHACO
(to Paraguay 1938)
ACRE
(to Bolivia, 1867)
AMAZONAS
PARA
MARANHAO
PIAUI
CEARA
BAHIA
GOIAS
MATO GROSSO
MINAS GERAIS
SAO PAULO
PARANA
SANTA CATARINA
RIO GRANDE DO SUL
RONDONIA
RIO BRANCO
AMAPA
NETH. GUIANA
FR. GUIANA
Falkland Islands
(Br. 1833)
BRITISH GUIANA
BOUNDARY
Scale 1:24,000,000 (384 miles=1 inch)
Statute Miles
0 100 200 300
Present Bdy. of British Guiana
Br. Guiana. Bdy. settlement 1899
Original Schomburgk Line
Extension of Schomburgk Line
Extreme Venezuelan Claim
Extreme British Claim
NORTH WEST
SOUTH AMERICA
Conflicting Territorial Claims
Scale 1:40,000,000 (640 miles=1 inch)
Statute Miles
0 200 400 600
Boundaries fixed by Treaty
The conflicting claims of the various states are shown by narrow bands of their respective colours
ACRE TERRITORY

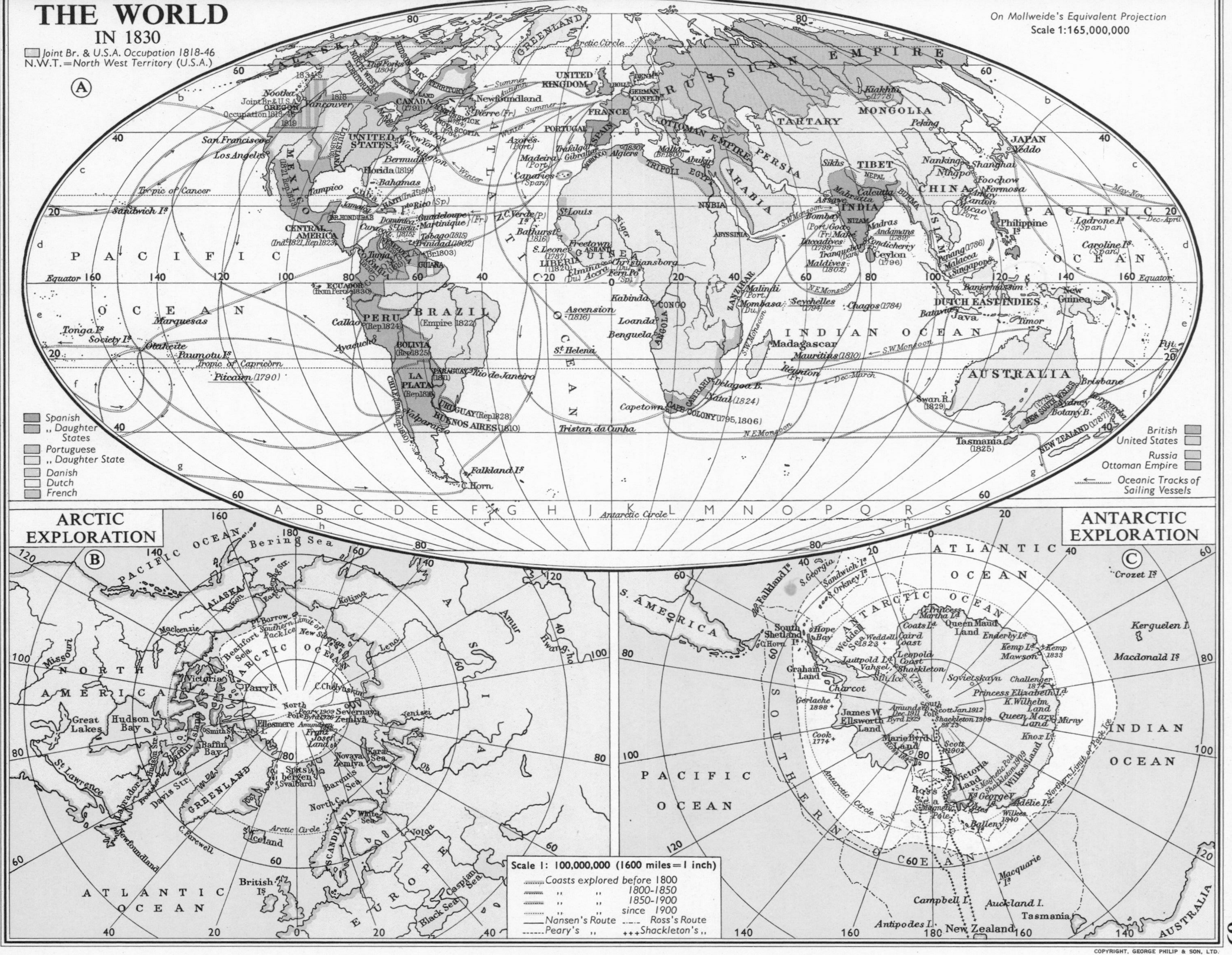
THE WORLD
IN 1830
Joint Br. & U.S.A. Occupation 1818-46
N.W.T.=North West Territory (U.S.A.)
On Mollweide's Equivalent Projection
Scale 1:165,000,000
A
Spanish
,, Daughter States
Portuguese
,, Daughter State
Danish
Dutch
French
British
United States
Russia
Ottoman Empire
Oceanic Tracks of Sailing Vessels
ARCTIC EXPLORATION
B
ANTARCTIC EXPLORATION
C
Scale 1: 100,000,000 (1600 miles=1 inch)
Coasts explored before 1800
,, ,, 1800-1850
,, ,, 1850-1900
,, ,, since 1900
Nansen's Route
Peary's ,,
Ross's Route
Shackleton's ,,

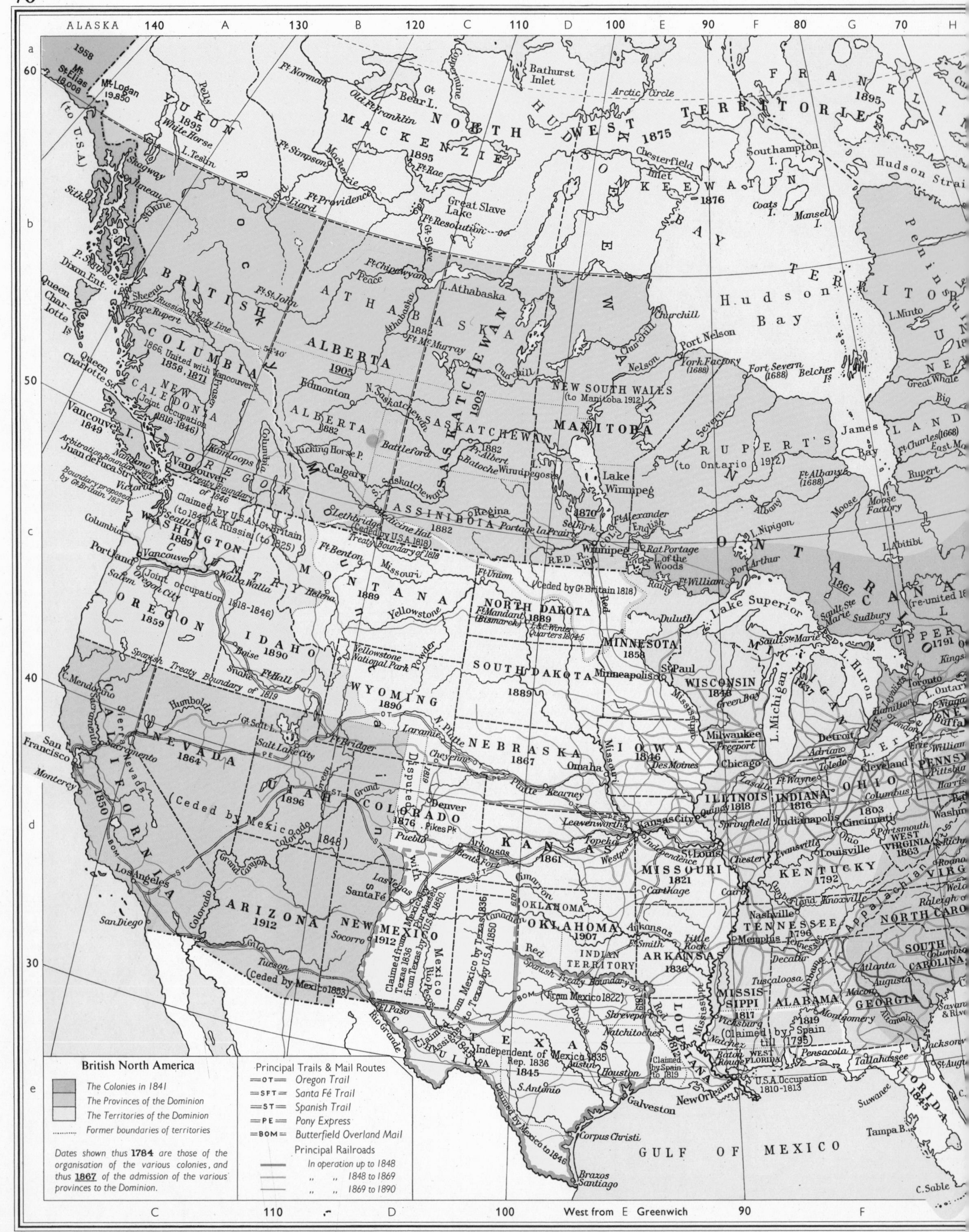
British North America
The Colonies in 1841
The Provinces of the Dominion
The Territories of the Dominion
Former boundaries of territories
Dates shown thus 1784 are those of the organisation of the various colonies, and thus 1867 of the admission of the various provinces to the Dominion.
Principal Trails & Mail Routes
OT Oregon Trail
SFT Santa Fé Trail
ST Spanish Trail
PE Pony Express
BOM Butterfield Overland Mail
Principal Railroads
In operation up to 1848
" " 1848 to 1869
" " 1869 to 1890
West from Greenwich
ALASKA
YUKON 1895
MACKENZIE 1895
NORTH-WEST TERRITORIES 1875
FRANKLIN 1895
KEEWATIN 1876
Hudson Bay
ATHABASKA 1882
ALBERTA 1905
ALBERTA 1882
SASKATCHEWAN 1905
SASKATCHEWAN 1882
ASSINIBOIA 1882
MANITOBA 1870
NEW SOUTH WALES (to Manitoba 1912)
RUPERT'S LAND (to Ontario 1912)
BRITISH COLUMBIA 1866 United with Vancouver 1858 1871
NEW CALEDONIA (Joint Occupation 1818-1846)
Vancouver I. 1849
OREGON COUNTRY
Claimed by U.S.A. (to 1846) & Russia (to 1825) G.t Britain
ONTARIO 1867
UPPER CANADA 1791
WASHINGTON 1889
OREGON 1859
IDAHO 1890
MONTANA 1889
WYOMING 1890
NORTH DAKOTA 1889
SOUTH DAKOTA 1889
MINNESOTA 1858
WISCONSIN 1848
MICHIGAN 1837
NEVADA 1864
CALIFORNIA 1850
UTAH 1896
COLORADO 1876
NEBRASKA 1867
IOWA 1846
ILLINOIS 1818
INDIANA 1816
OHIO 1803
KANSAS 1861
MISSOURI 1821
KENTUCKY 1792
WEST VIRGINIA 1863
ARIZONA 1912
NEW MEXICO 1912
OKLAHOMA 1907
INDIAN TERRITORY
ARKANSAS 1836
TENNESSEE 1796
MISSISSIPPI 1817
ALABAMA 1819
GEORGIA
SOUTH CAROLINA
NORTH CAROLINA
TEXAS Independent of Mexico 1835 Rep. 1836 1845
LOUISIANA
FLORIDA 1845
(Ceded by Mexico 1848)
(Ceded by Mexico 1853)
Spanish Treaty Boundary of 1819
Treaty Boundary of 1818
(Ceded by G.t Britain 1818)
GULF OF MEXICO

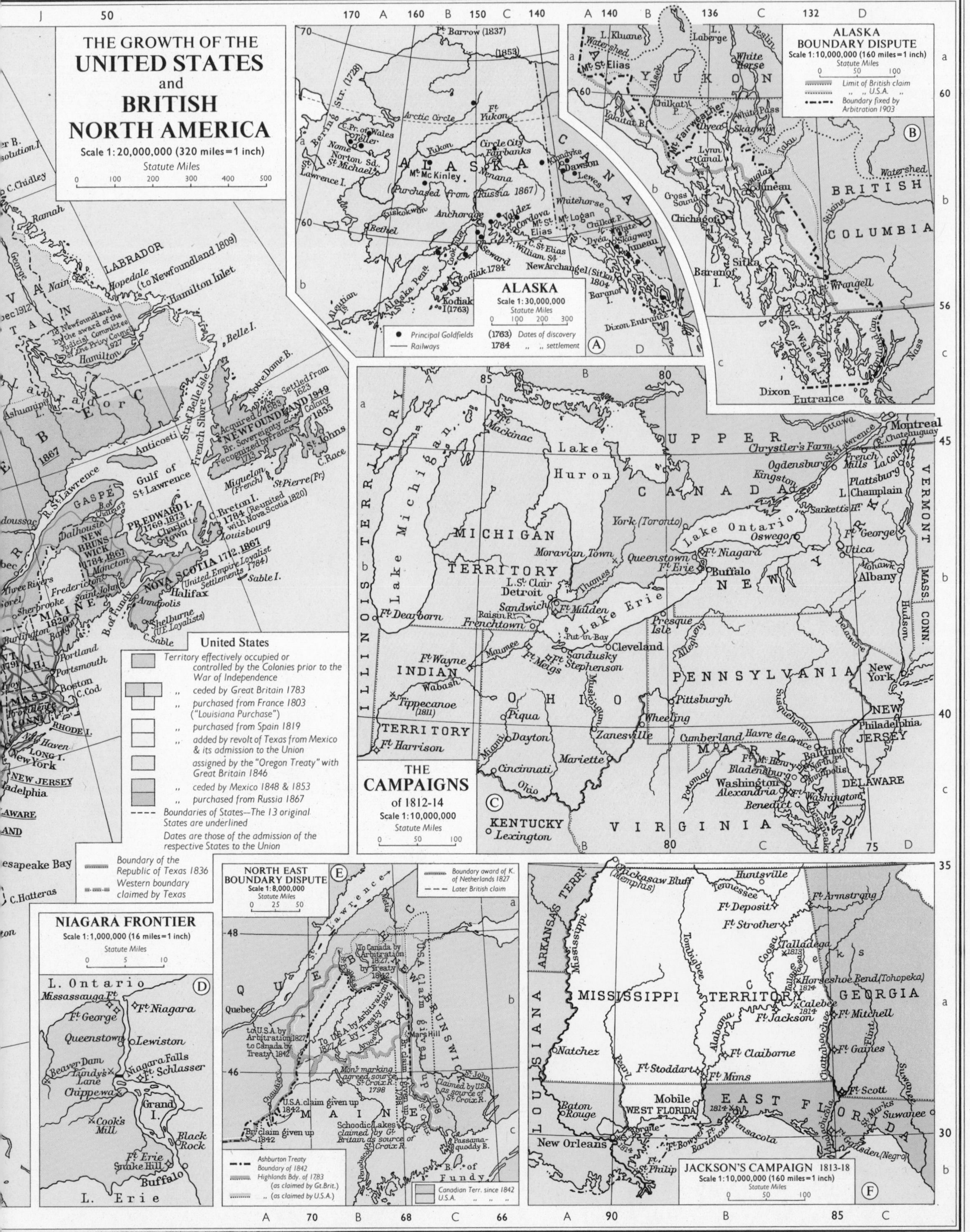
THE GROWTH OF THE UNITED STATES and BRITISH NORTH AMERICA
Scale 1: 20,000,000 (320 miles = 1 inch)
Statute Miles
0 100 200 300 400 500
United States
Territory effectively occupied or controlled by the Colonies prior to the War of Independence
,, ceded by Great Britain 1783
,, purchased from France 1803 ("Louisiana Purchase")
,, purchased from Spain 1819
,, added by revolt of Texas from Mexico & its admission to the Union
,, assigned by the "Oregon Treaty" with Great Britain 1846
,, ceded by Mexico 1848 & 1853
,, purchased from Russia 1867
Boundaries of States–The 13 original States are underlined
Dates are those of the admission of the respective States to the Union
Boundary of the Republic of Texas 1836
Western boundary claimed by Texas
LABRADOR
NEWFOUNDLAND 1949
Gulf of St Lawrence
NEW BRUNSWICK 1784, 1867
NOVA SCOTIA 1712, 1867
PR. EDWARD I. 1769, 1873
ALASKA
Scale 1: 30,000,000
Statute Miles
0 100 200 300
Principal Goldfields
Railways
(1763) Dates of discovery
1784 ,, ,, settlement
(Purchased from Russia 1867)
ALASKA BOUNDARY DISPUTE
Scale 1: 10,000,000 (160 miles = 1 inch)
Statute Miles
0 50 100
Limit of British claim
,, ,, U.S.A. ,,
Boundary fixed by Arbitration 1903
BRITISH COLUMBIA
YUKON
THE CAMPAIGNS of 1812-14
Scale 1: 10,000,000
Statute Miles
0 50 100
UPPER CANADA
MICHIGAN TERRITORY
INDIAN TERRITORY
ILLINOIS TERRITORY
OHIO
PENNSYLVANIA
NEW YORK
VIRGINIA
KENTUCKY
NIAGARA FRONTIER
Scale 1: 1,000,000 (16 miles = 1 inch)
Statute Miles
0 5 10
L. Ontario
L. Erie
NORTH EAST BOUNDARY DISPUTE
Scale 1: 8,000,000
Statute Miles
0 25 50
Boundary award of K. of Netherlands 1827
Later British claim
Ashburton Treaty Boundary of 1842
Highlands Bdy. of 1783 (as claimed by Gt. Brit.)
,, (as claimed by U.S.A.)
Canadian Terr. since 1842
U.S.A. ,, ,,
QUEBEC
MAINE
NEW BRUNSWICK
JACKSON'S CAMPAIGN 1813-18
Scale 1: 10,000,000 (160 miles = 1 inch)
Statute Miles
0 50 100
MISSISSIPPI TERRITORY
GEORGIA
EAST FLORIDA
WEST FLORIDA
LOUISIANA
ARKANSAS TERR.

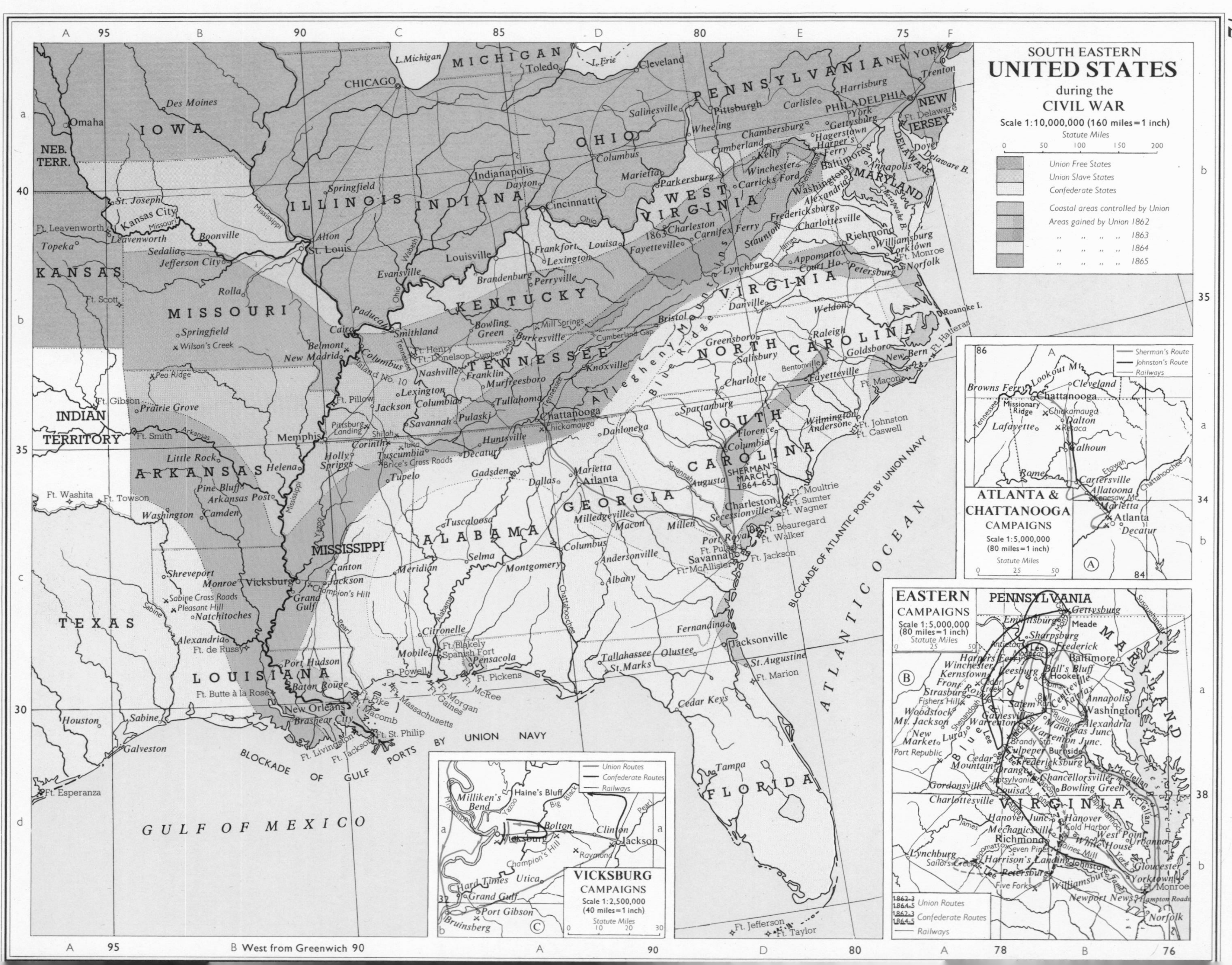
SOUTH EASTERN
UNITED STATES
during the
CIVIL WAR
Scale 1:10,000,000 (160 miles=1 inch)
Statute Miles
0 50 100 150 200
Union Free States
Union Slave States
Confederate States
Coastal areas controlled by Union
Areas gained by Union 1862
" " " " 1863
" " " " 1864
" " " " 1865
ATLANTA & CHATTANOOGA CAMPAIGNS
Scale 1:5,000,000
(80 miles=1 inch)
Statute Miles
Sherman's Route
Johnston's Route
Railways
EASTERN CAMPAIGNS
Scale 1:5,000,000
(80 miles=1 inch)
Statute Miles
Union Routes
Confederate Routes
Railways
VICKSBURG CAMPAIGNS
Scale 1:2,500,000
(40 miles=1 inch)
Statute Miles
Union Routes
Confederate Routes
Railways
BLOCKADE OF ATLANTIC PORTS BY UNION NAVY
BLOCKADE OF GULF PORTS BY UNION NAVY
ATLANTIC OCEAN
GULF OF MEXICO
SHERMAN'S MARCH 1864-65
West from Greenwich 90

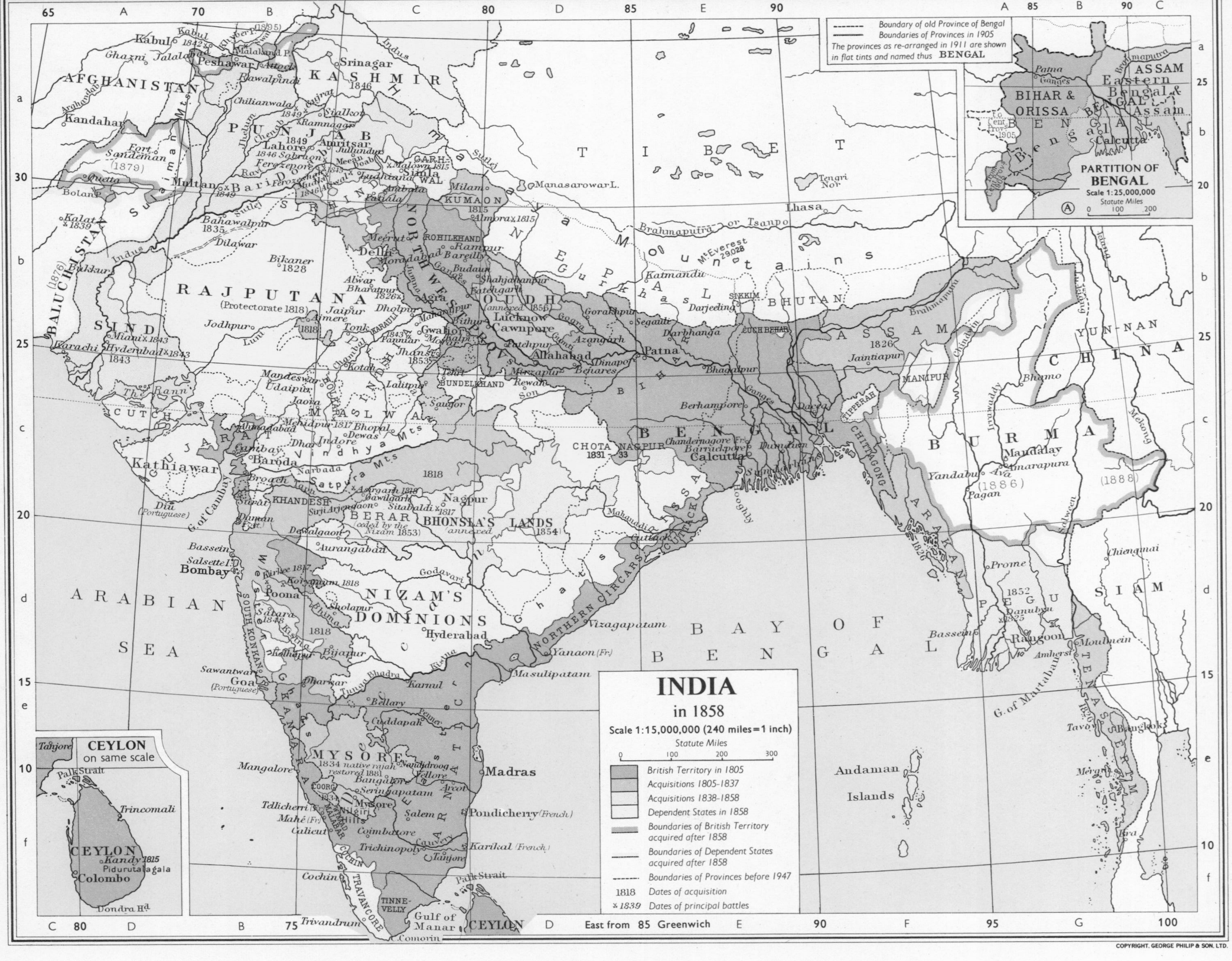
INDIA
in 1858
Scale 1:15,000,000 (240 miles=1 inch)
Statute Miles
British Territory in 1805
Acquisitions 1805-1837
Acquisitions 1838-1858
Dependent States in 1858
Boundaries of British Territory acquired after 1858
Boundaries of Dependent States acquired after 1858
Boundaries of Provinces before 1947
1818 Dates of acquisition
x 1839 Dates of principal battles
East from 85 Greenwich
PARTITION OF BENGAL
Scale 1:25,000,000
Boundary of old Province of Bengal
Boundaries of Provinces in 1905
The provinces as re-arranged in 1911 are shown in flat tints and named thus BENGAL
CEYLON
on same scale
ARABIAN SEA
BAY OF BENGAL
RAJPUTANA
NIZAM'S DOMINIONS
MYSORE
BURMA
TIBET
AFGHANISTAN
BALUCHISTAN
KASHMIR
PUNJAB
SIND
ASSAM
BENGAL
CHINA
SIAM
Madras
Calcutta
Bombay
Hyderabad
Delhi

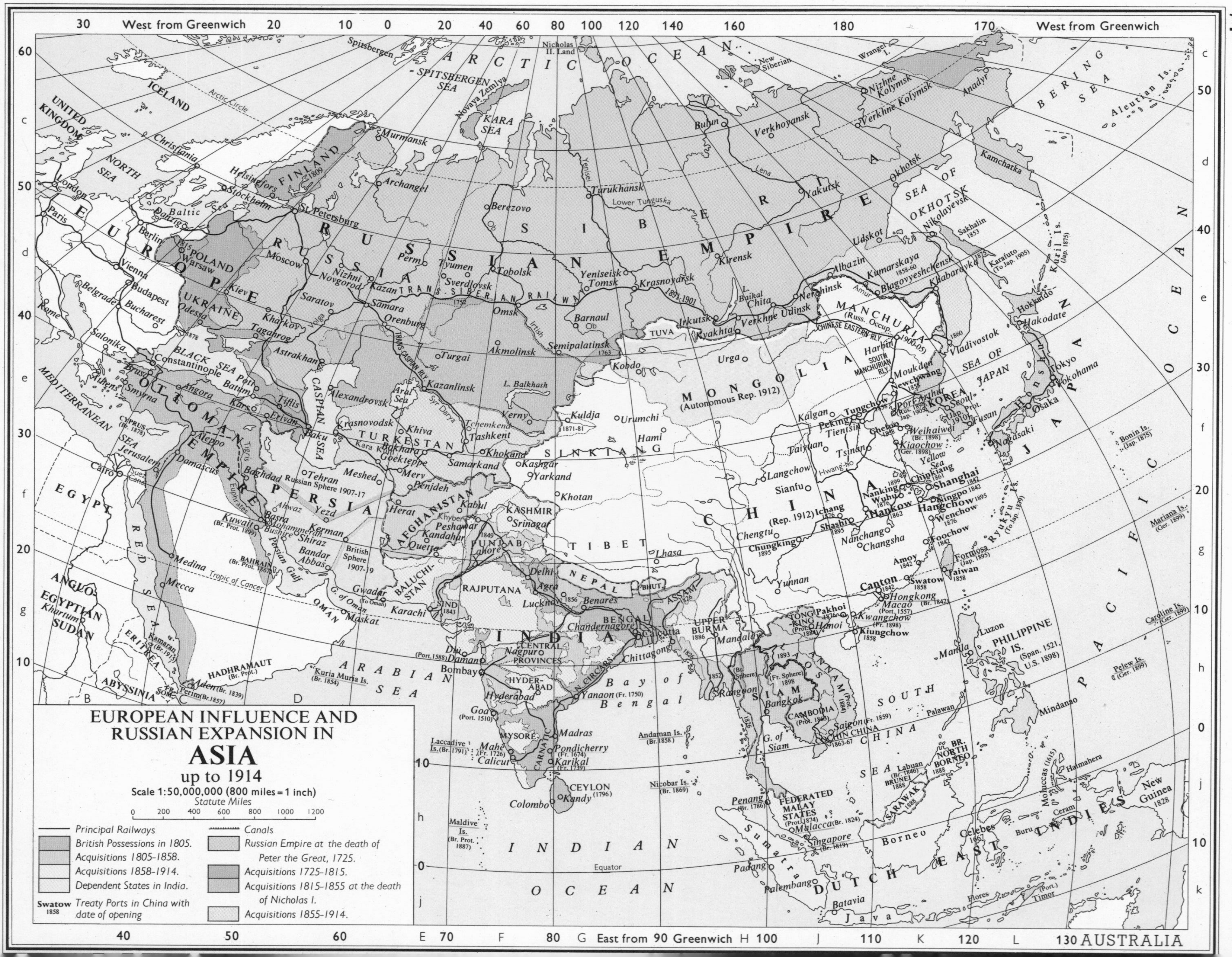
EUROPEAN INFLUENCE AND RUSSIAN EXPANSION IN
ASIA
up to 1914
Scale 1:50,000,000 (800 miles = 1 inch)
Statute Miles
0 200 400 600 800 1000 1200
Principal Railways
British Possessions in 1805.
Acquisitions 1805-1858.
Acquisitions 1858-1914.
Dependent States in India.
Swatow 1858 Treaty Ports in China with date of opening
Canals
Russian Empire at the death of Peter the Great, 1725.
Acquisitions 1725-1815.
Acquisitions 1815-1855 at the death of Nicholas I.
Acquisitions 1855-1914.
West from Greenwich
East from 90 Greenwich
ARCTIC OCEAN
PACIFIC OCEAN
INDIAN OCEAN
RUSSIAN EMPIRE
SIBERIA
MONGOLIA
CHINA
INDIA
PERSIA
OTTOMAN EMPIRE
JAPAN
DUTCH EAST INDIES
AUSTRALIA

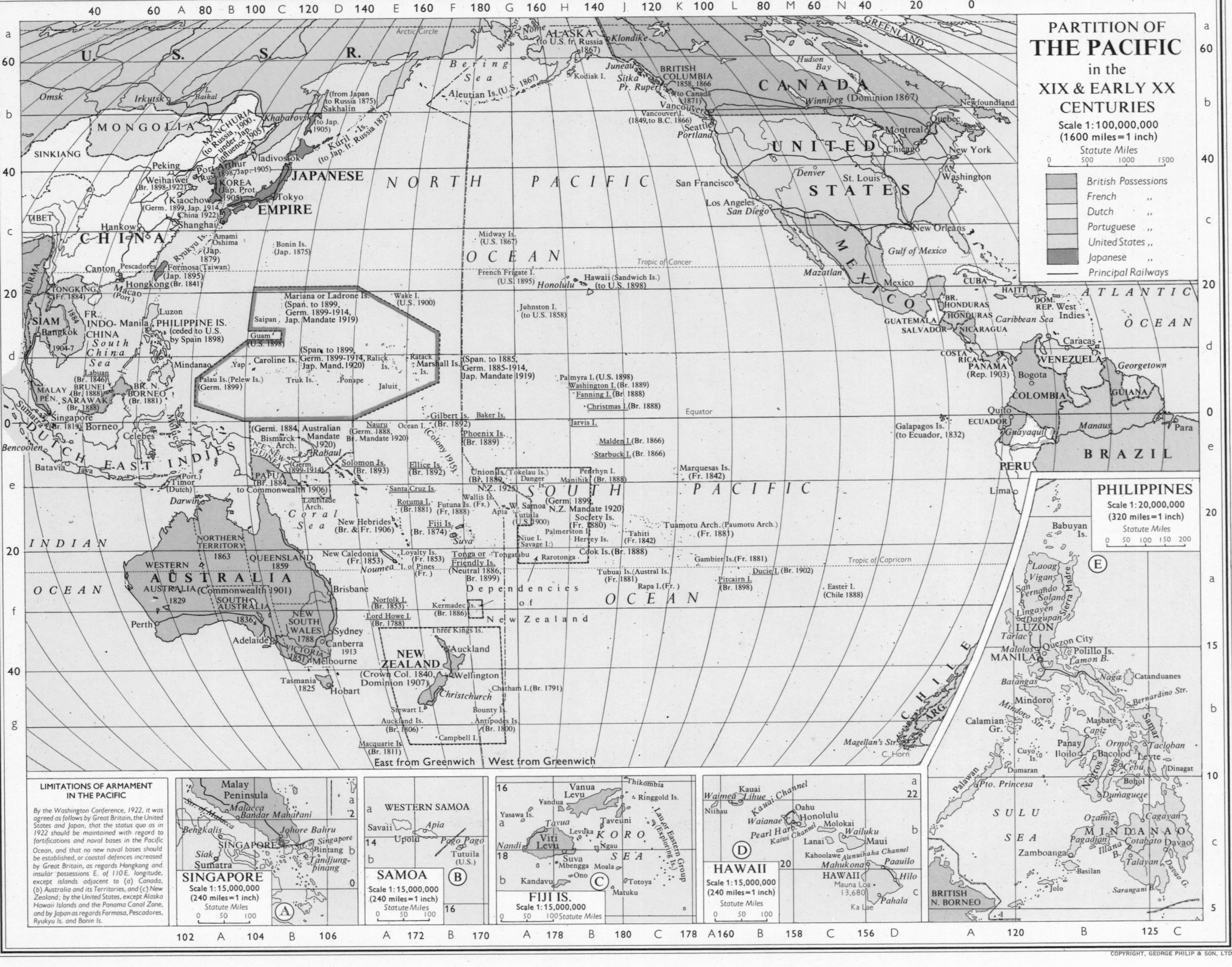

PARTITION OF
THE PACIFIC
in the
XIX & EARLY XX
CENTURIES
Scale 1:100,000,000
(1600 miles=1 inch)
Statute Miles
0 500 1000 1500
British Possessions
French
Dutch
Portuguese
United States
Japanese
Principal Railways
U. S. S. R.
MONGOLIA
MANCHURIA (to Russia 1900, under Jap. influence 1905)
SINKIANG
CHINA
KOREA (Jap. Prot. 1905)
JAPANESE EMPIRE
Tokyo
Port Arthur (Russ. 1898, Jap. 1905)
Weihaiwei (Br. 1898-1922)
Kiaochow (Germ. 1899, Jap. 1914, China 1922)
Shanghai
Hankow
Canton
Hongkong (Br. 1841)
Macao (Port.)
Formosa (Taiwan) (Jap. 1895)
Ryukyu Is.
Amami Oshima (Jap. 1879)
Bonin Is. (Jap. 1875)
Sakhalin (from Japan to Russia 1875)
Kuril Is. (to Jap. fr. Russia 1875)
Vladivostok
Khabarovsk
TONGKING (Fr. 1884)
SIAM
Bangkok
FR. INDO-CHINA
BURMA
TIBET
PHILIPPINE IS. (ceded to U.S. by Spain 1898)
Luzon
Manila
Mindanao
MALAY PEN.
Singapore (Br. 1819)
Labuan (Br. 1846)
BRUNEI (Br. 1888)
SARAWAK (Br. 1888)
BR. N. BORNEO (Br. 1881)
Borneo
Celebes
Moluccas
Sumatra
Java
Batavia
Bencoolen
DUTCH EAST INDIES
Mariana or Ladrone Is. (Span. to 1899, Germ. 1899-1914, Jap. Mandate 1919)
Saipan
Guam (U.S. 1898)
Caroline Is. (Span. to 1899, Germ. 1899-1914, Jap. Mand. 1920)
Palau Is. (Pelew Is.) (Germ. 1899)
Yap
Truk Is.
Ponape
Ralick Is.
Ratack Is.
Marshall Is. (Span. to 1885, Germ. 1885-1914, Jap. Mandate 1919)
Jaluit
Wake I. (U.S. 1900)
Midway Is. (U.S. 1867)
French Frigate I. (U.S. 1895)
Hawaii (Sandwich Is.) (to U.S. 1898)
Honolulu
Johnston I. (to U.S. 1858)
Palmyra I. (U.S. 1898)
Washington I. (Br. 1889)
Fanning I. (Br. 1888)
Christmas I. (Br. 1888)
Jarvis I.
Malden I. (Br. 1866)
Starbuck I. (Br. 1866)
Gilbert Is. (Br. 1892)
Baker Is.
Ocean I.
Nauru (Germ. 1888, Br. Mandate 1920)
Phoenix Is. (Br. 1889)
Ellice Is. (Br. 1892)
(Colony 1915)
(Germ. 1884, Australian Mandate 1920)
Bismarck Arch.
NEW GUINEA
Rabaul
PAPUA (Br. 1884, to Commonwealth 1906)
Solomon Is. (Br. 1893)
Timor (Port.) (Dutch)
Darwin
Louisiade Arch.
Coral Sea
Santa Cruz Is.
Rotuma I. (Br. 1881)
New Hebrides (Br. & Fr. 1906)
Futuna Is. (Fr. 1888)
Wallis Is. (Fr.)
Fiji Is. (Br. 1874)
Suva
New Caledonia (Fr. 1853)
Noumea
Loyalty Is. (Fr. 1853)
I. of Pines (Fr.)
Tonga or Friendly Is. (Neutral 1886, Br. 1899)
Tongatabu
Union Is. (Tokelau Is.) (Br. 1889, N.Z. 1925)
Danger Is.
W. Samoa
Apia
Tutuila (U.S. 1900)
(Germ. 1899, N.Z. Mandate 1920)
Niue I. (Savage I.)
Palmerston I.
Hervey Is.
Rarotonga
Cook Is. (Br. 1888)
Manihiki
Penrhyn I. (Br. 1888)
Society Is. (Fr. 1880)
Tahiti (Fr. 1842)
Marquesas Is. (Fr. 1842)
Tuamotu Arch. (Paumotu Arch.) (Fr. 1881)
Gambier Is. (Fr. 1881)
Tubuai Is. (Austral Is.) (Fr. 1881)
Rapa I. (Fr.)
Pitcairn I. (Br. 1898)
Ducie I. (Br. 1902)
Easter I. (Chile 1888)
Kermadec Is. (Br. 1886)
Norfolk I. (Br. 1853)
Lord Howe I. (Br. 1788)
Dependencies of New Zealand
Three Kings Is.
NEW ZEALAND (Crown Col. 1840, Dominion 1907)
Auckland
Wellington
Christchurch
Chatham I. (Br. 1791)
Bounty Is.
Antipodes Is. (Br. 1800)
Stewart I.
Auckland Is. (Br. 1806)
Campbell I.
Macquarie Is. (Br. 1811)
AUSTRALIA (Commonwealth 1901)
WESTERN AUSTRALIA 1829
NORTHERN TERRITORY 1863
QUEENSLAND 1859
SOUTH AUSTRALIA 1836
NEW SOUTH WALES 1788
VICTORIA 1851
Tasmania 1825
Perth
Adelaide
Melbourne
Canberra 1913
Sydney
Brisbane
Hobart
INDIAN OCEAN
NORTH PACIFIC OCEAN
SOUTH PACIFIC OCEAN
Tropic of Cancer
Equator
Tropic of Capricorn
Arctic Circle
East from Greenwich
West from Greenwich
Bering Sea
Aleutian Is. (U.S. 1867)
Nome
ALASKA (to U.S. fr. Russia 1867)
Klondike
Kodiak I.
Juneau
Sitka
Pr. Rupert
BRITISH COLUMBIA 1858, 1866 (to Canada 1871)
Vancouver
Vancouver I. (1849, to B.C. 1866)
Seattle
Portland
GREENLAND
Hudson Bay
CANADA
Winnipeg (Dominion 1867)
Newfoundland
Quebec
Montreal
Chicago
New York
Washington
UNITED STATES
Denver
St. Louis
San Francisco
Los Angeles
San Diego
New Orleans
Gulf of Mexico
MEXICO
Mazatlan
Mexico
CUBA
HAITI
DOM. REP.
West Indies
Caribbean Sea
BR. HONDURAS
HONDURAS
GUATEMALA
SALVADOR
NICARAGUA
COSTA RICA
PANAMA (Rep. 1903)
Caracas
VENEZUELA
Georgetown
GUIANA
Bogota
COLOMBIA
Quito
ECUADOR
Guayaquil
Galapagos Is. (to Ecuador, 1832)
PERU
Lima
BRAZIL
Manaus
Para
CHILE
ARG.
Magellan's Str.
C. Horn
ATLANTIC OCEAN
PHILIPPINES
Scale 1:20,000,000
(320 miles=1 inch)
Statute Miles
0 50 100 150 200
Babuyan Is.
Laoag
Vigan
San Fernando
Solano
Sierra Madre
Lingayen
Dagupan
LUZON
Tarlac
Malolos
Quezon City
MANILA
Polillo Is.
Lamon B.
Naga
Catanduanes
Batangas
Mindoro
Mindoro Str.
Bernardino Str.
Samar
Calamian Gr.
Masbate
Capiz
Panay
Iloilo
Ormoc
Tacloban
Leyte
Bacolod
Negros
Cebu
Dinagat
Cuyo Is.
Dumaran
Palawan
Pto. Princesa
Bohol
Dumaguete
SULU SEA
Ozamiz
Cagayan
MINDANAO
Pagadian
Illana B.
Cotabato
Davao
Talayan
Davao G.
Zamboanga
Basilan
Jolo
Sarangani B.
BRITISH N. BORNEO
LIMITATIONS OF ARMAMENT IN THE PACIFIC
By the Washington Conference, 1922, it was agreed as follows by Great Britain, the United States and Japan, that the status quo as in 1922 should be maintained with regard to fortifications and naval bases in the Pacific Ocean, and that no new naval bases should be established, or coastal defences increased by Great Britain, as regards Hongkong and insular possessions E. of 110E. longitude, except islands adjacent to (a) Canada, (b) Australia and its Territories, and (c) New Zealand; by the United States, except Alaska Hawaii Islands and the Panama Canal Zone, and by Japan as regards Formosa, Pescadores, Ryukyu Is. and Bonin Is.
Malay Peninsula
Malacca
Bandar Maharani
Str. of Malacca
Bengkalis
Johore Bahru
SINGAPORE
Str. of Singapore
Bintang
Tandjung-pinang
Siak
Sumatra
SINGAPORE
Scale 1:15,000,000
(240 miles=1 inch)
Statute Miles
0 50 100
WESTERN SAMOA
Savaii
Upolu
Apia
Pago Pago
Tutuila (U.S.)
SAMOA
Scale 1:15,000,000
(240 miles=1 inch)
Statute Miles
0 50 100
Vanua Levu
Yandua
Thikombia
Ringgold Is.
Yasawa Is.
Tavua
Taveuni
Viti Levu
Levuka
Nandi
KORO SEA
Lau or Eastern Group (Exploring Is.)
Ngau
Suva
Mbengga
Moala
Ono
Totoya
Kandavu
Matuku
FIJI IS.
Scale 1:15,000,000
0 50 100 Statute Miles
Kauai
Waimea
Lihue
Kauai Channel
Niihau
Oahu
Waianae
Honolulu
Pearl Harb.
Kaiwi Channel
Molokai
Lanai
Wailuku
Maui
Kahoolawe
Alenuihaha Channel
Mahukona
Paauilo
HAWAII
Mauna Loa 13,680
Hilo
Ka Lae
Pahala
HAWAII
Scale 1:15,000,000
(240 miles=1 inch)
Statute Miles
0 50 100

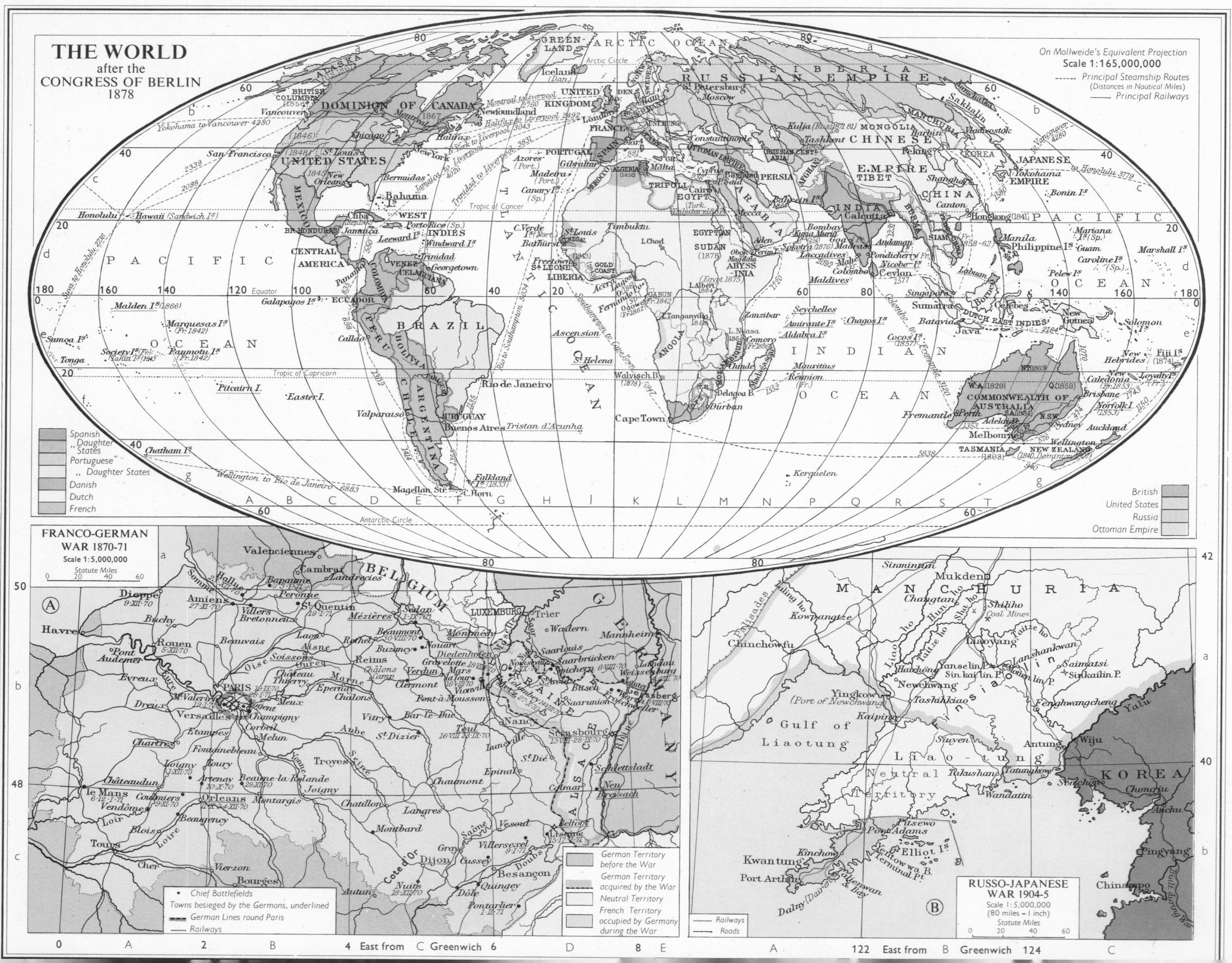
THE WORLD
after the
CONGRESS OF BERLIN
1878
On Mollweide's Equivalent Projection
Scale 1:165,000,000
Principal Steamship Routes
(Distances in Nautical Miles)
Principal Railways
Spanish
,, Daughter States
Portuguese
,, Daughter States
Danish
Dutch
French
British
United States
Russia
Ottoman Empire
RUSSIAN EMPIRE
SIBERIA
DOMINION OF CANADA
UNITED STATES
CHINESE EMPIRE
JAPANESE EMPIRE
INDIA
BRAZIL
ARGENTINA
COMMONWEALTH OF AUSTRALIA
PACIFIC OCEAN
ATLANTIC OCEAN
INDIAN OCEAN
ARCTIC OCEAN
FRANCO-GERMAN
WAR 1870-71
Scale 1:5,000,000
Statute Miles
Chief Battlefields
Towns besieged by the Germans, underlined
German Lines round Paris
Railways
German Territory before the War
German Territory acquired by the War
Neutral Territory
French Territory occupied by Germany during the War
BELGIUM
GERMANY
LUXEMBURG
PARIS
ALSACE
LORRAINE
RUSSO-JAPANESE
WAR 1904-5
Scale 1:5,000,000
(80 miles = 1 inch)
Statute Miles
Railways
Roads
MANCHURIA
KOREA
Gulf of Liaotung
Liao-tung
Neutral Territory
Port Arthur
Mukden
East from Greenwich

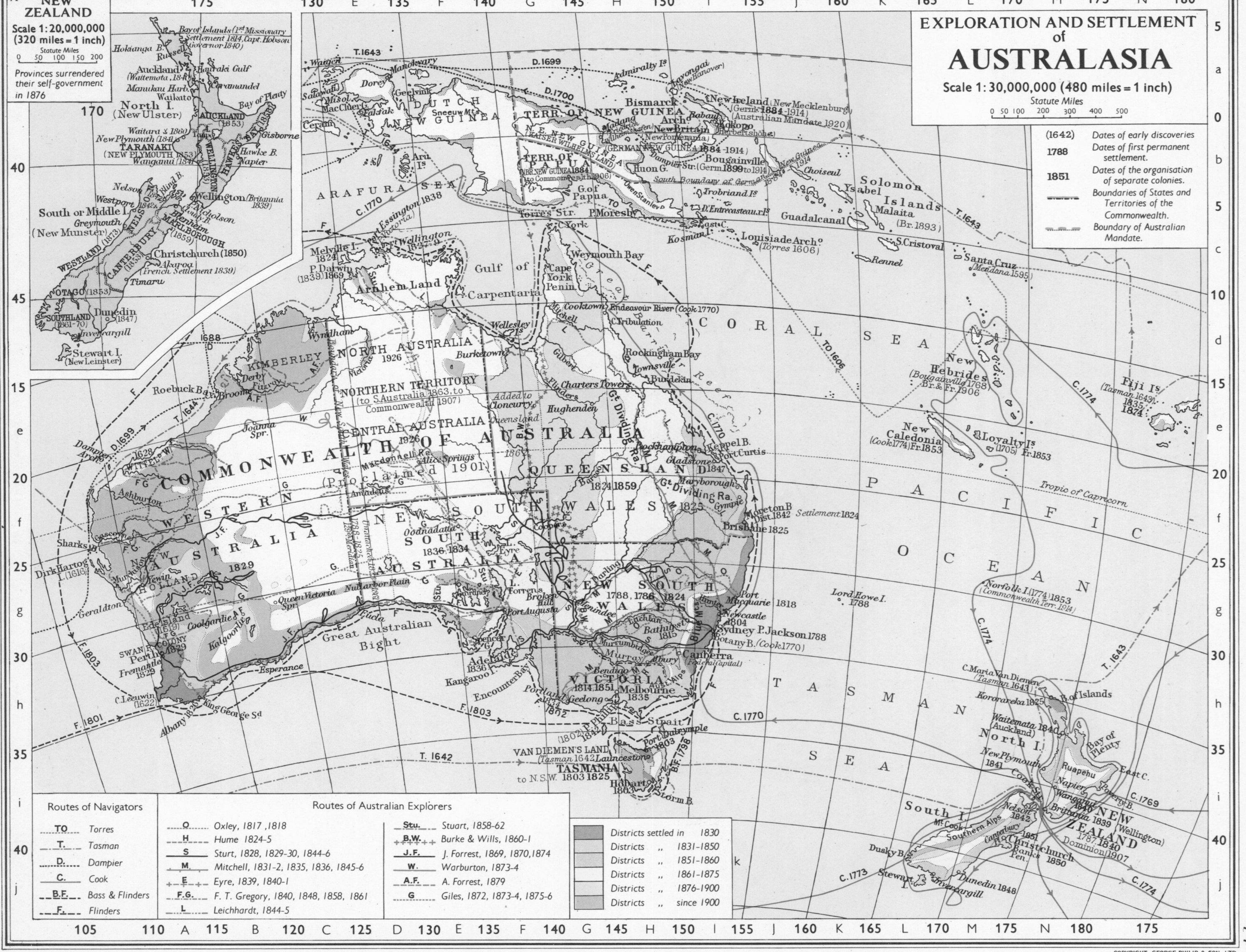

EXPLORATION AND SETTLEMENT of AUSTRALASIA
Scale 1:30,000,000 (480 miles = 1 inch)
Statute Miles
(1642) Dates of early discoveries
1788 Dates of first permanent settlement.
1851 Dates of the organisation of separate colonies.
Boundaries of States and Territories of the Commonwealth.
Boundary of Australian Mandate.
NEW ZEALAND
Scale 1:20,000,000 (320 miles = 1 inch)
Provinces surrendered their self-government in 1876
Routes of Navigators
TO Torres
T. Tasman
D. Dampier
C. Cook
B.F. Bass & Flinders
F. Flinders
Routes of Australian Explorers
O Oxley, 1817, 1818
H Hume 1824-5
S Sturt, 1828, 1829-30, 1844-6
M Mitchell, 1831-2, 1835, 1836, 1845-6
E Eyre, 1839, 1840-1
F.G. F. T. Gregory, 1840, 1848, 1858, 1861
L Leichhardt, 1844-5
Stu. Stuart, 1858-62
B.W. Burke & Wills, 1860-1
J.F. J. Forrest, 1869, 1870, 1874
W. Warburton, 1873-4
A.F. A. Forrest, 1879
G Giles, 1872, 1873-4, 1875-6
Districts settled in 1830
Districts ,, 1831-1850
Districts ,, 1851-1860
Districts ,, 1861-1875
Districts ,, 1876-1900
Districts ,, since 1900
COMMONWEALTH OF AUSTRALIA (Proclaimed 1901)
WESTERN AUSTRALIA 1829
NORTH AUSTRALIA 1926
NORTHERN TERRITORY (to S.Australia 1863, to Commonwealth 1907)
CENTRAL AUSTRALIA 1926
QUEENSLAND 1824 1859
NEW SOUTH WALES 1788, 1786
SOUTH AUSTRALIA 1836 1834
VICTORIA 1814 1851
VAN DIEMEN'S LAND (Tasman 1642)
TASMANIA to N.S.W. 1803 1825
NEW ZEALAND 1787 1840 Dominion 1907
CORAL SEA
TASMAN SEA
PACIFIC OCEAN
ARAFURA SEA
Great Australian Bight
Gulf of Carpentaria
Tropic of Capricorn
DUTCH NEW GUINEA
TERR. OF NEW GUINEA
TERR. OF PAPUA
Solomon Islands (Br. 1893)
New Hebrides (Bougainville 1768) Br. & Fr. 1906
New Caledonia (Cook 1774) Fr. 1853
Fiji Is (Tasman 1643) 1835 1874
Sydney P. Jackson 1788
Botany B. (Cook 1770)
Canberra (Federal Capital)
Melbourne 1835
Adelaide 1836
Brisbane 1825
Hobart 1803
Perth 1829
Dunedin 1848
Christchurch 1850

BALKAN PENINSULA
1800-1914
Scale 1:6,000,000 (96 miles=1 inch)
Statute Miles
0 50 100
Ottoman Boundary in 1800
Ottoman Boundary in 1900
Bulgarian Boundary proposed by Treaty of San Stefano 1878, amended by Treaty of Berlin 1878
Boundaries of the Balkan States as modified by the Treaties of London and Bucharest 1913 and by subsequent agreements.
States are coloured as in 1878, with later acquisitions in lighter tints.
THE SLAVONIC and BULGARIAN POWERS in the BALKAN PENINSULA
Scale 1:20,000,000
Bulgarian power in XIV C. (before Turkish Invasion)
Bulgarian power at its widest extent (IX C.)
K. of Serbia in 1350 under Stephen Dushan
Extent of S.W. Slavonic or Serbian Settlements in VIII C. (Slavs, Serbs, Croats & Crovats).
Vienna
Drave
Save
Belgrade
Danube
SERBIA
BULGARIA
Tirnova
Ragusa
Serdica
Philippopolis
Adrianople
Constantinople
Uskub
Okhrida
Durazzo
Salonica
Janina
Athens
A
CRETE
(Autonomous 1898)
(To Greece 1908)
Continuation of Main Map on same scale
C. Malia
Cerigo
Suda
Canea
Candia
Mt Ida
AUSTRIA HUNGARY
RUSSIA
BESSARABIA
(To Russia 1812)
JEDISAN
(to Russia 1791)
BUKOVINA
to Austr. 1777
MOLDAVIA
(Autonomous 1822)
TRANSYLVANIA
RUMANIA
(united state 1858/61)
WALACHIA
(Autonomous 1822)
DRAGASHAN
DOBRUJA
BOSNIA
(Austrian Protectorate 1878, annexed 1909)
HERZEGOVINA
DALMATIA
Dinaric Alps
MONTENEGRO
SERBIA
Autonomous 1817
To Serbia (1878)
BULGARIA 1878
EASTERN RUMELIA
(To Bulgaria 1885)
ALBANIA
(Ind. Principality 1913)
MACEDONIA
THRACE
THESSALY
(To Greece 1881-'97)
LIVADIA
GREECE
MOREA
IONIAN IS.
(To Greece 1863)
English Prot. 1814-'63
ASIA MINOR
ADRIATIC SEA
IONIAN SEA
ÆGEAN SEA
BLACK SEA
Sea of Marmara
Sporades
Cyclades
Dodecanese
(Italian Occupation 1912)
Choczim
Czernowitz
Balta
Dniester
Sereth
Pruth
Jassy
Kishinev
Bender
Akerman
to Moldavia 1856
retroceded to Russia 1878
Kilia
Kilia Mouth
Sulina
Danube Delta
Focsani
Galatz
Ismail
Braila
Tulcea
Hirsova
Trajan's Wall
Constanta
Bucharest
Oltenitza
Silistra
Kutchuk Kainarji
Bazarchik
Balchik
Varna
Kamchik
Maros
Hermannstadt
Alt
Temesvar
Mehadia
Orsova
Iron Gate
Craiova
Dragasani
Aluta
Citatea
Widin
Danube
Giurgevo
Simnitza
Ruschuk
Nicopolis
Sistova
Rasgrad
Shumla
Pravadi
Brod
Save
Bosna
Banyaluka
Semlin
Belgrade
Chabats
Passarowitz
Semendria
Sokol
Drina
Morava
Travnik
Sarajevo
Kraguyevats
Oujitsa
Krushevatz
Nish (Nissa)
Pirot
Spalato
Mostar
Narenta
Novibazar
Kossovo
Prishtina
Vrania
Tsaribrod
Slivnitza
Sofia
Dubnik
Plevna
Lovcha
Tirnova
Isker
Yantra
Shipka Pass
Gabrova
Koprivshtitza
Karlovo
Kazanlik
Stara Zagora
Tunja
Burgas
Ragusa
Castelnuovo
Cattaro
Cetinje
Tuzi
Diakova
Ristovatz
Kumanovo
Kustendil
Egri Palanka
Uskub (Skoplje)
Scutari (Skodra)
Antivari
Dulcigno
Drin
Kotchana
Philippopolis
Maritza
Balak
Tamrush
Mustapha Pasha
Kirk Kilisse
Adrianople
Midia
Strumnitza
Struma
Vardar
Durazzo
Skhumbi
Okhrida
Monastir (Bitolia)
Doiran
Seres
Kavalla
Mesta
Dimotika
Lule Burgas
Chatalja
Bosporus
Constantinople
Scutari
Rodosto
S. Stefano
Dedeagach
Enos
Thasos
Samothrace
Gallipoli
Bulair
Gemlik
Brussa
Lampsacus
Valona
Veria
Salonica
Imbros
Lemnos
Dardanelles
Tenedos
Servia
Elassona 1881
Metsovo
Janina
Corfu
Parga
Arta
Larissa
Volos
Mitylene
Preveza
Leucas
Scyros
Psara
Chios
Manissa
Smyrna
Livadia
Lepanto
Egripo
Negroponte
Cephalonia
Argostolion
Missolonghi
Trib. Prince 1829
G. of Corinth
Patras
Kalavryta
Athens
Karystos
Andros
Tinos
Samos
Aidin
Zacynthos (Zante)
Zante
Corinth
Argos
Piraeus
Egina
Nauplia
Kingdom 1830
Ruphia
Karytena
Tripolitza
Cythnos
Hydra
Spezzia
Seriphos
Paros
Naxos
Sparta
Kalamata
Navarino
Modon
Koroni
Amorgos
Cos
Malvasia
C. Malia
Milos
Cerigo
C. Matapan
Santorin
Rhodes
East from Greenwich

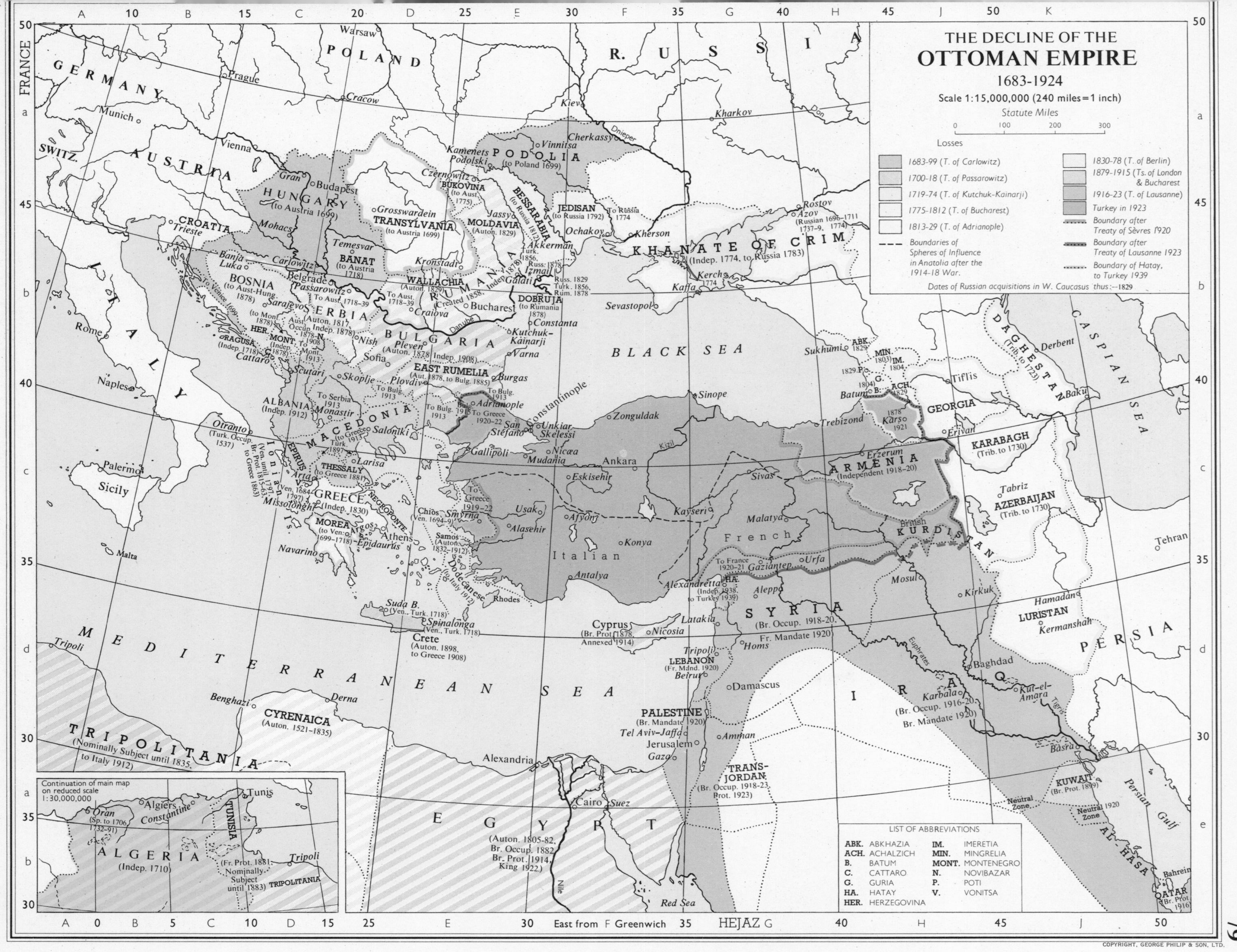
THE DECLINE OF THE
OTTOMAN EMPIRE
1683-1924
Scale 1:15,000,000 (240 miles=1 inch)
Statute Miles
0 100 200 300
Losses
1683-99 (T. of Carlowitz)
1700-18 (T. of Passarowitz)
1719-74 (T. of Kutchuk-Kainarji)
1775-1812 (T. of Bucharest)
1813-29 (T. of Adrianople)
Boundaries of Spheres of Influence in Anatolia after the 1914-18 War.
1830-78 (T. of Berlin)
1879-1915 (Ts. of London & Bucharest)
1916-23 (T. of Lausanne)
Turkey in 1923
Boundary after Treaty of Sèvres 1920
Boundary after Treaty of Lausanne 1923
Boundary of Hatay, to Turkey 1939
Dates of Russian acquisitions in W. Caucasus thus:—1829
LIST OF ABBREVIATIONS
ABK. ABKHAZIA
ACH. ACHALZICH
B. BATUM
C. CATTARO
G. GURIA
HA. HATAY
HER. HERZEGOVINA
IM. IMERETIA
MIN. MINGRELIA
MONT. MONTENEGRO
N. NOVIBAZAR
P. POTI
V. VONITSA
RUSSIA
POLAND
GERMANY
AUSTRIA
ITALY
HUNGARY (to Austria 1699)
TRANSYLVANIA (to Austria 1699)
PODOLIA (to Poland 1699)
BESSARABIA (to Russia 1812)
MOLDAVIA (Auton. 1829)
WALLACHIA (Auton. 1829)
JEDISAN (to Russia 1792)
KHANATE OF CRIM (Indep. 1774, to Russia 1783)
BANAT (to Austria 1718)
BOSNIA (to Aust-Hung. 1878)
SERBIA
BULGARIA (Auton. 1878 Indep. 1908)
EAST RUMELIA (Aut. 1878, to Bulg. 1885)
DOBRUJA (to Rumania 1878)
MACEDONIA
ALBANIA (Indep. 1912)
GREECE (Indep. 1830)
BLACK SEA
CASPIAN SEA
DAGHESTAN (Trib. to 1723)
GEORGIA
KARABAGH (Trib. to 1730)
AZERBAIJAN (Trib. to 1730)
ARMENIA (Independent 1918-20)
KURDISTAN
SYRIA (Br. Occup. 1918-20. Fr. Mandate 1920)
LEBANON (Fr. Mdnd. 1920)
PALESTINE (Br. Mandate 1920)
TRANS-JORDAN (Br. Occup. 1918-23. Prot. 1923)
IRAQ (Br. Occup. 1916-20. Br. Mandate 1920)
LURISTAN
PERSIA
KUWAIT (Br. Prot. 1899)
AL-HASA
QATAR (Br. Prot. 1916)
MEDITERRANEAN SEA
EGYPT (Auton. 1805-82, Br. Occup. 1882, Br. Prot. 1914, King 1922)
CYRENAICA (Auton. 1521-1835)
TRIPOLITANIA (Nominally Subject until 1835, to Italy 1912)
Cyprus (Br. Prot. 1878, Annexed 1914)
Crete (Auton. 1898, to Greece 1908)
Continuation of main map on reduced scale 1:30,000,000
ALGERIA (Indep. 1710)
TUNISIA (Fr. Prot. 1881. Nominally Subject until 1883)
East from Greenwich
HEJAZ

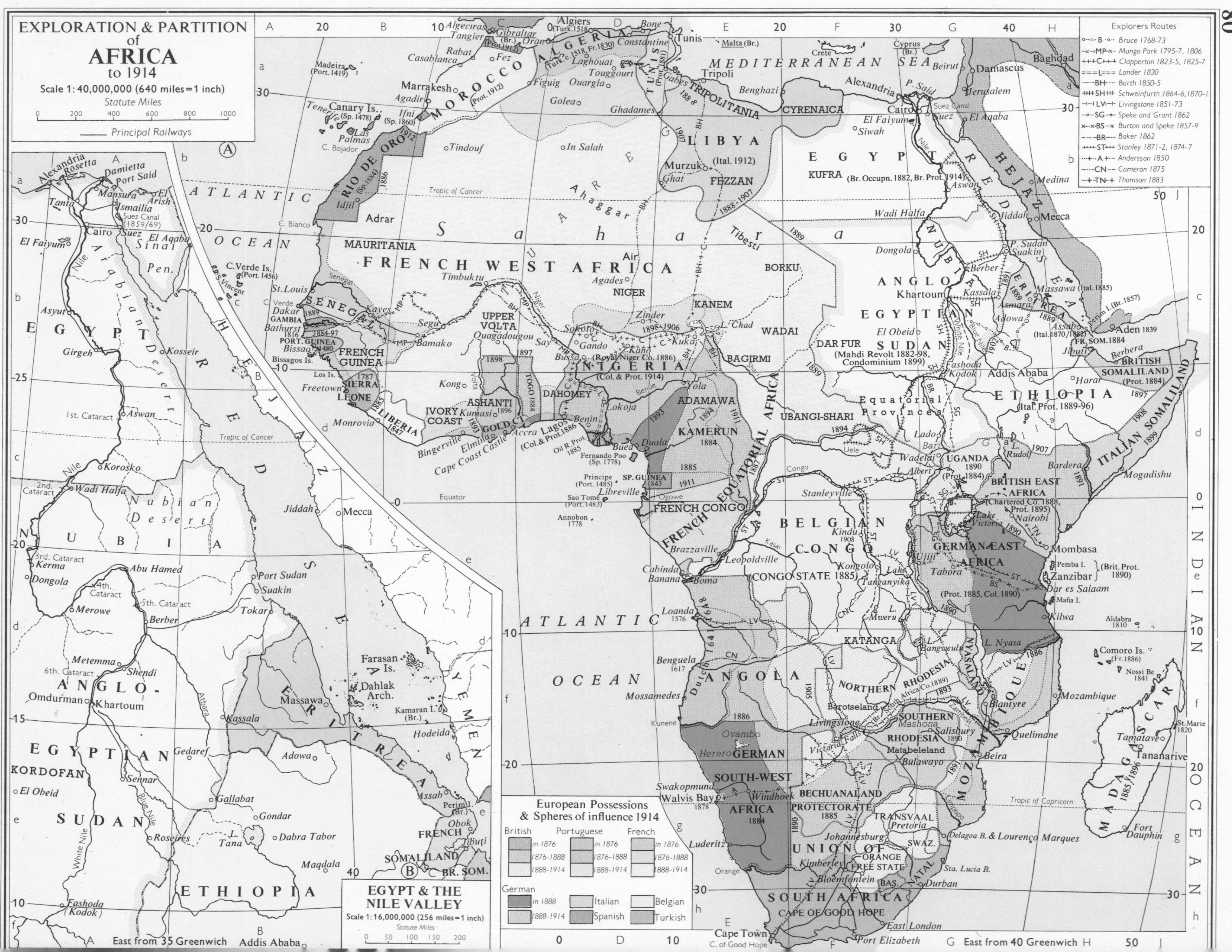

EXPLORATION & PARTITION of AFRICA to 1914
Scale 1: 40,000,000 (640 miles = 1 inch)
Statute Miles
0 200 400 600 800 1000
Principal Railways
Explorers Routes
B Bruce 1768-73
MP Mungo Park 1795-7, 1806
C Clapperton 1823-5, 1825-7
L Lander 1830
BH Barth 1850-5
SH Schweinfurth 1864-6, 1870-1
LV Livingstone 1851-73
SG Speke and Grant 1862
BS Burton and Speke 1857-9
BR Baker 1862
ST Stanley 1871-2, 1874-7
A Andersson 1850
CN Cameron 1875
TN Thomson 1883
European Possessions & Spheres of influence 1914
British
Portuguese
French
in 1876
1876-1888
1888-1914
German
in 1888
1888-1914
Italian
Spanish
Belgian
Turkish
MEDITERRANEAN SEA
ATLANTIC OCEAN
INDIAN OCEAN
RED SEA
MOROCCO (Prot. 1912)
ALGERIA
TUNIS (Prot. 1881)
TRIPOLITANIA
CYRENAICA
LIBYA (Ital. 1912)
FEZZAN
EGYPT
KUFRA (Br. Occupn. 1882, Br. Prot. 1914)
RIO DE ORO
MAURITANIA
FRENCH WEST AFRICA
Sahara
SENEGAL
GAMBIA
PORT. GUINEA
FRENCH GUINEA
SIERRA LEONE
LIBERIA 1847
IVORY COAST
GOLD CT.
ASHANTI 1896
UPPER VOLTA
TOGO 1884
DAHOMEY
NIGERIA (Col. & Prot. 1914)
NIGER
KANEM
BORKU
WADAI
BAGIRMI
DAR FUR
ANGLO EGYPTIAN SUDAN (Mahdi Revolt 1882-98, Condominium 1899)
NUBIA
ERITREA
ETHIOPIA (Ital. Prot. 1889-96)
BRITISH SOMALILAND (Prot. 1884)
FR. SOM. 1884
ITALIAN SOMALILAND
UBANGI-SHARI
EQUATORIAL AFRICA
ADAMAWA
KAMERUN 1884
SP. GUINEA 1843
FRENCH CONGO
BELGIAN CONGO (CONGO STATE 1885)
UGANDA 1890 (Prot. 1884)
BRITISH EAST AFRICA (Chartered Co. 1888, Prot. 1895)
GERMAN EAST AFRICA (Prot. 1885, Col. 1890)
Zanzibar (Brit. Prot. 1890)
ANGOLA
KATANGA
NORTHERN RHODESIA
SOUTHERN RHODESIA
NYASALAND
MOZAMBIQUE
GERMAN SOUTH-WEST AFRICA 1884
BECHUANALAND PROTECTORATE 1885
TRANSVAAL
ORANGE FREE STATE
SWAZ.
BAS.
NATAL
UNION OF SOUTH AFRICA
CAPE OF GOOD HOPE
MADAGASCAR 1885/1896
Tropic of Cancer
Equator
Tropic of Capricorn
East from 40 Greenwich
EGYPT & THE NILE VALLEY
Scale 1:16,000,000 (256 miles = 1 inch)
Statute Miles
0 50 100 150 200
EGYPT
NUBIA
ANGLO-EGYPTIAN SUDAN
KORDOFAN
ERITREA
ETHIOPIA
YEMEN
HEJAZ
FRENCH SOMALILAND
BR. SOM.
Arabian Desert
Nubian Desert
Sinai Pen.
East from 35 Greenwich

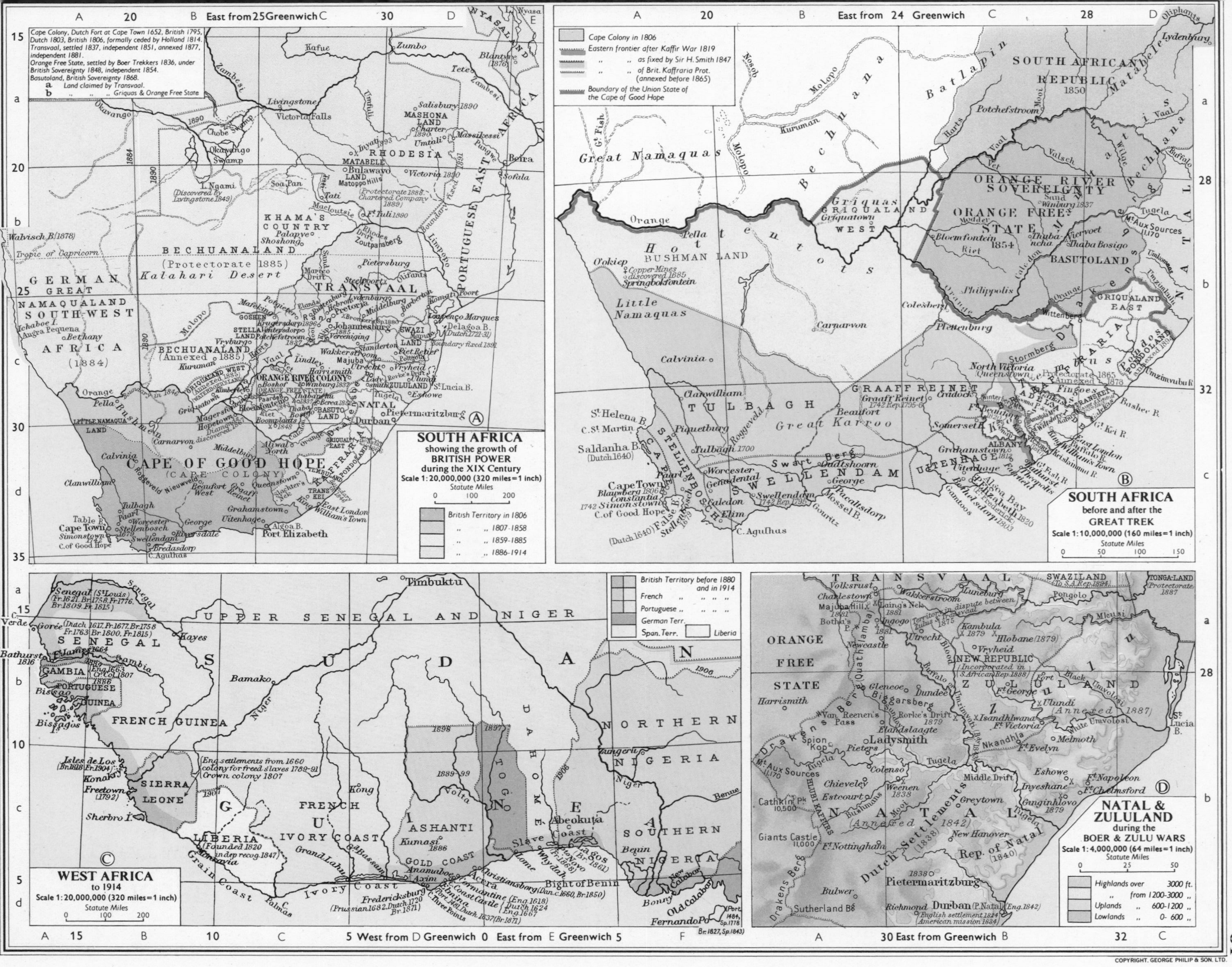
Cape Colony, Dutch Fort at Cape Town 1652, British 1795, Dutch 1803, British 1806, formally ceded by Holland 1814. Transvaal, settled 1837, independent 1851, annexed 1877, independent 1881. Orange Free State, settled by Boer Trekkers 1836, under British Sovereignty 1848, independent 1854. Basutoland, British Sovereignty 1868.
a Land claimed by Transvaal.
b „ „ „ Griquas & Orange Free State
SOUTH AFRICA
showing the growth of
BRITISH POWER
during the XIX Century
Scale 1:20,000,000 (320 miles=1 inch)
British Territory in 1806
„ „ 1807-1858
„ „ 1859-1885
„ „ 1886-1914
Cape Colony in 1806
Eastern frontier after Kaffir War 1819
„ „ as fixed by Sir H. Smith 1847
„ „ of Brit. Kaffraria Prot. (annexed before 1865)
Boundary of the Union State of the Cape of Good Hope
SOUTH AFRICA
before and after the
GREAT TREK
Scale 1:10,000,000 (160 miles=1 inch)
British Territory before 1880 and in 1914
French
Portuguese
German Terr.
Span. Terr.
Liberia
WEST AFRICA
to 1914
Scale 1:20,000,000 (320 miles=1 inch)
NATAL & ZULULAND
during the
BOER & ZULU WARS
Scale 1:4,000,000 (64 miles=1 inch)
Highlands over 3000 ft.
„ from 1200-3000 „
Uplands „ 600-1200 „
Lowlands „ 0-600 „
COPYRIGHT, GEORGE PHILIP & SON, LTD.

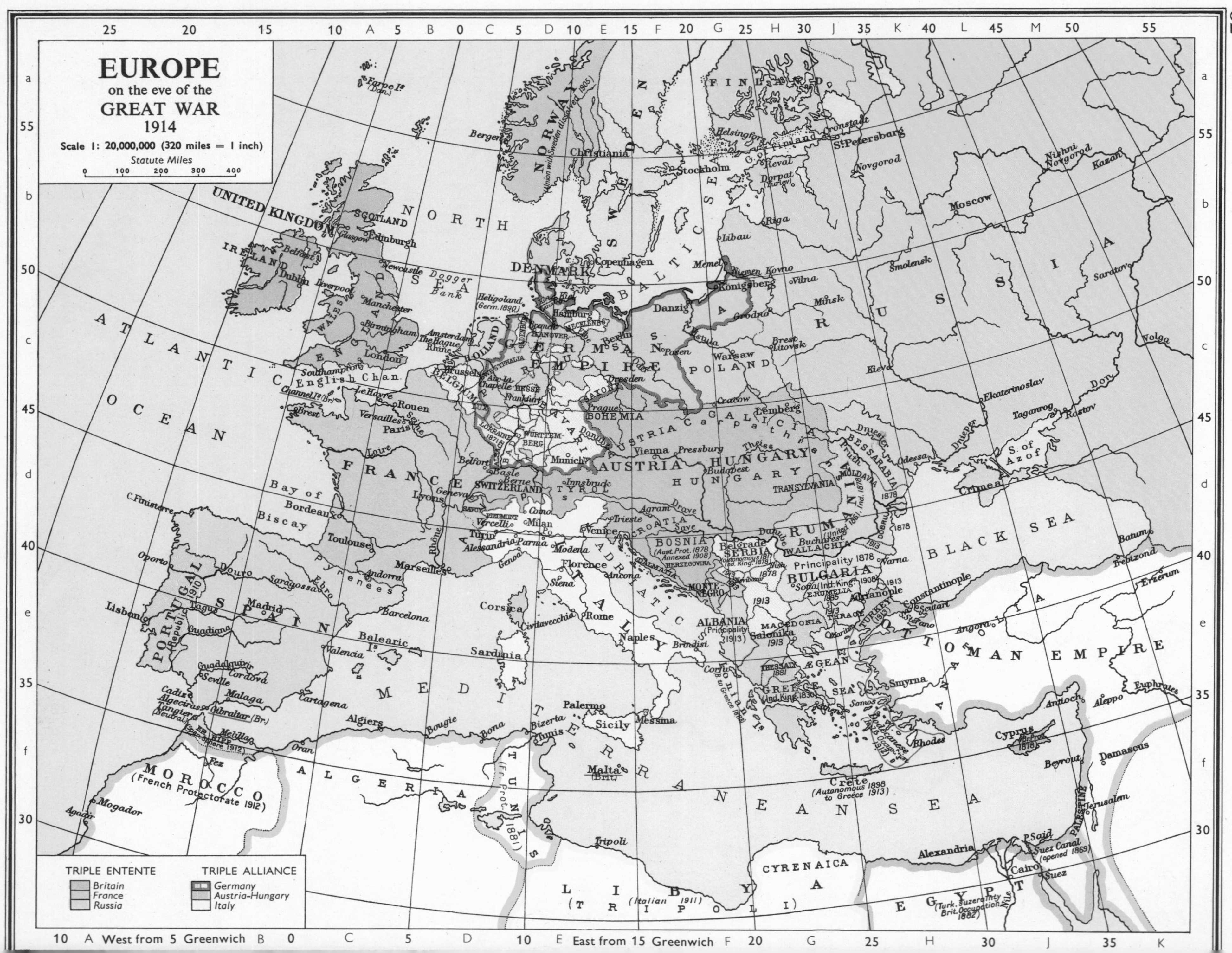
EUROPE
on the eve of the
GREAT WAR
1914
Scale 1: 20,000,000 (320 miles = 1 inch)
Statute Miles
0 100 200 300 400
TRIPLE ENTENTE
Britain
France
Russia
TRIPLE ALLIANCE
Germany
Austria-Hungary
Italy
West from 5 Greenwich
East from 15 Greenwich
ATLANTIC OCEAN
NORTH SEA
BALTIC SEA
BLACK SEA
MEDITERRANEAN SEA
UNITED KINGDOM
IRELAND
SCOTLAND
ENGLAND
WALES
FRANCE
SPAIN
PORTUGAL
NORWAY
SWEDEN
FINLAND
DENMARK
GERMAN EMPIRE
AUSTRIA HUNGARY
RUSSIA
ITALY
SWITZERLAND
BULGARIA
RUMANIA
SERBIA
ALBANIA
GREECE
OTTOMAN EMPIRE
MOROCCO
(French Protectorate 1912)
ALGERIA
TUNIS
LIBYA
(Italian 1911)
(TRIPOLI)
CYRENAICA
EGYPT
(Turk. Suzerainty Brit. Occupation 1882)
Bay of Biscay
English Chan.
Dogger Bank
Moscow
St. Petersburg
London
Paris
Berlin
Vienna
Rome
Madrid
Constantinople
Lisbon
Stockholm
Christiania
Copenhagen
Warsaw
Budapest
Belgrade
Bucharest
Athens
Crete
(Autonomous 1898 to Greece 1913)
Cyprus
Malta (Brit.)
Gibraltar (Br.)
Heligoland (Germ. 1890)

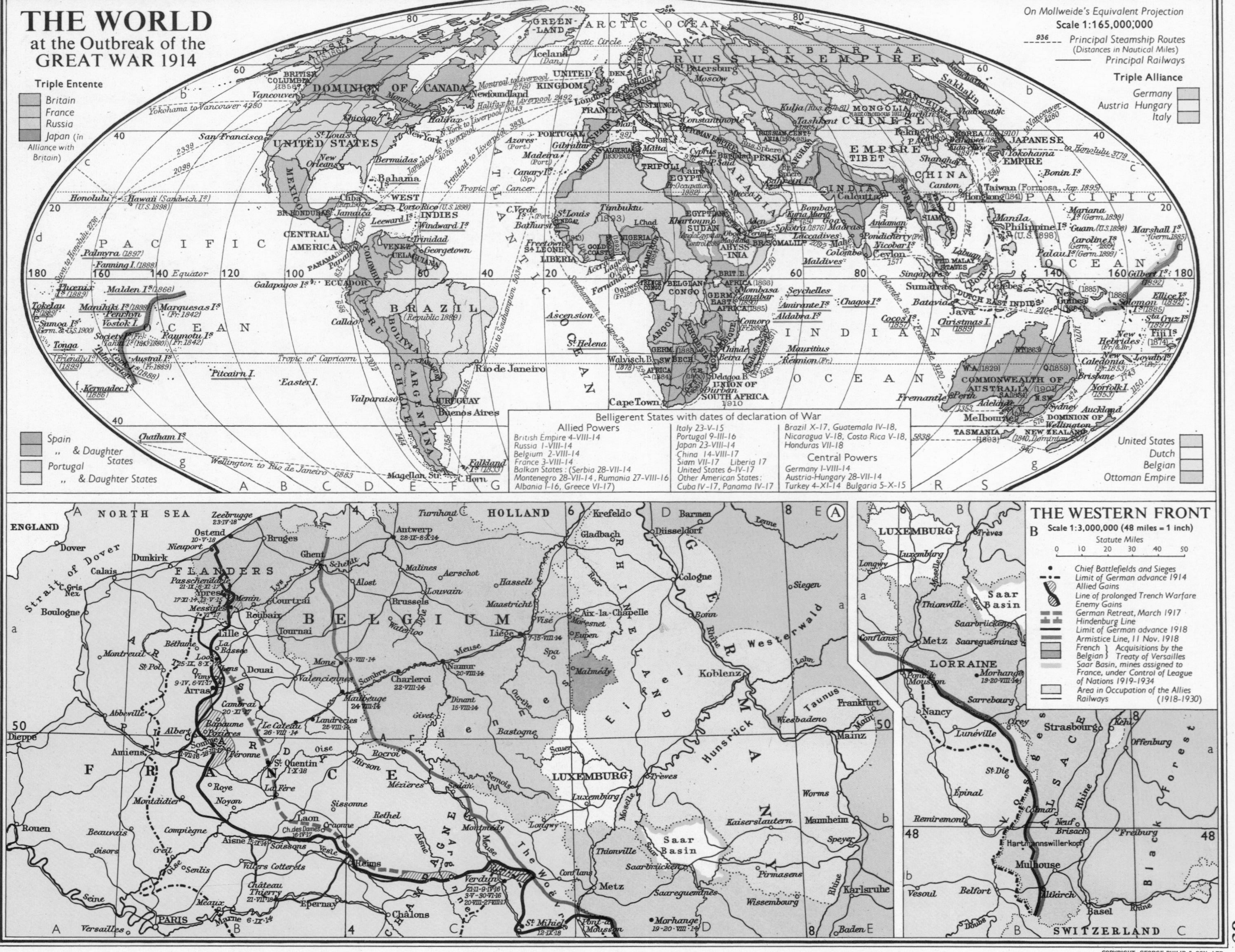
THE WORLD
at the Outbreak of the
GREAT WAR 1914
On Mollweide's Equivalent Projection
Scale 1:165,000,000
936 Principal Steamship Routes
(Distances in Nautical Miles)
Principal Railways
Triple Entente
Britain
France
Russia
Japan (in Alliance with Britain)
Triple Alliance
Germany
Austria Hungary
Italy
Spain
" & Daughter States
Portugal
" & Daughter States
United States
Dutch
Belgian
Ottoman Empire
Belligerent States with dates of declaration of War
Allied Powers
British Empire 4-VIII-14
Russia 1-VIII-14
Belgium 2-VIII-14
France 3-VIII-14
Balkan States: (Serbia 28-VII-14
Montenegro 28-VII-14, Rumania 27-VIII-16
Albania 1-16, Greece VI-17)
Italy 23-V-15
Portugal 9-III-16
Japan 23-VIII-14
China 14-VIII-17
Siam VII-17 Liberia 17
United States 6-IV-17
Other American States:
Cuba IV-17, Panama IV-17
Brazil X-17, Guatemala IV-18,
Nicaragua V-18, Costa Rica V-18,
Honduras VII-18
Central Powers
Germany 1-VIII-14
Austria-Hungary 28-VII-14
Turkey 4-XI-14 Bulgaria 5-X-15
THE WESTERN FRONT
Scale 1:3,000,000 (48 miles = 1 inch)
Statute Miles
0 10 20 30 40 50
Chief Battlefields and Sieges
Limit of German advance 1914
Allied Gains
Line of prolonged Trench Warfare
Enemy Gains
German Retreat, March 1917
Hindenburg Line
Limit of German advance 1918
Armistice Line, 11 Nov. 1918
French } Acquisitions by the
Belgian } Treaty of Versailles
Saar Basin, mines assigned to France, under Control of League of Nations 1919-1934
Area in Occupation of the Allies (1918-1930)
Railways

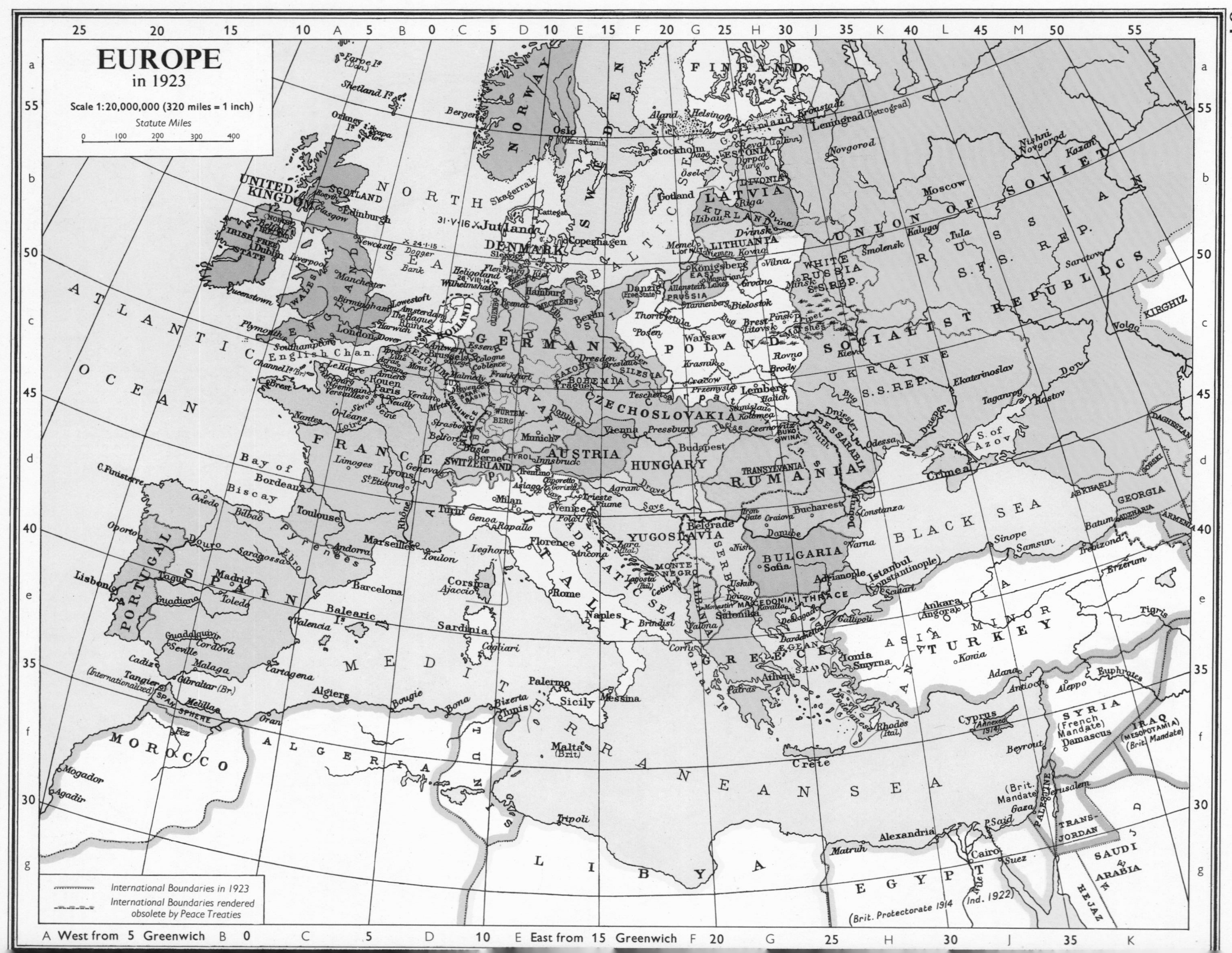
EUROPE
in 1923
Scale 1:20,000,000 (320 miles = 1 inch)
Statute Miles
0 100 200 300 400
International Boundaries in 1923
International Boundaries rendered obsolete by Peace Treaties
West from 5 Greenwich
East from 15 Greenwich
ATLANTIC OCEAN
NORTH SEA
BALTIC SEA
BLACK SEA
MEDITERRANEAN SEA
ADRIATIC SEA
Bay of Biscay
UNITED KINGDOM
IRISH FREE STATE
FRANCE
SPAIN
PORTUGAL
GERMANY
POLAND
CZECHOSLOVAKIA
AUSTRIA
HUNGARY
SWITZERLAND
ITALY
YUGOSLAVIA
RUMANIA
BULGARIA
ALBANIA
GREECE
TURKEY
NORWAY
SWEDEN
FINLAND
DENMARK
ESTONIA
LATVIA
LITHUANIA
UNION OF SOVIET SOCIALIST REPUBLICS
R.S.F.S.R.
UKRAINE S.S.REP.
WHITE RUSSIA S.S.REP.
GEORGIA
ALGERIA
TUNIS
LIBYA
EGYPT
(Brit. Protectorate 1914
Ind. 1922)
MOROCCO
SYRIA (French Mandate)
IRAQ (MESOPOTAMIA) (Brit. Mandate)
PALESTINE (Brit. Mandate)
TRANS-JORDAN
HEJAZ
SAUDI ARABIA

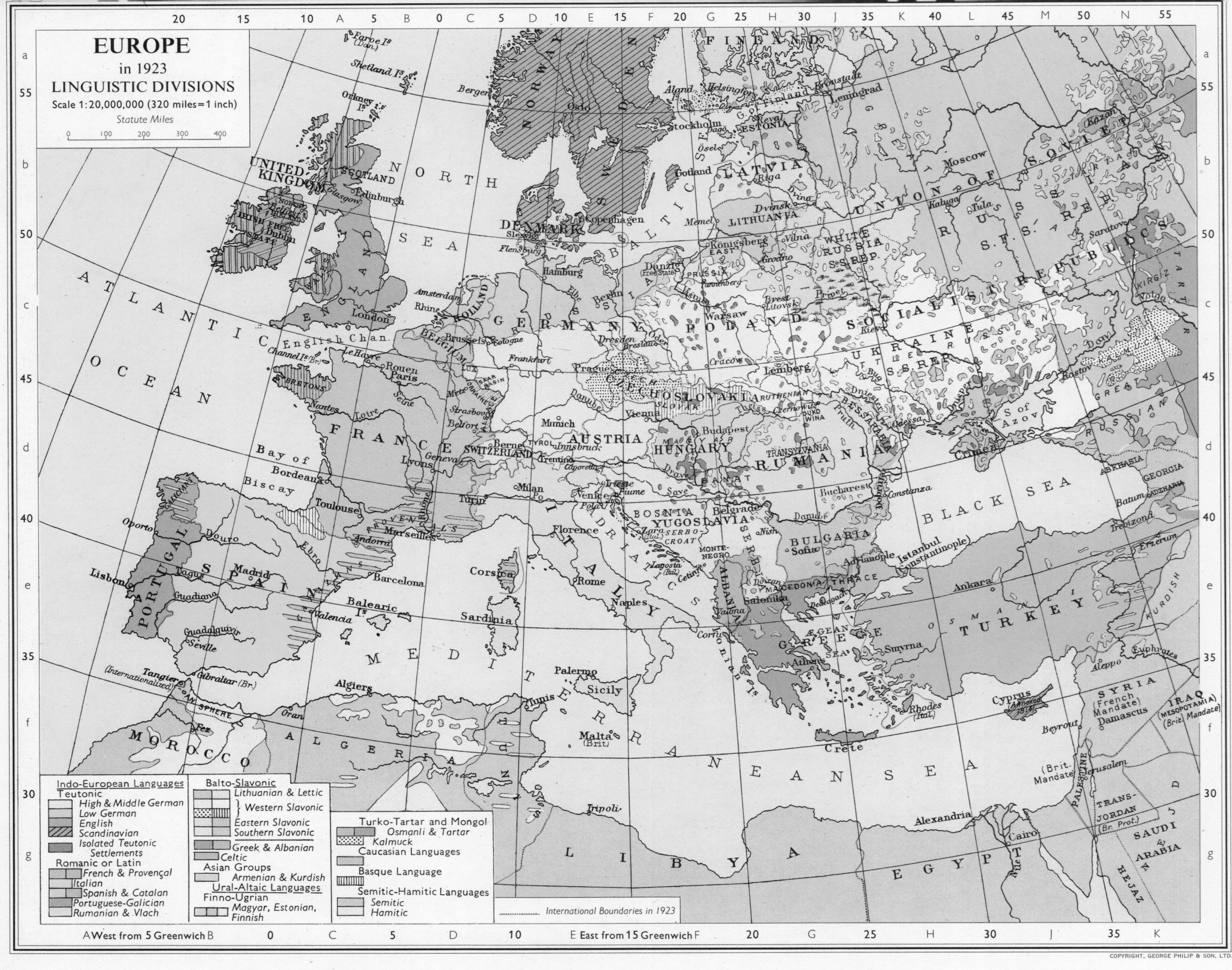

EUROPE
in 1923
LINGUISTIC DIVISIONS
Scale 1:20,000,000 (320 miles=1 inch)
Statute Miles
0 100 200 300 400
Indo-European Languages
Teutonic
High & Middle German
Low German
English
Scandinavian
Isolated Teutonic Settlements
Romanic or Latin
French & Provençal
Italian
Spanish & Catalan
Portuguese-Galician
Rumanian & Vlach
Balto-Slavonic
Lithuanian & Lettic
Western Slavonic
Eastern Slavonic
Southern Slavonic
Greek & Albanian
Celtic
Asian Groups
Armenian & Kurdish
Ural-Altaic Languages
Finno-Ugrian
Magyar, Estonian, Finnish
Turko-Tartar and Mongol
Osmanli & Tartar
Kalmuck
Caucasian Languages
Basque Language
Semitic-Hamitic Languages
Semitic
Hamitic
International Boundaries in 1923
A West from 5 Greenwich B
E East from 15 Greenwich F
ATLANTIC OCEAN
NORTH SEA
BALTIC SEA
BLACK SEA
MEDITERRANEAN SEA
UNITED KINGDOM
NORWAY
SWEDEN
FINLAND
DENMARK
GERMANY
POLAND
FRANCE
SPAIN
PORTUGAL
ITALY
AUSTRIA
HUNGARY
RUMANIA
YUGOSLAVIA
BULGARIA
ALBANIA
GREECE
TURKEY
UNION OF SOVIET SOCIALIST REPUBLICS
MOROCCO
ALGERIA
LIBYA
EGYPT
SYRIA
IRAQ

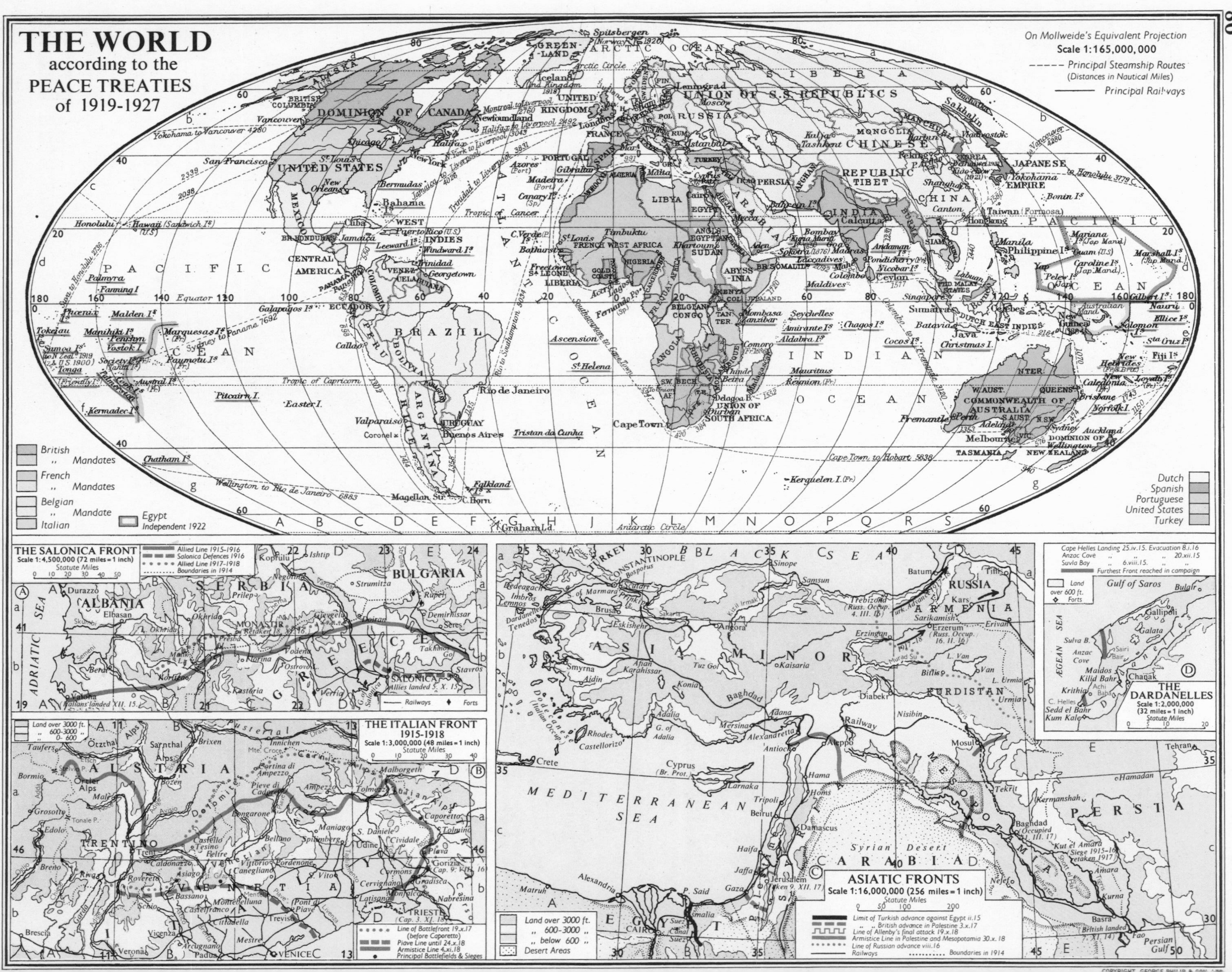
THE WORLD
according to the
PEACE TREATIES
of 1919-1927
On Mollweide's Equivalent Projection
Scale 1:165,000,000
Principal Steamship Routes
(Distances in Nautical Miles)
Principal Railways
British
" Mandates
French
" Mandates
Belgian
" Mandate
Italian
Egypt
Independent 1922
Dutch
Spanish
Portuguese
United States
Turkey
THE SALONICA FRONT
Scale 1:4,500,000 (72 miles = 1 inch)
Statute Miles
Allied Line 1915-1916
Salonica Defences 1916
Allied Line 1917-1918
Boundaries in 1914
Railways
Forts
THE ITALIAN FRONT
1915-1918
Scale 1:3,000,000 (48 miles = 1 inch)
Statute Miles
Land over 3000 ft.
600-3000
0-600
Line of Battlefront 19.x.17
(before Caporetto)
Piave Line until 24.x.18
Armistice Line 4.xi.18
Principal Battlefields & Sieges
ASIATIC FRONTS
Scale 1:16,000,000 (256 miles = 1 inch)
Statute Miles
Limit of Turkish advance against Egypt ii.15
British advance in Palestine 3.x.17
Line of Allenby's final attack 19.x.18
Armistice Line in Palestine and Mesopotamia 30.x.18
Line of Russian advance viii.16
Railways
Boundaries in 1914
Land over 3000 ft.
600-3000
below 600
Desert Areas
Cape Helles Landing 25.iv.15. Evacuation 8.i.16
Anzac Cove 20.xii.15
Suvla Bay 6.viii.15.
Furthest Front reached in campaign
Land over 600 ft.
Forts
THE DARDANELLES
Scale 1:2,000,000
(32 miles = 1 inch)
Statute Miles

CENTRAL
EUROPE
in 1939
Scale 1:10,000,000 (160 miles=1 inch)
Statute Miles
0 50 100 150 200
Boundary of Czechoslovakia 1937
Sudetenland to Germany Oct. 1938
To Hungary Nov. 1938
To Hungary March 1939
Boundary between Germany and Russia 28th. Sept. 1939
NORWAY
SWEDEN
FINLAND
ESTONIA
LATVIA
LITHUANIA
Annexed by U.S.S.R. 1940
NORTH SEA
BALTIC SEA
DENMARK
NETHERLANDS
BELGIUM
LUX.
FRANCE
GERMANY
EAST PRUSSIA
POLAND
WHITE RUSSIA
U.S.S.R.
German-Soviet Non-aggression Pact 23rd August 1939
UKRAINE
PROT. OF BOHEMIA-MORAVIA March 1939
SLOVAKIA Indep. March 1939
CARPATHIAN-RUTHENIA
AUSTRIA To Germany March 1938
SWITZERLAND
HUNGARY
RUMANIA
ITALY
YUGOSLAVIA
BULGARIA
BLACK SEA
To Germany March 1939
To Lith. Sept. 1939
Teschen To Poland Oct. 1938
Bergen
Stavanger
Egersund
Kristiansand
Oslo
Göteborg
Norrkoping
Stockholm
Gotland
Oland
Aland Is.
Turku
Helsinki
Viipuri
Gulf of Finland
Leningrad
Tallinn
Hiiumaa
Saaremaa
G. of Riga
Tartu
L. Peipus
Pskov
Riga
Liepaja
Dvina
Memel
Kaunas
Wilno
Königsberg
Gdynia
Danzig
Neman
Minsk
Vitebsk
Smolensk
Moscow
Aarhus
Copenhagen
Malmo
Bornholm
Heligoland
Kiel
Kiel Canal
Hamburg
Bremen
Stettin
Elbe
Weser
Hanover
Brunswick
Berlin
Oder
Magdeburg
Groningen
Amsterdam
The Hague
Rotterdam
Arnhem
Rhine
Munster
Dortmund
Essen
Antwerp
Brussels
Cologne
Godesberg
Leipzig
Chemnitz
Dresden
Liége
Frankfurt
Mainz
Reims
Chalons
Verdun
Metz
Nancy
Saarbrucken
Nürnberg
Stuttgart
Strasbourg
Danube
Munich
Prague
Plzen
Poznan
Vistula
Warsaw
Lodz
Brest
Lublin
Breslau
Czestochowa
Cracow
Przemysl
Lvov
Kiev
Zhitomir
Dnepr
Kharkov
Dnepropetrovsk
Cernauti
Dnestr
Iasi
Odessa
Linz
Vienna
Salzburg
Inn
Innsbruck
Brenner P.
Basle
Zurich
Berne
Lyons
Budapest
Debrecen
Szeged
Timisoara
Galati
Sevastopol
Milan
Turin
Verona
Po
Venice
Trieste
Zagreb
Genoa
Bologna
Marseilles
Rhone
Zara
Belgrade
Bucharest
Constanta
East from 20 Greenwich

EUROPE
at the height of
AXIS POWER
October 1942
Scale 1:22,500,000 (360 miles = 1 in)
Statute Miles
0 100 200 300 400
Germany, principal Axis Power under direct rule of Hitler
Italian Empire
German and Axis Satellites
States occupied by Germany 1942
Furthest limit of German Advance October, 1942
Extended limit of German Advance December, 1941
United Kingdom, British Empire and Mandates
Countries in Military Occupation of United Nations
Neutral Countries
Boundary of Czechoslovakia in 1938
East from 5 Greenwich

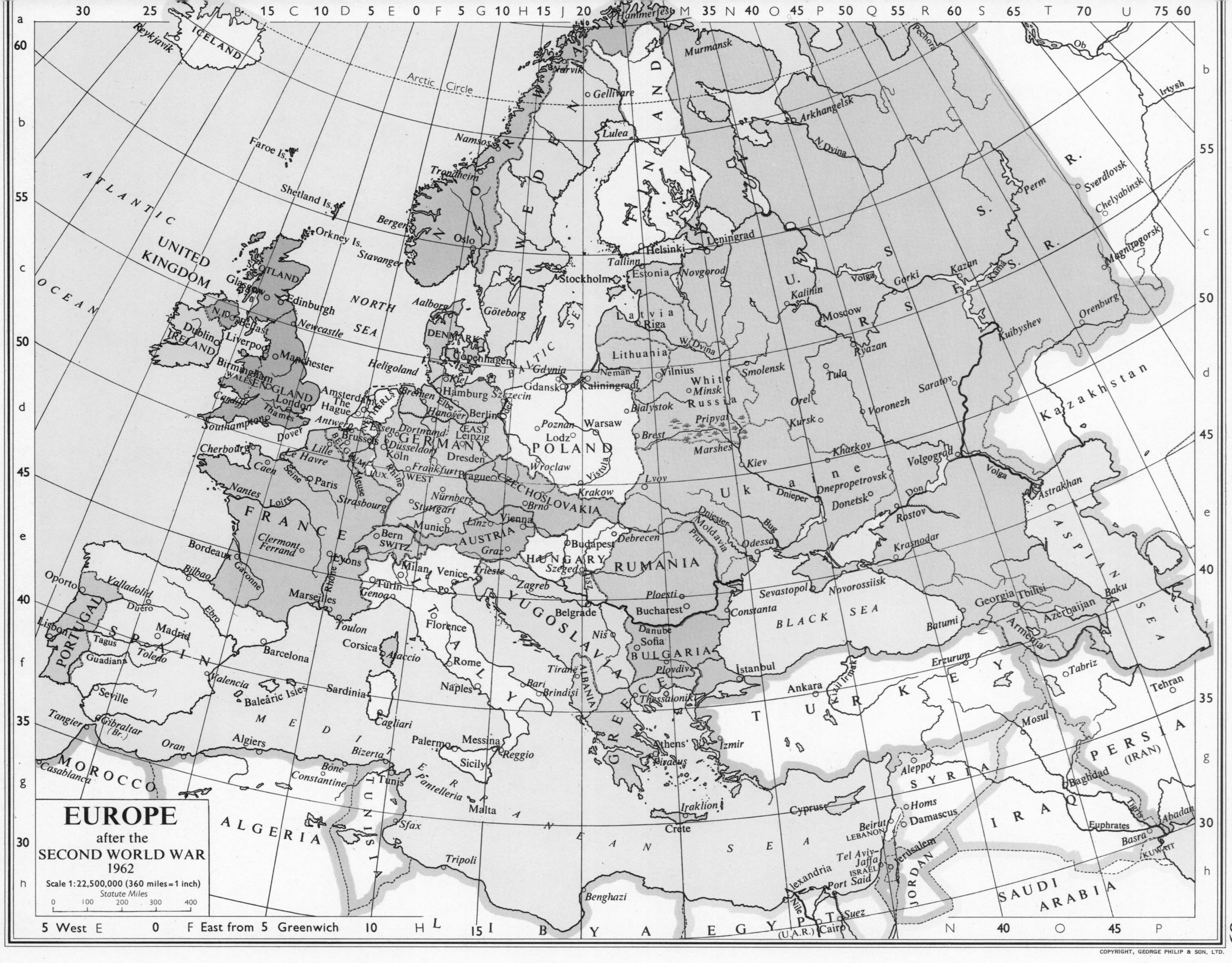
EUROPE
after the
SECOND WORLD WAR
1962
Scale 1:22,500,000 (360 miles=1 inch)
Statute Miles
5 West
East from 5 Greenwich
Arctic Circle
ATLANTIC OCEAN
NORTH SEA
BALTIC SEA
BLACK SEA
CASPIAN SEA
MEDITERRANEAN SEA
ICELAND
UNITED KINGDOM
IRELAND
NORWAY
SWEDEN
FINLAND
DENMARK
POLAND
EAST GERMANY
WEST GERMANY
FRANCE
SPAIN
PORTUGAL
ITALY
SWITZ.
AUSTRIA
CZECHOSLOVAKIA
HUNGARY
RUMANIA
YUGOSLAVIA
ALBANIA
BULGARIA
GREECE
TURKEY
U.S.S.R.
Kazakhstan
PERSIA (IRAN)
IRAQ
SYRIA
LEBANON
ISRAEL
JORDAN
SAUDI ARABIA
KUWAIT
EGYPT (U.A.R.)
LIBYA
TUNISIA
ALGERIA
MOROCCO
COPYRIGHT, GEORGE PHILIP & SON, LTD.

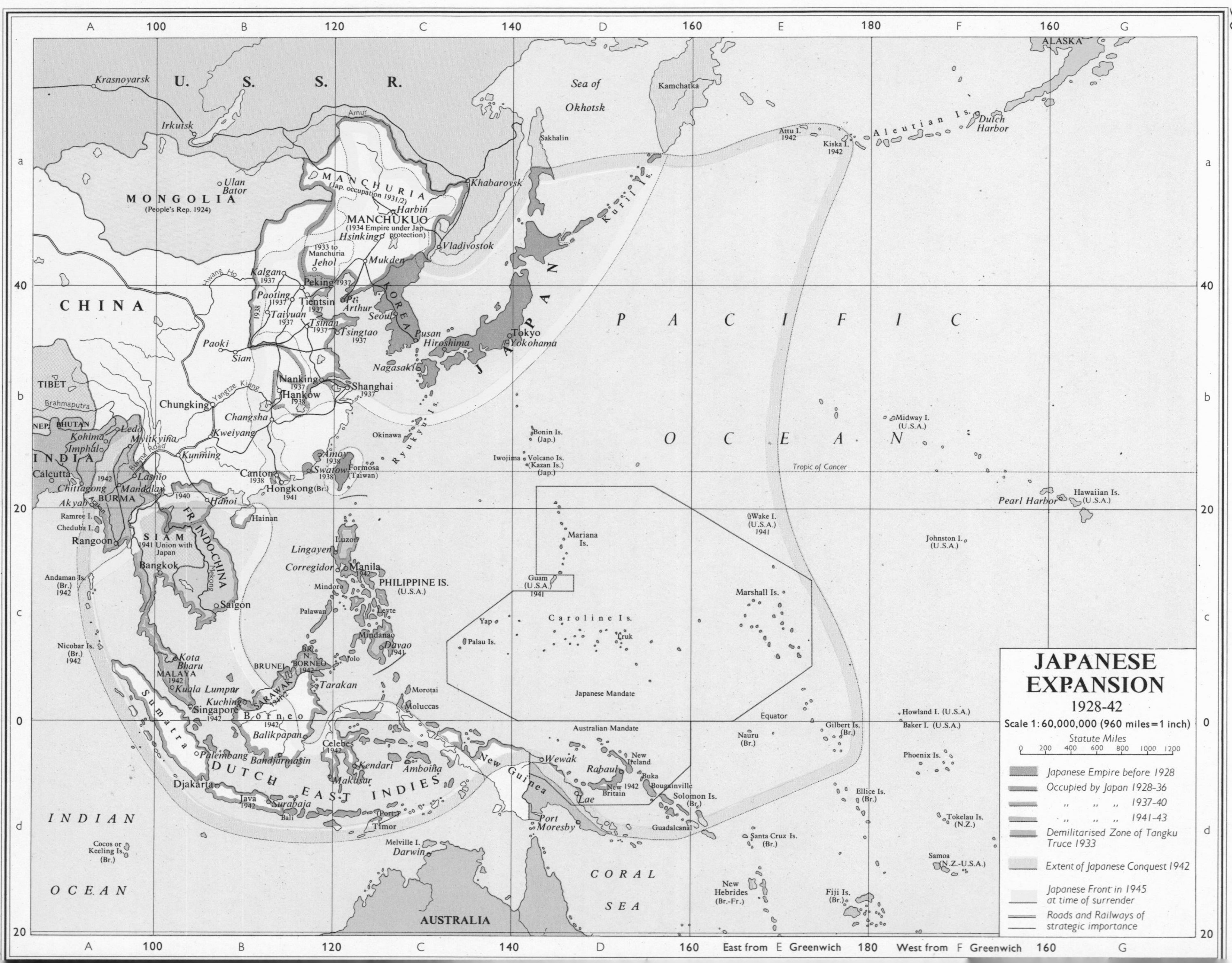
JAPANESE EXPANSION
1928-42
Scale 1: 60,000,000 (960 miles = 1 inch)
Statute Miles
0 200 400 600 800 1000 1200
Japanese Empire before 1928
Occupied by Japan 1928-36
" " " 1937-40
" " " 1941-43
Demilitarised Zone of Tangku Truce 1933
Extent of Japanese Conquest 1942
Japanese Front in 1945 at time of surrender
Roads and Railways of strategic importance
East from E Greenwich
West from F Greenwich
U. S. S. R.
MONGOLIA (People's Rep. 1924)
CHINA
MANCHURIA (Jap. occupation 1931/2)
MANCHUKUO (1934 Empire under Jap. protection)
KOREA
JAPAN
PACIFIC OCEAN
INDIAN OCEAN
CORAL SEA
AUSTRALIA
PHILIPPINE IS. (U.S.A.)
DUTCH EAST INDIES
FR. INDO-CHINA
SIAM 1941 Union with Japan
BURMA
INDIA
TIBET
Sea of Okhotsk
Japanese Mandate
Australian Mandate
Tropic of Cancer
Equator
Pearl Harbor
Hawaiian Is. (U.S.A.)
Midway I. (U.S.A.)
Wake I. (U.S.A.) 1941
Guam (U.S.A.) 1941
Attu I. 1942
Kiska I. 1942
Aleutian Is.
Dutch Harbor
ALASKA
Kamchatka
Sakhalin
Kurile Is.
Ryukyu Is.
Okinawa
Bonin Is. (Jap.)
Volcano Is. (Kazan Is.) (Jap.)
Iwojima
Mariana Is.
Caroline Is.
Marshall Is.
Truk
Yap
Palau Is.
Gilbert Is. (Br.)
Nauru (Br.)
Ellice Is. (Br.)
Solomon Is. (Br.)
Guadalcanal
Bougainville
Buka
New Ireland
New Britain 1942
Rabaul
Lae
Wewak
New Guinea
Port Moresby
Santa Cruz Is. (Br.)
New Hebrides (Br.-Fr.)
Fiji Is. (Br.)
Samoa (N.Z.-U.S.A.)
Tokelau Is. (N.Z.)
Phoenix Is.
Howland I. (U.S.A.)
Baker I. (U.S.A.)
Johnston I. (U.S.A.)
Tokyo
Yokohama
Hiroshima
Nagasaki
Pusan
Seoul
Mukden
Harbin
Hsinking
Khabarovsk
Vladivostok
Jehol
1933 to Manchuria
Peking 1937
Tientsin 1937
Pt. Arthur
Kalgan 1937
Paoting 1937
Taiyuan 1937
Tsinan 1937
Tsingtao 1937
Nanking 1937
Hankow 1938
Shanghai 1937
Sian
Paoki
Chungking
Changsha
Kweiyang
Kunming
Canton 1938
Hongkong (Br.) 1941
Amoy 1938
Swatow 1938
Formosa (Taiwan)
Hainan
Hanoi
Saigon
Bangkok
Rangoon
Mandalay
Lashio
Myitkyina
Ledo
Kohima
Imphal
Calcutta
Chittagong
Akyab
Ramree I.
Cheduba I.
Burma Road
Andaman Is. (Br.) 1942
Nicobar Is. (Br.) 1942
Irkutsk
Krasnoyarsk
Ulan Bator
Amur
Hwang Ho
Yangtze Kiang
Mekong
Brahmaputra
NEP.
BHUTAN
Luzon
Lingayen
Corregidor
Manila 1942
Mindoro
Palawan
Leyte
Mindanao
Davao 1941
Jolo
Kota Bharu
MALAYA 1942
Kuala Lumpur
Singapore 1942
Kuching
SARAWAK
BRUNEI
BR. N. BORNEO 1942
Borneo
Tarakan
Balikpapan 1942
Bandjarmasin
Sumatra
Palembang
Djakarta
Java 1942
Surabaja
Bali
Celebes 1942
Kendari
Makasar
Amboina
Morotai
Moluccas
Timor
Melville I.
Darwin
Cocos or Keeling Is. (Br.)

EASTERN
ASIA
1945-1962
Scale 1:30,000,000 (480 miles=1 inch)
Statute Miles
0 100 200 300 400 500
Principal Railways
East from 110 Greenwich
U. S. S. R.
Omsk
Novosibirsk
Barnaul
Stalinsk
Irkutsk
L. Baikal
Ulan Ude
Chita
Aleksandrovsk Sakhalin
Karaganda
Semipalatinsk
L. Balkhash
Alma Ata
Khabarovsk
Ulan Bator
MONGOLIA
People's Republic 1924
Urumchi
Harbin
(Pinkiang)
Kirin
Changchun
Hsi-Liao
Vladivostok
Fushun
Mukden
(Shenyang)
INNER MONGOLIA
SINKIANG-UIGUR
CHINESE REPUBLIC
People's Republic 1949
Paotow
Peking
Tientsin
Taiyuan
Dairen
Pt. Arthur
North KOREA South
Cease Fire Line, July 1953
38th. Parallel
Seoul
Pusan
SEA OF JAPAN
JAPAN
Hokkaido
Sapporo
Hakodate
Honshu
Sendai
Niigata
Kanazawa
Tokyo
Yokohama
Nagoya
Kyoto
Kobe
Osaka
Hiroshima
Fukuoka
Nagasaki
Kumamoto
Kagoshima
Tsinan
Tsingtao
Yellow Sea
Lanchow
Sian
Cease Fire Line 1949
LADAKH
KASHMIR
Indus
TIBET
Invaded by Chinese forces 1950
Sutlej
Nanking
Shanghai
Wuhan
Hangchow
EAST CHINA SEA
Chengtu
Chungking
Nanchang
Changsha
Delhi
NEPAL
Katmandu
Lhasa
Tsangpo
SIK.
Punakha
BHUTAN
Disputed Area
Brahmaputra
Lucknow
Kanpur
Varanasi (Benares)
Ganga
INDIA
Br. Dom. 1947
Rep. within Commonwealth 1950
E. PAK.
Dacca
Calcutta
Howrah
Chittagong
Myitkyina
BURMA ROAD
Kunming
Kweiyang
Foochow
Amoy
Quemoy
Taipei
FORMOSA (Taiwan)
Nationalist China 1950
Tainan
Ryukyu Is.
Okinawa
(Under U.S. Control 1952)
Canton
Hongkong (Br.)
Macao (Port.)
Nanning
Si-Kiang
Mandalay
BURMA
Union of Burma, Indep. Rep. 1948
Irrawaddy
Salween
Mekong
North
Hanoi
Luang Prabang
LAOS
Vientiane
VIETNAM
Cease Fire Line, July 1954
Hue
Hainan
PACIFIC OCEAN
Nagpur
Godavari
Bay of Bengal
Rangoon
Moulmein
Chiangmai
SIAM (THAILAND)
Bangkok
CAMBODIA
Indep. 1945/54
Pnom Penh
South
Saigon-Cholon
Luzon
PHILIPPINES
Indep. 1946
Manila
Samar
Madras
Pondicherry (To India 1954)
Andaman Is. (Indian)
Gulf of Siam
SOUTH CHINA SEA
Palawan
Mindanao
Davao
CEYLON
Br. Dom. 1948
Colombo
Nicobar Is. (Indian)
Jesselton
Labuan
BRUNEI
NORTH BORNEO
SARAWAK
Kuching
Borneo
Celebes Sea
Penang
MALAYA
Federation 1948, Indep. within Commonwealth 1957
Kuala Lumpur
Malacca
Singapore
Medan
Sumatra
Simeulve
Nias
Padang
Siberut
Palembang
Halmahera
Moluccas
New Guinea
(Disputed Netherlands Indonesia)
Ceram
Buru
INDIAN OCEAN
Kalimantan
Sulawesi (Celebes)
Bandjarmasin
INDONESIA
Indep. Republic 1949
JAVA SEA
Djakarta
Semarang
Surabaja
Djokjakarta
Java
Sunda Sea
Sumbawa
Flores
Sumba
Timor
(Port.)
Arafura Sea

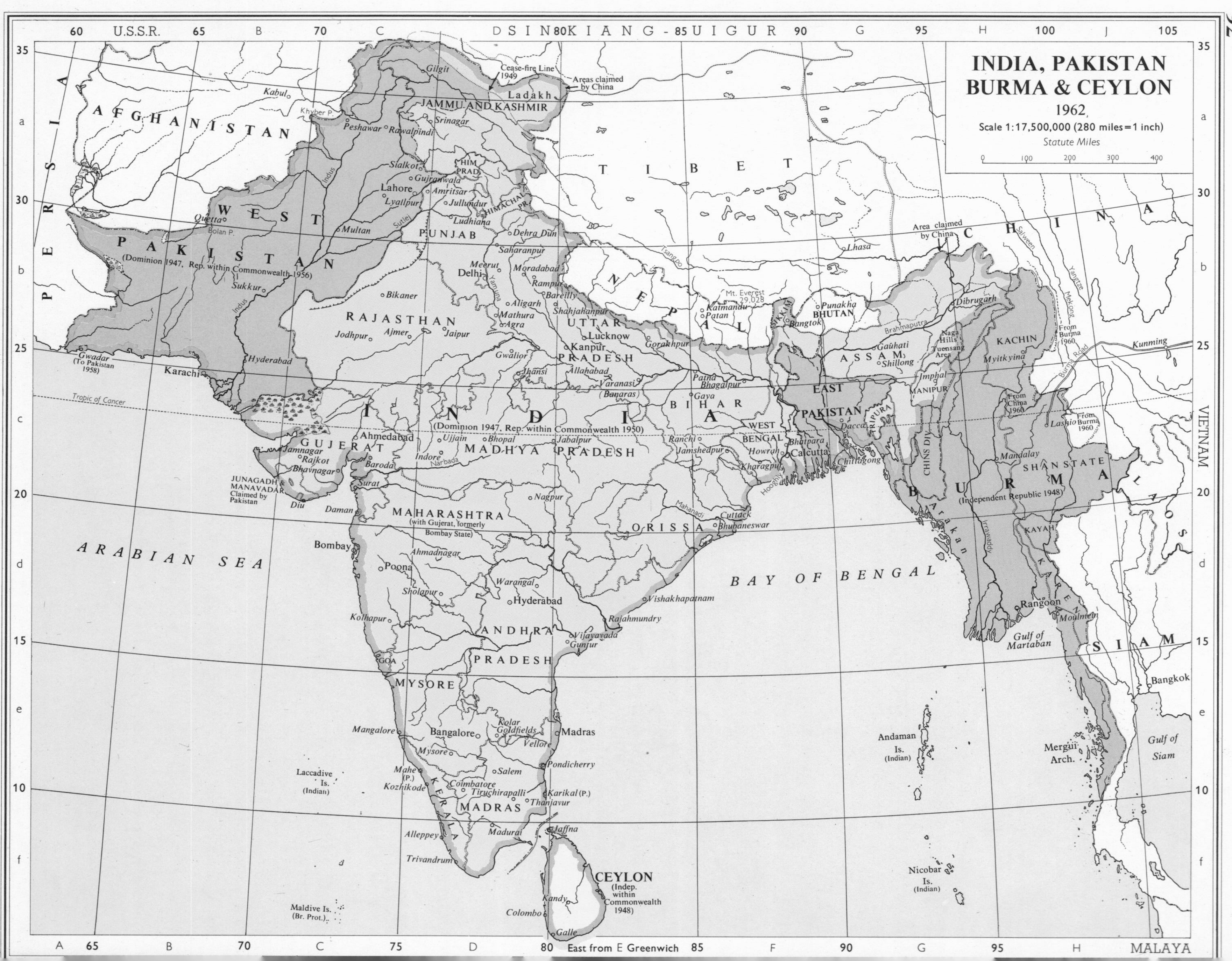
INDIA, PAKISTAN
BURMA & CEYLON
1962
Scale 1:17,500,000 (280 miles=1 inch)
Statute Miles
0 100 200 300 400
U.S.S.R.
SINKIANG-UIGUR
VIETNAM
MALAYA
PERSIA
AFGHANISTAN
TIBET
CHINA
NEPAL
BHUTAN
SIKKIM
WEST PAKISTAN
(Dominion 1947, Rep. within Commonwealth 1956)
EAST PAKISTAN
INDIA
(Dominion 1947, Rep. within Commonwealth 1950)
BURMA
(Independent Republic 1948)
SIAM
LAOS
CEYLON
(Indep. within Commonwealth 1948)
JAMMU AND KASHMIR
Ladakh
Cease-fire Line 1949
Areas claimed by China
Area claimed by China
HIM PRAD
HIMACHAL PR.
PUNJAB
RAJASTHAN
UTTAR PRADESH
BIHAR
WEST BENGAL
ASSAM
MADHYA PRADESH
GUJERAT
MAHARASHTRA
(with Gujerat, formerly Bombay State)
ORISSA
ANDHRA PRADESH
MYSORE
MADRAS
KERALA
GOA
KACHIN
SHAN STATE
KAYAH
KAREN
CHINS DIV.
MANIPUR
TRIPURA
Naga Hills Tuensang Area
JUNAGADH & MANAVADAR Claimed by Pakistan
Gwadar (To Pakistan 1958)
From China 1960
From Burma 1960
Mt. Everest 29,028
ARABIAN SEA
BAY OF BENGAL
Gulf of Martaban
Gulf of Siam
Andaman Is. (Indian)
Nicobar Is. (Indian)
Laccadive Is. (Indian)
Maldive Is. (Br. Prot.)
Mergui Arch.
Tropic of Cancer
East from E Greenwich
Burma Road
Khyber P.
Bolan P.
Indus
Sutlej
Yamuna
Narbada
Mahanadi
Hooghly
Brahmaputra
Irrawaddy
Salween
Mekong
Yangtze
Tsangpo
Kabul
Peshawar
Rawalpindi
Srinagar
Gilgit
Sialkot
Gujranwala
Lahore
Amritsar
Lyallpur
Jullundur
Ludhiana
Quetta
Multan
Sukkur
Hyderabad
Karachi
Dehra Dun
Saharanpur
Meerut
Delhi
Moradabad
Rampur
Bareilly
Aligarh
Mathura
Agra
Bikaner
Jodhpur
Ajmer
Jaipur
Shahjahanpur
Lucknow
Kanpur
Gorakhpur
Gwalior
Jhansi
Allahabad
Varanasi (Banaras)
Patna
Bhagalpur
Gaya
Katmandu
Patan
Gangtok
Punakha
Lhasa
Dibrugarh
Gauhati
Shillong
Imphal
Myitkyina
Kunming
Lashio
Mandalay
Dacca
Chittagong
Ahmedabad
Jamnagar
Rajkot
Bhavnagar
Baroda
Surat
Diu
Daman
Ujjain
Bhopal
Indore
Jabalpur
Ranchi
Jamshedpur
Bhatpara
Howrah
Calcutta
Kharagpur
Nagpur
Cuttack
Bhubaneswar
Bombay
Poona
Ahmadnagar
Sholapur
Kolhapur
Warangal
Hyderabad
Vishakhapatnam
Rajahmundry
Vijayavada
Guntur
Mangalore
Bangalore
Kolar Goldfields
Vellore
Madras
Mysore
Mahe (P.)
Kozhikode
Coimbatore
Salem
Pondicherry
Tiruchirapalli
Karikal (P.)
Thanjavur
Madurai
Alleppey
Trivandrum
Jaffna
Kandy
Colombo
Galle
Rangoon
Moulmein
Bangkok

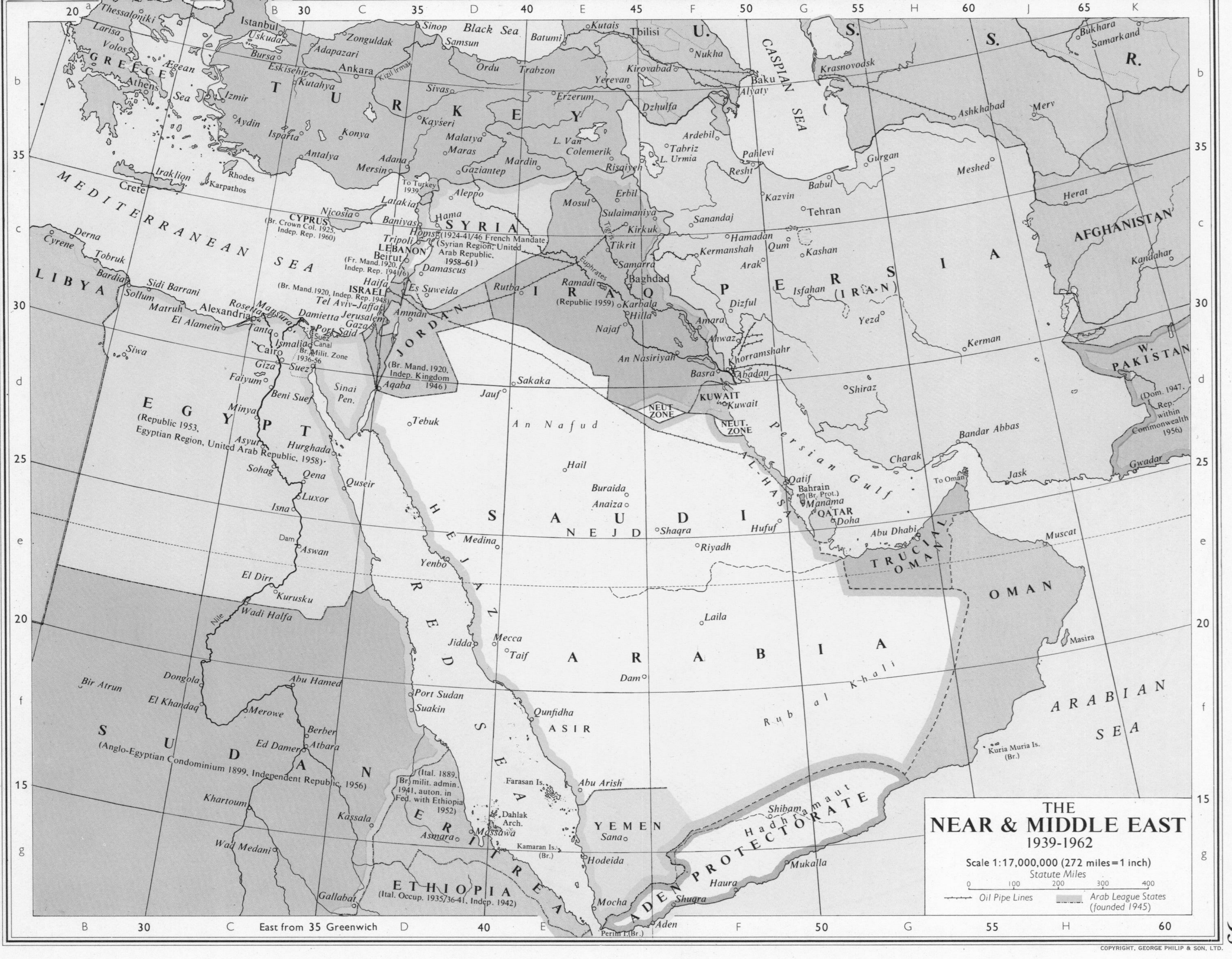
THE
NEAR & MIDDLE EAST
1939-1962
Scale 1:17,000,000 (272 miles=1 inch)
Statute Miles
0 100 200 300 400
Oil Pipe Lines
Arab League States (founded 1945)
East from 35 Greenwich
MEDITERRANEAN SEA
Black Sea
CASPIAN SEA
RED SEA
ARABIAN SEA
Persian Gulf
TURKEY
U.S.S.R.
GREECE
CYPRUS (Br. Crown Col. 1925, Indep. Rep. 1960)
SYRIA (1924-41/46 French Mandate (Syrian Region, United Arab Republic, 1958-61)
LEBANON (Fr. Mand. 1920, Indep. Rep. 1941/6)
ISRAEL (Br. Mand. 1920, Indep. Rep. 1948)
JORDAN (Br. Mand. 1920, Indep. Kingdom 1946)
IRAQ (Republic 1959)
PERSIA (IRAN)
AFGHANISTAN
W. PAKISTAN (Dom. 1947, Rep. within Commonwealth 1956)
EGYPT (Republic 1953, Egyptian Region, United Arab Republic, 1958)
LIBYA
SUDAN (Anglo-Egyptian Condominium 1899, Independent Republic, 1956)
ERITREA (Ital. 1889, Br. milit. admin. 1941, auton. in Fed. with Ethiopia 1952)
ETHIOPIA (Ital. Occup. 1935/36-41, Indep. 1942)
SAUDI ARABIA
KUWAIT
NEUT. ZONE
QATAR
Bahrain (Br. Prot.)
TRUCIAL OMAN
OMAN
YEMEN
ADEN PROTECTORATE
Hadhramaut
NEJD
HEJAZ
ASIR
AL-HASA
An Nafud
Rub al Khali
Sinai Pen.
Suez Canal Br. Milit. Zone 1936-56
To Turkey 1939
Thessaloniki
Larisa
Volos
Athens
Aegean Sea
Istanbul
Uskudar
Bursa
Eskisehir
Kutahya
Izmir
Aydin
Isparta
Antalya
Zonguldak
Adapazari
Ankara
Kizil Irmak
Konya
Sinop
Samsun
Ordu
Trabzon
Sivas
Kayseri
Malatya
Maras
Adana
Mersin
Gaziantep
Mardin
Erzerum
L. Van
Colemerik
Batumi
Kutais
Tbilisi
Yerevan
Kirovabad
Nukha
Dzhulfa
Baku
Alyaty
Krasnovodsk
Ashkhabad
Merv
Bukhara
Samarkand
Rhodes
Karpathos
Iraklion
Crete
Nicosia
Latakia
Baniyas
Aleppo
Hama
Homs
Tripoli
Beirut
Damascus
Haifa
Tel Aviv-Jaffa
Jerusalem
Gaza
Es Suweida
Amman
Aqaba
Rutba
Mosul
Erbil
Sulaimaniya
Kirkuk
Tigris
Euphrates
Tikrit
Samarra
Baghdad
Ramadi
Karbala
Hilla
Najaf
An Nasiriyah
Amara
Basra
Abadan
Khorramshahr
Ahwaz
Dizful
Rizaiyeh
Tabriz
L. Urmia
Ardebil
Pahlevi
Resht
Babul
Gurgan
Kazvin
Tehran
Sanandaj
Hamadan
Kermanshah
Qum
Arak
Kashan
Isfahan
Yezd
Kerman
Meshed
Herat
Kandahar
Shiraz
Bandar Abbas
Charak
Jask
Gwadar
Derna
Cyrene
Tobruk
Bardia
Sollum
Sidi Barrani
Matruh
El Alamein
Alexandria
Rosetta
Mansura
Damietta
Port Said
Tanta
Ismalia
Cairo
Giza
Suez
Faiyum
Beni Suef
Minya
Asyut
Hurghada
Sohag
Qena
Luxor
Isna
Quseir
Dam
Aswan
El Dirr
Kurusku
Nile
Wadi Halfa
Siwa
Bir Atrun
Dongola
El Khandaq
Abu Hamed
Merowe
Berber
Atbara
Ed Damer
Khartoum
Wad Medani
Kassala
Gallabat
Port Sudan
Suakin
Asmara
Massawa
Dahlak Arch.
Farasan Is.
Kamaran Is. (Br.)
Sakaka
Jauf
Tebuk
Hail
Buraida
Anaiza
Shaqra
Riyadh
Hufuf
Qatif
Manama
Doha
Abu Dhabi
To Oman
Muscat
Masira
Kuria Muria Is. (Br.)
Medina
Yenbo
Mecca
Jidda
Taif
Laila
Dam
Qunfidha
Abu Arish
Sana
Hodeida
Mocha
Perim I. (Br.)
Aden
Shuqra
Haura
Mukalla
Shibam

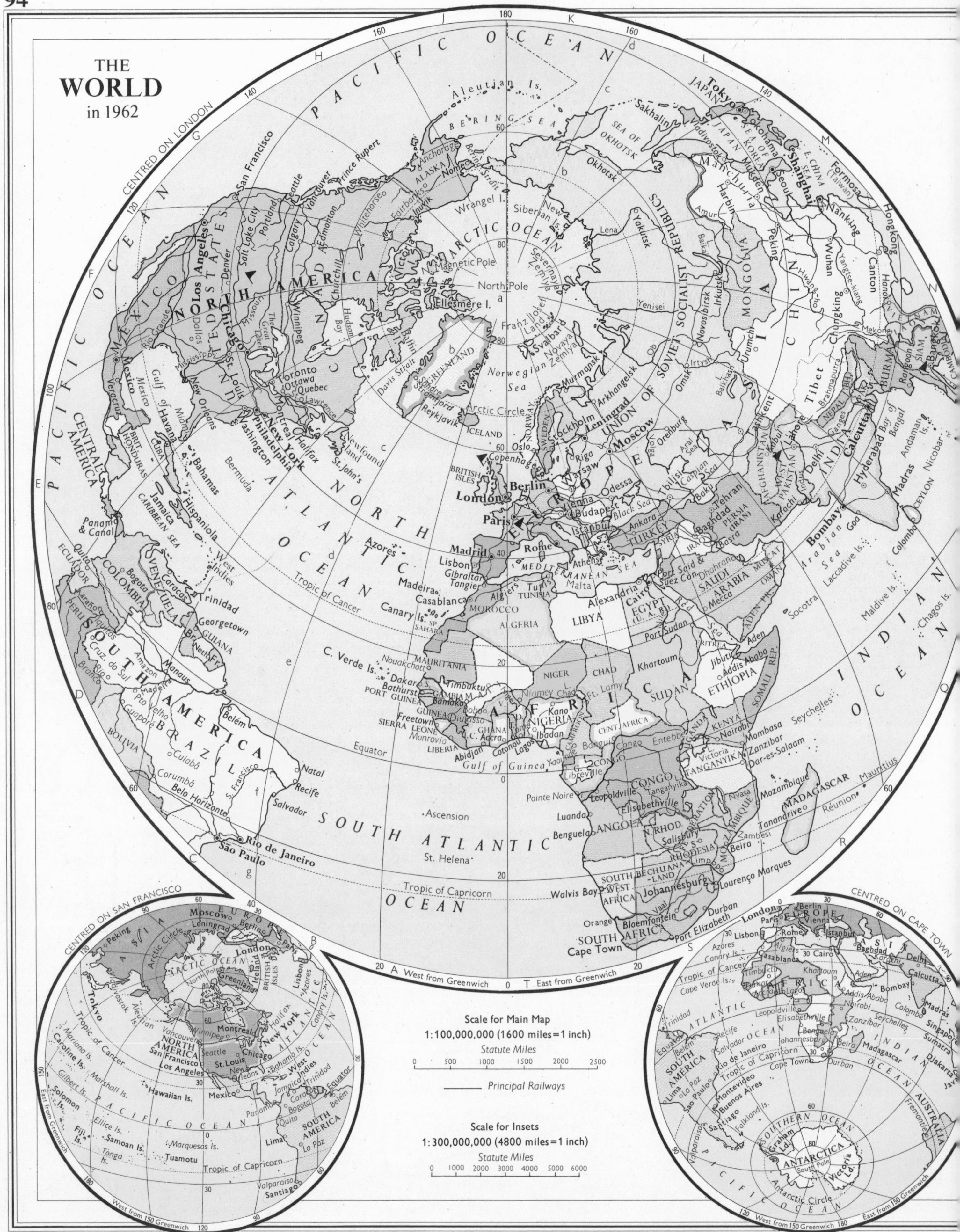

THE
WORLD
in 1962
CENTRED ON LONDON
PACIFIC OCEAN
ARCTIC OCEAN
NORTH ATLANTIC OCEAN
SOUTH ATLANTIC OCEAN
INDIAN OCEAN
NORTH AMERICA
SOUTH AMERICA
EUROPE
AFRICA
ASIA
UNITED STATES
CANADA
MEXICO
CENTRAL AMERICA
UNION OF SOVIET SOCIALIST REPUBLICS
CHINA
MONGOLIA
INDIA
BRAZIL
North Pole
Magnetic Pole
Arctic Circle
Tropic of Cancer
Equator
Tropic of Capricorn
Gulf of Guinea
MEDITERRANEAN SEA
Norwegian Sea
BERING SEA
SEA OF OKHOTSK
Arabian Sea
Bay of Bengal
Caribbean Sea
Gulf of Mexico
Hudson Bay
Davis Strait
Aleutian Is.
GREENLAND
ICELAND
BRITISH ISLES
London
Paris
Berlin
Madrid
Rome
Moscow
Leningrad
Tokyo
Shanghai
Peking
Calcutta
Bombay
Cairo
Johannesburg
Cape Town
New York
Chicago
Los Angeles
San Francisco
Rio de Janeiro
São Paulo
West from Greenwich
East from Greenwich
Scale for Main Map
1:100,000,000 (1600 miles=1 inch)
Statute Miles
0 500 1000 1500 2000 2500
Principal Railways
Scale for Insets
1:300,000,000 (4800 miles=1 inch)
Statute Miles
0 1000 2000 3000 4000 5000 6000
CENTRED ON SAN FRANCISCO
CENTRED ON CAPE TOWN
SOUTHERN OCEAN
ANTARCTICA
South Pole
Antarctic Circle
AUSTRALIA

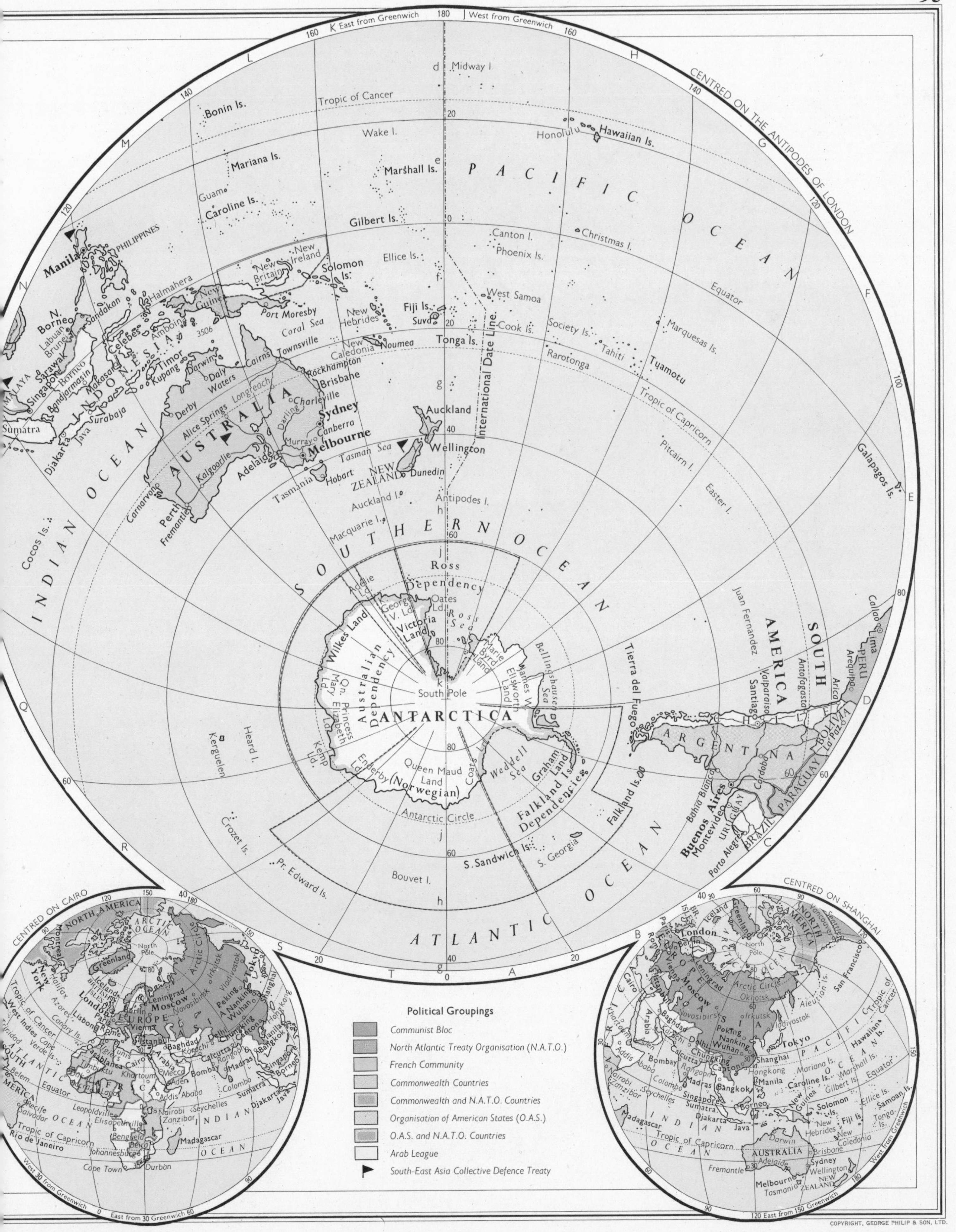
CENTRED ON THE ANTIPODES OF LONDON
East from Greenwich
West from Greenwich
PACIFIC OCEAN
INDIAN OCEAN
SOUTHERN OCEAN
ATLANTIC OCEAN
Tropic of Cancer
Equator
Tropic of Capricorn
Antarctic Circle
International Date Line
Midway I.
Bonin Is.
Wake I.
Hawaiian Is.
Honolulu
Mariana Is.
Marshall Is.
Guam
Caroline Is.
Gilbert Is.
Canton I.
Phoenix Is.
Christmas I.
Ellice Is.
Manila
PHILIPPINES
New Ireland
New Britain
Solomon Is.
New Guinea
Halmahera
Port Moresby
West Samoa
Fiji Is.
Suva
New Hebrides
Coral Sea
Cook Is.
Society Is.
Tahiti
Marquesas Is.
Rarotonga
Tuamotu
N. Borneo
Sandakan
Labuan
Brunei
Celebes
Amboina
Sarawak
Borneo
Singapore
Bandjarmasin
Makasar
INDONESIA
Timor
Kupang
Darwin
Daly Waters
Cairns
Townsville
New Caledonia
Noumea
Tonga Is.
Rockhampton
Brisbane
Charleville
Longreach
Alice Springs
Derby
AUSTRALIA
Darling
Sydney
Canberra
Murray
Melbourne
Adelaide
Kalgoorlie
Carnarvon
Perth
Fremantle
Sumatra
Djakarta
Java
Surabaja
MALAYA
Auckland
Wellington
Tasman Sea
NEW ZEALAND
Dunedin
Tasmania
Hobart
Auckland I.
Antipodes I.
Macquarie I.
Pitcairn I.
Easter I.
Galapagos Is.
Cocos Is.
Ross Dependency
Adelie Ld.
George V. Ld.
Oates Ld.
Ross Sea
Victoria Land
Wilkes Land
Australian Dependency
Qn. Mary Ld.
Princess Elizabeth Ld.
South Pole
ANTARCTICA
Marie Byrd Land
James W. Ellsworth Land
Bellingshausen Sea
Kemp Ld.
Enderby Ld.
Queen Maud Land (Norwegian)
Coats Ld.
Weddell Sea
Graham Land
Falkland Is. Dependencies
Falkland Is.
S. Sandwich Is.
S. Georgia
Bouvet I.
Pr. Edward Is.
Crozet Is.
Kerguelen
Heard I.
Juan Fernandez
Tierra del Fuego
SOUTH AMERICA
Callao
Lima
PERU
Arequipa
Arica
Antofagasta
Valparaiso
Santiago
CHILE
BOLIVIA
La Paz
ARGENTINA
Cordoba
PARAGUAY
Bahia Blanca
Buenos Aires
Montevideo
URUGUAY
Porto Alegre
BRAZIL
CENTRED ON CAIRO
NORTH AMERICA
ARCTIC OCEAN
North Pole
Greenland
New York
Montreal
Halifax
Azores
Canary Is.
Iceland
BRITISH ISLES
London
Paris
Lisbon
Berlin
Vienna
EUROPE
Leningrad
Moscow
Novosibirsk
Irkutsk
Vladivostok
Tokyo
Peking
Nanking
Wuhan
Shanghai
Hong Kong
Chungking
Canton
Manila
Bangkok
Singapore
Delhi
Calcutta
Rangoon
Bombay
Madras
Colombo
Karachi
Baghdad
Istanbul
Tunis
Algiers
Casablanca
Cairo
Mecca
Aden
Khartoum
Addis Ababa
Timbuktu
Dakar
Lagos
Leopoldville
Elisabethville
Nairobi
Zanzibar
Seychelles
Madagascar
Benguela
Beira
Johannesburg
Durban
Cape Town
Cape Verde Is.
West Indies
Belem
Recife
Salvador
Rio de Janeiro
Trinidad
Sumatra
Djakarta
Java
Borneo
INDIAN OCEAN
ATLANTIC OCEAN
Tropic of Capricorn
West 30 from Greenwich
0 East from 30 Greenwich 60
CENTRED ON SHANGHAI
Vancouver
Seattle
San Francisco
Aleutian Is.
Okhotsk
Arctic Circle
Hawaiian Is.
Mariana Is.
Marshall Is.
Caroline Is.
Gilbert Is.
Ellice Is.
Samoan Is.
Solomon Is.
Fiji Is.
Tonga Is.
New Hebrides
New Caledonia
Brisbane
Sydney
Wellington
Melbourne
Tasmania
NEW ZEALAND
Adelaide
Darwin
Fremantle
Arabia
Addis Ababa
Aden
Nairobi
Zanzibar
PACIFIC OCEAN
120 East from 150 Greenwich
West from Greenwich
Political Groupings
Communist Bloc
North Atlantic Treaty Organisation (N.A.T.O.)
French Community
Commonwealth Countries
Commonwealth and N.A.T.O. Countries
Organisation of American States (O.A.S.)
O.A.S. and N.A.T.O. Countries
Arab League
South-East Asia Collective Defence Treaty

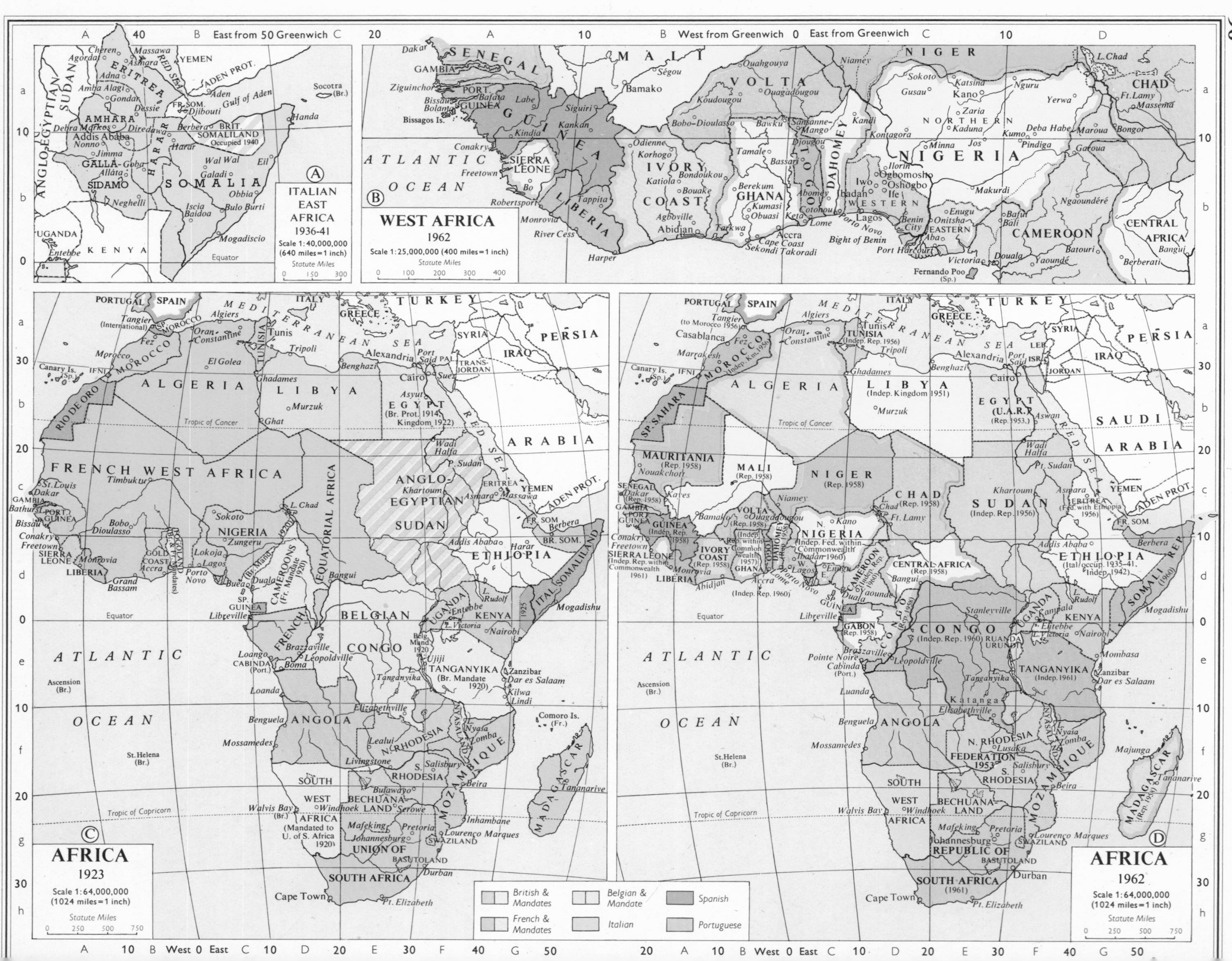

A
ITALIAN EAST AFRICA
1936-41
Scale 1:40,000,000 (640 miles=1 inch)
Statute Miles
B
WEST AFRICA
1962
Scale 1:25,000,000 (400 miles=1 inch)
Statute Miles
C
AFRICA
1923
Scale 1:64,000,000 (1024 miles=1 inch)
Statute Miles
D
AFRICA
1962
Scale 1:64,000,000 (1024 miles=1 inch)
Statute Miles
British & Mandates
French & Mandates
Belgian & Mandate
Italian
Spanish
Portuguese

INDEX

Note.—Each map in the Atlas is divided into squares by the lines of latitude and longitude, and these squares are indicated by Reference Letters in the borders of the map. These Reference Letters follow each name in the Index after the Map Number, and indicate in which square each place will be found. Thus: 'Aargau, 29B, Ca' shows that Aargau will be found on Map 29B, in the square indicated by the Reference Letters 'Ca'.

ABBREVIATIONS

Abp. – *Archbishopric*
Arch. – *Archipelago*
B. – *Bay*
Bp. – *Bishopric*
Bur. – *Burgraviate*
C. – *Cape*
Cal. – *Caliphate*
Co. – *County*
D. – *Duchy*
Dist. – *District*
Eccl. – *Ecclesiastical*
Elec. – *Electorate*
G.D. – *Grand Duchy*
I.(s) – *Island(s)*
King. – *Kingdom*
L. – *Lake*
Ld. – *Land*
Land. – *Landgraviate*
M. – *March, Mark*
Marg. – *Margraviate*
Marq. – *Marquisate*
Mt.(s) – *Mount, Mountain(s)*
Mte. – *Monte*
Oc. – *Ocean*
Pr. – *Principality*
Prot. – *Protectorate*
Prov. – *Province*
Pt. – *Point*
R. – *River*
Reg. – *Region*
Rep. – *Republic*
S. – *Seigneurie*
Sd. – *Sound*
St. – *State*
Terr. – *Territory*
V. – *Viscounty*

AACHEN, 8, Da; 12, Fd; 38, Gc
Aalborg, 26, Db; 88, Gb
Aalen, 30, Hd; 53, Hc
Aar, R., 29B, Ba
Aarau, 29B, Ca
Aargau, canton, 29B, Ca
Aargau, reg., 10, Ce
Aarhus, 26, Db
Aba, 96B, Cb
Abadan, 93, Fc
Abancay, 68, Bd
Abbasid Caliphate, 8, He
Abbendone (Abingdon), 13, Ee
Abbéville, 38, Dc; 83A, Aa
Abbotsbury, 36, Dg
Abedesberie (Abbotsbury), 13, Df
Abenaki, 56, Fa
Abensberg, 29A, Da
Abeokuta, 81C, Ec
Aberdeen, 14, Fb; 37A, Cb
Aberdeen, co., 37A, Cb
Aberfeldy, 37A, Cb; 49A, Cb
Aberfoyle, 37A, Bb; 48B, Aa
Abergavenny, 27, Ce
Abergwili, 27, Be; 28A, Bc
Aberlleiniog, 13, Bc
Abernethy, 14, Ec
Abidjan, 96B, Bb
Abingdon, 27, Ee
Abitibi, L., 45A, Ba
Abkhazia, 79, Hb
Åbo, 26, Fa
Abomey, 96B, Cb
Abone (Sea Mills), 3A, De
Abotrites, 8, Ea
Aboukir B., 64, Jf
Abraham, Heights of, 56A
Abrantes, 63, Ac
Abruzzi, reg., 32A, Ec
Abruzzo, 22, Ec
Abu Arish, 93, Ef
Abu Dhabi, 93, Ge
Abu Hamed, 80B, Ad
Abus Fl. (The Humber), 3A, Gc
Abydos, 19, Dd
Abydus, 4B, Hc
Abyssinia (Habesh), 6, Ed
Acadia, 45A, Ea; 55B, Db
Acajutla, 55B, Be
Acapulco, 43A, Cc
Accia, 22, Dc
Accompong, 43A, Ec
Accra, 81C, Dc
Acerenza, 22, Fc
Acerenza, eccl. prov., 22, Fc
Achaia, 1, Ed
Achaia, Pr. of, 19, Ce
Achalzich, 79, Hb
Achi Baba, 86D
Achill I., 15, Ac
Achonry, 15, Cb
Achusi (Pensacola), 43A, Da
Acklin I., 43A, Eb
Acqui, 20, Hf; 23B, Bb
Acra (Acre), 13, Gd
Acre, 16, Kf
Acre, terr., 68, Bc
Acre (Akko), 18C, Cf
Acton Burnell, 27, Dd
Actune (Acton), 13, Dc
Adalia, 6, Eb; 86C, Bb
Adalia, G. of, 86C, Bb
Adamawa, 80A, Ed
Adana (Aden), 1, Gf
Adana, Turkey, 18C, Ca
Adapazari, 93, Ca
Adda, R., 5, Bb
Addis Ababa, 96A, Ab
Adelaide, Australia, 77, Fl
Adelaide, S. Africa, 81B, Cc
Adélie Land, 69C
Adelingi (Athelney), 13, De
Adelsberg, 39, Lf
Aden, 80A, Hc; 93, Fg
Aden, G. of, 96A, Ba
Aden Prot., 93, Fg
Adige, R., 5, Cb; 86B, Bd
Adirondack Mts., 57, Ea
Admiralty Is., 77, Hb
Adna, 96A, Aa
Adour, R., 11, Ce; 63, Ea
Adowa, 80B, Be
Adramyttium, 19, De
Adrar, 80A, Bb
Adrian, 70, Fc
Adrianople, 78, Fe
Adriatic Sea, 5, Ec
Adwalton Moor, 48A, Cc
Adzharia, 84, Ld
Ægean Sea, 78, Ef
Ægean Theme, 9, He
Ægina, 78, Dg
Ægyptus, 2, Jg
Aerschot, 83A, Ca
Aesica (Great Chesters), 3C
Aesium, 5B, Bb
Afghan Supremacy, 59A, Ba
Afghanistan, 61B, Bb; 92, Aa
Afiun Karahissar, 86C, Bb
Africa, 2, Eg; 4B, Dd
Africa, Exarchate of, 4B, Cd
Afyon, 79, Fc
Agades, 80A, Dc
Agadir, 80A, Ba; 82, Af
Agali, 22, Bc
Agamenticus (York), 45B, Db
Agawam (Ipswich), 45B, Db
Agboville, 96B, Bb
Agde, 11, Ee
Agder, 12, Fb
Agemundrenesse (Amunderness), 18, Dc
Agen, 11, Dd; 17A, Cd
Agenais, 17, Ff
Aggershuus (Christiania), 34, Ea
Aghadoe, 15, Bd
Aghlabids, 8, Dd
Aghlabids, King. of, 6B, Ca
Aghmat, 6, Ab
Agincourt, 28D, Da
Agnadello, 32A, Cb
Agordat, 96A, Aa
Agra, 73, Cb
Agraca, Mte., 63B
Agram, 21, Mf; 39, Lf
Agrigentum (Girgenti), 5, Df
Aguilar, 23D, Ca
Agulhas, C., 81B, Bc
Ahaggar, 80A, Db
Ahausen, 29A, Da
Ahmadabad, 73, Bc
Ahmadnagar, 59A, Bd; 92, Cd
Ahrensböck, 65F, Ba
Ahwaz, 6A, Db; 93, Fc
Aidin, 78, Fg; 86C, Ab
Aigle, 29B, Ab
Aiguesmortes, 20, Fg
Aiguillon, 53, De
Aila, 6A, Bc; 18C, Cj
Ailech, 7A, Aa
Ailsa Craig, 49A, Bc
Aimargues, 38, Fg
Ain, R., 29A, Ab
Aintab, 18C, Ea
Air, 80A, Dc
Airds Moss, 49A, Bc
Aire, Flanders, 17, Gc
Aire, Gascony, 22, Bc
Aire, R., 7C, Cb
Airgialla, 7A, Ba
Aisne, R., 17, Hd; 83A, Bb
Aix, 11, Fe
Aix la Chapelle, 10, Bc
Ajaccio, 30, Hg; 84, Dd
Ajmere, 73, Bb
Ajnadain, 6A, Ab
Akaroa, 77A
Akeman Street, 3A, Ee
Akerman, 51, Gd; 78, Hb
Akhaltsikh, 61, Ff
Akhlat, 19, Ge
Akko (Acre), 18C, Cf
Akmolinsk, 74, Fc
Akpatok I., 71, Ha
Akyab, 90, Ac
al Anbar, 6A, cb
al Dahna, 6, Fc
Al-Hasa, 79, Je
al Jawf, 6, Ec
al Kufah, 6A, Cb
al Mahdiyah, 6, Cb
al Nufud, 6, Fc
al Raqqah, 6A, Ba
al Ruha, 6A, Ba
Alabama, R., 56, Bd; 57A, Bc
Alabama, st., 72, Cc
Alagoas, 68, Fc
Alais, 30, Ff
Åland Is., 26, Ea
Alamanni, 7A, Fb
Alani, 2, Ld
Alans, 6, Fa; 19, Gd
Alarcos, 23C, Cc
Alasehir, 79, Ec
Alaska, 69B; 71A, Ba
Alaska Pen., 71A, Bb
Alatri, 22A
Alauna (Maryport), 3A, Cb
Alava, 23C, Da
Alba, 5, Ab
Alba de Tormes, 63, Cb
Alban, 7C, Aa; 14, Dc
Albania, 78, Be
Albanian Pr., 24, Fe
Albanians, 18B, Cb
Albano, 22A
Albany, Georgia, 72, Dc
Albany, New York, 57, Eb
Albany, W. Australia, 77, Bl
Albany, reg., 81B, Cc
Albany, R., 70, Fb
Albara, 18C, Dc
Albaracin, 22, Bc; 23C, Eb
Albazin, 74, Lc
Albemarle, 45B, Ae
Albemarle Sd., 57, Ce
Albert, 83A, Ba
Albert, L., 80A, Fd
Alberta, 70, Cb
Albi, 11, Ee; 22, Dc
Albiac, 38, Df
Albis, R., 2, Fc
Albistan, 19, Fe
Albon, 30, Ff
Albret, 17, Ef
Albret, S. of, 30, Cf
Albuera, 23D, Bc; 63, Bc
Albury, 77, Hi
Alcacer do Sal, 23C, Ac
Alcala, 22, Bc; 63, Db
Alcala de Henares, 23C, Db
Alcaniz, 63, Eb
Alcantara, Brazil, 68, Ec
Alcantara, Spain, 23C, Bc; 63, Bc
Alcazar, 34, Be
Alchester, 3A, Ee
Alcira, 23C, Ec
Alclyde, 7B, Aa
Alclyde (Dumbarton), 14, Dd
Alcobaça, 22, Ad
Aldabra, 80A, He
Aldbury, 36, Ff
Aldea de Ponte, 63, Bb
Alderney, 17, Dd
Aleksandrovsk, 91, Ha
Alemquer, 63B
Alemtejo, 23C, Ac; 63, Bc
Alençon, 11, Db
Alençon, D. of, 30, Dd
Alenuihaha Chan., 75D, Cb
Aleppo (Haleb), 18C, Eb
Aleria, 5, Bc; 53, Bf
Alessandria, 32A, Cb
Alet, 11, Bb; 53, Ef
Aleutian Is., 71A, Ab
Alexandretta, 18C, Db
Alexandria, Egypt, 80B, Aa
Alexandria, Louisiana, 72, Bc
Alexandria, Virginia, 57, Cd
Alexandrovsk, 74, Dd
Alford, 37A, Cb
Algarve, 23C, Ad; 63, Ad
Algarve de Alem Mar, 47, Ae
Algeciras, 23C, Cd; 63A
Algeria, 24, Cf; 80A, Da
Algeria, Pashalik of, 47, Ce
Algiers, 34, Ce; 80A, Da
Algiers, Sultanate of, 34, De
Algoa B., 81B, Cc
Algonkins, 45A, Ca
Alhandra, 63B
Alicante, 23C, Ec; 63, Ec
Alice Springs, 77, Ef
Alids, King. of, 6B, Ga
Alife, 21A, Cb; 23B, Ed
Aligarh, 59C, Cb; 92, Db
Aliwal, 73, Ca
Aliwal North, 81A, Cd
Aljubarrota, 23D, Ac
Aljustro, 23C, Ad
Alkmaar, 46A, Db
Allahabad, 73, Db
Allata, 96A, Ab
Allatoona, 72A, Aa
Allegheny Mts., 57, Bd
Allegheny, R., 45A, Bb
Allemania, 8, Db
Allemanni, 2, Ed; 4A, Db
Allen, Bog of, 15, Ec
Allen, L., 15, Cb
Allenstein, 84, Gb
Alleppey, 92, Df
Aller, R., 10, Cb; 55A, Hb
Allerdale, 28B, Bc
Allier, R., 11, Ed
Allstedt, 39C, Bb
Allumette Is., 45A, Ba
Alma Ata, 91, Ab
Almada, 23D, Ac
Almalik, 25, Hb
Almanza, 47, Be; 63, Ec
Almaraz, 63, Cc
Almeida, 23C, Bb; 63, Bb
Almeria, 22, Bd; 23C, Dd
Almina, C., 63A
Almissa, 22, Fc
Almohad Empire, 18A, Ac
Almonacid, Aragon, 63, Eb
Almonacid, New Castile, 63, Dc
Almora, 73, Cb
Almoravids, 16, Be
Aln, R., 28B, Db
Alnwick, 13, Ea
Alost, 46A, Cd
Alpes, 1, Cc; 2, Fd
Alps, The, 5, Ca; 10, De
Alpuente, 23C, Ec
Alresford, 27, Ee
Alsace, 10, Bd; 39B, Db
Alsace-Lorraine, 65D, Ab
Alsebruge (Axbridge), 13, De
Alsek, R., 71B, Ba
Alsen, 60B, Ba; 65F, Aa
Alsen Sd., 65F, Aa
Alsh, L., 49A, Bb
Alston, 13, Db
Alt, R., 78, Ec
Alt Breisach, 39B, Db
Altenburg, 10, Fd; 21, Kc
Altenkirchen, 53, Gb
Altkirch, 39B, Dc; 83B, Bb
Altmark, 30, Jb; 60A, Cb
Altomünster, 22, Eb
Alton, England, 27, Fe
Alton, Illinois, 72, Cb
Altona, 51, Bc; 65F, Ab
Altorf, 29B, Cb
Altranstadt, 50, Cc
Aluta, R., 19, Cd; 78, Ec
Alvarado, 43A, Cc
Alvertune (Allerton, Northallerton), 13, Eb
Alwar, 73, Cb
Alwinestune (Carisbrooke), 13, Ef
Alyaty, 93, Fb
Alyth, 37A, Cb
Amadeus, L., 77, Ef
Amalfi, 5, Ed
Amami-Oshima, 75, Dc
Amapa, 68, Db
Amara, 86C, Ec; 93, Fc
Amarante, 63, Ab
Amarapura, 73, Gc
Amasia, 9, Kd
Amasra, 24, Je
Amastris, 19, Ed
Amatola Mts., 81B, Cc
Amazon, R., 68, Dc
Amazonas, 68, Cc
Amba Alagi, 96A, Aa
Ambala, 73, Ca
Amberg, 29A, Da
Amboina, 52C, Cb; 90, Cd
Amboise, 11, Dc
Ambra, 32E, Bb
Ambresberie (Amesbury), 13, Ee
Ambur, 59D
Ameland, 46A, Ea
Amelia, 57, Ce
Ameria, 5B, Bb
Amersfoort, 46A, Eb
Amersham, 27, Fe
Amhara, 96A, Aa
Amherst, 73, Gd
Amichel, 43A, Cb
Amida, 2, Mf; 6A, Ca
Amida (Diarbekr), 33A, Fc
Amiens, 11, Eb; 83A, Bb
Amirante Is., 83, Me
Amisus, 18B, Fb; 24, Ke
Amiterno, 21A, Ba
Amman, 79, Gd
Amorgos, 78, Fg
Amorium, 9, Je
Amoy, 91, Ed
Ampezzo, 86B, Ca
Ampurias, 23C, Ga
Amritsar, 73, Ba
Amsterdam, 31A, Ca; 46A, Db
Amsterdam, I., 42B
Amu Darya, R., 61B, Ba
Amur, R., 25, Ma; 91, Fa
An Nafud, 93, Ed
An Nasiriyah, 93, Fc
Anadirsk, 42, Aa
Anadyr, 74, Qb
Anagni, 22A; 32A, Ed
Anahuac, 43A, Cc
Anaiza, 93, Ed
Anamaboe, 81C, Dc
Anapa, 61, Ef
Anas, R., 2, Bf
Anatolia, 33A, Dc; 64, Jf
Anatolic Theme, 9, Je
Ancénis, 20, Ce
Anchialus, 8, Hc
Anchorage, 71A, Ca
Anchu, 76B, Cb
Ancona, 5, Dc
Ancona, M. of, 21, Kg
Ancud, 68, Bg
Ancyra, 2, Ke; 8, Jd
Andalusia, 23C, Cd; 63, Cd
Andaman Is., 73, Fe
Andastes, 45B, Bc
Andechs, 20, Je
Anderida (Pevensey), 3A, Gf
Anderida Silva, 3A, Ff
Andernach, 10, Bc
Anderson, 72, Ec
Andersonville, 72, Dc
Andes, 68, Bc
Andhra, 1, Kf
Andhra Pradesh, 92, Dd
Andorra, 30, Dg; 63, Fa
Andover, 27, Ee
Andredsweald (The Weald), 13, Ge
Andria, 21A, Db
Andros, I., 78, Eg
Andros Is., 43A, Eb
Androscoggin, R., 45B, Da
Andrusov, 50, Gc; 54, Jb
Andujar, 23C, Cc; 63, Cc
Angara, R., 91, Da
Angermanland, 26, Ea
Angers, 11, Cc; 17, Ee
Anghalle, 37B, Dc
Angles, 2A, Ba; 4A, Ba
Anglesey, 27, Bc
Angli, 2, Ec
Anglo-Egyptian Sudan, 80A, Fc
Angol, 68, Bf
Angola, 80A, Ef
Angora, 19, Ee; 86C, Bb
Angostura (Ciudad Bolivar), 68, Cb

Angoulême, 11, Dd; 17A, Cd
Angoulême, Co. of, 11, Dd
Angoumois, 17, Ef; 38, Df
Angra Pequena, 81A, Ac
Anguilla, 43A, Fc
Angus, 14, Fc
Anhalt, 20, Jc; 30, Jc
Ani, 9, Ld
Anjala, 51, Fa
Anjou, 28C, Bc; 38, Ce
Anjou, Co. of, 11, Dc; 17, Ee
Ankara, 79, Fb
Anklam, 26, Dc
Ann, 45B, Ad
Annale, R., 49B, Db
Annaly, 15, Dc
Annam, 25, Kd; 74, Jg
Annan, 49A, Cc
Annandale, 14, Ed; 28B, Bb
Annapolis, Maryland, 57, Cd; 72B, Ba
Annapolis (Port Royal), 45A, Db; 71, Hc
Annecy, 30, Gf
Annobon, 80A, De
Annonay, 30, Ff
Annone, 23B, Bb
Ansbach, 38, Jd
Ansbach, Pr., 53, Jc
Anstruther, 49A, Cb
Antalya, 79, Fc
Antarctic Ocean, 69C
Antarctica, 95, Ak
Antequera, 23D, Cd
Antibes, 38, Gg
Anticosti, 45A, Ea
Antietam, 72B, Ba
Antigua, 43A, Fc
Antioch, 6A, Ba; 18C, Db
Antioch, Pr. of, 18C, Dc
Antiochia, 16, He
Antipodes I., 69C, 75, Fg
Antivari, 22, Fc; 78, Bd
Antofagasta, 68, Be
Antofagasta, st., 68, Ce
Antoing, 46A, Cd
Antrim, co., 37C; 49B, Eb
Antrim, Mts. of, 15, Eb
Antung, 76B, Ca
Antwerp, 17A, Ea; 46A, Dc
Anzac Cove, 86D
Aosta, 5, Ab
Apalachee, 56, Cd
Apalachicola, R., 71F, Ba
Apamea (Famia), 18C, Dc
Apcher, 30, Ef
Apennines, 5, Dc
Apia, 75B, Ba
Appalache, 43A, Da
Appalache Bay, 43A, Db
Appalachian Mts., 70, Fd
Appenzell, 29B, Da
Appenzell, canton, 29B, Da
Appin, 49A, Bb
Appleby, 13, Db; 27, Db
Appledore, 7C, Dc
Appomattox Court House, 72, Eb
Appomattox, R., 72B, A6
Apt, 22, Dc; 30, Fg
Apulia, 4B, Fc; 5, Ed
Apulia, D. of, 16, Fd
Apure, R., 43A, Ed
Apurimac, R., 41B, Be
Aqaba, 93, Dd
Aquae (Buxton), 3A, Ec
Aquae Sulis (Bath), 3A, De
Aquidaban, 68, De
Aquila, 23B, Dc; 39, Kg
Aquileia, 5, Db
Aquileia, eccl. prov., 22, Eb
Aquino, 21A, Bb; 22, Ec
Aquinum, 5B, Bc
Aquitaine, 4A, Cc
Aquitaine, D. of, 17, Fe
Aquitania, 2, Dd; 8B, Bb
Ar, 65B, Aa
Arabia, 1, Ge; 6, Fc
Arabia Deserta, 1, Ge
Arabia Felix, 1, Fe
Arabian Desert, 80B, Ab
Arabian Sea, 25, Fe
Aracaju, 68, Fd
Aracena, 23D, Bd
Arachosia, 1, Jd
Arad, 33C, Eb
Arafura Sea, 77, Ec; 91, Fg
Aragon, 23C, Ea; 63, Eb
Aragon, King. of, 23C, Eb
Araguaia, R., 68, Dd
Arak, 93, Fc
Arakan, 73, Fc; 92, Gd
Aral, L., 6, Ga; 25, Eb
Aralskoje, 61B, Ba
Aran I., 15, Ca
Aran Is., 15, Bc
Aranda, 63, Db
Aranjuez, 63, Db
Ararguez, 54, Be
Aras, R., 19, He
Aravalli Ra., 59C, Bb
Arbe, 22, Ec
Arbo, 23B, Eb
Arboga, 26, Eb
Arborea, 23B, Bd
Arbre Croche, 56, Ca
Arbroath, 37A, Cb
Arc, 28D, Ec
Arcenefeld (Archenfield), 13, De
Arces, 5B, Bc
Archa, 18C, Dd
Arcole, 29A, Dc
Arcos, 23C, Bb
Arcot, 59D; 73, Ce
Arctic Ocean, 69B
Arcugnano, 86B, Bb
Ardagh, 15, Dc
Ardagh, bp., 15A, Bb
Ardebil, 19, He; 93, Fb
Arden, 7B, Cb
Arden, Forest of, 3A, Ed
Ardennes, 11, Fb; 83A, Ca
Ardfert, 15, Bd
Ardfinnan, 15, Dd
Ardgour, 14, Cc
Ardnamurchan Pt., 49A, Ab
Ardoch, 49A, Cb
Ardstraw, bp., 15A, Ba
Arelate (Upper King. of Burgundy), 10, Bf
Aremberg, 53, Gb
Aremburg, 65B, Aa
Arequipa, 68, Bd
Arevallo, 63, Cb
Arezzo, 21, Jg; 32E, Bb
Argaon, 59C, Cc
Argentan, 17, Fd
Argentina, 68, Ce; 83,Ff
Argentine Confederation, 68, Cf
Argentine Rep., 68, Cf
Argenton, 38, De
Arghandab, R., 73, Aa
Argonne, 83A, Cb
Argos, 78, Dg
Argostolion, 78, Cf
Arguin, 35, Hc; 52, Jc
Argyle, bp., 14A, Bb
Argyll, 14, Cc
Argyll, co., 49A, Bb
Argyll and Tarbert, co., 37A, Bb
Aria, 1, Jd
Ariano, 21A, Cb
Arica, 68, Bd
Ariminum (Rimini), 5, Db
Arinos, R., 68, Dd
Arinsol, 23C, Cd
Arisaig, 49A, Bb
Arizona, 70, Cd
Arizona Terr., 67D, Bb
Arkansas, 72, Bc
Arkansas Post, 72, Bc
Arkansas, R., 70, Dd
Arkansas Terr., 67C, Db
Arkhangelsk, 61, Fb; 88, Oa
Arklow, 15, Ed
Arlberg Pass, 29A, Db
Arles, 11, Fe; 17A, Ee
Arles, King. of, 20, Ff
Armagh, 15, Eb
Armagh, co., 37C; 49B, Eb
Armagnac, Co. of, 11, Ce
Armenia, 19, Ge; 79, Hc
Armenia, King. of, 19, Ee
Armeniac Theme, 9, Kd
Armenians, 18C, Ca
Armentieres, 46A, Bd
Armorica, 2, Cd; 4A, Bb
Armstrong, 28B, Bb
Arnhem, 46A, Eb
Arnhem Land, 77, Ed
Arnis, 65F, Aa
Arno, R., 5, Cc; 21B, Bd
Arnsberg, 20, Hc; 38, Hc
Arnstadt, 38, Jc
Arnswalde, 21, Lb
Aroche, 23D, Bd
Aroostook, R., 71E, Bb
Arpinum, 5B, Bc
Arques, 20, Dd
Arran, 14, Cd
Arras, 17, Gc; 46A, Bd
Arroyo de los Molinos, 63, Bc
Arsamosata, 9, Ke
Arsuf, 18C, Bf
Arta, 64, Gf; 78, Cf
Artaxata, 1, Gc
Artenay, 76A, Ab
Artois, 17, Gc; 83A, Ba
Aru Is., 77, Ec
Aruba, 41B, Cb
Arundel, England, 27, Ff
Arundel, Maryland, 45B, Ad
Arve, R., 29B, Ab
Arwystli, 13, Cd
Arzobispo, 63, Cc
Ascalon, 6A, Ab; 18C, Bg
Ascension, 40, Je; 96C, Ae
Aschaffenburg, 29A, Ca
Ascoli, 5, Dc
Ashanti, 81C, Dc
Ashburton, 27, Cf
Ashburton, R., 77, Bf
Ashby-de-la-Zouch, 48A, Cc
Ashdown, 7B, Cc
Ashkhabad, 93, Hb
Ashridge, 36, Ff
Ashuanipi, L., 71, Hb
Asia, cont., 94, Pc
Asia, diocese, 2, Kf
Asia, reg., 1, Ed
Asia Minor, 86C, Bb
Asiago, 84, Ec; 86B, Bb
Asir, 93, Ef
Asirgarh, 73, Cc
Askeaton, 37B, Cd; 49B, Cd
Asmara, 80A, Gc; 93, Df
Asoka Empire, 1, Ke
Aspadana, 1, Hd
Aspern, 29A, Ga
Aspinwall (Colon), 43D, Ed; 68, Bb
Aspromonte, 32C, Ee
Aspropotamos, R., 78, Cf
Assab, 80B, Ce
Assam, 25, Jd; 73, Fb
Assandun, 12, Ed
Assassins, 18C, Dc
Assaye, 59C, Cc; 69A, Nc
Assiette, Col d', 29A, Bc
Assiniboia, 70, Db
Assisi, 5, Dc
Assuan, 6, Ec
Assynt, 14, Ca
Astarac, Co. of, 11, De
Asterabad, 61, Hg
Asti, 5, Bb; 32A, Cb
Astico, R., 86B, Bb
Astorga, 23C, Ba; 63, Ba
Astrakhan, 19, Hc
Astrakhan, reg., 61, Hd
Asturias, 23C, Ca; 63, Ba
Asuncion, 68, De
Aswan, 80B, Ac; 96D, Fb
Aswan Dam, 93, Ce
Asyut, 80B, Ab
Atacama Desert, 68, Be
Atapuerca, 23C, Da
Atbara, 93, Cf
Atbara, R., 80B, Bd
Atelkuza, 9, Hc
Atella, 32A, Fd
Ath, 46A, Cd; 53, Eb
Athabaska, 70, Cb
Athabaska L., 70, Db
Athabaska, R., 70, Cb
Athboy, 49B, Ec
Athelney, 7C, Bc; 36, Df
Athenae, 2, Hf
Athenry, 37B, Cc; 49B, Cc
Athens, 78, Df
Athens, Barony of, 18B, Cc
Athens, D. of, 19, Ce
Athlone, 15, Dc
Atholl, 14, Dc
Athos, Mt., 9, Gd; 18B, Cb
Athy, 15, Ed
Atlanta, 72A, Ab
Atlantic Ocean, 35, Hd
Atrato, R., 43A, Ed
Atrebates, 3A, Ee
Atrek, R., 61, Jg
Atri, 21, Kg
Atropatene, 2, Nf
Attalia, 19, Ee
Attock, 73, Ba
Attu, I., 90, Ea
Aube, R., 76A, Cb
Auberoche, 28C, Cd
Aubigny, 53, Ed
Auch, 11, De
Auch, eccl. prov., 22, Bc
Auchterarder, 49A, Cb
Auckland, 75, Ff; 77A
Auckland, prov., 77A
Auckland (Waitemata), 77, Ml
Auckland I., 69C; 75, Fg
Auerstädt, 65B, Ba
Aughrim, 49B, Cc
Augsburg, 10, Dd
Augusta (Fort Cornwallis), 57D, Ab
Augusta, Georgia, 72, Dc
Augusta, Maine, 67B, Ca
Augusta Taurinorum (Turin), 5, Ab
Auldearn, 37A, Cb
Aumale, 17, Fd
Aunis, 30, Ce
Aurangabad, 73, Cd
Auray, 28C, Ac; 55A, Be
Aureliani, 2, Dd
Aurillac, 17, Gf; 30, Ef
Aussig, 31, Lc
Aust, 7A, Cb
Austerfield, 7B, Cb
Austerlitz, 29A, Ga
Austin, 70, Ed
Austral (Tubual) Is., 75, Hf; 83, Bf
Australia, 69A, Qf
Australia, Commonwealth of, 77, Ff
Australian Alps, 77, Hl
Australian Dependency, 95, PJ
Australasia, 7A, Eb; 8, Da
Austria, 50, Dd; 65A, Cb
Austria, reg., Italy, 5, Cb
Austria, March of, 10, Fd
Austria-Hungary, 82, Fc
Austrian Empire, 62, Fc; 65B, Cb
Austrian Netherlands, 54, Db
Austrian Silesia, 60A, Fc
Autun, 8B, Bb; 11, Fc
Auvergne, 11, Ed; 20, Ef
Auvergne, Co. of, 11, Ed
Auxerre, 11, Ec
Auximum, 5B, Bb
Auximum (Osimo), 5, Dc
Auxonne, 30, Fe
Ava, 41A, Gb; 73, Gc
Avalon, 45A, Ga
Avars, 8, Gb; 9, Fc
Aveiro, 22, Ac
Aventine, 5A
Aversa, 32A, Fd
Avesnes, 46A, Cd
Avignon, 11, Fe; 17, Hf
Avila, 22, Bc; 63, Cb
Avisio, R., 86B, Ba
Avlona, 18A, Ba
Avoca, R., 15, Ed
Avon, R., Bristol, 27, De
Avon, R., Hants., 27, Ef
Avon, R., Warwick, 27, Ed
Avondale, 28B, Ab
Avranches, 8B, Ab; 11, Cb
Avretone (Overton, Richard's Castle), 13, Dd
Awe, L., 14, Ce
Ax, 11, Ce
Axbridge, 27, De
Axel Heiberg Land, 44, Fa
Axim, 40, Jd; 81C, Dc
Ayacucho, 68, Bd; 69A, Fe
Ayas, 19, Fe
Aydin, 19, De; 93, Bb
Aylesbury, 7A, Cb; 48A, Cd
Aylesford, 7B, Dc
Ayr, 14, Dd
Ayr, co., 37A, Bc; 49A, Bc
Ayr, R., 14, Dd
Ayton, 37A, Cc
Ayubale, 56, Cd
Ayubites, Empire of the, 18B, Ed
Azangarh, 73, Db
Azerbaijan, 79, Jc; 89, Pe
Azores, 55B, Hc
Azov, 24, Kd; 79, Ga
Azov, Sea of, 19, Fc
Aztec Kingdom, 35, Dc
Aztecs, 43A, Bb

BAALBEK, 6A, Bb
Baalbek (Heliopolis), 18C, De
Babul, 93, Gb
Babuyan Is., 75E, Ba
Babylon, 2, Mg
Bacalhaos, 40, Gb.
Bachan, 52C, Cb
Bacharach, 29A, Ba
Bacolod, 75E, Bb
Bactria, I, Jd
Badajoz, 22, Ad; 63, Bc
Badakshan, 61B, Cb
Bade (Bath), 13, De
Baden, 20, Hd; 29B, Ca
Baden, Marg. of, 30, Hd
Baden Baden, 29A, Ca
Badenoch, 14, Eb; 37A, Bb
Badissin, 31, Lc
Baentone (Bampton), 13, Cf
Baeza, 23C, Dd
Bafata, 96B, Aa
Baffin Bay, 44, Ha; 69B
Baffin I., 44, Ga
Bafut, 96B, Db
Bage, 20, Fe
Baghdad, 6A, Cb; 9, Lf
Baghdad, Caliphate of, 18A, Gc
Baghdad Railway, 86C, Bb
Bagirmi, 80A, Ec
Bagnolo, 32D, Bb
Bahama Is., 43A, Eb
Bahawalpur, 73, Bb
Bahia (Salvador), 68, Fd
Bahia, st., 68, Ed
Bahia Blanca, 68, Cf
Bahn, 60A, Eb
Bahrein, 6, Gc; 79, Ke
Baikal, L., 25, Ka; 91, Da
Baker, I, 90, Fd
Bakewell, 7C, Cb
Bakhchisarai, 51, Ge
Baku, 19, Hd; 79, Jb
Balaguer, 23C, Fb
Balaklava, 61, Df
Balasore, 59A, Ec
Balassaghun, 25, Gb
Balaton, L., 31, Me; 33c, Db
Balch, 61B, Bb
Balchik, 78, Gd
Baleares Insulae, 2, Df
Balearic Is, 23C, Gc; 63 Gc
Bali, 96B, Db
Balidon Hill, 28B, Cb
Balikpapan, 90, Bd
Balkans, 78, Ed
Balkh, 6, Hb; 25, Fc
Balkhash, L., 25, Gb; 91, Ab
Ballachulish, 49A, Bb
Ballater, 49A, Cb
Balleny Is., 69C
Ballinamuck, 49B, Dc
Balliol, 28B, Db
Ball's Bluff, 72B, Ba
Ballycastle, 49B, Ea
Ballymena, 49B, Eb
Ballymore, 49B, Dc
Ballyshannon, 49B, Cb
Balneum Regis, 5B, Bb
Balta, 51, Fd; 78, Gb
Baltic Sea, 22, Ea; 26, Eb
Baltimore, Maryland, 57, Cd; 72 B, Ba
Baluchistan, 61B, Bc; 74 Ef
Bamako, 80A, Cc; 81C, Cb
Bamberg, 10, Dd
Bamborough, 27, Ea
Banana, 80A, Ee
Banaras (Varanasi), 92, Eb
Banat of Craiova, 33C, Ec
Banat of Temesvar, 33C, Eb
Banbury, 27, Ed
Banda Is, 52 C, Cb
Banda Oriental, 68, Df
Bandar Abbas, 93, Hd
Bandar Maharani, 75A, Aa
Bandjarmasin, 91, Eg
Bandon, 49B, Ce
Bandon, R., 15, Ce
Banff, co., 37A, Cb; 49A, Cb
Bangalore, 73, Ce
Bangaya Is., 52C, Bb
Bangkok, 73, Ge; 92, Je
Bangor, Caernarvon, 13, Bc; 36, Bd
Bangor, Flint, 7A, Ca; 13, Dc
Bangor, Ireland, 37B, Fb
Bangor, Maine, 71, Hc
Bangor, bp, 36, Be
Bangtok, 92, Fb
Bangui, 96D, Dd
Bangweulu, L., 80A, Gf
Baniyas, 93, Db
Banjermassim, 69A, Pe
Bankot, 59A, Bd
Banks I., 44, Ba
Banks Pen., 77, MJ
Bann, R., 15, Eb; 37C
Bannaventa (Whilton Lodge) 3A, Ed
Bannockburn, 28B, Aa
Bannow, B., 15, Ed
Bantam, 41A, He
Bantry, 49B, Be
Bantry B., 15, Be
Banwelle (Banwell), 13, De
Banyaluka, 39, Mf; 78, Ac
Bapaume, 30, Ec; 83A, Ba
Bar, 17A, Eb; 39B, Bb
Bar, D. of, 30, Fd; 39B, Ba
Bar-le-Duc, 17, Hd; 29A, Aa
Bar-sur-Aube, 11, Fb
Bar-sur-Seine, 11, Fb
Bar Hill, 3A, Ba
Baramahal, 59C, Ce
Baranof I., 71B, Cb
Baranow, 26, Fc
Barataria Bay, 43A, Db
Barawa, 40, Md; 41A, Bd
Barbados, 43A, Gc
Barbarike, I, Je
Barbary, 40, Kc
Barbastro, 22, Cc
Barberton, 81A, Dc
Barbuda, 43A, Fc
Barcastro, 23C, Fa
Barcelona, Spain, 23C, Gb; 63, Gb
Barcelona, Venezuela, 68, Ca
Barcelona, Co. of, 23C, Ga
Barcelona, Co. of (Spanish March), 11, De
Barcelonnette, 38, Gf
Barcelos, 68, Cc
Barcoo, R., 77, Gg
Bardera, 80A, Hd
Bardia, 93, Ac
Bardney, 36, Fd
Bardsey, I., 7C, Ab
Bareilly, 73, Cb
Barents Sea, 69B
Barfleur, 28C, Bb; 55A, Cd
Bari, Africa, 80A, Gd
Bari, Italy, 5, Fd; 32A, Gd
Bari Doab, 73, Ba
Barka, 6, Db; 9, Gf
Barking, 13, Ge; 36, Gf
Barletta, 32A, Gd
Barlings, 36, Fd
Barmen, 83A, Da
Barnard Castle, 27, Eb
Barnaul, 91, Ba
Barnestable (Barnstaple), 13, Be

Barnet, 27, Fe
Barnstaple, England, 27, Ce
Barnstaple, Massachusetts, 45B, Dc
Baroda, 73, Bc
Barotseland, 80A, Ff
Barra, 43A, Ec
Barra, I., 14, Ac
Barrackpore, 73, Ec
Barranquilla, 68, Ba
Barrois Mouvant, 39B, Bb
Barrosa, 63, Bd
Barrow, Pt., 71A, Ba
Barrow, R., 15, Ed; 37B, Ed
Bartenstein, 60B, Ha
Barth, 31, Ka
Barton-on-Humber, 27, Fc
Bartzo, 23B, Fc
Baruth, 39C, Da
Bärwalde, 39, Lb; 60A, Dc
Basel (Basle), 29B, Ba
Bashee B., 81B, Dc
Basilan, 75E, Bc
Basilicata, 5, Fd
Basing, 7C, Cc; 48A, Cd
Basinges (Basingstoke), 13, Ee
Basingstoke, 27, Ee
Basle (Basel), 29B, Ba
Basle, canton, 29B, Ba
Basle, Bp. of, 29B, Ba
Basques, 8C, Bb
Basra, 6A, Db
Basra (Bassorah), 41A, Ba
Bass Rock, 28B, Ca
Bass Str., 77, Hi
Bassano, 32D, Bb; 86B, Bb
Bassari, 96B, Cb
Basse, Fontaine, 22, Cb
Bassein, Burma, 73, Fd
Bassein, India, 73, Bd
Bassignano, 32B, Bb; 51, Bd
Bassigny, 39B, Bb
Bassorah, 33A, Gd
Bassorah (Basra), 41A, Ba
Bastarnae, 2, Jc
Bastia, 20, Hg
Bastogne, 83A, Ca
Basutoland, 81B, Db
Batak, 78, Ee
Batangas, 75E, Bb
Batanta, 52C, Db
Batavia, 74, Jj
Batavian Rep., 51, Bc
Bath, England, 27, De
Bath, N. Carolina, 56, Dc
Bath and Wells, bp., 36, Cf
Bathurst, C. Prov., 81B, Cc
Bathurst, Gambia, 81C, Ab
Bathurst, New South Wales, 77, Hh
Bathurst Inlet, 70, Da
Batlapin, 81B, Ca
Batoche, 70, Db
Baton Rouge, 56, Ad
Batouri, 96B, Db
Battle, 12, Ed; 36, Gg
Battleford, 70, Db
Batuchina, 52B, Aa
Batum, 33A, Fb; 79, Hb
Batum, reg., 79, Hb
Batumi, 88, Oe
Baturin, 50, Gc
Baugé, 28D, Bc
Baugy, 38, Ee
Bautzen, 10, Fc; 53, Lb
Bavaria, 10, Ed; 21, Ke
Bavaria, D. of, 30, Jd
Bavaria-Landshut, D. of, 31, Kd
Bavaria-Munich, D. of, 30, Jd
Bavarians, 4A, Eb
Bawku, 96B, Ba
Bay Is., 43B, Bc
Bayeux, 11, Cb
Baylen, 62, Be; 63, Dc
Bayonne, 11, Ce; 63, Ea
Bayreuth, 20, Jd; 53, Jc
Bayreuth, pr., 38, Jc
Baza, 23C, Dd
Bazarchik, 78, Fd
Bazas, 11, Cd
Beachy Hd., 55A, Dc
Beacon Hill, 56B
Beacons, 27, Ce
Béarn, V. of, 11, Ce
Beaucaire, 17, Hg
Beaufort, France, 38, Ce
Beaufort, Georgia, 57D, Ab
Beaufort, S. Africa, 81B, Bc
Beaufort, Syria, 18C, Ce
Beaufort Bay, 44, Aa
Beaufort Sea, 69B
Beaufort West, 81A, Bd
Beaugency, 20, De; 76A, Ac
Beaujeu, 11, Fc
Beaujeu, S. of, 20, Fe
Beaulieu, England, 36, Eg
Beaulieu, France, 22, Cb
Beauly, 49A, Bb
Beaumaris, 27, Bc
Beaumont, 30, Ed; 76A, Cb
Beaune, 30, Fe
Beaune-la-Rolande, 76A, Bb
Beaupréau, 53, Cd
Beauséjour, 45A, Ea
Beauvais, 11, Eb; 83A, Bb
Beauvais, Co. of, 11, Eb
Beauvale, 36, Ed
Beauvoir, 38, Be
Beaver Dam, 71D
Bebbanburh (Banburgh), 13, Ea
Bec, 17, Fd; 22, Cb
Beccles, 13, Hd
Bechuana, 81B, Ba
Bechuanaland, 81A, Bb; 96, Eg
Bechuanaland Prot., 80A, Fg; 81A, Bc
Bedale, 27, Eb
Bedeforde (Bedford), 13, Fd
Bedefordscire (Bedfordshire), 13, Fd
Bedford, England, 27, Fd
Bedford, Virginia, 57, Be
Bedford, co., 27, Fd
Bedlington, 27, Ea
Bednore, 59C, Ce
Bedr, 6, Ec
Bedvinde (Great Bedwyn), 13, Ee
Bedwin, 27, Ee
Beeston Castle, 48A, Bc
Bega, 6, Ec
Beilan, 64, Kf
Beira, 81A, Da
Beira, prov., 63, Ab
Beirut, 79, Gd; 80A, Ga
Beisan, 18C, Cf
Beja, 23C, Bc
Belata, 23C, Ac
Belbuck, 22, Fa
Belcher Is., 70, Fb
Belchite, 63, Eb
Belem, 22, Ad
Belem (Para), 41B, Ed; 68, Ec
Belfast, 37B, Fb; 49B, Fb
Belfort, 29A, Bb; 39B, Cc
Belgae, 3A, De
Belgard, 21, Mb
Belgian Congo, 80A, Fe
Belgium, 83A, Ca; 87, Ab
Belgrade, 78, Cc
Belin, 38, Cf
Belinas (Paneas), 18C, Ce
Belize, 43A, Dc
Bellary, 73, Cd
Belle I., Canada, 71, Jb
Belle I., France, 11, Bc
Belle Isle, Str. of., 71, Jb
Belleek, 49B, Cb
Bellegarde, 53, Ef
Bellême, 11, Db; 17, Fd
Belley, 11, Fd; 22, Db
Bellingshausen Sea, 95, Ej
Bellingtun (Bedlington), 13, Ea
Bellinzona, 5, Ba; 29B, Db
Belluno, 5, Da; 86B, Ca
Belmont, U.S.A., 72, Cb
Belo Horizonte, 68, Ee
Belturbet, 49B, Db
Belvedoir (Belvoir), 13, Fd
Belvoir, England, 36, Fe
Belvoir, Syria, 18C, Cf
Belyi, 61, Dc
Bemis Heights, 57, Eb
Benares, 25, Hd; 73, Db
Benauges, 11, Cd
Benavente, 63, Ca
Benbecula, 14, Ab
Benburb, 49B, Eb
Bencoolen, 52, Qe; 75, Ce
Bender, 50, Fd; 78, Gb
Bendigo, 77, Gi
Benedict, 71C, Cc
Benevento (Beneventum), 5, Ed
Benevento, D. of, 23A, Ec
Beneventum (Benevento), 5, Ed
Beneventum, D. of, 4B, Fc
Benfleet, 7C, Dc
Bengal, 25, Hd; 73, Ec
Bengal, Bay of, 25, He
Benghazi, 80A, Ea
Bengkalis, 75A, Ab
Benguela, 80A, Ef
Beni Suef, 93, Cd
Benin, 81C, Fc
Benin City, 96B, Cb
Benin, Bight of, 81C, Ed
Bennington, 57, Eb
Benon, 30, Ce
Bensington, 7B, Cc
Bent's Fort, 70, Dd
Bentheim, 20, Gb
Bentheim, Co. of, 46C, Ca
Bentonville, 72, Eb
Benue, R., 81C, Fc
Beorn, 12, Dc
Berar, 73, Cc
Berat, 86A, Ab
Berber, 80B, Ad
Berbera, 96A, Ba
Berberati, 96B, Db
Berbers, 6, Bc
Berbice, reg., 41B, Dc
Berbice, R., 68B, Ba
Berchamstede (Berkhamsted), 13, Fe
Berchelai (Berkeley), 13, De
Berchtesgaden, 21, Ke
Bere, 28A, Cb
Bere I., 15, Be
Berea, 81A, Cc
Berekum, 96B, Bb
Beresina, R., 50, Fc
Berewic (Berwick), 13, Da
Berezovo, 74, Eb
Berg, Co. of, 20, Gc
Berg, D. of, 38, Gc; 46C, Cb
Bergamo (Bergamum), 5, Bb
Bergen, Nassau, 29A, Ca
Bergen, Netherlands, 46A, Db
Bergen, Norway, 26, Ca
Bergen, Rügen, 22, Ea
Bergen op Zoom, 46A, Dc
Bergerac, 20, Df; 28C, Cd
Bergues, 53, Eb
Berhampore, 73, Ec
Berhampur, 59A, Dd
Beri (Berry Pomeroy), 13, Cf
Bering Sea, 74, Qc
Bering Str., 69B
Berkeley, England, 27, De
Berkeley, Maryland, 45B, Ae
Berkeley, reg., 45A, Bd
Berkhamsted, 27, Fe
Berkshire, 27, Ee
Berkshire Hills, 57, Eb
Berlad, 33A, Ca
Berlin, 21, Kb
Bermejo, R., 68, Ce
Bermuda Hundred, 45B, Ae
Bermuda I., 55B, Dc
Bermudas (Somers Is.), 43A, Fa
Bernardino Pass, 5, Ba
Bernburg, 53, Jb
Berne, 10, Be; 29B, Bb
Berne, canton, 29B, Bb
Bernicia, 7B, Ca; 12, Dc
Bernina, 29A, Db
Berrochescire (Berkshire), 13, Ee
Berry, 17A, Cc
Berry, D. of, 30, Ee
Berthier, 56, Ea
Bervie, 49A, Cb
Berwick, 14, Fd
Berwick, co., 37A, Cc
Berwick upon Tweed, 28B, Cb
Besalú, 22, Cc
Besançon, 11, Gc; 29A, Bb
Besançon, eccl. prov., 22, Db
Beshbalik, 25, Jb
Bessarabia, 50, Fd; 78, Gb
Bessin, 8, Bb
Bessingen, 20, Hd
Betanzos, 63, Aa
Bethany, 81A, Ac
Bethel, 71A, Aa
Bethelsdorp, 81B, Cc
Bethesda, Pool of, 18D
Bethlehem, 18C, Cg
Béthune, 28B, Ba; 46A, Bd
Betwa, R., 52A, Bb
Beuthen, 21, Nc
Beverley, 27, Fc
Beverley Manor, 56, Dc
Beverlie (Beverley), 13, Fc
Bewcastle, 7B, Ba; 13, Da
Beyrout, 6A, Bb; 18C, Ce
Béziers, 11, Ee; 17A, De
Bhagalpur, 73, Eb
Bhamo, 73, Gc
Bharatpur, 73, Cb
Bhatpara, 92, Fc
Bhavnagar, 92, Cc
Bhima, R., 73, Cd
Bhonsla's Lands, 73, Cc
Bhopal, 59C, Cc; 73, Cc
Bhubaneswar, 92, Fc
Bhutan, 73, Fb
Bialystok, 51, Ec
Biar, 23C, Ec
Biberach, 20, Hd
Bicocca, 32A, Cb
Bidar, 59C, Cd
Bidassoa, R., 63, Ea
Biddeford, 57, Fb
Bideford, 48A, Ad
Biel (Bienne), 29B, Ba
Biel, L., 29B, Ba
Bielefeld, 30, Hb; 53, Ha
Bielgorod, 19, Fb
Biella, 32A, Cb
Bielostok, 26, Fc; 84, Gb
Bielsk, 61A, Bb
Bienne, 65A, Ab
Bienne (Biel), 29B, Ba
Big, R., 70, Gb
Big Black, R., 72C, Aa
Biggarsberg, 81D, Bb
Bigorre, 17, Fg
Bigorre, Co. of, 11, De
Bihacs, 31, Lf; 39, Lf
Bihar, 73, Eb
Bihar and Orissa, 73A, Bb
Bijapur, 52A, Bc; 73, Cd
Bijayah, 6, Bb
Bikaner, 73, Bb
Bilbao, 23D, Da; 63, Dd
Billungs, Lds. of the, 10, Db
Billungs, M. of the, 10, Ea
Biloxi, 56, Bd
Binche, 46A, Dd
Bingerville, 80A, Cd
Binkath, 6, Ha
Bintang, 75A, Bb
Bir Atrun, 93, Bf
Birkenfeld, 39B, Da; 65D, Ab
Birmingham, 64, Bc
Birr, 15, Dc
Birthen, 10, Bc
Biscay, B. of, 11, Bd
Bischofsheim, 20, Jc
Bishop's Stortford, 27, Ge
Bisignano, 21A, Dc
Bismarck (Fort Mandant), 70, Dc
Bismarck Arch., 77, Hb
Bissagos Is., 81C, Ab; 96B, Aa
Bissao, 81C, Ab
Bissau, 96B, Aa
Bistritz, 24, Gd
Bitervum, 5B, Bb
Bithur, 73, Db
Bithynia, 2, Ke; 16, Jd
Bitlis, 9, Le; 86C, Db
Bitolia (Monastir), 78, Ce
Bitonto, 32B, Fd; 54, Fd
Bitsch, 76A, Db
Bizerta, 34, De
Black Castle, 15, Ed
Black Elster, R., 39C, Db
Black Forest, 10, Cd; 29A, Bb
Black Mts., 27, Ce
Black, R., 57, Db
Black River, 43A, Dc
Black Rock, 71D
Black Russia, 50, Ec
Black Sea, 4A, Jc; 19, Ed
Black Umvolosi, R., 81D, Bb
Blacksod B., 49B, Ab
Blackstocks, 57D, Aa
Blackwater, R., Meath. 49B, Ec
Blackwater, R., Munster, 15, Cd
Blackwater, R., Ulster, 15, Db
Bladensburg, 71C, Cc
Blagovyeshchensk, 74, Lc
Blair Atholl, 37A, Cb; 49A, Cb
Blairgowrie, 37A, Cb
Blakeney, 27, Gd
Blamont, 30, Gd; 39B, Cb
Blanc, Mt., 29A, Bc
Blanchegarde, 18C, Bg
Blanco, C., Africa, 80A, Bb
Blanco, C., Oregon, 67C, Aa
Blanco (North), C., 55B, Kc
Blandford, 27, Df
Blankenberghe, 46A, Cc
Blantyre, 80A, Gf; 81A, Ea
Blatno, 9, Fc
Blatobulgium, (Birrens), 3A, Ca
Blauwberg, 81B, Ac
Blaye, 17, Ef
Bleichfeld, 10, Dd
Blekinge, 26, Eb
Bléneau, 53, Ed
Blenheim, Germany, 29A, Da
Blenheim, New Zealand, 77A
Bletchingley, 27, Fe
Blewfields, 43B, Bc
Blida (Blyth), 13, Ec
Blind B., 77A
Bloemfontein, 81B, Cb
Blois, 11, Dc
Blois, Co. of, 11, Dc
Blood, R., 81D, Ba
Bloody Foreland, 49B, Ca
Blore Heath, 27, Dd
Blue Mts., 77, Ih
Blue Nile, R., 80B, Ae
Blue Ridge Mts., 57, Be
Bluestack, 15, Cb
Blumenau, 68, Ee
Blunkenburg, 30, Jc
Bo, 96B, Ab
Bobbio, 22, Dc
Bobo-Dioulasso, 96B, Ba
Boca de Navios, 43A, Gd
Boca del Toro, 43A, Dd
Bochingeham (Buckingham), 13, Fe
Bochingehamscire (Buckinghamshire), 13, Fe
Böckelheim, 10, Bd
Bodele (Bootle), 13, Cb
Bodmin, 27, Bf
Bodotria Aest. (Firth of Forth), 3A, Da
Bogesund, 26, Db
Boggerah Mts., 15, Bd
Bogota, 68, Bb
Bohemia, King of, 21, Ld
Bohemia-Moravia, Prot. of, 87, Dc
Bohemian Forest, 60A, Dd
Bohemond, 16, Fd
Bohemond, Castle of, 18E
Bohol, 75E, Bc
Bohun, 28A, Cc
Bohns, 26, Db
Behuslan, 50, Cb
Bois le Duc, 46A, Ec
Boisdale, L., 49A, Ab
Boise, 70, Cc
Bojador, C., 55B, Jd
Bokhara, I, Jd; 6, Hb
Bokhara, Khanate of, 61B, B6
Bolama, 96B, Aa
Bolan Pass, 73, Ab; 92, Bb
Bolchen, 39B, Ca
Bolerium Prom., 3A, Af
Bolinbroc (Bolingbroke), 13, Gc
Bolingbroke, 27, Fc
Bolivar, 68, Cf
Bolivia, 68, Cd
Bologna (Bononia), 5, Cb
Bolsena, L., 32A, Dc
Bolsover, 13, Ec
Bolton, England, 48A, Bc
Bolton, Mississippi, 72C, Aa
Bolton Abbey, 36, Ed
Bolton Castle, 48A, Cb
Bolzen, 5, Ca
Boma, 80A, Ee
Bombay, 73, Bd
Bona, 16, De; 47, De
Bonacca, 43A, Dc
Bonar Bridge, 49A, Bb
Bonaventure, 45A, Ea
Bonavista, B., 45A, Ga
Bonavista, C., 45A, Ga
Bondoukou, 96B, Bb
Bone, 80A, Da
Bongor, 96B, Da
Boni, 52C, Bb
Bonifacio, 23A, Dc; 53, Bf
Bonin Is., 74, Nf; 90, Db
Bonn, 10, Bc; 83A, Da
Bonny, 81C, Fd
Bononia, 5B, Aa
Booma Pass, 81B, Cc
Boomplaats, 81A, Cc
Boonesboro, 57A, Cb
Boonesborough, 56, Cc
Boonville, 72, Bb
Boothia Pen., 44, Ea
Bopfingen, 20, Jd
Boppard, 20, Gc
Bordeaux, 11, Cd
Bordeaux, eccl. prov., 22, Bb
Bordesley, 36, Ee
Börglum, 26, Cb
Borgne, L., 71F, Ba
Borisov, 62, Hb
Borku, 80A, Ec
Bormio, 29B, Eb; 32A, Ba
Borne (Eastbourne), 13, Gf
Borneo, 40, Pd; 91, Ef
Borneo (Java Major), 35, Pd
Bornholm, 26, Eb
Bornhöved, 20, Ja
Borodino, 62, Ka
Boroughbridge, 27, Eb
Borthwick, 37A, Cc
Boshof, 81A, Cc
Bosna, R., 78, Bc
Bosnia, 21, Mf; 78, Ac
Bosporus, 78, Ge; 86C, Aa
Bosra, 6A, Bb
Boston, England, 27, Fd
Boston, Massachusetts, 45B, Db; 56B
Boston Neck, 56B
Bostra, 18C, Df
Bosworth, 27, Ed
Botany B., 77, Ih
Botha's Pass, 81D, Aa
Bothnia, G. of, 26, Fa
Bothwell, 28B, Ab
Bothwell Bridge, 49A, Bc
Botzen, 10, De
Bouake, 96B, Bb
Boudonitza, 19, Ce
Bougainville, 77, Ic; 90, Dd
Bouillon, 46A, Ee; 53, Fc
Boulogne, 11, Da
Boulonnais, 53, Db
Boundi, 59C, Cb
Bounty I., 75, Fg
Bourbon, 17, Ge; 42, Mf
Bourbon, Co. of, 11, Ec
Bourbon, S. of, 20, Ee
Bourbon l'Ancy, 30, Ee
Bourbon l'Archambault, 53, Ed
Bourbonnais, 17, Ge
Bourg, Guyenne, 20, Cf
Bourg, Savoy, 30, Fe
Bourganeuf, 30, Df
Bourges, 11, Ec
Bourges, eccl. prov., 22, Cb

Bourges, V. of, 11, Ec
Bourgneuf Bay, 28C, Ac
Bourne, 36, Fe
Boutières, 38, Ff
Bouvet I., 95, Th
Bouvines, 17, Gc; 46A, Cd
Bovino, 22, Fc
Bowes, 13, Db
Bowling Green, Kentucky, 72, Cb
Bowling Green, Virginia, 57, Cd
Bowness, 3C
Boxley, 36, Gf
Boxtel, 46A, Ec
Boyata, 68, Bb
Boyne, R., 15, Ec; 37B, Ec
Brabant, 46A, Dd
Brabant, D. of, 17, Hc; 46, Bb
Bracciano, 39, Kg
Brackley, 27, Ed
Bradeford (Bradford-on-Avon), 13, De
Bradenstock, 36, Ef
Bradford, Wilts., 27, De
Bradford, Yorks., 48A, Cc
Bradninch, 27, Cf
Bradock Down, 48A, Ad
Braemar, 37A, Cb; 49A, Cb
Braga, 22, Ac; 63, Ab
Braga, eccl. prov., 22, Ac
Braganca, Brazil, 68, Ec
Bragança, Portugal, 63, Bb
Brahmaputra (Tsanpo), R., 73, Eb
Braila, 51, Fd; 78, Fc
Bramber and Steyning, 27, Ff
Brampton, 49A, Cc
Branco, R., 68, Cc
Brancepeth, 27, Eb
Brandenburg, Germany, 10, Eb
Brandenburg, Kentucky, 72, Cb
Brandenburg, M. of, 21, Kb
Brandon, 45B, Ae
Brandon B., 49B, Ad
Brandon Hill, 15, Ad
Brandy Station, 72B, Ba
Brandywine, R., 57, Dd
Branford, 45B, Cc
Brännkyrka, 26, Eb
Branodunum (Brancester), 3A, Gd
Bras d'Or, L., 45A, Ea
Brashear City, 72, Bd
Brasilia, 68, Ed
Braunau, 21, Kd; 29A, Ea
Braunsberg, 26, Ec; 39, Na
Bravo del Norte (Rio Grande), R., 43A, Bb
Bravoniacum (Kirkby Thore), 3A, Db
Bravonium (Leintwardine), 3A, Dd
Brazil, 41B, Ee; 68, Dd
Brazos, R., 70, Ed
Brazos Santiago, 70, Ee
Brazzaville, 80A, Ee
Brechin, 14, Fc
Brecon, 27, Ce
Breda, 46A, Dc
Breda, Barony of, 46C, Bb
Bredasdorp, 81A, Bd
Brederode, 46A, Db
Breedevoort, 46A, Fc
Breedon, 7B, Cb
Breeds Hill, 56B
Breffny, 15, Db
Breisach, 29A, Ba; 38, Gd
Breisgau, 30, Ge; 38, Ge
Breitenfeld, 39, Kc
Breitenwang, 20, Je
Brembre (Bramber), 13, Ff
Bremen, 10, Cb
Bremen, eccl. prov., 22, Da
Bremen, Abp. of, 30, Hb
Bremenium (High Rochester), 3A, Da
Bremerhaven, 55A, Hb; 65D, Aa
Bremetennacum (Ribchester), 3A, Dc
Brenner Pass, 5, Ca; 10, De
Breno, 86B, Ab
Brenta, R., 5, Cb; 86B, Bb
Brentford, 48A, Cd
Brescello, 32D, Bb
Brescia, 5, Cb; 29A, Dc
Breslau, 21, Mc
Bresse, 17A, Ec; 38, Fe
Bressuire, 20, Ce
Brest, 30, Ad
Brest Litovsk, 26, Fc
Breteuil, 11, Eb; 30, Dd
Bretigny, 24, Cd; 28C, Cb
Bretlinton (Bridlington), 13, Fb
Breton C., 45A, Fa
Bretons, 85, Bc
Breuckelen, 45B, Cc
Briançon, 20, Gf
Briansk, 26, Hc
Briar Creek, 57D, Ab
Brice's Cross Roads, 72, Cc
Brideport (Bridport), 13, Df
Bridgetown, 43A, Gc
Bridgnorth, 27, Dd
Bridgwater, 27, De
Bridiers, 20, De
Bridlington, 36, Fc
Bridport, 27, Df
Brieg, 31, Mc; 39, Mc
Brienne, 11, Fb
Brienz, 29B, Bb
Brienz, L., 29B, Bb
Briey, 20, Fd; 39B, Ba
Brig, 29B, Bb
Brigantes, 3A, Db
Brighton, 48B, Cd
Brignoles, 20, Gg
Brihuega, 63, Db
Brill, 46A, Dc
Brindisi (Brindisium), 5, Fd
Brioude, 11, Ed
Brisbane, 77, Ig
Brissac, 53, Cd
Bristol, England, 27, De
Bristol, Rhode I., 57, Fe
Bristol, Tennessee, 72, Db
Bristol, bp., 36, Df
Bristol Channel, 27, Ce
Bristou (Bristol), 13, De
Britain, 2A, Aa
Britannia, 2, Cc
Britannia (Brittany), 8B, Ab
British Columbia, 70, Bb
British East Africa, 80A, Gd
British Guiana, 43D, Gd; 68B, Bb
British Honduras, 55B, Ae
British Isles, 69B
British Kaffraria, 81B, Db
British New Guinea (Terr. of Papua), 77, Gc
British North Borneo, 74, Kh; 90, Bc
British Somaliland, 96A, Bb
British South Africa Company, 80A, Ff
Brittania (Wellington), 77, Nj
Brittany, 7A, Cb
Brittany, Co. of, 11, Bb
Brittany, D. of, 30, Bd
Brive, 20, Df
Briwetone (Bruton), 13, De
Brixen, 10, De; 20, Je
Brixworth, 7B, Cb
Broach, 73, Bc
Broad, R., 57D, Aa
Brocavum (Brougham), 3A, Db
Brocolitia (Carrowburgh), 3c
Brod, 78, Ac
Brodick, 37A, Bc
Brody, 50, Fc; 84, Hb
Broken Hill, 77, Gh
Bromberg, 54, Fb; 60A, Fb
Brömsebro, 47, Fa; 50, Db
Bromsgrove, 27, Dd
Bromyard, 27, Dd
Brondolo, 32D, Cb
Bronker's Spruit, 81A, Cc
Brookline, 56B
Brooklyn, 57B
Broom, L., 14, Cb
Broome, 77, Ce
Brosna, R., 15, Dc
Brouage, 53, Ce
Brough, 13, Db; 28B, Cc
Brougham, 28B, Cc
Browns Ferry, 72A, Aa
Bruchhausen, 20, Hb
Bruck, 21, Le
Bruffe, 49B, Cd
Bruges, 17, Gc; 46A, Cc
Bruinsberg, 72C, Ab
Brunanburh, 7C, Ba
Brundisium, 2, Ge
Brunei, 91, Ff
Brunig Pass, 29B, Cb
Brunkeberg, 26, Eb
Brünn, 21, Md; 29A, Ga
Brunnen, 29B, Cb
Brunswick, Georgia, 56, Cd
Brunswick, Germany, 10, Db; 38, Hb
Brunswick, Maine, 57, Gb
Brunswick-Lüneburg, D. of, 20, Jb
Brunswick-Wolfenbüttel, D. of, 30, Hb
Brusa, 19, Dd; 86c, Aa
Brussa, 6, Da
Brussels, 28D, Ea; 46A, Dd
Bruttium, 4B, Fd; 5, Fe
Bryansk, 88, Mc
Brycheiniog, 7B, Bc; 13, Ce
Byron, I., 45A, Ea
Bucaramanga, 68, Bb
Bucellas, 63B
Bucfestre (Buckfastleigh), 13, Cf
Buch, 17, Ef
Buchan, 14, Fb
Buchanan, 48B, Aa
Bucharest, 78, Fc
Buchau, 20, Hd
Buchhorn, 20, He; 53, Hd
Buchy, 76A, Ab
Buckingham, 27, Fe
Buckingham, co., 27, Fe
Buckland (Cornwall), 36, Bg
Buckland (Somerset), 36, Cf
Buczacz, 50, Fd
Buda, 39, Ne
Budapest, 33C, Db; 87, Dc
Budaun, 73, Cb
Budge Budge, 59A, Ec
Budua, 22, Fc
Budweis, 21, Ld; 29A, Fa
Buea, 80A, Dd
Buelit, 7B, Bb; 13, Cd
Buen Ayre, 43A, Fc
Buenaventura, 41B, Bc
Buenos Aires, 68, Df
Buffalo, 71C, Cb
Buffalo, R., C. Prov., 81B, Cc
Buffalo (Umzimyati), R., 81D, Bb
Bug, R., Poland, 26, Fc; 39, Qb
Bug, R., Ukraine, 9, Jc; 50, Gd
Bugey, 38, Fe
Bugia, 34, De
Builth, 27, Cd
Bujids, King. of, 6B, Gb
Buka, 90, Dd
Bukellarian, Theme, 9, Jd
Bukhara, 93, Jb
Bukkur, 73, Ab
Bukovina, 33C, Fb
Bulair, 78, Fe; 86D
Bulawayo, 81A, Cb
Bulgar, 9, Mb; 19, Ha
Bulgaria, 78, Ed
Bulgaria, King. of, 19, Cd
Bulgarians, 8, Jb
Bulgarians of Kazan, 61, Gd
Bulgars, 8C, Db; 25, Da
Bull Run, 72B, Ba
Bull Run, R., 72B, Ba
Bulo Burti, 96A, Bb
Bulun, 74, La
Bulwer, 81D, Ab
Bundelkhand, 73, Cc
Bundoran, 49B, Cb
Bungay, 27, Hd
Bunker Hill, 56B
Bunzlau, 21, Lc
Buraburg, 8A, Ca
Buraida, 93, Ed
Burdas, 9, Mb
Burdekin, R., 77, He
Burdigala, 2, Ce
Burdwan, 59A, Ec; 59B
Burford, 7B, Cc; 27, Ee
Burg, 39, Kb
Burg (Peterborough), 13, Fd
Burgas, 78, Fd
Burgau, 20, Jd
Burgdorf, 29B, Ba
Burgh by Sands, 3C
Burgh on Sands, 28B, Bc
Burgos, 22, Bc; 63, Da
Burgos, eccl. prov., 22, Bc
Burgundia, 8B, Cb
Burgundian Kingdom, 4A, Db
Burgundians, 2A, Bb; 8C, Bb
Burgundiones, 2, Fd
Burgundy, Co. of, 10, Be; 11, Fc
Burgundy, D. of, 11, Fc
Burgundy, King. of (Arelate), 11, Fd
Burhampur, 59C, Cc
Burke (De Burgh), 37B, Cc
Burkesville, 72, Cb
Burketown, 77, Fe
Burlington, New Jersey, 45B, Bc
Burlington, Vermont, 57, Ea
Burma, 73, Gc
Burma (Mien), 25, Jd
Burma Road, 91, Cd
Burpham, 7C, Cc
Burrium (Usk), 3A, De
Bursa, 93, Ba
Burton upon Trent, 36, Ee
Burtone (Burton), 13, Ed
Buru, 52C, Cb; 91, Fg
Bury St. Edmunds, 27, Gd
Busaco, 63, Ab
Bushman Land, 81B, Ab
Bushmans, R., 81D, Ab
Bushmen, 81A, Ac
Bushy Run, 57, Bc
Bussa, 80A, Dc
Bute, 14, Cd
Bute, co., 37A, Bc
Butera, 21A, Cd
Butler, 37B, Dd
Butley, 36, He
Buton, 52C, Bb
Bütow, 31, Ma
Butte des Mortes, 56, Bb
Butterworth, 48B, Cc
Buttington, 7C, Bb
Buxar, 59A, Db
Buxtehude, 26, Cc
Buzakha, 6, Fc
Buzancy, 76A, Cb
Buzzard B., 45B, Dc
Byblos (Gibelet), 18C, Cd
Bydgoszcz, 31, Nb
Byelgorod, 61, Ed
Byland, 36, Ec
Byzantine Empire, 9, Ge
Byzantium, 1, Ec

CABELLUM, 5B, Aa
Cabinda, 80A, Ee
Cabinda, col., 96C, De
Cabot Str., 45A, Fa
Cacabellos, 63, Ba
Caceres, 23C, Bc
Cachoeira, 68, Fd
Caconda, 52, Ke
Cadore, 32A, Ea
Cadiz, 23C, Bd; 63, Bd
Cadodachos, 43A, Ca
Cadzand, 46A, Cc
Caen, 11, Cb
Caer Gai, 3A, Cd
Caer Segeint, 7B, Ab
Caer Segont, 13, Bc
Caer Sws, 3A, Cd
Caerdydd (Cardiff), 13, Ce
Caerlaverock, 28B, Bb
Caerleon, 13, De; 28A, Dc
Caerphilly, 27, Ce; 28A, Cc
Caesar Augusta, 2, Ce
Caesarea, Africa, 2, Df; 4A, Cd
Caesarea, Km. of Jerusalem, 18C, Bf
Caesarea, Syria, 18C, Dc
Caesarea, Turkey, 6, Eb; 19, Fe
Caffraria, 69A, Lf
Cagayan, 75E, Bc
Cagliari, 23A, Bd; 32B, Be
Cagliari, eccl. prov., 22, Dd; 23A, Bd
Cahokia, 56, Ac
Cahors, 11, Dd; 17A, Cd
Caicos, 43A, Eb
Caird Coast, 69C
Cairns, 95, Lf
Cairo (Fustat), 6A, Ab
Cairo, Egypt, 80B, Ab
Cairo, Illinois, 72, Cb
Caistor, Lincs., 3A, Fc
Caistor, Norfolk, 7B, Db
Caithness, 14, Da
Cajamarca, 41B, Bd
Calabria, 5, Fd; 21A, Dc
Calabria Theme, 9, Fe
Calahorra, 22, Bc; 23C, Da
Calais, 17A, Ca; 30, Dc
Calamian Group, 75E, Ab
Calatafimi, 32C, De
Calatayud, 23C, Db; 63, Eb
Calatrava, 22, Bd; 23C, Dc
Calcaria (Tadcaster), 3A, Ec
Calcutta, 59B
Caldera, 68, Be
Caldiero, 29A, Dc
Caldonazzo, 86B, Bb
Calebee, 71F, Ba
Caledon, 81B, Ac
Caledon, R., 81B, Cb
Caledonia, 2, Bb; 14, Eb
Calgary, 70, Cb
Calhoun, 72A, Aa
Cali, 68, Bb
Calicut, 73, Ce
California, 43A, Ab; 70, Cd
California, G. of, 43A, Ab
Callander, 49A, Bb
Callao, 68, Bd
Calleva Atrebatum (Silchester), 3A, Ee
Callinicum, 2, Lf; 4B, Kd
Calmar, 26, Eb
Calmar, Union of, 35, Ka
Calne, 27, De
Caltabellotta, 21A, Bd
Caltanisetta, 21A, Cd
Calvi, 53, Bf
Calvinet, 38, Ef
Calvinia, 81B, Ab
Camaldoli, 22, Ec; 23A, Cb
Camarinal, C., 63A
Cambay, 35, Nc; 73, Bc
Cambay, G. of, 73, Bc
Cambodia, 91, De
Camboglanna (Birdoswald), 3C
Cambolu, 35, Pb
Cambrai, 46A, Cd
Cambrai, Bp of, 46C, Ab
Cambrésis, 46A, Cd
Cambridge, England, 27, Gd
Cambridge, Massachusetts, 45B, Db, 56B
Cambridge, co., 27, Gd
Cambridge (Charles), R., 56B
Cambuskenneth, 14, Ec
Camden, Arkansas, 72, Bc
Camden, S. Carolina, 57D, Ab
Camelon, 3A, Ca
Camerino, 5, Dc
Cameron, 37A, Bb
Cameroon, 96D, Dd
Cameroons, 96C, Dd
Cameta, 68, Ec
Camisards, 54, Cd
Campagna, 32A, Ed
Campaldino, 32E, Bb
Campania, 5, Dd
Campbell, 28B, Aa; 37A, Bb
Campbell I., 69C; 75, Fg
Campbeltown, 49A, Bc
Campeche, 43A, Cc
Campeche, st., 43A, Cc
Campeche, G. of, 43A, Cb
Camperdown, 55A, Fb
Campinas, 68, Ee
Campo Formio, 65A, Bb
Campobasso, 32A, Fd
Campos, 68, Ee
Camulodunum (Colchester), 3A, Ge
Canada, 45A, Ba; 69A, Fb
Canadian, R., 70, Dd
Canal Zone, 68, Ab
Canary Is., 80A, Bb
Canaveral, C., 70, Fe
Canberra, 77, Hi
Cancelleria, 5A
Candia, 19, De; 78, Eh
Canea, 78, Dh
Canigou, 22, Cc
Canna, 15, Bb
Cannae, 21A, Db
Cannanore, 59A, Ce
Cannes, 30, Gg
Canossa, 23B, Cb
Canovium (Caerhun), 3A, Cc
Canso, C., 45A, Ea
Cantabria, 4A, Bc; 8, Bc
Cantabrian Mts., 63, Ca
Canterbury, England, 27, He
Canterbury, N.Z., 77A
Canterbury, bp., 36, Gf
Canterbury, eccl. prov., 22, Ba
Canterbury Plain, 77, Mj
Cantii, 3A, Ge
Canton, China, 25, Ld; 91, Ed
Canton, Mississippi, 72, Bc
Cantuaria (Canterbury), 13, He
Cantware, 7A, Db
Canusium, 5, Fd
Cão, 35, Kf
Cap Francois, 43A, Ec
Capdenac, 38, Ef
Cape, 81B, Ac
Cape Ann (Gloucester), 45B, Db
Cape Breton I., 71, Hc
Cape Breton I. (Ile Royale), 45A, Ea
Cape Coast, 96B, Bb
Cape Coast Castle, 81C, Dc
Cape Cod B., 45B, Dc
Cape Colony, 69A, Lf
Cape Colony (Cape of Good Hope), 81A, Bd
Cape Fear, R., 57, Bf; 57D, Ba
Cape Fear (Charles), R., 45A, Bc
Cape of Good Hope (Cape Colony, 81A), Bd
Cape Porpoise, 45B, Db
Cape Town, 81B, Ac
Caper Verde Is., 80A, Ac
Cape York Pen., 77, Gd
Capetown, 52, Kf
Capitanata, 32A, Fd
Capitol, 5A
Capiz, 75E, Bb
Capo d'Istria, 22, Eb; 32D, Cb
Cappadocia, 2, Lf
Cappadocia Theme, 9, Je
Caporetto, 84, Ec; 86B, Da
Caprera I., 32C, Bd
Capri, 5, Ed
Capsa, 6, Bb
Capua, 5, Ed; 32A, Fd
Capua, D. of, 23A, Ec
Capua, Pr. of, 21A, Cb
Caqueta, R., 68, Bc
Carabobo, 68, Cb
Caracas, 41B, Cc; 68, Cb
Caradeña, 22, Bc
Caralis, 2, Ef
Caramania, 33A, Dc
Caravaggio, 32D, Ab
Carberry House, 37A, Cc
Carbisdale, 37A, Bb
Carcassonne, 11, Ee
Cardaillac, 38, Df
Cardiff, 3A, Ce; 27, Ce
Cardigan, 13, Db; 28A, Bb
Cardigan, co., 27, Bd
Cardigan B., 27, Bd
Carelia, 26, Ha; 47, Ja
Carentan, 38, Cd
Carhaix, 11, Bb
Carham, 14, Fd
Caribbean Sea, 43A, Ec
Caribs, 43A, Fd
Carignano, 29A, Bc; 30, Gf

Carinthia, D. of, 10, Fe; 21, Ke
Carisbrooke Castle, 48B, Cd
Carlat, 17, Gf; 30, Ef
Carleol (Carlisle), 13, Db
Carlingford, 49B, Eb
Carlisle, England, 27, Db
Carlisle, N. America, 57, Cc
Carlisle, bp., 36, Dc
Carlow, 15, Ed
Carlow, co., 37C; 49B, Ed
Carlowitz, 33C, Db; 79, Ca
Carlsbad, 64, Ec; 65C, Ba
Carlsruhe, 65A, Ab
Carmania, 1, He
Carmarthen, 27, Be; 36, Bf
Carmarthen, co., 27, Be; 28A, Bc
Carmel, Mt., 18C, Cf
Carmona, 6, Ab; 23C, Cd
Carnarvon, Australia, 95, Ng
Carnarvon, S. Africa, 81B, Bb
Carnarvon, Wales, 27, Bc
Carnarvon, co., 27, Bd
Carnatic, 73, Ce
Carnero Pt., 63A
Carnic Alps, 29A, Eb; 86B, Ca
Carnifex Ferry, 72, Db
Carniola, 10, Ff
Carniola, D. of, 21, Lf
Carnsore Pt., 15, Ed
Carolina, 45A, Ad
Caroline Is., 74, Mg; 90, Dc
Carolines, 40, Rd
Carpathian Mts., 8, Gb; 50, Ed
Carpathian Ruthenia, 87, Ec
Carpatus Mons, 2, Hd
Carpentaria, G. of, 77, Fd
Carpentras, 22, Dc
Carpi, 32A, Db
Carrantuohill, 15, Be
Carrara, 32B, Cb
Carrick, Galloway, 14, Dd
Carrick, Leitrim, 49B, Cc
Carrick, Tipperary, 49B, Dd
Carrickfergus, 37B, Fb; 49B, Fb
Carricks Ford, 72, Eb
Carriden, 3A, Ca
Carrig a Foyle, 49B, Bd
Carse of Gowrie, 28B, Ba
Carso, 86B, Db
Cartagena, Columbia, 43A, Ec
Cartagena, Spain, 4A, Bd 23C, Ed; 63, Ed
Cartago, 41B, Bc
Cartersville, 72A, Aa
Carthage, 4A, Ed; 9, Ee
Carthage, U.S.A., 70, Ed
Carthago, 2, Ff
Carthago Nova, 2, Cf
Cartmel, 28B, Cc; 36, Dc
Carumnassa, R., 59A, Db
Casablanca, 80A, Ca; 96D, Ba
Casale, 32A, Cb
Casalmaggiore, 32D, Bb
Casco B., 57, Fb
Casco (Fort Loyal) (Falmouth), 45B, Db
Caseros, 68, Df
Cashel, 15, Dd
Caspe, 23C, Eb; 23D, Eb
Caspian Sea, 19, Hd; 25, Eb
Cassanitae, 1, Ge
Cassano, Calabria, 22, Fd
Cassano, Lombardy, 29A, Cc
Cassel, Flanders, 20, Fc
Cassel, Thuringia, 20, Hc
Cassett, 30, Ee
Castalla, 63, Ec
Castamon, 18A, Ea
Castanheira, 63B
Castel Branco, 22, Ad
Castel Jaloux, 38, Df
Castel Sardo, 23B, Bd
Castelbaldo, 32D, Bb
Castelfranco, 86B, Bb
Castell Collen, 3A, Cd
Castellamare, 32C, Ed
Castello, 22A
Castello Branco, 63, Bc
Castello Tesino, 86B, Ba
Castellon Alani (Richmond), 13 Eb
Castellon Harundel (Arundel), 13, Ff
Castellon Warham (Corfe Castle), 13 Df
Castelnau, 20, Dg
Castelnaudary, 30, Dg
Castelnuovo, 78, Bd
Castelorizo, 86C, Ab
Castelsagrat, 38, Df
Castets, 38, Cf
Castiglione, Lombardy, 29A, Dc
Castiglione, Tuscany, 20, Jg
Castile, King. of, 23C, Cb
Castilla do Oro, 43A, Dd
Castillon, 11, Cd
Castle I., 56B
Castle Dermot, 49B, Ed
Castle Donglas, 49A, Cc
Castle Flemish, 3A, Be
Castle of St. Angelo, 5A
Castle Rising, 48A, Dc
Castlebar, 49B, Bc
Castlecary, 3A, Ca
Castledykes, 3A, Ca
Castlefinn, 49B, Db
Castlehill, 3A, Ba
Castlejordan, 15, Dc
Castlekevin, 37B, Ec
Castlereagh, 49B, Cc
Castleroe, 37B, Ea
Castles, B. of the, 55B, Ea
Castlesteads, 3C
Castleton, 57, Eb
Castletown, 48A, Ab
Castra Exploratum (Netherby), 3A, Ca
Castres, 20, Eg; 22, Cc
Castro, 22, Ec; 32B, Cc
Castro Giovanni, 23A, Ef
Castrum Felicitatis, 5B, Bb
Cat I., 43A, Eb
Catalans, 85, Cd
Catalonia, 23C, Fb; 63, Fb
Catalonia, Pr. of, 16, Cd
Catamarca, 68, Ce
Catanduanes, 75E, Bb
Catania, 21A, Cd; 22, Fd
Catanzaro, 22, Fd
Cataractonium (Catterick Bridge), 3A, Eb
Cateau Cambrésis, 34, Cb
Cathay, 25, Kc
Cathkin Peak, 81D, Ab
Catóche, C., 43A, Db
Catric (Catterick), 13, Eb
Catrone, 22, Fd
Catskill Mts., 57, Db
Cattaro, 22, Fc; 78, Bd
Cattegat, 84, Ea
Catterick, 7A, Ca
Catuvellauni, 3A, Fe
Cauca, R., 68, Bb
Caucasus, 19, Gd; 33A, Fb
Caucasus Mons, 2, Me
Caudebec, 20, Dd
Cauna (Calne), 13, De
Causennae (Ancaster), 3A, Fd
Caus, 13, Dd; 28A, Db
Causse, 38, Eg
Cauvery, R., 73, Ce
Cavan, 49B, Dc
Cavan, co., 37C; 49B, Dc
Cavour, 32C, Ab
Cawnpore, 73, Db
Cawood Castle, 48A, Cc
Cayenne, 43B, Ed; 68, Db
Cayman Is., 43A, Dc
Cayo Romano, 43A, Eb
Cayoan, 52B, Aa
Cayugas, 45A, Bb
Ceara, 41B, Fd
Ceara (Fortaleza), 68, Fc
Ceara, st., 68, Fc
Cebu, 75E, Bb
Cebu, I., 75E, Bb
Ceccanum, 5B, Bc
Cedar Creek, 72B, Aa
Cedar Keys, 72, Dd
Cedar Mountain, 72B, Aa
Cedar Rapids, 57, Ea
Cefalu, 21A, Cc; 22, Ed
Celebes, 52C, Bb; 74, Lj
Celebes (Sulawesi), 91, Eg
Celebes Sea, 91, Ff
Celle, 30, Jb
Celorico, 63, Bb
Celtic Lands, 4A, Aa
Celts, 8C, Aa
Cembala, 19, Ed
Ceneda, 22, Eb
Central Africa, rep., 96D, Dd
Central America, rep., 69A, Ed
Central Australia, 77, Ef
Central Provinces, India, 74, Ff
Centreville, 72B, Ba
Cephallenia Theme, 9, Ge
Cephalonia, 78, Cf
Cephalonia, Co. of, 24, Gf
Ceprano, 23B, Dd
Ceram, 52C, Cb; 77, Db; 91, Fg
Cerami, 23A, Ef
Ceramix, 21A, Cd
Cerdagne, 30, Dg
Cerdana, 23C, Ga
Ceredigion (Cardigan), 7B, Ab; 13, Bd
Ceri, 13, Cd
Cerignola, 32A, Fd
Cerigo, 18B, Cc; 78, Dg
Cerisolo, 29A, Bc
Cernauti, 87, Fc
Cerne, 36, Dg
Cerneli (Cerne Abbas), 13, Df
Cerralvo, 43A, Cb
Cerro de Pasco, 68, Bd
Certesyg (Chertsey), 13, Fe
Cervera, 63, Fb
Cervignano, 86B, Db
Cesena, 32A, Eb
Cesenae, 5B, Ba
Cesme, 51, Ff
Cestre (Chester), 13, Dc
Cestrescire (Cheshire), 13, Dc
Cetinje, 78, Bd
Cette, 30, Eg
Ceuta, 23C, Ce; 34, Ac; 63A
Cevennes, 11, Ed
Ceylon, 73, Df
Ceylon (Seilan), 25, Hf
Chabats, 78, Bc
Chablais, 29B, Ab
Chacabuco, 68, Bf
Chaco, 68, Ce
Chad, L., 96B, Da
Chad, rep., 96D, Dc
Chads Ford, 57, Dd
Chagos Is., 69A, Ne; 94, Qf
Chagres, 43A, Ed
Chalcedon, 2, Je; 8, Hc
Chalchuites, 43A, Bb
Chalcis, 4B, Kd
Chaldea Theme, 9, Kd
Chaldiran, 33A, Fb
Chaleur B., 45A, Da
Chalgrove Field, 48A, Cd
Challon, 29B, Ab
Chalon, 11, Fc
Chalôns, 11, Fb; 83A, Cb
Châlons Camp, 76A, Cb
Chaluz, 17, Ff
Cham, 21, Kd
Chambal, R., 73, Cb
Chambersburg, 72, Eb
Chambéry, 20, Ff; 30, Ff
Chambly, 56, Ea
Champa, 25, Ke
Champagne, 11, Eb; 83A, Cb
Champagne, Co. of, 20, Fd
Champigny, 76A, Bb
Champion's Hill, 72C, Aa
Champlain L., 57, Ea
Chanak, 86D
Chancellorsville, 72B, Ba
Chandax, 9, He
Chandernagore, 59B
Chandière, R., 71E, Ac
Chang-an, 1, Nd
Changchow, 41A, Jb
Changchun, 91, Fb
Changsha, 91, Ed
Changtan, 76B, Ba
Channel Is., 11, Bb
Chantoceaux, 20, Ce
Chapelle St. Lambert, 46B
Charak, 93, Gd
Charcot I., 69C
Chard, 27, Df; 48A, Bd
Charente, R., 17, Ef
Charing Cross, 27A
Charleroi, 46A, Dd
Charles, C., 45B, Be
Charles, King. of, 8A, Bc
Charles (Cambridge), R., 56B
Charles (Cape Fear), R., 45A, Bc
Charles City, 45B, Ae
Charles Fort, 45A, Ad
Charles Town, 45A, Ad
Charleston, Massachusetts, 45B, Db
Charleston, S. Carolina, 57D, Bb
Charleston, W. Virginia, 72, Db
Charleston (Stephen's Fort), 57, Eb
Charlestown, Massachusetts, 56B
Charlestown, Natal, 81D, Aa
Charleville, Australia, 95, Lg
Charleville, France, 53, Fc
Charlotte, 57, Af
Charlottesville, 57, Be; 72B, Ab
Charlottetown, 71, Hc
Charolais, 30, Fe; 38, Fe
Charolles, 17, He
Charolles, Co., 31A, Bd
Charost, 53, Ed
Charroux, 22, Cb
Charsianon Theme, 9, Je
Charter, 81A, Da
Charters Towers, 77 Hf
Chartres, 11, Db; 17A, Cb
Chartreux, 11 Fd
Chatalja, 78, Ge
Château Chinon, 30, Ee
Château Dauphin, 53, Ge
Château d'If, 38, Fg
Château des Dames, 83A, Bb
Château Gaillard, 20, Dd
Château Neuf, 20, Ee
Château Thierry, 17, Gd
Châteaubriant, 38, Ce
Châteaudun, 11, Db
Châteaugay, R., 71C, Da
Châteauroux, 17, Fe
Châteauroux, S. of, 20, De
Châtellerault, 11, Dc
Chatham, 55A, Dc
Chatham I., 75, Gg
Châtillon, 38, Cd; 76A, Cc
Chattahoochee, R., 72, Cc
Chattanooga, 72A, Aa
Chaudière, R., 56, Ea
Chaumont, 20, Fd; 76A, Cb
Chaves, 23C, Bb; 63, Bb
Cheat, R., 57, Bd
Cheduba I., 90, Ac
Chefoo, 74, Le
Chegar, R., 59D
Chelm, 26, Fc; 33C, Ea
Chelmsford, 27, Ge
Chelsea, 56B
Chelyabinsk, 89, Sb
Chelyuskin, C., 69B
Chemnitz, 31, Kc; 53, Kb
Chenab, R., 73, Ba
Chenaresburg (Knaresborough), 13, Eb
Chengtu, 25, Kc; 91, Dc
Chenth (Kent), 13, Ge
Chepstow, 27, De
Cher, R., 11, Dc; 17, Ge
Chera, 1, Kf
Cherasco, 32B, Ab; 47, Dd
Cheraw, 57D, Ba
Cherbourg, 28D, Bb; 30, Cd
Cherchebi (Kirkby Lonsdale), 13, Db
Cheren, 96A, Aa
Cheriton, 48A, Cd
Cherkassy, 79, Fa
Cherna, R., 86A, Ca
Chernigov, 19, Eb; 26, Hc
Cherokees, 45A. Ac
Cherry Valley, 57, Db
Cherso, 23B, Eb
Cherson, 2A, Eb; 19, Ed
Cherson Theme, 9, Jd
Chertsey, 36, Ff
Chesapeake B., 57, Cd
Chester, England, 27, Dc
Chester, Illinois, 70, Fd
Chester, Pennsylvania, 57, Dd
Chester (Fort New Korsholm), 45B, Bd
Chester, bp., 36, Dd
Chester, Co. Palatine of, 27, Dc
Chesterfield Inlet, 70, Ea
Chesterford, 3A, Gd
Chester-le-Street, 3A, Eb; 7C, Ca
Chetsteven (Kesteven), 13, Fd
Cheviot Hills, 27, Da; 28B, Cb
Cheyenne, 70, Dc
Chiangmai, 91, Ce
Chiao Chow, 1, Oe
Chiapas, 43A, Cc
Chiavenna, 5, Ba; 23B, Bd
Chiavenna, Co. of, 29B, Db
Chicacole, 59A, Dd
Chicago, 56, Bb
Chichagof I., 71B, Cb
Chichester, 27, Ff
Chichester, bp., 36, Fg
Chickamauga, 72A, Aa
Chickasaw Bluff (Memphis), 71F, Aa
Chickasaws, Alabama, 43A, Da,
Chickasaws, W. Virginia, 45A, Ac
Chiclayo, 68, Bc
Chicoa, 43A, Da
Chidambaram, 59D
Chidley, C., 71, Ha
Chiem L., 29A, Eb
Chiemsee, 22, Eb
Chiengmai, 73, Gd
Chiese, R., 5, Cb; 86B, Ab
Chieti, 5, Ec
Chieveley, 81D, Ab
Chigirin, 50, Gd
Chignecto, C., 45A, Ea
Chihuahua, 43A, Bb
Chikishlyar, 61B, Ab
Chile, 42, Ff; 68, Be
Chilianwala, 73, Ba
Chilkat B., 71B, Bb
Chillan, 68, Bf
Chillicothe, 56, Cc
Chiloe I., 68, Bg
Chiltern Hills, 27, Fe
Chilternsaetan, 7B, Cc
Chimay, 30, Fc; 46A, Dd
Chimkent, 61B, Ba
China, 41A, Ja; 74, Je
China Sea, 25, Le
Chinampo, 76B, Cb
Chincha Is., 68, Bd
Chinchowfu, 76B, Aa
Chinde, 83, Le
Chindwin, R., 73, Gb
Chinese Eastern Railway, 74, Ld
Chinese Empire, 83, Oc
Chinese Rep., 91, Dc
Ching Chow, 1, Oe
Chingleput, 59D
Chingkiang, 25, Lc; 74, Le
Chinon, 17, Fe; 28C, Cc
Chins Division, 92, Gc
Chinsura, 59B
Chiny, 20, Fd
Chioggia, 32D, Cb
Chios, 24, Hf; 78, Ef
Chippenham, 7C, Bc; 27, De
Chippewa, 71D
Chipping Norton, 27, Ee
Chirbury, 13, Cd
Chirk, 27, Cd
Chisholm, 37A, Bb
Chita, 91, Ea
Chitaldroog, 59A, Ce
Chitor, 25, Gd; 52A, Bb
Chittagong, 92, Gc
Chittagong, st., 73, Fc
Chiusi, 5, Cc
Chobe Swamp, 81A, Ba
Choctaws, 56, Bd
Choczim, 50, Fd; 54, Hc
Choiseul, E. Indies, 77, Jc
Choiseul, France, 53, Fc
Chola, 1 Kf
Cholas, 25, Ge
Cholula, 43A, Cc
Chongju, 76B, Cb
Chonos Arch., 68, Bg
Chorasmia, 1, Jc
Chorlu (Tzurulum), 19, Dd
Chota Nagpur, 73, Dc
Chotusitz, 29A, Fa
Chowan, R., 45B, Ae
Christchurch, England, 27, Ef
Christchurch, N.Z., 77A
Christiania, 50, Cb; 54, Ea
Christiansand, 26, Cb
Christiansborg, 69A, Kd; 81C, Dc
Christianstad, 51, Cb
Christmas I., Indian Ocean, 83, Pe
Christmas I., Pacific Ocean, 75, Hd
Christopolis, 19, Cd
Chrysopolis, 2, Je; 18E
Chrystler's Farm, 71C, Ca
Chu, R., 91, Ab
Chubut (Rawson), 68, Cg
Chubut, R., 68, Cg
Chudes, 9, Ha
Chulak, 61B, Ba
Chungking, 91, Dd
Chur, 5, Ba; 29B, Db
Church, States of the, 32A, Ec
Church of the Holy Sepulchre, 18D
Churchill, 70, Eb
Churchill, R., 70, Db
Cibalae, 2, Gd
Cibyrrhaeot Theme, 9, Je
Cicestre (Chichester), 13, Ff
Cilgerran, 28A, Bb
Cilicia, 2A, Ec; 18C, Cb
Cilicia Theme, 2, Kf
Cilli, 21, Le
Cilurnum (Chesters), 3C
Cimarron, R., 70, Ed
Cin, Sea of, 25, Md
Cinbretune (Kinderton), 13, Dc
Cincinnati, 57A, Cb; 71C, Bc
Cintra, 23C, Ac; 63B
Circassia, 61, Ff
Circesium, 2, Mg; 4A, Ld
Circle City, 71A, Ca
Cirencester, 27, Ee
Cirencestre (Cirencester), 13, Ee
Cirey, 83B, Ba
Cirta, 2, Ef
Cisalpine (Italian) Rep., 65A, Ab
Citatea, 78, Dc
Citeaux, 11, Fc
Citra, 32A, Fd
Citronelle, 72, Cc
Citta di Castello, 32A, Ec
Cittadella, 86B, Bb
Cittavecchia, 22, Fc
City Pt., 57, Ce
Ciudad Bolivar (Angostura), 68, Cb
Ciudad Real, 23C, Ce; 63, Dc
Ciudad Rodrigo, 23C, Bb; 63, Bb
Ciudad Victoria, 43A, Cb
Ciudadela, 22, Cc
Cividale, 21, Ke; 86B, Da
Civita, 23B, Bd
Civita Vecchia, 5, Cc
Civitate, 21A, Cb
Civitella, 32A, Ec
Clackmannan, co., 37A, Cb; 49A, Cb
Cladyford, 49B, Db
Clair-sur-Epte, 11, Db
Clairac, 22, Cc; 38, Df
Clairvaux, 11, Fb
Clanoventa (Ravenglass), 3A, Cb
Clanwilliam, 81B, Ac
Clara (Clare), 13, Gd
Clare, England, 27, Gd
Clare, Ireland, 37B, Cd
Clare, Wales, 28A, Cc

Clare, co., Ireland, 37C; 49B, Cd
Clare, R., 15, Cc
Clarendon, England, 17, Ec
Clarendon, N. Carolina, 45A, Bd
Classis, 23A, Da
Clausentum (Bitterne), 3A, Ef
Claverhouse, 37A, Cb
Clear, C., 15, Be
Cleeve, 36, Cf
Clermont, Auvergne, 8B, Bb; 11, Ed
Clermont, Champagne, 39B, Ba; 76A, Cb
Clermont, Co. of, 20, Ed; 39B, Ba
Clermont Ferrand, 53, Ee
Cleve, Netherlands, 46A, Fc
Cleve, Co. of, Netherlands, 46A, Fc
Cleveland, Ohio, 71C, Bb
Cleveland, Tennessee, 72A, Aa
Cleves, 53, Gb
Clew B., 15, Bc; 49B, Bc
Clifford, Scotland, 28B, Cc
Clifford, Wales, 13, Cd
Clifford, Co. of., Wales, 28A, Cb
Clifton, 49A, Cc
Clinton, 72C, Aa
Clisson, 28C, Bc
Clissow, 50, Ec
Clogher, 15, Db
Clonard, 15, Dc
Cloncurry, 77, Gf
Clones, 37B, Db; 49B, Db
Clonfert, 15, Cc; 49B, Cc
Clonlish, 49B, Bd
Clonmacnoise, 15, Dc
Clonmel, 37B, Dd; 49B, Dd
Clontarf, 12, Cc; 49B, Ec
Cloudy B., 77A
Cloyne, 15, Ce
Clun, 27, Cd; 28A, Cb
Cluny, 11, Fc
Clydesdale, 14, Ed; 28B, Bb
Clyde, R., 14, Ed; 28B, Ab
Clyde, Firth of, 14, Dd
Clyveland (Cleveland), 13, Eb
Coahuila, 70, Dd
Coats I., 70, Fa
Coats Land, 69C
Cobh (Queenstown), 49B, Ce
Cobija, Bolivia, 68, Cd
Cobija, Chile, 68, Be
Coblenz, 10, Bc; 38, Gc
Coburg, 30, Jc
Cochem, 20, Gc
Cochin, 59A, Ce; 73, Cf
Cochin, st., 59C, Ce; 73, Ce
Cochin China, 74, Jg
Cockburn Chan., 68, Bh
Cockermouth, 27, Cb
Cocos (Keeling) Is., 83, Oe; 90, Ad
Cod, C., 45B, Db
Coevorden, 46A, Fb
Coggeshall, 36, Gf
Cognac, 38, Df
Cohoes, 57, Eb
Coiba I., 43A, Dd
Coigny, 53, Cc
Coimbatore, 73, Ce
Coimbra, 22, Ac; 63, Ab
Colchester, 27, Ge
Cold Harbor, 72B, Bb
Coldstream, 36, Db; 37A, Cc
Colecestra (Colchester), 13, Ge
Colemerik, 93, Eb
Colenso, 81D, Ab
Coleraine, 49B, Ea
Coleroon, R., 52A, Cc; 59D
Colesberg, 81B, Cb
Coligny, 20, Fe
Colima, 43A, Bc
Coll, 14, Bc
Colle, 32E, Bb
Colleton, 45A, Ad
Collioure, 23D, Ga; 53, Ef
Colmar, 8A, Cb; 10, Bd
Colmars, 53, Ge
Cologne, 10, Bc; 83A, Da
Cologne, Abp. of, 46C, Cb
Cologne, eccl. prov., 22, Da
Colombey, 76A, Db
Colombia, 68, Bb
Colombia, Confederation of, 43D, Fd
Colombia, Rep. of, 68, Bb
Colombia, U.S. of, 68, Bb
Colombo, 73, Cf
Colon (Aspinwall), 43D, Ed
Colonea Theme, 9, Kd
Colonia, 68, Df
Colonia Agrippina, 2, Ec
Colonia del Sacramento, 41B, Dg
Colonna, C., 23A, Fd
Colonsay, 14, Bc
Colooney, 49B, Cb
Colorado, R., Argentina, 68, Cf
Colorado, R., U.S.A., 44, Ee
Colorodo, st., 70, Dd
Colorado Terr., 67D, Cb
Colosseum, 5A
Columbia, S. Carolina, 57D, Aa
Columbia, Tennessee, 72, Cb
Columbia, Virginia, 56, Dc
Columbia, R., 70, Cb
Columbus, Kentucky, 72, Cb
Columbus, Ohio, 72, Db
Colwyn, 28A, Cb
Comacchio, 5, Db
Combermere, 36, De
Comeragh Mts., 15, Dd
Comfort Pt., 67A, Cb
Comiaclum, 5B, Ba
Cominges, 17, Fg; 20, Dg
Cominges, Co. of, 11, De
Commercy, 39B, Bb
Comminges, 22, Cc
Como, 5, Bb; 29A, Cc
Como, L., 5, Ba
Comorin, C., 73, Cf
Comoro Is., 80A, Hf
Compiègne, 17, Gd; 31A, B
Compludo, 22, Ac
Compoalla, 43A, Cc
Compostela, 43A, Bb
Compostella, 16, Ad
Conakry, 96B, Ab
Concepcion, Chile, 68, Bf
Concepcion, Paraguay, 68, De
Concepcion, Uruguay, 68, Df
Concord, 45B, Db
Concordia, 68, Df
Conde, 46A, Cd
Condeixa, 63, Ab
Condercum (Benwell), 3C
Condom, 53, Df
Conegliano, 86B, Cb
Conflans, 30, Ed; 83A, Cb
Congaree, R., 57D, Ab
Congo, rep., (formerly Belgian) 96D, Ee
Congo, rep. (formerly French) 96D, De
Congo, R., 80A, Fd
Congo State, 80A, Fe
Coni, 20, Gf
Coningesburg (Conisborough), 13, Ec
Conisborough, 27, Ec
Conjeeveram, 59D
Connacht, 15, Cc
Connaught, 37B, Cc; 49C
Connecticut, 45B, Cc
Connecticut, R., 45A, Cb
Conn, L., 15 Bb; 37B, Bc
Connor, 15, Eb; 49B, Eb
Consentia (Cosenza), 5, Fe
Constance, 10, Ce; 29B, Da
Constance, L. of, 29B, Da
Constanta, 78, Gc
Constantia, 81B, Ac
Constantine, 80A, Da
Constantinople, 18E; 78 Ge
Constantinopolis (Byzantium), 2, Je
Constantsa, 24, He
Constitucion, 68, Bf
Conti, 53, Ec
Convent Garden, 27A
Conversano, 21A, Db
Conway, 27, Cc
Conza, 22, Fc
Cooch Behar, 59C, Eb
Cook Inlet, 71A, Bb
Cook Is., 75, Hf
Cook, Mt., 77, Lj
Cook Str., 77, Mj
Cook's Mill, 71D
Cooktown, 77, Ge
Coolgardie, 77, Ch
Coombe, 36, Ee
Cooper's Creek, 77, Gg
Coorg, 73, Ce
Coosa, R., 56, Bd
Copenhagen, 26, Db
Copiapo, 41B, Bf; 68, Be
Coppermine, R., 70, Ca
Coquet, R., 28B, Db; 48A, Bb
Coquimbo, 68, Bf
Coral Sea, 77, Je; 90, Dd
Corato, 21A, Db
Corbach, 60A, Bc
Corbeil, 11, Eb
Corbet, 28A, Db
Corbie, 11, Eb; 22, Ca
Corbridge, 27, Ea
Cordoba, 68, Cf
Cordova, Alaska, 71A, Ca
Cordova, Spain, 22, Bd; 63, Cd
Cordova, Emirate of, 8, Bd
Corduba, 2, Cf
Corfe Castle, 27, Df
Corfu, 78, Bf
Coria, 22, Ac; 63, Bc
Coringa, 59C, Dd
Corinium (Cirencester), 3A, Ee
Corinth, Greece, 2, Hf
Corinth, U.S.A., 72, Cc
Corinth, G. of, 78, Df
Coritani, 3A, Fc
Cork, 15, Ce
Cork, co., 37C; 49B, Ce
Cork Harbour, 37B, Ce
Cormantine, 81C, Dc
Cormons, 86B, Db
Cornbie (Carn Brea), 13, Af
Corneto, 22A; 23B, Cc
Cornouaille, Co. of, 11, Bb
Cornovii, 3A, Dd
Cornvalge (Cornwall), 13, Bf
Cornwall, Canada, 57, Da
Cornwall, co., 27, Bf
Coro, 43A, Fc
Coromandel, 77A
Coromandel Coast, 59A, De
Coron, 19, Ce
Coronel, 86, Ff
Corpus Christi, 70, Ee
Correggio, 32A, Db
Corregidor, 90, Cc
Corrib, L., 15, Bc; 37B, Bc
Corrientes, 68, De
Corrientes, C., Cuba, 43A, Db
Corrientes, C., Mexico, 43A, Bb
Corrieyairack Pass, 49A, Bb
Corsewall Pt., 49A, Bc
Corsica, 5, Bc
Corstopitum (Corbridge), 3C
Cortenuova, 20, Hf
Cortina di Ampezzo, 86B, Ca
Cortona, Bruttium, 5, Fe
Cortona, Florence, 21, Kg
Corumba, 68, Dd; 94, Cf
Corunna, 23D, Aa; 63, Aa
Corvey, 22, Da; 65B, Aa
Cos, 78, Fg
Cosenza, 23A, Fd
Cosenza (Consentia), 5, Fe
Cossacks, 50, Gd
Cossimbazar, 59B
Costa Rica, 43D, Dc
Cotabato, 75E, Bc
Côte d'Or, 76A, Cc
Coteau du Lac, 57, Da
Cotentin, 8, Bb; 17, Ed
Cotonou, 94, Te; 96B, Cb
Cotrone, 23A, Fd
Cotswold Hills, 27, De
Cottian Alps, 29A, Bc
Couci, 11, Eb
Couci, S. of, 20 Ed
Coudres, I. aux, 45A, Ca
Coulmiers, 76A, Ac
Countisbury, 7C, Bc
Coupland, 28B, Bc
Couserans, 22, Cc
Courantyne, 68, Db
Courtrai, 28C, Da; 46A, Cd
Coutances, 11, Cb
Coutras, 38, Cf
Covadonga, 22, Bc
Covelong, 59D
Coventreu (Coventry), 13, Ed
Coventry, 27, Ed
Cowal, 14, Cd
Cowans Ford, 57, Af
Cowpens, 56, Cc; 57D, Aa
Cozumel, 43A, Db
Crac de la Pierre (Krak), 18C, Cg
Cracow, 21, Nc
Cracow, Rep. of, 64, Gc
Cradock, 81B, Cc
Craigmillar, 37A, Cc
Crail, 49A, Cb
Craiova, 54, Gd; 78, Dc
Cramond, 3A, Ca
Craon, 20, Ce
Craonne, 83A, Bb
Crati, R., 21A, Dc
Crave (Craven), 13, Db
Craven, 45A, Bd
Crawford, 37A, Cc
Crecy, 28C, Ca
Crediton, 27, Cf; 36, Cg
Creeks, 56, Bd; 71F, Ba
Crefeld, 46A, Fc
Creil, 83A, Bb
Crema, 32D, Ab
Cremona, 5, Cb
Creneburne (Cranborne) 13, Bf
Crépy, 53, Ec
Crespy, 38, Ed
Creta, 2, Jf
Crete, 19, Ce; 78, Eh
Crevant, 28D, Dc
Crewkerne, 48B, Bd
Criccieth, 28A, Bb
Crichelade (Cricklade), 13, Ee
Crickhowell, 28A, Cc
Cricklade, 27, Ee
Crieff, 49A, Cb
Crim, Khanate of, 79, Ga
Crim Tartary, 33A, Ea
Crimea, 50, Gd
Croagh Patrick, 15, Bc
Croatan I., 45A, Bc
Croatia, 21, Lf
Croats, 9, Fc
Croce, Mte., 86B, Ca
Croceraguel, 36, Bb
Crococalana (Brough), 3A, Fc
Croisic, 55A, Be
Cromarty, 37A, Bb; 49A, Bb
Cromarty, co., 37A, Bb
Cromarty Firth, 14, Db
Cropredy Bridge, 48A, Cc
Cross Sd., 71B, Bb
Crossen, 31, Lb
Croton, 57, Ec
Crowland, 7B, Cb; 7C, Cb 36, Fe
Crown Point, 57, Eb
Crown Princess Martha Land, 69C
Crows Nest Pass, 44, Cd
Croxton, 36, Fe
Crozet Is., 69C
Cruces (Venta Cruz), 43A, Ed
Cruilande (Crowland), 13, Fd
Crussol, 20, Ff
Cruz, C. de, 43A, Ec
Cruzeiro do Sul, 94, Df
Csanad, 19, Cc
Ctesiphon, 1, Gd; 6A, Db
Cuba, 43A, Db
Cuch Behar, 73, Eb
Cucui, 68, Cb
Cucuta, 68, Bb
Cuddalore, 59D
Cuddapah, 73, Ce
Cuenca, Ecuador, 68, Bc
Cuenca, Spain, 22, Bc
Cuiaba, 68, Dd
Cuillins, 14, Bb
Cujavia, 26, Ec; 39, Nb
Culebra B., 43A, Dc
Culiacan, 43A, Bb
Cullen, 49A, Cb
Culloden, 49A, Bb
Culpeper, 72B, Ba
Cumana, 43A, Fc
Cumans, 19, Dc
Cumberland, 71C, Cc
Cumberland, co., 27, Cb
Cumberland Gap, 72, Db
Cumberland House, 44, Dc
Cumberland Mts., 56, Cc
Cumberland, R., 56, Bc
Cumberland Sd., 70, Ha
Cumbria, 7B, Ba; 13, Db
Cumbrian Hills, 27, Cb
Cumnock, 37A, Bc; 49A, Bc
Cuncacestre (Chester-le-Street), 13, Eb
Cuneo, 32A, Bb
Cunetio (Mildenhall), 3A, Ee
Cunningham, 14, Dd
Cupar, 37A, Cb
Curcura, 23B, Fc
Curico, 68, Bf
Curitiba, 68 Ee
Curzola, 22, Fc
Cushendun, 49B, Ea
Cussey, 76A, Cc
Custozza, 32C, Cb
Cutch, 73, Ac
Cuttack, 73, Ec
Cuttack, st., 73, Ec
Cuxhaven, 55A, Hb; 60B, Bb
Cuyo Is., 75E, Bb
Cuyuni, R., 68B, Ba
Cuzco, 68, Bd
Cyclades, 78, Eg
Cydewain, 13, Cd
Cydnus, R., 18C, Ba
Cynllaith, 13, Cd
Cyprus, 2, Kg; 4A, Je; 6A, Ab
Cyprus, King. of, 18A, Eb
Cyprus Theme, 9, Je
Cyrenaica, 1, Ed; 80A, Fa
Cyrene, 2, Hg; 4A, Ge; 93, Ac
Cythnos, 78, Eg
Cyzicus, 6, Da,; 8, Hc
Czarnikow, 31, Mb
Czartorysk, 51, Fc
Czaslau, 60A, Ed
Czech, 8C, Cb; 85, Fc
Czechoslovakia, 84, Fc
Czechs, 8, Fb
Czernowitz, 33C, Fb; 78, Ea
Czerwinsk, 26, Fc
Czestochowa, 21, Nc; 87, Db

DABRA TABOR, 80B, Be
Dacca, 59B; 73, Fc
Dachstein, 29A, Eb
Dacia, 2, He
Dacre, 7C, Ba
Dadisleia (Tickhill), 13, Ec
Daghestan, 79, Jb; 84, Md
Dagö, 26, Fb
Dagsburg, 39B, Db
Dagupan, 75E, Ba
Dahlak Arch., 80B, Cd
Dahlonega, 72, Dc
Dahomé, 81C, Ec
Dahomey, 96B, Cb
Daibul, 6, Hc
Dairen, 91, Fd
Dairen (Dalny), 76B, Ab
Daix, R., 1, Hb
Dakar, 80A, Bc; 96B, Aa
Dakota Terr., 67D, Ca
Dal, 26, Db
Dal Arridhe, 15, Eb
Dalecarlia, 26, Da
Dalhousie, 71, Hc
Dalkeith, 37A, Cc; 48A, Bb
Dalkey, 37B, Ec
Dallas, Georgia, 72, Dc
Dallas, Texas, 94, Ed
Dalmally, 49A, Bb
Dalmatia, 32A, Gc; 78, Ad
Dalnaspidal, 49A, Bb
Dalny (Dairen), 76b, Ab
Dalriada, 14, Cc; 15, Ea
Dalriada Scots, 7B, Aa
Dalriada Ulaid, 7A, Ba
Dalry, Ayrshire, 37A, Bc
Dalry, Kirkcudbright, 49A, Bc
Dalton, 72A, Aa
Daltune (Dalton), 13, Cb
Dalwhinnie, 49A, Bb
Daly Waters, 95, Mf
Dam, 93, Ee
Daman, 73, Bc
Damariscotta, 45B, Ea
Damascus, 2, Lg; 18C, De
Damascus, Emirs of, 18C, De
Damietta, 6A, Ab; 9, Jf
Damm, 50, Cc
Dammartin, 20, Ed
Damme, 17, Gc, 55, Ec
Damnonii, 3A, Ba
Dampier Arch., 77, Bf
Dampier Str., 77, Hc
Dampierre, 20, Fd
Damvillers, 39B, Ba; 53, Fc
Dan, R., 57, Be
Danes, 2A, Ca; 7A, Fa; 8, E
Danewerk, 65F, Aa
Danilovski, 61, Eb
Danish Mercia, 7C, Cb
Danishmend, 16, Ke
Dankov, 61, Ed
Danube, R., 21, Me; 33C, Ec
Danubius, R., 1, Ec; 2, He
Danubyu, 73, Gd
Danum, (Doncaster), 3A, Ec
Danville, 57, Be
Danzig, 21, Na
Danzig, Rep. of, 60B, Ga
Dar es Salaam, 80A, Ge
Dar Fur, 80A, Fc
Daras, 4B, Ld
Darbhanga, 73, Eb
Dardanelles, 78, Fe; 86D
Dargun, 22, Ea
Darien, Central America, 43A, Ed
Darien, Georgia, 56, Cd
Darien, G. of, 43A, Ed
Darjeeling, 73, Eb
Darley, 36, Ee
Darling, R., 77, Gh
Darmstadt, 29A, Ca
Daroca, 23C, Eb
Dartford, 36, Gf
Dartmoor, 27, Cf
Dartmouth, England, 27, Cf
Dartmouth, Nova Scotia, 45A, Eb
Dartmouth College, 57, Eb
Darum, 18C, Bg
Darwin, 90, Cd
Dassel, 20, Hc
Dauphiné, 20, Ff; 30, Ff
Davao 75E, Cc
Davao G., 75E, Cc
Davenport, 7C, Bb
David Comnenus, 18B, Eb
David Street, 18D
David's Gate, 18D
David's Tower, 18D
Davis Str., 44, Jb,; 69B
Davos, 29B, Db
Dawson, 71A, Da
Dax, 22, Bc; 28C, Be; 30, Cg
Dayton, 71C, Bc; 72, Db
De Aveiro, 36, Kd
De Burgh (Burke), 37B, Cc
De Courcy, 17, Ba
De Leuwin, 42B
De Witts Land, 42, Qe
Deabolis, 18A, Ca
Dead Sea, 18C, Cg
Deal, 27, He
Dean, Forest of, 3A, De
Deba Habe, 96B, Da
Debra Markos, 96A, Aa
Debrecen, 87, Ec
Debreczin, 33C, Eb
Decatur, Alabama, 72, Cc
Decatur, Georgia, 72A, Ab
Deccan, 41A, Ec; 73, Cd
Deceangli, 3A, Cc
Decies, 15, Dd
Deddington, 27, Ed
Dedeagach, 78, Ee; 86C, Aa
Dee, R., Aberdeenshire, 14, Fb
Dee, R., Galloway, 36, Bb
Dee, R., Wales, 27, Dc
Deer I., 56B
Deerfield, 45B, Cb

Deganwy, 13, Cc; 28A, Ca
Deheubarth, 13, Be; 17, Cc
Dehra Dun, 92, Da
Deira, 7B, Ca
Delagoa B., 81A, Dc
Delaware B., 45B, Bd; 57, Dd
Delaware, R., 45B, Bc; 57, Dc
Delft, 30, Fb; 46A, Db
Delgado, C., 58, Me
Delhi, 25, Gd; 73, Cb
Delhi, Sultanate of, 25, Gd
Demerara (Georgetown), 43D, Gd
Demerara, R., 68B, Ba
Demetae, 3A, Bd
Demirhissar, 86A, Ea
Demmin, 21, Kb; 39, Kb
Demotika, 9, Hd
Denain, 54, Cb
Denbigh, 27, Cc
Dendermonde, 46A, Dc
Dene (Dean), 13, De
Denia, 23C, Fc; 63, Fc
Denmark, 12, Gc
Denmark, King. of, 26, Db
Denmark and Norway, 54, Da
Dennewitz, 60B, Dc
D'Entrecasteaux Is., 77, Ic
Denver, 70, Dd
Deogir, 25, Gd
Déols, 11, Dc
Depenbech, 13, Dc
Deptford, 13, Ge
Derbent, 6, Fa; 19, Hd
Derby, Connecticut, 45B, Cc
Derby, England, 13, Ed
Derby, W. Australia, 77, Ce
Derby, co., 27, Ec
Derbyscire (Derbyshire), 13, Ec
Derevlyans, 9, Hb
Derg, L., 15, Cc
Derg, R., 15, Db
Derlington (Darlington), 13, Eb
Derna, 79, Dd
Derry, 15, Db
Derwent, R., 27, Ec; 48A, Cc
Des Moines, 70, Ec
Deshima, 52, Rc
Desmond, 15, Be
Desna, R., 9, Jb; 61A, Db
Dessie, 96A, Aa
Dessau, 31, Kc; 39, Kc
Desterro (Florianopolis), 68, Ee
Detmold, 10, Cc; 60B, Bc
Detroit, 45A, Ab
Dettingen, 54, Dc; 60A, Bc
Deutsch Brod, 31, Ld
Deva (Chester), 3A, Dc
Devenescire (Devon), 13, Cf
Deventer, 22, Da; 46A, Fb
Devernaki Pass, 78, Dg
Deveron, R., 14, Fb
Devikottai, 59D
Devizes, 27, De
Devol, R., 86A, Bb
Devon, 27, Cf
Devonport, 55A, Ac
Dewalgaon, 73, Cc
Dewas, 73, Cc
Dewsland, 27, Ae
Dhahran, 94, Rd
Dhar, 73, Cc
Dharwar, 73, Cd
Dholpur, 73, Cb
Diakova, 78, Cd
Diamantina, 68, Ed
Diarbekr, 19, Fe
Diarbekr (Amida), 33A, Fc
Dibrugarh, 92, Hb
Die, 11, Fd; 22, Dc; 38, Ff
Diedenhofen (Thionville), 10, Bd; 76A, Cb
Diepholz, 30, Hb
Dieppe, 30, Dd; 83A, Ab
Dieren, 46A, Fb
Dieulacres, 36, Dd
Digne, 22, Dc; 38, Gf
Dijon, 11, Fc
Dilawar, 73, Bb
Dimotika, 78, Fe
Dinagat, 75E, Cb
Dinan, 11, Bb
Dinant, 46A, Dd
Dinapore, 73, Db
Dinaric Alps, 78, Ac
Dinas, 28A, Cb
Dinas Bran, 28A, Cb
Dindigul, 59A, Ce
Dinevor, 13, Be
Dingle, 49B, Ad
Dingle B., 15, Ad
Dingwall, 14, Db
Dinkelsbühl, 53, Jc
Dioclea, 9, Fd
Diocletian, Baths of, 5A
Dioscoridis I., 1, Hf
Diredawa, 96A, Bb
Direlton, 28B, Ca
Dirk Hartog I., 77, Ag
Disentis, 20, He; 29B, Cb
Ditmarsh, 26, Cc
Diu, 73, Bc
Dixmude, 46A, Bc
Dixon Entrance, 71B, Cc
Dizful, 93, Fc
Djagatai Empire, 25, Hb
Djakarta, 91, Dg
Djerba, 16, Ef
Djibouti, 96A, Ba
Djokjakarta, 91, Eg
Djougou, 96B, Cb
Dnieper, R., 50, Gc; 87, Gc
Dniester, R., 8, Hb; 87, Fc
Doab, The, 59A, Db
Dobb's Ferry, 57, Ec
Doberan, 22, Ea
Dobruja, 78, Gc
Dobrzyn, 21, Nb
Dobunni, 3A, De
Doce Leguas, Cays de, 43A, Eb
Dodecanese, 79, Ec
Dodinga, 52B, Aa
Dogger Bank, 82, Cb
Doha, 93, Gd
Doiran, 78, De
Dol, 11, Cb; 30, Cd
Dôle, 20, Fe; 38, Fe
Dolforwyn, 28A, Cb
Dolomites, 86B, Ba
Dolores, 43C, Ab
Dolwyddelan, 28A, Ca
Dombes, 53, Fd
Domfront, 17, Ed
Dominica, 43A, Fc
Dömitz, 38, Jb
Domrémy, 28D, Eb
Don, R., Russia, 16, Lc; 19, Fb
Don, R., Scotland, 14, Fb
Don Cossacks, 61, Fe
Donauwörth, 29A, Da
Doncaster, 27, Ec
Dondra Hd., 73, Df
Donegal, co., 37C; 49B, Cb
Donegal Abbey, 37B, Cb
Doneham (Dunham Massey), 13, Dc
Donets, R., 19, Fc; 61, Ee
Donetsk, 89, Nd
Dongola, 80B, Ad
Donnington Castle, 48B, Cd
Donzy, 17, Ge; 31A, Bd
Dora Baltea, R., 5, Ab
Dorat, 53, Dd
Dorcestre (Dorchester), 13, Df
Dorchester, Dorset, 27, Df
Dorchester, Massachusetts, 45B, Db; 56B
Dorchester, New Jersey, 45B, Bd
Dorchester, Oxon., 3A, Ee; 7B, Cc
Dorchester Heights, 56B
Dorchester Neck, 56B
Dorchester Pt., 56B
Dordogne, R., 11, Dd
Dore, 7B, Cb
Dorey, 77, Eb
Dordrecht, 26, Bc; 53, Fb
Dornach, 29B, Ba
Dornoch, 37A, Bb; 49A, Cb
Dornoch, bp., 14A, Bb
Dornoch Firth, 14, Eb
Dorostol, 9, Hd
Dorpat, 26, Gb
Dorset, 27, Df
Dorsete (Dorset), 13, Df
Dort, 46A, Dc
Dortmund, 10, Bc
Dorylaeum, 9, Je
Douai, 30, Ec; 46A, Cd
Doubs, R., 11, Fc; 29A, Bb
Douglas, Alaska, 71B, Cb
Douglas, Scotland, 37A, Cc
Douglas, clan, 28B, Ab
Douglas Castle, 28B, Bb
Dourdan, 38, Ed
Douro, R., 22, Ac; 63, Bb
Dover, Delaware, 57, Dd
Dover, England, 27, He
Dover, New England, 45B, Db
Dover, Str. of., 11, Da
Dovere (Dover), 13, He
Down, 15, Fb
Down, co., 37C; 49B, Eb
Downham Market, 48B, Dc
Downpatrick, 37B, Fb; 49B, Fb
Downpatrick, bp., 15A, Ca
Downs, The, 55A, Dc
Downton, 27, Ee
Dragasani, 78, Ec
Dragashan, 78, Ec
Draguignan, 20, Gg; 30, Gg
Draheim, 60A, Fb
Drakens Berg (Quathlamba), 81D, Ab
Drakensberg, 81B, Db
Drangiana, 1, Jd
Draper's Meadow, 56, Cc
Drave, R, 8, Fb; 21, Le
Dregoviches, 9, Gb
Drenthe, 46A, Fb
Dresden, 21, Kc; 31, Kc
Dreux 11, Db; 76A, Ab
Dreznik, 33C, Dc
Drina, R., 78, Bc
Drogheda, 37B, Ec; 49B, Ec
Droitwich, 27, Dd
Dromore, 49B, Eb
Dromore, bp., 15A, Ba
Drumburgh, 3C
Drumclog, 49A, Bc
Dryslwyn, 28A, Bc
Duala, 80A, Dd; 96B, Db
Dubawnt L., 44, Db
Dubienka, 51, Ec
Dubitza, 54, Fc
Dublin, 15, Ec
Dublin, abp., 15A, Bb
Dublin, co., 37C; 49B, Ec
Dübnik, 78, Ed
Dubris (Dover), 3A, He
Ducatus Venetianus, 23B, Db
Ducie I., 75, Jf
Dudelei (Dudley), 13, Dd
Dudley, 27, Dd
Duero, R., 22, Bc; 63, Cb
Duich, L., 49A, Bb
Duisburg, 20, Gc; 46A, Fc
Duiveland, 46A, Cc
Dulce, R., 41B, Cf
Dulcigno, 22, Fc; 78, Be
Duleek, 15, Ec
Duluth, 70, Ec
Dumaguete, 75E, Bc
Dumaran, 75E, Ab
Dumbarton, 37A, Bc; 48A, Ab
Dumbarton, co., 37A, Bb; 49A, Bc
Dumdum, 73, Ec
Dumfries, 28B, Bb; 36, Cb
Dumfries, co., 37A, Cc; 49A, Cc
Dumio, 22, Ac
Dumnonii, 3A, Bf
Dun, 20, Ee
Dun Laoghaire (Kingstown), 49B, Ec
Düna, 26, Gb
Dünaburg, 26, Gb
Dunbar, 14, Fc
Dunblane, 14, Ec; 49A, Cb
Duncannon, 49B, Ed
Duncansby Hd., 14, Ea; 49A, Ca
Dundalk, 37B, Ec; 49B, Ec
Dundee, Natal, 81D, Bb
Dundee, Scotland, 28B, Ca; 48A, Ba
Dundonald Castle, 28B, Ab
Dundrennan, 14, Ee
Dundrum, 37B, Fb
Dunedin, 77A
Dunewic (Dunwich), 13, Hd
Dunfermline, 14, Ec
Dungannon, 49B, Eb
Dungarvan, 37B, Dd; 49B, Dd
Dungeness, 55A, Dc
Dungiven, 49B, Eb
Dunhevet (Dunheved, Launceston), 13, Bf
Dunholm (Durham), 13, Eb
Dunkeld, 14, Ec
Dunkeswell, 36, Cg
Dunkirk, 46A, Bc
Dunlavin, 49B, Ec
Dunmore Hd., 15, Ad
Dunnet Hd., 14, Ea
Dunnottar, 37A, Cb
Dunois, 30, Dd
Dunrobin, 37A, Cb
Dunrobin Castle, 49A, Cb
Duns, 37A, Cc; 48A, Bb
Dunstable, 27, Fe
Dunstaffnage, 49A, Bb
Dunstanburgh, 27, Eb
Dunster, 27, Ce; 48A, Bd
Dunvegan, 49A, Ab
Dunwich, 27, Hd; 36A
Duppel, 65F, Aa
Dupplin Moor, 28B, Ba
Durance, R., 11, Fe; 29A, Ad
Durango, 43A, Bb
Duras, 53, De
Durazzo, 78, Be
Durban (Port Natal), 81D, Bb
Düren, 20, Gc
Durham, England, 27, Eb
Durham, New Hampshire, 57, Fb
Durham, Bb. of, 28B, Dc; 36, Db
Durham, Palatinate of. 27, Eb
Durinish, 14, Bb
Durlach, 38, Gd
Durnkrüt, 19, Bc
Durness, 14, Da
Durnovaria (Dorchester), 3A, Df
Durobrivae (Rochester), 3A, Ge
Durobrivae (Water Newton), 3A, Fd
Durocobrivae (Dunstable), 3A, Fe
Durolipons (Cambridge), 3A, Gd
Durotriges, 3A, Df
Durovernum (Canterbury), 3A, He
Durovigatum (Godmanchester), 3A, Fd
Dürrenstein, 29A, Fa
Dürres, 88, Je
Dusky B., 77, Lk
Düsseldorf, 38, Gc; 83A, Da
Dutch Brazil, 41B, Ed; 42, He
Dutch East Indies, 74, KJ; 90, Bd
Dutch Harbor, 90, Fa
Dutch New Guinea, 77, Fb
Duxbury, 45B, Db; 57, Fb
Dvina, R., (N.), 61, Fb; 88, Oa
Dvina, R., (W.), 50, Fb; 64, Hb
Dvinsk, 84, Ha
Dyea, 71B, Cb
Dyfed, 7B, Ac; 13, Be
Dyle, R., 46B; 83A, Ca
Dynefwr, 28A, Bc
Dyrrhachium, 2, Ge; 4A, Fc
Dzhulfa, 93, Fb

Ealondscire, (Islandshire), 13, Ea
Eamont, 7C, Ba
Earn, L., 14, Dc
Easby, 7B, Ca
East C., Asia, 69B
East C., New Zealand, 77, Nl
East, Pref. of the., 2, Kf
East Angles, 7A, Da
East Anglia, 7B, Db; 12, Ec
East China Sea, 91, Fd
East Florida, 71F, Ba
East Franconia, 10, Dd
East Friesland, Co. of, 30, Gb
East Germany, 89, Hc
East London, 81B, Cc
East Main, R., 70, Gb
East March, 28B, Cb
East Mark, 8A, Db
East of March, 27, Cd
East Pakistan, 92, Gc
East Prussia, 39, Pb
East Roman Empire, 2, Kf
East Saxons, 7A, Db
Easter I., 75, Kf
Eastern, prov., Nigeria, 96B, Cb
Eastern Association, 48A, Dc
Eastern Bengal and Assam, 73A, Cb
Eastern Ghats, 73, Dd
Eastern Roman Empire, 8, Gd
Eastern Rumelia, 78, Ed
Eastham, 45B, Dc
Easthampton, 45B, Cc
Easton, 57, Dc
Eastphalia, 10, Db
Ebbsfleet, 36, Hf
Ebenezer, 57D, Ab
Eboracum (Evrvic) (York), 13, Eb
Ebro, R., 22, Bc; 63, Da
Eburacum (York), 3A, Ec
Ecbatana, 1, Gd; 6, Fb
Ecclefechan, 49A, Cc
Ecclesia de Labataille (Battle), 13, Gf
Echallar, 63, Ea
Echallens, 29B, Ab
Ecija, 6, Ab
Eckernförde, 65F, Aa
Eckmühl, 65B, Bb
Ecuador, 68, Bc
Edam, 46A, Eb
Eddisbury, 7C, Bb
Edelsland, 42B; 77, Bh
Eden, R., 7C, Ba; 27, Db
Edenton, 57, Ce
Edessa, 2, Lf; 6, Eb; 19, Fe
Edessa, Co. of, 16, Ke
Edeyrnion, 13, Cd
Edge Hill, 48A, Cc
Edgecot, 27, Ed
Edinburgh (Dunedin), 14, Ed
Edinburgh, co., 49A, Cc
Edington, 36, Df
Edisto, R., 57D, Ab
Edmonton, 70, Cb
Edolo, 86B, Aa
Eecloo, 46A, Cc
Efferding, 31, Kd
Eger, Bohemia, 21, Kc
Eger, Hungary, 33C, Eb
Eger, R., 21, Kc
Egersund, 87, Ba
Eggmühl, 29A, Ea
Egisheim, 39B, Db
Egitama, 22, Ad
Eglesham (Eynsham), 13, Ee
Egmont, 22, Ca; 46A, Db
Egremont, 27, Cb
Egri Palanka, 78, Dd
Egripo, 78, Df
Egypt, 80A, Fb; 93, Bd
Egypt (Misr), 6, Dc
Egyptian Sudan, 83, Ld
Ehrenbreitstein, 51, Bc
Eia (Eye), 13, Hd
Eichsfeld, 20, Hc
Eichstadt, 10, Dd
Eider, R., 60B, Ba; 65F, Aa
Eifel, 83A, Da
Eigg, 14, Bc
Eight Emirates, 24, Jf
Eil, 96A, Bb
Eilean Donan, 49A, Bb
Einsiedeln, 22, Db; 29B, Ca
Eire, 49B, Dc
Eisenach, 20, Jc; 39C, Ac
Eisenburg, 39C, Bc
Eisenburg (Vasvar), 29A, Gb
Ekaterinoslav, 64, Kd
El Agheila, 88, Jg
El Alamein, 93, Bc
El Aqaba, 80B, Ab
El Arish, 80B, Aa
El Bodon, 63, Bb
El Damer, 93, Cf
El Dirr, 93, Ce
El Dorado, 43A, Fd
El Faiyum, 80B, Ab
El Golea, 96C, Ca
El Khandaq, 93, Cf
El Morro, 43A, Db
El Obeid, 80A, Fc
El Paso, 70, Dd
Elands, R., 81A, Cc
Elandslaagte, 81D, Ab
Elassona, 78, Df
Elba, 5, Cc
Elbasan, 86A, Ba
Elbe, R., 10, Cb; 60A, Ec
Elberfeld, 53, Gb; 60B, Ac
Elbeuf, 28C, Cb; 38, Dd
Elbing, 21, Na; 39, Na
Elburz, 19, Je
Elche, 23C, Ec
Elchingen, 22, Eb; 29A, Da
Elderslie, 28B, Ab
Electoral Palatinate, 30, Hd
Eleuthera I., 43A, Eb
Elfael, 13, Cd
Elfsborg, 50, Cb
Elgin, 37A, Cb
Elgin, bp., 14A, Cb
Elgin, co., 49A, Cb
Elgin and Forres, co., 37A, Cb
Elim, 81B, Ac
Elizabeth, New Jersey, 45B, Bc
Elizabeth, Virginia, 45B, Ae
Elizabeth, C., 45B, Db
Elizabethtown, 57B
Elizabethville, 96C, Ef
Elk Hill, 57, Be
Elkton, 57, Dd
Ellandun, 7B, Cc
Ellesmere, 28A, Db
Ellesmere I., 44, Ga
Ellice Is., 90, Ed
Ellichpur, 52A, Bb
Elliot, 28B, Cb
Elliot Is., 76B, Bb
Ellwangen, 22, Eb
Elmeslae (Helmsley), 13, Eb
Elmet, 7A, Ca
Elmham, 7B, Db; 36A
Elmham, bp., 36A
Elmina, 35, Jd; 81C, Dc
Elmshorn, 65F, Ab
Elne, 11, Ee
Elnestow (Elstow), 13, Fd
Elphin, 15, Cc
Elster, R., 10, Ec
Elstow, 36, Fe
Elten, 65A, Aa
Elvas, 23C, Bc; 63, Bc
Ely, 27, Gd
Ely, bp., 36, Ge
Ely, I. of, 27, Gd
Elyg (Ely), 13, Gd
Embrun, 11, Gd
Emden, 38, Gb; 65D, Aa
Emesa, 9, Ke
Emilia, 32A, Db
Emirs of Damascus, 18C, De
Emly, 15, Cd
Emmitsburg, 72B, Ba
Empingham (Losecoat Field), 27, Fd
Empire, The, 16, Dc; 54, Eb
Ems, 60B, Ac
Ems, R., 10, Bb; 38, Gb
Enaghdun, 15, Bc
Encounter B., 77, Fl
Endeavour R., 77, He
Enderby Land, 69C
Engadi, 18C, Cg
Engadin, 29B, Eb
Engelberg, 10, Ce
Engelberg, Abbey of, 29B, Cb
Engern, 10, Cb
Enghien, 46A, Dd
England, 34, Bb; 55A, Cb

England, King. of, 20, Cc
English, R., 70, Eb
English Channel, 7B, Cc
English Mercia, 7C, Bb
Enkhuizen, 46A, Eb
Enköping, 26, Eb
Ennis, 49B, Cd
Enniscorthy, 15, Ed
Enniskillen, 49B, Db
Enns, R., 29A, Fb
Enos, 78, Fe
Entebbe, 96C, Fd
Entschede, 46A, Fb
Enugu, 96B, Cb
Eperjes, 33C, Eb
Épernay, 83A, Bb
Ephesus, 8, Hd
Epidaurus, 79, Dc
Epidium Prom., 3A, Aa
Epila, 23D, Eb
Épinal, 20, Gd; 83B, Ba
Epirus, 1, Ed; 79, Dc
Epirus, Despotate of, 19, Ce
Eppenstein, 10, Fe
Epworth, 36, Fd
Equatorial Provs., 80A, Fd
Erbach, 38, Hd
Erbil, 93, Eb
Erfurt, 10, Dc; 39C, Bc
Eriboll, 49A, Ba
Ericht, L., 49A Bb
Erie, 70, Fc
Erie, L., 45A, Ab
Eries, 45A, Ab
Eriska, 49A, Ab
Eritrea, 80B, Ce; 96A, Aa
Erivan, 61, Ff; 79, Hb
Erlau, 31, Pe; 33A, Ba
Ermeland, 39, Pb
Ermine Street, 3A, Fd
Erne, L., 15, Db
Erne, Upper L., 49B, Db
Errigal, 15, Ca
Erz Gebirge, 10, Ec
Erzerum, 6, Fb; 79, Hc
Erzingan, 86C, Cb
Es Suweida, 93, Dc
Escewelle (Ashwell), 13, Gd
Escomb, 7B, Ca
Eshowe, 81D, Bb
Eskdale, 14, Ed
Eskisehir, 79, Fc
Eskishehr, 86C, Bb
Esla, R., 63, Cb
Esmeraldas, 68, Bb
Esopus, 45B, Cc
Española (Hispaniola), 43A, Ec
Esperance, 77, Ch
Esperance, C.d', 45A, Ea
Espinosa, 63, Da
Espirito Santo, 68, Ed
Essek, 33C, Db
Essen, 53, Gb; 87, Bb
Essequibo, 41B, Dc
Essequibo, R., 68, Db
Essex, 27, Ge
Essling, 29A, Ga
Esslingen, 30, Hd
Essonnes, 38, Ed
Est-Treding (East Riding), 13, Fc
Estavayer, 29B, Ab
Estcourt, 81D, Ab
Este, 23B, Cb; 32D, Bb
Este (D. of Ferrara), 32A, Db
Este (D. of Modena), 32A, Db
Esthonia, 26, Gb
Esthonians, 9, Ha
Estonia, 87, Fa
Estrella, Sierra d', 63, Bb
Estremadura, Portugal, 63, Ac
Estremadura, Spain, 63, Bc
Etampes, 11, Eb; 17, Gd
Étaples, 30, Dc
Ethandun, 7C, Bc
Ethiopia, 80A, Gd
Etna, Mt., 5 Ef
Etowah, R., 72A, Aa
Ettlingen, 65A, Ab
Ettrick, R., 14, Ed
Ettrick Forest, 28B, Bb
Eu, 11, Db; 17, Fd; 30, Dc
Eucla, 77, Dh
Eugubium, 5B, Bb
Eupàtoria (Kozlov), 50, Gd
Eupen, 83A, Da
Euphrates, R., 2, Mg; 6A, Cb
Eure, R., 76A, Ab
Europa Pt., 63A
Eustria, 8, Cb
Eutaw Springs, 57D, Ab
Evansville, 72, Cb
Evaux, 30, Ee
Everest, Mt., 73, Eb; 92, Fb
Everglades, 43A, Db
Evesham, 13, Ed; 27, Ed
Evora, 22, Ad; 63, Bc
Evora, eccl. prov., 22, Ad
Evreux, 11, Db; 17, Fd
Evrvicscire (Yorkshire), 13, Eb
Ewias, 13, De
Ewisdale, 28B, Bb
Ewyas, 7C, Bc
Ewyas Lacy, 28A, Dc
Exarchate, 5, Cb
Exe, R., 27, Cf; 48B, Bd
Exeter, England, 27, Cf
Exeter, New Hampshire, 45B, Db
Exeter, bp., 36, Bg
Exilles, 38, Gf
Exmoor, 27, Ce
Exonia (Exeter), 13, Cf
Exploring Is. (Lau Group), 75C, Ca
Exsessa (Essex), 13, Ge
Eye, 27, Hd
Eylau, 60A, Ha; 60B, Ha
Eyre, L., 77, Fg

Faenza, 5, Cb
Faesulae, 5, Cc
Fair Hd., 49B, Ea
Fairbanks, 71A, Ca
Fairfax, 72B, Ba
Fairfield, Connecticut, 45B, Cc
Fairfield, S. Africa, 81B, Cc
Faiyum, 93, Cd
Fakfak, 77, Eb
Falaise, 11, Cb
Falkenburg, 39B, Ca
Falkenstein, Austria, 33C, Cb
Falkenstein, Swabia, 10, Cd
Falkirk, 28B, Bb; 49A, Cc
Falkland Is., 68, Dh
Falkland Is. Dependencies, 95, Cj
Falköping, 26, Db
Falmouth, England, 55A, Ac
Falmouth, Maine, 57, Fb
Falmouth (Casco) (For Loyal), 45B, Db
False B., 81B, Ac
Falsterbo, 26, Db
Falun, 26, Ea
Famagusta, 16, Je
Famia (Apamea), 18C, Dc
Fanning I., 75, Hd
Fano, 32A, Ec
Fanum, 5B, Bb
Fao, 86C, Ec
Farasan Is., 80B, Cd
Fareham 27, Ef
Farewell, C., 69B
Farmingham, 45B, Cc
Farnea, Is. (Farne Is.), 13, Ea
Farnham, 27, Fe
Faro, 22, Ad
Faroe Is., 12, Ca; 82, Aa
Farquharson, 37A, Cb
Farrukhabad, 59C, Cb
Fars, 6, Gb
Fashoda (Kodak), 80B, Ae
Fast Castle, 28B, Cb
Fatehgarh, 73, Cb
Fatehpur, 73, Db
Fatimite anti-Caliphate, 6B, Ba
Fatimite Caliphs, 16, Jg
Faucigny, 30, Ge
Faventia, 5B, Aa
Faversham, 27, Ge
Fayetteville, N. Carolina, 57, Bf
Fayetteville, W. Virginia, 72, Db
Fayum, 6A, Ac
Fear, C., 57D, Bb
Fécamp, 11, Db
Federal District, Brazil, 68, Bd
Federated Malay States, 74, Jh
Fehmarn, 60B, Ca; 65F, Ba
Fehrbellin, 60A, Db
Felipinas, Islas (Philippine Is.), 41A, Kc
Feltre, 5, Ca; 86B, Ba
Fenestrelles, 53, Ge
Fenghwangcheng, 76B, Ca
Fentsch, 39B, Ba
Fer, Pointe au, 57, Ea
Ferette, 31A, Dd
Fergana, 61B, Ca
Ferghana, 6, Ja
Fergus, R., 15, Cd
Ferle (Firle), 13, Gf
Fermanagh, 49B, Db
Fermanagh, co., 37C
Fermo (Firmum), 5, Dc
Fermoy, 49B, Cd
Fernandina, 72, Dc
Fernando Poo, 80A, Dd
Ferns, 15, Ed
Ferozepore, 73, Ba
Ferozeshah, 73, Ba
Ferrara, 5, Cb; 29A, Dc
Ferrara, D. of (Este), 32A, Db
Ferreus (Orontes), R., 18C, Dc
Ferrol, 55B, Kb; 63, Aa
Ferry Land, 45A, Ga
Ferrybridge, 27, Ec
Feurs, 11, Fd
Fez, 9, Bf; 40, Jc; 80A, Ca
Fez, Sultanate of (Watasios), 34, Be
Fezensac, Co. of, 11, De
Fezzan, 6, Cc; 80A, Eb
Fiesole, 32A, Dc
Fife, 14, Ec
Fife, co., 37A, Cb; 49A, Cb
Fifth Cataract, 80B, Ad
Figeac, 17, Gf
Figueira da Foz, 63, Ab
Figueras, 63, Ga
Figuig, 80A, Ca
Fiji Is., 75C; 77, Ne
Filey, 3A, Fb
Finale, 54, Dd
Findhord, 49A, Cb
Findhorn, R., 37A, Cb
Findon, 49A, Cb
Fingoes, 81B, Dc
Finisterre, C., 63, Aa
Finland, 26, Ga; 88, La
Finland, G. of, 26, Gb
Finnish Peoples, 19, Ca
Finsiaolin, 76B, Ba
Finsteraarhorn, 29B, Cb
Finstingen, 39B, Db
Firmana, 23A, Db
Firmum (Fermo), 5, Dc
First Cataract, 80B, Ac
Fischhausen, 26, Ec
Fishers Hill, 72B, Aa
Fishguard, 55A, Ac
Fishkill, 57, Ec
Fitero, 22, Bc
Fitzalan, 28A, Db; 28B, Dc
Fitzgerald, 37B, Ec
Fitzgibbon, 37B, Cd
Fitzmaurice, 37B, Bd
Fitzroy, R., 77,Ce
Fiume, 39, Lf
Five Forks, 72B, Bb
Fivizzano, 32A, Db
Flanders, 46A, Bd
Flarchheim, 10, Dc
Flatbush, 57B
Flattery, C., 67C, Aa
Flavigny, 22, Cb
Fleet, R., 27A
Flensburg, 26, Cc; 60B, Ba
Fleurus, 38, Fc; 46B
Fleury, Languedoc, 53, Ef
Fleury, Sens, 22, Cb
Flinders, R., 77, Gf
Flint, 28A, Ca
Flint, co., 28A, Ca
Flint, R., 71F, Ca
Flodden, 28B, Cb
Flodden Field, 37A, Cc
Florchingen, 39B, Ca
Florence, Italy, 32E, Bb
Florence, U.S.A., 72, Ec
Florence, Rep. of, 32A, Dc
Flores, Azores, 55B, Hc
Flores, E. Indies, 52C, Bc
Florianopolis (Desterro), 68, Ee
Florida, 56, Bd; 72, Dd
Florida, C., 55B, Bd
Florida Terr., 67C, Ec
Florina, 86A, Cb; 88, Ke
Fluelen, 29B, Cb
Flushing, 46A, Cc
Fochabers, 37A, Cb
Focsani, 51, Fd; 78, Fc
Foggia, 23B, Ed; 32A, Fd
Föhr, 65F, Aa
Foix, 11, De; 17 ,Fg
Folchingeham (Folkingeham), 13, Fd
Folkstone, 13, He; 27, He
Fondi, 21A, Bb; 22, Ec
Fonseca, G. of, 43A, Dc
Fontaine, 46B
Fontainebleau, 47, Cc
Fontanet, 8A, Bb
Fontenay, 30, Ce
Fontenoy, 46A, Cd; 54, Cb
Fontevrault, 17, Ee
Font-Marigny, 22, Cb
Foochow, 25, Ld; 91, Ed
Forbach, 39B, Ca
Forbes, 37A, Cb
Forcalquier, 20, Fg; 30, Fg
Forchheim, 8, Eb, 22, Eb
Ford, 36, Cg
Forden, 3A, Cd
Foresta, 13, De
Forewic (Fordwich), 13, He
Forez, Co. of, 11, Ed
Forfar, 49A, Cb
Forfar, co., 37A, Cb
Forks, The, 69A, Da
Forli, 32A, Eb
Forlimpopoli, 21, Kf
Formentera, 23C, Fc
Formigny, 28D, Bb
Formosa (Taiwan), 91, Fd
Fornbi (Formby) 13, Cc
Fornovo, 32A, Db
Forres, 37A, Cb
Fort, 81D, Bb
Fort Albany, 70, Fb
Fort Alexander, 70, Eb
Fort Amsterdam, 45B, Bc
Fort Ann, 57, Eb
Fort Argyll, 56, Cd
Fort Armstrong, Mississippi Terr., 71F, Ba
Fort Armstrong, Pennsylvania, 57, Bc
Fort Assomption, 57C, Ab
Fort Assumption (Memphis), 56, Bc
Fort Augusta, Georgia, 56, Cd
Fort Augusta, Pennsylvania, 56, Db
Fort Augustus, 37A, Bb
Fort Bard, 65B, Ab
Fort Bariancas, 71F, Ba
Fort Barraux, 38, Ff
Fort Beafort, 81B, Cc
Fort Beauharnais, 56, Ab
Fort Beauregard, 72, Dc
Fort Bedford, 57, Bd
Fort Benton, 70, Cc
Fort Bird, 56, Db
Fort Blakely, 72, Cc
Fort Boise, 44, Cd
Fort Bowyer, 71F, Ba
Fort Brewerton, 57, Cb
Fort Bridger, 70, Cc
Fort Bull, 57, Db
Fort Bute (Manchac), 56, Ad
Fort Butte à la Rose, 72, Bc
Fort Caroline, 43A, Da
Fort Caswell, 72, Ec
Fort Chambly, 57, Ea
Fort Charlotte, 56, Bd
Fort Chartres, 56, Ac
Fort Chelmsford, 81D, Bb
Fort Chequemagon, 56, Ba
Fort Chipewyan, 70, Cb
Fort Chiswell, 57, Ae
Fort Christina (Newcastle), 45B, Bd
Fort Claiborne, 71F, Ba
Fort Clinton, New York, 57, Dc
Fort Clinton, Vermont, 57, Eb
Fort Cornwallis (Augusta), 57D, Ab
Fort Crèvecoeur, 56, Ab
Fort Crown Point, 56, Eb
Fort Cumberland, 57, Bd
Fort Dauphin, Canada, 44, Ec
Fort Dauphin, Madagascar, 80A, Hg
Fort de la Presentation, 56, Db 57, Da
Fort de Russy, 72, Bc
Fort Dearborn, 71C, Ab
FortDelaware, 72, Eb
Fort Deposit, 71F, Ba
Fort des Abitibis, 45A, Ba
Fort Detroit, 56, Cb
Fort Dobbs, 56, Cc
Fort Donelson, 72, Cb
Fort Dummer (Hinsdale), 57, Eb
Fort Duquesne (Fort Pitt), 57, Bc
Fort Edward, 57, Eb
Fort Erie, 71C, Cb; 71D
Fort Esperanza, 72, Ad
Fort Evelyn, 81D, Bb
Fort Frédéric, 56, Eb
Fort Frederica, 56, Cd
Fort Frederick (Port Elizabeth), 81B, Cc
Fort Frontenac, 57, Ca
Fort Gadsden (Negro), 71F, Ba
Fort Gaines, Alabama, 72, Cc
Fort Gaines, Georgia, 71F, Ca
Fort George, British Columbia, 44, Bc
Fort George, Natal, 81D, Bb
Fort George, New York, 57, Eb
Fort George, Ontario, 71D
Fort George, Oregon, 67C, Aa
Fort George, Scotland, 49A, Bb
Fort Gibson, 72, Ab
Fort Granby, 57D, Ab
Fort Halifax, 56, Fb
Fort Hall, 70, Cc
Fort Harris, 57, Cc
Fort Harrison, 71C, Ac
Fort Hatteras, 72, Eb
Fort Henry, Ohio, 56, Cc
Fort Henry, Tennessee, 72, Cb
Fort Herkimer, 57, Db
Fort Hunter, 56 Eb
Fort Independence, 57, Eb
Fort Jackson, Georgia, 72, Dc
Fort Jackson, Louisiana, 72, Cd
Fort Jackson, Mississippi Terr., 71F, Ba
Fort James, 81C, Ab
Fort Jefferson, 72, De
Fort Johnston, 72, Ec
Fort King George, 56, Cd
Fort la Baye, 56, Bb
Fort la Galette, 56, Db
Fort La Reine, 44, Ed
Fort Lamotte, 45A, Cb
Fort Lamy, 96B, Da
Fort Laramie, 67C, Ca
Fort Lawrence, 45A, Ea
Fort le Boeuf, 57, Bc
Fort Leavenworth, 72, Bb
Fort Lee, 57B
Fort Lifou, 52C, Bc
Fort Ligonier, 57, Bc
Fort Livingston, 72, Cd
Fort Loudoun, 56, Cc
Fort Louis, 56, Bd
Fort Loyal (Casco) (Falmouth), 45B, Db
Fort McAllister, 72, Dc
Fort McHenry, 71C, Cc
Fort Mackinac, 56, Ca
Fort McMurray, 70, Cb
Fort Macomb, 72, Cc
Fort Macon, 72, Ec
Fort McRee, 72, Cc
Fort Malden, 71C, Bb
Fort Mandant (Bismarck), 70, Dc
Fort Marion, 72, Dd
Fort Massac, 56, Bc
Fort Massachusetts, 72, Cc
Fort Maurepas, 44, Ec
Fort Meigs, 71C, Bb
Fort Miami, 56, Cb
Fort Mims, 71F, Ba
Fort Mitchell, 71F, Ca
Fort Monroe, 72, Eb
Fort Montgomery, 57, Dc
Fort Moore, 56, Cd
Fort Morgan, 72, Cc
Fort Motte, 57D, Ab
Fort Moultrie, 57D, Bb
Fort Mufflin, 57, Dd
Fort Napoleon, 81D, Bb
Fort Nassau, Moluccas, 52B, Aa
Fort Nassau, New Jersey, 45B, Bd
Fort Nassau (Fort Orange), 45B, Cb
Fort Necessity, 57, Bd
Fort New Elfsborg, 45B, Bd
Fort New Gothenburg, 45B, Bd
Fort New Korsholm (Chester), 45B, Bd
Fort Niagara, 57, Bb
Fort Norman, 70, Ba
Fort Nottingham, 81D, Ab
Fort Ontario, 57, Cb
Fort Orange (Fort (Nassau), 45B, Cb
Fort Orleans, 56, Ac
Fort Oswego, 57, Cb
Fort Pentagöet (Penobscot), 45B, Ea
Fort Pickens, 72, Cc
Fort Pike, 72, Cc
Fort Pillow, 72, Cb
Fort Pitt (Fort Duquesne), 57, Bc
Fort Pitt (Pittsburgh), 57A, Ca
Fort Powell, 72, Cc
Fort Presqu'ile, 57, Ab
Fort Prince George (Savannah), 56, Cd
Fort Providence, 70, Ca
Fort Prudhomme, 56, Bc
Fort Pulaski, 72, Dc
Fort Quiatanon, 57A, Ba
Fort Rae, 70, Ca
Fort Resolution, 70, Ca
Fort Richelieu, 45A, Ca
Fort Rouille (Fort Toronto), 56, Db
Fort Royal, 43A, Fc
Fort St. David, 59D
Fort St. Esprit (La Pointe), 56 Aa
Fort St. George, 59D
Fort St. Jean, 57, Ea
Fort St. John, 70, Bb
Fort St. Joseph, L. Huron, 45A Ab
Fort St. Joseph, L. Michigan, 56, Bb
Fort St. Louis, Illinois, 56, Bb
Fort St. Louis, Nova Scotia, 45A, Db
Fort St. Louis, Texas, 43A, Cb
Fort St. Philip, 72, Cd
Fort St. Philippe, 57A, Bd
Fort St. Therese, 45A, Ca
Fort Sandeman, 73, Aa
Fort Sandusky, 56, Cb
Fort Schlosser, 57, Bb
Fort Schuyler, 57, Db
Fort Scott, Georgia, 71F, Ca
Fort Scott, Kansas, 72, Bb
Fort Severn, 70, Fb
Fort Shevchenko, 61B, Aa
Fort Simpson, 70, Ba
Fort Smith, 72, Bb

Fort Snelling, 67C, Da
Fort Stanwix, 57, Db
Fort Stephenson, 71C, Bb
Fort Stoddard, 71F, Ba
Fort Strother, 71F, Ba
Fort Sumter, 72, Ec
Fort Taylor, 72, De
Fort Ticonderoga, 56, Eb
Fort Tombécbé (Fort York), 56, Bd
Fort Toronto (Fort Rouille), 56, Db
Fort Toulouse, 56, Bd
Fort Towson, 72, Ac
Fort Tuli, 81A, Cb
Fort Union, 70, Dc
Fort Vancouver, 44, Bd
Fort Venango, 57, Bc
Fort Victoria, Canada, 44, Bd
Fort Victoria, Natal, 81D, Bb
Fort Wagner, 72, Dc
Fort Walker, 72, Dc
Fort Washington, Maryland, 71C, Cc
Fort Washington, New Jersey, 57B
Fort Washita, 72, Ac
Fort Watson, 57D, Ab
Fort Wayne, 71C, Ab
Fort Wellington, 77, Ed
Fort Western, 56, Fb
Fort William, Bengal, 59C, Ec
Fort William, Canada, 70, Fc
Fort William, Scotland, 37A, Bb
Fort William Henry, 57, Eb
Fort Wiltshire, 81B, Cc
Fort Wrangell, 71B, Cb
Fort York (Fort Tombécbé), 56, Bd
Fort Yukon, 71A, Ca
Fortaleza (Ceara), 68, Fc
Forteviot, 49A, Cb
Forth, R., 28B, Aa
Forth, Firth of, 14, Fc
Fortore, R., 21A, Cb
Fossalta, 20, Jf
Fosse Way, 3A, Ed
Fotheringhay, 27, Fd
Fougères, 20, Cd; 28D, Bb
Fountains, 36, Ec
Four Cantons, L. of the, 29B, Cb
Fourth Cataract, 80B, Ad
Fowey, 48B, Ad
Foyle, L., 15, Da
Foyle, R., 37B, Db
Framlingham, 27, Hd
France, I. de, Indian Ocean, 58, Me
France, King of, 20, De
France Antarctique, 41B, Ef
Franche Comté, 30, Fe
Franci, 2, Ec
Francia, 8B, Bb; 11, Eb
Franconia, 10, Cc
Frankenthal, 38, Hd
Frankfort, U.S.A., 72, Db
Frankfurt, R. Main, 10, Cc
Frankfurt, R. Oder, 21, Lb
Frankfurt, G.D. of, 65B, Aa
Frankish Empire, 8, Cb
Frankish Kingdom, 4A, Cb
Franklin, 72, Cb
Franklin, terr., 70, Ga
Franks, 2A, Ba; 8C, Ba
Franz Josef Land, 69B
Frascati (Tusculum), 22A
Fraser, R., 70, Bb
Fraserburgh, 49A, Cb
Fraustadt, 31, Mc
Fraxinet, 11, Ge
Fraxinetum, 23A, Ab
Fray Bentos, 68, Df
Frazer, 37A, Bb
Fredericia, 65F, Aa
Frederick, 72B, Ba
Fredericksburg, Virginia, 72B, Ba
Fredericksburg, W. Africa, 81C, Dd
Frederickstown, 57, Cd
Fredericton, 56, Fa; 71, Hc
Frederiksstein, 50, Cb
Fredrikshald, 51, Cb
Fredrikshamn, 62, Ha
Freeman's Farm, 57, Eb
Freeport, 70, Fc
Freetown, 81C, Bc
Freiberg, 53, Kb
Freiburg, Germany, 31, Kc
Freiburg, Switzerland, 10, Be; 29A, Ba
Freising, 10, Dd; 31B, Cb
Fréjus, 22, Dc; 38, Gg
Fremantle, 77, Bh
Fremington, 27, Be
French, R., 45A, Aa
French Congo, 80A, Ee
French Empire, 62, Cc
French Equatorial Africa, 80A, Ed
French Frigate I., 75, Gc
French Guiana, 68, Db
French Guinea, 81C, Bb
French Indo-China, 90, Bc
French Ivory Coast, 81C, Cc
French Mills, 57, Da
French Post, 57A, Bc
French Rep., 51, Bd
French Somaliland, 80B, Ce
French West Africa, 80A, Cc
Frenchtown, 71C, Bb
Fresnillo, 43A, Bb
Frew, Ford of, 49A, Bb
Fribourg (Freiburg), 29B, Bb
Fribourg, canton, 29B, Bb
Friedberg, Austria, 31, Me
Friedberg, Germany, 53, Hb
Friedland, Bohemia, 47, Fb
Friedland, East Prussia, 60A, Ha
Friedrich Wilhelmshafen (Madang), 77, Hc
Friedrichstadt, 65F, Aa
Friendly (Tonga) Is., 75, Gf
Friesach, 21, Le
Friesland, 46A, Ea
Frio, C., 68, Ee
Frisia, 8, Da; 20, Gb
Frisian Is., 55A, Fb
Frisians, 2A, Ba; 7A, Ea
Frisii, 2, Ec
Fritzlar, 8, Da; 10, Cc
Friuli, 5, Da
Friuli, M. of, 23B, Da
Frobisher, B., 71, Ha
Frome, 7B, Bc
Fronsac, 11, Cd; 20, Cf
Front Royal, 72B, Aa
Frontenai, 20, Ce
Froschweiler, 76A, Db
Frotesham (Frodsham), 13, Dc
Frutigen, 29B, Bb
Fuego, vol., 43A, Cc
Fuente Guinaldo, 63, Bb
Fuenterrabia, 23C, Ea; 63, Ea
Fuentes, de Onoro, 63, Bb
Fukuoka, 91, Gc
Fulda, 10, Cc
Fulda, R., 10, Cc; 20, Hc
Fulford, 13, Ec
Fulham, 7C, Cc
Funchal, 55B, Jc
Fundy, B. of, 45A, Da
Fünen, 51, Cb; 65F, Ba
Fünfkirchen, 22, Fb; 39, Ne
Furka Pass, 29B, Cb
Furnes, 46A, Bc
Furness, 36, Cc
Fürstenberg, 30, He
Fürstenwalde, 22, Ea
Fürth, Bavaria, 38, Jd
Fürth, Bohemia, 29A, Ea
Fusan, 74, Le
Fushun, 91, Fb
Füssen, 29A, Db
Futhernesse (Furness), 13, Cb
Futuna Is., 75, Fe
Fyne, L., 14, Cc
Fyvie, 37A, Cb

GABARAS B., 45A, Fa
Gabarret, 20, Dg
Gabbards, 55A, Dc
Gabes, 6, Cb; 80A, Da
Gabon, 96D, De
Gabrova, 78, Ed
Gabun, 76, Kd
Gadara, 18C, Cf
Gades, 2, Bf
Gadsden, 72, Cc
Gaeta, 5, Dd
Gaikas, 81B, Cc
Gaikwar, 59A, Bc
Gaines Mill, 72B, Bb
Gainesburg (Gainsborough), 13, Fc
Gainesville, 72B, Ba
Gainsborough, 48A, Cc
Gairloch, 49A, Bb
Galadi, 96A, Bb
Galapagos Is., 75, Le
Galata, 86D
Galati, 61, Be
Galatia, 2, Kf
Galatz, 51, Fd; 78, Fc
Galekas, 81B, Dc
Galford, 7B, Ac
Galich, 19, Cc
Galicia, Poland, 33C, Eb
Galicia, Spain, 63, Ba
Galicians, 85, Ad
Galilee, Sea of, 18C, Cf
Galitch, 19, Ga
Galla, 80A, Gd
Gallabat, 80B, Be
Galla-Sidamo, 96A, Ab
Galle, 92, Ef
Gallegos, 68, Ch
Gallia, 2, Dd
Gallinas, C., 43A, Ec
Gallipoli, Italy, 21A, Eb
Gallipoli, Turkey, 78, Fe
Galloway, 14, Db
Gallura, 23B, Bd
Galtellia, 23B, Bd
Galty Mts., 15, Cd
Galveston, 72, Bd
Galway, 37B, Bc; 49B, Bc
Galway, co., 37C; 49B, Bc
Galway B., 37B, Bc
Gamalama, 52B, Aa
Gambia, 81C, Ab; 96B, Aa
Gambia, R., 81C, Bb
Gambier Is., 75, Jf
Gandersheim, 10, Cc
Gandhara, 1, Kd
Gandia, 23D, Ec
Gando, 80A, Dc
Ganga, R., 91, Bd
Ganganorum Prom., 3A, Bd
Ganges, R., 25, Hd; 73, Ec
Gangra, 16, Jd
Gap, 22, Dc; 30, Gf; 38, Gf
Garamantes, 6, Cc
Garda, L., 5, Cb
Gardelegen, 20, Jb
Gardner, L., 77, Fh
Garfagna, 32E, Ba
Gargano, Mte., 5, Fd
Garhwal, 73, Ca
Garlannonum (Burgh Castle), 3A, Hd
Garigliano, R., 5, Dd
Garonne, R., 11, Dd
Garoua, 96B, Db
Gartagnana, 23B, Cb
Gartz, 31, Lb; 39, Lb
Gascony, D. of, 11, Ce
Gascoyne, R., 77, Af
Gaspé, 45A, Da
Gaspé, C., 45A, Ea
Gaspereau, 45A, Ea
Gassentino, 32E, Bb
Gastein, 21, Ke
Gatesheved (Gateshead), 13, Eb
Gatinais, 17, Gd
Gatinais, Co. of, 11, Eb
Gatton, 27, Fe
Gauhati, 92, Gb
Gaul, Pref. of, 2, Dd
Gaur, 52A, Cb
Gava, 92, Fc
Gavle, 50, Da
Gavre, 46A, Cd
Gawilgarh, 73, Cc
Gaza, 9, Jf; 18C, Bg; 79, Fd
Gaziantep, 79, Gc
Gdansk, 89, Jc
Gdow, 33C, Eb
Gdynia, 87, Db
Gedaref, 80B, Be
Gedrosia, 1, Je
Geelong, 77, Gl
Geelvink, B., 77, Fb
Geestemünde, 65D, Aa
Gefle, 26, Ea
Geissberg, 76A, Eb
Gelderland, 46A, Eb
Geldern, 20, Gc
Gelligaer, 3A, Ce
Gellivare, 88, Ka
Gelnhausen, 20, Hc; 65A, Aa
Gemar, 39B, Db
Gembloux, 46B
Gemlik, 78, Ge
Gemmi Pass, 29B, Bb
Genadental, 81B, Ac
Genappe, 46B
Generality, Lands of the, 46A, Dc
Geneva, 11, Gc; 29B, Ab
Geneva, L. of, 29B, Ab
Gengenbach, 53, Hc
Genoa (Genova), 5, Bb
Genoa, eccl. prov., 22, Dc
Genoa, G. of, 5, Bb
Genoa, Rep. of, 32A, Cb
Genova (Genoa), 5, Bb
George, 81B, Bc
George, L., 45A, Cb; 57, Eb
George, R., 71, Hb
Georgetown (Demerara), 43D, Gd; 68B, Ba
Georgetown, Delaware, 57, Dd
Georgetown, S. Carolina, 57D, Bb
Georgia, U.S.A., 43C, Ca; 56, Cd
Georgia, U.S.S.R., 19, Gd; 25, Db; 79, Hb
Georgian B., 45A, Aa
Gepidae, 2, Hd : 4A, Gb
Gera, 21, Kc; 65B, Ba
Gerace, 22, Fd
Geraldton, 77, Ag
Gerba, 6, Cb
Geringswalde, 22, Ea
German Confederation, 69A, Kb
German East Africa, 80A, Ge
German Flats, 57, Db
German New Guinea, 77, Hc
German South-West Africa, 81A, Ac
Germani, 1, Db
Germanna, 56, Dc
Germantown, 57, Dc
Germany, 87, Cb
Germany, King of, 16, Db; 20, Jc
Germiyan, 19, Ee
Gernemutha (Yarmouth), 13, Hd
Gerolstein, 53, Gb
Gerona, 11, Ef; 63, Gb
Gerresheim, 22, Da
Gerrha, 1, He
Gerrhael, 1, Ge
Gersau, 29B, Ca
Gerstungen, 10, Cc
Gertruidenberg, 46A, Dc
Gesoriacum (Boulogne), 3A, Hf
Gettysburg, 72B, Ba
Gévaudan, Co. of, 11, Ed
Gèvres, 53, Dc
Gex, 38, Fe
Ghadames, 80A, Da; 96C, Cb
Ghana, 96B, Bb
Ghassanids, 6A, Bb
Ghat, 80A, Eb
Ghazni, 25, Fc; 73, Aa
Ghent, 17, Gc; 46A, Cc
Gheria, 59A, Ec
Gheriah, 59A, Bd
Ghillinges (Gilling), 13, Eb
Ghomera, 6, Ab
Giants Castle, 81D, Ab
Gibelet (Byblos), 18C, Cd
Gibelin, 18C, Bg
Gibraltar, Europe, 23D, Cd; 63A
Gibraltar, S. America, 43A, Ed
Gibraltar, Str. of, 63A
Glen, 17, Gc; 30, Ee
Giengen, 20, Jd; 38, Jd
Giessen, 60B, Bc
Gifford, 28A, Bc
Gijon, 23D, Ca
Gila, R., 67D, Bb; 70, Cd
Gilbert Is., 90, Ed
Gilbert, R., 77, Ge
Gildeford (Guildford), 13, Fe
Gilgit, 92, Ca
Gilolo, 52C, Ca
Gimborn, 60A, Ac
Gingee, 59D
Ginginhlovo, 81D, Bb
Giornico, 29B, Cb
Giovenazzo, 21A, Db
Gipewiz (Ipswich), 13, Hd
Girgeh, 80B, Ab
Girgenti (Agrigentum), 5, Df
Gironde, R., 17, Ef; 28C, Bd
Girvan, 49A, Bc
Gisborne, 77A
Gisors, 20, Dd; 83A, Ab
Gitschin, 39, Lc
Giurgevo, 78, Ed
Givelcestre (Ilchester), 13, Df
Givet, 53, Fb; 83A, Ca
Giza, 93, Cd
Gjevgelu, 86A, Da
Gladbach, 83A, Da
Gladstone, 77, If
Glama, R., 12, Ga
Glamorgan, Lordship of, 27, Ce
Glandève, 20, Gg; 22, Dc
Glarus, 29B, Da
Glarus, canton, 29B, Db
Glasgow, 14, Dd
Glasgow, bp., 14A, Bc
Glastingeberie (Glastonbury), 13, De
Glastonbury, 27, De
Glatz, 21, Mc; 39, Mc
Glatz, co., 39, Mc
Glauchau, 39C, Cc; 53, Kb
Gleichen, 39C, Ac
Glen Affric, 14, Db
Glen Coe, 49A, Bb
Glen Elchaig, 49A, Bb
Glen Finnan, 49A, Bb
Glen Garry, 14, Dc
Glen Lyon, 49A, Bb
Glen Moriston, 14, Db
Glen Orchy, 49A, Bb
Glen Shiel, 49A, Bb
Glen Spean, 14, Dc
Glencoe, Natal, 81D, Bb
Glendalough, 15, Ec
Glenlochar, 3A, Bb
Glenluce, 36, Bc; 49A, Bc
Glenmore, 14, Db
Glevum (Gloucester), 3A, De
Glogau, 21, Mc
Glokhov, 19, Eb
Gloucester, England, 27, De
Gloucester, Virginia, 45B, Ae
Gloucester (Cape Ann), 45B, Db; 57, Fb
Gloucester, bp., 36, Df
Gloucester, co., 27, De
Glowecestre (Gloucester), 13, De
Glowecestrescire (Gloucestershire), 13, De
Glücksburg, 65F, Aa
Glückstadt, 38, Hb
Glywising, 7B, Bc
Gmünd, 20, Hd; 38, Hd
Gmunden, 39, Ke
Gnesen, 21, Mb
Gnesen, eccl. prov., 22, Fa
Goa, 73, Bd
Goba, 96A, Ab
Gobbio, 23B, Dc
Godavari, R., 25, He; 73, Cd
Godesberg, 87, Bb
Godfrey of Bouillon, 16, Gd
Gödöllö, 33C, Db
Godwin, 12, Dd
Goes, 46A, Cc
Gogra, R., 73, Db
Golas, 68, Dd
Goias, st., 68, Ed
Gok Tepe, 61, Jg
Gokcha, L., 19, Hd
Golconda, 52A, Bc
Golconda Coast, 52A, Cc
Gold Coast, 81C, Dc
Goldelminge, (Godalming), 13, Fe
Golden Gate, Constantinople, 18E
Golden Gate, Jerusalem, 18D
Golden Horde, 25, Da; 61, Fe
Golden Horde, Khanate of the, 19, Gb
Golden Horn, 18E
Golden Vale, 15, Cd
Goldenkron, 22, Eb
Goldsboro, 72, Eb
Goldsborough, 3A, Fb
Golea, 80A, Da
Göllersdorf, 39, Md
Gollheim, 29A, Ba
Gollnow, 26, Ec
Golspie, 49A, Bb
Gommern, 39C, Ba
Gonave, 43A, Ec
Gondar, 80B, Be; 96A, Aa
Gondrecourt, 39B, Bb
Gondwana, 52A, Cb
Gonzaga, 20, Jf
Gonzaga (Marq. of Mantua), 32A, Db
Good Hope, C. of (Tormentoso), 35, Kf; 81B, Ac
Gooshland, 57, Ce
Gooty, 59A, Cd
Gorakhpur, 73, Db
Gordon, 37A, Bc; 37A, Cb
Gordon Castle, 37A, Cb
Gordonsville, 57, Bd; 72B, Aa
Gorée, 81C, Ab
Gorinchem, 46A, Dc
Gorizia, 23B, Db; 84, Ec
Görlitz, 21, Lc
Gorski, 84, Ld
Görz, 21, Kf; 39, Ke
Görz, Co. of, 39, Ke
Gorze, 39B, Ba
Goshen, 81A, Bc
Goslar, 10, Dc
Gosselies, 46B
Göteborg, 87, Ca
Gotha, 30, Jc; 54, Eb
Gothenburg, 47, Ea; 50, Cb
Gothia, Marq. of, 11, Ee
Gotland, 26, Eb; 34, Ea
Gottesgab, 39C, Cc
Göttingen, 26, Dc; 38, Hc
Gottorp, 51, Bc
Gourdon, 17, Ff
Gouritz, R., 81B, Bc
Governors I., 56B
Gower, 27, Be
Gowna, L., 15, Dc
Goya, 68, De
Graaff Reinet, 81B, Cc
Graaff Reinet, dist., 81B, Cc
Gracias á Dios, C., 43A, Dc
Gradisca, 32A, Eb; 86B, Db
Grado, 32D, Cb
Grafenau, 31, Kd
Graham, 37A, Bb
Graham Land, 69C
Grahamstown, 81B, Cc
Graian Alps, 29A, Bc
Grain Coast, 81C, Bc
Grammont, 22, Ca; 46A, Cd
Grampians, 14, Dc
Gran, 22, Fb; 39, Ne
Gran, eccl. prov., 22, Fb
Gran, R., 31, Nd
Gran Chaco, 68, Ce
Granada, Nicaragua, 43A, Dc
Granada, Spain, 23C, Dd; 63, Dd
Granada, eccl. prov., 22, Bd
Granada, King of, 23C, Dd
Granadine Confederation, 68, Bb
Granard, 15, Dc
Grand Canal, 25, Lc
Grand Canyon, 70, Cd

Grand Gulf, 72C, Aa
Grand I., New York, 71D
Grand I., Vermont, 57, Ea
Grand Lahu, 81C, Cc
Grand Portage, 44, Ed
Grand Pré, 45A, Ea
Grand, R., 70, Dd
Grand Tartary, 42, Ob
Grande Chartreuse, 22, Db
Grande Gette, R., 46B
Grandpré, 30, Fd
Grandson, 29B, Ab
Granson, 30, Ge
Grant, 37A, Bb
Grantham, 13, Fd
Grantown, 49A, Cb
Granville, 55A, Cd
Grappa, Mt., 86B, Bb
Grasse, 22, Dc
Graudenz, 62, Fb
Grauer Bund, 29B, Db
Graus, 23C, Fa
Grave, 46A, Ec
Gravelines, 46A, B c
Gravelotte, 76A, Cb
Gravesend, 45B, Cc; 57B
Gravina, 21A, Db
Gravosa, 39, Ng
Gray, 38, Fe; 76A, Cc
Grays Inn, 27A
Graz, 21, Le; 29A, Fb
Great Abaco I., 43A, Eb
Great Australian Bight, 77, Dh
Great Bahama I., 43A, Eb
Great Bear L., 70, Ca
Great Belt, 65F, Ba
Great Bridge, 57, Ce
Great Bulgaria, 19, Jb
Great Cayman, 43A, Dc
Great Dividing Ra., 77, Hf
Great Exuma, 43A, Eb
Great Fish, R., Cape Prov., 81B, Cc
Great Fish, R., S.W. Africa, 81B, Aa
Great Inagua, 43A, Eb
Great Karroo, 81B, Bc
Great Kei, R., 81B, Dc
Great Lakes, 69B
Great Manitoulin I., 45A, Aa
Great Marlow, 48A, Cd
Great Namaqualand, 81A, Ac
Great Namaquas, 81B, Aa
Great Ouse, R., 27, Gd
Great Pedee, R., 45A, Bd
Great Poland, 39, Mb
Great Russian, 85, Kb
Great St. Bernard Pass, 29A, Bc
Great Salt L., 70, Cc
Great Slave L., 70, Ca
Great Slave, R., 70, Ca
Great Whale, R., 70, Gb
Great Zab, R., 6A, Ca
Greater Antilles, 43A, Ec
Greece, 78, Dg
Green B., 56, Ba
Green Mts., 45A, Cb
Green, R., 70, Cd
Green Bay, 70, Fc
Greenbrier, R., 57, Ad
Greencastle, 37B, Eb
Greenland, 69B
Greenlaw, 48A, Bb
Greenock, 49A, Bc
Greensboro, 72, Eb
Greenwich, 45B, Cc
Greifswald, 22, Ea; 39, Ka
Greiz, 39C, Cc; 53, Kb
Grenada, 43A, Fc
Grenadines, 43A, Fc
Grenoble, 11, Fd
Grentebrige (Cambridge), 13, Gd
Grentebrigescire (Cambridgeshire), 13, Gd
Gretna, 28B, Bb; 49A, Cc
Greymouth, 77A
Greytown, 81D, Bb
Grèzes, 17A, Dd
Griffen, 39, Le
Griffin's Wharfe, 56B
Grimesbi (Grimsby), 13, Fc
Grimsby, 27, Fc
Grimsel Pass, 29B, Cb
Grinstead, 27, Fe
Griqualand East, 81B, Db
Griqualand West, 81B, Bb
Griquas, 81B, Bb
Griquatown, 81B, Bb
Gris Nez, C., 55A, Dc
Grisingen, 30, Hd
Grisons (Rhaetian Leagues), 29B, Db
Grobe, 22, Ea
Gröbming, 31, Ke; 39, Ke
Grodno, 26, Fc; 60A, Jb
Groll, 46A, Fb
Groningen, 46A, Fa
Groningen, prov., 46A, Fa
Grosmont, 28A, Dc
Grosotto, 86B, Aa
Gross Jägersdorf, 51, Ec
Gross Mariazell, 22, Fb
Grossbeeren, 60B, Db
Grosseto, 20, Jg; 22, Ec
Grosswardein, 33C, Eb
Grotska, 33C, Ec; 51, Ee
Grozny, 88, Pe
Gruffyd ap Llywelyn, Pr. of, 12, Dc
Gruyères, 29B, Bb
Guadalajara, Mexico, 43A, Bb
Guadalajara, Spain, 63, Db
Guadalcanal, 77, Jc; 90, Dd
Guadalquivir, R., 63, Cd
Guadalupe, 22, Ad
Guadarrama, Sierra de, 63, Db
Guadeloupe, 43A, Fc
Guadenhutten, 56, Cb
Guadiana, R., 63, Bd
Guadix, 22, Bd; 23C, Dd
Guam, 40, Qd; 90, Dc
Guanahani, 40, Fc
Guanajuato, 43A, Bb
Guapora, R., 68, Cd
Guaporé, 94, Df
Guarda, 22, Ac; 63, Bb
Guastalla, 32A, Db
Guatemala, 43A, Cc
Guatulco, 42, Ed
Guaviare, R., 68, Cb
Guayaquil, 68, Ac
Guben, 31, Lc
Guelders, 60A, Ac
Guelders, Co. of, 46C, Ba
Guelders, D. of, 31A, Cb
Gueldres, 46A, Fc
Guérande, 30, Be
Gueret, 30, De
Guerminstre (Warminster), 13, De
Guernsey, 17, Dd
Guiana, 68, Db
Guienne, D. of (Aquitaine), 11, Dd
Guildford, 27, Fe
Guilford, 45B, Cc
Guilford Court House, 57, Be
Guillon, 28C, Ec
Guimaraes, 23D, Ab
Guinea, 81C, Dc; 96B, Aa
Guinea, G. of, 94, Te
Guinegate, 30, Ec
Guines, 11, Da; 17, Fc
Guingamp, 22, Bb; 38, Bd
Guipuzcoa, 23C, Da
Guise, 17, Gd; 30, Ed; 53, Ec
Guitres, 22, Db
Gujarat, 25, Gd; 73, Bc
Gujranwala, 92, Ca
Gujrat, 73, Ba
Gumti, R., 73, Db
Gundwana, 59A, Cc
Güns, 39, Me
Guntur, 59A, Cd; 92, Ed
Gurev, 61, He
Gurgan, 93, Gb
Guria, 79, Hb
Gurk, 22, Eb
Gurkhas, 73, Db
Gurramkonda, 59A, Ce
Gurupa, 41B, Dd
Gusau, 96B, Ca
Güstrow, 39, Kb
Guthrum's King., 7C, Db
Guyenne, 20, Df; 28C, Cd
Gwadar, 92, Ab
Gwalior, 25, Gd; 73, Cb
Gwent, 28A, Dc
Gwynedd, 13, Bc; 28A, Dc
Gympie, 77, Ig
Gyrwe (Jarrow), 13, Eb

HAARLEM, 46A, Db
Habesh (Abyssinia), 6, Ed
Habitancum (Risingham), 3A, Da
Habsburg, 11, Gc; 29B, Ca
Hackensack, 57B
Haddeby, 12, Gc
Haddington, 49A, Cc
Haddington, co., 49A, Cc
Hadhramaut, 93, Ff
Hadjach, 50, Gc
Hadrianopolis, 2, Je
Hadrian's Wall, 3C
Hafir, 6, Fc
Hafrsfjord, 12, Fb
Hafsids, 24, Eg
Hafsids (Sultanate of Tunis), 34, De
Hagenau, 20, Gd; 29A, Ba
Hagerstown, 72, Eb
Hague, C. de la, 55A, Cd
Hague, The, 46A, Db
Hagustalham (Hexesham) (Hexham), 13, Db
Haifa, 18C, Cf; 93, Cc
Hail, 93, Ed
Hailes, 36, Ef
Hainan, 25, Ke; 91, De
Hainau, 60B, Ec
Hainaut, 10, Ac; 46A, Cd
Haine, R., 46B
Haine's Bluff, 72C, Aa
Haingeham (Hedingham), 13, Gd
Haiti, 43A, Ec
Hakodate, 91, Hb
Halberstadt, 10, Dc
Haleb (Aleppo), 18C, Eb
Halesowen, 36, De
Halifax, England, 48A, Cc
Halifax, N. Carolina, 57, Ce
Halifax, Nova Scotia, 45A, Eb
Hall, 20, Hd; 53, Hc
Halland, 26, Db; 47, Ea
Halle, 10, Ec; 31B, Ca
Hallue, 76A, Bb
Halmahera, 91, Ff
Halmstad, 26, Db
Halton, 27, Dc
Halys, R., 18A, Ea; 24, Jf
Ham, 30, Ed
Hama, 18C, Dc; 93, Db
Hamadan, 6A, Db; 93, Fc
Hamar, 26, Da
Hamburg, 10, Cb
Hamdan, 6, Fd
Hamdanids, King of, 6B, Fa
Hami, 74, Hd
Hamid, 19, Ee
Hamilton, Canada, 70, Fc
Hamilton, Scotland, 37A, Bc
Hamilton Inlet, 71, Jb
Hamilton, R., 71, Hb
Hamm, 60A, Ac
Hammadids, 16, Ce
Hampshire, 27, Ec
Hampton, New Hampshire, 45B, Db
Hampton, Virginia, 45B, Ae
Hampton Roads, 72B, Bb
Hamton, 7B, Cc
Han Dominions, 1, Od
Hanau, 29A, Ca; 30. Hc
Hanchong, 76B, Ba
Han-chung, 1, Nd
Handa, 96A, Ca
Hangchow, 74, Lf; 91, Ec
Hangchow (Quinsay) (Lingan), 25, Mc
Hanging Rock, 57D, Aa
Hankow, 74, Ke; 90, Bb
Hanoi, 25, Kd; 91, Dd
Hanover, Germany, 26, Cc
Hanover, Virginia, 57, Ce; 72B, Bb
Hanover, El., 53, Ha
Hanover Junction, 72B, Bb
Hantescire (Hampshire), 13, Ee
Hantune (Southampton), 13, Ef
Harar, 96A, Bb
Harar, prov., 96A, Bb
Harbin (Pinkiang), 90, Ca; 91, Fb
Harcourt, 17, Fd; 53, Cc
Hard Times, 72C, Aa
Hardangerfjord, 12, Fb
Hardknot, 3A, Cb
Harenc, 18C, Db
Harfleur, 30, Dd; 53, Dc
Harlech, 27, Bd
Harmazia, 1, He
Harold, 12, Dd
Harper, 96B, Bb
Harper's Ferry, 56, Dc; 72B, Ba
Harran, 6A, Ba
Harris, 14, Bb; 37A, Ab
Harrisburg, 72, Ea
Harrismith, 81A, Cc; 81D, Ab
Harrison's Landing, 72B, Bb
Harrodsburg, 56, Cc
Hartford, 45B, Cc
Hartland, 36 Bg
Hartmannswillerkopf, 83B, Bb
Harts, R., 81A, Cc
Harvard College, 56B
Harwich, 27, He
Harz, 60A, Cc
Harz, mts., 10, Dc
Harzburg, 10, Dc
Hasselt, 26, Cc; 83A, Ca
Hastenbeck, 60A, Bb
Hastings, 27, Gf
Hastinges (Hastings), 13, Gf
Hatay, 79, Gc
Hatfield, 7B, Cc
Hatteras, C., 45A, Bf; 57, Df
Hattin, 18C, Cf
Haughmond, 36, De
Haura, 93, Fg
Hauraki, G., 77A
Hauterive, 22, Db
Havana, 43A, Db
Havelberg, 10, Eb; 30, Kb
Haverfordwest, 27, Ae
Haverhill, 45B, Db
Havre, 76A, Ab
Havre de Grâce (Le Havre), 38, Dd
Havre de Grace, Maryland, 71C, Cc
Haw, R., 57, Be
Hawaii, 75D, Cc
Hawaiian Is., 90, Gb
Hawarden, 13, Cc; 27, Cc
Hawke B., 77A
Hawkes Bay, 77A
Hawick, 28B, Cb
Hay, 28A, Cb
Hayingen, 30, Hd
Haymarket, 27A
Heard I., 95, Qh
Heathfield, 7A, Ca
Hebrides, 37A, Ab; 49A, Ab
Hebron, Palestine, 18C, Cg
Hebron, Transvaal, 81A, Cc
Hechingen, 60B, Cc; 65B, Ab
Heda (Hythe), 13, He
Hedgley Moor, 27, Da
Hedmark, 12, Ga
Hedon, 27, Fc
Heidelburg, 29A, Ca
Heilbronn, 29A, Ca
Heiligenkreuz, 22, Fb
Heiligerlee, 46A, Fa
Heilsberg, 26, Fc; 60A, Ha
Heinsberg, 46C, Cb
Hejaz, 6, Fc; 80B, Bc
Hejer, 6, Fc
Helder, 46A, Db
Heldernesse (Holderness), 13, Fc
Helena, Arkansas, 72, Bc
Helena, Montana, 70, Cc
Heletune (Halton), 13, Dc
Heligoland, 55A, Ga; 60A, Aa
Heligoland Bight, 55A, Ga
Heliopolis (Baalbek), 18C, De
Hellas, 9, Ge
Helles, C., 86D
Hellespont, 34, He
Hellespontus, 2, Jf
Helluland, 35, Gb
Helmsdale, 49A, Ca
Helsingborg, 26, Db
Helsingfors, 26, Fa
Helsingland, 26, Ea
Helsingor, 26, Db
Helsinki, 87, Ea
Helston, 27, Af
Helvetian Rep., 65A, Ab
Hemmingstedt, 26, Cc; 30, Ha
Hempstead, 45B, Cc
Hendaye, 53, Cf
Hengistdun, 7B, Ac
Hennebont, 28C, Ac; 55A, Be
Hennersdorf, 60A, Ec
Henrico, 45B, Ae
Henry, C., 45B, Be
Heppenheim, 65C, Ab
Heraclea, Iconium, 16, Je
Heraclea, Nicaea, 19, Ed
Heraklea, 18C, Ba
Herat, 25, Fc; 61B, Bb
Herbertshöhe (Kokopo), 77, Ib
Herculis Prom., 3A, Be
Herdeslege, (Eardisley). 13, Dd
Hereford, 13, Dd
Hereford, bp., 36, De
Hereford, Co., 27, Dd
Herefordscire (Herefordshire), 13, Dd
Hereke, 33A, Cb
Herero, 80A, Ef
Héricourt, 31A, Dd
Héristal, 7A, Eb; 8, Da
Herjedalen, 26, Da
Hermannstadt (Sibin), 19, Cc
Hermannstadt, Hungary, 24 Gd; 78, Ec
Hermitage, 28B, Cb
Hermon, Mt., 18C, De
Hernösand, 26, Ea
Hersfeld, 10, Cc; 30, Hc
Herteforde (Hertford), 13, Fe
Hertefordscire (Hertfordshire), 13, Fe
Hertford, 27, Fe
Hertford, co., 27, Fe
Heruli, 2, Kd
Hervey Is., 75, He
Herzegovina, 39, Mg; 78, Ad
Hesdin, 53, Eb
Hesse, 10, Cc
Hesse, G. D. of, 65C, Aa
Hesse, Land. of, 30, Hc
Hesse-Cassel, Land., 38, Hc
Hesse-Darmstadt, Land., 38, Hc
Hessen, 60B, Bc
Hevellians, 10, Eb
Heversham, 7B, Ba
Hexham, 27, Db; 36A
Heytesbury, 27, De
Hibernia, 2, Bc
Hierapolis, 2, Lf; 4B, Kd
Hierosolyma, 1, Fd
High Bridge, 49A, Bb
High Street, 3A, Db
Hiiumaa, 87, Ea
Hildburghausen, 39C, Ac
Hildesheim, 10, Cb
Hilla, 93, Ec
Hillsborough, 57, Be
Hilo, 75D, Dc
Himachal Pradesh, 92, Da
Himalaya Mts., 73, Ca
Hims, 6A, Bb
Hindon, 27, De
Hindu Kush, 59A, Ba
Hindu States, 25, Ge
Hindustan, 40, Nc
Hingham, 45B, Db
Hinsdale (Fort Dummer), 57, Eb
Hippo, 4A, Dd; 8, Dd
Hippo Regius, 2, Ef
Hira, 6A, Cb
Hiroshima, 91, Gc
Hirschau, 22 Db
Hirschberg, 39, Lc; 60A, Ec
Hirson, 83A, Cb
Hirsova, 78, Fc
Hispania, 2, Be
Hispaniola (Española), 43A, Ec
Hit, 6A, Cb
Hitchin, 36, Ff
Hlobane, 81D, Ba
Hlubi Kaffirs, 81D, Ab
Hobart, 77, Hj
Hobkirk's Hill, 57D, Aa
Hoboken, 45B, Bc
Hochkirch, 60A, Ec
Hochschwab, 29A, Fb
Höchst, 38, Hc
Höchstadt, 29A, Da
Hodeida, 80B, Ce; 93, Eg
Hofburg, 20, Gd
Hog I., 56B
Hohe Tauern, 29A, Eb
Höhen, 10, Ec
Hohenburg, Bavaria, 20, Jd
Hohenburg, Swabia, 20, Hd
Hohenfriedeberg, 60A, Fc
Hohenlinden, 29A, Da
Hohenlohe, 20, Jd
Hohenzollern, 38, Hd
Hohnstein, 60A, Cc
Hokianga B., 77A
Hokkaido, 91, Hb
Holborn, 27A
Holkar, 73, Cc
Holkar and Sindhia, 59A, Cc
Hollabrünn, 29A, Ga
Holland, Co. of, 17, Hb; 46A, Db
Holland, dist., England, 13, Gd
Holland, King. of, 65B, Aa
Holly Springs, 72, Cc
Holme Cultram, 36, Cc
Holme St. Benet, 36, He
Holstein, 10, Ca
Holt, 28A, Da; 48B, Bc
Holy I., 12, Dc; 36, Eb
Holy Roman Empire, 20, Jd
Holy Sepulchre, Church of the, 18D
Holyhead, 3A, Bc
Holyrood, 14, Ed
Homburg, 30, Gc; 39B, Ca
Home, 28B, Cb
Homildon Hill, 27, Da
Homs, 18C, Dd; 79, Gd; 93, Dc
Honduras, 43D, Dc
Honduras, C., 43B, Bc
Honduras, G. of, 43A, Dc
Honfleur, 28D, Cb; 55A, Dd
Hongkong, 91, Ed
Honiton, 27, Cf
Honolulu, 75, Hc; 75D, Cb
Honshu, 91, Gc
Hooghly, 59B
Hooghly, R., 59B; 92, Fc
Hoogstraeten, 46A, Dc
Hoorn, 30, Fc; 46A, Eb
Hope, 28A, Ca
Hope Bay, 69C
Hopedale, 71, Hb
Hopetown, 81A, Bc
Hopton Heath, 48A, Bc
Horburg, 39B, Db
Hordaland, 12, Fa
Horgen, 29B, Ca
Horn, 46C, Bb
Horn, C., 68, Ch
Horncastle, 3A, Fc
Horseshoe Bend (Tohopeka), 71F, Ba
Horsham, 27, Fe
Horta, 5B,, Bb
Hostatrich 63, Gb
Hottentots, 81B, Bb
Houdan, 38, Dd
Housatonic, R., 45B, Cc
Houston, 72, Ad
Hovedene (Howden), 13, Fc
Howland I., 90, Fc
Howrah, 92, Fc
Howth, 49B, Ec

Howth Hd., 15, Ec
Hoy, 49A, Ca
Hoya, 20, Hb
Hoysalas, 25, Ge
Hradisch, 22, Fb
Hsi-Liao, R., 91, Fb
Hsinking, 90, Ca
Hsu Chow, 1, Od
Huanuco, 68, Bc
Huaras, 68, Bc
Hubbariton, 57, Eb
Hubertusburg, 60A, Dc
Hudson B., 70, Fb
Hudson, R., 57, Dc
Hudson (North), R., 45B, Bc
Hudson Str., 70, Ga
Hudson Bay Company, 58, Eb
Hudson Bay Company Terr., 44, Eb
Hué, 91, De
Huelgas, 22, Bc
Huelva, 23C, Bd
Huesca, Granada, 23D, Dd
Huesca, Saragossa, 23C, Ea
Hufuf, 93, Fd
Hughenden, 77, Gf
Huillier, Fort d', 56, Ab
Hull, 27, Fc
Hulme, 48B, Bc
Hulst, 46A, Dc
Humana, 5B, Bb
Humanita, 68, De
Humber, 27, Gc
Humboldt, R., 70, Cc
Hume Castle, 28B, Cb
Hungarian Ore Mts., 50, Dd
Hungary, 33C, Db; 87, Dc
Hungary, King. of, 16, Fc
Hungshui-Ho, R., 91, Dd
Hun-ho, R., 76B, Ba
Hüningen, 53, Gd
Hunni, 2, Ld
Huns, 2A, Fb
Hunsrück, 83A, Db
Huntcliff, 3A, Fb
Huntedun (Huntingdon), 13, Fd
Huntedunscire (Huntingdonshire), 13, Fd
Hunter, R., 77, Ih
Huntingdon, 27, Fd
Huntingdon, co., 27, Fd
Huntly, 37A, Cb; 49A, Cb
Huntsville, 72, Cc; 71F, Ba
Huon G., 77, Hc
Hurghada, 93, Cd
Huron, L., 45A, Ab
Huron Mission, 45A, Ab
Hurons, 45A, Ab
Hush, 54, Hc
Hussinetz, 31, Ld
Husum, 65F, Aa
Huy, 53, Fb
Hvitramannaland, 35, Fc
Hwang-ho, R., 25, Lc
Hwicce, 7B, Bc
Hy (Iona), 14, Bc
Hyderabad, Nizam's Dominions, 73, Cd
Hyderabad, Sind, 73, Ab
Hydra, 78, Dg
Hyères, 30, Gg
Hyères, Is. d', 53, Gf
Hyrcania, 1, Hd
Hythe, 27, He

IAL, 13, Cc
Iambia, 1, Fe
Iarum (Yarm), 13, Eb
Iasi, 87, Fc
Iazyges, 1, Ec
Ibadan, 96B, Cb
Ibelim, 18C, Bg
Iberia, 19, Gd
Iberus, R., 2, Ce
Ica, 68, Bd
Icaria, 19, De
Iceland, 88, Ba
Iceni, 3A, Gd
Ichaboe I., 81A, Ac
Ichang, 74, Ke
Icknield Way, 3A, Fe
Iconium (Konieh), 18A, Eb; 19, Ee
Iconium (Seljuk Sultanate of Rum), 16, Je
Ida, Mt., 78, Eh
Idaho, 70, Cc
Idaho Terr., 67D, Ba
Idjil, 80A, Bb
Idrisids, 8, Ae
Idrisids, King. of, 6B, Aa
Idstedt, 65F, Aa
Ife, 96B, Cb
Ifni, 80A, Bb
Ifni, col., 96C, Ab
Iganie, 64, Gc
Iglau, 31, Ld; 39, Ld
Ikshids, King. of, 6B, Eb
Ilchester, 27, De
Ile Bouchard, 38, e
Ilfracombe, 48B, Ad
Ilha, 41B, Ee
Ilheus, 68, Fd
Ili, R., 91, Ab
Ilkhan Empire, 25, Ec
Ilkley, 7B, Cb
Ill, R., 39B, Db
Illana B., 75E, Bc
Illapel, 68, Bf
Iller, R., 10, Dd; 29A, Db
Illinois, 56, Bc; 72, Cb
Illinois, R., 56, Bb
Illinois Terr., 71C, Ab
Illyria, King. of, 65C, Bb
Illyria, Pref. of, 2, Hf
Illyrian Prov., 62, Ec
Illyricum, 4A, Gc
Illyricum, Diocese, 2, Gd
Ilmen, L., 26, Hb
Iloilo, 75E, Bb
Ilorin, 96B, Cb
Imbros, 78, Ee
Imeretia, 79, Hb
Imperial Hungary, 39, Me
Imphal, 92, Gc
In Salah, 80A, Db
Inca King., 35, Fe
Inchcolm, 14, Ec
Inde, 43A, Bb
Independence, 70, Ed
India, 92, Dc
Indian Ocean, 35, Ne
Indian Terr., 67D, Db
Indiana, 72, Cb
Indiana Terr., 67B, Aa
Indianapolis, 72, Cb
Indies, 42, Oc
Indonesia, 91, Eg
Indore, 73, Cc
Indraprastha, 1, Ke
Indus, R., 1, Kd; 73, Ab
Ingelheim, 10, Cd
Ingogo, 81D, Aa
Ingolstadt, 22, Eb; 29A, Da
Ingria, 26, Gb; 47, Ha
Inhambane, 96C, Fg
Inis Cathy, 15, Bd
Inishannon, 49B, Ce
Inn, R., 20, Je; 29A, Db
Inn Quarter, 33C, Cb; 53, Kc
Inner Mongolia, 91, Eb
Innichen, 86B, Ca
Innsbruck, 29A, Db
Inny, R., 15, Dc
Inter Ripam et Mersham, 13, Dc
Interlaken, 29B, Bb
Inuvik, 94, Gb
Inveraray, 37A, Bb; 49A, Bb
Inveravon, 3A, Ca
Invercargill, 77A
Inveresk, 3A, Ca
Inverey, 49A, Cb
Invergarry, 49A, Bb
Invergordon, 49A, Bb
Inverkeithing, 37A, Cb; 48B, Ba
Inverlochy, 49A, Bb
Inverness, 14, Db
Inverness, co., 37A, Bb; 49A, Bb
Inverurie, 49A, Cb
Invola, 32A, Db
Inyati, 81A, Ca
Inyeshane, 81D, Bb
Iona (Hy), 14, Bc; 49A, Ab
Ionia, 84, He
Ionian Is., 62, Ge; 78, Cf
Ionian Sea, 78, Bf
Iowa, 70, Ec
Iowas, 56, Bb
Ipswich (Agawam), 45B, Db; 57, Fb
Ipswich, England, 27, Hd
Iquique, 68, Be
Iquitos, 68, Bc
Iraklion, 88, Lf; 93, Bb
Iran (Persia), 89, Pg; 93, Gc
Iraq, 6A, Db; 79, Hd
Irchester, 3A, Fd
Ireland, 15; 49A
Irish Free State, 84, Ab
Irish Sea, 15, Fc; 28B, Ac
Irkutsk, 91, Da
Iron Gate, 78, Dc
Iroquois, 45A, Bb
Irrawaddy, R., 73, Gc; 92, Hd
Irtapan, 43A, Cc
Irthing, R., 28B, Cc
Irtysh, R., 25, Ga; 91, Aa
Irun, 63, Ea
Irvine, 49A, Bc
Isabella, 43A, Ec
Isandhlwana, 81D, Bb
Isar, R., 10, Ed
Isauria, 2, Kf
Isca (Caerleon), 3A, De
Isca Dumnoniorum (Exeter), 3A, Cf
Ischia, 32B, Dd
Iscia Baidoa, 96A, Bb
Isère, R., 11, Fd; 32A, Bb
Isernia, 22, Ec
Isfahan, 25, Ec; 93, Gc
Ishtip, 86A, Da
Isker, R., 78, Dd
Island Number Ten, 72, Cb
Islands, B. of, 77A
Islay, 14, Bd
Isle of France, 38, Ed
Isles, King. of the, 14, Bb
Isles, The, bp., 14A, Ab
Ismail, 51, Fd; 78, Gc
Ismailia, 80B, Aa; 86C, Bc
Isna, 93, Cd
Isny, 30, Je
Isola, 32D, Bb
Isonzo, 2A, Cb
Isonzo, R., 5, Db; 86B, Da
Ispahan, 6, Gb
Isparta, 93, Cb
Israel, 89, Mg; 93, Cc
Issoire, 30, Ef
Issoudun, 11, Dc
Istanbul, 93, Ba
Istria, 5, Db; 10, Ef
Isurium (Aldborough), 3A, Eb
Italia, 2, Fe
Italian (Cisalpine) Rep., 65A, Ab
Italian Somaliland, 80A, Hd
Italy, 88, He
Italy, Exarchate of, 4B, Ec
Italy, King. of, 20, Jf
Italy, Pref. of, 2, Fe
Itil, 9, Mc
Ituna Aest. (Solway Firth), 3A, Cb
Itzehoe, 65F, Ab
Iuka, 72, Cc
Iviza, 23C, Fc; 63, Fc
Ivory Coast, 81C, Cd
Ivrea, 5, Ab
Ivry, 38, Dd
Iwo, 96B, Cb
Iwojima, 90, Db
Izborsk, 9, Ha
Izmir, 93, Bb

JABALPUR, 92, Ec
Jabia, 6A, Bb
Jablunkau, 39, Nd
Jaca, 22, Bc; 23C, Ea
Jackson, Mississippi, 72C, Aa
Jackson, Tennessee, 72, Cb
Jacksonville, 72, Dc
Jaen, 22, Bd; 23C, Dd
Jaffa, 86C, Bc
Jaffa (Joppa), 18C, Bf
Jaffna, 92, Ef
Jagellons, Lands of the, 31, Md
Jagerndorf, 31, Mc; 33C, Da
Jaintiapur, 73, Fb
Jaipur, 73, Cb
Jaipur, st., 59C, Cb
Jajce, 39, Mf
Jalalabad, 73, Ba
Jalangi, R., 59B
Jalayas, Dominions of the, 24, Mf
Jaleswar, 59B
Jaluit, 75, Fd
Jamaica, 45B, Cc
Jamaica, I., 43A, Ec
Jamaica B., 57B
James B., 70, Fb
James, R., 57, Ce; 72B, Ab
James City, 45B, Ae
James W. Ellsworth Land, 69C
Jamestown, 45B, Ae
Jammu and Kashmir, 92, Da
Jamnagar, 92, Cc
Jamshedpur, 92, Fc
Jamtland, 12, Ha
Janer, 31, Mc
Janina, 78, Cf
Jankau, 38, Ld
Jaora, 73, Cc
Japan, 91, Gc
Japan (Zipangu), 25, Nc
Japan, Sea of, 91, Gc
Japanese Empire, 75, Ec
Japura, R., 68, Cc
Jargeau, 28D, Dc
Jarnac, 38, Cf
Jaroslau, 26, Fc
Jaroslavl, 19, Fa
Jarrow, 36, Ec
Jarvis I., 75, He
Jask, 93, Hd
Jassy, 50, Fd; 78, Fb
Jativa, 23C, Ec
Jats, 59A, Cb
Jauf, 93, Dd
Java, 42B; 91, Dg
Java Major (Borneo), 35, Pd
Java Minor (Sumatra), 35, Oe
Java Sea, 91, Eg
Jaxartes, R., 1, Jc
Jebel Hamrin, 19, Ge
Jebel Tarik, 9, Ae
Jedburgh, 14, Fd
Jeddah, 6, Ec
Jedisan, 50, Gd; 78, Gb
Jefferson City, 72, Bb
Jehol, 90, Ba
Jehoshophat's Gate, 18D
Jelling, 12, Gc
Jemappes, 46A, Cd; 62, Cb
Jemmingen, 46A, Ga
Jemtland, 26, Ed
Jena, 30, Jc; 38, Jc; 62, Eb
Jericho, 18C, Cg
Jersey, 17, Dd
Jerusalem, 6A, Bb; 18C, Cg
Jerusalem, King. of, 18C, Cf
Jervaulx, 36, Ee
Jesselton, 91, Ef
Jessore, 59B
Jever, 30, Gb; 38, Gb
Jhansi, 73, Cb
Jhelum, R., 73, Ba
Jibuti, 80B, Ce; 94, Re
Jiddah, 80B, Bc
Jimma, 96A, Ab
Jitomir, 50, Fc
Joanna Spring, 77, Cf
Jodhpur, 73, Bb
Johannesburg, 81A, Cc
Johore, 58, Pd
Johore Bahru, 75A, Bb
Johnston, 28B, Bb
Johnston I., 90, Fc
Johnstone, 28B, Bb
Joigny, 11, Ec
Joinville, 17, Hd; 20, Fd
Jolo, 75E, Bc
Jönköping, 26, Db
Joppa, 18A, Ec
Joppa (Jaffa), 18C, Bf
Jordan, 89, Ng; 93, Dc
Jordan, R., 18C, Cf
Jos, 96B, Cb
Joscelin, Lordship of, 18C, Eb
Josselin, 30, Be
Joux, 53, Gd
Juan de Fuca Str., 70, Bc
Juan Fernandez Is., 68, Bf
Jucar, R., 23C, Ec
Juggernaut, 59A, Ed
Jujuy, 41B, Cf
Julian Alps, 86B, Da
Jülich, 20, Gc; 46A, Fd
Jülich, D. of, 46A, Fd
Juliers, Co. of, 46C, Cb
Jullundur, 73, Ca
Jumièges, 22, Cb
Jumna, R., 73, Cb
Junagadh and Manavadar, 92, Cc
Juneau, 71B, Cb
Junin, Argentina, 68, Cf
Junin, Peru, 68, Bd
Junto, Mte., 63B
Jura, I., 14, Cc
Jura, mts., 11, Gc
Jura, Sd. of, 14, Cd
Jurjan, 6, Gb
Jurua, R., 68, Cc
Jussy, 29B, Ab
Justingen, 30, Hd
Jüterbog, 53, Kb
Jutes, 4A, Ba; 7A, Fa
Juti, 2, Eb
Jutland, 55B, La; 84, Da
Juzajan, 6, Hb

KA LAE, pt., 75D, Dc
Kaanbaligh (Peking), 25, Lc
Kabul, 6, Hb; 25, Fc; 73, Aa
Kabul, R., 73, Aa
Kabusi, R., 81B, Cc
Kachin, 92, Hb
Kadisiya, 6A, Cb
Kaduna, 96B, Ca
Kaffa, 19, Fd; 25, Cb
Kaffraria, 81A, Cd
Kafiristan, 61B, Cb
Kagoshima, 91, Gc
Kahoolawe, 75D, Cb
Kaifeng, 25, Lc
Kaiping, 76B, Ba
Kairwan, 8, Ed
Kaisaria, 33A, Ec; 86C, Cb
Kaiser Wilhelm Land, Antarctica, 69C
Kaiser Wilhelms Land (North-East New Guinea), 77, Gc
Kaiserslautern, 29A, Ba
Kaiserswerth, 10, Bc
Kaiwi Chan., 75D, Cb
Kalahari Desert, 81A, Bb
Kalamata, 78, Dg
Kalat, 73, Ab
Kalau, 39C, Db
Kalavryta, 78, Df
Kalgan, 74, Kd; 90, Ba
Kalgoorlie, 77, Ch
Kalimantan, 91, Eg
Kalinga, 1, Lf
Kaliningrad, 89, Kc
Kalinjar, 52A, Cb
Kalisz, 21, Nc; 31, Nc
Kalka, 19, Fc
Kalmuck, 85, Lc
Kalocsa, 22, Fb; 24, Fd
Kalocsa, eccl. prov., 22, Fc
Kalpi, 73, Cb
Kaluga, 24, Kc; 50, Hc
Kama, R., 19, Ja; 88, Qb
Kamakura, 25, Nc
Kamaran, 40, Md
Kamaran I., 80B, Cd; 93, Ef
Kambula, 81D, Ba
Kamchatka, 74, Oc; 90, Da
Kamchik, R., 78, Fd
Kamenets Podolski, 79, Ea
Kamerun, 80A, Ed
Kaminiec, 50, Fd
Kamloops, 70, Bb
Kammin, 21, Lb
Kammin, Bp. of, 31, Ma
Kamp, 22, Da
Kampala, 96D, Fd
Kanara, 59A, Be; 73, Be
Kanauj, 25, Hd
Kanawha, R., 57, Ad
Kanazawa, 91, Gc
Kandahar, 61B, Bb; 73, Aa
Kandavu, 75C, Bb
Kandi, 96B, Ca
Kandy, 73, Df
Kanem, 80A, Ec
Kangaroo I., 77, Fi
Kanizsa, 39, Me
Kankan, 96B, Ba
Kano, 96B, Ca
Kanpur, 92, Eb
Kansas, 70, Ed
Kansas, R., 44, Ee
Kansas City, 72, Bb
Kansas Terr., 67D, Cb
Kapolna, 33C, Eb
Kappel, 29B, Ca
Kaprivshtitza, 78, Ed
Kara Kum, 61B, Ab
Kara Kuyunli, 24, Lf
Kara Sea, 74, Ea
Karabagh, 79, Jc
Karachi, 73, Ab
Karafuto, 74, Nd
Karaganda, 91, Ab
Karakakua B., 58, Bd
Karakoram Mts., 59A, Ca
Karakorum, 25, Kb
Karaman, Amirate of, 19, Ee
Karansebes, 33C, Eb
Kara-shahr, 1, Lc
Karassi, 33A, Cc
Karauli, 73, Cb
Karawanken, 29A, Fb
Karbala, 79, Hd
Kardis, 50, Fb; 54, Ha
Karen, 92, Hd
Kargopol, 61, Eb
Karikal, 59D
Karlovo, 78, Ed
Karlsbad, 31B, Ca
Karlskrona, 51, Db; 54, Fa
Karlsruhe, 83A, Eb
Karmati, King. of, 6B, Fb
Karnul, 73, Cd
Karpathos, 93, Bb
Kars, 19, Gd; 61, Ff; 79, Hb
Karystos, 78, Ef
Karytaena, 78, Dg
Kasai, R., 80A, Ee
Kasalinsk, 61B, Ba
Kaschau, 31, Pd; 50, Ed
Kashan, 93, Gc
Kashgar, 1, Kd
Kashmir, 1, Kd; 73, Ca
Kaskaskia, 56, Bc
Käsmark, 21, Pd
Kasogs (Cherkesses), 9, Lc
Kassa, 33C, Eb
Kassala, 80B, Bd
Kastamuni, 33A, Db
Kastoria, 86A, Cb
Kasvin, 19, He
Kat, R., 81B, Cc
Katanga, 80A, Ff; 96D, Ee
Kathiawar, 73, Bc
Katif, 6, Gc
Katiola, 96B, Bb
Katmandu, 73, Eb
Katrine, L., 14, Dc
Katsina, 96B, Ca
Kattegat, 12, Gb
Katwa, 59B
Kauai, 75D, Ba
Kauai Chan, 75D, Bb
Kaufbeuren, 20, Je
Kaunas, 87, Ea
Kavalla, 78, Ee; 84, Gd
Kawita, 56, Cd
Kayah, 92, Hd
Kayes, 81C, Bb
Kayseri, 79, Gc
Kaysersburg, 39B, Db
Kazam, 19, Ha
Kazan Is., 90, Db
Kazanlik, 78, Ed
Kazanlinsk, 74, Ed
Kazvin, 6, Fb; 93, Gb
Ke Chow, 1, Od
Kearney, 70, Ec
Kecskemet, 33C, Db

Kedgeree, 59B
Keeling (Cocos) Is., 90, Ad
Keewatin, 70, Ea
Kehl, 39B, Db; 65B, Ab
Kei Is., 52C, Dc
Keiskamma, R., 81B, Cc
Keith, 37A, Cb
Kells, 15, Ec; 49B, Ec
Kelly, 72, Eb
Kelso, 14, Fd; 37A, Cc
Kemi, 26, Fa
Kemp Land, 69C
Kempten, 20, Je
Kenauj, 59C, Cb
Kendal, 27, Db
Kendari, 90, Cd
Kenesaw Mt., 72A, Aa
Kenilworth, 27, Ed
Kenmare, R., 15, Be
Kennebec, R., 45A, Da
Kennedy, 28B, Ab
Kent, co., 27, Ge
Kent I., 45B, Ad
Kentucky, 72, Cb
Kenya, 96C, Fd
Keppel B., 77, If
Kerala, 92, De
Kerbela, 6A, Cb
Kerch, 9, Kc; 79, Ga
Kerguelen I., 69C, 76, Ng
Kerma, 80B, Ad
Kermadec Is., 75, Gf
Kerman, 25, Ed; 93, Hc
Kermanshah, 79, Jd
Kermian, 33A, Cc
Kernstown, 72B, Aa
Kerrera I., 14, Cc
Kerry, co., 37C; 49B, Bd
Kerulen, R., 91, Eb
Kesselsdorf, 60A, Dc
Keta, 96B, Cb
Kexholm, 50, Ga
Key West, 43A, Db
Keynsham, 36, Df
Khabarovsk, 91, Gb
Khama, 88, Kf
Khama's Country, 81A, Cb
Khanate, 50, Gd
Khandesh, 73, Bc
Kharagpur, 92, Fc
Kharda, 59C, Cd
Kharkov, 9, Kc
Khartoum, 80B, Ad; 96D, Fc
Khazar Empire, 9, Lc
Khazars, 9, Lc
Kherson 8, Jc; 50, Gd
Khiva, 6, Ga; 61B, Ba
Khiva, Khanate of, 61B, Aa
Khmer Empire, 25, Ke
Khmyelnik, 19, Cb
Khodzhent, 61B, Ba
Khojand, 6, Ja
Khokand, 25, Gb; 61B, Ca
Kholm, 61A, Bb
Khorasan, 6, Gb; 25, Ec
Khorramshahr, 93, Fc
Khotan, 1, Ld
Khuzistan, 6, Gb
Khwarizm, 6, Ha; 25, Eb
Khyber Pass, 73, Ba; 74, Fe
Kiakhta, 69A, Pb
Kiaochow, 74, Le
Kichinef, 51, Fd
Kicking Horse Pass, 70, Cb
Kidderminster, 27, Dd
Kidwelly, 27, Be; 28A, Bc
Kiel, 26, Dc; 51, Bc; 60B, Ca
Kiel Canal, 87, Bb
Kielce, 21, Pc
Kiev, 19, Eb; 50, Gc; 82, Jb
Kilcullen, 37B, Ec
Kildare, 15, Ec; 49B, Ec
Kildare, co., 37C; 49B, Ec
Kildrummy, 49A, Cb
Kilfenora, 15, Bd; 49B, Bd
Kilia, 51, Fd; 78, Gc
Kilia Mouth, 78, Gc
Kilid Bahr, 86D
Kilimane, 40, Le
Kilkenny, 15, Dd
Kilkenny, co., 37C
Killala, 15, Bb
Killaloe, 15, Cd
Killarney, 49B, Bd
Killarney, Lakes of, 15, Bd
Killiecrankie Pass, 14, Ec
Killybegs, 49B, Cb
Kilmacduagh, 15, Cc
Kilmacrenan, 49B, Da
Kilmallock, 37B, Cd
Kilrush, 49B, Bd
Kilsyth, 37A, Bc; 48B, Ab
Kilwa, 80A, Ge; 96C, Fe
Kimberley, S. Africa, 81A, Bc
Kimberley, W. Australia, 77, De
Kinburn, 51, Gd; 61, De
Kincardine, co., 37A, Cb
Kinchow, 76B, Ab
Kindah, 6, Fc
Kindia, 96B, Aa
Kindu, 80A, Fe
King George Sd., 77, Bi
King George V. Land, 69C
King William's Town, 81B, Cc
King's Co., 37C; 49B, Dc
Kings Lynn, 24, Cc; 48A, Dc
Kings Mountain, 56, Cc
Kingston, Canada, 71C, Cb
Kingston, England, 27, Fe
Kingston, Georgia, 56, Cd
Kingston, Jamaica, 43A, Ec
Kingston, New York, 57, Ec
Kingston upon Hull, 36, Fd
Kingstown (Dun Laoghaire), 49B, Ec
Kingswood, 36, Df
Kington, 27, Cd
Kinloss, 14, Eb
Kinross, 37A, Cb
Kinross, co., 49A, Cb
Kinsale, 37B, Ce; 49B, Ce
Kintore, 37A, Cb
Kintyre, 14, Cd
Kintyre, Mull of, 49A, Bc
Kipchaks (Polovtsi), 19, Gc
Kippure, 15, Ec
Kirchhayn, 30, Hc
Kirensk, 74, Jc
Kirgiz, 25, Ja; 61, Je
Kirin, 91, Fb
Kirk Kilisse, 78, Fe
Kirkcaldy, 49A, Cb
Kirkcudbright, 28B, Bc
Kirkcudbright, co., 37A, Bc
Kirkee, 73, Bd
Kirkham, 36, Fc
Kirkpatrick, 28B, Bb
Kirkstall, 36, Ed
Kirkstead, 36, Fd
Kirkuk, 79, Hc
Kirkwall, 37A, Ca
Kirman, 6, Gc
Kirmisin, 6A, Db
Kirovabad, 93, Fa
Kirriemuir, 37A, Cb
Kishinev, 78, Gb
Kiska I., 90, Ea
Kistna, R., 1, Kf; 73, Cd
Kittery, 45B, Db
Kiungchow, 74, Kg
Kiutayeh, 64, Jf
Kizil Ahmadli, Amirate of, 19, Ed
Kizil Irmak, R., 19, Ed
Kizil Kum, 61B, Ba
Kladrau, 21, Kd
Klagenfurt, 29A, Fb
Klattau, 21, Kd; 53, Kc
Klausenburg (Kolosvar), 33C, Eb
Klein Schnellendorf, 60A, Fc
Klip, R., 81A, Cc
Klondyke, 71A, Da
Kloster Zeven, 60A, Bb
Klostergrab, 39, Kc
Klosterneuburg, 22, Fb
Kluane, L., 71B, Ba
Knapdale, 14, Cd; 37A, Bc
Knäred, 50, Cb
Knaresborough, 27, Eb
Knights of the Sword, 34, Ga
Knights Templar, Hospital of the, 18D
Knin, 22, Fc
Knocke, 46A, Bd
Knockin, 28A, Db
Knockmealdown Mts., 15, Cd
Knocktopher, 49B, Dd
Knoidart, 14, Cb
Knox Land, 69C
Knoxville, 72, Db
Kobdo, 74, Hd
Kobe, 91, Gc
Koblenz, 83A, Da
Kodiak, 71A, Bb
Kodiak I., 71A, Bb
Kodok (Fashoda), 80B, Ae
Kohima, 90, Ab
Kokenhusen, 26, Gb
Kokopo (Herbertshöhe), 77, Ib
Kola, 42, La; 61, Ea
Kolar, 59A, Ce; 59D
Kolar Goldfields, 92, De
Kolberg, 21, La
Kolhapur, 73, Bd
Kolima, R., 69B
Kolin, 29A, Fa; 31, Lc
Kölln, 26, Dc
Köln, 89, Gc
Kolomea, 84, Gc
Kolomna, 19, Fa
Kolozsvar (Klausenburg), 33C, Eb; 34, Gc
Komati Poort, 81A, Dc
Kommotau, 21, Kc
Komorn, 39, Ne
Konakry, 81C, Bc
Kong, 80A, Cd; 81C, Dc
Kongolo, 80A, Fe
Konia, 24, Jf
Konieh (Iconium), 18A, Eb
Königgratz, 21, Lc; 60A, Ec
Königsau, R., 65F, Aa
Königsberg, Bavaria, 39C, Ac
Konigsberg, E. Prussia, 21, Pa
Königstein, 65B, Ba
Konitz, 21, Mb
Konkan, 1, Kf
Konkans, 59A, Bd
Kontagora, 96B, Ca
Konya, 79, Fc
Koonap, R., 81B, Cc
Koporje, 26, Gb
Köprulü, 86A, Ca
Kora, 59A, Db
Korcë, 88, Ke
Kordofan, 80B, Ae
Korea, 91, Fc
Korhogo, 96B, Bb
Koritza, 86A, Bb
Koro Sea, 75C, Ba
Koroni, 78, Cg
Kororareka, 77, Mi
Korosko, 80B, Ac
Korygaum, 73, Bd
Kosas, 81B, Cc
Kosel, 60A, Gc; 65B, Ca
Koselsk, 19, Fb
Koslin, 31, Ma; 54, Fb
Kosman, I., 77, Id
Kosseir, 80B, Ab
Kossovo, 24, Ge; 78, Cd
Kossovopolye, 50, Ee
Kostroma, 24, Lb; 61, Fc
Kota Bharu, 90, Bc
Kotah, 59C, Cb; 73, Cb
Kotchana, 78, De
Köthen, 39C, Bb
Kottbus, 21, Lc; 31, Lc
Koudougou, 96B, Ba
Kovno, 26, Fb
Kowpangtze, 76B, Aa
Kozhikode, 92, De
Kozlov, 61, Fd
Kozlov (Eupatoria), 50, Gd
Kra, 73, Ge
Kraguyevats, 78, Cc
Krak, 18C, Dd
Krak (Crac de la Pierre), 18C, Cg
Krakow, 88, Kd
Kranganur, 59A, Ce
Krasnik, 26, Fc; 84, Gb
Krasnodar, 89, Nd
Krasnovodsk, 61, Hf; 93, Ga
Krasnoyarsk, 74, Hc; 90, Aa
Krefeld, 83A, Da
Kremnitz, 21, Nd
Krems, 10, Fd
Kremsier, 31, Md; 65C, Cb
Kremsmünster, 22, Eb
Kressenbrunn, 21, Md
Kreuznach, 29A, Ba
Kreuzschanze, 46A, Dc
Kriechingen, 39B, Ca
Krim Tartars, 61, Ee
Krishnagar, 59B
Kristiansand, 87, Ba
Krithia, 86D
Kriviches, 9, Ha
Kroja, 19, Bd
Kronstadt, Hungary, 34, Hc
Kronstadt, Russia, 51, Ga
Krossen, 21, Lb
Krugersdorp, 81A, Cc
Krumau, 39, Ld
Krushevatz, 78, Cd
Kuala Lumpur, 91, Df
Kuban, R., 19, Fc
Kubans, 16, Lc
Kublai Khan, Empire of, 25, Kc
Kucha, 1, Lc
Kuching, 91, Ef
Kufra, 80A, Fb
Kufstein, 39, Ke
Kuibyshev, 88, Qc
Kuka, 80A, Ec
Kuldja, 74, Gd
Kulikovo, 19, Fb
Kulm, Poland, 21, Nb
Kulm, Saxony, 60B, Dc
Kum Kale, 86D
Kuma, R., 33A, Gb
Kumamoto, 91, Gc
Kumanovo, 78, Cd
Kumaon, 73, Ca
Kumarskaya, 74, Lc
Kumasi, 81C, Dc; 96B, Bb
Kumo, 96B, Da
Kunene, R., 80A, Ef
Kunersdorf, 54, Eb; 60A, Eb
Kunming, 91, Dd
Kuopio, 61, Cb
Kupang, 95, Mf
Kur, R., 33A, Gb
Kura, R., 19, Hd
Kurdish, 85, Le
Kurdistan, 79, Hc
Kurdla, 59A, Cd
Kuria Muria Is., 93, Hf
Kuril Is., 74, Od; 90, Da
Kurland, 26, Fb
Kurna, 86C, Ec
Kursk, 19, Fb; 88, Nc
Kuruman, 81A, Bc
Kuruman, R., 81B, Ba
Kuruska, 93, Ce
Kushan Dominions, 1, Jd
Kuskokwim, R., 71A, Ba
Kuskuskie, 57, Ac
Kustendil, 78, Dd
Küstrin, 31, Lb
Kut-el-Amara, 79, Jd
Kutahya, 33A, Cc; 93, Cb
Kutais, 33A, Fb; 93, Ea
Kutchuk Kainarji, 78, Fd
Kuttenberg, 31, Ld
Kuwait, 79, Je; 93, Fd
Kwangchow, 74, Kf
Kwangtung, 76B, Ab
Kweiyang, 91, Dd
Kyakhta, 74 Jc
Kyburg, 29B, Ca
Kyle, 14, Dd
Kyoto, 25, Nc; 91, Gc
Kyritz, 26, Dc

La Bahia, 43C, Bb
La Balize, 56, Be
La Bassee, 83A, Ba
La Belle Alliance, 46B
La Charité, 28D, Dc; 38 Ee
La Colle, 71C, Db
La Colombe, 22, Cb
la Conception, 45A, Ab
La Fère, 28D, Db; 83A, Bb
La Ferté, 22, Db
La Ferté Vidame, 38, Dd
La Garnache, 38, Ce
La Guaira, 43A, Fc
La Haye Sainte, 46B
La Higuera, 23D, Dd
La Hougue, 55A, Cd
La Mancha, 23D, Dc; 63, Dc
La Manche (English Channel), 55A, Dc
La Marche, 39B, Bb
La Marche, Co. of, 11, Dc
La Motte, I., 57, Ea
La Paz, 68, Cd
La Plata, Argentina, 68, Df
La Plata, Bolivia, 41B, Ce
La Plata, dist., 41B, Cf; 42, Ff
La Plata, rep., 69A, Ff
La Plata, Rio de, 68, Df
La Plata, United Provs. of, 68, Cf
La Pointe (Fort St. Esprit), 56, Aa
La Réole, 17, Ff
La Roche, 53, Cd
La Roche Bernard, 38, Be
La Roche Derien, 28C, Ab
La Rochelle, 11, Cc; 53 Cd
La Serena, 68, Bf
La Teste de Buch, 28C, Bd
La Tour, 30, Ef
La Trappe, 22, Cb
La Tremouille, 30, De
Labe, 96B, Aa
Laberge, L., 71B, Ca
Labiau, 39, Pa; 50, Ec
Labrador, 71, Hb
Labrador, Pen. of, 71, Hb
Labuan, 91, Ef
Laccadive Is., 92, Ce
Lachine, 57, Ea
Lachlan, R., 77, Hh
Lactodorum (Towcester), 3A, Ed
Lacy, 17, Bb
Ladakh, 92, Da
Lade, 12, Ga
Lado, 80A, Gd
Ladoga, 19, Ea
Ladoga, L., 26, Ha
Ladrones, 40, Rd
Ladysmith, 81D, Ab
Lae, 90, Dd
Lafayette, 72A, Aa
Lafayetteville, 56, Dc
Lagan, R., 15, Fb
Lagen, R., 12, Ga
Lagentium (Castleford), 3A, Ec
Laghouat, 80A, Da
Lagos, Nigeria, 80, Dc; 81C, Ec
Lagos, Portugal, 4B, Ad; 23C, Ad
Lagosta, 84, Fd
Laguna, 68, Ee
Lahave, 45A, Eb
Lahn, R., 10, Cc; 83A, Ea
Lahore, 25, Gc; 73, Ba
Lahr, 30, Gd
Laibach, 10, Fe
Laighin (Leinster), 15, Ed
Laila, 93, Fe
Laing's Nek, 81D, Aa
Lakhmids, 6A, Cb
Lalitpur, 73, Cc
Lamballe, 17, Dd; 20 Bd
Lambertville, 57, Dc
Lambeth, 27A
Lamego, 22, Ac; 23C, Bb
Lammermuir Hill, 14, Fd
Lamon B., 75E, Bb
Lampadar, 27, Bd
Lampsacus, 78, Fe
Lamu, 40, Me
Lanai, 75D, Cb
Lanark, 28B, Bb
Lanark, co., 37A, Cc; 49A, Cc
Lancaster, England, 3A, Db; 27, Db
Lancaster, Pennsylvania, 57, Cc
Lancaster, clan, 28B, Db
Lancaster, lordship, 28A, Bc
Lancaster, Co. Palatine of, 27, Dc
Lancaster Sd., 44, Ga
Lanchow, 91, Dc
Landau, 29A, Ca; 76A, Eb
Landeck, 20, Je
Landeshut, 60A, Ec
Landrecies, 46A, Cd
Landriano, 32A, Cb
Land's End, 55A, Ac
Landsberg, Brandenburg, 21, Lb
Landsberg, Osterland, 21, Kc
Landsberg, Styria, 31, Le
Landshut, 21, Kd
Landstuhl, 39B, Da
Lanercost, 36, Dc
Langarone, 86B, Ca
Langeac, 20, Ef
Langeland, 65F, Ba
Langensalza, 39C, Ab; 60B, Cc
Langford House, 48B, Cd
Langholm, 28B, Bb
Langobardi, 2, Fc
Langport, 27, De
Langres, 11, Fc
Langside, 37A, Bc
Languedoc, 17A, De; 20, Eg
Lanporth (Langport), 13, De
Lansdown, 48A, Bd
Lanshankwan, 76B, Ba
Lanstavetone (Launceston), 13, Bf
Lanthony, 36, Df
Laoag, 75E, Ba
Laodicea, 2, Lf; 18, Cc
Laon, 11, Eb; 83A, Bb
Laos, 91, De
Lapland, 61, Ca
Laprairie, 56, Ea
Laramie, 70, Dc
Larantuka, 52C, Bc
Larche, Col de, 29A, Bc
Laredo, 43A, Cb
Largs, 14, Dd; 37A, Bc
Larino, 22, Ec
Larissa, 19, Ce; 78, Df
Larnaka, 86C, Bc
Laron, 20, Df
Las Navas de Tolosa, 23C, Dc
Las Palmas, 80A, Bb
Las Vegas, 44, Ce; 70, Dd
Lasalle, 70, Fc
Lashio, 92, Hc
Lastingham, 7B, Ca
Laswari, 59C, Cb
Latakia, 79, Gc
Lateran, 5A
Lathom, 48A, Bc
Latin States, 24, Gf
Latins, 8C, Bb
Latisana, 86B, Db
Latvia, 87, Fa
Lau (Eastern) Group, 75C, Ca
Lau Group (Exploring Is.), 75C, Ca
Lauder, 49A, Cc
Lauderdale, 28B, Cb
Laudenburg, Holstein, 20, Jb; 65F, Bb
Lauenburg, Pomerania, 21, Ma
Lauenburg, D., 65F, Bb
Lauenstein, 39C, Dc
Laufen, 29B, Ba
Laun, 39, Kc
Launceston, England, 27, Bf
Launceston, Tasmania, 77, Hj
Laund, 36, Fe
Laupen, 29B, Bb
Laurencekirk, 49A, Cb
Lausanne, 11, Gc; 29B, Ab
Lausitz, 10, Ec
Lausitz, M. of, 21, Lc
Lauter, R., 76A, Eb
Lautrec, 20, Eg
Lavagna, 20, Hf
Laval, 20, Cd
Lavant, 22, Eb
Lavatrae (Bowes), 3A, Eb
Lavaur, 20, Dg
Lavongai (New Hanover), 77, Ib
Lavoro, Terra de, 32A, Fd
Lawes (Lewes), 13, Ff
Lawless, 37B, Bb
Lazica, 19, Gd
Le Cateau, 83A, Ba
Le Creuzot, 88, Fd
Le Havre (Havre de Grace), 38, Dd; 89, Fd

Le Mans, 11, Dc
Le Puiset, 17, Fd
Le Puy, 11, Ed
Lea, R., 7C, Cc
Leaf, R., 70, Gb
League of God's House, 29B, Db
League of Ten Jurisdictions, 29B, Db
Lealui, 96C, Ef
Leavenworth, 70, Ed; 72, Bb
Lebanon, 18C, Ce; 79, Gd
Lebu, 68, Bf
Lebus, 21, Lb; 60A, Eb
Lecce, 5, Gd
Lech, R., 10, De; 30, Jd
Leck, R., 46A, Dc
Lectoure, 11, De
Ledbury, 27, Dd
Ledecestre (Leicester), 13, Ed
Ledecestrescire (Leicestershire), 13, Ed
Ledo, 90, Ab
Lee, R., 15, Ce
Leeds, Kent, 27, Ge; 36, Gf
Leeds, Yorks, 48A, Cc
Leer, 30, Gb
Leesburg, 57, Cd; 72B, Ba
Leeuwarden, 46A, Ea
Leeuwin, C., 77, Bh
Leghorn, 23B, Cc; 32E, Bb
Legnago, 29A, Dc; 62, Ec
Legnano, 20, Hf
Leicester, 27, Ed
Leicester, co., 27, Ed
Leicester, diocese, 36A
Leighlin, 15, Dd
Leinster, 37B, Dd; 49C
Leinster (Laighin), 15, Ed
Leinster Irish, 49C
Leipzig, 10, Ec
Leire, 12, Gc
Leiria, 23C, Ac; 63, Ac
Leith, 37A, Cc; 48A, Bb
Leitmeritz, 21, Lc
Leitrim, 17, Ba; 49B, Cc
Leitrim, co., 37C; 49B, Cb
Leix, 37B, Dd
Lemberg, 26, Fd; 33C, Eb
Lemnos, 19, De; 78, Ef
Lena, R., 25, Ma; 91, Da
Leningrad, 87, Ga
Lenne, R., 83A, Da
Lennox, 14, Dd
Lens, 17, Gc; 83A, Ba
Lenteurde (Leintwardine), 13, Dd
Lenton, 36, Ee
Leoben, 29A, Fb; 65A, Cb
Leofminstre (Leominster), 13, Dd
Leofric, 12, Dc
Leominster, 27, Dd; 48B, Bc
Léon, France, 11, Ab
Leon, Nicaragua, 43A, Dc
Leon, Spain, 63, Ca
Leon, King. of, 23C, Ba
Leon, prov., 63, Cb
Leon and Castile, King. of, 23C, Cb
Leona, C., 63A
Leonine City, 5A
Leontini, 5, Ef
Leopold Coast, 69C
Leopoldville, 80A, Ee
Lepanto, 18B, Cc; 78, Cf
Lepontine Alps, 29A, Cb
Leptis, 6, Cb
Lerida, 23D, Fb; 63, Fb
Les Clairets, 22, Cb
Lesbos, 19, De
Lescar, 11, Ce
Lesgians, 19, Hd
Lesina, 22, Fc
Lesina, I., 23B, Fc
Lesna, 54, Jb
Lesser Antilles, 43A, Fc
Lesser Armenia, 25, Cc
Lessines, 46A, Cd
Lethbridge, 70, Cc
Lethington, 37A, Cc
Letocetum (Wall), 3A, Ed
Letterkenny, 49B, Db
Leucadia, 64, Gf
Leucas, 62, Ge; 78, Cf
Leuchtenburg, 21, Kd
Leuk, 29B, Bb
Leuthen, 54, Fb; 60A, Fc
Leutkirch, 53, Hd
Leutschau, 19, Cc; 31, Pd
Leven, L., Inverness, 14, Cc
Leven, L., Kinross, 14, Ec
Levis, 57C, Ba
Levis, Pt., 56A
Levuka, 75C, Ba
Lewes, 27, Gf
Lewes, R., 71A, Da
Lewis, 14, Ba
Lewiston, 71D
Lexington, Kentucky, 56, Cc
Lexington, Massachusetts, 57, Fb
Lexington, Tennessee, 72, Cb
Leyden, 46A, Db
Leyen, 65B, Ab
Leyre, 22, Bc
Leyte, 75E, Bb
Lhasa, 25, Jd; 73, Fb
Liang Chow, 1, Nd
Liao-ho, R., 76B, Ba
Liao-tung, 76B, Ba
Liaotung, G. of, 76B, Aa
Liaoyang, 76B, Ba
Liard, 70, Ba
Liard, R., 70, Ba
Libau, 26, Fb
Libava, 51, Eb
Liberia, 81C, Cc
Libreville, 80A, Dd
Libya, 80A, Eb; 93, Ac
Licata, 21A, Bd
Licefelle (Lichfield), 13, Ed
Lichfensteig, 29B, Da
Lichfield, 27, Ed
Lichfield, bp., 36, De
Lichsfeld, bp., 30, Jc
Lichtenberg, 39B, Db
Lida, 26, Gc
Liddisdale, 14, Fd; 28B, Cb
Lideforde (Lidford), 13, Bf
Liechtenstein, 65A, Ab
Liège, 46A, Ed
Liège, Bp. of, 46A, Ed
Liegnitz, 19, Bb; 21, Mc
Lienz, 31, Ke
Liepaja, 87, Ea
Lier, 46A, Dc
Lierkenshoek, 46A, Dc
Liffey, R., 15, Ec
Lifford, 37B, Db
Liger, R., 2, Dd
Ligny, Belgium, 46B
Ligny, France, 39B, Bb
Liguria, 5, Bb; 32C, Bb
Lihue, 75D, Bb
Lille, 28D, Da; 46A, Cd
Lillebonne, 17, Fd
Lillo, 46A, Dc
Lilybaeum, 5, Df
Lima, 68, Bd
Limasol, 18A, Ec
Limburg, Germany, 60A, Bd
Limburg, Netherlands, 46A, Ed
Limburg, Co. of, 46C, Bb
Limerick, 15, Cd
Limerick, co., 37C; 49B, Cd
Limia, 23C, Ab
Limoges, 11, Dd; 84, Cc
Limousin, V. of, 11, Dd
Limoux, 20, Eg
Limpopo, R., 81A, Db
Lincluden, 36, Cb
Lincolescire (Lincolnshire), 13, Fc
Lincolla (Lincoln), 13, Fc
Lincoln, 7B, Cb; 27, Fc
Lincoln, bp., 36, Fe
Lincoln, co., 27, Fc
Lincoln, lordship, 28A, Ca
Lincoln Wolds, 27, Fc
Lincolns Inn, 27A
Lindau, 30, He
Lindi, 96C, Fe
Lindinis (Ilchester), 3A, De
Lindisfarna (Lindisfarne), 13, Ea
Lindisfarne, 36, Eb; 36A
Lindley, 81A, Cc
Lindsay, 28B, Ca; 37A, Cb
Lindsey, 7B, Cb
Lindum (Lincoln), 3A, Fc
Lingan (Quinsay) (Hangchow), 25, Mc
Lingayen, 75E, Ba
Lingen, 60A, Ab
Lingen, co., 38, Gb
Linköping, 26, Eb
Linlithgow, 28B, Bb
Linlithgow, co., 37A, Cc
Linnhe, L., 14, Cc
Linz, 10, Fd; 33C, Cb
Lion, G. of the, 17, Gg
Lipari Is., 5, Ee
Lippa, 33C, Eb
Lippe, 65D, Aa
Lippe, Co., 30, Hc
Lippe, R., 20, Gc
Lisaine, 76A, Dc
Lisbon, 22, Ad; 23C, Ac; 63B
Lisbon, eccl. prov., 22, Ad
Lisburn, 49B, Eb
Lisieux, 11, Db
Liskeard, 27, Bf
L'Isle Jourdain, 30, Dg
Lismore, Ireland, 15, Dd
Lismore, Scotland, 14, Cc
Lismore, bp., 14A, Bb
Lissa, 32C, Fc
Lithuania, 50, Fc; 87, Ea
Lithuania, G.D. of, 26, Gc
Lithuanians, 9, Ga
Little Belt, 65F, Aa
Little Harbour (Rye), 45B, Db
Little Minch, 14, Bb
Little Namaqua Land, 81A, Ac
Little Namaquas, 81B, Ab
Little Poland, 39, Pc
Little Rock, 72, Bc
Little Russia, 51, Gc
Little Russian, 85, Jc
Little St. Bernard Pass, 5, Ab
Littlechester, 3A, Ed
Litus Saxonicum, 3A, Hd
Livadia, 78, Df
Livenza, R., 86B, Cb
Liverpool, 27, Dc
Livingstone, 81A, Ca
Livonia, 26, Gb
Livonians, 9, Ga
Livorno, 32A, Dc
Livron, 38, Ff
Lixheim, 29A, Ba; 39B, Db
Lizard, 55A, Ac
Llanbadarn, 28A, Bb
Llanbadarn Fawr, 13, Bd
Llandaf (Llandaff), 13, Ce
Llandaff, 27, Ce
Llandaff, bp., 36, Cf
Llandovery, 3A, Cd; 27, Ce
Llanelwy, 13, Cc
Llanfaes, 7B, Ab
Llangollen, 48B, Bc
Llanio, 3A, Bd
Llano Estacado, 44, De
Llanthony, 36, Cf
Llantwit, 28A, Cc
Loanda, 80A, Ee
Loango, 96C, De
Loano, 29A, Cc; 38, Hf
Lobenstein, 39C, Bc
Lobositz, 54, Eb; 60A, Ec
Locarno, 29B, Cb
Loch Inver, 49A, Ba
Lochaber, 14, Dc
Loches, 11, Dc; 17, Fe
Lochmaben, 28B, Bb
Lochnannagh, 49A, Bb
Lockerbie, 49A, Cc
Locri, 5, Fe
Löcse, 39, Pd
Lodève, 11, Ee
Lodi, 32A, Cb
Lodz, 87, Db; 89, Jc
Logan, Mt., 70, Aa
Logans, 56, Cc
Logia Sinus, 3A, Ab
Logrono, 23D, Da; 63, Da
Logstown, 57, Ac
Logudoro, 23B, Bd
Loigny, 76A, Ab
Loir, R., 11, Dc
Loire, R., 11, Cc; 22, Cb
Loitz, 31, Ka
Loja, 68, Bc
Lokoja, 80A, Dd; 96C, Cd
Lombard Alps, 29A, Dc
Lombard King., 5, Bb; 8B, Cb
Lombards, 4A, Fb
Lombardy, 20, Hf; 32C, Bb
Lombardy, King. of, 23A, Ba
Lombartzyde, 46A, Bc
Lombers, 20, Eg
Lome, 81C, Ec; 94, Te
Lomond, L., 14, Dc
Lonato, 32D, Bb
Loncastre (Lancaster), 13, Db
Londinium (London), 3A, Fe
London, Canada, 70, Fc
London, England, 27, Fe
London, bp., 36, Gf
London Bridge, 27A
Londonderry, co., 37C; 49B, Eb
Long B., 57D, Bb
Long I., Bahamas, 43A, Eb
Long I., Massachusetts, 56B
Long I., New York, 45B, Cc; 56, Eb
Long Island Sound, 57, Ec
Long, L., 14, Dc
Longford, co., 37C; 49B, Dc
Longibardia, 9, Fd
Longjumeau, 38, Ed
Longone, 32B, Cc
Longreach, 95, Lg
Longtown, 49A, Cc
Longueuil, 57, Ea
Longueville, 20, Dd
Longwy, 39B, Ba; 83A, Cb
Lookout Mt., 72A, Aa
Loop Hd., 15, Bd
Loos, 83A, Ba
Lopadium, 19, Dd
Lorch, 8, Eb
Lörchingen, 39B, Db
Lord Howe I., 77, Jh
Loreto, 21, Kg
Lorient, 53, Bd; 55A, Be
Loritello, 21A, Cb
Lorne, 14, Cc
Lorne, Firth of, 14, Cc
Lorraine, 83B, Ba
Lorraine, C. de, 45A, Ea
Lorraine, D. of, 20, Gd; 39B, Cb
Lorris, 20, Ee
Lorsch, 8, Db
Los, Is. de, 81C, Bc
Los Adaes, 43A, Ca
Los Angeles, 70, Cd
Los Diabolos, 40, Fc
Los Tiburones, I. de, 40, Be
Losecoat Field (Empingham), 27, Fd
Lostwithiel, 27, Bf
Lot, R., 11, Dd; 22, Cc
Lothar, King. of, 8A, Dc
Lotharingia, 8A, Ca
Lotharingia, D., 10, Ac
Lothian, 14, Ed
Lothian, co., 37A, Cc
Loudoun Hill, 3A, Ba
Loudun, 20, De
Loughbrickland, 49B, Eb
Loughrea, 37B, Cc; 49B, Cc
Louis, King. of, 8A, Db
Louisa, 72, Db; 72B, Aa
Louisburg, 45A, Fa
Louise, 57, Cd
Louisiade Arch., 77, Id
Louisiana, 56, Bd
Louisiana, st., 72, Bc
Louisville, 72, Cb
Lourenço Marques, 81A, Dc
Lourmarin, 38, Fg
Louth, England, 27, Fc
Louth, Ireland, 37B, Ec
Louth, co., 37C; 49B, Ec
Louvain, 46A, Dd
Lovat, R., 19, Ea
Lovcha, 78, Ed
Lowell, 45B, Db
Lower Alsace, Land. of, 20, Gd
Lower Austria, 65C, Cb
Lower Burgundy (Regnum Provinciae), 11, Fd
Lower California, 42, Dc; 43D Ab
Lower Canada, 71, Gc
Lower Doab, 59C, Db
Lower Lausitz, Marg. of, 31, Lc
Lower Lorraine, 20, Fc
Lower Lotharingia, 10, Ac
Lower Palatinate, 34, Dc; 38, Hd
Lower Peru, 41B, Be
Lower Silesia, 60A, Fc
Lower Tunguska, R., 74, Hb
Lowestoft, 54, Cb; 55A, Db
Loyalty Is., 77, Lf
Loyang, 1, Od
Luang Prabang, 91, Dd
Lübben, 39C, Db
Lubeck, 10, Db
Lublin, 26, Fc
Lucca, 5, Cc
Lucca, Rep. of, 32A, Dc
Luce, B., 14, De
Lucena, 23D, Cd
Lucera, 5, Ed
Lucerne, 10, Ce; 29B, Ca
Lucerne, canton, 29B, Ca
Luckenwalde, 60A, Db
Lucknow, 73, Db
Luçon, 20, Ce; 47, Bc
Lucy, 28B, Bc
Luderitz, 80A, Eg
Ludes (Louth), 13, Fc
Ludgershall, 27, Ee
Ludhiana, 73, Ca
Ludlow, 13, Dd; 27, Dd
Lug, R., 28A, Db
Lugano, 29B, Cb
Lugdunum, 2, Dd
Lugnaquillia, 15, Ed
Lugo, 23C, Ba; 63, Ba
Luguvalium (Carlisle), 3C
Luitpold Land, 69C
Lujan, 68, Cf
Lu-kiang, R., 73, Gb
Lule Burgas, 78, Fe
Lulea, 88, Ka
Luna, 20, Jf
Lund, 16, Ea; 26, Db
Lund, eccl. prov., 22, Ea
Lundonia (London), 13, Ge
Lundy's Lane, 71D
Lune, R., 48B, Bb
Lüneburg, Germany, 10, Db
Luneburg, Transvaal, 81D, Ba
Lunel, 38, Fg
Lunenburg, 45A, Eb
Lunéville, 10, Bd; 39B, Cb
Lung-Hsi, 1, Nd
Luni, R., 73, Bb
Lunigiana, 32E, Ba
Lünstadt, 20, Gd
Luray, 72B, Aa
Luristan, 79, Jd
Lusatia (Lausitz), 10, Fc
Lusatia, M. of, 16, Eb
Lusatians, 10, Eb
Lusignan, 11, Dc
Lussac, 28C, Cc
Lussina, 23B, Eb
Lutetia, 2, Dd
Lutsk, 19, Db
Lutter, 38, Jc
Lutterberg, 60A, Bc
Lutterworth, 27, Ed
Lützelburg, 39B, Db
Lützelburg (Luxemburg), Co. of, 20, Fd
Lützen, 38, Jc; 60B, Dc
Luvre (Oswestry), 13, Cd
Luxembourg, 31A, Dc; 46A, Fe
Luxemburg (Lützelburg), Co. of, 20, Fd
Luxemburg, D., 46A, Ee
Luxeuil, 10, Be; 39B, Cc
Luxor, 93, Cd
Luynes, 53, Dd
Luzon, 75E, Ba
Lvov, 87, Ec
Lyallpur, 92, Ca
Lycia, 1, Fd
Lydda (St. George), 18C, Bg
Lydenburg, 81B, Da
Lydford, 7C, Ac; 27, Bf
Lydia, 2, Jf
Lykandos, 9, Ke
Lym (Lyme Regis), 13, Df
Lyme Regis, 27, Df
Lynchburg, 57, Be; 72B, Ab
Lynn, 17, Fb; 27, Gd
Lynn Canal, 71B, Cb
Lyonnais, 17, Hf; 38, Ef
Lyons, 11, Fd
Lyons, eccl. prov., 22, Cb
Lyons, Co. of, 11, Fd
Lys, R., 46A, Cd
Lyubech, 9, Jb

Maabar, 35, Nd
Maas, R., 20, Fc; 30, Fc
Maastricht, 83A, Ca
Macae, 1, He
MacAllister, 37A, Bc
Macao, 91, Ed
Macapa, 68, Db
Macaria, 22, Fc
Macassar, 52C, Ac
McCarthy, 15, Cd
MacCluer G., 77, Eb
MacDonald, 37A, Ab
Macdonald Is., 69C
MacDonald of Clanranald, 37A, Bb
MacDonald of Glencoe, 37A, Bb
MacDonald of Glengarry, 37A, Bb
MacDonald of Inverlochy, 37A, Bb
MacDonald of Keppoch, 37A, Bb
McDonnell, 37B, Ea
Macdonnell Ra., 77, Ef
McDouall, 28B, Ac
Macedonia, 2, Hf; 78, De
Maceio, 68, Fc
Macerata, 22, Ec
Macfie, 37A, Ab
Macgillicuddys Reeks, 15, Bd
McGillipatrick, 15, Dd
Macgregor, 28B, Aa
McGuire, 37B, Db
Machecoul, 30, Ce
Macintosh, 37A, Bb
Mackay, 37A, Ba
MacKenzie, clan, 37A, Bb
Mackenzie, district, 70, Ca
Mackenzie, R., 44, Bb
McKinley, Mt., 71A, Ba
Maclachlan, 37A, Bb
Maclean, 37A, Bb
MacLeod, 37A, Aa
Macloutsie, R., 81A, Cb
MacMahon, 37B, Bd
McMahon, 37B, Eb
MacMurrough, 15, Ed
McMurrough, 37B, Ed
Macnab, 28B, Aa
Mâcon, France, 11, Fc
Macon, U.S.A., 72, Dc
Macpherson, 37A, Bb
Macquarie Is., 69C; 75, Eg
Macroom, 49B, Ce
Mactan, 40, Qd
Macziewice, 51, Ec
Madagascar, 80A, Hf
Madang (Friedrich Wilhelmshafen), 77, Hc
Maddy, L., 49A, Ab
Madeira, 80A, Ba
Madeira, R., 41B, Ce; 68, Cc
Madhya Pradesh, 92, Dc
Madras, 59D
Madras, st., 92, De
Madre de Dios I., 68, Bh
Madrid, 23C, Db; 63, Db
Madura, 25, Gf; 59A, Cf
Madurai, 92, Df
Maelienydd, 13, Cd
Maelor, 13, Dc
Maeotis Palus, 2, Ld
Maestricht, 46A, Ed
Mafeking, 81A, Cc; 96C, Eg
Mafia I., 80A, Ge

Mafra, 63B
Magadha, I., Le
Magdala, 83, Ld
Magdalen Is., 45A, Ea
Magdalena, R., 68, Bb
Magdalena (Rio Grande), R., 43A, Ed
Magdeburg, 10, Db; 21, Jb
Magdeburg, eccl. prov., 22, Ea
Magdeburg, Abp. of, 30, Jb
Magellan's Str., 68, Bh
Magennis, 37B, Eb
Magenta, 29A; Cc; 32C, Bb
Magersfontein, 81A, Bc
Maggiore, L., 5, Bb
Maghreb, 9, Bf
Maghreb-al-Aqsa, 6, Ab
Maghreb-al-Awsat, 6, Bb
Magnano, 29A, Bc
Magnis (Carvoran), 3C
Magnis (Kenchester), 3A, Dd
Magnitogorsk, 88, Rc
Magnus Portus (Portsmouth Harb.), 3A, Ef
Magog, 57C, Ab
Maguelonne, 11, Ee
Magus Muir, 37A, Cb
Magyar, 85, Fc
Magyars, 8, Hb; 9, Hc
Mahanadi, R., 73, Dc
Maharajpur, 73, Cb
Maharashtra, 92, Dc
Mahé, 73, Ce
Mahon, 63, Hc
Mahra, 6, Gd
Mahratta, 69A, Nc
Mahukona, 75D, Cb
Maida, 62, Fe
Maidenhead, 48B, Cd
Maidos, 86D
Maidstone, 48A, Dd
Maikop, 88, Oe
Maillezais, 22, Bb; 38, Ce
Main, R., Germany, 10, Cd
Main, R., Ireland, 15, Eb
Maine, prov., France, 38, Dd
Maine, st., U.S.A., 71E, Bc
Maine, terr., N. America, 45A, Cb
Maine, Co. of., 11, Cb
Mainland, 49A, Ca
Mainz, 10, Cd; 83A, Eb
Mainz, abp., 30, Hc
Mainz, eccl. prov., 22, Ea
Maipu, 68, Bf
Majapahit, 40, Pe
Majorca, 23C, Gc; 63, Gc
Majorca, King. of, 23D, Gc
Majuba Hill, 81D, Aa
Majunga, 96D, Gf
Makasar, 90, Cd
Makran, 6, Hc
Makurdi, 96B, Cb
Makyan, 52B, Aa
Malabar Coast, 59A, Ce
Malacca, 75A, Aa; 91, Df
Malacca, Str. of, 75A, Aa
Malaga, 23C, Cd; 63, Cd
Malaita, 77, Kc
Malakand Pass, 73, Ba
Malamocco, 32D, Cb
Malatya, 79, Gc
Malay Pen., 75, Cd
Malaya, 91, Df
Malborgeth, 86B, Da
Malchin, 31, Kb
Malden I., 75, He
Malden, R., 56B
Maldive Is., 92, Cf
Maldon, 27, Ge; 48A, Dd
Maldonado, 68, Df
Malduna (Maldon), 13, Ge
Male, 86B, Aa
Mali, 96D, Bc
Malia, C., 78, Dg
Malik L., 86A, Bb
Malin Hd., 15, Da
Malindi, 69A, Me
Malines, 51, Ac; 83A, Ca
Malling, 36, Gf
Mallow, 49B, Cd
Malmédy, 46A, Kd; 83A, Da
Malmesberie (Malmesbury), 13, De
Malmesbury, 27, De; 48A, Bd
Malmö, 26, Db; 60B, Da
Maloja Pass, 29B, Db
Malolos, 75E, Bb
Malown, 73, Ca
Malpas, 27, Dc
Malplaquet, 46A, Cd; 54, Cb
Malta, 8, Ed; 34, Ee
Malton, 27, Fb
Malvasia, 18B, Cc; 78, Dg
Malvern, England, 36, De
Malvern, Virginia, 57, Ce
Malwa, 1, Ke; 73, Cc
Mamecastre (Manchester), 18, Dc
Mameln, 38, Hb
Mameluke Sultans, 24, Hg
Mamelukes, 25, Cc
Mamistra, 18C, Ca
Mamore, R., 68, Cd
Mamucium (Manchester), 3A, Dc
Man, I. of, 7B, Aa; 34, Bb
Managua, 43D, Dc
Manama, 93, Gd
Manassas Junction, 72B, Ba
Manau, 14, Dc
Manaus, 68, Dc
Manbedj, 18C, Eb
Manchac (Fort Bute), 56, Ad
Manchester, England, 7C, Bb
Manchester, New York, 57, Eb
Manchu, 42, Qb
Manchukuo, 90, Ca
Manchuria, 74, Ld; 90, Ca
Mandalay, 73, Gc
Mandan Village, 44, Dd
Mandeswar, 73, Cc
Manfredonia, 32A, Fd
Mangalore, 73, Be
Mangi, 35, Pc
Mangi (Song Empire), 25, Kd
Manhattan I., 45B, Cc; 57B
Maniago, 86B, Ca
Manihiki, 75, He
Manila, 75E, Bb
Manipur, 73, Fc
Manissa, 78, Ff
Manitoba, 70, Eb
Mannheim, 29A, Ca; 83A, Eb
Manokvary, 77, Eb
Manresa, 23C, Fb; 63, Fb
Mansel, I., 70, Fa
Mansfeld, 20, Jc; 60A, Cc
Mansura, Egypt, 80B, Aa
Mansura, India, 6, Hc
Mansurabad, 6A, Db
Mansurah, 18A, Ec
Mantatis, 81B, Da
Mantes, 17, Fd
Mantua, 5, Cb; 22, Eb
Mantua, Marq. of (Gonzaga), 32A, Db
Manukau Harbour, 77A
Manzanares, 63, Dc
Manzanillo, 43D, Bc
Manzikert, 16, Le
Maputa, R., 81A, Dc
Maqdala, 80B, Be
Mar, 14, Fb
Mar del Plata, 68, Df
Maracaibo, 43A, Ec
Maracaibo, L., 43A, Ed
Marajo I., 68, Ec
Maranhão, 41B, Ed
Maranhao (Sao Luis), 68, Ec
Maranhao, st., 68, Ec
Marañon, R., 68, Bc
Marans, 38, Ce
Marar, G. of, 73, Cf
Maras, 93, Db
Marash, 18C, Da
Maratha, 59A, Cc
Marbella, 23D, Cd
Marble Head, 57, Fb
Marburg, 20, Hc
March, R., 21, Md
Marches, The, 32A, Ec
Marchfield, 21, Md
Marcianopolis, 4A, Hc
Marcomanni, 2, Gd
Mardin, 18A, Gb; 93, Eb
Mare Adriaticum, 2, Ge
Mare Ægæum, 2, Jf
Mare Cantabricum, 1, Bc
Mare Caspium, 1, Gc
Mare Internum, 1, Cd
Mare Ionium, 2, Gf
Mare Suevicum, 2, Gb
Mare Tyrrhenum, 2, Ff
Maree, L., 14, Cb
Marengo, 29A, Cc; 62, Dd
Margam, 7B, Bc
Margarita, 43A, Fc
Margiana, 1, Jd
Margidunum (Castle Hill), 3A, Fd
Maria, 63, Eb
Maria Van Diemen, C., 77, Mh
Mariana Is., 74, Ng; 90, Dc
Marib, 6, Fd
Marico Drift, 81A, Cb
Marie Byrd Land, 69C
Marie Galante, 43A, Fc
Marienbourg, 46A, Dd
Marienburg, 21, Na
Marienthal, 22, Ea
Marienwalde, 22, Fa
Marienwerder, 21, Nb
Marietta, Georgia, 72A, Ab
Marietta, Ohio, 56, Cc
Mariette, 71C, Bc
Marignano, 32A, Cb
Marinids, 24, Ag
Maritime Alps, 29A, Bc
Maritza, 78, Ed
Maritza, R., 78, Fe
Mark, 12, Ga
Mark, Co. of, 20, Gc; 46C, Cb
Market Drayton, 48B, Bc
Markirch, 39B, Db
Markland, 35, Fb
Marlborough, England, 27, Ee
Marlborough, N.Z., 77A
Marle, 11, Eb
Marlow, 27, Fe
Marmande, 30, Df
Marmara, Sea of, 78, Ge
Marmolada, 29A, Eb
Marmoutier, 22, Cb
Marne, R., 11, Eb
Maros, R., 33C, Eb; 78, Dc
Maroua, 96B, Da
Marquesas Is., 75, Je
Marra, 18C, Dc
Marrakesh, 80A, Ca; 96D, Ba
Marrana, 23B, Cc
Marroqui, C., 63A
Mars Hill, 71E, Cb
Mars la Tour, 76A, Cb
Marsaglia, 29A, Cc
Marsal, 39B, Cb
Marsala, 32C, De
Marsalquivir, 34, Be
Marseilles, 11, Fe; 29A, Ad
Marshall Is., 90, Ec
Marshfield, 45B, Db
Marsi, 21A, Bb
Marsia, 23A, Dc
Marsico, 21A, Cb; 22, Fc
Marston Moor, 48A, Cc
Martaban, G. of, 73, Gd
Martello, The, 86B, Cb
Martha's Vineyard, 45B, Dc
Martigny, 29B, Bb
Martinique, 43A, Fc
Martirano, 21A, Dc
Martyropolis, 4B, Ld
Marvejols, 38, Ef
Maryborough, Australia, 77, Ig
Maryborough, Ireland, 49B, Dc
Maryland, 57, Cd; 72B, Ba
Masan-daran, 61B, Ab
Masbate, 75E, Bb
Mascarenhas, 40, Mf
Mashona, 80A, Gf
Mashona Land, 81A, Da
Masira, 93, He
Mask, L., 15, Bc
Maskat, 41A, Cb; 74, Df
Masmünster, 39B, Dc
Mason and Dixon's Line, 56, Dc
Masovia, 26, Fc
Masper, 45B, Cc
Massa, 22, Ec; 32A, Db
Massachusetts, 45B, Db
Massagetae, 1, Hc
Massawa, 80B, Bd
Massema, 96B, Da
Massikessi, 81A, Da
Massilia, 2, Ee
Masulipatam, 73, Dd
Masurian Lakes, 84, Gb
Matabele, 81B, Da
Matabeleland, 81A, Ca
Matagorda Bay, 43A, Cb
Matamoros, 43A, Cb
Matanzas, 43A, Db
Matapan, C., 78, Dg
Matatana, 40, Mf
Matera, India, 59C, Db
Matera, Italy, 21A, Db
Mathura, 92, Db
Mato Grosso (Villa Bella), 68, Cd
Mato Grosso, prov., 68, Dd
Matoppo Hills, 81A, Cb
Matruh, 84, Hf; 93, Bc
Mattapony, R., 72B, Ba
Matuku, 75C, Bb
Maturin, 68, Cb
Maubeuge, 46A, Cd
Maui, 75D, Cb
Mauléon, 20, Cg
Maumee, R., 57A, Ca; 71C, Bb
Mauna Loa, 75D, Dc
Mauretania, 2, Df
Mauriac, 20, Ef
Mauritania, 80A, Bc
Mauritania, rep., 96D, Ac
Mauritia (Pernambuco), 42, He
Mauritius, 42, Mf; 69A, Ne
Mauvezin, 38, Dg
Mawddach, R., Bb
Mawson, 69C
Maxen, 60A, Dc
Maxwell, 28B, Bb; 37A, Cc
May, C., 45B, Bd
May, I. of, 28B, Ca
Maya, 63, Ea
Mayas, 43A, Cc
Maybole, 28B, Ab
Mayence, 33C, Bb
Mayenne, 17, Ed
Mayenne, R., 53, Cc
Maynooth, 49B, Ec
Mayo, 15, Bc
Mayo, co., 37C; 49B, Bc
Mayorga, 63, Ca
Mazagan, 42, Jc
Mazapil, 43A, Bb
Mazaltan, 43A, Bb
Mazovia, 39, Pb
Mazzara, 21A, Bd; 22, Ed
Mbengga, 75C, Bb
Meander, R., 19, De
Mearns, 14, Fc
Meath, 17, Bb; 37B, Dc
Meath (Midhe), 15, Dc
Meath, co., 49B, Ec
Meaux, England, 36, Fd
Meaux, France, 11, Eb
Mecca, 6, Fc; 25, Dd; 80B, Bc
Mechanicsville, 72B, Bb
Mechlin, 46A, Dc
Mecklenburg, 10, Db
Mecklenburg, D. of, 10, Db
Medan, 91, Cf
Medellin, Colombia, 68, Bb
Medellin, Spain, 63, Cc
Medelpad, 26, Ea
Medeltune (Melton Mowbray), 13, Fd
Media, I., Gd
Medicine Hat, 70, Cb
Medina, 25, Dd; 93, De
Medina (Yathreb), 6, Fc
Medina de Rio Seco, 63, Cb
Medina Sidonia, 23C, Cd
Mediolanum (Milan), 5, Bb
Mediterranean Sea, 8, Fd
Meean Doab, 73, Ca
Meerut, 73, Cb
Mehadia, 78, Dc
Mehdiya, 9, Ee
Mehidpur, 73, Cc
Meiningen, 20, Jc; 30, Jc
Meirionydd (Merioneth), 13, Db
Meisenheim, 60B, Ad
Meissen, 10, Ec
Meissen, March of, 10, Fc
Mejillones, 68, Be
Mekong, R., 25, Ke; 91, De
Melandra Castle, 3A, Ec
Melbourne, 77, Hi
Melcombe Regis, 27, Df
Meldorf, 20, Ha
Melfi, 21A, Cb; 22, Fc
Melilla, 34, Be; 40, Jc
Melinde, 41A, Be
Melite I., 2, Ff
Melitene, 6A, Ba
Melk, 21, Ld
Mellrichstadt, 10, Dc
Melmoth, 81D, Bb
Melnik, 19, Cd
Meloria I., 24, De
Melrose, 14, Fd; 28B, Cb
Melton Mowbray, 27, Fd
Melun, 11, Eb; 17, Gd
Melville I., Australia, 77, Ed
Melville I., Canada, 44, Ca
Melville Pen., 44, Fb
Memel, 26, Fb; 60A, Ha
Memel, R., 26, Fb
Memleben, 10, Dc
Memmingen, 20, Jd; 29A, Da
Memphis, Egypt, 2, Kh
Memphis, U.S.A., 72, Bb
Memphis (Chickasaw Bluff), 71F, Aa
Memphis (Fort Assumption), 56, Bc
Menado, 52C, Ba
Mende, 11, Ed; 17, Gf
Menderes, R., 24, Hf
Mendip Hills, 27, De
Mendocino, C., 70, Bc
Mendoza, 68, Cf
Mendrisio, 29B, Cc
Menin, 46A, Cd; 53, Eb
Menindee, 77, Gh
Mentana, 32C, Dc
Menteith, 14, Dc
Menteshe, 19, De
Menzies, 37A, Bb
Meonware, 7A, Cb
Meppen, 20, Gb
Mequinenza, 23C, Fb; 63, Fb
Meran, 10, De; 86B, Ba
Mercia, 7B, Cb; 12, Dc
Mercians, 7A, Ca
Mere, 27, De
Meresberie (Maesbury), 13, Cd
Merevale, 36, Ee
Mergui, 73, Ge
Mergui Arch., 92, He
Merida, Spain, 63, Bc
Merida, Venezuela, 43A, Ed
Meridian, 72, Cc
Merioneth, co., 27, Cd
Merleberge (Marlborough), 13, Ee
Meroe, 35, Ld
Merowe, 80B, Ad
Merrimac, R., 45B, Db
Merry Mount (Quincey), 45B, Db
Merse (Mersea I.), 13, Ge
Merse, The, 14, Fd
Mersea, 7C, Dc
Merseburg, 10, Dc; 39C, Bb
Merseburg, M. of, 10, Ec
Mersen, 8A, Ca; 9, Db
Mersey, R., 27, Dc
Mersha, R. (Mersey), 13, Cc
Mersin, 93, Cb
Mersina, 86C, Bb
Mertola, 23C, Bd
Merton, 36, Ff
Merv, 6, Hb; 25, Fc; 61B, Bb
Mesembria, 8, Hc
Meseritz, 22, Fa; 31, Lb
Meshed, 61B, Ab; 93, Hb
Mesopotamia, 1, Gd; 6A, Ca
Messana, 2, Gf
Messina, 5, Ee
Messina, eccl. prov., 22, Ed
Messines, 83A, Ba
Mesta, R., 78, Ee
Mestre, 86B, Cb
Meta, R., 43A, Ed; 68, Cb
Metaris Aest. (The Wash), 3A, Gc
Metemma, 80B, Ad
Methone, 9, Ge
Methven, 28B, Ba
Metis, R., 71E, Ba
Metsovo, 78, Cf
Metz, 10, Bd; 83A, Db
Metz, Bp. of, 30, Gd; 39B, Ca
Meuse, R., 10, Ac, 17, Hc
Meuse, Mouth of the, 46A, Cc
Mexico, city, 43A, Cc
Mexico, st., 43A, Bb
Mexico, G. of, 43A, Cb
Mezen, R., 61, Ga
Mézières, 46A, De, 53, Fc
Miami, 94, Ed
Miami, R., 71C, Bc
Miamis, 45A, Ab; 56, Bb
Miani, 73, Ab
Michigan, 70, Fc
Michigan, L., 56, Bb
Michigan Terr., 67C, Da
Michillimackinac I., 45A, Aa
Michoacan, 43A, Bc
Micmacs, 45A, Da
Mics, 31, Kd
Middelburg, C. of Good Hope, 81A, Bd
Middelburg, Netherlands, 46A, Cc
Middelburg, Transvaal, 81A, Cc
Middelfart, 65F, Aa
Middle I. (South I., N.Z.), 77A
Middle Angles, 7A, Ca
Middle Drift, 81D, Bb
Middle March, 28B, Bb
Middle Saxons, 7A, Cb
Middleham, 27, Eb
Middlesex, 27, Fe
Middleton, 37A, Cb
Middletown, Connecticut, 45B, Cc
Middletown, New Jersey, 45B, Bc
Midelsexe (Middlesex), 13, Fe
Midhe (Meath), 15, Dc
Midhurst, 27, Fe
Midia, 78, Ge
Midnapore, 59A, Ec; 59B
Midway I., 90, Fb
Miedniki, 26, Fb
Mien (Burma), 25, Jd
Mierdyk, 46A, Dc
Milam, 73, Da
Milan (Mediolanum), 5, Bb
Milan, eccl. prov., 22, Db
Milan, D. of, 32A, Cb
Milazzo, 21A, Cc; 32C, Ee
Milborne Port, 27, Df
Mileburne (Milborne Port), 13, Df
Miletus, 19, De
Milford, Connecticut, 45B, Cc
Milford, Wales, 27, Ae
Milford Haven, 55A, Ac
Milhau, 11, Ed
Mill Springs, 72, Db
Milledgeville, 72, Dc
Millen, 72, Dc
Millikens Bend, 72C, Aa
Milos, 78, Eg
Milton, 7C, Dc
Milwaukee, 70, Fc
Milzienians, 10, Fc
Min Yueh, 1, Oe
Minaei, 1, Gf
Minas Gerais, 68, Ed
Minch, The, 14, Bb
Mincio, R., 5, Cb
Mindanao, 75E, Bc
Mindelheim, 53, Jc
Minden, 10, Cb
Minden, Bp. of, 60A, Bb
Mindoro, 75E, Bb
Mindoro Str., 75E, Bb
Mingrelia, 61, Ff; 79, Hb
Minho, 63, Ab
Minho, R., 63, Ba
Minna, 96B, Cb
Minneapolis, 70, Ec

Minnesota, 70, Ec
Minnesota Terr., 67D, Da
Minorca, 23C, Gb; 63, Gb
Minsk, 26, Gc; 87, Fb
Minster, 7B, Dc
Minto, L., 70, Gb
Minya, 93, Cd
Miquelon, 45A, Fa
Mirabeau, 17, Fe
Mirabel, 18C, Cf
Mirambeau, 20, Cf
Miramichi B., 45A, Ea
Miranda, Brazil, 68, De
Miranda, Portugal, 22, Ac; 63, Bb
Miranda, Spain, 63, Da
Mirande, 53, Df
Mirandola, 32A, Db
Mirepoix, 22, Cc; 38, Dg
Mirny, 69C
Mirzapur, 59B; 73, Db
Misilmeri, 21A, Bd
Miskolcz, 31, Pd
Misol, 52C, Cb; 77, Eb
Misr (Egypt), 6, Dc
Missassauga Fort, 71D
Missenden, 36, Ff
Missionary Ridge, 72A, Aa
Mississippi, R., 56, Ab; 70, Ec
Mississippi, st., 70, Fd
Mississippi, Delta of the, 43A, Db
Mississippi Terr., 67B, Bb; 71F, Ba
Missolonghi, 78, Cf
Missouri, R., 70, Ec; 72, Bb
Missouri, st., 72, Bb
Missouri Terr., 67C, Ca
Missunde, 65F, Aa
Mistassini, L., 70, Gb
Mistra, 19, Ce
Misurata, 88, Jg
Mitau, 50, Eb; 61A, Ba
Mitchell, R., 77, Ge
Mitchelstown, 49B, Cd
Mittelmark, 31, Kb; 60A, Db
Mitylene, 78, Ef
Mizen Hd., 15, Be
Mkusi, R., 81D, Ba
Mlava, 21, Pb
Moala, 75C, Bb
Mobile, 56, Bd; 67C, Eb
Mocha, 93, Eg
Modbury, 27, Cf
Modder, R., 81B, Cb
Modena, 8A, Dc
Modena (Mutina), 5, Cb
Modena, D. of (Este), 32A, Db
Modon, 78, Cg
Modrusch, 2, Fb
Moesia, 1, Ec; 4A, Gc
Moffat, 37A, Cc
Mogador, 82, Af
Mogadiscio (Mogadishu), 96A, Bb
Mogadishu, 80A, Hd; 96C, Gd
Mogul Empire, 52A, Bb
Moguntiacum, 2, Ec
Mohacs, 33C, Db; 39, Ne
Mohammed Abtin, Dominions of, 24, Kf
Mohawk, R., 57, Db
Mohawks, 45A, Cb; 57, Db
Mohi, 19, Cc
Mohilev, 26, Hc; 50, Gc
Moidart, 14, Cc; 49A, Bb
Mojaisk, 19, Fa
Mold, 27, Cc
Moldau, R., 21, Ld
Moldavia, 50, Fd; 78, Fb
Molème, 22, Cb
Molfetta, 23B, Fd
Molina, 23D, Eb
Molins de Rey, 63, Gb
Molise, 23B, Ed; 32A, Fd
Mollendo, 68, Bd
Molloy, 37B, Dc
Mollwitz, 60A, Fc
Molokai, 75D, Cb
Molopo, R., 81B, Ba
Molotov, 88, Rb
Moloyaroslavetz, 62, Ka
Molucca Passage, 52C, Ca
Moluccas, 52C, Cb; 91, Ff
Mölzen, 10, Ec
Mombasa, 80A, Ge; 96D, Fe
Momonia (Mumha) (Munster), 15, Cd
Mömpelgard, 39B, Cc
Mon, I. (Anglesey), 7B, Ab; 13, Bc
Mona (Angelsey), 3A, Bc
Mona Passage, 43A, Fc
Monaco, 32A, Bc
Monaghan, 49B, Eb
Monaghan, co., 37C; 49B, Eb
Monastir (Bitolia), 78, Ce
Monavia (I. of Man), 3A, Bb
Monclova, 43A, Bb
Moncton, 71, Hc
Mondego, R., 63, Ab
Mondoñedo, 22, Ac
Mondovi, 29A, Cc
Mondovia, 32A, Bb
Monemude (Monmouth), 13, De
Monemvasia, 19, Ce
Monfalcone, 86B, Db
Monflanquin, 38, Df
Monforte, 22, Ac
Monghyr, 59A, Eb
Mongol Il-Khans, Empire of the, 19, He
Mongolia, rep., 91, Db
Monks Bretton, 36, Ed
Monks Corner, 57D, Ab
Monmouth, 27, De
Monmouth Court House, 56, Eb; 57, Dc
Monnow, R., 28A, Dc
Monocacy, 72B, Ba
Monocacy, R., 72B, Ba
Monomotapa, 52, Lf
Monongahela, R., 45A, Bb
Monopoli, 32A, Gd
Monreal (Mons Regalis), 18C, Ch
Monreale, 21A, Bc; 22, Ed
Monreale, eccl. prov., 22, Ed
Monroe, 72, Bc
Monrovia, 81C, Bc
Mons, 46A, Cd
Mons Regalis (Monreal), 18C, Ch
Mont Cenis Pass, 5, Ab
Mont de Marsan, 38, Cg
Mont Genèvre Pass, 32A, Bb
Mont Louis, 53, Ef
Mont St. Jean, 46B
Mont St. Michel, 17, Ed
Mont Valerien, 76A, Ab
Montacute, 27, Df
Montagnais, 45A, Ca
Montagud (Montacute), 13, Df
Montalto, 39, Kg
Montana, 70, Dc
Montana Terr., 67D, Ba
Montaperto, 23B, Cc
Montargis, 17, Gd; 38, Ed
Montauban, Provence, 20, Ff
Montauban, Toulouse, 11, Dd
Montaut, 38, Dg
Montbard, 76A, Cc
Montbazon, 53, Dd
Montbéliard, 20, Ge
Montbrison, 30, Ff
Montcenis, 38, Fe
Montdidier, 31A, Bc; 83A, Bb
Monte Cassino, 5, Dd
Monte Peloso, 21A, Db
Monte Redondo, 63B
Monte San Angelo, 21A, Db
Montebello, Milan, 29A, Cc
Montebello, Pavia, 29A, Cc
Montecatini, 32E, Bb
Montefeltro, 32A, Ec
Monteleone, 21A, Dc
Montélimar, 30, Ff
Montendre, 38, Cf
Montenegro, 39, Ng; 78, Bd
Montenotte, 29A, Cc
Montepulciano, 32E, Bb
Montereau, 28D, Db; 31A, Bc
Monterey, California, 70, Bd
Monterey, Mexico, 43A, Bb
Montescaglioso, 21A, Db
Montevideo, 68, Df
Montfaucon, 22, Db
Montferrat, Marq. of, 32A, Cb
Montfort, 11, Db; 30, Dd
Montgomery, Alabama, 72, Cc
Montgomery, Wales, 27, Cd
Montgomery, family, 28B, Ab
Montiel, 23D, Dc
Montlaur, 30, Ef
Montlhéry, 30, Ed; 31A, Bc
Montluçon, 53, Ed
Montmédy, 29A, Aa; 83A, Cb
Montmorency, 53, Ec
Montpellier, 11, Ee
Montpensier, 30, Ee
Montreal, 45A, Ca; 57, Ea
Montreuil, 11, Da; 83A, Aa
Montrose, 49A, Cb
Montserrat, 22, Cc
Montserrat, I., 43A, Fc
Monza, 4B, Eb; 5, Bb
Monzon, 63, Fb
Mooi, R., 81A, Cc
Mook, 46A, Ec
Moore's Creek, R., 57D, Ba
Moorfields, 27A
Moorfoot Hills, 28B, Bb
Moors, 2A, Ac
Moose, R., 70, Fb
Moose Factory, 70, Fb
Moquegua, 68, Bd
Mora, 26, Da
Moradabad, 73, Cb
Morant, 43A, Ec
Morar, 73, Cb
Morar, L., 14, Cc
Morat, 29B, Bb; 31A, Dd
Morava, R., 78, Cc
Moravia, 8A, Eb; 33C, Db
Moravia, M. of, 21, Md
Moravian Empire, 9, Fc
Moravian Town, 71C, Bb
Moravians, 8, Fb
Moray, 14, Db; 37A, Bb
Moray Firth, 14, Eb
Morea, 78, Dg
Morecambe B., 27, Cc
Morella, 23C, Eb
Morena, Sierra, 63, Cc
Moresnet, 83A, Da
Moret, 20, Ed
Moreton B., 77, Ig
Morgannwg, 7C, Bc; 12, Dd
Morgannwg (Glamorgan), 13, Ce
Morgarten, 29B, Ca
Morhange, 83B, Ba
Moriah, 18D
Moridunum (Carmarthen), 3A, Be
Morimont, 22, Db
Morlaix, 28C, Ab; 38, Bd
Moro, 52B, Aa
Morocco, 96C, Ba
Morocco, King., 80A, Ca
Morotai, 90, Cc
Morpeth, 13, Ea
Morrisburg, 57, Da
Morristown, 57, Dc
Mors, 60A, Ac
Mortagne, 11, Db; 30, Dd
Mortain, 11, Cb
Mortara, 32C, Bb
Mortemart, 53, Dd
Mortie, 52C, Ca
Mortimer, Ireland, 37B, Dd
Mortimer, Wales, 28A, Bc
Mortimers Cross, 27, Dd
Morven, 14, Cc
Mosbach, 20, Hd
Moscow, 19, Fa
Moscow, Pr. of, 24, Kb
Moselle, R., 10, Bd; 39B, Cb
Mosquito Coast, 43A, Dc
Mossamedes, 80A, Ef
Mossel B., 81B, Bc
Mostar, 39, Mg; 78, Ad
Mosul, 6A, Ca; 25, Dc
Motien lin Pass, 76B, Ba
Motir, 52B, Aa
Motrone, 32E, Bb
Moulins, 30, Ee
Moulmein, 73, Gd; 92, Hd
Mount Desert I., 45B, Ee
Mount Grace, 36, Ec
Mount Jackson, 72B, Aa
Mount Vernon, 57, Cd
Mountmellick, 49B, Dc
Moura, 23C, Bc
Mourne Mts., 15, Eb
Mourne, R., 15, Db
Moutiers, 11, Gd
Mouzon, 22, Db
Moy, 49A, Bb
Moyenvic, 39B, Cb
Mozambique, 80A, Hf
Mozambique, col., 80A, Gf
Mozdok, 61, Ff
Mozhaisk, 88, Nb
Mscislaw, 51, Gc; 61A, Db
Mstof, 26, Ec
Muck, 14, Bc
Mudania, 79, Eb
Mudki, 73, Ba
Mugello, 32E, Bb
Mügeln, 39C, Db
Mühlberg, 34, Eb; 39C, Db
Mühldorf, 10, Ed
Mühlhausen, 20, Jc
Muiden, 46A, Eb
Muilrea, 15, Bc
Mukalla, 93, Fg
Mukden, 76B, Ba
Mukden (Shenyang), 91, Fb
Mulde, R., 39C, Cb
Mulgrave, 27, Fb
Mulhausen, 30, Ge
Mulhouse, 29A, Bb; 83B, Bb
Mulkaid, 52A, Bc
Mull, 14, Cc
Mullingar, 49B, Dc
Multan, 25, Gc; 73, Ba
Multun, 6, Jb
Mumha (Momonia, Munster), 15, Cd
Muncaster, 13, Cb
Münchengrätz, 60B, Ec
Münden, 53, Hb
Mundelsheim, 29A, Ca
Munich, 29A, Da
Munkacz, 50, Ed; 54, Gc
Münster, Germany, 10, Bc
Munster, Ireland, 37B, Cd
Munster (Mumha, Momonia), 15, Ca
Münster, Bp. of, 30, Gb
Munster Irish, 49C
Munster Thal, 29B, Eb
Münsterberg, 31, Mc
Mur, R., 21, Le
Murad Su, R., 19, Ge
Murat, 30, Ef
Murbach, 20, Ge; 39B, Dc
Murchison, R., 77, Bg
Murcia, 22, Bd; 63, Ed
Murcia, prov., 63, Ec
Muret, 11, De; 22, Cc
Murfreesboro, 72, Cb
Muri, 29B, Ca
Murmansk, 74, Bb; 88, Ma
Murom, 19, Ga
Murom-Riazan, 19, Fb
Murray, 28B, Ba; 37A, Ba
Murray, R., 77, Hi
Murrumbidgee, R., 77, Hh
Mursa, 2, Gd
Murshidabad, 59A, Ec
Murten, 30, Ge
Murviedro, 23C, Ec
Murzuk, 80A, Eb; 96C, Db
Muscat, 40, Mc; 93, He
Muscovy, 35, Mb; 61, Fc
Muskingum, R., 71C, Bb
Musselburgh, 49A, Cc
Mustapha Pasha, 78, Fe
Muta, 6A, Bb
Mutina (Modena), 5, Cb
Muziris, 1, Kf
Mweru, L., 80A, Fe
Myitkyina, 92, Hb
Mynyw (St. David's), 13, Ae
Myriocephalon, 18A, Eb
Mysore, 59A, Ce; 73, Ce
Mysore, st., 59D; 73, Ce
Mystic, R., 56B
Myton, 28B, Dc

NAARDEN, 46A, Eb
Naas, 49B, Ec
Nablus, 18C, Cf
Nabresina, 86B, Db
Nachod, 33C, Da
Nafels, 29B, Da
Naga, 75E, Bb
Naga Hills, 92, Gb
Nagasaki, 91, Fc
Nagoya, 91, Gc
Nagpur, 73, Cc
Nagy Sarlo, 33C, Db
Nahuas, 43A, Bc
Naiman, 25, Hb
Nain, 71, Hb
Nairn, 37A, Cb
Nairn, co., 37A, Cb; 49A, Cb
Nairn, R., 37A, Cb
Nairobi, 80A, Ge
Naissus, 2, He; 4A, Gc
Najaf, 93, Ec
Najera, 23D, Da; 28C, Ae
Nakhijevan, 9, Me
Namsos, 88, Ha
Namur, 28D, Ea; 46A, Dd
Namur, Co. of, 46C, Bb
Nanaimo, 70, Bc
Nanchang, 91, Ed
Nancy, 10, Bd; 39B, Cb
Nandi, 75C, Aa
Nandidroog, 73, Cc
Nanking, 91, Ec
Nanning, 91, Dd
Nantasket, 45B, Db
Nantes, 11, Cc; 17, Ee
Nantes, Co. of, 11, Cc
Nantucket, 45B, Ec
Nantwich, 48A, Bc
Napier, 77A
Naples (Neapolis), 5, Ed
Naples, King. of, 32A, Fd
Napo, R., 68, Bc
Narbada, R., 25, Gd; 73, Cc
Narberth, 28A, Bc
Narbo, 2, De
Narbonne, 11, Ee
Narbonne, eccl. prov., 22, Cc
Narenta, R., 78, Ad
Narew, R., 31, Pb; 39, Qb
Narke, 50, Db
Narnia, 5B, Bb
Naro, 21A, Bd
Narragansett B., 45B, Dc
Narragh, 15, Ec
Narva, 26, Gb; 54, Ha
Narvik, 88, Ja
Naseby 48B, Cc
Nashborough (Nashville), 56, Bc
Nashville (Nashborough), 56, Bc
Nass, R., 71B, Dc
Nassau, 43A, Eb
Nassau, Co. of, 20, Hc
Natal, Brazil, 68, Fc
Natal, Rep. of, 81D, Bb
Natchez, 56, Ad
Natchitoches, 70, Ed
Nauders, 29A, Db
Naugard, 31, Lb
Naumburg, 21, Jc; 38, Jc
Naumkeag (Salem), 45B, Db
Naupactus, 19, Ce
Nauplia, 78, Dg
Nauplis, 18A, Cb
Nauru, 90, Ed
Nauta, 68, Bc
Navan, 49B, Ec
Navarino, 78, Cg
Navarre, 63, Ea
Navarreins, 38, Cg
Navio (Brough), 3A, Ec
Naworth, 27, Db
Naxos, 78, Eg
Naxos, D. of, 24, Hf; 34, Ge
Naxouat, 56, Fa
Nay, 38, Cg
Nazareth, Italy, 22, Fc
Nazareth, Palestine, 18C, Cf
Naze, The, 55A, Dc
Neagh, L., 15, Eb
Neapolis, 2, Fe
Neapolis (Naples), 5, Ed
Neath, 28A, Bc
Neath, R., 28A, Bc
Nebbio, 22, Dc
Nebraska, 70, Dc
Nebraska Terr., 67D, Ca
Neckar, R., 10, Cd
Neerwinden, 53, Fb
Negapatam, 59D
Neghelli, 96A, Ab
Negotin, 86A, Da
Negrepelisse, 38, Df
Negro (Fort Gadsden), 71F, Ba
Negro, R., Argentina, 68, Cf
Negro, R., Brazil, 68, Cc
Negroponte, 78, Ef
Negros, 75E, Bb
Nehavend, 6A, Db
Neisse, 21, Mc
Neisse, R., 10, Fc; 60A, Ec
Neiva, 41B, Bc
Nejd, 6, Fc; 84, Kg; 93, Ed
Nejef, 86C, Dc
Nejran, 6, Fd
Nellore, 52A, Cc
Nelson, 77A
Nelson, prov., 77A
Nelson, R., 70, Eb
Neman, R., 87, Eb
Nemirov, 51, Fd
Nemours, 30, Ed
Nemours, D. of, 30, Ed
Nen, R., 27, Gd; 36, Ge
Nenagh, 37B, Cd; 49B, Cd
Nenana, 71A, Ca
Neocaesarea, 18A, Fa
Nepal, 73, Db
Nephin, 15, Bb
Nepi, 22A
Nepomuk, 22, Eb
Nérac, 38, Df
Nerchinsk, 52, Qb; 74, Kc
Neresheim, 65A, Bb
Nesle, 20, Ed
Ness, L., 14, Db
Nesse, 13, De
Nessib, 64, Kf
Netherby, 28B, Bb
Netherlands, 46A; 53, Fb
Netherlands, King. of the, 64, Dc
Netherlands Guiana, 68, Db
Netley, 36, Eg
Netz, 65A, Ca
Netze R., 31, Me; 39, Mb
Neu Breisach, 76A, Db
Neu-Sandec, 39, Pd
Neuburg, 38, Jd; 47, Ec
Neuchâtel, 10, Be; 29B, Aa
Neuchâtel, canton, 29B, Aa
Neuchâtel, L. of, 29B, Ab
Neuenburg, 20, Ge
Neuf Brisach, 83B, Ba
Neufchâteau, 29A, Aa
Neufchâtel, 53, Dc
Neuhaüsel, 33C, Db
Neuilly, 84, Cc
Neumark, 31, Lb
Neumarkt, 29A, Db
Neumünster, 65F, Aa
Neuse, R., 57, Cf
Neuss, 46A, Fc
Neustadt, Austria, 21, Me
Neustadt, Hungary, 33C, Db
Neustadt, Moravia, 51, Dd
Neustadt, Palatinate, 39B, Ea
Neustadt, Saxony, 38, Jc
Neustria, France, 4A, Bb
Neustria, Italy, 5, Bb
Neutra, 21, Nd
Neuwerk, 65D, Aa
Neuwied, 53, Gb
Neva, R., 19, Ea
Nevada, 70, Cd
Nevada, Sierra, Spain, 63, Dd
Nevada, Sierra, U.S.A., 70, Bd
Nevada Terr., 67D, Ba
Nevers, 11, Ec
Nevers, Co. of, 11, Ec
Neville, 28B, Cc
Neville's Cross, 27, Eb
Nevis, 43A, Fc
Nevis, L., 49A, Bb
Nevyansk, 61, Kc
New Albion, 42, Dc

New Amsterdam, Guiana, 68B, Ba
New Amsterdam, N. America, 42, Fb
New Archangel (Sitka), 71A, Db
New Biscay, 43A, Bb
New Britain, Canada, 71, Hb
New Britain, I., 90, Dd
New Britain (New Pomerania), I., 77, Ib
New Brunswick, Canada, 71, Hc
New Brunswick, New Jersey, 57, Dc
New Calabar, 81C, Fd
New Caledonia, 70, Bb
New Caledonia, I., 77, Lf
New Castile, 63, Dc
New Dorp, 45B, Bc
New East Prussia, 60A, Hb
New England, 45B, Db
New France, 52, Fb
New Galicia, 43A, Bb
New Granada, Captain-Generalship of, 41B, Bc
New Granada, Rep., 68, Bb
New Granada, U.S. of, 68, Bb
New Guinea, 90, Dd
New Guinea, Terr. of, 77, Hb
New Hampshire, 45B, Db
New Hanover, 81D, Bb
New Hanover (Lavongai), 77, Ib
New Haven, 45B, Cc
New Hebrides, 77, Le
New Holland, 42B; 77, Bg
New Ireland, 90, Dd
New Ireland (New Mecklenburg), 77, Ib
New Jersey, 45A, Cc; 57, Dc
New Leinster (Stewart I.), 77A
New Leon, 43A, Cb
New London, 45B, Cc
New Madrid, 72, Cb
New Market, 72B, Aa
New Mecklenburg (New Ireland), 77, Ib
New Mexico, 70, Dd
New Mexico Terr., 67D, Cb
New Munster (South I., N.Z.), 77A
New Navarre, 43A, Aa
New Netherland, 45B, Bc
New Orleans, 56, Ae
New Plymouth, 77A
New Point Comfort, 45B, Ae
New Pomerania, 60B, Da
New Pomerania (New Britain), 77, Ib
New Providence, 43A, Eb
New Republic, 81D, Ba
New Ross, 49B, Ed
New Santander, 43C, Bb
New Siberian Is., 74, Na
New Silesia, 60A, Gc
New South Wales, Australia, 77, Hh
New South Wales, Canada, 70, Eb
New Sweden, 45B, Bd
New Toledo, 41B, Ce
New Ulster (North I., N.Z.), 77A
New York, 57B
New York, st., 57, Db
New Zealand, 77, Nj
Newark, England, 27, Fc
Newark, New York, 57B
Newbattle, 14, Ed
Newbern, 56, Dc
Newburn, 48A, Cb
Newbury, England, 27, Ee
Newbury, Massachusetts, 45B, Db
Newburyport, 56, Eb
Newcastle, Delaware, 57, Dd
Newcastle, England, 27, Eb
Newcastle, Leinster, 37B, Ec
Newcastle, Limerick, 49B, Bd
Newcastle, Natal, 81D, Aa
Newcastle, New South Wales, 77, Ih
Newcastle, Ulster, 37B, Ea
Newcastle, Wales, 28A, Bb
Newcastle (Fort Christina), 45B, Bd
Newcastle-under-Lyme, 27, Dc
Newchwang, 74, Ld; 76B, Ba
Newerche (Newark), 13, Fc
Newfoundland, 45A, Fa
Newmarket, 48B, Dc
Newport, I. of W., 27, Ef
Newport, Monmouth, 28A, Cc
Newport, Rhode I., 45B, Dc
Newport, Wales, 28A, Bb
Newport News, 45B, Ae
Newport Pagnell, 48A, Cc
Newry, 49B, Eb
Newstead, 36, Ed
Newtown, 48B, Bc
Newtown Butler, 49B, Db
Newtownards, 49B, Fb
Ngami, L., 81A, Bb
Ngaoundéré, 96B, Db
Ngau, 75C, Ba
Nguru, 96B, Da
Niagara, 70, Gc
Niagara Falls, 57, Bb; 71D
Niamey, 96B, Ca
Nias, 91, Cf
Nicaea, 2, Je; 19, Dd; 79, Eb
Nicaea, Empire of, 19, De
Nicaragua, 43D, Dc
Nicaragua, L., 43D, Dc
Nicastro, 21A, Dc
Nice, 5, Ac; 11, Ge
Nice, Co. of, 38, Gg
Nicholas II Land, 74, Ga
Nickerie, 68B, Ba
Nicobar Is., 92, Gf
Nicomedia, 2, Ke; 19, Ed
Nicopolis, Bulgaria, 78, Ed
Nicopolis, Turkey, 19, Fd
Nicopolis Theme, 9, Ge
Nicosia, 18A, Ec
Nicoya, G. of, 43A, Dd
Nidaros (Trondheim), 26, Da
Nidda, 20, Hc
Nidum (Neath), 3A, Ce
Niebla, 23C, Bd
Niemen, R., 19, Ca; 50, Fc
Nieuport, 46A, Bc
Nieuwveld, 81A, Bd
Niger, rep., 96D, Cc
Niger, R., 81C, Fc
Niger, terr., 80A, Dc
Nigeria, 80A, Dc; 96B, Cb
Nigeria, Federation of, 96D, Cd
Nigritia, 52, Kd
Niigata, 91, Gc
Niihau, 75D, Ab
Nijni Kamchatsk, 52, Sb
Nikolayevsk, 74, Nc
Nikolsburg, 33C, Db; 39, Md
Nile, R., 25, Cd; 80B, Ab
Nilgiri Hills, 73, Ce
Nîmes, 11, Fe
Nimwegen, 20, Fc; 46A, Ec
Ninety Six, 57D, Aa
Ningpo, 41A, Kb; 74, Lf
Ninus, 2, Mf; 4A, Ld
Niort, 30, Ce
Nipigon, L., 70, Fb
Nipissing, L., 45A, Ba
Niš, 88, Ke
Nish (Nissa), 78, Cd
Nishapur, 25, Ec; 61B, Ab
Nishni Novgorod, 19, Ga
Nisibis, 2, Mf; 6A, Ca
Nissa, 8, Gc
Nissa (Nish), 78, Cd
Nith, R., 36, Cb
Nithsdale, 14, Ed; 28B, Bb
Niue (Savage) I., 75, Ge
Nive, R., 63, Ea
Nivelles, 46B
Nivernais, 17, Ge
Nizam's Dominions, 73, Cd
Nizhne Kolymsk, 74, Pb
Nkandhla, mts., 81D, Bb
Noce, R., 86B, Aa
Nocera, 22, Ec
Noddles I., 56B
Nogais, 61, Ee
Nogent le Roi, 30, Dd
Nogent-le-Rotrou, 38, Dd
Nogent-sur-Marne, 76A, Bb
Nogent-sur-Seine, 30, Ed
Noirmoutier, 9, Bc; 53, Bd
Noisseville, 76A, Db
Noix, I. aux, 57, Ea
Nola, 22, Ec
Noli, 23A, Ba
Nomadic Arab Tribes, 16, Fg
Nombre de Dios, Mexico, 43A, Bb
Nombre de Dios, Panama, 43A, Ed
Nome, 71A, Aa
Nomeny, 39B, Cb
Nona, 22, Fc
Nonette, 20, Ef
Nonno, 96A, Ab
Nootka, 69A, Cb
Norden, 10, Bb
Nordfulc (Norfolk), 13, Gd
Nordgau, Marg. of, 10, Dd
Nordhausen, 10, Dc
Nordheim, 10, Cc
Nördlingen, 29A, Da
Nordmark, 10, Eb
Nordreys, 12, Cb; 14, Bb
Nore, 55A, Dc
Nore, R., 15, Dd
Norfolk, 45B, Ae; 72B, Bb
Norfolk, co., 27, Hd
Norfolk I., 77, Lg
Norham, 27, Da; 28B, Cb
Norhamscire (Norhamshire), 13, Da
Noric Alps, 29A, Fb
Noricum, 2, Fd; 2A, Cb
Norman King., 18A, Bb
Normands, Îles, 17, Dd
Normandy, D. of, 11, Cb
Norrköping, 51, Db; 54, Fa
North C., 69B
North Chan., 14, Cd; 37A, Bc
North I. (New Ulster), 77A
North Pt., 71C, Cc
North (Hudson), R., 45B, Bc
North Sea, 12, Eb; 55A, Eb
North Anna, R., 72B, Bb
North Atlantic Ocean, 94, Cd
North Australia, 77, Ee
North Berwick, 49A, Cb
North Borneo, 91, Ef
North Dakota, 70, Dc
North Downs, 27, Ge
North Dvina, R., 89, Oa
North-East New Guinea (Kaiser Wilhelms Land), 77, Gc
North Esk, R., 14, Fc
North Foreland, 55A, Dc
North Frisian Is., 65F, Aa
North Kanara, 52A, Bc
North Konkan, 52A, Bc
North Korea, 91, Fb
North Pacific Ocean, 75, Gc
North Platte, R., 70, Dc
North Pole, 69B
North Potomac, R., 57, Bd
North Saskatchewan, R., 70, Cb
North Somerset I., 44, Ea
North Uist, 14, Ab
North Victoria (Queenstown), 81B, Cb
North Vietnam, 91, Dd
North Wales, 36A
North West Provs., 73, Cb
North West Terr., 67B, Ba
North-West Terrs., 70, Ea
Northallerton, 27, Eb
Northampton, England, 27, Fd
Northampton, Massachusetts, 45B, Cb
Northampton, co., 27, Fd
Northantone (Northampton), 13, Fd
Northantonescire (Northamptonshire), 13, Fd
Northern, prov., Nigeria, 96B, Ca
Northern Circars, 73, Dd
Northern Hiung-nu, 1, Kb
Northern Ireland, 49B, Eb
Northern Nigeria, 81C, Fc
Northern Rhodesia, 80A, Ff
Northern Slav Peoples, 8C, Ca
Northern Terr., Australia, 77, Ee
Northfield, 57, Eb
Northumbria, 7B, Ba
Northymbraland (Northumberland), 13, Da
Norton Sd., 71A, Aa
Nor-Treding (North Riding, Lincolnshire), 13, Fc
Nor-Treding (North Riding, Yorkshire), 13, Eb
Norway, 12, Ga; 82, Aa
Norway, King. of, 26, Da
Norwegian Sea, 94, Tb
Norwic (Norwich), 13, Hd
Norwich, 27, Hd
Norwich, bp., 36, He
Nosob, R., 81B, Ba
Nossi Be, 80A, Hf
Nöteborg, 26, Hb
Notley, 36, Ff
Noto, 21A, Cd
Notre Dame B., 71, Jc
Notre Dame de la Grasse, 22, Cc
Nottingham, 7C, Cb; 27, Ed
Nottingham, co., 27, Ec
Nouakchott, 96D, Ac
Nouart, 76A, Cb
Noumea, 75, Ff
Nova Coimbra, 41B, De
Nova Foresta (New Forest), 13, Ef
Nova Scotia, 45A, Eb
Novae, 2, Je; 4A, Hc
Novantae, 3A, Bb
Novara, 5, Bb
Novaya Zemlya, 74, Da
Novempopulana (Gascony), 8B, Ac
Novgorod, Poland, 47, Hb
Novgorod, Russia, 26, Hb
Novgorod, Pr., 61, Eb
Novgorod, Rep. of, 19, Ga
Novgorod Severski, 50, Gc
Novi, 29A, Cc
Novibazar, 78, Cd
Noviomagus (Chichester), 3A, Ff
Novo Alexandrovsk, 61B, Aa
Novogrodek, 26, Gc
Novorossiisk, 88, Ne
Novosibirsk, 91, Ba; 94, Pc
Noyon, 11, Eb; 83A, Bb
Nubia, 80B, Ac
Nubian Desert, 80B, Ac
Nubians, 6, Ec
Nugent, 37B, Dc
Nuits, 76A, Cc
Nukha, 93, Fa
Nullarbor Plain, 77, Dh
Numidia, 1, Cd; 4B, Dd
Nuneaton, 36, Ee
Nuremberg, 10, Dd
Nuremburg, Bur. of, 30, Jd
Nürnberg, 87, Cc
Nursia, 5, Dc; 23B, Dc
Nyasa, L., 80A, Gf
Nyasaland, 80A, Gf
Nyköping, 26, Eb
Nymphaeum, 19, De
Nymphenburg, 53, Jc
Nyons, 38, Ff
Nystad, 51, Ea; 61, Bb
OAHU, 75D, Cb
Oakham, 27, Fd
Oates Land, 95, KJ
Oaxaca, 43A, Cc
Ob, R., 25, Fa; 61, Lb; 91, Ba
Obbia, 96A, Bb
Ober Seik, 65F, Aa
Oberehnheim, 39B, Db
Oberland, 29B, Bb
Obi, 52C, Cb
Obidos, Brazil, 68, Dc
Obidos, Portugal, 63, Ac
Obok, 80B, Ce; 83, Ld
Obotrites, 10, Db
O'Brien, 15, Cd; 37B, Bd
Obuasi, 96B, Bb
O'Byrne, 37B, Ec
Ocaña, Colombia, 68, Bb
Ocaña, Spain, 62, Be; 63, Dc
O'Carroll, 15, Db
Ocean I., 75, Fe
Oceanus Atlanticus, 2, Ad
Oceanus Germanicus, 2, Dc
Oceanus Hibernicus (Irish Sea), 3A, Bc
Ochakov, 51, Gd
Ochementone (Okehampton) 13, Bf
Ochil Hills, 28B, Ba
O'Connor, 15, Cc; 37B, Cc
Ocrinum Prom., 3A, Af
Octapitarum Pr., 3A, Ae
O'Dempsey, 15, Dc
Odenburg, 16, Fc
Odense, 26, Db; 65F, Ba
Oder, R., 21, Lb; 31, Lb
Oderberg, 39, Nd
Odessa, 50, Gd; 51, Gd
Odessus, 4B, Gc
Odienne, 96B, Bb
Odiham, 27, Fe
Odoacer, King. of, 2A, Cb
O'Doherty, 37B, Da
O'Donnell, 37B, Cb
O'Donovan, 37B, Ce
O'Dowd, 15, Bb
Oels, 31, Mc
Oenaeum, 19, Fd
Oettingen, 39B, Ca
Ofen, 22, Fb
Ofen Pass, 29B, Eb
Offaly, 15, Dc
Offa's Dyke, 7B, Bb; 13, Cc
Offenburg, 38, Gd; 83B, Ba
O'Flaherty, 15, Cc
O'Flynn, 37B, Eb
Ogbomosho, 96B, Cb
Ogdensburg, 57, Da
Ogeechee, R., 57D, Ab
Oglio, R., 5, Cb
Ogmore, 27, Ce
Ogowe, R., 80A, Ed
O'Hanlon, 37B, Eb
Ohio, 72, Da
Ohio, R., 45A, Ab; 56, Bc
Ohod, Mt., 6, Fc
Oil River Prot., 80A, Dd
Oirghealla (Uriel), 15, Db
Oise, R., 11, Eb
Ojibways, 56, Ba
Oka, R., 61, Fc
Okavango, R., 81A, Aa
Okavango Swamp, 81A, Ba
Okehampton, 27, Bf
O'Kelly, 15, Cc
Okfuskee, 56, Bd
Okhotsk, 42, Qb; 74, Nc
Okhotsk, Sea of, 74, Nc
Okhrida, 78, Ce
Okinawa, 91, Fd
Oklahoma, 70, Ed
Oklahoma Indian Territory, 70, Ed
Öland, 26, Eb
Olavarria, 68, Cf
Old Bridge, 49B, Ec
Old Calabar, 81C, Fd
Old Castile, 63, Db
Old Castle, 37B, Db
Old Charles Town, 45A, Bd
Old Fort Franklin, 70, Ba
Old Head of Kinsale, 15, Ce
Old Kilpatrick, 3A, Ba
Old Orsova, 33C, Ec
Old Point Comfort, 45B, Ae
Old Providence I., 43A, Dc
Old Sarai, 25, Db
Old Sarum, 27, Ee
Oldenburg, 20, Hb; 30, Hb
Oldenburg, Co. of, 38, Hb
Oldenzaal, 46A, Fb
Oléron, 11, Cd
Olicana (Ilkley), 3A, Ec
Olifants, R., 81A, Db
Oliva, 21, Na
Olivenza, 64, Af
Olmütz, 21, Md; 33C, Db
Olonets, 26, Ha
Oloron, 11, Ce; 38, Cg
Öls, 39, Mc
Oltenitza, 78, Fc
Olustee, 72, Dc
Omagh, 37B, Db; 49B, Db
Omaha, 70, Ec
O'Malley, 37B, Bc
Oman, 6, Gc; 25, Ed; 93, He
Oman, G. of, 74, Df
Ombai, 52C, Bc
Omdurman, 80B, Ad
Ominitae, 1, Hf
Ommeyad Emirate, 6B, Aa
Omont, Co. of, 11, Fb
O'More, 37B, Dd
Omsk, 91, Aa
Oneida, L., 57, Cb
Oneidas, 45A, Bb
Onega, L., 26, Ja
Oneglia, 38, Hg
O'Neill, 15, Db
Onitsha, 96B, Cb
Onnum (Halton), 3C
Ono, 75C, Bb
Onondagas, 45A, Bb
Ontario, 70, Fc
Ontario, L., 57, Cb
Oodnadatta, 77, Fg
O'okiep, 81B, Ab
Opland, 12, Ga
Oporto, 23C, Ab; 63, Ab
Oppeln, 21, Mc
Opsikion, 9, Hd
Optimaton, 9, Jd
Oran, 16, Be; 33B, Aa; 80, Ca
Orange, France, 11, Fd
Orange, Virginia, 72B, Aa
Orange, R., 81B, Ab
Orange Free State, 81B, Cb
Orange River Colony, 81A, Cc
Orange River Sovereignty, 81B, Cb
Orangeburg, 57D, Ab
Oranmore, 49B, Cc
Orbe, 9, Dc; 29B, Ab
Orbetello, 32B, Cc; 38, Jg
Orchies, 46A, Cd
Ordovices, 3A, Cd
Ordu, 93, Da
Ordzhonikidze, 88, Oe
Ore Mts., 60A, Dc
Örebro, 26, Eb
Oregon, 70, Bc
Oregon City, 70, Bc
Oregon Country, 70, Cc
Oregon Terr., 67D, Aa
O'Reilly, 15, Dc
Orel, 61, Ed; 88, Nc
Orenburg, 61, Jd; 89, Rc
Orenburg Cossacks, 61, Jd
Orense, 23C, Ba; 63, Ba
Orewyn Bridge, 27, Cd
Orford, 13, Hd, 27, Hd
Oria, 21A, Db
Orientis, 2, Lg
Origny, 22, Cb
Orinoco, Delta of the, 43A, Fd
Orinoco, R., 68, Cb
Oriskany, 57, Db
Orissa, 25, Hd; 73, Ec
Oristano, 22, Dd
Oristano, eccl. prov., 22, Dd
Orizaba, 43A, Cc
Orkney, co., 37A, Ca
Orkney Is., 14, Fa
Orléanais, 38, De
Orléans, 11, Dc; 28C, Dc
Orléans, D. of, 30, Ee
Orléans, I. d', 57C, Ba
Orlov, 61, Jc
Ormoc, 75E, Bb
Ormond, 15, Cd
Ormskirk, 48A, Bc
Ormuz, 25, Ed
Orneau, R., 46B
Orontes, R., 6A, Ba; 18A, Fc
Orontes (Ferreus), R., 18C, Dc
Oropesa, 63, Cc
O'Rourke, 15, Cb
Oroya, 68, Bd
Orsova, 78, Dc
Orsoy, 53, Gb
Orta, 23B, Bb
Ortegal, C., 63, Aa
Ortenau, 33C, Bb

Orthez, 30, Cg; 63, Ea
Ortles, 29A, Db
Ortona, 21, Lg
Oruba, 43A, Fc
Oruro, 68, Cd
Orvieto, 5, Dc
Osaka, 91, Gc
Ösel, 26, Fb
Osero, 22, Ec
O'Shaughnessy, 15, Cc
Oshogbo, 96B, Cb
Osiek, 26, Fc
Osimo, 21, Kg
Osimo (Auximum), 5, Dc
Oslo, 26, Db; 84, Ea
Osma, 22, Bc
Osmanli, 85, Je
Osnabrück, 10, Cb
Ossory, 15, Dd
Ostend, 46A, Bc; 47, Cb
Öster-Götland, 26, Eb
Ostheim, 39C, Ac
Ostia, 5, Dd; 22A
Ostmark, 10, Ec
Ostrach, 29A, Cb
Ostrogothi, 2, Jd
Ostrogothic Kingdom, 4A, Eb
Ostrogoths, 2A, Db
Ostrolenka, 60B, Hb; 64, Gc
Ostrovo L., 86A, Cb
Oswego, 70, Gc; 71C, Cb
Oswestry, 13, Cd; 27, Cd
Otadini, 3A, Da
Otago, 77A
Otaheite, 69A, Be
Otchakov, 54, Jc
Otford, 7B, Dc
Othona (Bradwell), 3A, Ge
O'Toole, 15, Ed; 37B, Ec
Otranto, 5, Gd; 32A, Gd
Otrar, 25, Fb
Ottawa, 70, Gc
Ottawa, R., 45A, Ba; 71C, Ca
Ottawas, 45A, Aa
Otterburn, 27, Da
Ottery St. Mary, 36, Cg
Ottoman Empire, 50, Ee
Ottoman Turks, 24, Hf
Ouagadougou, 96B, Ba
Ouahgouya, 96B, Ba
Ouargla, 80A, Da
Oudenarde, 46A, Cd; 54, Cb
Oudh, 73, Db
Oudon, 20, Ce
Oudtshoorn, 81B, Bc
Ouiatanon, 56, Bb
Oujitsa, 78, Bd
Ourcq, R., 76A, Bb
Ourique, 23C, Ad
Ourthe, R., 83A, Ca
Ouse, R., 27, Ec; 36, Fd
Ovambo, 80A, Ef
Översee, 65F, Aa
Overton, 27, Ee
Overyssel, 46A, Fb
Oviedo, 23C, Ca; 63, Ca
Owen Stanley Ra., 77, Hc
Ox Mts., 15, Cb
Oxeneford (Oxford), 13, Ee
Oxenefordscire (Oxfordshire), 13, Ee
Oxford, England, 27, Ee
Oxford, Maryland, 45B, Ad
Oxford, bp., 36, Ef
Oxford, co., 27, Ee
Oxus, R., 1, Jd; 6, Hb; 25, Fc
Oyster Bay, 45B, Cc
Ozamiz, 75E, Bc

PAARDE BERG, 81A, Cc
Paarl, 81B, Ac
Paauilo, 75D, Db
Pacaltsdorp, 81B, Bc
Pachacamac, 41B, Be
Pacific Ocean, 40, Cd; 75
Padang, 91, Dg
Paderborn, 10, Cc
Padua (Patavium), 5, Cb; 86B, Bb
Paducah, 72, Cb
Paestum, 5, Ed
Pagadian, 75E, Bc
Pagan, 25, Jd; 73, Gc
Pago Pago, 75B, Bb
Pahala, 75D, Dc
Pahang, 41A, Hd
Pahlevi, 93, Fb
Paithan, 1, Kf
Pakhoi, 74, Jf
Palace, Constantinople, 18E
Palapye, 81A, Cb
Palar, R., 59D
Palatine, 5A
Palato, eccl. prov., 22, Fc
Palau Is., 90, Cc
Palawan, 75E, Ac; 90, Bc
Palazzo di Venezia, 5A
Palembang, 91, Dg
Palencia, 22, Bc
Palenque, 43A, Cc
Palermo, eccl. prov., 22, Ed
Palermo (Panormus), 5, De
Palestine, 6A, Ab; 79, Gd
Palestrina, 22A
Palma, 22, Cd; 23C, Gc
Palmas, C., 81C, Cd
Palmella, 23C, Ac
Palmerston I., 75, He
Palmyra, 2, Lg; 4A, Ke
Palmyra I., 75, Hd
Palos, 23D, Bd
Pamiers, 17, Fg; 22, Cc
Pamir, 59A, Ba; 61B, Cb
Pampeluna, 23D, Ea
Pamlico, R., 57, Cf
Pamlico Sound, 45B, Af
Pamphylia, 2, Jf
Pamplona, 22, Bc; 23C, Ea
Panama, 43A, Ed; 68, Bb
Panay, 75E, Bb
Pandhya, 1, Kf
Pandyas, 25, Ge
Paneas (Belinas), 18C, Ce
Panganga, R., 59A, Cd
Panipat, 59A, Cb
Panniar, 73, Cb
Pannonia, 2, Gd; 9, Fc
Panormus (Palermo), 5, De
Pantelleria, 88, Hf
Pantheon, 5A
Panton, 57, Ea
Panuco, 43A, Cb
Panuco, R., 43A, Cb
Paoki, 90, Bb
Paoting, 90, Bb
Paotow, 91, Eb
Papal States, 32B, Dc; 34, Ed
Paphlagonia, 2, Ke; 9, Jd
Papua, G. of, 77, Gc
Papua, Terr. of (British New Guinea), 77, Gc
Para (Belem), 41B, Ed; 68, Ec
Para, st., 68, Dc
Paradies, 22, Fa
Paraguay, 68, De
Paraguay, Jesuit Mission State of, 41B, Df
Paraguay, R., 41B, De
Paraiba, 68, Fc
Paraiba, st., 68, Fc
Paramaribo, 68, Db
Parana, 68, Cf
Parana, R., 41B, Df; 68, De
Parana, st., 68, De
Paranagua, 68, Ee
Parchim, 21, Jb
Parenzo, 22, Eb; 23B, Db
Parga, 54, Ge; 78, Cf
Paria, G. of, 43B, Dc
Parintins, 68, Dc
Paris, 11, Eb; 17, Gd
Parisi, 3A, Fc
Parkersburg, 72, Db
Parma, 5, Cb; 38, Jf
Parma, D. of, 38, Jf; 54, Dd
Parnaiba, 68, Ec
Parnaiba, R., 68, Ec
Paros, 78, Eg
Parret, R., 7B, Bc
Parry Is., 69B
Parthenay, 11, Cc
Parthia, 1, Hd
Parthian Empire, 1, Hd
Partenkirchen, 22, Eb
Passamaquoddy B., 45A, Da; 71E, Cc
Passaro, C., 32B, Ee
Passarowitz, 33C, Ec; 78, Cc
Passau, 10, Ed
Passchendaele, 83A, Ba
Passo Fundo, 68, De
Pasto, 68, Bb
Patagonia, 68, Cg
Pataliputra, 1, Le
Patan, 92, Fb
Patavium (Padua), 5, Cb
Patay, 28D, Cb
Patchefstroom, 81A, Cc
Patiala, 73, Ca
Patillos, 68, Be
Patna, 73, Eb
Patras, 78, Cf
Patriarch's Pond, 18D
Patrimonium, 23B, Dd
Patrimony of St. Peter, 16, Ed; 32A, Ed
Patti, 22, Fd
Patzinaks (Pechenegs), 9, Jc
Pau, 30, Cg
Paumotu Arch. (Tuamotu Arch.), 69A, Ce; 75, He
Pavia, 6, Ba; 8B, Cb
Pavia (Picinum), 5, Bb
Pawtucket, 45B, Dc
Paxo, 62, Ge
Paxton, 57, Cc
Paysandu, 68, Df
Pea Ridge, 72, Bb
Peace, R., 44, Cc; 70, Cb
Peak, The, 27, Ec
Pearl, R., 71F, Ea; 72C, Aa
Pearl Coast, 43A, Fc
Pearl Harbor, 75D, Bb; 90, Gb
Pearl Is., 43A, Ed
Peciers (Peak), 13, Ec
Pecos, R., 44, De
Pecs, 19, Bc; 33C, Db
Pedee, R., 57D, Ba
Pedir, 40, Od
Peebles, 49A, Cc
Peebles, co., 37A, Cc; 49A, Cc
Peekskill, 57, Ec
Pegu, 25, Je; 73, Gd
Peipus, L., 26, Gb
Peishwa, 59A, Bd
Peking, 91, Ec
Peking (Kaanbaligh), 25, Lc
Pelagonia, 19, Cd
Pelew Is., 74, Mh
Pella, 81B, Ab
Pelly, R., 70, Aa
Peloponnesus, 9, Ge
Pelotas, 68, Df
Pelplin, 22, Fa
Pelusium, 18A, Ec
Pelvoux, Mt., 29A, Bc
Pemaquid, 45A, Db; 45B, Eb
Pemba I., 80A, Ge
Pembroke, 27, Be
Pembroke, Co. Palatine of, 27, Be
Pelim, 61, Kc
Penafiel, 23D, Cb
Peñan de Alger, 34, Ce
Penang, 91, Df
Penay, 29B, Ab
Penbroc (Pembroke), 13, Be
Pendennis, 48A, Ad
Penedo, 68, Fd
Peneverdant (Penwortham), 13, Dc
Peniscola, 23D, Fb
Penjdeh, 61B, Bb; 74, Ee
Penkridge, 13, Dd
Pennal, 3A, Cd
Penner, R., 59D; 73, Ce
Pennine Alps, 29A, Bb
Pennine Chain, 27, Db; 28B, Cc
Pennsylvania, 57, Cc; 72B, Ba
Penobscot (Fort Pentagöet), 45B, Ea
Penobscot B., 45B, Ea
Penobscot, R., 45A, Da; 71E, Bc
Penrith, 27, Db
Penryn, 48A, Ad
Penrhyn I., 75, He
Pensacola, 56, Bd; 67B, Bb
Pensacola (Achusi), 43A, Da
Penselwood, 7B Bc
Pentapolis, Africa, 2, Hg; 4B, Ge
Pentapolis, Italy, 5, Dc
Pentegoet, 56, Fb
Penthièvre, 17, Dd
Pentland Firth, 14, Ea
Pentland Hills, 14, Ed
Penukonda, 52A, Bc
Penza, 61, Fd
Peoria, 56, Bb
Pera, 18E; 19, Dd
Perambakan, 59D
Perche, 17, Fd; 30, Dd
Perekop, 51, Gd; 61, De
Perekop, G. of, 61, De
Pereyaslav, 19, Eb
Pergamum, 9, He; 18A, Db
Perigord, Co. of, 11, Dd
Perigueux, 11, Dd
Perim I., 80B, Ce
Perm, 61, Jc; 89, Rb
Pernambuco (Mauritia), 42, He
Pernambuco (Recife), 68, Fc
Pernambuco, st., 68, Fc
Pernau, 26, Fb
Péronne, 11, Eb; 83A, Bb
Perovsk, 61B, Ba
Perpignan, 11, Ee
Perryville, 72, Db
Persarum Regnum, 2, Og
Persepolis, 1, Hd
Pershore, 27, Dd
Persia, 6, Gb; 33A, Hd; 74, De
Persia (Iran), 89, Pg; 93, Gc
Persian Empire, 2A, Fc
Persian Gulf, 6, Gc; 93, Gd
Persis, 1, Hd
Persore (Pershore), 13, Dd
Perth, Scotland, 14, Ec
Perth, W. Australia, 77, Bh
Perth, co., 37A, Cb; 49A, Cb
Peru, 68, Bd
Peru, Viceroyalty of, 41B, Be; 42, Ee
Perugia, 5, Dc; 21, Kg
Perusia, 5B, Bb
Pesaro, 8A, Dc; 21, Kg
Pesaro (Pisaurum), 5, Dc
Pescadores, 75, Cc
Pescara, 32A, Fc
Peschiera, 29A, Dc; 32D, Bb
Peshawar, 25, Gc; 73, Ba
Pessinus, 2, Kf
Pest, 39, Ne
Peterborough, 36, Fe
Peterborough, bp., 36, Fe
Peterhead, 37A, Db
Petersburg, 57, Ce; 72B, Bb
Petersfield, 27, Ef; 48A, Cd
Peterwardein, 50, Dd
Petra, 6A, Bb
Petrianae, 3A, Cb
Petropavlovsk, 58, Rb
Petropolis, 68, Ee
Petsamo, 88, Ma
Pettau, 9, Fc
Petuaria (Brough), 3A, Fc
Pevenesel (Pevensey), 13, Gf
Pevensey, 27, Gf
Pfaffenhofen, 65A, Bb
Pfalzburg, 39B, Db
Pfävers, 29B, Db
Pfirt, 39B, Dc
Pfullendorf, 53, Hd
Pharsalus, 9, Ge
Philadelphia, Nicaea, 19, De
Philadelphia, Pennsylvania, 57, Dd
Philiphaugh, 37A, Cc; 48B, Bb
Philippeville, 46A, Dd
Philippine Is., 74, Lg
Philippine Is. (Felipinas, Islas), 41A, Kc
Philippines (St. Lazaro Arch.), 40, Qd
Philippolis, 81B, Cb
Philippopolis, 2, Je; 78, Ed
Philippsburg, 29A, Ca
Philipstown, 49B, Dc
Philomelion, 18A, Eb
Phoenicia, 1, Fd
Phoenix Is., 90, Fd
Phrygia, 2, Jf
Piacenza (Placentia), 5, Bb
Piaui, 68, Ec
Piave, R., 5, Db; 86B, Cb
Picardy, 28D, Db; 83A, Bb
Pichincha, 68, Bc
Picinum (Pavia), 5, Bb
Pickawillany, 56, Cb
Pickering, 27, Fb
Pickeringham (Pickering), 13, Fb
Picquigny, 30, Ed
Picti, 2, Cb
Picts, 7B, Ba
Pidurutalagala, 73, Df
Piedmont, 32A, Bb
Piedmont, Pr. of, 38, Gf
Piedra, 22, Bc
Piet Retief, 81A, Dc
Pietermaritzburg, 81D, Bb
Pieters, 81D, Ab
Pietersburg, 81A, Cb
Pietra Santa, 38, Jg
Pieve di Cadore, 86B, Ca
Pike's Peak, 70, Dd
Pilar, 68, De
Pilcomayo, R., 68, Ce
Pilica, 60A, Hc
Pilica, R., 31, Pc; 33C, Ea
Pillau, 39, Na
Pillnitz, 60A, Dc
Pilsen, 10, Ed; 39, Kd
Pilten, 26, Fb
Pilton, 7C, Ac
Piltune (Pilton), 13, Be
Pinar del Rio, 43A, Db
Pindari, 73, Cb
Pindiga, 96B, Db
Pindus, 50, Ee
Pine Bluff, 72, Bc
Pinerolo, 32A, Bb
Pines, I. of, 75, Ff
Piney, 53, Fc
Ping Chow, 1, Od
Pingyang, 76B, Cb
Pinktang (Harbin), 91, Fb
Pinkie, 37A, Cc
Pinneberg, 38, Hb
Pinos, I. de Cuba, 43A, Db
Pinos, I. de, Panama, 43A, Ed
Pinsk, 34, Hb; 50, Fc; 84, Hb
Piombino, 5, Cc
Pippli, 59B
Piqua, 71C, Bb
Piquetberg, 81B, Ac
Piraeus, 78, Dg; 88, Kf
Pirapora, 68, Ed
Pirmasens, 83A, Db
Pirna, 31, Kc; 39C, Dc
Pirot, 78, Dd
Pisa, 5, Cc; 8A, Dc
Pisaurum, 5B, Bb
Pisaurum (Pesaro), 5, Dc
Piscataqua B. (Portsmouth), 45B, Db
Pisco, 68, Bd
Pisek, 21, Ld; 60A, Ed
Pisidia, 2, Kf
Pisino, 22, Eb
Pistoia, 32E, Ba
Pisuerga, R., 63, Ca
Pitcairn I., 75, Jf
Pitiqui, 43C, Ab
Pitsewo, 76B, Bb
Pittsburg Landing, 72, Cb
Pittsburgh, 71C, Cb
Pittsburgh (Fort Pitt), 57A, Ca
Pityus, 2, Me
Piura, 68, Ac
Placentia, 45A, Ga; 52, Gb
Placentia (Piacenza), 5, Bb
Plaine Selve, 22, Bb
Plancenoit, 46B
Plasencia, 22, Ac; 63, Bb
Plassey, 59A, Ec
Pläswitz, 62, Fb
Platte, R., 70, Dc
Plattsburg, 57, Ea
Plauen, 21, Kc
Plava, 86B, Da
Pleasant Hill, 72, Bc
Plenty, B. of, 77A
Pleshey, 27, Ge
Pless, 31, Nd; 39, Nd
Plessis-les-Tours, 30, De
Plettenburg, 81B, Cb
Pleven, 79, Db
Plevna, 78, Ed
Plintone (Plympton), 13, Bf
Plock, 21, Nb
Ploërmel, 20, Be
Ploesti, 88, Ld
Plön, 65F, Ba
Ploughed Hill, 56B
Plovdiv, 79, Db
Plunket, 37B, Ec
Plymouth, England, 27, Bf
Plymouth, Massachusetts, 45B, Dc
Plympton, 27, Bf; 36, Bg
Plzen, 87, Cc
Pnom Penh, 91, De
Po, R., 5, Cb; 21B, Bc; 38, Gf
Poblet, 22, Cc
Poclinton (Pocklington), 13, Fc
Podiebrad, 31, Lc
Podlesia, 50, Fc
Podolia, 50, Fd
Poetovia, 2, Gd
Poggibonsi, 32E, Bb
Pohlde, 10, Dc
Pointe Noire, 96D, De
Poissy, 11, Db; 38, Ed
Poitiers, 11, Dc
Poitou, 30, Ce
Poitou, Co. of, 11, Cc
Pola, 5, Db
Poland, 50, Ec; 87, Eb
Poland, King. of, 21, Nc
Poles, 8, Hb; 9, Fb
Polesina, 32D, Bb
Policastro, 32A, Fd
Poligny, 30, Fe
Polillo Is., 75E, Bb
Polling, 10, De
Polotsk, 26, Gb
Polotsk, Pr. of, 19, Db
Polovtsi (Kipchaks), 19, Gc
Poltava, 50, Gd
Polygars, 52A, Bc
Pombal, 63, Ac
Pomerania, D. of, 21, Mb
Pomeranian, 8, Fa
Pomerelia, 19, Bb; 31, Na
Pompadour, 53, De
Ponape, 75, Ed
Pondicherry, 59D
Pondoland, 81B, Db
Pondos, 81B, Db
Ponferrada, 63, Ba
Pongolo, R., 81D, Ba
Poniec, 50, Dc
Pons, 20, Cf
Pons Aelius (Newcastle), 3C
Pont à Mousson, 39B, Cb
Pont Audemer, 20, Dd
Pont di Piave, 86B, Cb
Pontarlier, 30, Ge; 76A, Dc
Pontecorvo, 32A, Ed
Pontefract, 27, Ec; 48A, Cc
Pontes (Staines), 3A, Fe
Pontevedra, 63, Aa
Ponthieu, Co. of, 11, Da
Pontica, 2A, Eb
Pontigny, 22, Cb; 28C, Dc
Pontivy, 38, Bd
Pontoise, 20, Ed
Pontremoli, 32A, Cb
Pontus, 2, Kf
Pontus Euxinus, 2, Ke
Pontvailain, 28C, Cc
Ponza, 32A, Ed
Pool, 28A, Cb
Poole, 27, Df
Poole, family, 28A, Cb
Poona, 73, Bd
Popayan, 68, Bb
Popocatopetl, 43A, Cc
Poprad, 31, Pd
Populonium, 5B, Ab
Porcestre (Porchester), 13, Ef
Porcien, Co. of, 11, Fb
Pordenone, 32D, Cb; 86B, Cb
Port Adams, 76B, Bb
Port Antonio, 43A, Ec
Port Arthur, Canada, 70, Fc
Port Arthur, China, 91, Fc

Port au Port, 45A, Fa
Port au Prince, 43C, Dc
Port Augusta, 77, Fh
Port aux Basques, 45A, Fa
Port Bonnel, 18C, Cb
Port Curtis, 77, If
Port Dalrymple, 77, Hj
Port Darwin, 77, Ed
Port Dieu, 29B, Bb
Port Elizabeth (Fort Frederick), 81B, Cc
Port Essington (Port Victoria), 77, Ed
Port Gibson, 72C, Ab
Port Harcourt, 96B, Cb
Port Hudson, 72, Bc
Port Jackson (Sydney), 77, Ih
Port Macquarie, 77, I h
Port Mahon, 54, Ce
Port Moresby, 77, Hc
Port Mouton, 45A, Eb
Port Natal (Durban), 81D, Bb
Port Nelson, 70, Eb
Port Nicholson, 77A
Port of Spain, 43A, Fc
Port Phillip, 77, Gi
Port Pleasant, 57A, Cb
Port Republic, 72B, Aa
Port Royal (Annapolis), 45A, Db
Port Royal (Stuart Town), 45A, Ad
Port Royal, Jamaica, 43A, Ec
Port Said, 80B, Aa
Port St. Julian, 41B, Ch
Port Simpson, 70, Ab
Port Sudan, 80B, Bd; 96D, Fc
Port Victoria (Port Essington), 77, Ed
Portadown, 49B, Eb
Portage la Prairie, 70, Eb
Portalegre, 22, Ad
Portarlington, 49B, Dc
Portland, England, 7C, Bc
Portland, Maine, 56, Eb
Portland, Oregon, 70, Bc
Portland, Victoria, 77, Gi
Portland Canal, 71B, Dc
Portloc (Porlock), 13, Ce
Porto, 22A
Porto Alegre, 68, Df
Porto Novo, India, 59D
Porto Novo, Dahomé, 81C, Ec
Porto Praya, 55B, He
Porto Rico, 43A, Fc
Porto Seguro, 68, Fd
Porto Seguro, prov., 41B, Ee
Porto Velho, 94, Df
Porto Viejo, 68, Ac
Portree, 49A, Ab
Portsmouth (Piscataqua B.), 45B, Db
Portsmouth, England, 27, Ef
Portsmouth, New Hampshire, 45B, Db
Portsmouth, Ohio, 70, Fd
Portsmouth, Rhode I., 45B, Dc
Portsmouth, Virginia, 57, Ce
Portsoy, 49A, Cb
Portugal, 63, Ac
Portugal, Co. of, 23C, Bb
Portugal, King. of, 23D, Bb
Portuguese East Africa, 81A, Db
Portuguese Guinea, 81C, Ab; 96B, Aa
Portus Adurni (Porchester), 3A, Ef
Portus Lemanis (Lympne), 3A, He
Posadas, 68, De
Poschiavo, 29B ,Eb
Posen, 21, Mb
Posen, reg., 60B, Fb
Potawatomis, 45A, Ab
Potchefstroom, 81B, Ca
Potgieter, 81A, Cc
Poti, 61, Ff; 79, Hb
Potomac, R., 57, Cd; 72B, Ba
Potosi, 68, Cd
Potsdam, 54, Eb; 60A, Db
Poughkeepsie, 57, Ec
Pounanen, 19, De
Poverty B., 77, Ni
Powder, R., 70, Dc
Powderham, 13, Cf
Powhatans, 45A, Bc
Powick Bridge, 48A, Bc
Powys, 7C, Bb; 13 Cd; 27, Cd
Pozières, 83A, Ba
Poznań, 61A, Ab; 87, Db
Praga, 51, Ec
Prague, 21, Lc
Prague, eccl. prov., 22, Fb
Prairie du Chien, 67C, Da
Prairie Grove, 72, Bb
Praslin, 53, Fc
Prato, 20, Jg; 32E, Bb
Prättigau, 29B, Db
Pravadi, 78, Fd
Prayaga, 52A Cb
Pregel, R., 60A, Ha
Prèmontrè, 22, Cb
Prenzlau, 21, Kb; 65B, Ba
Presba L., 86A, Cb
Presidios, 32B, Cc; 38, Jg
Preslav, 9, Hd
Presque Isle, 71C, Bb
Presqu'Ile, 56, Cb
Pressburg, 10, Gd
Preston, 27, Dc
Prestonpans, 49A, Cc
Prestune (Preston), 18, Dc
Pretoria, 80A, Fg; 81A, Cc
Prettin, 39C, Cb
Preveza, 78, Cf
Priegnitz, 31B, Ca; 60A, Cb
Prilep, 19, Cd; 86A, Ca
Prince Albert, 70, Db
Prince Edward I., 71, Hc
Prince Edward I. (Ile de St. Jean), 45A, Ea
Prince Edward Is., 95, Sh
Prince of Wales, C., 71A, Aa
Prince of Wales I., Alaska, 71B, Cc
Prince of Wales I., Canada, 44, Ea
Prince Rupert, 70, Bb
Prince Willem's Is., 42B
Prince William Sd., 71A, Ca
Princess Elizabeth Land, 69C
Princeton, 57, Dc
Principato, 32A, Fd
Principato Salerno, 21A, Cb
Principe, 80A, Dd
Prinkipo Is., 86C, Aa
Pripet, R., 50, Fc
Pripet Marshes, 84, Hb
Prishtina, 78, Cd
Pritzwalk, 21, Kb
Prizren, 19, Cd
Prome, 25, Je; 73, Gd
Prospect Hill, 56B
Prosperous, 49B, Ec
Provencals, 85, Cd
Provence, 8A, Cc; 9, Dd
Provence, Co. of, 11, Gd
Provence, Marq. of, 20, Ff
Providence, Maryland, 45B, Ad
Providence, Rhode I., 45B, Dc
Provincia, 2A, Bb
Provins, 17, Gd
Prüm, 20, Gc
Prussia, 51, Dc; 65A, Ba
Prussians, 8, Ga
Pruth, R., 50, Fd; 78, Fb
Przemysl, 26, Fd; 87, Ec
Psara, 78, Ef
Pskov, 26, Gb
Pueblo, 70, Dd
Puerto Bello, 43A, Ed
Puerto Cabello, 68, Ca
Puerto de Caballos, 43A, Dc
Puerto Deseado, 68, Cg
Puerto Madryn, 68, Cg
Puerto Montt, 68, Bg
Puerto Princesa, 75E, Ac
Puerto Principe, 43A, Eb
Pularoon, 52C, Cb
Pulaski, 72, Cb
Pulaway, 52C, Cb
Pulicat, 59D
Pulicat, L. of, 59D
Pultusk, 31, Pb; 54, Gb
Punakha, 92, Gb
Pungwe, R., 81A, Da
Punjab, 73, Ba; 74, Fe
Puno, 68, Bd
Punta Arenas, 68, Bh
Purdysburg, 57D, Ab
Purnea, 59A, Eb
Purus, R., 68, Cc
Pusan, 91, Fc
Pustat (Cairo), 6A, Ab
Pustertal, 29A, Db; 86B, Ca
Put-in-Bay, 71C, Bb
Putivl, 19, Eb
Puttlingen, 20, Gd; 39B, Da
Putumayo, R., 68, Bc
Puylaurens, 38, Eg
Pwllheli, 28A, Bb
Pyatigorsk, 88, Oe
Pyrenæ Montes, 2, De
Pyrenees, 11, De; 63, Fa
Pyritz, 10, Fb

QATAR, 93, Gd
Qatif, 93, Gd
Qena, 93, Cd
Qivira, 44, Ee
Quadi, 2, Gd
Quatford, 13, Dd
Quathlamba (Drakens Berg), 81D, Ab
Quatre Bras, 46B; 62, Cb
Quebec, 45A, Ca; 56A; 57C, Ba
Quebec, prov., 56, Da
Quedlinburg, 10, Dc; 65A, Ba
Queen Charlotte Is., 70, Ab
Queen Charlotte Sd., 70, Bb
Queen Mary Land, 69C
Queen Maud Land, 69C
Queen Victoria Spring, 77, Ch
Queen's Co., 37C; 49B, Dd
Queensferry, 49A, Cc
Queensland, 77, Gf
Queenstown (Cobh), 49B, Ce
Queenstown (North Victoria), 81B, Cb
Queenstown, Canada, 71C, Cb
Queenstown, Cape Colony, 81A, Cd
Quelimane, 80A, Gf
Quemoy, 91, Ed
Quensanfu, 25, Kc
Quercy, 17, Ff; 28C, Cd
Quetta, 61B, Bb; 73, Aa
Quezon City, 75E, Bb
Quiberon, 53, Bd; 55A, Be
Quilon, 59A, Cf
Quimper, 11, Ab
Quimperlé, 22, Bb; 28D, Ac
Quincey (Merry Mount), 45B, Db
Quincy, 70, Ed
Quingey, 76A, Cc
Quinsay (Lingan, Hangchow), 25, Mc
Quito, 68, Bc
Qum, 93, Gc
Qunfidha, 93, Ef
Quseir, 93, Cd

RAAB, 21, Me
Raab, R., 31, Me; 39, Me
Raasay, 49A, Ab
Rabast, C. de, 45A, Ea
Rabat, 80A, Ca
Rabaul, 77, Ib; 90, Dd
Raby, 27, Eb
Raccoon Ford, 57, Cd
Race, C., 45A, Ga
Radcot Bridge, 27, Ee
Raddenore (Radnor), 13, Cd
Radicofani, 23B, Cc
Radimiches, 9, Jb
Radnor, 27, Cd
Radom, 31, Pc; 39, Pc
Radstadt, 21, Ke
Radzyn, 51, Ec
Raeburnfoot, 3A, Ca
Rageneia (Rayleigh), 13, Ge
Raglan, 48A, Bd
Ragnit, 26, Fb
Ragusa, 39, Ng; 78, Bd
Ragusa, eccl. prov., 22, Fc
Ragusa, Rep. of, 54, Fd
Rain, 29A, Da
Rainy, R., 70, Ec
Rais, 17, Ee; 30, Ce
Raisin, R., 71C, Bb
Rajahahan, 59B
Rajahmundry, 92, Ed
Rajasthan, 92, Cb
Rajkot, 92, Cc
Rajputana, 73, Bb
Rakka, 18A, Fb
Rakonitz, 39, Kc
Raleigh, 57, Bf
Raleigh's Virginia Colony, 45A, Bc
Ralick Is., 75, Fd
Ralph, 12, Dc
Ramadi, 93, Ec
Ramah, 71, Hb
Ramesyg (Ramsey), 13, Fd
Ramillies, 46A, Dd
Ramle, 18C, Bg
Ramleh, 6A, Ab
Rammekens, 46A, Cc
Ramnagar, 73, Ba
Rampur, 73, Cb
Ramree I., 90, Ac
Ramsay's Mills, 57, Bf
Ramsbury, 36A
Ramsey, 36, Fe
Ranchi, 92, Fc
Rand, 81A, Cc
Rangoon, 73, Gd; 92, Hd
Rann, The, 73, Bc
Rannoch, L., 49A, Bb
Rannoch Moor, 49A, Bb
Rapa I., 75, Hf
Rapallo, 32A, Cb
Raphoe, 15, Db
Rappahannock, R., 57, Cd
Rapperswyl, 29B, Ca
Rappoltstein, 39B, Db
Raquette, R., 57, Da
Rarotonga, 75, Gf
Ras el Ain, 6A, Ca
Rasgrad, 78, Fd
Raslawice, 51, Ec
Rastatt, 29A, Ca
Rat Portage, 70, Ec
Ratack Is., 75, Fd
Ratae (Leicester), 3A, Ed
Rathfarnham, 49B, Ec
Rathlin I., 15, Ea
Rathmines, 49B, Ec
Rathmore, 37B, Ec
Rathmullan, 49B, Da
Ratibor, 21, Nc
Ratisbon, 8A, Db
Ratisbon (Regensburg), 10, Ed
Ratzeburg, 22, Ea; 30, Jb
Ravenglass, 48B, Bb
Ravenna, 5, Db; 23B, Cb
Ravenna, eccl. prov., 22, Ec
Ravensberg, Co. of, 30, Hb
Ravensburg, 20, He; 30, He
Ravenscar, 3A, Fb
Ravenspur, 27, Gc
Ravenstein, 46A, Ec
Ravi, R., 73, Ba
Rawa, 21, Pc
Rawalpindi, 73, Ba
Rawson (Chubut), 68, Cg
Raymond, 72C, Aa
Raymond of Toulouse, 16, Fd
Ré, I. de, 17, Ee
Reading, England, 27, Fe
Reading, Massachusetts, 57, Cc
Reate, 5, Dc
Recife (Pernambuco), 68, Fc
Recklinghausen, 20, Gc
Reculver, 7B, Dc
Red, R., Canada, 70, Ec
Red, R., U.S.A., 70, Ed
Red River Colony, 70, Ec
Red Russia, 50, Ed
Red Sea, 6, Ec; 25, Cd
Redarians, 10, Eb
Redesdale, 13, Da; 28B, Cb
Redinges (Reading), 13, Ee
Redinha, 63, Ab
Redstone (Fort Burd), 57, Bc
Ree, L., 15, Dc
Regensburg, 8, Eb; 31B, Cb
Reggio (Rhegium), Bruttium, 5, Ee
Reggio (Rhegium), Lombardy, 5, Cb
Reggio, eccl. prov., 22, Fd
Regina, 70, Db
Regni, 3A, Ff
Regulbium (Reculver), 3A, He
Rehdaniya, 33A, Dd
Rei, 19, Je
Reichenau, 22, Db
Reichenbach, 33C, Ca
Reigate, 27, Fe
Reims, 11, Fb; 83A, Cb
Reims, eccl. prov., 22, Cb
Remagen, 20, Gc
Remington, 57, Cd
Remiremont, 39B, Cb
Rendsburg, 38, Ha; 65F, Aa
Renfrew, 14, Dd
Renfrew, co., 37A, Bc
Rennel, 77, Kd
Rennes, 11, Cb
Reno, R., 5, Cb; 29A, Dc
Rense, 30, Gc
Rensselaerwyk, 45B, Cb
Requena, 63, Ec
Rerigonius Sinus, 3A, Ba
Resaca, 72A, Aa
Resht, 93, Fb
Resino, 22, Fc
Resolution I., 71, Ha
Rethel, 20, Fd; 31A, Cc
Retford, 27, Fc; 48A, Cc
Réunion, 69A, Mf
Reuss, 39C, Cc
Reuss, Co. of, 30, Kc; 38, Jc
Reuss, R., 29B, Ca
Reutlingen, 20, Hd
Reval, 26, Gb; 54, Ga
Revesby, 36, Fd
Rewah, 73, Dc
Reykjavik, 88, Aa
Reynosa, 63, Ca
Rha, R., 1, Gc
Rhaetia, 2, Fd; 8, Db
Rhætian Alps, 29A, Cb
Rhætian Leagues (Grisons), 29B, Db
Rhagae, 1, Hd
Rhayader, 28A, Cb
Rhegium (Reggio), Bruttium, 5, Ee
Rhegium (Reggio), Lombardy, 5, Cb
Rheinau, 29B, Ca
Rheinberg, 46A, Fc
Rheinfelden, 29A, Bb
Rhenus, R., 2, Ed
Rhine, R., 10, Bc; 46A, Db
Rhine, Confederation of the, 62, Ec
Rhine Prov., 60B, Ac
Rhineland, 83A, Da
Rhodanus, R., 2, De
Rhode Island, 45B, Dc
Rhodes, 78, Gg
Rhodes Drift, 81A, Cb
Rhodesia, 81A, Da; 83, Le
Rhodesia and Nyasaland, Federation of, 96D, Ef
Rhodope, 9, Gd; 50, Ee
Rhodri Mawr, Pr. of, 7C, Bb
Rhodus, 2, Jf
Rhône, R., 11, Fd; 30, Ff
Rhos, 13, Cc
Rhuddlan, 27, Cc
Rhufoniog, 13, Cc
Riade, 10, Ec
Ribacoa, 23D, Bb
Ribagorza, 23C, Fa
Ribble, R., 27, Dc
Ribe, 12, Gc; 65F, Aa
Riccall, 12, Dc
Richard's Castle, 28A, Db
Richelieu, 47, Cc; 53, Dd
Richelieu, R., 45A, Ca
Richmond, Canada, 57, Ea
Richmond, Natal, 81D, Bb
Richmond, Surrey, 48B, Cd
Richmond, Virginia, 57, Ce
Richmond, Yorkshire, 27, Eb
Ried, 65B, Bb
Rieneck, 53, Hb
Rienzi, House of, 5A
Riet, R., 81B, Cb
Rieti, 32C, Dc
Rieux, 22, Cc
Riez, 22, Dc
Riga, 26, Fb
Riga, eccl. prov., 22, Ga
Riga, G. of, 26, Fb
Rimini (Ariminum), 5, Db
Rincoede (Ringwood), 13, Ef
Ringgold Is., 75C, Ca
Rio Branco, 94, Df
Rio Branco, prov., 68, Cb
Rio de Janeiro, 68, Ee
Rio de la Hacha, 43A, Ec
Rio de Oro, 80A, Bb
Rio Grande, 68, Df
Rio Grande (Bravo del Norte), R., 43A, Bb
Rio Grande (Magdalena), R., 43A, Ed
Rio Grande, R., Central America, 43A, Dc
Rio Grande do Norte, prov., 68, Fc
Rio Grande do Sul (San Pedro do Rio Grande), 41B, Dg
Rio Grande do Sul, prov., 68, De
Rio Pardo, 68, De
Rio Pecos, R., 70, Dd
Rio Salado, 23D, Bd
Rioja, 23C, Da
Riom, 17, Gf; 20, Ef
Ripa, R. (Ribble), 18, Dc
Ripoll, 22, Cc
Ripon, 27, Eb
Ripuarian Franks, 8B, Cb
Ripuarii, 2, Ec
Ripun (Ripon), 13, Eb
Risalyeh, 93, Eb
Risti, 22, Ec
Ristovatz, 78, Cd
Ritzebüttel, 30, Hb; 38, Hb
Riva, 20, Jf; 32D, Bb
Rivaulx, 36, Ec
River Cess, 96B, Bb
Riversdale, 81A, Bd
Riviera, 29A, Cc
Rivière du Loup, 45A, Da
Rivoli, Piedmont, 29A, Bc
Rivoli, Veneto, 29A, Dc
Riyadh, 93, Fe
Rjörneborg, 26, Fa
Roanne, 38, Fe
Roanoke, 70, Gd
Roanoke I., 45B, Bf
Roanoke, R., 45A, Bc
Roanoke Sd., 55B, Cc
Robe, R., 15, Bc
Robert of Flanders, 16, Ed
Robertsbridge, 36, Gg
Robertson, 37A, Bb
Robertsport, 96B, Ab
Robogdium Prom., 3A, Aa
Roca, C. da, 63, Ac
Rocca San Casiano, 32E, Ba
Roccasecca, 32A, Ed
Roche, 36, Ed
Rochefort, 30, Cf; 53, Ce
Rochefoucauld, 53, De
Rochester, 27, Ge
Rochester, bp., 36, Gf
Rochingeham (Rockingham), 13, Fd
Rochlitz, 39, Kc; 39C, Cb
Rockhampton, 77, If
Rockhill, 57, Af
Rockingham, 27, Fd
Rockingham B., 77, He
Rockingham Forest, 3A, Fd
Rocky Mount, 57D, Aa
Rocky Mts., 70, Bb
Rocourt, 46A, Ed
Rocroy, 38, Fd
Rodemackern, 39B, Ca
Rodez, 11, Ed
Rodney and de Grasse, 55B, De
Rodosto, 8, Hc; 78, Fe
Roebuck B., 77, Ce
Roelant (Rhuddlan), 13, Cc
Roer, R., 83A, Da
Roeskilde, 26, Db

Rogaland, 12, Fb
Roger's Rock, 57, Eb
Roggeveld, 81B, Bc
Rohan, 17, Dd
Rohilkhand, 73, Cb
Roleca, 63, Ac
Rolla, 72, Bb
Röm, 65F, Aa
Roma (Rome), 2, Fe; 5, Dd
Romagna, 20, Jf; 32A, Ec
Roman Empire, 1, Dc; 4A, Jd
Roman Empire (under Syagrius), 2A, Bb
Romaniola, 23B, Cb
Rome (Roma), 5, Dd
Rome, U.S.A., 72A, Aa
Rome, eccl. prov., 22, Ec
Romenel (Romney), 13, Gf
Romesey (Romsey), 13, Ef
Romney, 27, Gf
Romsey, 36, Eg
Roncaglia, 10, Cf; 20, Hf
Roncesvalles, 8, Bc; 22, Bc
Roncesvalles Pass, 63, Ea
Ronciglione, 39, Kg
Ronda, 23C, Cd; 63, Cd
Rondonia, 68, Cd
Roosebeke, 28D, Da
Roraima, 68B, Aa
Rorke's Drift, 81A, Dc; 81D, Bb
Rosa, Mte., 29A, Bc; 29B, Bc
Rosario, 68, Cf
Rosas, 63, Ga
Roscommon, 15, Cc
Roscommon, co., 37C; 49B, Cc
Roscrea, 37B, Dd; 49B, Dd
Rose Castle, 28B, Bc
Roseires, 80B, Ae
Rosellae, 5B, Ab
Rosemarkie, bp., 14A, Bb
Rosenheim, 53, Kd
Rosetta, 6A, Ab; 80B, Aa
Rosheim, 39B, Db
Rosnay, 11, Fb
Rosoy, 38, Ed
Ross, England, 27, De
Ross, Ireland, 15, Be
Ross, co., 37A, Bb
Ross, dist., 14, Db
Ross Dependency, 95, Kj
Ross Sea, 69C
Rossano, 22, Fd
Rossbach, 60A, Cc
Rosslyn, 36, Cb
Rostock, 21, Ka; 22, Ea
Rostov (-on-Don), 19, Fc; 79, Ga
Rostov, Suzdal, 19, Fa
Rosyth, 84, Ba
Roteland (Rutland), 13, Fd
Rothbury, 28B, Db
Rothenburg, 20, Jd; 60A, Eb
Rothesay, 37A, Bc
Rotterdam, 46A, Dc
Rotterdam, I., 42B
Rottweil, 20, Hd; 30, Hd
Rotuma I., 75, Fe
Roubaix, 83A, Ba
Roucy, 20, Ed; 30, Ed
Rouecestre (Rochester), 13, Ge
Rouen, 11, Db; 83A, Ab
Rouen, eccl. prov., 22, Cb
Rouergue, Co. of, 11, Ed; 28C, De
Rough Castle, 3A, Ca
Roundway Down, 48A, Cd
Rouses Pt., 57, Ea
Roussillon, Co. of, 11, Ee
Rouvray, 28D, Cb
Roveredo, 32D, Bb
Rovereto, 38, Jf; 86B, Bb
Rovigno, 23B, Db; 32B, Db
Rovigo, 32D, Bb
Rovno, 84, Hb
Rowley, 45B, Db
Rowton, 48B, Bc
Roxburgh, 14, Fd
Roxburgh, co., 37A, Cc; 49A, Cc
Roxbury, 56B
Roxolani, 1, Fc
Royal Niger Company, 80A, Dc
Royal Palace, Jerusalem, 18D
Royale, I. (Cape Breton I.), 45A, Ea
Royan, 38, Cf
Roye, 20, Ed; 81A, Bb
Ruanda-Urundi, 96D, Ee
Ruapehu, 77, Ni
Rub al Khali, 93, Gf
Rueda, 63, Cb
Rufford, 36, Ed
Rudolf, L., 80A, Gd
Rudolstadt, 30, Jc; 39C, Bc
Rügen I., 10, Ea
Rügenwalde, 31, Ma
Rugii, 2, Fc; 2, Hd
Ruhr, R., 10, Bc
Rullion Green, 49A, Cc
Rum, I., 14, Bc
Rum, Seljuk Sultanate of (Iconium), 16, Je
Rum or Iconium, King. of, 18A, Fb
Rumania, 78, Ec
Rumelia, 50, Ee
Runcorn, 7C, Bb
Runnymede, 27, Fe
Rupel, 86A, Ea
Rupel Pass, 19, Cd
Rupert, R., 70, Gb
Rupert's Land, 45A, Ba; 70, Fb
Ruphia, R., 78, Cg
Ruppin, 21, Kb
Ruremonde, 46A, Ec
Rus, King. of, 16, Jb
Ruschuk, 78, Ed
Russell, 77A
Russia, 26, Hb; 34, Ja
Russia, Prs. of, 19, Ga
Russian Central Asia, 83, Mc
Russian Empire, 62, Hb; 74, Gc
Russian Soviet Federal Socialist Rep., 84, Lb
Russian States, 24, Kb
Rustenburg, 81A, Cc
Rutba, 93, Ec
Ruthenian, 85, Gc
Rutherglen, 49A, Bc
Ruthin, 27, Cc
Ruthven, 37A, Cb
Ruthwell, 7B, Ba
Rutland, 27, Fd
Rutli, 29B, Cb
Rüttgen, 39B, Ca
Rutupiae (Richborough), 3A, He
Ryazan, 19, Fb; 88, Nc
Rye, 13, Gf; 27, Gf
Rye (Little Harbour), 45B, Db
Ryknield Way, 3A, Ed
Rymnik, 61, Ae
Ryswyk, 46A, Db
Ryukyu Is., 91, Fd
Rzeszow, 26, Fc
Rzhev, 61, Dc; 88, Mb

SAALE, R., 10, Dc; 39C, Bb
Saalfeld, 20, Jc; 39C, Bc
Saanen, 29B, Bb
Saar, R., 39B, Ca; 83A, Db
Saar Basin, 83A, Db
Saarbrücken, 10, Bd; 83A, Db
Saareguemines, 83A, Db
Saaremaa, 87, Ea
Saarlonis, 53, Gc; 76A, Db
Saarumon, 76A, Db
Saarwerden, 39B, Db
Saaz, 21, Kc
Saba, 43A, Fc
Sabancuy, 43A, Cc
Sabina, 32A, Ec
Sabina, bp., 22A
Sabine, 72, Bd
Sabine, R., 72, Bc
Sabine Cross Roads, 72, Bc
Sabinensis, 5B, Bb
Sabino, 45B, Eb
Sable, C., Florida, 70, Fe
Sable, C., Nova Scotia, 45A, Db
Sable I., 71, Jc
Sabrina Aest. (Severn), 3A, Ce
Sabugal, 63, Bb
Sachsenburg, 53, Kd
Sacile, 29A, Ec
Säckingen, 22, Db; 29B, Ba
Saco, 45B, Db
Saco, R., 45B, Db
Sacramento, California, 70, Bd
Sacramento, Uruguay, 42, Gf
Sacramento, R., 70, Bd
Sadowa, 60B, Ec
Saffarids, King. of, 6B, Hb
Sagan, 31, Lc; 39, Lc
Saginaw B., 45A, Ab
Sagitta (Sidon), 18C, Ce
Sagona, 20, Hg
Sagres, 35, Jc
Saguenay, R., 45A, Ca
Sahagun, 22, Ac; 63, Ca
Sahara, 80A, Db
Saharanpur, 92, Db
Saigon, 90, Bc
Saigon-Cholon, 91, De
Sailors Creek, 72B, Ab
Saimatsi, 76B, Ca
St. Achebrannus, 13, Af
St. Aignan, 53, Dd
St. Albans, 27, Fe
St. Amand, 46A, Cd; 46B
St. Amand-Montrond, 38, Ee
St. Andrew I., 43A, Dc
St. Andrews, 14, Fc; 37, Cb
St. Andrews, bp., 14A, Cb; 36, Db
St. Angelo, Castle of, 5A
St. Anne, Church of, 18D
St. Anns, 43A, Ec
St. Antonin, 38, Df
St. Asaph, 27, Cc
St. Asaph, bp., 36, Ce
St. Augustine, 72, Dd
St. Austell, 48B, Ad
St. Avold, 76A, Db
St. Bartholomew, 43A, Fc
St. Bees, 36, Cc
St. Benedictus de Holme (St. Benedict's Abbey), 13, Hd
St. Bernard, Hospice of, 22, Db
St. Berrione (St. Buryan), 13, Af
St. Bertrand, 38, Dg
St. Blazey, 48B, Ad
St. Brieuc, 11, Bb
St. Carentochus (Crantock), 13, Af
St. Cast, 55A, Bd
St. Charles, 56, Ac
St. Charles, R., 56A
St. Christopher, 43B, Dc; 55B, De
St. Clair, 45A, Ab
St. Clair, L., 45A, Ab
St. Claude, 20, Fe
St. Croix, R., 45A, Da; 56, Fa
St. Cuthbertes-Lond, 13, Eb
St. David's, 27, Ae
St. David's, bp., 36, Ce
St. Denis, France, 22, Cb
St. Denis, Louisiana, 56, Bc
St. Dié, 22, Db; 83B, Ba
St. Dizier, 76A, Cb
St. Edmundi (Bury St. Edmunds), 13, Gd
St. Elias, C., 71A, Ca
St. Elias, Mt., 71B, Aa
St. Eustatius, 43A, Fc
St. Fargeau, 20, Ee
St. Flour, 20, Ef; 22, Cc
St. Francis, L., Quebec, 57C, Bb
St. Francis, L., St. Lawrence R., 57, Da
St. Francis, R., 71E, Bb
St. Francis de Sales Mission, 45A, Ca
St. Gall, 10, Ce; 29B, Da
St. Gallen, 29B, Da
St. Geneviève, 56, Ac
St. George (Lydda), 18C, Bg
St. George, Str. of, 18E
St. George's B., 45A, Bd
St. Germain, 53, Dc; 84, Cc
St. Germain, C., 45A, Fa
St. Germans, 36, Bg
St. Germanus, 13, Bf
St. Giles, 27A
St. Gilles, Languedoc, 20, Fg
St. Gilles, Poitou, 53, Cd
St. Goar, 22, Da
St. Gotthard, 29A, Gb; 33C, Db
St. Gotthard Pass, 29B, Cb
St. Helena, 40, Je; 96C, Bf
St. Helena B., 81B, Ac
St. Helens, 55A, Cc
St. Hyacinthe, 57, Ea
St. Ignace Mission, 45A, Aa
St. Ives, Cornwall, 55A, Ac
St. Ives, Hunts, 13, Fd; 48A, Cc
St. Jacob, 30, Ge
St. James Church, Jerusalem, 18D
St. Jean, I. de, (Prince Edward I.), 45A, Ea
St. Jean d'Angely, 20, Cf
St. Jean de Luz, 63, Ea
St. Jean de Maurienne, 11, Gd
St. Jean Pied de Port, 30, Cg; 63, Ea
St. Jehan, I., 45A, Da
St. John, 45A, Da
St. John, Hospital of, 18D
St. John, I., 43A, Fc
St. John, L., 71, Gc
St. John, R., 45A, Da; 71E, Cc
St. John the Baptist, Church of, 18D
St. John's (San Juan), 56, Cd
St. John's, Newfoundland 45A, Ga
St. Johns, Quebec, 56, Ea
St. John's R., 43A, Da
St. Joseph, 72, Bb
St. Jullian, B. de, 45A, Fa
St. Kitts, 43A, Fc
St. Lawrence, G. of, 45A Ea
St. Lawrence I., 71A, Aa
St. Lawrence, R., 45A, Da; 57, Da
St. Lazaro Arch. (Philippines), 40, Qd
St. Lizier, 11, De
St. Lo, 22, Bb; 28C, Bb
St. Louis (Senegal), 81C, Aa
St. Louis, Missouri, 56, Ac; 57A, Ab
St. Louis, W. Africa, 80A, Bc; 96C, Ac
St. Loys, C., 45A, Ea
St. Lucia, 43A, Db
St. Lucia B., 81D, Bb
St. Lucia, I., 43A, Fc; 43C, Ec
St. Maixent, 22, Bd; 38, Ce
St. Malo, 20, Cd; 28C, Ab
St. Maria in Mt. Zion, 18D
St. Marie, 80A, Hf
St. Marks, 71F, Ca; 72, Dc
St. Martin, 43A, Fc
St. Martin, C., 81B, Ac
St. Martin, Church of, 18D
St. Mary Magdalen, Church of, 18D
St. Mary's (Santa Maria), 56, Cd
St. Mary's, Canada, 45A, Ba; 56, Db
St. Mary's, Maryland, 45B, Ad
St. Mary's Hospital, 18D
St. Maur, 30, Ed
St. Maurice, R., 57C, Aa
St. Michael (St. Michael's Mount), 13, Af
St. Michael, Alaska, 71A, Aa
St. Mihiel, 83A, Cb
St. Moritz, 29B, Ab
St. Neots, 36, Fe
St. Neotus, 13, Bf
St. Omer, 22, Ca; 46A, Bd
St. Osyth, 36, Hf
St. Paul, France, 22, Cc; 53, Fe
St. Paul, Minnesota, 70, Ec
St. Pauls, 27A
St. Peter, Church of, Jerusalem, 18D
St. Peter's, Rome, 5A
St. Petersburg, 51, Gb; 61, Dc
St. Philippe, 56, Be
St. Pieranus (St. Piran), 13, Af
St. Pierre, 45A, Fa
St. Pierre, L., 57C, Aa
St. Pol, 46A, Bd
St. Pol, prov., 46A, Bd
St. Pol de Leon, 17, Cd
St. Pölten, 21, Ld
St. Probus (Probus), 13, Bf
St. Quentin, 11, Eb; 83A, Bb
St. Regis, 57, Da
St. Riquier, 17, Gc
St. Sauveur, 45A, Db
St. Seurin, 22, Bc
St. Sever, 22, Cc
St. Simon's I., 56, Cd
St. Sophia, 18E
St. Stephen's Gate, 18D
St. Symeon (Seleucia), 18C, Cb
St. Thomas, 43A, Fc
St. Thomas' Tomb, 35, Od
St. Trond, 22, Da; 46A, Ed
St. Urban, 29B, Ba
St. Vaast, 22, Ca; 28C, Bb
St. Valery en Caux, 55A, Dd
St. Valery sur Somme, 28C, Ca
St. Veit, 21, Le
St. Vincent, 80A, Ac
St. Vincent, C., 63, Ad
St. Vincent, I., 43A, Fc
Ste. Foy, 38, Df
Ste. Katherine, 45A, Ga
Saintes, 11, Cd; 30, Cf
Saintonge, 38, Cf
Saintonge, Co. of, 11, Cd
Saipan, 75, Ed
Sajits, King. of, 6B, Fa
Sakaka, 93, Ec
Sakaria, R., 86C, Ba
Sakas, 1, Ke
Sakhalin, 91, Ha
Saladin and the Ayubites, Empire of, 18A, Ee
Salado, R., N. Argentina, 68, Ce
Salado, R., S. Argentina, 68, Cf
Salamanca, 23C, Cb; 63, Cb
Salamis, 9, Je
Salawati, 52C, Db; 77, Eb
Salces, 23D, Ga; 53, Ef
Saldanha, 63, Ca
Saldanha B., 81B, Ac
Salem (Naumkeag), 45B, Db
Salem (Varkinskil), 45B, Bd
Salem, India, 59C, Ce
Salem, Massachusetts, 57, Fb
Salem, Oregon, 70, Bc
Salem, Virginia, 72B, Ba
Salemi, 32C, De
Salerno (Salernum), 5, Ed
Salerno, D. of, 23A, Ec
Salerno, Pr. of, 21A, Cb
Salernum (Salerno), 5, Ed
Salian Franks, 8B, Ba
Salii, 2, Ec
Salinae (Droitwich), 3A, Dd
Salinesville, 72, Da
Salins, 20, Fe; 31A, Cd
Salisbury, England, 27, Ee
Salisbury, New Hampshire, 45B, Db
Salisbury, North Carolina, 57, Af
Salisbury, Rhodesia, 81A, Da
Salisbury, bp., 36, Ef
Salm, Alsace, 20, Gd
Salm, Luxemburg, 20, Fc
Salm, king., 65B, Aa
Salmon Falls, 45B, Db
Salo, 29A, Dc
Salobrena, 23C, Dd
Salom, 2A, Cb
Salona, Dalmatia, 23B, Fc
Salona, Greece, 19, Ce
Salonae, 2, Ge
Salonica, 78, De
Salonica, G. of, 86A, Db
Salonica, King. of, 19, Cd
Salsette I., 73, Bd
Salt Lake City, 70, Cc
Salt Lakes, 59B
Salta, 68, Ce
Saltillo, 43A, Bb
Salto, 68, Df
Saluda, R., 57D, Aa
Saluzzo, 32A, Bb
Saluzzo, Marq. of, 32A, Bb
Salvador, 43D, Dc
Salvador (Bahia), 68, Fd
Salvatierra, 28C, Ae
Salween, R., 25, Jd; 73, Gc
Salza, 20, Jc
Salzach, R., 29A, Eb
Salzburg, 10, Ee
Salzburg, eccl. prov., 22, Eb
Salzburg, Abp. of, 31, Ke
Salzwedel, 10, Db; 26, Dc
Samana, C., 43A, Fc
Samandar, 9, Md
Samanids, King. of, 6B, Ha
Samar, 75E, Cb
Samara, 61, Hd
Samarkand, 6, Hb; 25, Fc
Samarra, 6A, Cb; 9, Lf
Sambre, R., 46A, Dd
Samoa, 90, Fd
Samoa Is., 83, Ae
Samogitia, 26, Fb
Samos, I., 78, Fg
Samos, theme, 9, He
Samosata, 8, Kd
Samothrace, 78, Ee
Samsun, 19, Fd; 93, Da
San, R., 19, Cb
San Agostino, 5A
San Ambrosio, 68, Be
San Antonio, 70, Ee
San Antonio Bay, 44, Ef
San Antonio, C., 43A, Db
San Bernardino Str., 75E, Bb
San Blas, G. of, 43A, Ed
San Cesareo, 5A
San Christobal, 43A, Cc
San Clemente, 5A
San Cosmo y Damiano, 22, Ac
San Cristoval, 77, Kd
San Daniele, 32D, Ca
San Diego, 70, Cd
San Domingo, 43A, Fc
San Domingo, st., 43A, Ec
San Felipe, Chile, 68, Bf
San Felipe, Venezuela, 43A, Fc
San Felix, 68, Ae
San Fernando, Philippines, 75E, Ba
San Fernando, Venezuela, 68, Cb
San Francisco, 70, Bd
San Germano, 23B, Dd
San Geronimo, 43A, Ba
San Geronimo de Yuste, 22, Ac
San Gimignano, 32E, Bb
San Giovanni, 29A, Cc
San Grisogono, 5A
San Ildefonso, 63, Db
San Jorge, G. de, 68, Cg
San José, 43A, Dd
San Juan (St. John's), 56, Cd
San Juan, Argentina, 68, Cf
San Juan, Mexico, 43A, Bb
San Juan, Porto Rico, 43A, Fc
San Juan de la Peña, 22, Bc
San Juan de los Remedios, 43A, Eb
San Juan de Nicaragua, 43A, Dc
San Juan de Ulloa, 43A, Cc
San Leopoldo, 68, De
San Lorenzo del Escorial, 22, Bc
San Lorenzo Fuori le Mura, 5A
San Lorenzo in Damaso, 5A
San Lorenzo in Lucina, 5A
San Lucas, Mexico, 43A, Bb
San Lucas, Spain, 23C, Bd
San Lucas, C., 43A, Ab
San Luis, Argentina, 42, Ge
San Luis, Brazil, 68, Cf
San Luis, Texas, 43A, Ca
San Luis de Caceres, 68, Dd

San Luis Potosi, 43A, Bb
San Marco, 21A, Dc; 22, Fd
San Marino, 32A, Ec
San Martin, Mexico, 43A, Bb
San Martin, Spain, 22, Cd
San Miguel de Piura, 41B, Bd
San Miniato, 32E, Bb
San Nicolas, 68, Cf
San Pablo, I., 40, Ce
San Pedro do Rio Grande (Rio Grande do Sul), 41B, Dg
San Pietro, 5A
San Prassede, 5A
San Quattro Coronati, 5A
San Rafael, 68, Cf
San Roque, 63A
San Salvador, 43A, Dc
San Salvador, I., 43A, Eb
San Salvador de Bahia, 41B, Fe
San Sebastian, Colombia, 43A, Ed
San Sebastian, Spain, 63, Ea
San Sepolcro, 32E, Cb
San Severina, 22, Fd
San Silvestro, 5A
San Sisto, 5A
San Stefano, Rome, 5A
San Stefano, Turkey, 78, Ge
San Susanna, 5A
San Thomé, 43B, Dd
San Vito, 32D, Cb; 86B, Cb
San Xavier, 43A, Ca
San Zoilo, 22, Bc
Sana, 6, Fd; 93, Ef
Sanandaj, 93, Fb
Sancerre, 17, Ge
Sand, R., 81A, Cb
Sandakan, 95, Ne
Sandal, 27, Ec
Sandalwood I. (Sumba), 52C, Bc
Sanday, 49A, Ca
Sandec, 31, Pd
Sandomir, 31, Pc
Sandusky, 71C, Bb
Sandwic (Sandwich), 13, He
Sandwich, England, 7B, Dc
Sandwich, Massachusetts, 45B, Dc
Sandwich, Michigan Terr., 71C, Bb
Sandwich Is., Antarctic Ocean, 69C
Sandwich Is., Pacific Ocean, 42, Bc
Sandy Hook, 57B
Sangarius, R., 19, Ed
Sangir Is., 52C, Ca
Sanguessa, 63, Ea
Sanquhar, 49A, Cc
Sansanne-Mango, 96B, Ca
Santa Agata, 5A
Santa Balbina, 5A
Santa Barbara, 43A, Bb
Santa Barbara Is., 42, Cc
Santa Catalina, 56, Cd
Santa Catarina, 68, Ee
Santa Catarina, st., 68, De
Santa Cecilia, 5A
Santa Croce, 5A
Santa Cruz, Argentina, 68, Ch
Santa Cruz, Bolivia, 68, Cd
Santa Cruz, Brazil, 41B, Fe
Santa Cruz, Canary Is., 55B, Jd
Santa Cruz, I., Pacific Ocean, 77, Ld
Santa Cruz, I., West Indies, 43A, Fc
Santa Elena B., 43D, Dc
Santa Fé, Argentina, 68, Cf
Santa Fé, Florida, 56, Cd
Santa Fé, New Mexico, 70, Dd
Santa Fé, Spain, 22, Bd
Santa Fé de Bogota, 41B, Bc
Santa Isabel, 68, Cc
Santa Lucia B., 80A Gg
Santa Maria, 68, De
Santa Maria (St. Mary's), 56, Cd
Santa Maria in Trastevere, 5A
Santa Maria Maggiore, 5A
Santa Marta, 43A, Ec
Santa Maura, 50, Ef
Santa Prisca, 5A
Santa Rosa, 43A, Bb
Santa Sabina, 5A
Santander, 23C, Da; 63, Da
Santarem, Brazil, 68, Dc
Santarem, Portugal, 63, Ac
Santarem, W. Africa, 35, Kd
Santas Creus, 22, Cc
Santee, R., 45A, Bd; 57D, Bb
Santiago, Chile, 68, Bf
Santiago, San Domingo, 43A, Ec
Santiago, Spain, 63, Aa
Santiago, eccl prov., 22, Ac
Santiago de Compostella, 8, Ac; 22, Ac; 23D, Aa
Santiago de Cuba, 43A, Ec
Santorin, 78, Eg
Santos, 68, Ee
Sao Borja, 68, De
Sao Francisco, 68, Ee
Sao Francisco, R., 68, Ec
Sao José de Rio Negro, 41B Dd
Sao Luis (Maranhao), 68, Ec
Sao Manuel, 68, Dc
Sao Paulo, 68, Ee
Sao Paulo, st., 68, Ee
Sao Tomé, 80A, Dd
São Vicente, Brazil, 41B, Ef
São Vicente, Portugal, 22, Ad
Saône, R., 11, Fc; 20, Fe
Sapporo, 91, Hb
Saragossa, 23C, Eb; 63, Eb
Saragossa, eccl. prov., 22, Bc
Sarai, 19, Hc; 25, Db; 61, Ge
Sarajevo, 39, Ng; 78, Bd
Saranac, R., 57, Da
Sarandi, 68, Df
Sarangani B., 75E, Cc
Saratoga, 57, Eb
Saratov, 61, Gd
Sarawak, 91, Ef
Sardes, 9, He
Sardica, 4B, Hc; 8, Gc
Sardinia, 5, Bd
Sardinia, King. of, 32B, Ad
Sardis, 18A, Db
Sarepta, 18C, Ce
Sargans, 29B, Da
Sargans, canton, 29B, Db
Sari Bair, 86D
Sarikamish, 86C, Da
Sarisberie (Salisbury), 13, Ee
Sark, 17, Dd
Sarkel, 9, Kc
Sarlat, 20, Df
Sarmatia, 1, Fb
Sarnem, 29B, Cb
Sarnthal Alps, 86B, Ba
Saros, G. of, 86D
Saros-Patak, 33C, Eb
Sarrebourg, 83B, Ba
Sarthe, R., 11, Cc
Sarukham, 33A, Cc
Sarum, 7A, Cb
Sarzana, 22, Dc; 32E, Aa
Saskatchewan, 70, Db
Sassbach, 29A, Ca
Satara, 73, Bd
Satpura Mts., 73, Cc
Saucourt, 9, Cb
Saudi Arabia, 93, Ed; 96D, Gb
Sauer, R., 83A, Cb
Saugerties, 56, Eb
Saugor, 73, Cc
Sault Ste. Marie, 45A, Aa
Saumur, 11, Cc
Saumurois, 53, Cd
Saurashtra, 1, Ke
Sauveterre, 38, Cg
Savage (Niue) I., 75, Ge
Savaii, 75B, Aa
Savana, 22, Ec
Savannah (Fort Prince George), 56, Cd
Savannah, Georgia, 56, Cd; 72, Dc
Savannah, Tenn., 72, Cb
Savannah, R., 56, Cd; 72, Dc
Save, R., 22, Fb; 78, Bc
Savona, 5, Bb
Savoy, 28C, Ed; 32A, Ab
Savoy, Co. of, 11, Fd; 20, Ff
Savoy, D. of, 32A, Bb
Sawantwari, 73, Bd
Sawley, 36, Dd
Saxe-Weimar, 51, Cc
Saxon States, 47, Eb
Saxones, 2, Ec
Saxonia, 8B, Ca; 12, Gc
Saxons, 4A, Ba; 7A, Fa
Saxony, 10, Cb; 60A, Dc
Saxony, Duchies of, 53, Jb
Saxony, Elec. of, 31, Kc
Say, 80A, Dc
Saybrook, 45B, Cc
Sayda, 39C, Dc
Sayn, 20, Gc
Sayn, Co. of, 30, Gc
Scalea, 21A, Cc
Scandalion, 18C, Ce
Scandia, 2, Fa
Scandinavia, 69B
Scania, 26, Db; 47, Ea
Scapa Flow, 55B, Ka; 84, Ba
Scarboro, 57, Fb
Scarborough, 3A, Fb; 27, Fb
Scardonia, 22, Fc
Scarpanto, 18B, Dc
Sceptesberie (Shaftsbury), 13, De
Schaffhausen, 29B, Ca; 65A, Ab
Schaffhausen, canton, 29B, Ca
Schärding, 21, Kd
Schässburg, 50, Ed
Schauenburg, 20, Hb
Schaumberg, 21, Kd
Schelde, R., 46A, Cd
Schemnitz, 31, Nd
Schenectady, 57, Eb
Schenk, 38, Gc
Schesel, 8, Ea
Schio, 86B, Bb
Schirmeck, 39B, Db
Schlei, R., 65F, Ba
Schleiz, 39C, Bc
Schleswig, 26, Cc; 65F, Aa
Schleswig, D., 30, Ha; 65F, Aa
Schleswig, M. of, 10, Ca
Schlettstadt, 20, Gd; 76A, Db
Schleusingen, 39C, Ac
Schmalkalden, 34, Eb
Schmölln, 39C, Cc
Schober Pass, 29A, Fb
Schönhausen, 60B, Cb
Schoodic Lakes, 71E, Bc
Schoonhoven, 46A, Dc
Schouwen, 46A, Cc
Schuylkill, R., 45B, Bc; 57, Dc
Schwarzburg, 39C, Ab
Schwarzburg, Pr., 38, Jc, 39C, Bc
Schwarzenberg, 39C, Cc
Schwarzenburg, 29B, Bb
Schwechat, 33C, Db
Schwedt, 39, Lb
Schweidnitz, 31, Mc; 39, Mc
Schweinfurt, 30, Jc; 38, Jc
Schwerin, 10, Db; 20, Jb
Schwerin, D., 38, Jb
Schwiebus, 39, Lb
Schwyz, 29B, Ca
Schwyz, canton, 29B, Ca
Scilly Is., 55B, Kb
Sciptone (Skipton), 18, Dc
Sciréburne (Sherborne), 13, Df
Scireburne (Sherburn), 13, Ec
Sciropesberie (Shrewsbury), 13, Dd
Sciropescire (Shropshire), 13, Dd
Scituate, 45B, Db
Scone, 14, Ec
Scopia, 16, Gd
Scoti, 2, Bc
Scotland, 12, Cb; 34, Ba
Scots, 15, Eb
Scott, 28B, Cb
Scutari, 78, Ge; 86C, Aa
Scutari (Skodra), 78, Bd
Scyros, 78, Ef
Scythia, 1, Kb
Seaford, 27, Gf
Seattle, 70, Bc
Sebago L., 45B, Db
Sebaste, 18C, Cf
Sebastea, 8, Kd; 9, Ke
Sebenico, 31, Lg; 32A, Fc
Secessionville, 72, Dc
Seckau, 22, Eb
Second Cataract, 80B, Ac
Sedalia, 72, Bb
Sedan, 29A, Aa; 88, Fd
Sedberuie (Sadberge), 13, Eb
Sedd el Bahr, 86D
Sedgemoor, 48B, Bd
Sées, 22, Cb
Segauli, 73, Eb
Segeberg, 22, Ea; 38, Jb
Segedunum (Wallsend), 3C
Segelocum (Littleborough), 3A, Fc
Segni, 22A
Segontium (Caernarvon), 3A, Bc
Segorbe, 22, Bd
Ségou, 96B, Ba
Segovia, 23D, Cb; 63, Cb
Segre, R., 20, Dh
Segu, 80A, Cc
Seilan (Ceylon), 25, Hf
Seine, R., 11, Db; 76A, Cb
Seistan (Sijistan), 6, Hb; 61B, Bb
Seisyllwg, 7C, Ab
Sekondi Takoradi, 96B, Bb
Selby, 36, Ed; 48A, Cc
Selenga, R., 91, Db
Seleucia, 8, Jd; 9, Ke
Seleucia (St. Symeon), 18C, Cb
Selgovae, 3A, Ca
Seljuk Empire, 16, Le
Seljuk Empire of Rum or Iconium, 18B, Ec
Seljuk Kingdom of Rum or Iconium, 19, Fe
Seljuk Turks, 24, Jf
Selkirk, Canada, 70, Eb
Selkirk, Scotland, 14, Fd
Selkirk, co., 37A, Cc
Selma, 72, Cc
Selsey, 7A, Cb; 36A
Selsey, diocese, 36A
Selwood, 7B, Bc
Selymbria, 19, Dd
Selz, 39B, Eb
Semarang, 91, Eg
Semendria, 78, Cc
Semeni, R., 86A, Ab
Semipalatinsk, 91, Ba
Semlin, 78, Cc
Semmering Pass, 29A, Fb
Semoy, R., 46A, Ee
Sempach, 29B, Ca
Sempringham, 36, Fe
Semur, 11, Fc; 30, Fe
Sendai, 91, Hc
Senecas, 45A, Bb
Seneffe, 46A, Dd
Senegal (St. Louis), 81C, Aa
Senegal, rep., 96, Ac
Senegal, terr., 81C, Bb
Senegal, R., 81C, Ba
Senez, 22, Dc
Senigallia, 39, Kg
Senlis, 11, Eb; 83A, Bb
Sennar, 80B, Ae
Senne, R., 46B
Senogalliae, 5B, Bb
Sens, 11, Eb; 17, Gd
Sens, eccl. prov., 22, Cb
Seoul, 91, Fc
Sept Iles, 45A, Da
Septimania, 4A, Cc; 8, Cc
Sequana, R., 2, Dd
Serai, 24, Md
Serampore, 59B
Serbia, 78, Cd
Serbia, King. of, 18B, Bb
Serbs, 9, Fd
Serdica, 2, He; 78A
Seres, 78, De; 86A, Ea
Sereth, R., 50, Fd; 78, Fb
Sergipe, 68, Fd
Seringapatam, 73, Ce
Seriphos, 78, Eg
Serowe, 96C, Eg
Serpa, 23D, Bd
Serpent's Mouth, 43B, Dc
Serres, 38, Ff
Serrey, 60A, Ja
Servia, 9, Fd; 78, De
Servian Princes, 24, Ge
Seseltre (Seasalter), 13, He
Sesia, R., 29A, Cc
Sessa, 22, Ec
Seteia Aest., 3A., Cc
Setif, 8, Dd
Seton, clan, 28B, Ba; 37A, Cb
Setubal, 63, Ac
Sevastopol, 51, Ge
Seven Pines, 72B, Bb
Severn, R., Britain, 36, De
Severn, R., Canada, 70, Eb
Severnaya Zemlya, 69B
Severski, 19, Eb
Severyans, 9, Jb
Seville, 23C, Cd; 63, Bd
Seville, eccl. prov., 22, Ad
Sèvres, 84, Cc
Seward, 71A, Cb
Seychelles, 69A, Me; 94, Rf
Sfax, 89, Hg
Shackleton, 69C
Shaftesbury, 27, Df
Shahjahanpur, 73, Db
Sha-ho, R., 76B, Ba
Shan State, 92, Hc
Shanghai, 91, Fc
Shangtu, 25, Lb
Shannon, R., 15, Cc; 37B, Cc
Shap, 36, Dc; 49A, Cc
Shaqra, 93, Fd
Shari, R., 80A, Ed
Sharks B., 77, Af
Sharpsburg, 72B, Ba
Shashi, 74, Ke
Shatt el Hai, R., 86C, Ec
Shawnees, 45B, Bc; 56, Bc
Sheelin, L., 15, Dc
Sheen, 36, Ff
Sheerness, 54, Cb
Sheffield, 27, Ec; 48A, Cc
Shelburne, 71, Hc
Shenandoah, R., 57, Bd; 72B, Aa
Shendi, 80B, Ad
Shenyang (Mukden), 91, Fb
Sheppey, 7C, Dc
Sherborne, 27, Df; 36, Df
Sherborne, diocese, 36A
Sherbro I., 81C, Bc
Sherbrook, 57C, Bb
Sherbrooke, 71, Gc
Sherburn, 48B, Cc
Sheriffmuir, 37A, Cb
Sherman's March, 72, Dc
Sherwood, 7B, Cb
Sherwood Forest, 3A, Ec
Shetland Is., 12, Da; 34, Ba
Shibam, 93, Ff
Shiel, L., 49A, Bb
Shiliho, 76B, Ba
Shillong, 92, Gb
Shiloh, 72, Cb
Shipka Pass, 78, Ed
Shiraz, 6, Gc; 93, Gd
Shirley, 45B, Ae
Shiz, 6A, Da
Shoeburyness, 7C, Dc
Sholanghur, 59A, Ce
Sholapur, 73, Cd
Shoreditch, 27A
Shoreham, England, 27, Ff
Shoreham, Vermont, 57, Eb
Shoshong, 81A, Cb
Shreveport, 70, Ed; 72, Bc
Shrewsbury, England, 27, Dd
Shrewsbury, New Jersey, 45B, Bc
Shropshire, 27, Dd; 28A, Db
Shumla, 62, Hd; 78, Fd
Shuqra, 93, Fg
Shushan (Susa), 6A, Db
Siak, 75A, Ab
Sialkot, 73, Ba
Siam (Thailand), 91, De
Siam, G. of, 91, De
Sian, 91, Dc
Sianfu, 74, Je
Siberia, 74, Jb; 83, Pa
Siberut, 91, Cg
Sibin (Hermannstadt), 19, Cc
Sibir, 25, Fa; 40, Na
Sibir, Khanate of, 25, Ga
Sibton, 36, He
Sicilia, 2, Ff
Sicily, 5, Df
Sicily, Co. of, 16, Ee
Sicily, King. of, 23B, Ed
Side, 19, Ee
Sidi Barrani, 93, Bc
Sidlaw Hills, 14, Ec
Sidnacester, 36A
Sidnacester, diocese, 36A
Sidon (Sagitta), 18C, Ce
Siegburg, 20, Gc
Siegen, 53, Hb; 83A, Ea
Siena, 5, Cc
Siena, Rep. of, 32A, Dc
Sieradz, 31, Nc
Sierra Leone, 81C, Bc
Sierra Madre, 43A, Bb
Siffin, 6A, Ba
Sigmaringen, 10, Cd; 60B, Cd
Sigüenza, 22, Bc
Siguiri, 96B, Ba
Sijilmasa, 6, Ab
Sijistan (Seistan), 6, Hb
Sikhs, 59C, Ba
Si-Kiang, R., 91, Ed
Sikkim, 73, Eb; 92, Fb
Sikri, 52A, Bb
Silesia, 33C, Db
Silesia, D. of, 21, Mc
Silistra, 78, Fc
Silistria, 19, Dd
Sillery, 45A, Ca
Silos, 22, Bc
Silures, 3A, Ce
Silves, 22, Ad
Simancas, 23C, Cb
Simbach, 29A, Ea
Simbirsk, 61, Gd
Simcoe, L., 45A, Bb
Simeulve, 91, Cf
Simla, 73, Ca
Simnitza, 78, Ed
Simonstown, 81B, Ac
Simplon Pass, 29B, Cb
Sinai, 6A, Ac
Sinai Peninsula, 18A, Ed; 80B, Ab
Sinaloa, 43A, Bb
Sinclair, 37A, Ca
Sind, 1, Je; 73, Ab
Sindhia, 73, Cc
Singapore, 75A, Bb; 91, Df
Singapore, Str. of, 75A, Bb
Singara, 2, Mf
Singidunum, 4A, Gc
Sinigaglia, 8A, Dc; 32A, Ec
Sin kai lin Pass, 76B, Ba
Sinkailin Pass, 76B, Ca
Sinkiang-Uigur, 91, Bc
Sinmintun, 76B, Ba
Sinope, 19, Fd; 79, Gb
Sinsheim, 29A, Ca
Sinus Arabicus, 1, Fe
Sinus Aualites, 1, Gf
Sinus Oxianus, 1, Hc
Sinus Persicus, 1, He
Sion, 11, Gc
Sion (Sitten), 29B, Bb
Siponto, 23B, Ed
Sirhind, 52A, Ba; 73, Ca
Sirji Arjengaon, 73, Cc
Sirmium, 2, Ge; 4A, Fc
Sis, 18C, Ca; 19, Fe
Siscia, 2, Gd
Sissek, 31, Mf; 33A, Aa
Sissonne, 83A, Bb
Sisteron, 22, Dc; 30, Ff
Sistova, 78, Ed
Sita, 19, Fa
Sitabaldi, 73, Cc
Sitcha, 61, De
Sitka, 71B, Cb
Sitka (New Archangel), 71A, Db
Sitten (Sion), 29B, Bb
Sitvatorok, 33C, Db

Siuyen, 76B, Ba
Sivas, 79, Gc
Siwah, 80A, Fb; 93, Bd
Siward, 12, Dc
Siwas, 16, Ke; 18A, Fb
Six Nations, 57, Cb
Sixth Cataract, 80B, Ad
Skagerrak, 12, Gb; 84, Da
Skagway, 71B, Cb
Skara, 26, Db
Skaw, The, 12, Gb
Skeena, R., 70, Bb
Skelleftea, 26, Fa
Skelton, 27, Fb
Skenesboro, 57, Eb
Skenfrith, 28A, Dc
Skeninge, 26, Db
Skhumbi, R., 78, Be
Skibbereen, 49B, Be
Skipsea, 13, Fc
Skipton, 27, Dc
Skiringssal, 12, Gb
Skodra (Scutari), 78, Bd
Skog, 50, Da
Skoplje (Uskub), 78, Cd
Skreen, 15, Ec
Skumbi, R., 86A, Aa
Skye, 14, Bb
Slachter's Nek, 81A, Cd
Slane, 49B, Ec
Slaney, R., 15, Ed; 37B, Ed
Slave Coast, 81C, Ec
Slavinia, 21B, Cb
Slavinia, D. of, 21, Lb
Slavonia, 39, Mf
Slavonic Peoples, 8A, Da
Slavs, 4A, Hb; 8, Ha
Sleat, 14, Cb
Sleat, Sd. of, 14, Cb
Slieve Bloom, 15, Dc
Slieve League, 15, Cb
Sligo, 37B, Cb; 49B, Cb
Sligo, co., 37C; 49B, Cb
Slivnitza, 78, Dd
Slovak, 85, Fc
Slovakia, 87, Ec
Slovenes, 9, Fc
Sluys, 28C, Da; 46A, Cc
Slyne Hd., 49B, Ac
Smaland, 26, Db
Small Saxon States, 65C, Ba
Smerwick, 49B, Ad
Smith Sd., 42, Ga; 69B
Smithfield, 57, Ce
Smithland, 72, Cb
Smolensk, 19, Eb; 26, Hc
Smolensk, Pr., 19, Ea
Smyrna, 78, Ff
Snake, R., 44, Cd; 70, Cc
Snake Hill, 71D
Sneeuw Mts., 77, Fb
Snotingeham (Nottingham), 13, Ed
Snotinghamscire (Nottinghamshire), 13, Fc
Snowdon, 27, Cc
Soa Pan, 81A, Cb
Soana, 23B, Cc
Sobral, 63B
Sobraon, 73, Ba
Sobrarbe, 23C, Ea
Society Is., 75, He
Socorro, 70, Dd
Socotra, 94, Re; 96A, Ca
Söderhamn, 26, Ea
Söderköping, 34, Fa; 50, Db
Södermanland, 26, Eb
Sodor and Man, bp., 36, Bc
Soest, 20, Hc
Sofala, 40, Le; 81A, Db
Sofia, 78, Dd
Sogdiana, 1, Jc; 6, Ha
Sognefjord, 12, Fa
Sohag, 93, Cd
Soignes, Forest of, 46B
Soignies, 46B
Soissons, 11, Eb; 83A, Eb
Sokol, 78, Bc
Sokoto, 96B, Ca
Sokotra, 41A, Cc; 83, Md
Solano, 75E, Ba
Soldaia, 19, Ed
Soldin, 21, Lb
Sole Bay, 55A, Db
Soleure (Solothurn), 29B, Ba
Solferino, 29A, Dc; 32C, Cb
Solikamsk, 61, Jc
Sollum, 93, Bc
Solms, 30, Hc
Solomon Is., 77, Kc; 90, Dd
Solothurn (Soleure), 29B, Ba
Solothurn, canton, 29B, Ba
Solsona, 22, Cc
Solway Firth, 14, Ee
Solway Moss, 37A, Cc
Somali Rep., 96D, Gd
Somalia, 96A, Bb
Somberete, 43A, Bb
Somers Is. (Bermudas), 43A, Fa
Somerset, 27, De
Somerset East, 81B, Cc
Somerton, 7B, Bc
Somme, R., 11, Eb; 83A, Bb
Somnath, 52A, Ab; 25, Gd
Somosierra, 63, Db
Son, R., 73, Dc
Sonchön, 76B, Cb
Soncino, 32D, Ab
Sonderburg, 65F, Aa
Sondershausen, 39C, Ab
Sondre Stromfjord, 94, Cb
Sondrio, 29B, Db
Song Empire (Mangi), 25, Kd
Sonora, 43A, Ab
Sonora, R., 43A, Ab
Soor, 60A, Ec
Sora, 5B, Bc
Sorauren, 63, Ea
Sorbs, 8, Ea
Sorel, 57C, Aa
Soria, 23C, Db; 63, Db
Sorrento, 5, Ed
Sorviodunum (Salisbury), 3A, Ee
Soule. 17, Eg; 30, Cg
Sources, Mont Aux, 81D, Ab
South (Middle) I. (New Munster), 77A
South Africa, Rep. of, 96D, Eh
South Africa, Union of, 80A Fg
South African Republic, 81B, Ca
South Anna, R., 72B, Bb
South Atlantic Ocean, 94, Af
South Australia, 77, Eg
South Beveland, 46A, Cc
South Carolina, 57D, Ab
South China Sea, 91, Ef
South Dakota, 70, Dc
South Downs, 27, Ff
South Esk, R., 14, Fc
South Georgia, 69C
South Ice, 69C
South Kanara, 52A, Bc
South Konkan, 73, Bd
South Korea, 91, Fc
South Manchurian Railway, 74, Ld
South Molton, 27, Cf
South Orkney Is., 69C
South Pacific Ocean, 75, He
South Pass, 44, Dd
South Pole, 69C
South Potomac, R., 57, Bd
South Prussia, 60A, Fb
South Ronaldsay, 49A, Ca
South Saskatchewan, R., 70, Db
South Saxons, 7A, Cb
South Sea, 40, Ed
South Shetland Is., 69C
South Shields, 3C
South Uist, 14, Ab
South Vietnam, 91, De
South West Africa, 96C, Dg
Southampton, England, 27, Ef
Southampton, Long I., 45B, Cc
Southampton I., 70, Fa
Southern Alps, N.Z., 77, Mj
Southern Hiung-nu, 1, Nc
Southern Nigeria, 81C, Fc
Southern Ocean, 69C
Southern Rhodesia, 80A, Ff
Southern Slavs, 8C, Cb
Southland, 77A
Southold, 45B, Cc
Southwark, 27, Fe; 27A
Southwell, 36, Fd; 48B, Cc
Southwold, 55A, Db
Souvigny, 22, Cb
Sovietskaya, 69C
Sozopolis, 18A, Eb
Sozusa, 4B, Ge
Spa, 46A, Ed
Spain, 34, Bd; 63, Db
Spalato, 5, Fc; 78, Ad
Spalding, 27, Fd
Spallinge (Spalding), 13, Fd
Spandau, 60A, Db
Spanish Fort, 72, Cc
Spanish Guinea, 80A, Dd
Spanish Main, 43A, Ec
Spanish March, 8, Cc
Spanish Morocco, 96C, Ba
Spanish Netherlands, 38, Fc
Spanish Sahara, 96D, Ab
Spanish Town, 43A, Ec
Sparta, 78, Dg
Spartanburg, 72, Dc
Spartel, C., 62, Ae; 63A
Spectacle I., 56B
Spencer G., 77, Fh
Sperrin Mts., 15, Db
Spey, R., 14, Eb
Speyer, 29A, Ca; 83A, Eb
Speyer (Spires), 20, Hd
Spezia, 32A, Cb
Spezzia, 78, Dg
Spichern, 76A, Db
Spilimberg, 86B, Ca
Spinalonga, 79, Ec
Spinis (Speen), 3A, Ee
Spion Kop, 81D, Ab
Spires (Speyer), 20, Hd
Spithead, 55A, Cc
Spitzbergen, 42, Ka; 74, Aa
Spitzbergen Sea, 74, Ba
Splügen Pass, 29B, Db
Spoleto (Spoletium), 5, Dc
Spoleto, D. of, 5, Dc; 21, Kg
Sponheim, 20, Gd
Sporades, 78, Df
Spotsylvania, 72B, Ba
Spree, R., 10, Eb
Springbokfontein, 81B, Ab
Springfield, Illinois, 72, Cb
Springfield, Massachusetts, 45B, Cb
Springfield, Missouri, 72, Bb
Spurn Hd., 55A, Db
Squillace, 5, Fe
Srinagar, 25, Gc; 73, Ca
Srivijaya, 25, Jf
Staaten Land, 42, Sf
Stade, 20, Hb
Stadford (Stafford), 13, Dd
Stadfordscire (Staffordshire), 13, Dd
Stadtlohn, 38, Gb
Staete Land, 42B
Staffarda, 29A, Bc; 50, Be
Stafford, 27, Dd
Stafford, co., 27, Dd
Stagno, 22, Fc
Stalingrad, 88, Od
Stalino, 88, Nd
Stalinsk, 91, Ba
Stamford, Connecticut, 45B, Cc
Stamford, England, 27, Fd
Stamford Bridge, 12, Dc
Standerton, 81A, Cc
Stanes (Staines), 13, Fe
Stanford (Stamford), 13, Fd
Stanfordbrycge (Stamford Bridge), 13, Fb
Stångebro, 26, Eb
Stanislau, 84, Gc
Stanleyville, 80A, Fd; 96D, Ed
Stantune (Long Stanton), 13, Dd
Stanwix, 3C
Stanz, 29B, Cb
Stara Zagora, 78, Ed
Staraya Russa, 61, Dc
Starbuck I., 75, He
Stargard, 21, Lb; 31, Kb
Starodub, 19, Ga; 61, Dd
Staten I., 45B, Bc; 57B
Stau (Stow), 13, Fc
Staufen, 10, Cd
Staunton, 56, Dc
Staunton, R , 57, Be
Stavanger, 12, Fb; 47, Da
Stavelot, 22, Da; 46A, Ed
Stavoren, 26, Cc
Stavropol, Astrakhan, 61, Fe
Stavropol, Kazan, 61, Gd
Stavros, 86A, Eb
Stavuchanak, 61, Ce
Stayninges (Steyning), 13, Ff
Steelpoort, 81A, Db
Steenkerque, 46A, Dd
Steenwyk, 46A, Fb
Steier, 21, Ld
Steinamanger, 21, Me
Steinau, 39, Mc
Stella Land, 81A, Bc
Stellenbosch, 81B, Ac
Stellenbosch, dist., 81B, Ac
Stelvio Pass, 29B, Eb
Stenay, 38, Fd
Stendal, 20, Jb
Stephen Dushan, Emp. of, 24, Ge
Stephen's Fort (Charleston), 57, Eb
Sternberg, 21, Lb
Stettin, 31, Lb; 39, Cb
Stewart, 28B, Ab; 37A, Bb
Stewart I. (New Leinster), 77A
Stikine, R., 71B, Db
Stillwater, 57, Eb
Stirling, 14, Ec; 37A, Cb
Stirling, co., 37A, Bb; 49A, Bb
Stockach, 29A, Cb
Stockholm, 26, Eb
Stoke Courcy, 27, Ce
Stolbova, 47, Ja; 50, Gb
Stollhofen, 29A, Ba
Stolp, 21, Ma
Stolpen, 39C, Eb
Stonehaven, 49A, Cb
Stonington, 45B, Dc
Stony Pt., 57, Dc
Storkow, 31, Kb
Storkyro, 50, Ea
Storm B., 77, Hj
Stormberg, 81B, Cb
Stornoway, 49A, Aa
Stoss Pass, 29B, Da
Stour, R., 27, Ge
Strabane, 49B, Db
Stradella, 29A, Cc
Stralsund, 26, Dc; 31B, Ca
Strand, 27A
Strängnäs, 26, Eb
Stranraer, 49A, Bc
Strasbourg, 7A, Eb; 83B, Ba
Strasburg, U.S.A., 72B, Aa
Strassburg, 10, Bd
Strata Florida, 36, Ce
Strata Marcella, 36, Ce
Stratford, 45B, Cc
Strath Earn, 14, Ec
Strath Spey, 14, Eb
Strathaven, 28B, Ab
Strathclyde, 14, Ed; 36A
Strathfillan, 49A, Bb
Strathmore, 14, Ec
Strathnaver, 14, Da
Stratton, 48A, Ad
Straubing, 39, Kd
Strelitz, 60B, Db; 65B, Ba
Striguil, 13, De; 28A, Dc
Stromness, 49A, Ca
Stronsay, 49A, Ca
Strumna, R., 78, De; 86A, Ea
Strumnitza, 78, De
Strymon, 9, Gd
Stuart Town (Port Royal), 45A, Ad
Stuhlweissenburg, 33C, Db
Stuhm, 39, Nb
Stuhmsdorf, 50, Dc
Stumitza, 86A, Da
Sturgeon L., 45A, Bb
Stuttgart, 29A, Ca
Styria, 10, Fe
Styria, D. of, 21, Le
Styrian Alps, 29A, Fb
Suakin, 80B, Bd
Suana, 5B, Ab
Subiaco, 22, Ec
Suck, R., 15, Cc
Sucre, 68, Cd
Suda Bay, 79, Dc
Sudan, reg., 81C, Db
Sudan, rep., 96D, Ec
Sudberie (Sudbury), 13, Gd
Sudbury, Canada, 70, Fc
Sudetes, 60A, Fc
Sudfulc (Suffolk), 13, Hd
Sudras, 59D
Sudreys, 12, Cb; 14, Bc
Sudrie (Surrey), 13, Fe
Sudsexe (Sussex), 13, Ff
Sud-Treding (South Riding), 13, Gc
Sudwelle (Southwell), 13, Ec
Sudwerca (Southwark), 13, Fe
Suevi, 2, Ed; 4A, Ac
Suez, 80B, Ab
Suez Canal, 80B, Aa
Suffolk, Virginia, 57, Ce
Suffolk, co., 27, Hd
Sugar Hill, 57, Eb
Suir, R., 15, Dd; 37B, Dd
Sukhumi, 79, Hb
Sukkur, 92, Bb
Sula Is., 52C, Bb
Sula Sea, 75E, Bc
Sulaiman Mts., 73, Aa
Sulaimaniya, 93, Fb
Sulawesi (Celebes), 91, Eg
Sulina, 78, Gc
Sullana, 68, Ac
Sullivan, 15, Be
Sully, 38, Ee
Sulzbach, 21, Jd
Sumatra, 35, Od
Sumatra (Java Minor), 35, Oe
Sumatra, I., 91, Dg
Sumba, 91, Fg
Sumba (Sandelwood I.), 52C, Bc
Sumbawa, 91, Eg
Sumorsete (Somerset), 13, Ce
Sunart, 14, Cc
Sunbury, 56, Dc
Sunda Sea, 91, Fg
Sundarbans, 59B, 73, Ec
Sunday, R., 81D, Bb
Sundgau, 30, Ge; 39B, Dc
Superior, L., 56, Ba; 70, Fc
Supplingenburg, 20, Jb
Sur (Tyre), 18C, Ce
Surabaja, 91, Eg
Surat, 73, Bc
Surinam, 41B, Dc; 42, Gd
Surrey, 7A, Cb; 27, Fe
Susa, Italy, 5, Ab
Susa, N. Africa, 6, Cb; 24, Ef
Susa (Shushan), 1, Gd; 6A, Db
Susquehanna, R., 45A, Bb; 57, Db
Sussex, 27, Ff
Sutherland, 14, Da
Sutherland Berg, 81D, Ab
Sutlej, R., 73, Da
Sutri, 21, Kg; 23B, Dc
Sutrium, 5, Dc
Suva, 75, Fe; 75C, Bb
Suvla B., 86D
Suwanee, 71F, Ca
Suwanee, R., 71F, Ca
Suzdal, 19, Ga
Suzdal, dist., 19, Ga
Suzzara, 29A, Dc
Svalbard, 94, Rb
Sveaborg, 51, Fa
Svendborg, 26, Db
Sverdlovsk, 74, Ec; 88, Sb
Sverdrup Is., 44, Da
Swaanendael, 45B, Bd
Swabia, 10, Ce; 20, He
Swabian Jura, 10, Cd
Swakopmund, 80A, Eg
Swale, R., 12, Dc
Swan River Colony, 77, Bh
Swanage, 7C, Cc
Swansea, Rhode I., 45B, Dc
Swansea, Wales, 27, Ce; 28A, Bc
Swart Berg, 81B, Bc
Swat, R., 73, Ba
Swatow, 74, Kf; 90, Bb
Swaziland, 80A, Gg; 81A, Dc
Sweden, 26, Ea; 47, Fa; 82, Ea
Sweden and Norway, 64, Ea
Swedish Pomerania, 51, Cc
Sweetheart Abbey, 36, Cc
Swellendam, 81B, Bc
Swellendam, dist., 81B, Bc
Sweyn, 12, Dd
Swilly L., 15, Da
Swiss Confederation, The, 29B; 30, He
Switzerland, 47, Dc; 54, Dc
Sycamore Shoals, 57A, Cb
Sydney (Port Jackson), 77, Ih
Sylt, 65F, Aa
Syr Darya, R., 25, Fb; 61B, Ba
Syracusae, 2, Gf
Syracuse (Syracusa), 5, Ef
Syracuse, New York, 57, Cb; 67B, Ca
Syria, 1, Fd; 6A, Bb; 79, Gc
Syriam, 40, Od
Syrian Desert, 86C, Cc
Syrtis Major, 2, Gg
Syrtis Minor, 2, Fg
Szabacs, 33C, Dc
Szathmar, 33C, Eb
Szcelankemen, 33C, Eb
Szczebrzeszyn, 26, Fc
Szczecin, 89, Hc
Szczekociny, 51, Ec
Sze Chow, 1, Od
Szeged, 87, Ec
Szegedin, 33C, Eb; 39, Pe
Sziget, 33C, Db

TABASCO, 43A, Cc
Tabatinga, 68, Cc
Table B., 81A, Ad
Taboga I., 43A, Ed
Tabor, 31, Ld; 33C, Cb
Tabora, 80A, Ge
Tabriz, 6, Fb; 19, He; 79, Jc
Tacloban, 75E, Bb
Tacna, Chile, 68, Bd
Tacna, Peru, 68, Cd
Tacuba, 43A, Cc
Tacutu, R., 68B, Bb
Tadcaster, 48A, Cc
Tadkin, R., 57, Ae
Tadmor, 6A, Bb; 9, Kf
Tadoussac, 45A, Da; 71, Hc
Tafosoho, 52B, Aa
Taganrog, 61, Ee
Taginae, 5, Dc
Tagliacozzo, 21, Kg
Tagliamento, R., 29A, Ec
Tagus, R., 23C, Cc; 63, Bc
Tahirids, King. of, 6B, Ga
Tahiti, 75, He
Tai Yuan, 1, Od
Taif, 6, Fc; 93, Ee
Taillebourg, 17, Ef
Tain, 37A, Bb; 49A, Bb
Tainan, 91, Fd
Taipei, 91, Fd
Taitze-ho, R., 76B, Ba
Taiwan, 74, Lf
Taiwan (Formosa), 91, Fd
Taiyuan, 91, Ec
Takhires Gol, L., 86A, Eb
Takrit, 6, Fb
Taku, R., 71B, Cb
Takushan, 76B, Bb
Talangama, 52B, Aa
Talavera, 62, Be; 63, Cc
Talayan, 75E, Bc
Talca, 68, Bf
Talcaguano, 68, Bf
Tali, 25, Kd
Talienwan, 76B, Ab
Talienwan B., 76B, Ab
Talikot, 52A, Bc
Taling Ho, R., 76B, Aa
Talladega, 71F, Ba
Tallahassee, 72, Dc
Tallapoosa, R., 71F, Ba
Tallard, 38, Gf
Tallinn, 87, Fa
Talmont, 20, Ce

Tamale, 96B, Bb
Tamar, R., 27, Bf
Tamatave, 80A, Hf
Tambof, 61, Fd
Tamesis (R. Thames), 3A, Ge
Tampa, 72, Dd
Tampa B., 44, Ff; 70, Fe
Tampico, 43A, Cb
Tamrush, 78, Ee
Tamworde (Tamworth), 13, Ed
Tamworth, 7B, Cb; 48A, Cc
Tana, India, 35, Nd
Tana, Russia, 19, Fc
Tana, L., 80B, Be
Tananarive, 80A, Hf
Tanaro, R., 29A, Bc
Tancrids Tower, 18D
Tandil, 68, Df
Tandjungpinang, 75A, Bb
Tanega Shima, 41A, La
Tanganyika, 96C, Fe
Tanganyika, L., 80A, Fe
Tangermünde, 30, Kb
Tangier, 23D, Ce; 63A
Tanjore, 59D
Tann, 29A, Ea
Tannenberg, 31, Pb; 84, Gb
Tanner's Gate, 18D
Tanta, 80B, Aa
Tantallon Castle, 28B, Ca
Tantone (Taunton), 13, Ce
Taormina, 21A, Cd
Taormina (Tauromenium), 5, Ef
Tapajos, 68, Dc
Tappita, 96B, Bb
Tapti, R., 73, Bc
Tara, 15, Ec
Tarakan, 90, Bc
Taranaki, 77A
Taranto, 32A, Gd
Taranto, G. of, 32B, Fd
Tarapaca, Chile, 68, Cd
Tarapaca, Colombia, 68, Cc
Tarascon, 38, Dg
Tarasp, 29B, Eb
Tarazona, 22, Bc; 23C, Eb
Tarbes, 11, Ce; 63, Fa
Tarentaise, 22, Db
Tarentaise, eccl. prov., 22, Db
Targowica, 51, Gd
Tarifa, 23D, Cd; 63A
Tarija, 68, Ce
Tarim, R., 25, Hb; 91, Bb
Tarki, 19, Hd
Tarkwa, 96B, Bb
Tarlac, 75E, Ba
Tarn, R., 11, Ed
Tarnof, 26, Fc
Tarnopol, 33C, Fb; 62, Hc
Tarnow, 33C, Ea
Taron, 18C, Ce
Tarraco, 2, De
Tarragona, 23C, Fb; 63, Fb
Tarragona, eccl. prov., 22, Cc
Tarsus, 6A, Ba; 18C, Bb
Tartar, 85, Mb
Tartary, 35, Nb; 69A, Nb
Tartas, 30, Cg
Tartu, 87, Fa
Tashihkiao, 76B, Ba
Tashkent, 25, Fb; 61B, Ba
Tasman Sea, 77, Kl
Tasmania, 77, Gj
Tateshale (Tanshelf), 13, Ec
Tati, 81A, Cb
Tati, R., 81A, Cb
Tattershall, 27, Fc
Tatungkow, 76B, Cb
Taufers, 86B, Aa
Taunton, England, 27, Ce
Taunton, Rhode I., 45B, Dc
Taunus, 83A, Ea
Taurica, 2, Kd
Tauroggen, 60A, Ja
Tauromenium (Taormina), 5, Ef
Taurus, 2, Kf; 19, Ee
Taus, 31, Kd
Tavastehus, 26, Fa
Tavestoche (Tavistock), 13, Bf
Taveuni, 75C, Ba
Tavira, 23C, Bd
Tavistock, 27, Bf
Tavoy, 73, Ge
Tavua, 75C, Aa
Taxila, 1, Kd
Tay, Firth of, 14, Fc
Tay, L., 14, Dc
Tay, R., 14, Ec
Tbilisi, 93, Ea
Tchirman, 33A, Cb
Tebuk, 93, Dd
Tecklenburg, 20, Gb
Tecklenburg, co., 46C, Ca
Tees, R., 27, Eb
Teesdale, 28B, Cc
Tefe, 68, Cc
Tegeingl, 13, Cc
Tegesta, 43A, Db
Tehama, 6, Fd
Tehran, 93, Gb
Tehri, 73, Cc
Tehuantepec, 43A, Cc
Tehuantepec, Isthmus of, 43A, Cc
Teifi, R., 27, Bd
Teith, R., 14, Dc
Tekke, Amirate of, 19, Ee
Tekrit, 86C, Dc
Tel Aviv-Jaffa, 79, Fd
Tell-basher (Turbessel), 18C, Eb
Teller, 71A, Aa
Tellicherri, 73, Ce
Tembuland, 81A, Cd
Tembus, 81B, Cb
Teme, R., 28A, Cb
Temesvar, 33C, Eb
Temple, Jerusalem, 18D
Temple, London, 27A
Temple Bar, 27A
Templeborough, 3A, Ec
Templin, 31, Kb
Temuco, 68, Bf
Tenasserim, 73, Ge
Tenby, 27, Be
Tenda, 32A, Bb
Tenda, Coc di, 29A, Bc
Tenedos, 78, Ef; 86C, Ab
Tenerife, 80A, Bb
Tenes, 16, Ce
Tengri Nor, L., 73, Fa
Tennessee, R., 56, Bd
Tennessee, st., 72, Cb
Tenterden, 27, Ge
Teodekesberie (Tewkesbury), 13, De
Teofilo-Otoni, 68, Ed
Tephrik, 16, Ke
Tepl, 22, Eb
Teplitz, 33C, Ca; 60B, Dc
Terek, R., 19, Hd; 61, Ff
Terek Cossacks, 61, Gf
Teresina, 68, Ec
Tergovist, 24, Hd
Terminal Pt., 76B, Bb
Termoli, 32A, Fc
Ternate, 52B, Aa
Terni, 22, Ec; 39, Kg
Terracina, 5, Dd; 22A
Terschelling, 46A, Ea
Tertry, 7A, Db; 8B, Bb
Teruel, 22, Bc; 23C, Eb
Teschen, 21, Nd; 87, Dc
Teslin, L., 70, Aa
Teslin, R., 71B, Ca
Tete, 42, Le; 81A, Da
Tetford (Thetford), 13, Gd
Tettenhall, 7C, Bb; 13, Dd
Tetuan, 16, Ae
Teupitz, 60A, Db
Teutonic Knights, 21B, Db; 26, Gb
Teviot, R., 48A, Bb
Teviotdale, 28B, Cb
Tewkesbury, 27, De; 36, Df
Texas, 70, Ed
Texel, 46A, Da
Tezcuco, 43A, Cc
Thaba Bosigo, 81B, Cb
Thabanchu, 81B, Cb
Thailand (Siam), 91, De
Thame, 36, Ff
Thames, R., Canada, 45A, Ab
Thames, R., Connecticut, 45B, Cc
Thames, R., England, 27, Ee
Thanet, 7B, Dc
Thanjavur, 92, De
Thann, 39B, Dc
Thapsus, 2, Ff
Thar Desert, 59A, Bb
Tharandt, 39C, Dc
Thasos, 78, Ee
The Forks, 69A, Da
The Hague, 46A, Db
Theanum, 5B, Bc
Thebes, 19, Ce
Theiss, R., 22, Gb; 33C, Eb
Thelwall, 7C, Bb
Theodosiopolis (Erzerum), 4A, Ld
Theopolis, 81B, Cc
Thérouanne, 22, Ca; 46A, Bd
Thessalonica, 8, Gc; 9, Gd
Thessalonica Theme, 9, Gd
Thessaly, 78, Df
Thetford, 7C, Db; 36, Ge
Thiers, 30, Ef
Thikombia, 75C, Ca
Thimer, 11, Db
Thionville, 29A, Ba; 83A, Db
Third Cataract, 80B, Ad
Thirsk, 27, Eb
Tholen, 46A, Dc
Tholey, 39B, Da
Thomar, 23C, Ac; 63, Ac
Thomastown, 49B, Cd
Thomond, 15, Cd
Thompsons I., 56B
Thorn, 21, Nb
Thorney, 36, Fe
Thouars, 11, Cc
Thousand Is., L. of, 57, Ca
Thrace, 8, Hc; 78, Fe
Thrace Theme, 9, Hd
Thracesian Theme, 9, He
Thracia, 2, Je
Threave, 14, Ee
Threave Castle, 28B, Ac
Three Kings I., 75, Ff
Three Points, C., 81C, Dd
Three Rivers, 57C, Aa
Thun, 29B, Bb
Thun, L., 29B, Bb
Thur, R., 29B, Ca
Thurgau, 10, Ce; 29B, Da
Thuringia, 10, Dc; 39C, Ac
Thuringia, Land. of, 21B, Cb
Thuringia, March of, 10, Fc
Thuringian Forest, 10, Dc
Thuringians, 4A, Ea; 7A, Fb
Thurles, 49B, Dd
Thurso, 37A, Ca
Tiber, R., 5, Dc; 32A, Ec
Tiberias, 18C, Cf
Tibesti, 80A, Eb
Tibet, 25, Hc; 92, Fa
Tiburon, C., 43A, Ec
Ticino, canton, 29B, Cb
Ticino, R., 5, Bb
Tickhill, 27, Ec
Ticonderoga, 57, Eb
Tidor, 52B, Aa
Tientsin, 74, Ke; 91, Ec
Tierra del Fuego, 68, Ch
Tierra Firme, 43A, Fd
Tiflis, 19, Gd; 79, Hb
Tigris, R., 2, Mg; 6A, Ca
Tikhvin, 88, Mb
Tikrit, 93, Ec
Till, R., 28B, Cb; 48A, Cb
Tilsit, 60A, Ha; 61, Bc
Timahoe, 15, Dd
Timaru, 77A
Timbuktu, 81C, Da
Timbuktu (Tombuto), 35, Jd
Timisoara, 87, Ec
Timor, 52C, Cc; 91, Fg
Timor Laut, 52C, Dc
Tinchebrai, 17, Ed
Tindouf, 80A, Cb
Tinemuthe (Tynemouth), 13, Ea
Tingitana, 2, Cg
Tinnevelly, 73, Cf
Tinos, 78, Eg
Tintagel, 13, Bf; 27, Bf
Tintern, 36, Df
Tioga, 56, Db
Tippecanoe, 71C, Ab
Tipperah, 73, Fc
Tipperary, 37B, Cd
Tipperary, co., 49B, Dd
Tippermuir, 37A, Cb
Tiranë, 88, Je
Tiree, 14, Bc
Tirlemont, 46A, Dd
Tirnova, 78, Ed
Tiruchirapalli, 92, De
Tisz, R., 89, Kd
Titicaca, L., 68, Cd
Titus, Baths of, 5A
Tiverton, 27, Cf
Tivoli, 22A; 32A, Ed
Tlaxcala, 43A, Cc
Tlemsen, 6, Ab; 9, Bf
Tmatarakhan, 9, Kc
Tobago, 43A, Fc
Tobermory, 49A, Ab
Tobolsk, 74, Ec
Tobruk, 93, Ac
Tocantins, R., 68, Ec
Toce, R., 29B, Cb
Togean Is., 52C, Bb
Toggenburg, 29B, Ca; 30, He
Toggenburg, canton, 29B, Da
Togo, 81C, Ec; 96B, Cb
Togoland, 96C, Cd
Tohopeka (Horseshoe Bend), 71F, Ba
Tokar, 80B, Bd
Tokat, 33A, Eb
Tokay, 33C, Eb
Tokelau Is., 83, Ae; 90, Fd
Tokelau (Union) Is., 75, Ge
Tokyo, 91, Gc
Toledo, Ohio, 70, Fc
Toledo, Spain, 23C, Cc; 63, Cc
Toledo, eccl. prov., 22, Bc
Toledo, Mts. of, 63, Cc
Toliman, 52B, Ab
Tollhuys, 53, Gb
Tolmezzo, 86B, Da
Tolmino, 86B, Da
Tolosa, 2, De
Tols, 53, Jd
Tolu, 43A, Ed
Tombigbee, R., 43A, Da
Tombuto (Timbuktu), 35, Jd
Tomen-y-mur, 3A, Cd
Tomini, Gulf of, 52C, Bb
Tomsk, 42, Ob; 74, Gc
Tonale Pass, 29A, Db
Tonbridge, 27, Ge
Tondern, 65F, Aa
Tonebridge (Tonbridge), 13, Ge
Tonga (Friendly) Is., 75, Gf
Tonga Land, 81D, Ca
Tongatabu, 75, Gf
Tongking, 74, Jf
Tongue, Kyle of, 49A, Ba
Tongueland, 36, Bc
Tonk, 73, Cb
Tonnai, 20, Cf
Tonnerre, 11, Fc; 17A, Dc
Tönning, 65F, Aa
Tonsberg, 26, Db
Toome, 37B, Eb
Topeka, 10, Ed
Tor B., 55A, Bc
Torchesey (Torksey), 13, Fc
Tordesillas, 23D, Cb; 63, Cb
Torgau, 21, Kc; 39C, Cb
Torjok, 19, Ea
Torksey, 7C, Cb
Tormentoso, C. (C. of Good Hope), 35, Kf
Tormes, R., 63, Bb
Torni (Thorney), 13, Fd
Toro, 23C, Cb; 63, Cb
Toronto, 70, Gc
Toronto (York), 71C, Cb
Toropets, 19, Ea
Torre, Devon, 36, Cg
Torre, Somerset, 13, Ce
Torrens, L., 77, Fh
Torres, 23B, Bd
Torres, eccl. prov., 22, Dc
Torres Str., 77, Gc
Torres Vedras, 63B
Torridon, L., 14, Cb
Torrington, 27, Bf
Tortola, 43A, Fc
Tortona, 5, Bb
Tortosa, 23C, Fb; 63, Fb
Tortue (Tortuga), 43D, Eb
Tortuga, I., Haiti, 43A, Eb
Tortuga, I., Venezuela, 43A, Fc
Tory I., 15, Ca
Tostar, 6A, Db
Toteberie (Tutbury), 13, Ed
Totenais (Totnes), 13, Cf
Totnes, 27, Cf
Totoya, 75C, Cb
Touggourt, 80A, Da
Toul, 10, Ad; 39B, Bb
Toulon, 11, Fe; 29A, Ad
Toulouse, 11, De
Toulouse, Co. of, 11, De
Touraine, 11, Dc
Tourcoing, 46A, Cd
Tournai, 46A, Cd
Tournon, 17, Hf; 38, Df
Tours, 11, Dc
Tours, eccl. prov., 22, Bb
Toury, 76A, Ab
Towcester, 7C, Cb; 48B, Cc
Tower, 27A
Townsville, 77, He
Towton, 27, Ec
Towy, R., 28A, Cb
Trabzon, 93, Da
Trafalgar, 55B, Kc; 69A, Jc
Trafalgar, C., 63A
Trajan's Wall, 78, Gc
Tralee, 37B, Bd; 49B, Bd
Trani, 32A, Gd
Tranquebar, 42, Od; 59D
Trans Tiberis, 5A
Trans-Caspian Railway, 74, Dd
Trans-Jordan, 79, Gd
Transkei, 81B, Dc
Transmarine Algarve, 35, Jc
Trans-Siberian Railway, 74, Ec
Transvaal, 81A, Cb
Transylvania, Europe, 33C, Eb
Transylvania, N. America, 57A, Bb
Transylvanian Alps, 50, Ed
Trapani, 5, De
Trapezus, 2, Le; 4A, Kc
Traquair, 28B, Bb
Tras os Montes, 63, Bb
Trasimene, L., 5, Dc
Trastamara, 23D, Aa
Trau, 22, Fc
Traungau, 10, Fd
Traunstein, 53, Kd
Trautenau, 60B, Ec
Travancore, 73, Cf
Travnik, 78, Ac
Trebbio, R., 5, Bb
Trebinje, 22, Fc
Trebizond, 19, Fd; 79, Gb
Trebizond, Empire of, 19, Fd
Trebnitz, 22, Fa
Tregony, 27, Bf
Tréguier, 11, Bb
Tremetone (Trematon), 13, Bf
Trencsen, 21, Nd
Trent, 5, Ca
Trent, Bp. of, 30, Je; 33C, Cb
Trent, R., 27, Fc
Trentino, 84, Ec; 86B, Aa
Trenton, 45A, Cb; 57, Dc
Tresch (Thirsk), 13, Eb
Trèves, 10, Bd; 83A, Db
Trèves, Abp. of, 22, Db; 46C, Cb
Treviglio, 32A, Cb
Treviso, 5, Db; 86B, Cb
Treviso, M. of, 23B, Cb
Trévoux, 53, Fe
Tribulation, C., 77, He
Tribur, 10, Cd
Trichinopoly, 59D
Triebl, 39, Kd
Trier, 31A, Dc; 76A, Db
Trieste, 5, Db
Triglav, 29A, Fb
Trim, 15, Ec; 49B, Ec
Trim, bp., 15A, Bb
Trimontium (Newstead), 3A, Da
Trincomali, 73, Df
Trinidad, Bolivia, 68, Cd
Trinidad, Cuba, 43A, Eb
Trinidad, I., 43A, Fc
Trinity B., 45A, Ga
Trinovantes, 3A, Ge
Tripoli, Libya, 6, Cb; 80A, Ea
Tripoli, Syria, 6A, Bb; 18C, Cd
Tripoli, Volhynia, 19, Dc
Tripoli, Co. of, 18C, Dd
Tripolis, 2, Fg
Tripolitana, 4B, Ee
Tripolitania, 80A, Ea
Tripolitza, 78, Dg
Tripura, 92, Gc
Trisameron, 4B, Dd
Trisanna, R., 29B, Ea
Tristan da Cunha, 69A, Jf
Trivadee, 59D
Trivandrum, 73, Cf
Trivento, 22, Ec
Trobriand Is., 77, Ic
Trocala, 5, Df
Troia, 21A, Cb
Troina, 21A, Cd
Troitskoye, 61, Ec
Trondelag, 12, Ga
Trondheim (Nidaros), 26, Da; 88, Ha
Trondhjem, 50, Ca
Trondhjem, prov., 50, Ca
Tronto, R., 21A, Ba
Troppau, 31, Md; 39, Md
Tropea, 22, Fd
Trostan, 15, Ea
Trotternish, 14, Bb
Troy, 57, Eb
Troyes, 2, Dd; 28D, Db
Troyes, Co. of, 11, Eb
Trucial Oman, 93, Ge
Trujillo, Peru, 68, Bc
Trujillo, Spain, 23C, Cc; 63, Cc
Trujillo, Venezuela, 68, Bb
Truk, 90, Dc
Truro, 27, Af
Truxillo, 43A, Dc
Tsang-Wu, 1, Oe
Tsanpo (Brahmaputra), R., 73, Eb
Tsaribrod, 78, Dd
Tschaslau, 31, Ld
Tsinan, 91, Ec
Tsingtao, 91, Fc
Tsympe, 33A, Cb
Tuam, 15, Cc
Tuamotu Arch. (Paumotu Arch.), 75, He
Tuareg, 80A, Db
Tübingen, 10, Cd; 64, Dd
Tubuai (Austral) Is., 75, Hf
Tucson, 70, Cd
Tucuman, 41B, Cf; 68, Ce
Tudela, 23C, Ea; 63, Ea
Tuder, 5, Dc
Tuensang Area, 92, Gb
Tugela, R., 81D, Bb
Tula, 84, Kb; 88, Nc
Tulbagh, 81B, Ac
Tulbagh, dist., 81B, Bc
Tulcea, 78, Gc
Tullagh, 37B, Ec
Tullahoma, 72, Cb
Tullamore, 49B, Dc
Tulle, 22, Cb; 30, Df
Tulunid Dominions, 9, Hf
Tulunids, King. of, 6B, Db
Tumbez, 68, Ac
Tummel, R., 49A, Bb
Tunga Bhadra, R., 73, Cd
Tungchow, 74, Kd
Tunis, 24, Df; 80A, Da
Tunis, prot., 80A, Da
Tunis, Pashalik of, 47, De
Tunis, Sultanate of (Hafsids), 34, De
Tunisia, 96C, Ca; 96D, Ca
Tunja, 68, Bb
Tunja, R., 78, Fd
Tupelo, 72, Cc

Turbessel (Tell-basher), 18C, Eb
Turenne, 11, Dd
Turenne, V. of, 11, Dd
Turgai, 74, Ed
Turkestan, 61B, Ba
Turkestan, reg., 61B, Ba
Turkey, 93, Db
Turkheim, 29A, Ba; 39B, Db
Turkish Hungary, 39, Ne
Turkomans, 24, Lf
Turks Is., 43A, Eb
Turku, 87, Ea
Turin, 20, Gf; 32C, Ab
Turin (Augusta Taurinorum), 5, Ab
Turnberry, 14, Dd
Turneffe, 43A, Dc
Turnham Green, 48A, Cd
Turnhout, 46A, Dc
Turov, 26, Gc
Turriff, 37A, Cb
Turukhansk, 74, Gb
Tus, 6, Gb
Tuscaloosa, 72, Cc
Tuscan Presidios, 47, Ed
Tuscana, 5B, Ab
Tuscany, 5, Ce
Tuscany, D. of, 23A, Cb
Tuscany, G. D. of, 32B, Cc; 38, Jg
Tuscaroras, 45A, Bc
Tusculum (Frascati), 22A
Tuscumbia, 72, Cc
Tutbury, 27, Ed
Tutuila, 75, Ge; 75B, Bb
Tuva, 74, Hc
Tuy, 22, Ac; 23C, Aa
Tuz Gol, L., 86C, Bb
Tuzi, 78, Bd
Tver, 19, Fa
Tvinam (Twineham, Christchurch), 13, Ef
Tweed, R., 14, Ed; 28B, Bb
Twelve Pins, 15, Bc
Two Sicilies, King. of, 18B, Bc; 21, Kg; 32B, Ed
Tyburn, 27A
Tyne, R., 27, Eb; 28B, Dc
Tynedale, 13, Db
Tynedale, Franchise of, 28B, Cb
Tynemouth, 27, Ea
Tyr Connell, 15, Cb
Tyr Owen, 15, Db
Tyras, R., 2, Jd
Tyre, 2, Lg; 16, Kf
Tyre (Sur), 18C, Ce
Tyrnau, 39, Md
Tyrol, 20, Je
Tyrol, Co. of, 20, Je
Tyrone, 37B, Db
Tyrone, co., 49B, Db
Tyrrell, 37B, Dc
Tyrrhenian Sea, 5, Dd
Tyumen, 74, Ec
Tzurulum (Chorlu), 19, Dd

UBANGI-SHARI, 80A, Fd
Ubeda, 23C, Dc
Uberaba, 68, Ed
Uberlingen, 20, He
Ucayali, R., 68, Bc
Uch, 25, Gd
Uckermark, 31B, Ca
Ucles, 23C, Dc
Udaipur, 73, Bc
Udine, 22, Eb; 29A, Eb
Udskot, 74, Mc
Uele, R., 80A, Fd
Uexküll, 26, Fb
Ufa, 61, Jd
Ufa, R., 19, Ka
Uganda, 80A, Gd
Uighur, 25, Hb
Uitenhage, 81A, Cd
Uitenhage, dist., 81B, Cc
Ujiji, 80A, Fe
Ujjain, 1, Ke; 92, Dc
Ukermark, 60A, Db
Ukraine, 19, Eb; 50, Gd
Ukraine Soviet Socialist Rep., 84, Jc
Ukrians, 10, Eb
Uladh (Ultonia, Ulster), 15, Db
Ulan Bator, 91, Db
Ulan Ude, 91, Da
Uleåborg, 61, Cb
Ullapool, 49A, Bb
Ulm, 10, Cd; 29A, Ca
Ulster, 37B, Db; 49C
Ulster (Uladh, Ultonia), 15, Db
Ulster Irish, 49C
Ultonia (Uladh, Ulster), 15, Db
Ulundi, 81D, Bb
Ülzen, 26, Dc
Umarkot, 52A, Ab
Umbria, 5, Dc; 32A, Ec
Umeå, 26, Fa
Umfraville, 28B, Cb
Unfuli, R., 81A, Ca
Umkomaas, R., 81B, Db
Umtali, 81A, Da
Umzimkulu, R., 81B, Db
Umzimvubu, R., 81B, Db
Umzimyati (Buffalo), R., 81D, Bb
Una, R., 33C, Dc
Ungava, 70, Gb
Ungava B., 44, Hc; 71, Hb
Union (Tokelau) Is., 75, Ge
Union of Soviet Socialist Republics, 94, Qc
United Arab Republic, 96D, Fb
United Kingdom, 64, Ab
United Provinces, Rep. of, 38, Fb
United States of America, 70–71
United States of Brazil, 68, Dd
Unkiar Skelessi, 79, Eb
Unterwalden, 29B, Cb
Upland, New Sweden, 45B, Bd
Upland, Sweden, 26, Ea
Upolu, 75B, Ba
Upper Alsace, 31A, Dd
Upper Alsace, Land. of, 20, Ge
Upper Austria, 65C, Bb
Upper Burgundy (Regnum Jurense), 11, Gc
Upper Burma, 74, Hf
Upper Canada, 71C, Ca
Upper Doab, 59C, Cb
Upper Lausitz, Marg. of, 31, Lc
Upper Lorraine, 20, Gd
Upper Lotharingia, 10, Bd
Upper Palatinate, 30, Jd
Upper Peru, 41B, Ce
Upper Senegal and Niger, 81C, Da
Upper Silesia, 60A, Fc
Upper Volta, 80A, Cc
Upsala, 26, Eb
Uraba, G. of, 43A, Ed
Ural Mts., 19, Ka
Ural, R., 19, Kb; 61, Hd
Uralsk, 61, Hd
Urbannia, 72B, Bb
Urbino, 5, Dc; 8A, Dc
Urbinum, 5B, Bb
Urfa, 79, Gc
Urga, 74, Jd
Urgel, 11, De; 23C, Fa
Urgenj, 25, Eb
Uri, 29B, Cb
Uriel, 37B, Eb
Uriel (Oirghealla), 15, Db
Urmia, 86C, Db
Urmia, L., 6A, Da
Urseren, 29B, Cb
Uruguaiana, 68, De
Uruguay, 68, Df
Uruguay, R., 68, De
Urumchi, 91, Bb
Usak, 79, Ec
Usedom, 10, Eb; 31, Kb
Ushant, 11, Ab
Usingen, 65B, Aa
Usk, 28A, Dc
Usk, R., 27, De; 28, Cb
Uskub (Skoplje), 78, Cd
Uskudar, 93, Ba
Ust Yurt, 61, Jf
Ustyug, 61, Gb
Utah, 70, Cd
Utah L., 44, Cd
Utah Terr., 67D, Bb
Utica, Mississippi, 72C, Aa
Utica, New York, 57, Db
Utrecht, Natal, 81D, Ba
Utrecht, Netherlands, 46A, Eb
Uitrecht, prov., 46A, Eb
Utrecht, Bp. of, 46C, Ca
Uttar Pradesh, 92, Eb
Uttoxeter, 48B, Cc
Uxbridge, 48B, Cd
Uyuni, 68, Ce
Uzés, 11, Fe
Uzes (Cumans), 9, Mc
Uznach, 29B, Da

VAAL, R., 81A, Cc
Vabres, 22, Cc
Vadstena, 26, Db
Vaduz, 38, He
Vahsel B., 69C
Vaigeu, 52C, Db
Vaison, 22, Dc
Val d'Aran, 23D, Fa
Val Leventina, 29B, Cb
Val Maggia, 29B, Cb
Valais, 29B, Bb
Valais, Co. of, 11, Gc
Valcour I., 57, Ea
Valdemoni, 21A, Cc
Valdez, 71A, Ca
Valdivia, 68, Bg
Vale Royal, 36, Dd
Valence, 11, Fd
Valence, family, 37B, Ed
Valencia, Spain, 63, Ec
Valencia, Venezuela, 68, Cb
Valencia, eccl. prov., 22, Bd
Valencia, prov., 63, Ec
Valenciennes, 46A, Cd
Valentia I., 49B, Ae
Valladolid, 23C, Cb; 63, Cb
Valle Crucis, 36, Ce
Valley Forge, 57, Dc
Vallombrosa, 32A, Dc
Valls, 63, Fb
Vallum Antonini, 3A, Ba
Valmy, 62, Cc
Valognes, 11, Cb
Valois, 17, Gd
Valois, Co. of, 11, Eb
Valona, 16, Fd; 78, Be
Valparaiso, 68, Bf
Valromey, 53, Fe
Valsainte, 29B, Bb
Valsch, R., 81B, Ca
Valtellina, 29B, Db
Valverde, 23D, Bc
Van, 19, Ge; 86C, Db
Van, L., 6A, Ca
Van Diemen's Land, 77, Gj
Van Reenen's Pass, 81D, Ab
Vancouver, Canada, 70, Bc
Vancouver, U.S.A., 70, Bc
Vancouver I., 70, Bc
Vandal Kingdom, 4A, Dd
Vandali, 2, Gc
Vandalia, 67C, Eb
Vandals, 2A, Ac
Vannes, 11, Bc
Vanua Levu, 75C, Ba
Var, R., 29A, Bd
Värälä, 51, Fa
Varanasi (Banaras), 92, Eb
Varazdin, 21, Me
Vardar, R., 78, De; 86A, Da
Varennes, 29A, Aa; 31A, Cc
Varey, 20, Ff
Varilhes, 38, Dg
Varkinskil (Salem), 45B, Bd
Varna, 78, Fd
Vasa, 26, Fa
Vasconia, 4A, Bc
Vassy, 38, Fd
Vasvar, 33C, Db
Vasvar (Eisenburg), 29A, Gb
Vaternish, 14, Bb
Vatersay, 49A, Ab
Vatican, 5A
Vatter, L., 26, Db
Vauclair, 22, Cb
Vaucouleurs, 28D, Eb
Vaud, 29B, Ab
Vaud, Co. of, 11, Gc
Vaudemont, 20, Fd; 39B, Cb
Vaudreuil, 57, Da
Vechte, R., 46A, Gb
Vectis (I. of Wight), 3A, Ef
Veglia, 22, Eb
Veile, 65F, Aa
Velay, Co. of, 11, Fd
Velikie Luki, 61, Dc
Velletri, 32B, Dd
Vellinghausen, 60A, Ac
Vellore, 59D
Venaissin, 30, Ff
Vendée, 53, Cd; 62, Bc
Venden, 26, Gb
Vendôme, 11, Dc
Venedae, 1, Fb
Vener, L., 26, Db
Venetia, 5, Db; 32C, Db
Venetian Alps, 29A, Dc
Venezuela, 43C, Ed; 68, Cb
Venezuela, G. of, 43A, Ec
Venice, 32D, Cb
Venice, D. of, 10, Ef
Venice, G. of, 29A, Ec
Venlo, 46A, Fc
Venonae (High Cross), 3A, Ed
Venta Belgarum (Winchester), 3A, Ee
Venta Cruz (Cruces), 43A, Ed
Venta Icenorum (Caister), 3A, Hd
Venta Silurum (Caerwent), 3A, De
Ventadour, 17, Gf; 53, Ee
Ventersdorp, 81A, Cc
Ventimiglia, 5, Ac; 20, Gg
Vera Cruz, 43A, Cc
Vera Cruz, Terra da, 40, He
Veragua, 43A, Dd
Veragua, prov., 43A, Dd
Vercelli, 5, Bb; 29A, Cc
Verchères, 57, Ea
Vercovicium (Housesteads), 3C
Verde, C., 80A, Bc; 81C, Ab
Verden, 10, Cb; 60A, Ac
Verden, Bp. of, 38, Hb
Verdon, R., 29A, Bd
Verdun, Gascony, 38, Dg
Verdun, Lotharingia, 10, Ad
Verdun, Bp. of, 39B, Ba
Vereeniging, 81A, Cc
Veria, 78, De
Verkhne Kolymsk, 74, Ob
Verkhne Udinsk, 74, Jc
Verkhoyansk, 74, Mb
Verkne Chusovoi, 61, Jc
Verlucio (Sandy Lane), 3A, De
Vermandois, Co. of, 11, Eb
Vermland, 26, Db
Vermont, 67C, Fa; 71, Gc
Vernemetum (Willoughby), 3A, Ed
Verneuil, 17, Fd
Verny, 74, Fd
Verona, 5, Cb; 32D, Bb
Verona, M. of, 10, Ef; 20, Jf
Verria, 86A, Db
Versailles, 53, Ec; 76A, Bb
Verterae (Brough), 3A, Db
Vertus, 30, Ed
Veruela, 22, Bc
Verulamium (St. Albans), 3A, Fe
Verviers, 46A, Ed
Vervins, 38, Ed
Vesle, R., 83A, Bb
Vesoul, 20, Ge; 83B, Bb
Vester-Götland, 26, Db
Vesterås, 26, Eb
Vesterbotten, 26, Fa
Vestmanland, 26, Eb
Veszprem, 21, Me
Vet (Sand), R., 81A, Cc
Vevey, 29B, Ab
Vexin, Co. of, 11, Db
Vexins, 38, Ce
Vézelay, 20, Ee; 31A, Bd
Vezeronce, 8B, Cb
Via Dolorosa, 18D
Viadua, R., 2, Gc
Vianen, 46A, Ec
Vianna, 23D, Ab; 63, Ab
Viatka, 19, Ha
Viborg, Denmark, 26, Cb
Viborg, Finland, 26, Ga
Vic, 39B, Cb
Vic Bigorre, 63, Fa
Vicenza, 5, Cb; 38, Jf
Vich, 11, Ef
Vichy, 88, Fd
Vicksburg, 72C, Aa
Victoria, British Columbia, 70, Bc
Victoria, Cameroon, 96B, Cb
Victoria, Rhodesia, 81A, Db
Victoria, dist., S. Africa, 81B, Cc
Victoria Falls, 81A, Ca
Victoria I., Canada, 44, Ca
Victoria, I., Moluccas, 52C, Cb
Victoria, L., 80A, Ge
Victoria Land, 69C
Victoria, R., 77, Ee
Victoria, st., 77, Gi
Vidin, 33A, Bb
Viedma, 68, Cg
Vienna, Austria, 10, Gd
Vienna, Gaul, 2, Dd
Vienne, 11, Fd; 17A, Ed
Vienne, eccl. prov., 22, Db
Vienne, R., 11, Dc; 30, De
Vientiane, 91, De
Viervoet, 81B, Cb
Vierzon, 28C, Dc; 76A, Bc
Vietnam, 91, De
Vigan, 75E, Ba
Vigo, 63, Aa
Viipuri, 87, Fa
Vijayanagar, 52A, Bc
Vijayanagar, king., 41A, Ec
Vijayavada, 92, Ed
Viken, 12, Gb
Vilagos, 33C, Eb
Vilaine, R., 30, Be
Vilkomir, 26, Fb
Villa Bella (Mato Grosso), 68 Cd
Villa do Conde, 63, Ab
Villa Dolores, 68, Cf
Villa St. Albani (St. Albans), 13, Fe
Villa Viciosa, Portugal, 63, Bc
Villa Viciosa, Spain, 63, Db
Villach, 10, Ee; 29A, Eb
Villafranca, Italy, 32C, Cb
Villafranca, Spain, 63, Ba
Villarrica, 68, De
Villefranche, Guyenne, 53, Ee
Villefranche, Lyonnais, 53, Fe
Villemaur, 31A, Bc
Villena, 23C, Ec; 63, Ec
Villeneuve, 20, Df
Villers Bretonneux, 76A, Bb
Villers Cotterets, 83A, Bb
Villersexel, 76A, Dc
Vilna, 26, Gc
Vilnius (Vilna), 88, Lc
Vimiero, 63, Ac
Viminacium, 2, He
Vimy, 83A, Ba
Vincennes, 56, Bc
Vinchy, 8B, Ba
Vindhya Mts., 73, Cc
Vindocladia (Badbury), 3A, Df
Vindolanda (Chesterholm), 3C
Vindomora (Ebchester), 3C
Vindovala (Rudchester), 3C
Vinegar Hill, 49B, Ed
Vinland, 35, Fb
Vinnitsa, 79, Ea
Vinovia (Binchester), 3A, Eb
Vionville, 76A, Cb
Vire, 53, Cc
Virgin Is., 43A, Fc
Virginia, 57, Ce; 72B, Bb
Virginia Colony, Raleigh's, 45A, Bc
Viroconium (Wroxeter), 3A, Dd
Visconti, Lands of, 24, Dd
Visé, 83A, Ca
Viseu, 23C, Ab
Vishakhapatnam, 92, Ed
Vishegorod, 19, Da
Visigothi, 2, Hd
Visigothic Kingdom, 4A, Bc
Viso, Mte., 29A, Bc
Visp, 29B, Bb
Vistula, R., 31, Pc; 33C, Ea
Vitebsk, 26, Hb
Viterbo, 5, Dc
Viti Levu, 75C, Aa
Vitichev, 9, Jb
Vitoria, Brazil, 68, Ee
Vitoria, Spain, 63, Da
Vitoria la Conguista, 68, Ed
Vitré, 20, Cd
Vitry, 11, Fb
Vitry, Co. of, 11, Fb
Vittoria, 4B, Bc
Vittorio, 86B, Cb
Viviers, 11, Fd; 17, Hf
Vizagapatam, 73, Dd
Vizcaya, 23C, Da
Vizeu, 22, Ac; 63, Bb
Vizianagram, 59A, Dd
Vizye, 19, Dd
Vlach, 8C, Db
Vlachs, 19, Dc
Vladikavkaz, 61, Ff
Vladimir, Poland, 26, Fc
Vladimir, Russia, 19, Ga
Vladimir Volinski, 19, Cb
Vladivostok, 91, Gb
Vlieland, 46A, Da
Vodena, 86A, Db
Vogtland, 21, Kc
Volcano Is., 90, Db
Volga, R., 19, Hc; 24, Md
Volgograd, 89, Od
Volhynia, 50, Fc
Volkovisk, 62, Gb
Volksrust, 81D, Aa
Volmeringen, 39B, Ca
Vologda, 19, Fa
Volos, 78, Df
Volta, 96B, Ba
Volta, R., 81C, Dc
Volterra, 32E, Bb
Volturno, R., 32C, Dd
Voltutara, 22, Fc
Vorarlberg, 33C, Cb
Voronezh, 61, Ed; 88, Nc
Vosges, 10, Bd; 83B, Ba
Vostok I., 83, Be
Votyaks, 19, Ja
Vouillé, 4A, Bb; 8B, Ab
Vrania, 78, Cd
Vryburg, 81A, Bc
Vryheid, 81A, Dc; 81D, Ba
Vyatiches, 9, Ka
Vyazma, 19, Ea

WAAG, R., 21, Nd
Waal, R., 46A, Ec
Wabash, R., 56, Bc; 57A, Bb
Wachefeld (Wakefield), 13, Ec
Wad Medani, 93, Cg
Wadai, 80A, Ec
Wadelai, 80A, Gd
Wadern, 76A, Db
Wadi Halfa, 80B, Ac
Wagram, 29A, Ga
Wagrians, 10, Da
Wahlstatt, 60B, Fc
Waianae, 75D, Bb
Waiblingen, 10, Cd
Waidhaus, 39, Kd
Waidhofen, 21, Le
Waigen, 77, Eb
Waikato, R., 77A
Wailuku, 75D, Cb
Waimea, 75D, Bb
Waitara, 77A
Waitemata (Auckland), 77, Mi
Waitzen, 22, Fb
Wake I., 90, Ec
Wakefield, 27, Ec
Wakkerstroom, 81D, Ba
Wal Wal, 96A, Bb
Walachia, 78, Ec
Walcheren, 46A, Cc
Waldeck, 30, Hc
Waldeck, co., 38, Hc
Walden, 36, Ge
Waldsassen, 22, Eb
Waledana (Saffron Walden), 13, Gd

Walenstadt, 29B, Da
Wales, 28A; 34, Bb; 55A, Bb
Wales, Pr. of, 27, Cd
Wales, The March of, 17, Dc
Walila, 6, Ab
Walingeford (Wallingford), 13, Ee
Walla Walla, 70, Cc
Wallhof, 50, Eb
Wallingford, 27, Ee
Wallis Is., 75, Ge
Walpole, 57, Eb
Walsingham, 36, Ge
Walsleben, 10, Db
Waltham, 13, Ge; 36, Gf
Walton Castle, 3A, He
Walvis Bay, 80A, Eg
Walvisch B., 81A, Ab
Wandatin, 76B, Bb
Wandiwash, 59D
Wangama, 77A
Wanganui, 77, Nj
Wangen, 30, He
Wantage, 7C, Cc; 48B, Cd
Warangal, 25, Ge; 92, Dd
Warberg, 26, Db
Wardha, R., 59C, Cc
Wardour Castle, 48A, Bd
Wareham, 27, Df
Wargaon, 59A, Bd
Warham (Wareham), 13, Df
Wark, 27, Da; 28B, Cb
Warkworth, 27, Ea
Warnabians, 10, Eb
Warneton, 46A, Bd
Warnstedt, 10, Dc
Warren, 28A, Ca
Warrenton, 72B, Ba
Warrenton Junction, 72B, Ba
Warrington, 3A, Dc; 48A, Bc
Warsaw, 21, Pb
Warsaw, G. D. of, 62, Gb
Warta, R., 21B, Db; 31, Db
Wartburg, 20, Jc; 39C, Ac
Warthe, R., 21, Lb; 22, Fa
Warwic (Warwick), 13, Ed
Warwick, England, 27, Ed
Warwick, Rhode I., 45B, Dc
Warwick, co., 27, Ed
Warwicscire (Warwickshire), 13, Ed
Wash, The, 27, Gd; 36, Ge
Washington, Arkansas, 72, Bc
Washington, Dist. of Columbia, 71C, Cc; 72B, Ba
Washington, st., 70, Bc
Washington I., 75, Hd
Washington Terr., 67D, Aa
Wasit, 6A, Db
Watasios (Sultanate of Fez) 34, Be
Watauga Association, 57A, Cb
Watchet, 27, Ce
Waterboer's Land, 81A, Bc
Wateree, R., 57D, Aa
Waterford, 15, Dd
Waterford, co., 49B, Dd
Waterloo, 46B
Watford, 48B, Cd
Watkins Pt., 45B, Be
Watling Street, 3A, Ed
Wattignies, 46A, Dd
Watton, 36, Fd
Waverley, 36, Ff
Wavre, 46A, Dd; 46B
Waxhaw Creek, 57, Af
Weardale, 28B, Cc
Weare, 27, De
Wearmouth, 36, Ec
Weddell Sea, 69C
Wedmore, 7C, Bc
Wedone (Weedon), 13, Ed
Weenen, 81D, Bb
Wehlau, 39, Pa; 50, Ec
Weiden, 38, Jd
Weihaiwei, 74, Le
Weil, 30, Hd; 38, Hd
Weilerthal, 39B, Db
Weimar, 10, Dc
Weinsberg, 10, Cd
Weissenburg, Alsace, 39B, Da
Weissenburg, Germany, 20, Jd; 29A, Da
Weissenfels, 39C, Bb
Weitburg, 65B, Aa
Welbeck, 36, Ed
Weldon, 72, Eb
Welfesholz, 10, Dc
Wella (Wells), 13, Gd
Welland, R., 27, Fd
Welle (Wells), 13, De
Wellesley, 37B, Ec
Wellesley Is., 77, Fe
Wellington, 75, Fg
Wellington (Brittania), 77, Nj
Wellington, prov., 77A
Wells, 27, De
Welshpool, 27, Cd
Wenchow, 74, Lf
Wendover, 27, Fe
Wener, L., 12, Hb
Wenloch (Wenlock), 13, Dd
Wenlock, 27, Dd
Weobley, 27, Dd; 28, Db
Werben, 10, Db; 38, Jb
Werc (Wark), 13, Da
Werdenfels, 53, Jd
Weremuthe (Wearmouth), 13, Eb
Werle, 21, Kb
Wernigerode, 60A, Cc
Werra, R., 10, Dc; 20, Hc
Wertheim, 53, Hc
Wes-Treding (West Riding, Lincolnshire), 13, Fc
Wes-Treding (West Riding, Yorkshire), 13, Ec
Wesel, 20, Gc; 60A, Ac
Wesel (Oberwesel), 20, Gc
Weser, R., 10, Cb; 30, Hb
Wessaugusset (Weymouth), 45B, Db
Wessex, 7B, Bc; 12, Dd
West Bengal, 92, Fc
West Dvina, R., 89, Lb
West Florida, 56, Bd
West Franconia, 10, Cd
West Germany, 89, Gd
West Indies, 55B, Dd
West Looe, 27, Bf
West March, 28B, Bb
West Meath, co., 49B, Dc
West New Jersey, 45A, Cc
West Pakistan, 92, Bb
West Point, 57, Dc; 72B, Bb
West Prussia, 31, Nb
West Roman Empire, 2, Fe
West Saxons, 7A, Cb
West Schelde, R., 54, Cb
West Virginia, 72, Db
West Wales, 7B, Ac; 36A
Westderbei (West Derby), 18, Dc
Wester Wald, 10, Cc
Western, prov., Nigeria, 96B, Cb
Western Australia, 77, Cg
Western Ghats, 73, Bd
Western Pomerania, 39, Kb
Western Samoa, 75, Ge; 75B
Westerwald, 83A, Da
Westland, 77A
Westmeath, co., 37C
Westminster, 27A; 36, Ff
Westminster, Palace of, 27A
Westminster Abbey, 27A
Westmonasterium (Westminster), 13, Fe
Westmorland, 27, Db
Westover, 45B, Ae; 57, Ce
Westphalia, 10, Bb; 20, Hc
Westport, Missouri, 70, Ed
Westport, New Zealand, 77A
Westray, 49A, Ca
Wetherby, 48B, Cc
Wethersfield, 45B, Cc
Wetter, L., 52C, Cc
Wettin, 10, Dc; 39C, Bb
Wettingen, 29B, Ca
Wetzlar, 10, Cc
Wewak, 90, Dd
Wexford, 15, Ed
Wexford, co., 37C; 49B, Ed
Wexio, 26, Db
Weymouth, 27, Df; 55A, Bc
Weymouth (Wessaugusset), 45B, Db
Weymouth B., 77, Gd
Whalley, 36, Dd
Wheeling, 57, Ac
Wherwell, 36, Ef
Whitby, 27, Fb
Whitchurch, 48B, Cd
White Castle, 28A, Dc
White Croats, 9, Gb
White Horse, 71B, Ca
White House, 72B, Bb
White Huns, 6, Ha
White Marsh, 57, Dc
White Mts., 45A, Cb
White Nile, R., 80B, Ae
White Pass, 71B, Cb
White Plains, 57, Ec
White Russia, 51, Gc
White Sea, 61, Ea
White Umvolosi, R., 81D, Bb
Whitehall, 27A
Whitern, 7B, Aa
Whithorn, 14, De
Whitland, 36, Bf
Whitsand B., 55A, Ac
Whydah, 81C, Ec
Wiceford (Witchford), 13, Gd
Wich (Nantwich), 13, Dc
Wiche (Droitwich), 13, Dd
Wick, 49A, Ca
Wicklow, 15, Ed
Wicklow, co., 37C; 49B, Ed
Wicklow Hd., 15, Ed
Wicklow Mts., 15, Ed
Wicumbe (High Wycombe), 13, Fe
Widin, 19, Cd; 78, Dc
Wied, 20, Gc
Wielun, 61A, Ab
Wiesbaden, 60B, Bc; 83A, Ea
Wiesloch, 38, Hd
Wigan, 3A, Dc; 27, Dc
Wigemor (Wigmore), 13, Cd
Wight, I. of, 27, Ef
Wigmore, 28A, Db
Wigtown, 14, De
Wigtown, co., 37A, Bc
Wigtown B., 28B, Ac
Wiht, Is. de (I. of Wight), 13, Ef
Wiju, 76B, Ca
Wildhaus, 29B, Da
Wildspitze, 29A, Db
Wilge, R., 81B, Da
Wilhelmshaven, 55A, Hb
Wilkes Land, 69C
Wilkesbarre, 56, Db
Willebroek, 46A, Dc
Willemstadt, 52B, Aa
Williamsburg, 57, Ce
Williamsport, 70, Gc
Willis Creek, 56B
Willmanstrand, 51, Fa
Willsboro, 57, Ea
Wilmington, Delaware, 57, Dd
Wilmington, North Carolina, 57D, Ba
Wilno, 87, Fb
Wilson's Creek, 72, Bb
Wiltberg, 20, Jc
Wilten, 10, De
Wiltescire (Wiltshire), 13, Ee
Wilton, 27, Ee
Wiltshire, 27, Ee
Wiltunie (Wilton), 13, Ee
Wiltzes, 8, Ea; 10, Eb
Wimborne, 7C, Cc
Wimpfen, 10, Cd
Winburg, 81A, Cc
Winburne (Wimborne Minster), 13, Ef
Winceby, 48A, Cc
Wincelcumbe (Winchcomb), 13, Ee
Winchelsea, 17, Fc; 27, Gf
Winchester, England, 27, Ee
Winchester, Virginia, 57, Bd
Winchester, bp., 36, Ef
Windau, 26, Fb
Windesores (Windsor), 13, Fe
Windhoek, 80A ,Eg
Windsheim, 22, Eb; 30, Jd
Windsor, Connecticut, 45B, Cc
Windsor, England, 27, Fe
Windward Passage, 43A, Ec
Winnebago, L., 56, Bb
Winnepesaukee, L., 45B, Db
Winnipeg, 70, Ec
Winnipeg, L., 70, Eb
Winnipegosis, L., 70, Eb
Winnisimet, 56B
Winnsboro, 57D, Aa
Winter Hill, 56B
Winterberg Mts., 81B, Cc
Winterthur, 29B, Ca
Wintonia (Winchester), 13, Ee
Wirecestre (Worcester), 13, Dd
Wirecestrescire (Worcestershire), 13, Dd
Wisbeche (Wisbech), 13, Gd
Wisby, 26, Eb
Wischehrad, 31, Lc
Wisconsin, 70, Ec
Wisconsin, R., 56, Bb
Wislica, 31, Pc
Wismar, 26, Dc; 31B, Ca
Wissembourg, 29A, Ba
Witebi (Whitby), 13, Fb
Witham, Essex, 7C, Dc
Witham, Wiltshire, 36, Df
Witham, R., 27, Fc
Witney, 27, Ee
Witteland, 42B
Witteland West, 77, Bf
Wittelsbach, 20, Jd
Wittenberg, 21, Kc; 31B, Ca
Wittenberg, mts., 81B, Cb
Wittgenstein, 30, Hc
Wittstock, 21, Kb
Wloclawek, 22, Fa
Woburn, 36, Ff
Woerden, 46A, Db
Woëvre, The, 83A, Cb
Wohlau, 39, Mc
Wolfenbüttel, 20, Jb
Wolgast, 21, Ka
Wollin (Jomsburg), 10, Fb
Wolmar, 50, Fb
Wölpe, 20, Hb
Woods, L. of the, 70, Ec
Woodstock, England, 27, Ee
Woodstock, Virginia, 72B, Aa
Wooler, 49A, Cc
Worcester, England, 27, Dd
Worcester, Massachusetts, 57, Fb
Worcester, S. Africa, 81B, Ac
Worcester, bp., 36, De
Worcester, co., 27, Dd
Wordingborg, 26, Db
Worksop, 36, Ed
Worms, 10, Cd; 83A, Eb
Wörth, 39B, Ea; 76A, Db
Wragby, 36, Ed
Wrangel I., 74, Qa; 94, Jb
Wrath, C., 14, Ca
Wrexham, 48B, Bc
Wroclaw, 89, Jc
Wuhan, 91, Ec
Wuhu, 74, Ke
Württemberg, 10, Cd; 20, Hd
Würzburg, 10, Cd; 29A, Da
Wurzburg, G. D. of, 65B, Ba
Wurzen, 39C, Cb
Wychwood, 7B, Cc
Wycombe, 27, Fe
Wye, R., 27, De; 36, De
Wymondham, 36, He
Wynaad Malabar, 73, Ce
Wyndham, 77, De
Wynendael, 46A, Bc
Wyoming, 57, Cc
Wyoming, st., 70, Dc

XANTEN, 46A, Fc
Xeres, 23C, Bd; 63, Bd
Xingu, R., 68, Dc

Y GAER, 3A, Cd
Yadavas, 25, Gd
Yakutat B., 71B, Bb
Yakutsk, 74, Lb
Yalu, R., 76B, Ca
Yamasees, 45A, Bc
Yamuna, R., 92, Db
Yanaon, 73, Dd
Yanbu, 6, Ec
Yandabu, 73, Gc
Yandua, 75C, Ba
Yang Chow, 1, Oe
Yangtze-Kiang, R., 91, Dc
Yanselin Pass, 76B, Ba
Yantra, R., 78, Ed
Yaoundé, 96B, Db
Yap, 90, Cc
Yaqui, Pico de, 43D, Ec
Yarkand, 1, Kd; 74, Fe
Yarm, 27, Eb
Yarmak, 6A, Bb
Yarmouth, I. of W., 27, Ef
Yarmouth, Maine, 57, Fb
Yarmouth, Massachusetts, 45B, Dc
Yarmouth, Norfolk, 27, Hd
Yarmouth, Nova Scotia, 56, Fb
Yasawa Is., 75C, Aa
Yathreb (Medina), 6, Fc
Yavanas, 1, Je
Yazoo, R., 56, Ad; 72C, Aa
Yecla, 63, Ec
Yeddo, 69A, Qc
Yekaterinburg, 61, Kc
Yekaterinoslav, 51, Gd
Yellow Ford, 49B, Eb
Yellow Sea, 91, Fc
Yellowhead Pass, 44, Cc
Yellowstone, R., 70, Dc
Yellowstone National Park, 70, Dc
Yemen, 6, Fd; 25, De; 93, Ef
Yenbo, 93, De
Yenisei, R., 25, Ha
Yeniseisk, 74, Hc
Yentowwa B., 76B, Bb
Yerevan, 93, Ea
Yerwa, 96B, Da
Yeu, 53, Bd
Yewin, 77, Bg
Yezd, 6, Gb; 93, Gc
Yih Chow, 1, Nd
Yingkow, 76B, Ba
Ynys Enlli, 7B, Ab
Yokohama, 91, Gc
Yola, 80A, Ed
Yonne, R., 11, Ec
York (Agamenticus), 45B, Db
York, England, 27, Ec; 36A
York, Maine, 57, Fb
York, Pennsylvania, 57, Cd
York (Toronto), 71C, Cb
York, abp., 36, Ed
York, C., 77, Gd
York, eccl. prov., 22, Ba
York, Norse King. of, 7C, Ca
York, R., 72B, Bb
York Factory, 70, Eb
York Moors, 27, Fb
York Wolds, 27, Fb
Yorkshire, 27, Eb
Yorktown, 57, Ce; 72B, Bb
Youghal, 37B, De; 49B, De
Ypres, 17, Gc; 46A, Bd
Ysabel, 77, Jc
Ystrad Towy, 7B, Ac
Ythancester, 7B, Dc
Yu Chow, 1, Od
Yucatan, 43A, Db
Yu-chang, 1, Oe
Yugoslavia, 84, Fd
Yukon, 71B, Ba
Yukon, R., 71A, Ba
Yunnan, 74, Jf
Yun-nan, prov., 73, Gb
Yverdon, 29B, Ab
Yxninga (Exning), 13, Gd

ZABERN, 38, Gd
Zablat, 39, Ld
Zacatecas, 43A, Bb
Zacatula, 43A, Bc
Zacynthos (Zante) I., 78, Cg
Zafra, 63, Bc
Zagreb, 16, Fc
Zahringen, 10, Bd; 20, Gd
Zaitun, 25, Ld; 35, Pc
Zallaca, 23C, Bc
Zambesi, R., 81A, Da
Zamboanga, 75E, Bc
Zamora, 23C, Cb; 63, Cb
Zamosc, 50, Ec; 62, Gb
Zanesville, 71C, Bc
Zante, 78, Cg
Zante (Zacynthos) I., 78, Cg
Zanzibar, 80A, Ge
Zapetra, 8, Kd
Zara, 5, Eb; 32A, Fb
Zara, eccl. prov., 22, Ec
Zaria, 96B, Ca
Zator, 31, Nd
Zduny, 26, Ec
Zealand, 65F, Ba
Zeebrugge, 83A, Ba
Zeeland, Denmark, 51, Cb
Zeeland, Netherlands, 46A, Cc
Zehdenick, 22, Ea
Zeila, 40, Md
Zeitz, 21, Kc; 39C, Cb
Zeitz, March of, 10, Ec
Zell, 53, Hc
Zengg, 21, Lf
Zenta, 33C, Eb
Zerbst, 21, Kc
Zettin, 33C, Db
Zevenbergen, 46A, Dc
Zhitomir, 87, Fb
Zidon, 18A, Fc
Ziegenhain, 20, Hc
Zierikzee, 46A, Cc
Ziguinchor, 96B, Aa
Zinder, 80A, Dc
Zion Gate, 18D
Zipangu (Japan), 25, Nc
Zips, 24, Gd; 33C, Eb; 50, Ed
Zirids, 16, Df
Zittau, 21, Lc
Ziyanids, 24, Cg
Znaim, 21, Md; 31B, Db
Zobor, 9, Fc
Zollern, 10, Cd; 30, Hd
Zomba, 96C, Ff
Zonguldak, 79, Fb
Zorndorf, 54, Eb; 60A, Eb
Zornoza, 63, Da
Zossen, 60A, Db
Zoutpansberg, 81A, Cb
Zug, 29B, Ca
Zug, canton, 29B, Ca
Zug, L., 29B, Ca
Zuider Zee, 46A, Eb
Zullichau, 60A, Eb
Zulpich, 4B, Da
Zulu, 81D, Bb
Zululand, 81D, Bb
Zumbo, 81A, Da
Zungeru, 81C, Fc; 96C, Cd
Zurawno, 50, Ed
Zürich, 10, Ce; 29B, Ca
Zürich, canton, 29B, Ca
Zürich, L. of, 29B, Ca
Zutphen, 46A, Fb
Zutphen, prov., 46A, Fb
Zvenigorod, 19, Dc
Zweibrücken, 29A, Ba
Zweibrucken, Pr. of, 53, Gc
Zwettl, 39, Ld
Zwickau, 21, Kc; 39C, Cc
Zwolle, 46A Fb

PRINTED IN GREAT BRITAIN BY GEORGE PHILIP AND SON, LIMITED. LONDON BFB